Economics of Farm Management
in a Global Setting

Economics of Farm Management in a Global Setting

Kent D. Olson

Department of Applied Economics
College of Food, Agriculture, and Natural Resource Sciences
University of Minnesota

WILEY

John Wiley & Sons, Inc.

VP and Publisher	George Hoffman
Acquisition Editor	Lacey Vitetta
Project Editor	Jennifer Manias
Senior Editorial Assistant	Emily McGee
Assistant Marketing Manager	Diane Mars
Marketing Assistant	Laura Finley
Production Manager	Janis Soo
Assistant Production Editor	Elaine S. Chew
Media Editor	Greg Chaput
Cover Designer	Seng Ping Ngieng
Cover Image	© Duncan Walker, iStockphoto®

This book was set in 10/12.5 Palatino Roman by Thomson Digital, Noida, India and printed and bound by Hamilton Printing Company. The cover was printed by Hamilton Printing Company.

This book is printed on acid free paper. ⊗

Library of Congress Cataloging-in-Publication Data
Olson, Kent D.
  Economics of farm management in a global setting / Kent Olson.
      p. cm.
  Includes index.
  ISBN 978-0-470-59243-4 (hardback)
  1. Farm management. 2. Agriculture—Economic aspects. I. Title.
  S561.O477 2010
  630.68—dc22

                                    2010042186

Printed in the United States of America
10 9 8 7 6 5 4 3 2 1

Dedicated to Linda,
my wonderful wife of over 30 years!

Brief Contents

Contents

Preface

The world has changed, is changing, and will continue to change. The world is much closer to us, and we to the world. In the future, farmers will have to consider world events and world markets much more than they have in the past. This is true whether they are involved directly in international trade or marketing to local consumers. The world is here physically, technologically, and competitively. It is a global economy, a global marketplace.

I have written this new book because the global economy and marketplace are forcing farmers to understand the impact of world events on the strategies needed on their farms as well as to learn new management tools and methods to respond to the increased competition from across the road and around the world. Besides the basics of farm management, this book has new and expanded sections designed to help farmers understand the greater economic integration of countries and markets around the world and the management options they have to deal with internationalization.

This book covers the basics of management, budgeting, financial analysis, whole-farm planning, investment analysis, land ownership and leasing, risk management, and human resource management. Also included are expanded chapters on topics relatively new to farm management texts: strategic management, operations management, quality management, and production contract evaluation. As products and marketing become more individualized and local, the idea of the marketing mix from general business (that is, the "four Ps": product, price, place, promotion) has been added to the chapter on marketing basics. Since the size and financial complexity of farm businesses have grown, this book also includes a new chapter on farm succession and the development of written plans to transfer the farm business from one generation to the next. In addition, this book includes background material on lessons from microeconomics and macroeconomics and a survey of major agricultural policies in countries around the world.

I have written for managers, not record keepers or producers. Managers need to understand and use records and financial statements, but, in this competitive world, a manager who emphasizes record keeping over managing may not be in business long. Similarly, the person who just produces because he or she "knows what needs to be done," but does not manage the farm, will have trouble surviving in the future.

Throughout this text, I use the term "manager" to refer to whoever makes decisions, whether that person is an owner, operator, partner, female, male, family, hired management, staff, supervisor, and so on. In a multi-operator farm, the management team is the "manager." The decision can be small or large, frequent or infrequent.

How to Use This Text

I have a few suggestions on how this book can be used for teaching farm management. For on-campus, classroom teaching, the book can be used in a beginning class and also for an advanced class in farm management. It can also be used as the reference book for a project class centered on the development of a business plan for an actual farm. In an adult education setting, the book can be used as a general background with chapter emphasis changing as the topic changes for different classes.

For a semester-length, beginning farm management class, I would emphasize only parts of this text. For an introduction, I would start with Chapter 2 and the basic economic concepts in Chapter 4 and then introduce strategic management through Chapter 7. Then I would spend considerable time on financial analysis and management in Chapters 12, 13, and 14. (For a beginning course, I would leave out the calculation steps in estimating the cost of credit.) Another major section of the course would be composed of enterprise budgets, partial budgets, and whole-farm budgeting (Chapters 15, 16, and 17). Investment analysis (Chapter 20) and land ownership and use (Chapter 21) would be next. Risk management (Chapter 22) would take several class periods, because I teach the basic methods and then return to earlier topics and work through how risk analysis and management can be incorporated into those decisions. I would then end the course with discussions on human resource management (Chapter 24) and business organization (Chapter 25). At many points, I would refer students to background material for them to read on their own (such as micro- and macro-economics) or push them to explore advanced topics (such as strategy) but I would not be testing them on these chapters.

I would structure an advanced class around the development of a business plan (Chapter 3). The advanced class would review, presumably, and apply to farming the lessons from micro- and macro-economics (Chapters 4 and 5) in anticipation of using this knowledge in a longer discussion of strategic management (Chapters 7–10). The expanded "Four Ps" of marketing (product, price, place, promotion in Chapter 11) would be used to develop a better marketing section for the business plan. Some details of financial analysis and management, budgets, planning, investment analysis, and land ownership and use (Chapters 12–17 and 20–21) would be reviewed very briefly, and expanded if needed in an advanced class. Since these topics will be critical for many farms in the future, considerable time would be spent on the details of operations management, quality management, and production contract evaluation (Chapters 18, 19, and 23). All these topics would be used for a very comprehensive analysis and management of risk using the concepts and tools in Chapter 22. An advanced class would also spend more time on human resource management, business organization, and the need for and process of developing a farm transfer and succession plan (Chapters 24–27).

For an activity-based project course, this book could be used as the core reference for students developing a business plan for an actual farm. The course would start with a discussion of business plans and examples from farms and general businesses. Then the students would be expected to work through the sections of the business plan, reading from this book as needed, obtaining information from outside sources and the farm itself. The goal of the course would be the writing of a business plan. The course could include short lectures on the material in this book needed for each section of the plan, or the students could be expected to do their own reading.

In an adult education setting, the topic or issue of the meeting(s) could be centered on a certain topic or current problem or issue faced by a group of farmers. The instructor could then suggest chapters to review in preparation for understanding and solving the problem or issue considered that night. The level of detail and the amount of work expected by the adult students would be determined by the students and instructor and the time available.

Supplemental Materials

I encourage you to check my Web site for my farm management class. The Web site includes study notes for each lesson, virtual field trips to real farms, more examples, new analyses, both updated and background information, and other additions that enhance this text. You can access the Web site through my Web page: http://www.apec.umn.edu/faculty/kolson/.

For instructors, PowerPoint© slides with notes, instruction notes, answers and solutions for chapter review questions, and text question banks (with answers) are also available.

Acknowledgments

Many, many people have helped me learn and explore farm management. What I said in my first text is still true: I have not learned, developed, and written in isolation. I thank them all, but I can only remember the names of a few. Let me start with my late father, Norris Olson, who gave me my first lesson in farm management when I was still a preteen. As we stood by the feedlot on our family farm near Eagle Grove, Iowa, he described how the whole farm could be thought of as a set of individual businesses that needed to be planned both separately and as part of the whole farm. From that lesson, I went on to learn more about farm management from R.V. Diggins, my first agriculture teacher in high school, and Earl Heady, Ray Beneke, Sydney James, and Ron Winterboer at Iowa State University. At the University of California, Davis, and the University of Minnesota, I benefitted greatly from many discussions with all my colleagues, especially Hal Carter, Robert Craven, Vernon Eidman, Ben French, Lee Garoyan, Warren Johnston, Gordon King, Karen Klonsky, Dale Nordquist, Vernon Ruttan, and Erlin Weness. I also thank Alison Bunge and Frank Trnka for their help editing, checking, and building supplemental materials for the book. And I thank George Lobell for his encouragement and many ideas for writing and marketing this book.

I also thank the reviewers for this book and acknowledge their many suggestions for content and improvement. While they cannot be held accountable for the content and writing I have done, I did learn from their comments and the book is better for their input. They are:

Pierre Boumtje, Southern Arkansas University
Craig Dobbins, Purdue University
D. Lynn Forster, The Ohio State University
Bert Greenwalt, Ph.D., Arkansas State University
Nicole Klein, South Dakota State University
James Kliebenstein, Iowa State University
Wayne A. Knoblauch, Cornell University
Michael Popp, Arkansas State University
Jefferey Stokes, University of Northern Iowa

Many farmers have taught me about farm management, starting with our immediate neighbors near Eagle Grove, Iowa, and those I came to know through school, 4-H, FFA, and other contacts. To the farmers and producers throughout California, Minnesota, and across the country and the world, who put up with my questions and who peppered me with questions, I say, ''Thank you.'' These farmers pressed me for answers and pushed me to explore new problems, conditions, and tools for management. I always enjoy these questions even when delivered with emotion. They, in turn, patiently endured many questions from me about what they were thinking, how they were making decisions, and why they did what they did. They are too numerous to mention by name, and there are many whose names I never knew.

Over the years, my students have kept me alert and not allowed me to stop learning. Their questions, ideas, and energies are always great. I always enjoy my classes. Thank you.

To my family, Linda, Erik, and Marie, thank you for all the help, support, and love you have given me through the years and especially for your patience during the last few months of finalizing this text. Once again, Eddie, our dog, helped by always being by my side and insisting on play time.

Success comes in many designs and shapes. I hope the ideas, tools, and techniques in this book help you achieve your definition of success. I wish only the best for you.

Thanks for reading.

1

Managing the Farm in an Integrated World Economy

In this chapter:

- A changed and changing world
- Overview of this book

Farm management has always been and will always be a complicated and demanding task. The farm business is surrounded by uncertainties, demands, and changing conditions in a very competitive environment. Today's farm manager has greater pressures than in the past due to greater financial requirements, increasing integration of the global economy, greater exposure to product and input price fluctuations, the development of new products, structural adjustments in the general economy, an increasing world population with changing demographics, and greater instability in critical areas in the world. Even though today's farm work and life may seem familiar in many ways to farmers when they are working in the field or with livestock, farmers are more connected with the world economy than ever before. News from around the world can affect farmers almost immediately. And the news doesn't even have to be about agriculture! All these factors create opportunities and challenges for farmers. They make for the best and worst of times.

A Changed and Changing World

The world has not gotten smaller physically, but it has certainly become closer in terms of communication and ease of travel and transportation. Technology has brought the world to us, and we to the world. Our products can be shipped—quickly if needed—to virtually every point on the globe. New communication tools allow us to monitor markets around the world. We can connect instantly to current and potential customers in almost any corner of the globe.

This global connectivity comes with many advantages and disadvantages. Improvements in communication and greater efficiencies in moving both physical and financial assets have allowed lower costs to consumers and increased profits to those farms that have been able to adapt. However, the tighter connections have also created a downside. The ability to obtain product quickly (relative to previous years) even from other countries and the ability to deliver quickly has allowed businesses to decrease inventory levels and thus reduce inventory costs—a good thing at face value. However, these lower inventories for cost control also mean a smaller inventory to absorb fluctuations in supply due to weather problems and other interruptions in the supply chain. The inability to absorb fluctuations causes greater volatility in prices and supplies compared to eras when slower responses meant larger inventories.

Although a farmer may enjoy the benefits of the global market when delivering a higher quality, lower priced product to a new customer, the farmer can also feel the pain of that market when a competitor delivers a higher quality, better priced product to the farmer's current customer. Improved technology and communication can help everyone and does not respect current customer relationships. If farmers are not aware of what is happening elsewhere in the world, they may find that competitors in other countries are taking customers away—customers who may be just down the road from their farms. However, for the same reasons, farmers may be able to expand their markets by becoming more efficient than other suppliers.

We have also learned that a seemingly unrelated or small event in one part of the world can cause economic waves across the world. A short list of recent examples includes:

1. The financial crisis in 2008–09, caused in large part by rampant speculation and financing followed by failure in U.S. housing prices, led to
   a. financial limits placed on many businesses including farms, and
   b. the subsequent worldwide recession and decreased demand for agricultural products.
2. Government instability and warfare, causing disruption in and concern about energy supplies and thus a quick rise in energy costs.
3. Disease outbreaks, causing embargoes on imports when the disease is directly related to agriculture (foot and mouth disease, for example) and even when the disease is unrelated to agriculture (H1N1 flu, for example).

A business can face opportunities and threats due to events that occur in a different industry, region, or country. The uncertainty and instability caused by geo-political events occurring far away can cause great disruptions that can affect local farms adversely and at the same time can provide great opportunities.

The business climate of farming has changed considerably in recent years. The banking troubles of 2008–09 and the subsequent worldwide recession have changed many aspects of the economy even though agriculture has not felt the full brunt of those changes. Farmers have faced more requirements for obtaining credit but interest rates have been kept low (so far) by federal banks so as to not hurt the economy more and to encourage investment as businesses strive to recover. Other parts of the world economy have been hurt more, but agriculture has not been directly affected as deeply. However, income and wealth have decreased drastically, unemployment has risen to historically high levels, governments have become more integrated in the economy, businesses and banks have failed, and consumers have decreased consumption due to their uncertainty of the future—even if they could afford to keep spending.

These changes have also caused exchange rates between currencies to fluctuate. These shifts in exchange rates can greatly affect the price we receive for exports and have to pay for imports without fundamental changes in the underlying supply and demand conditions. For instance, a weak U.S. dollar means U.S. products are cheaper for a person in another country. However, a weak U.S.

dollar also means that imports such as fertilizers are more expensive for farmers in the United States. Similar stories can be told for other countries as their exchange rates fluctuate.

World trade in agricultural products continues to increase. Although growth in China, India, and other Southeast Asian countries has slowed due to the recession of 2008–09, growth of personal income in those countries has spurred their demand for grains and meat. Most of the increase in trade has been in the traditional distribution channels in which farmers sell their products locally and leave the logistics of global trade, distribution, and relationships to other businesses.

Other farmers have found opportunities in making global connections to market their products directly. These farmers face the challenges of trade regulations, GMO concerns, trade constraints due to disease (e.g., mad cow disease), and different cultural customs. However, many farmers have been successful and have learned new skills to take advantage of these opportunities.

At the same time, the interest in local food production and consumption is increasing as well. This appears to be close to but not directly connected to the interest in organic food. Even though the total demand is a small part of the whole food market, this interest in local and organic food has created an opportunity for many farmers to take advantage of new distribution channels that may include direct marketing to consumers and retailers.

Ethanol (from corn and sugar cane) and diesel from soybeans and other oil crops have created tremendous excitement and opportunity for many firms and farmers. But we have also seen how sensitive the biofuel market is to the oil market. What was a rapidly expanding industry quickly stopped as the price of oil (its chief substitute) fell, and credit for construction and operation disappeared when the financial troubles began in 2008–09. The biofuel industry has also had to deal with the debate over food versus fuel, since its main input is also used as food directly or as feed for livestock. This debate centers around the question of whether using grain and oilseeds for fuel is decreasing the supply of food by competing either directly or indirectly in terms of the use of land and other inputs—even if the land is in other regions of the same country or in other countries.

Climate change and other environmental concerns will have a major effect on farming in the future. These concerns include land degradation, water quality, open space, and odor issues, to name a few. The ethanol industry in particular has been faced with environmental concerns over the use of inputs for producing corn and the real and potential pollution those inputs cause. The public and environmental groups are asking for improved environmental quality and better production practices. The resulting political pressure may lead to regulations controlling what farmers can and cannot do. Farmers in environmentally-sensitive areas may have to change production practices, change the crops or livestock they grow, change location, or even stop production. Other areas of production may benefit from these changes in sensitive areas, and new products (such as eco-tourism) may benefit those who have to change.

Societal concerns such as animal welfare issues have and will change production practices in the future. European regulations already affect how animals are taken care of on the farm. In the United States, recent passage of an initiative dictates new regulations on how California producers can treat animals and run their livestock operations. However, greater pressure may come from processors and retailers as they respond to consumer pressure and seek suppliers who conform to certain practices regarding use of medications and hormones given to farm animals and the treatment of the animals.

Other changes are coming from suppliers and farmers themselves as they innovate and adopt technology to improve their productivity and efficiencies. Technology is being developed quickly. Our ability to harness the power of the computer and wireless communication in production is increasing rapidly. Those who do not adopt new productivity-enhancing technology may be left behind. Increased farm size is seen as essential to take full advantage of the new technologies and to avoid the cost of obsolescence by being able to replace machinery or other equipment as soon as new technological advances are introduced.

Changing demographics (that is, the change in the makeup of the people of a country and the world) can lead to tremendous changes in what is demanded from farmers. As the population ages in many countries, the type of food the population wants changes. Food consumed away from home increases and decreases directly as income and wealth increases and decreases. Different ethnicities have different choices in the food they eat. Food tastes of younger generations are different from those of older generations, so as younger people increase their buying power and become a larger percentage of a country's population, food demands will change.

With all these changes, the prudent farm manager in the future will have to have a strong external focus as well as maintain a strong internal focus on the farm. If we are not aware of what is happening beyond the farm and fail to adjust to those changes, the changes will come to our farm in ways we do not like.

Overview of the Book

The first section of this book is an introduction to farm management. This first chapter discusses managing the farm in an integrated world economy by looking at our changed and changing world, the farming environment, and the major opportunities and challenges that many farmers face. Chapter 2 is an overview of management that looks at goals; management activities; farmers as general managers; the management functions of planning, organizing, directing, and controlling; business functions; strategic versus operations management; human resource management; management skills inventory; and decision processes. Chapter 3 introduces the business plan, its basic outline, and an example business plan.

The second section of the book summarizes the basic lessons from economics and explains policy differences around the world that farmers should know so they can understand events and trends in the general economy and world and be better able to adapt quickly to changes. Chapter 4 covers lessons and points from microeconomics a farm manager needs to know in order to understand his or her business and the business decisions of others. Chapter 5 summarizes important lessons and points from macroeconomics that are key to understanding changes and trends in the national economy and the rest of the world. To help a farmer understand events and discussions in other countries, Chapter 6 is a summary of major types of policies and their impact on world farming and trade.

The third major section of the book covers strategic management and marketing. Chapter 7 introduces strategic management and then concentrates on strategic planning: identification of stakeholders; management values; and vision, mission, and objectives. Chapter 8 explains external analysis of the competitive environment, including Porter's five forces, and internal analysis of the farm's operating environment with an assessment of the farm's strengths, weaknesses, opportunities, and threats. Chapter 9 shows how strategy is crafted by starting with a description of generic strategies and continuing with complementary strategic actions, specific strategies for specific situations, tests for evaluating strategies, improving strategic planning, using scenarios in crafting strategy, and incorporating risk management into crafting strategy. Chapter 10 finishes strategic management with a discussion of strategy execution and control. It includes developing an organization, motivating people, allocating resources, strategic project plans and programs; the balanced score card; monitoring key indicators; corrective actions; and strategic product versus strategic process. Chapter 11 ends this section with a summary of marketing basics.

The fourth section covers financial analysis and management. Chapter 12 introduces and explains the main financial statements: balance sheet, income statement, statement of owner's equity, and statement of cash flows. It focuses on the format and structure of these statements as described by the Farm Financial Standards Council. Chapter 13 contains the core of financial analysis, including the major measures of financial position and performance for solvency, profitability, liquidity, repayment capacity, and financial efficiency. It also explains the processes for initial analysis, benchmarking, enterprise analysis, and diagnostic analysis. Chapter 14 is an introduction to financial management covering the time value of money, estimating the discount rate, sources and uses of capital, calculating loan payments, estimating the cost of credit, preparation of the cash flow budget, and financial control.

The fifth section introduces farm planning and quality management. This section starts with enterprise budgets in Chapter 15, including how they are developed from whole-farm records and from economic engineering and examples of crop and livestock enterprise budgets. Chapter 16 describes how partial budgets can be used to analyze changes in the plan and includes several examples. Chapter 17 describes whole-farm planning, including enterprise selection, development of the whole-farm budget, and projection of the cash flow budget and pro forma financial statements. Chapter 18 is a summary of lessons from operations management and includes process mapping; improving processes; and scheduling operations using sequencing and dispatching rules, project management, and input supply management. This section ends with Chapter 19 explaining quality management and control. The chapter starts with defining quality and includes product and process quality, the costs of quality, quality management, lessons from the quality gurus, total quality management (TQM), ISO 9000 standards, hazard analysis and critical control point (HACCP), developing process control systems, and tools for process improvement.

The sixth section covers capital asset management. It starts with Chapter 20 on investment analysis (or capital budgeting), which includes economic profitability versus financial feasibility, payback period, net present value (NPV), internal rate or return (IRR), and several examples of investment analyses. Chapter 21 covers land use and control, including ownership, leasing and renting alternatives, and some points and procedures for rent negotiation and determining a fair rent.

Section seven explains risk management. Chapter 22 explains the sources of risk and the basics of risk management: making risky decisions, payoff and regret matrices, decision trees, probability of success; and scenarios for risk management planning. The chapter includes an appendix on estimating probabilities. The concept of risk management is expanded in Chapter 23 by looking at production contract evaluation, including the types of production contracts, a process for evaluating production contracts, and a production contract evaluation checklist. An example contract is included at the end of the chapter.

The last major section of the book covers human resources, business organization, and succession planning. Chapter 24 introduces human resource management, starting with a discussion of human and employee needs as well as future labor force diversity and then describing the basic steps of human resource management: assessment of needs, job descriptions, matching employees to jobs, recruiting, interviewing, hiring, training, motivating, leading, directing, evaluating performance, and compensating (cash wages, benefits, incentives). The chapter ends with some ideas for improving communication for family and non-family management and employees and improving labor efficiency. Chapter 25 introduces business organization, including the business organization chart, board of advisors, legal business structures (sole proprietorship, partnership, general and limited partners, limited liability partnership, subchapter-C corporation, subchapter-S corporation, limited liability company, joint ventures, cooperatives) and some legal and tax implications. Chapter 26 introduces the concepts and basic tools for succession planning on farms, starting with a discussion of the farm business life cycle (entry, growth, and exit) and some ways to start farming, and then looks at the process of farm succession: transferring between generations, farming together or separately, multi-person operations, and communications among stakeholders.

The book ends with a look at some possible views of farming in the future in Chapter 27. The chapter discusses specialization, moving up and down the supply chain, contracting and vertical integration, redesigning the production system, and the need for broader management skills.

Summary

- Farm management is a complicated and demanding task.
- Farmers are increasingly connected to the global economy through technology, communications, and markets.
- Global connections can provide both opportunities and threats.
- The interest in local food production and consumption is increasing at the same time as international trade is increasing.
- Higher oil prices have created opportunities in biofuel production.
- Climate change, environmental concerns, and societal concerns are affecting farming now and into the future.
- The successful farm manager in the future will have to have a strong external focus as well as maintain a strong internal focus.

Review Questions

1. Compared to ten years ago, how has farming changed?
2. How has the producer of a commodity (such as wheat, beef, maize, and so on) been affected by an increasingly global market?
3. How have the opportunities presented by local markets affected farming?
4. Would you describe the changes you identified in the first three questions as positive or negative? Why?
5. Identify some ways you see farming coming closer to and being affected by the world economy in the future.
6. Describe some examples of threats and opportunities a farm may face due to increasing global connectivity.
7. Is society's concern over how farmers treat the environment and animals a threat or an opportunity? Why?
8. Describe some trends and changes that will affect farming aside from those mentioned in the text.

2

Management

In this chapter:

- Management activities
- The economic environment of the farm
- Management functions; business functions
- Farmers as general managers, not plant managers
- Management skills
- The decision process

What does a manager do? Managers do and are responsible for many things. Ultimately, they are responsible for making sure the business or organization accomplishes what it is supposed to accomplish. Most likely, they need to work with and through other people to achieve the desired results.

A business manager's job can be defined as the art and science that combines ideas, methods, and resources to produce and market a product profitably. This view limits the goal of the business to making a profit, but other goals are just as legitimate. Other goals are maximizing wealth, avoiding debt, reducing labor requirements, having family time, improving the natural environment, contributing to the community, and many more. To include these and other goals, a manager's job can be described as the allocation, direction, and control of limited resources to achieve the goals of the firm efficiently. This definition also recognizes that money, land, labor, and other resources are always limiting.

In this general view, farmers are no different from any other managers, so let us call them farm managers. They have a complicated job in a complicated world. The *Encyclopedia Britannica* first defines farm management as "making and implementing the decisions involved in organization and operating a farm for maximum production and profit." Later in the same article, the encyclopedia broadens the goals of profit and production by saying that "farmers manage the resources under their control and in ways to obtain as much satisfaction as possible from their decisions and actions." The second definition is a better fit for what farm managers and their families strive to do in today's environment.

These definitions may help us understand management, but a list of a manager's activities and duties provides a glimpse of the width and depth of management (Table 2.1). A farm manager needs to integrate information from the biological, physical, and social sciences. A farm manager needs to acquire, direct, and control resources. These include financial, physical,

Table 2.1   What Does a Manager Do?

Definitions provide an idea of what management is, but do they provide a good description of what managers do? Not really. Managers do many things; they are responsible for everything. Being a manager is no small task. A sample of what managers do is listed below.

- Set goals and objectives
- Seek, sort, compile, integrate, and use information from many sources
- Consider and analyze alternative courses of action
- Forecast the future
- Anticipate change
- Make decisions
- Carry out decisions
- Take action
- Acquire resources
- Organize the use of resources
- Communicate with creditors, employees, government agencies, etc.
- Train themselves, family members, and employees
- Buy and sell inputs and products
- Establish the timing of operations
- Monitor operations
- Recognize and identify problems and opportunities
- Respond and act when problems occur
- Mediate fights
- Evaluate results of decisions and actions
- Monitor financial conditions
- Monitor progress toward goals and objectives
- Accept responsibility
- Check on everything

Adapted from R. A. Milligan, and B. F. Stanton, "What Do Farm Managers Do?" *1989 Yearbook of Agriculture: Farm Management.* United States Department of Agriculture, p. 3.

and human resources. Depending on the type of farm, a farm manager must understand many kinds of knowledge, including soil structure, soil microbiology, livestock genetics, crop and animal nutrition and growth, weed and insect management, plant and animal diseases, ecology, machinery management, economics, financial management, international food markets, leadership, human psychology, business organization, business law, communication, strategic and operations management, and much more.

Many people and businesses have more than one goal that they strive to maximize or, at least satisfy. For farmers, multiple goals are due in part to the fact that farming is often both a production and consumption activity—life and work are closely intertwined. Some goals can be achieved together; some may conflict with one another. Goals can also be nested within other goals. For instance, a person may want to maximize income within the limits of time for family and protecting the environment. Goals may also be expressed as satisfaction, not maximization. People may choose alternatives to satisfy income needs and maximize net worth, for example. Many people balance their income goals with their environmental concerns, community and family activities, and their ethics and morals in all their decisions. Others may strive to never violate certain basic ethical

Table 2.2 Professional Farm Management

The goal of many farm managers is to manage their own farm, but this is not the only career possible in farm management. Many professional farm managers manage farms for land owners who choose to not be involved in the farm directly. The land owner may live far from the land, may lack the knowledge and technical skill about agriculture, may be retired, or may have another job and view the land as an investment. Many banks, investors, churches, colleges, charities, and other institutions employ professional farm managers. These professional farm managers represent their clients in the management of the firm. Depending on the needs of their clients, the professional farm manager may take care of all aspects of farm management or selected parts. Besides the tasks listed in Table 2.1, professional farm managers do many other tasks, including but not limited to the following:

- Select the most capable farm operator available
- Estimate the benefits and costs of alternative leases
- Negotiate lease terms
- Visit the farm to ensure good management is being practiced
- Consult with and make recommendations to the operator and owner
- Oversee construction of buildings and land improvements
- Supervise product marketing and, if necessary, input purchases
- Pay all authorized expenses
- Check on and apply for insurance and government programs
- Prepare reports on production progress and results, financial statements, asset conditions, and other topics for the owner
- Project budgets for the next year
- Provide information and help in income, estate, and tax planning

Depending on the situation and their qualifications, professional farm managers may offer other services such as real estate appraisals, custom farming, consulting, and real estate sales and purchases.

Professional farm managers may work independently or be part of a small, local office or even part of a regional or national farm management company.

principles, but then balance their goals by making a personal tradeoff between, say, income, family, and community time. Of course, the different weights or importance put on the different goals and thus the tradeoffs are the source of many conflicts within families and management teams. So conflict resolution skills are also needed by a farm manager.

Because the required knowledge and skills are so varied, consultants and advisors are available so a manager does not need to be an expert in all these fields. In fact, a person does not need to own land to be a farm manager; many land owners hire professional farm managers to manage their farms (Table 2.2). This text is an introduction to the skills needed to bring all this knowledge to bear on the management of one farm business.

The Farming Environment

A farm does not operate in isolation. A farmer has to consider many factors outside of the physical farm itself. We will look at this more closely as we develop process maps in Chapter 16, but for now we can think of this larger arena for the farm as its environment. This environment can be described

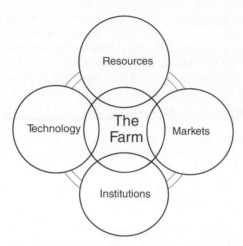

Figure 2.1　The Economic Environment of the Farm

as having four main components: resources, markets, institutions, and technology (Figure 2.1). Let's look at each of these components in more detail.

Resources.　A farm's available resources define the farm. Resources include the usual list of land, labor, capital (such as machinery, buildings, livestock, and supplies) and management skills as well as credit available and the farm's climate and weather. Information sources are also part of the farm's resources, and include magazines, newsletters, marketing clubs, consultants, management services, extension staff and other advisors, and the World Wide Web. A farmer's own entrepreneurial ability is a critical resource. Perhaps the first resource or asset that should be listed is the manager and his or her skills and knowledge.

Markets.　The markets are where products and inputs are bought and sold, and where prices are discovered. Although agricultural markets are regulated to some extent depending on the commodity, prices are not set and known. Prices are discovered through producers, processors, consumers, buyers and sellers talking together, sharing information, and settling on the price for that moment and place. Together these players determine the proximity, size, and price level of the market. Competition from neighbors, other countries, other food sources, and other products competing for the consumers' money can affect farmers' profit margins and thus managerial choices.

Institutions.　Many institutions affect a farmer's choices. The federal government is often seen as the biggest institution affecting farmers. However, institutions also include state and local government policies and regulations, credit policies, land use regulations, and contractual obligations. Environmental regulations are institutional constraints. Banks and other credit institutions have a large impact on how farms are managed and the options they have. Even social institutions, such as the community groups and churches farmers belong to and the coffee shop they go to, affect the alternatives considered and ultimately chosen.

Technology.　Technology is more than machines—it includes physical, mechanical, and biological processes and techniques as well as the information and management knowledge required to use those processes and techniques. Engineers, plant breeders, soil scientists, animal scientists, geneticists, plant pathologists, system analysts, economists, management scientists, and many other scientists give us technology. Past, current, and future technology choices affect the productivity and, thus, the viability of the farm.

A farm manager has to be concerned with and aware of the entire environment. At times, one area may be emphasized—say, technology at the time of a building program—but over time a balance is needed. The manager cannot be looking at one component (say, the market) almost exclusively and ignore other components. Changes can happen that create challenges and opportunities. If these changes are missed, the problems may become larger or the missed opportunities prove costly in terms of what is not gained.

The Functions of Management

Management can also be understood through four major functions:

- Planning
- Organizing
- Directing
- Controlling

These are separate yet intertwined functions. In any well-managed business, these four functions are occurring simultaneously with some variation over time in the attention paid to each function. When the business is in full swing, organizing and directing can dominate a manager's time and attention. However, planning and controlling can be just as critical to the success of the business as day-to-day operations are.

Planning

Planning is the determination of the intended strategy and course of action (that is, the plan) for the business. The basic process of planning generally involves the following steps:

1. Appraising the goals and objectives of the business owners and operators
2. Assessing the industry in which the farm will operate
3. Preparing an inventory of the farm resources available and analyzing the farm's situation within the industry
4. Selecting alternatives to be analyzed
5. Determining physical inputs and probable production for each alternative
6. Selecting prices to apply to the input and production data
7. Calculating expected costs and returns for each alternative
8. Estimating the potential range of costs and returns due to variability of prices, costs, and yields
9. Analyzing the probable results of the alternatives
10. Developing an operating plan based on probable results and the goals and objectives of the business manager and/or owner

Part of planning also is the establishment of control standards—the benchmarks by which the manager wants to evaluate how well the plan is being carried out. Another part of planning is the response to past results—that is, feedback control. Because of feedback, plans may need to be modified since prior results have not been at the desired level.

Tools of the planning process include budgets, economic analysis tools, and information on the physical needs and responses of plants and animals. Larger farms, more complex farms, and more people will increase the need to use these tools formally with written results.

Budgets report the quantified estimates of expected results due to carrying out a specific plan or set of actions. Four main types of budgets are listed below.

- Enterprise budgets: expected costs and returns for specific enterprises
- Whole farm budgets: expected costs and returns for a specific combination of enterprises
- Cash flow budgets: a projection of cash transfers into and out of the business listed by specific period
- Partial budgets: a listing of only those costs and returns expected to change due to a proposed change in the business

Economic analysis tools help a manager understand trends and issues in the general economy, as well as estimate the financial impact of alternative choices. These tools include microeconomic and macroeconomic principles, investment analysis and other financial tools, price forecasting, operations scheduling, risk management, and other techniques explained in this text.

Obviously, the result of planning is a plan. Plans will vary depending on the length of planning horizon, problem, or part of the business involved. Usually, a plan will include some general policies, procedures, or strategies to be carried out, and specific methods to be followed. Effective plans have several common elements:

1. They are based on attainable goals and objectives.
2. They reflect the manager's knowledge, skills, and interests.
3. They consider the quantity and quality of land, labor, and capital resources available to the manager.
4. They consider information about comparable operations and the past performance of the ranch or farm, but they are unique to a specific farm or ranch rather than being copies of other operations or models.
5. They are based on expectations for the future, not mere repetition of past practices.
6. They include short-, intermediate-, and long-term components.
7. They include strategies for managing production, marketing, finances, and personnel.
8. They provide methods for monitoring and evaluating situations and results (that is, the "control" function of management).
9. They are kept current, and are designed so they can be modified when objectives, resources, knowledge, expectations, or conditions change.

Policy and procedure statements are also the result of planning. These statements are guidelines to operational or short-run decision making. They provide established routine and thus operational efficiency for a business. Policy and procedure statements communicate decisions between individuals and through time. Although they need to be reevaluated as conditions and knowledge change, policy and procedure statements help avoid "reinventing the wheel" each time a decision is faced. The chosen feeding program on a livestock farm is an example of a policy and procedure statement. By deciding beforehand how and what to feed animals at different weights and stages, the daily feeding routine is quicker and more efficient than evaluating prices and nutritional needs every day. Whether these policy and procedure statements are formally written or informally discussed depends on the size and complexity of the business.

Organizing

Organizing involves the acquisition and organization of the necessary land, labor, machinery, livestock, capital, and management resources. It includes the negotiation of the terms necessary for resource acquisition. Organizing involves deciding who is responsible for what in the business and who reports to whom—that is, the organization chart. Organizing includes recruiting, hiring, and training employees as well as the management team. Organizing involves finding the right person to do the work that needs to be done and deciding whether that means using a current employee, hiring a new employee, or hiring a consultant or other resource for a specific job. Organizing also involves choosing whether the business will be a sole proprietorship, partnership, corporation, or other legal form.

Directing

Directing the chosen plan involves the coordination of the land, labor, machinery, livestock, capital, and management resources. It involves directing of physical activities; scheduling production and marketing; and motivating and directing labor resources. An effective director uses leadership, supervision, delegation, communication, motivation, and personnel development as primary management tools.

Controlling

Controlling the farm's performance consists of two parts: (1) evaluating the results of implementing the chosen plan by comparing them to the farm's initial goals and objectives and (2) taking corrective actions, if needed. Evaluation is usually done with budgets, records, and financial statements. ''Keeping the books,'' although important, is only part of control management. Many farmers are interested in ''keeping the books'' only as a ''scorecard,'' to find out how much money they made or because they are required to file income tax forms; they realize it is too late to influence the results, so ''keeping the books'' is, for most, a boring activity. Thus an important part of control management is the development of alternative measures or clues that can predict good or poor results while it is still possible to change, alter, or correct plans.

Once evaluation has pointed out problem areas, the manager needs to determine possible causes for these problems. Causes may be improper planning or implementation, improper setting of norms and standards, or changes in external forces, such as the economy, weather, or government policy. Finally, the manager must decide what actions are necessary to regain control of the situation. Even if the problems are not correctable or external and permanent, the manager must also decide what actions are necessary to regain control. A control plan will have the corrective actions specified for situations in which the measured variable falls outside the ''in-control'' range.

The control function completes a circle that began with planning. A farm manager may deal with all four functions on any given day if the business is small. On large farms, these functions may be divided between partners and/or employees. In either case, communication is needed between the functions for the farm to meet goals as effectively as possible.

Business Functions

The management functions just described should not be confused with business functions. Business functions include production, marketing, finance, human resource management, and so on, which are found in different parts of the business. Management functions are not isolated in different parts of the business but are carried out in each of the business functions. Crop production, for example, needs planning to decide which crops to grow, organizing to gather the inputs, directing to produce and market the crop, and controlling to decide whether an insecticide application is needed. In the same manner, financial management needs planning to decide how much credit is needed, organizing to obtain credit, directing to use the credit when needed, and controlling to check that the correct credit terms have been used.

Farmers as General Managers, Not Plant Managers

In general business terms, a farm manager needs to be a general manager—that is, a manager who is responsible for all management functions and all business functions even though the manager may not personally do all of them. A plant manager is responsible for operating the factory to meet the goals set by upper management, but the plant manager does not participate extensively in marketing, finance, strategy, and other functions. Just as technology, markets, and institutions have changed over time, the management requirements for the farm have changed and in the future will require a general manager, not a plant manager. In addition to the technical skills of the plant manager for producing crop and livestock products, the top farmer also needs skills in finance, marketing, human resource management, external relations, and other functions. The farmer may hire people with these skills, but the farmer needs to understand them as well.

The general manager sees the business as a whole, whereas the plant manager has a very defined set of tasks within the business. The differences between plant and general managers can also be seen in the issues that each works on within each of the four management functions (Table 2.3).

A general manager spends a significant amount of time and energy on strategic management, as well as on plant management. As explained in Chapters 7–10, strategic management involves looking at the bigger picture of the general economy and the farm's resources and capabilities and then choosing the best strategy for success in achieving the goals of the stakeholders in the long term. Plant management involves implementing the chosen strategy on a year-to-year, season-to-season, and day-to-day basis to achieve the goals of the stakeholders. These tasks are covered in several chapters.

The general manager needs to be responsible for human resource management on the farm. The importance of managing people cannot be understated for successful management, whether the farm is a one-person, sole-owner farm with no employees or a multi-person partnership or corporation with one or more employees. The need for human resource management skills is obvious on farms with multiple operators and employees, but these skills are also needed by the one-person farm owner who hires a custom operator for some tasks and also, just as important, for interaction with other suppliers and buyers to ensure efficient coordination of activities. The details of human resource management are covered in Chapter 22.

Table 2.3 Example Issues for Plant and General Managers

Management Function	Plant Manager	General Manager
Planning	• Developing improved production methods • Identifying tasks to be completed during the day	• Determining which products to produce • Developing a marketing strategy for products • Developing a strategy for farm growth • Selecting capital investments
Organizing	• Ensuring that input supplies are available when needed • Developing a machinery maintenance program	• Selecting production technologies that will be used • Developing a joint venture to lower the cost of acquiring inputs • Hiring the needed employees
Directing	• Developing training programs for new employees • Developing programs for motivating employees • Making day-to-day work assignments	• Developing and communicating a common vision for the business • Developing the employee • Developing human resource management practices
Controlling	• Ensuring that expenditures stay within budget • Ensuring that quality standards are being met • Monitoring various stages of production to be sure that production is proceeding within accepted tolerance levels	• Establishing the operating budget • Determining the critical items that need to be monitored from the perspective of the whole business • Monitoring the activities of competitors

Source: Dobbins, Boehlje, and Miller, 2000.

Management Skills

What skills will be needed for managing a farm successfully in the future? Based on his personal observation of executives, the well-respected management expert Peter Drucker (1967) concluded that effective executives differ in their personalities, strengths, weaknesses, values, and beliefs but share the ability to get the right things done. These "right things" include utilizing time efficiently, focusing on contribution to the goal, making strengths productive, doing first things first, and making effective, rational decisions. A much more recent study found very similar results. In their study of CEOs in general businesses, Kaplan, Klebanov, and Sorensen (2008) found that success and performance were more strongly correlated with execution-related skills than with interpersonal and team-related skills. Although team building and relationships are important to getting things done, the focus on execution and completion of the goals and objectives were more critical. Kaplan and colleagues noted that their findings were consistent with Bolton et al. (2008), who they quoted as saying that more "resolute, steadfast CEOs who stick to their guns tend to be better leaders than 'good listeners'." All these studies point to the need to focus on executing and getting things done. Other skills are needed, but if execution is lacking, so is success.

A more specific look at skills for managing a farm is provided by Wilson and Knorr (2008) and Boehlje, Dobbins, and Miller (2001). The broad set of skills needed by farm managers also can be seen in the list of ideas adapted from Wilson and Knorr's "20 Secrets of the Best Managed Farms" (Table 2.4).

Table 2.4   20 Secrets of the Best Managed Farms

1. Draw up a marketing plan—don't rely on the crystal ball, make a plan.
2. Sell ahead—sell some product before harvest.
3. Build storage—storage gives you marketing flexibility.
4. Sell more than your physical product—"Give the customer what he wants, when he wants it, and how he wants it, and they'll throw money at you."
5. Track results—sell the crop to your marketing profit center at harvest time and keep records on how well your marketing skills produce a better price.
6. Know your break-even costs—know when setting a price sets a profit or loss.
7. Switch to managerial accounting—obtain much more and better information than traditional cash-based accounting.
8. Make employee meetings pay off—use written agendas, check the "to do" list from the last meeting, and make a new one.
9. Think like a CEO—agriculture is a business, and every business needs a CEO to think about the big issues.
10. Hire the right people—great people make the difference between good and great results.
11. Buy inputs and store on-farm—storage capacity allows you to take advantage of pricing opportunities for inputs like you would with product storage.
12. Make one fuel fit all—shorten the list of inputs needed, start with using one kind of fuel in all vehicles on the farm, search for more ways to decrease the number of inputs purchased.
13. Rethink nitrogen rates—always look for ways to improve efficiency, and seek new information such as the new recommendations for nitrogen fertilizer.
14. Find equipment efficiencies—look for equipment that will be more efficient in labor hours and in fuel usage.
15. Upgrade to a laptop—desktop computers are perhaps cheaper but they aren't portable, they can't be taken to meetings so the manager can keep up with news and do additional analysis.
16. Adapt auto steer technology—look for new technology that lowers input costs, increases productivity, and reduces labor costs.
17. Manage your operating loan wisely—use the operating loan for operating expenses as designed, and obtain credit for other capital purchases.
18. Divide and conquer—divide your business into profit centers and cost centers, compare costs of internal operations with available external operators that could be hired for trucking, harvest, and so on.
19. Get expert financial help—an outside expert brings additional knowledge plus a third-person view without emotional ties to the business.
20. Well bought is half sold—market effectively at both the purchase and sale end of the livestock feeding.

Source: Wilson and Knorr, 2008.

In their excellent discussion of management skills, Boehlje, Dobbins, and Miller identified eight management areas and indicators of strong management skills for each managerial function (Table 2.5). They have also included self-assessment tools to help managers determine how well they are equipped for management in the future and where they need more training or to hire managerial help to cover a specific area. Evaluating the management skills of the manager or management team will help determine whether more training is needed and in what areas. It can also help evaluate the need to hire another person with the needed management skills. Anyone who needs to increase their skill level in any area can read the specific chapter in this book, read the references at the end of each chapter, or check for classes with their local extension office, university, and school.

Table 2.5 Farm Business Management Skills (and Their Indicators) for the 21st Century

1. Production management skills:
   - Completing operations in a timely manner
   - Choosing the technology best-suited for a particular situation, not just the newest or most popular technology
   - Consistently realizing efficiencies that are better than those achieved by others
   - Consistently achieving a volume of business per person that is above that achieved by others
   - Consistently achieving a volume of business per dollar invested that is greater than that achieved by others
   - Organizing production processes so that work flows smoothly
2. Procurement and selling skills:
   - Developing written purchase and sale plans
   - Buying with a purchasing agent mentality—understanding the value of features and services provided in addition to the product
   - Selling with a marketing agent mentality—understanding how to provide value to a customer in excess of product value
   - Consistently receiving product prices that are higher than others without taking increased risks
   - Consistently taking advantage of opportunities to transfer price risk for a fair cost
   - Understanding the merchandising environment for your product
3. Financial management skills:
   - Having profitability, liquidity, solvency, and financial efficiency ratios that are stronger than those of your competitors
   - Negotiating competitive interest rates, repayment terms, and collateral requirements
   - Having positive business relationships with lenders
   - Managing the business tax burden for maximum long-term benefits
   - Properly insuring life, health, and property
   - Maintaining a proper level of liability insurance
   - Preparing a multi-year plan for capital expenditures
   - Maintaining effective financial accounting and control systems
   - Making efficient use of working capital
   - Selecting the most profitable alternative for utilizing equity capital
   - Estimating the rate of return on capital investments
4. Human resource management skills:
   - Knowing how to listen effectively
   - Giving clear directions
   - Delegating appropriate authority and responsibility
   - Motivating employees to high performance
   - Providing a work environment that results in low employee turnover
   - Preparing job descriptions and performance evaluations
   - Managing the workforce to obtain high levels of labor productivity
   - Matching employee skills to job requirements
   - Providing employee training and advancement opportunities
   - Providing safe working conditions
   - Providing competitive compensation and benefits
5. Strategic management skills:
   - Being open to new ideas
   - Being able to develop a clear vision of what the business will become
   - Continually looking for ways to improve the overall performance of the business
   - Focusing on opportunities
   - Identifying the strengths and weaknesses of the farm business
   - Maintaining a long-term perspective
   - Identifying ways to take advantage of emerging markets
   - Analyzing the strategies of competitors
   - Developing a method for obtaining business advice from professionals outside the business

(continued)

Table 2.5   *(continued)*

6. Relationship skills:
   - Developing personal relationships
   - Quickly resolving conflicts that arise
   - Developing win/win solutions to problems
   - Quickly and accurately assessing individual strengths and weaknesses
   - Motivating people
   - Clearly communicating ideas to other people
   - Practicing active listening
7. Leadership skills:
   - Providing a clear sense of direction for the business
   - Continuing to learn about management
   - Serving as an officer of volunteer organizations
   - Helping motivate others to improve their skills
   - Continually looking for new ideas that will improve the business and the people associated with the business
   - Striving to build strong relationships with employees and business associates
   - Monitoring progress of strategy implementation
8. Risk management skills:
   - Establishing appropriate levels of liability, life, and health insurance
   - Developing contingency plans
   - Collecting information about important trends in the world economy
   - Understanding the size of the financial, human, and legal risks that the business faces
   - Developing backup management that could replace the principal manager in the case of an emergency

Source: Boehlje, Dobbins, and Miller, 2001.

The Decision Process

A standard section in most farm management texts over the past five decades is a list of five to eight decision-making steps (Table 2.6). Since these steps are seen visually as a linear list both here and in the original texts, they are often thought of as a linear set of steps that one follows in a definite sequence from beginning to end. However, these steps are not always followed in a straight, sequential process. The decision-making process has also been described as a ''groping, cyclical process.'' A decision process usually has many loops and feedback steps as new information is obtained and consequences are estimated and considered.

Based on interviews with farmers, this traditional model of **decision making** was revised (Öhlmér, Olson, and Brehmer, 1998). Instead of being described as a set of eight functions, the decision process is

Table 2.6   A ''Too Linear'' Model of Decision Making

1. Determination of values and setting of goals
2. Problem detection
3. Problem definition
4. Observation
5. Analysis
6. Development of intention
7. Implementation
8. Responsibility bearing

Table 2.7   A Revised Conceptual Model of the Decision-Making Process

Phase	Subprocess			
	Searching and Paying Attention	Planning	Evaluating and Choosing	Bearing Responsibility
Problem Detection	Information scanning Paying attention		Consequence evaluation Problem?	Checking the choice
Problem Definition	Information search Finding options		Consequence evaluation Choice of options to study	Checking the choice
Analysis and Choice	Information search	Planning	Consequence evaluation Choice of option	Checking the choice
Implementation	Information search Clues to outcomes		Consequence evaluation, Choice of corrective action(s)	Bearing responsibility for final outcome Feed forward information

Source: B. Öhlmér, K. Olson, and B. Brehmer, 1998.

described as a combination of four phases and four subprocesses. The phases are problem detection; problem definition; analysis and choice; and implementation. The four subprocesses are information search and paying attention; planning; estimating consequences, evaluation, and choice; and bearing responsibility. This revised model is best viewed as a matrix, not as a list of functions (Table 2.7). A list of functions implies a linear movement; a matrix better reflects the nonlinear process of making decisions.

In this revised model, some functions in the traditional model are changed. A farmer's values and goals are not listed in the matrix but should be understood to be developed before any decision process is started. Observation is included in the subprocess of searching for information and paying attention and is, thus, part of every phase of the revised model. A farmer does not separate observation from problem detection, for example. Searching for information and paying attention is a critical part of detecting problems; observation is not done only after a problem is detected. Development of intention to implement is not a phase by itself; instead, it is part of the subprocess of bearing responsibility and checking the choice. Bearing responsibility is also seen in all phases; it is not something done only after the decisions are made and implemented. A farmer knows that he or she is responsible for meeting values and goals; this concern is what starts the process. Bearing responsibility is the driving force behind searching for problems and opportunities; defining the problem and solution alternatives; analyzing and choosing the best alternative; and implementing the decision.

Besides revising the traditional model, these researchers saw five characteristics in farmers' decision making. First, farmers continually update their problem perceptions, ideas of options, plans, and expectations when new information is obtained. Second, farmers often use a qualitative approach to forming expectations and estimating consequences expressed in directions from the current condition. Third, in many situations, farmers prefer a "quick and simple" decision approach over a detailed, elaborate approach. Fourth, farmers prefer to collect information and avoid risk through small tests and incremental implementation. Fifth, during implementation, farmers continually check clues to form their evaluation of long-run actions in a feed forward and compensation approach, rather than a post-implementation evaluation.

Table 2.8   Three Kinds of Problems: Analysis, Management, and Design

System Component	Problem Type		
	Analysis	Management	Design
Inputs	given	unknown	given
Outputs	unknown	given	given
Structure	given	given	unknown

Another approach to decision making is to define the problem (or opportunity) as an analysis problem, a management problem, or a design problem (Table 2.8). These three types of problems are defined based on what is not known. Three components (inputs, outputs, and structure) are used to view a farm as a system. Inputs are land, labor, fertilizer, new equipment, animals, money, and so on. Outputs are the products: corn, milk, calves, vegetables, custom work, and so on. The structure is the people, processes, rules, current equipment, and so on that interact to create the outputs from the inputs.

Knowing what type of problem is being faced can help focus a manager's attention and resources on what needs to be done. In **analysis problems**, the task is to predict output based on given inputs and structure. Examples of analysis problems are the common "what-if" questions, building budgets, and forecasting prices and yields. In **management problems**, the task is to identify a feasible set of controllable inputs that will produce the desired output given the structure. Examples of management problems are annual plans, production schedules, and marketing plans. In **design problems**, the task is to choose a structure that will produce the desired output from the available inputs. Examples of design problems are facility and building designs, incentive pay systems, and organizational design.

Also, with so many duties and activities plus all the other potential things to do, how can a manager decide what to do at a particular point in time? Part of the answer to this question is addressed in the section on dispatching rules in Chapter 16, Operations Management. However, the manager can also use a simple sorting process that classifies what is important versus not important and then again what is urgent versus not urgent, as shown in Table 2.9. When asked what he thought was the

Table 2.9   Examples of Classifying Activities as Important versus Not Important and Urgent versus Not Urgent

	Urgent	Not Urgent
Important	**I**	**II**
	Crises	Planning
	Meetings	Communication
	Repairs	Relationships
	Deadlines	Organization
	Daily activities	Quality
		Evaluation
		Process improvement
Not important	**III**	**IV**
	Interruptions	Junk mail
	Mail	Busy work
	Reports	Coffee breaks
		Trivia and escape activity

one lesson he had learned from his study of history, the historian Arthur Toynbee responded, "The urgent is the enemy of the important." Farm managers (and all of us) can take that lesson to heart and decide what is really important and make the—perhaps hard—decision to forgo the urgent when something else is more important but not clamoring as noisily for attention. This is not to belittle the importance of dealing with crises, but many of the important but not urgent activities will have a much larger payoff in the long run. Thus, most of a manager's time should be spent in quadrant II as shown in the figure. Time in quadrants III and, especially, IV should be minimized.

The main point to learn from this discussion of the decision process is that there is not one, linear process that has to be followed. Early steps in the choice of alternatives likely involve simple analysis, while later steps will need more detailed analysis. The need for execution, as noted in the previous section, and Toynbee's comment about urgent versus important reminds the manager to continually classify and then prioritize those activities and decisions that are important and not urgent.

Summary

- Farm management is the allocation, direction, and control of limited resources to achieve the goals of the farm and farm family.
- People have many goals that may conflict with each other, so tradeoffs may need to be made between goals.
- The economic environment of the farm includes resources, markets, institutions, and technology.
- The four major functions of management are planning, organizing, directing, and controlling. These management functions are not the same as the business functions of production, marketing, financing, personnel management, and so on.
- Planning is the determination of the intended strategy and course of action.
- Organizing is the acquisition and organization of the necessary land, labor, machinery, livestock, capital, and management resources.
- Directing is the coordination of those resources (including motivation of people) to produce the chosen products.
- Controlling consists of comparing actual results to expected results and taking corrective actions when needed.
- Farmers are general managers, not plant managers.
- Peter Drucker, a famous management expert, recognized that all effective executives have the ability to get the right things done, including utilizing time efficiently, focusing on contribution to the goal, making strengths productive, doing first things first, and making effective, rational decisions.
- The quality of management skills can be evaluated by several indicators to determine the need for more training or hiring to meet the needs identified.
- Making decisions is not a linear process. It involves many iterative steps and feedback loops to earlier steps.
- Four phases of the decision process are problem detection, problem definition, analysis and choice, and implementation.
- Four subprocesses of decision making are information search and paying attention; planning; estimating consequences, evaluation, and choice; and bearing responsibility.

- There are three types of problems: analysis, management, and design.
- Classifying tasks by urgent versus not urgent and by important versus not important helps a manager decide which tasks should be given high priority.

Review Questions

1. What do you think are the most important things farm managers do? Use the list in Figure 2.1 and develop your own ideas.
2. Describe farm management in your own words.
3. Is profit maximization the only goal of farmers? If it isn't the only goal, what are five other, common goals that farmers may have?
4. Do a person's goals change over time? Why can two generations have different goals?
5. Describe and contrast the four functions of management: planning, organizing, directing, and controlling.
6. How would you describe an effective farm manager? How would you know whether a manager was effective?
7. How would you describe the decision-making process?
8. One psychologist developed a theory of decision making called the "garbage can theory" because problems and solutions seemed to meet by chance. How does that description fit with the decision-making process described in this chapter?

Further Reading

Boehlje, Michael, Craig Dobbins, Alan Miller, Janet Bechman, and Aadron Rausch. 2000. "Checking Your Farm Business Management Skills." ID-237, Purdue Extension, Purdue University, West Lafayette, Indiana.

Boehlje, Michael, Craig Dobbins, and Alan Miller. 2001. "Are Your Farm Business Management Skills Ready for the 21st Century?" ID-244, Purdue Extension, Purdue University, West Lafayette, Indiana.

Bolton, Patrick, Markus Brunnermeier, and Laura Veldkamp. 2008. "Leadership, Coordination and Mission-Driven Management," Columbia University working paper, quoted in Kaplan et al., 2008.

Dobbins, Craig, Michael Boehlje, and Alan Miller. 2000. "Farmers as Plant Managers and General Managers: Which Hat Do You Wear?" ID-236, Purdue Extension, Purdue University, West Lafayette, Indiana.

Drucker, Peter. 1967. *The Effective Executive*. New York: Harper Collins.

Kaplan, Steven N., Mark M. Klebanov, and Morten Sorensen, 2008. "Which CEO Characteristics and Abilities Matter?" Swedish Institute for Financial Research Conference on the Economics of the Private Equity Market; AFA 2008 New Orleans Meetings paper. Accessed at http://ssrn.com/abstract=972446 on September 13, 2009.

Klinefelter, D. 2005. "Twenty-Five Attributes of the 21st Century Farm Executive." College Station, Texas Cooperative Extension, Texas A&M University System, B-6168, p. 10–14, accessed at http://tepap.tamu.edu/TwentyfiveAttributes.htm on September 13, 2009.

Öhlmér, B., K. Olson, and B. Brehmer. 1998. "Understanding Farmers' Decision-Making Processes and Improving Managerial Assistance." *Agricultural Economics*, 18, 273–290.

Wilson, Mike, and Bryce Knorr. 2008 (March). "20 Secrets of the Best Managed Farms." farmfutures .com.

3

Business Plans

In this chapter:

- Reasons for a business plan
- Sample business plan outline
- An example executive summary from a business plan

Few managers can afford large speculative agricultural and economic experiments. Most people would consider it wiser to assess the economic consequences and risks of alternative actions on paper before implementation than in grim reality afterward. Yet knowing what to put on paper to produce these assessments is no easy task.

The common method of assessing, compiling, and reporting a manager's assessment of alternatives and the final choices is the preparation of a business plan. Preparing a written business plan not only forces a manager to make and defend choices, but also provides a document to show to creditors, investors, and customers. The act of writing a business plan will improve thinking, decisions, communication, and memory.

Every farm should have a written business plan as a record of why decisions were made and as a guide for current and future decisions. The size and complexity of the business will determine how detailed the plan is. A farm with more than two operators, partners, or owners will benefit from the communication required to prepare, discuss, and accept a written plan. Leaving out some details and assuming everyone knows what needs to be done may be the beginning of communication problems that lead to business problems. A major expansion of the business obviously requires a major effort to prepare a plan that will stand up to intense scrutiny by potential creditors or partners. Even a smaller operation or a part-time farm can benefit from a written plan.

If the actual results are not as planned, a written record can help any manager evaluate what went wrong, whether decisions could have been made to correct problems, how the business could have protected itself better, and so on. Without a written record, incorrect memories may cause incorrect changes.

Sample Business Plan Outline

The standard parts of a business plan include an executive summary supported by a more detailed analysis of the industry, the farm's position within that industry, and the farm's plans for marketing, production, organizing, staffing, and financing. A sample outline is listed in Table 3.1. An individual farm may not need to complete every part of this outline. A major investment or expansion will require a more complete plan. However, by considering every section, the farmer will have considered everything that is necessary to prepare for the future.

The business plan starts with the executive summary, which is a reader-friendly explanation of the details in the subsequent sections. In his classic article (1997) in *Harvard Business Review*, Sahlman argues that most business plans "waste too much ink on numbers and devote too little to the information that really matters to intelligent investors" (or to lenders, for most farmers). According to Sahlman, the business plan and especially the executive summary should focus on four points: (1) the people involved, (2) the opportunity, (3) the context, and (4) the risks and rewards. Numbers are needed to show that the principal people have thought through the impacts of uncertainties and have tested their assumptions about performance and behavior. However, Sahlman says, the numbers should be placed at the end of the plan, not at the front.

Describing the people is critical. Without the right team for the plan, all other aspects of the plan will not matter. What do the people know? Whom do they know? And how well are they known by others? The answers to these three questions will explain how well the people know the business and industry, their experience, and their education; how well they are connected in the industry in terms of suppliers and buyers; and how well others in the industry know and respect them as people and managers. Sahlman lists 14 questions that need to be answered about the people involved in the business (Table 3.2). While the long-time lender in a small community may know the farmer and family, the regional or corporate lender will probably not and, thus, will have to rely on the information in the business plan.

The opportunity is simply what the farm wants or plans to do. It may be expansion, incorporation of the next generation, or simply the continuation of the business. Describing the opportunity includes describing the business model and the strategy. The business model is simply a story or description of how the farm plans to make money. It may be copied from other farms, or it may be new. The strategy is what makes one farm different from others and provides a sustainable, competitive edge for the future. For instance, many farms have the business model of producing feed for the dairy herd and selling the milk to make money. One strategy would be to drive all costs down and be a cost leader in the industry. Another strategy would be to locate near a major market and cultivate a direct marketing opportunity with a grocery store or other buyer of milk. Another strategy that would also make the farm different from others is to convert to organic production. Yet another strategy would be to alter the business model to buy all the feed required, sell all calves, buy all replacements, and focus solely on the milking herd. Each of these example strategies is much more complex than these simple sentences convey, but they each follow the basic business model of a dairy farm; the strategy differentiates them from other farms.

Part of describing the opportunity includes a discussion of how large the market is for the farm's product(s) and how fast the market is growing. An investor or lender will also want to know whether the industry is structurally attractive—that is, whether the industry allows a firm to make a

Table 3.1   Sample Business Plan Outline

1. Executive Summary
   a. The people
   b. The opportunity
   c. The context
   d. The risks and rewards
2. General Description of the Farm
   a. Type of business
   b. Products and services
   c. Market description
   d. Location(s), legal descriptions
   e. History of the farm and operators
   f. Owners, partners, operators
3. Strategic Plan
   a. Vision, mission, goals, and objectives
   b. External analysis, summary
   c. Internal analysis, summary
   d. Chosen business strategy
   e. Strategy evaluation and control
4. Marketing Plan
   a. The target market: who are the customers?
   b. Pricing strategy
   c. Quality management and control of marketing
   d. Inventory and delivery timetables
   e. Market risk and control management
5. Production and Operations Plan
   a. Production process
      i. Product choice
      ii. Product and process design
      iii. Technology choice
      iv. Quality management and control of product and processes
      v. Environmental considerations
   b. Raw materials, facilities, and equipment
   c. Location of production
   d. Production risk and control management
   e. A production and operations schedule
6. Organization and Staffing Plan
   a. Personnel needs
   b. Sources of personnel
      i. Owner and other family labor
      ii. Hired employees
      iii. Consultants
   c. Structure and responsibilities
      i. Business organization
      ii. Brief job descriptions

(continued)

Table 3.1   (*continued*)

     d. Basic personnel policies
        i. Compensation
        ii. Evaluation
        iii. Training
     e. Workforce risk and control management
7. Financial Plan
     a. Financial statements: historical and projected including ratio analysis
     b. Capital needed
     c. Investment analysis
     d. Financial risk and control management

reasonable profit. Sahlman has also developed a set of questions to help a manager describe the opportunity for lenders and investors (Table 3.3). Most of these questions and points will be addressed in the external and internal analyses in the planning phase of strategic management (Chapter 8).

The context is a summary of the macro-environment in which the farm operates or will operate. This includes the macroeconomic forces at the national and international levels as well as the governmental rules and regulations at the local and national levels. Within the context section, the business plan should explain the impact of potential changes in the macro-environment and describe how the farm plans to respond if these potential changes occur. This information is also addressed in the external and internal analyses in the planning phase of strategic management (Chapter 8).

The business plan and especially the executive summary should be very explicit about the risks and rewards that the farm—and thus any lender and investor—will face. Sahlman argues that the people, opportunity, and context should be discussed from several angles. As will be discussed later

Table 3.2   Who Are These People, Anyway?

   1. Where are the owners and managers from?
   2. Where were they educated?
   3. Where have they worked or for whom?
   4. What have they accomplished, professionally and personally, in the past?
   5. What is their reputation within the business community?
   6. What experience do they have that is directly relevant to the opportunity they are pursuing?
   7. What skills, abilities, and knowledge do they have?
   8. How realistic are they about the venture's chances for success and the tribulations it will face?
   9. Who else needs to be on the team?
 10. Are they prepared to recruit high-quality people?
 11. How will they respond to adversity?
 12. Will they be able to make the inevitable hard choices?
 13. How committed are they to this venture?
 14. What are their motivations?

Source: Adapted from Sahlman, p. 101.

Table 3.3 Is This the Opportunity of a Lifetime?

1. Who are the customers?
2. How do the customers make decisions about buying the product or service?
3. How compelling is the product or service to the customer?
4. How will the product or service be priced?
5. How much does it cost to produce and deliver the product or service?
6. How much does it cost (in time and resources) to acquire a customer?
7. How easy is it to retain a customer?
8. When does the farm have to buy resources such as inputs, supplies, raw materials, etc., and hire people?
9. When does the farm have to pay for these resources?
10. How long before the customer sends the farm a check?
11. How much capital equipment is required?
12. Who are the current competitors?
13. What are their strengths and weaknesses?
14. What are their likely decisions and moves in the future?
15. How can the farm respond to their competitors' changes?
16. Who else may enter the industry and become a competitor?
17. Can alliances be formed with actual and potential competitors?

Source: Adapted from Sahlman, pp. 102–4.

in strategic management, the use of scenarios can be a powerful way to show the risks and rewards under different views of what the future holds. Lenders and investors will want to know how management will be able to change the distribution of potential outcomes to include more success and fewer problems. The plan should describe the tools that will be used to mitigate the risk of low product prices, high input prices, and uncertain markets. A lender may react positively to a frank discussion of what the risks are and how the farm is and will respond to these risks. One way of handling risk in a business plan is to identify and list major risks for the industry and this business (Example 3.1).

Example 3.1. Handling Risk in the Business Plan

Describing the plan and reporting potential profit can be the exciting parts of writing a business plan. However, assessing risk is an equally important part. Even though financial performance is difficult to predict, many people strive to make the financial plan very precise and predict what will happen in the future. Efforts to predict the future perfectly are usually met with imperfect results, so plans that rely on the imperfect predictions will likely have trouble as the future unfolds in unexpected ways. A more realistic approach is to plan for the future using reasonable estimates of what will most likely happen. "Once this reasonable financial plan has been completed, the task moves to the search and control of the risks associated with the business" (Brown and Painter, 2009). The next steps involve identifying the major sources of risk for the industry and for the specific business; searching for and discovering the few critical variables related to the sources of risk in the business plan and estimating their impact on the

(continued)

(*continued*)

financial performance of the business; determining how these risks can be controlled; and if they are uncontrollable, developing contingency plans.

Source: W. J. Brown and M. Painter, 2009. "Handling Risk in a Farm Business Plan." Peer-reviewed paper at the 17th International Farm Management Congress, Illinois State University, Bloomington/Normal, Illinois, July 19–24, 2009, accessed on January 30, 2010, at http://www.ifmaonline.org/pdf/congress/ 09_Brown&Painter.pdf.

Two simple graphs can show a lot of information about the risks and rewards (Sahlman, 1997). The first graph shows the depth of cash outflow, length of time before a positive cash flow is reached, and size of the positive cash flow after that date (Figure 3.1). This graph is especially applicable to a business plan seeking major new funding for a new venture such as a new livestock facility or a new planting of perennial crops. The second graph shows the potential distribution of the rate of return on investment (Figure 3.2). This graph shows the reality that one estimate is not guaranteed, but it also shows how well the farm's plan will likely perform under a range of scenarios of the future. Most lenders and investors know the future is uncertain and will welcome a frank depiction of how the business model and strategy perform in different situations. If the owners and managers of the farm do not want to show this information because it looks bad, they should realize that most lenders and investors will be suspicious and likely not provide funds.

As stated earlier, the executive summary is very critical for a successful business plan. The rest of the plan is only supporting material. Note too that the numbers are left to the end—even though they may take the most time to prepare for the report. Let's look at each of the remaining sections of the outline.

The general description of the farm is a short summary of where the farm is economically, physically, and historically. Any creditor will want to know the names of the owners, partners, and operators to provide both a human side to the management and the reputation of the people involved.

The strategic plan lays out the farm's vision and direction. It describes the farm's view of its chosen industry and how the farm is seen fitting into that industry. This section shows how and why the strategy was chosen and how it will be evaluated.

The marketing plan shows how the farm's products will be marketed physically and the initial plan for pricing. The plans for monitoring market conditions and for changing the marketing plan should be spelled out. For instance, if the plan is to use options to price corn, what indicators will be monitored to make buy and sell decisions? What are the contingency plans for sudden market shifts? The marketing

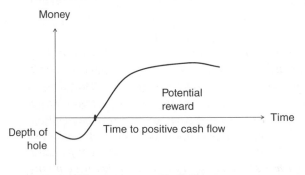

Figure 3.1 Time to Positive Cash Flow

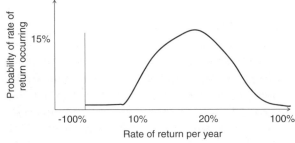

Figure 3.2 Distribution of the Rate of Return on Investment

plan should also include some discussion of the purchasing plan for inputs such as fertilizer and feed. Are advance purchases needed? Do feed requirements need to be hedged on the futures market?

The production and operations plan will probably take the most time to prepare and, if prepared well, save the most time during organizing and directing. In this section, the reasons for choosing certain production processes over alternatives are given. The amount and timing of raw materials such as equipment, fertilizer, seed, feed, and livestock are listed. The plans for controlling quality are described. Contingency plans for bad weather or equipment breakdowns are spelled out.

The next section describes the plan for organizing and staffing the business. Again, the size and detail of this section will depend on the size and complexity of the farm business. However, even a sole proprietorship needs to consider whether additional labor and additional knowledge (such as consultants) are needed. Writing and discussing job descriptions can be very helpful for employees and bosses and even for family members and long-time partners. Just saying (or worse, thinking), "We'll do it," can be detrimental to obtaining credit, the long-term success of the business, and family harmony.

The final section presents the financial plan, including historical and projected financial statements. Capital requirements and timing are shown. The plans and steps taken to protect the business financially need to be listed. Although it is usually seen as extremely painful and time consuming, the time put into the marketing plan and the production plan should make the preparation of the financial statements a matter of assembling numbers in the right places. Then interpretation of the statements can take precedence over preparation.

An Example Executive Summary

As an example of an executive summary from a business plan, let's consider the ideas and plans that Dave and Louise Gable and their son Jake have for their dairy farm. Space keeps us from showing the full plan here, but parts of the plan are sprinkled through other chapters; for example, the cropping plan and pro forma financial statements are in Chapter 15. The following paragraphs are examples of what the Gables could include in their business plan. Although the Gables wrote the plan, they often refer to themselves in the third person because they know some readers will not know them.

The people:

We are Dave and Louise Gable. We have had a dairy farm for 27 years and have increased it from humble beginnings of 53 lactating cows and 220 tillable crop acres to its current size of 600 lactating cows (with appropriate numbers of calves, replacement heifers, and dry cows) plus we own 1,250 tillable crop acres. We own all the machinery necessary to farm this many acres although we do hire some of the primary tillage in the fall.

Dave Gable graduated from the University 27 years ago with a degree in dairy science and started farming that same year. While attending classes at the University, he worked in the University dairy facilities both with the animals and in the office collecting and analyzing performance data. He has attended many classes, meetings, workshops, and training sessions in the years since. The formal classes are listed in his resume; they include dairy production and breeding; crop and milk marketing; pesticide application training; and managerial accounting. Dave Gable has served on and been president of the local cooperative board, state dairy improvement association, state milk producers association, his family's church, and their local community's business improvement committee. The specific years of membership and the other offices he has held are included in his resume. He has also been very active as a leader in 4-H and other youth organizations.

Louise Gable received a degree in nursing and worked at a local doctor's office for the first years of marriage and farming. When their first child was born, Louise gave up her nursing career but took on the record-keeping duties on the farm. These duties have expanded to monitoring markets and participating in grain and marketing decisions as well as long-run planning for the farm. She has attended many classes and meetings on marketing and accounting; the formal classes are listed in her resume and include dairy production records, crop and milk marketing, and accounting, including managerial accounting. Louise Gable has served on the state milk producers executive committee, the local school board, and the family's church council. The specific years of membership and the offices she has held are included in her resume. She too has been very active as a leader in 4-H and other youth organizations.

Jake Gable has just graduated from the University with a double degree in dairy science and business management. Currently he is working as a feed consultant at the local feed elevator and working the Gable farm part-time with both the dairy and crops. He plans to participate full-time in the farming business as expansion plans allow. While attending the University, he worked in the University's dairy facilities handling the cows and in the office managing the flow of data and information in the computer system. During two summers, he worked for a large dairy close to the University, helping them install and operate a new computer management system for their dairy productivity records. Jake Gable was president of his 4-H youth club during high school and was a member and officer in several organizations while in college; these are listed in his resume.

The Gables are well known and respected in their town, state, and across the nation. In the attached letter, Mr. Peter Giesler, long-time banker for the Gables, writes, "The Gables have always had a financial plan, knew what they wanted, and paid off all loans on time. They are among the most respected business people in our community. Dave has served on several boards and been the president of most of those boards. People know he will deliver what he says. The Gables weathered the financial troubles of the 1980s by tightening their belts and delaying further expansion plans without being told." Dr. Alice Fuhrman, the Gables' veterinarian, writes in her letter, "The Gables have subscribed to our health maintenance program for their dairy herd for 18 years. They follow our recommendations and have a very healthy, productive herd. I track their milk production and have watched it increase consistently year after year as they make genetic and management improvements."

The opportunity:

We, Dave and Louise Gable, plan to bring our son, Jake Gable, into our farming operation and pass the management and eventually the ownership to him as we move into retirement over the next 10–15 years. He has recently graduated in dairy science and business management from the University and wants to return to farming as the fifth generation on this farm.

Our current operation includes 600 lactating cows averaging 20,000 lb of milk per cow (305-day average). As the records show, our cost of production last year was $16.66 per 100 lb, which is about $2 below the area average according to the farm record association. We sell our milk to the United Milk Processors, who built a new, larger facility two years ago just 25 miles away from our farm. With Jake's new knowledge and the help of our veterinarian's health maintenance program, our first goals are to increase the herd to 700 lactating cows, increase milk production to 25,000 lb per cow, and lower the cost of production to $14.00 per 100 lb in the next three years. The pro forma financial statements for next year show a positive cash flow and increasing cash reserves as we increase production per cow.

In the next 10 years, we plan to expand our herd to 2,500 cows. These plans are now on hold until the milk price improves or other signals indicate that profitability will improve in the future. Our plans also include the gradual decrease of the crop enterprise of our farm business. The decrease will mirror the increase in the cow herd. It will be done through renting out the land to neighboring farmers and contracting to buy their production for our cows and to dispose of the animal waste. Some land will be sold to finance the building of the new dairy facilities. Further details on our expansion plans will be developed as our productivity improves and as the market improves profit potential.

The context:

For many years, total U.S. milk production has slowly increased due to increased production per cow even though the number of cows has decreased. The number of dairy farms has also decreased consistently. The current recession and weak U.S. dollar has caused both dairy exports and domestic milk consumption to decrease. According to the latest USDA outlook information, "Milk production during the second quarter of 2009 was up one-tenth of 1 percent from the second quarter of 2008, even though herd size was 53,000 head smaller than the corresponding quarter last year" (Quanbeck and Johnson, 2009). The USDA also forecasts feed prices to decline, so pressure on profits from low milk prices will decrease some. Since milk production is declining very slowly in response to decreased demand, prices will not be increasing quickly, so profit potential will not return rapidly either. Increased supplies of dry milk powder in Europe do not signal an immediate rise in profitability. The current USDA forecast is for (a) 2010 exports to be higher than 2009 levels but below 2008 levels, (b) domestic production to slow, and, (c) as a result, the Class III milk price to average $10.70–10.90 per cwt in 2009 and rise to an average of $13.75–$14.75 per cwt in 2010.

The risks and rewards:

The risk of financial ruin is rather high right now if we were to initiate an expansion with a high level of financing. Thus, we are planning to increase the cow herd (but maintain the physical facilities at their current size), improve profitability through improving productivity, and maintain current debt obligations. As we noted earlier, the cash flow is expected to be positive, but if the milk price drops to approximately $16 per 100 lb, cash flow becomes negative. This is why we are striving to increase production per cow and lower costs of production per unit of milk. If the price does not drop this much, the reward is a higher cash balance.

Although profit potential appears to be improving after next year, we, the Gables, do not anticipate that the potential will improve enough for us to initiate the building phase of our expansion plan. Further improvements need to be made both in the milk supply and demand conditions and in the general U.S. and world economies before the picture is clear enough for us. The rewards of an expansion in the future are greater, sustainable profit margins from a new facility using the latest technology.

Developing and writing a good business plan is an involved and probably complicated task. However, if a person, family, or business wants to turn a dream into reality, writing a business plan is an essential task. The outline and ideas presented in this chapter can help produce a plan that will provide good information to lenders and other stakeholders. The remaining chapters of this book will help complete all the parts of the outline.

Summary

- The common method of assessing, compiling, and reporting a manager's assessment of alternatives and the final choices is the preparation of a business plan.

- Preparing a business plan provides a structured approach for planning and helps ensure that important points are considered.
- The standard parts of a business plan include an executive summary supported by a more detailed analysis of the industry, the farm's position within that industry, and the farm's plans for marketing, production, organizing, staffing, and financing.
- The business plan and especially the executive summary should focus on four points: (1) the people involved, (2) the opportunity, (3) the context, and (4) the risks and rewards.
- Describing the people is critical in a business plan. What do the people know? Whom do they know? And how well are they known by others?
- The opportunity is simply what the farm wants or plans to do.
- The context is a summary of the macro-environment.
- The risk and rewards should be written very explicitly so a reader will realize that the business has anticipated the right uncertainties.
- Two simple graphs that show a lot of numerical information about risk and rewards are one showing the time to a positive cash flow and another one showing the distribution of the rate of return.

Review Questions

1. Why is a business plan needed? What size of farm needs to prepare a written business plan?
2. What four ingredients are more important in a business plan than a listing of financial numbers? Describe each of these ingredients.
3. Why do the people need to be described in a business plan even though they are dealing with a local lender?
4. Why are numbers still needed in a business plan?
5. What are the major sections in a typical business plan outline? Describe what is included in each section.
6. What two graphs can show a lot of information about potential risks and rewards? What does each graph show? Why should a farmer show the potential risks to a lender or potential partner?
7. Reread the example executive summary of the Gables' plan. Do you understand who is involved and what their plan is? What else would you like to know if you were the lender considering their request for a line of credit for next year?

Further Reading

Mullins, John W. 2006. *The New Business Road Test*. 2nd ed. Harlow, England: Financial Times Prentice Hall, 305 pp.

Sahlman, William A. 1997. "How to Write a Great Business Plan." *Harvard Business Review* July–August 1997, pp. 98–108.

Quanbeck, Kathryn, and Rachel J. Johnson. 2009. "Livestock, Dairy, and Poultry Outlook." LDP-M-182, Economic Research Service, USDA, August 19.

4

Lessons from Microeconomics

In this chapter:

- Basic concepts and terms
- Production planning
- Farm size
- Markets and market structure

This chapter is a summary of lessons and points from microeconomics that farm managers should know in order to understand their business and the business decisions of others. **Microeconomics** is the study of the behavior of individual persons, individual businesses and organizations, and the markets they participate in. Macroeconomics, the topic of the next chapter, is the study of national and international economies and trade between nations.

The chapter starts by explaining some basic microeconomic concepts and terms. The next section covers the economic concepts for planning production. Then we look at what determines farm size and why sizes can vary between different industries, times, and geographical areas. The final section explains several economic concepts in markets and market structure that are useful for strategic management.

Basic Microeconomic Concepts and Terms

In this section, we review several concepts and terms used in microeconomics that are useful to a farm manager for making decisions on the farm, for understanding the workings of the economy, and for understanding why people and companies respond to different market conditions.

Scarcity

We start with one very basic concept in economics: scarcity or limited resources. We do not have enough resources to satisfy all our needs and wants. We do not have enough land, labor, and capital or money to make or buy everything we need and want. This is true whether the ''we'' is individual people, a family, a business, a society or country, or the world. That means we have to make choices or tradeoffs. We have to decide which needs and wants have greater value or satisfaction for us and then decide how to use our limited resources to satisfy those needs and wants.

In the market, we buy goods and services that are used to satisfy needs and wants. Since resources are limited, we cannot have all the goods and services we would like. We have to choose some and forgo others, and we have to make tradeoffs. Each of us evaluates our resources, compares the values we place on different goods and services, competes in the market with other people, and finally chooses the mix of goods and services we can afford and that maximizes our satisfaction.

Most readers are astute enough to already see where the impact of scarcity and limited resources is heading: prices!

Prices

A price is the amount of money or goods that is asked or offered in exchange for something else. A price is also thought of as the cost of obtaining something.

Everyone is different in that we each have different needs and wants and different sets of limited resources. We rank, or place higher values on, satisfying some needs and wants over others. We are willing to use more of our limited resources to satisfy some needs and wants than we are willing to use for others. Because of all these variables, we have different prices at which we will sell (or buy) the same item.

These differences are easy to see when watching an auction. As the price increases, some people quit bidding because the price increases beyond the value they have placed on the item or they don't have enough resources to pay the higher price. At the end of the auction, the person who values the item enough and has sufficient resources to pay the final price takes ownership of the item being auctioned. The buyer is satisfied because the price is less than or equal to the value they had placed on the item, and the seller is satisfied because the price is greater to or equal to the value they had placed on the item. This example auction is the marketplace where the buyer and seller discovered the price at which both were satisfied and a transaction was made. Other potential buyers decided the tradeoff between the auction item and other goods and services was great enough to make them quit bidding and forgo the auction item.

If more of the same item were offered for sale in the auction, each of the final prices would be less than or equal to the value each buyer placed on the item and greater than or equal to the value each seller placed on the item. The number of items offered for sale and subsequently sold depends on the quantity each seller is willing to offer for sale and the quantity each buyer is willing to buy at the auction price. A higher price would give more value to more sellers, but a higher price would be greater than the value perceived by more buyers; so they would not buy the additional quantity. A lower price would decrease the value given to sellers so they would offer a lower quantity for sale, but a lower price would be lower than the value perceived by more buyers so they would want to buy a larger quantity and bid the price up and sellers would offer more for sale.

A retail store is not an auction, but similar principles operate in the store. The store owner (the seller) sets a price equal to or greater than the value to the seller. That value is the seller's cost and desired profit. (For the moment, we'll ignore the ideas of sales prices, cost leaders, and so on.) The customer (the potential buyer) sees the posted price and decides whether the price is equal to or less than the value they place on the item. If the price is equal to or less than the customer's value, the customer buys the product. If the store's price is greater than the customer's value, the customer does not buy.

In both the auction and the retail store, the number of items sold and bought depends on the price. This brings us to the concepts of supply and demand.

Supply and Demand

In ordinary conversation, **supply** is the amount of product or service offered (or could be offered) for sale in the market. This is slightly different from the view of a **supply schedule** or curve in economics. In ordinary conversation, supply is thought of as what is available. In economics, the supply schedule or curve represents how suppliers will adjust the quantity produced as price changes. The product or service may be supplied by a person, business, or organization. A rational supplier will produce and offer only that amount of the product or service that costs less than or equal to the price in the market. When the price of the product is low, less will be provided than when the price is high because the cost of producing more increases due to needing more resources to produce more. For example, if we keep other inputs constants (and don't use too much), more fertilizer is needed to increase crop production, more feed is needed to increase milk per cow, more land is needed to increase grain production, more labor is required to produce more hogs, and so on. At higher prices, a producer supplies more of a product when the increase in the price is higher than the increase in the cost of producing the additional amount. Also, at higher prices, a higher cost producer, who was not producing at the previous price, may start producing. For example, the cost of production on lower quality land may be higher than the market price in one time period so the land is not used for production. But a change in market conditions may raise the product price above the costs required to produce on that land and the farmer decides to use the land to produce the crop. When this response of increasing supply as the price increases is placed on a graph, we see an upward-sloping **supply curve**, such as S_1 in Figure 4.1.

In ordinary conversation, **demand** is the amount of product or service that a person, business, or organization is willing to purchase at a certain price. In economics, the **demand schedule** or curve represents how buyers will adjust the quantity demanded as price changes. As more product or service is purchased and consumed, the benefit or value of the additional consumption decreases. For example, the first apple may be very satisfying, but the second apple eaten immediately after the first is not as satisfying; it has less value to the person than the first apple. A third apple would have even less value than the second. (This is the law of diminishing returns, which we'll discuss more later.) Thus, a person would be willing to pay less for the second apple and even less for the third (if the apples could not be stored for a later meal). At some point, additional apples would be refused, and the value and thus the potential apple price would be zero for this person. When this response of

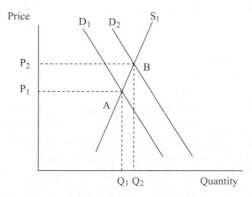

Figure 4.1 Supply and Demand Curves

decreasing value as quantity increases is graphed we see a downward-sloping **demand curve**, such as D_1 in Figure 4.1.

Where the supply and demand curves meet or cross is called the equilibrium point (A in Figure 4.1), and the **equilibrium price** (P_1) and **equilibrium quantity** (Q_1) are determined at that point. Although this simple graph assumes a lot of stability and common information between buyers and sellers in the market, the concept of the market finding the equilibrium price and quantity through the equalization of the benefit to the producer and to the consumer is a very useful and powerful mental model to have.

Suppose the demand for the product shifts to the right due to a new market being opened, new advertising for the product, or the failure of a competing product. This shift to the right is represented by the second demand curve, D_2. A new equilibrium point, B, is found that determines a new equilibrium price, P_2, and a new equilibrium quantity, Q_2. With no shift in the supply of the product, the current suppliers and new suppliers could increase production and sell more for a higher price. The sellers could afford to pay for more inputs to increase production because the product price would be higher. Economists call this change in supply a movement along the supply curve rather than a shift in the supply curve.

This example can be seen in the real increase or shift in demand for maize and oil crops caused by the increase in biofuel production that was caused by increased oil prices, subsidies by governments concerned about energy security, and improvements in technology. Farmers have been able to increase production on current land by using more inputs and receiving a higher price to cover the higher costs. Other land that was previously used for other uses has also been switched to production for biofuels. Farmers have also seen how the shift in demand can quickly move the other way, causing a lower price and thus a need to cut production to keep costs in line with market prices.

Supply and demand are important concepts. Both connect price and quantity. Supply and demand curves show how buyers and sellers adjust quantities as prices change. A recent example of an industry needing to rebalance supply and demand is the dairy industry in the United States (Example 4.1).

Example 4.1. Balancing Supply and Demand

The recent economic troubles and, for some, devastation of income and equity for many dairy farmers can be traced to the tremendous drop in milk prices and rise in feed costs starting in 2008. The drop in milk prices in the United States was due in large part to the rapid drop in exports of dairy products, which pushed down total demand while supply stayed at previous levels. The obvious result was the drop in milk price for farmers.

The supply has been slow to decline due to rigidities in dairy facilities and the reluctance to make quick decisions to stop production. Even so, many dairies did close and sold their cows. A weekly average of 50,000 dairy cows was being slaughtered during late 2009.

However, the signal to sell cows and cut production is a difficult signal to act on for an individual producer. If one producer does so, he loses because he has less milk to sell, but the remaining ones who did not cut production can enjoy a higher price for all the uncut production.

To help solve the problems of too much milk being produced and those individuals who cut production being hurt financially, the National Milk Producers Federation in the United States runs Cooperatives Working Together (CWT). CWT is a program that pays retiring dairy farmers to have their cows slaughtered. The program kicks in when supply outstrips demand, which it did in 2008 and 2009 when it paid to have more than 250,000 cows killed (about 10% of what is normally sold for meat), according to a *Washington Post* story. The Federation said that CWT was the only way the industry could do something collectively to help correct the imbalance between supply and demand.

As of 2010, prices and incomes began to improve with the decrease in total supply and the partial recovery of demand.

Source: D. Ramde, "Hope Returns after Year of Steep U.S. Dairy Losses," *The Washington Post*, February 3, 2010. Accessed on February 4, 2010, at http://www.washingtonpost.com/wp-dyn/content/article/2010/02/03/AR2010020300131.html.

Elasticity

One of the first adjustments to the simple supply and demand graph is due to the realization that not all supply and demand curves have the same slope and shape as drawn in Figure 4.1. Different products have supply curves with steeper slopes due to rapid increases in costs as production increases or more gradual slopes if the increase in costs is not as rapid. Consumers have demand curves with either steeper or more gradual slopes depending on how rapidly their value of the product changes as consumption increases. Economists refer to the responsiveness of demand to price change as the **price elasticity** of demand and supply.

As an example, consider the demand for ground beef compared to the demand for high-quality steak. While the general demand for all beef can remain fairly constant from a farmer's perspective, the quantity demanded of the different beef products can change quickly as the prices for these products change relative to each other. For example, if the price for high-quality steak increased and the price for ground beef did not change, consumers would likely decide that ground beef is a better value even though they might consider the steak to be higher in quality. In a mirror image, if the price for steak dropped, more consumers would switch from ground beef to steak. The responsiveness of the demand for steak as its price changes is called its "own price elasticity of demand." It is calculated as the percentage change in quantity demanded divided by the percentage change in its own price. The responsiveness of the demand for ground beef as the price of steak changes is called "cross price elasticity of demand." The cross price of demand is calculated as the percentage change in quantity demanded for a product divided by the percentage change in the price of another product.

Changes in the ability to supply a product can also change over time. For example, before planting occurs, the supply curve for wheat may resemble the supply curve S_{bp} in Figure 4.2. However, after harvest the supply of wheat becomes much more known and fixed. In fact, the supply of wheat (at a particular point in time) may change only because producers and consumers will change their storage plans. The more fixed supply of wheat is shown in a steeper supply curve such as S_{ah}.

Before planting, the supply curve is S_{bp} and previously known demand is represented by D_1, thus the equilibrium is discovered at point A with the equilibrium price for wheat at P_1 and the equilibrium quantity at Q_1.

Now suppose the demand for wheat were to increase by shifting right to the curve D_2. Before planting, the market would reach a new equilibrium at point B with a new equilibrium price of P_2 and quantity Q_2. However, if the shift in demand were to occur after harvest, the same shift in demand would yield the higher equilibrium price, P_3, but the quantity supplied would increase only to Q_3. Before planting, the farmers are more flexible in their response and can increase the

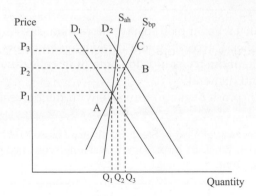

Figure 4.2   Supply Curves before Planting and after Harvest

supply by planting more acres or applying more fertilizer and other inputs. After harvest, farmers and other holders of wheat have a fixed supply and are not as flexible because harvest is done and the supply of wheat cannot be changed as easily. Higher prices may entice farmers to sell more now and store less for the future, but the total supply available cannot be changed after harvest (unless imports increase). Visually, we can easily see that the percentage change in price divided by the percentage change in quantity is greater if the same demand shift occurred before planting than after harvest. The price elasticity of supply is greater before planting than after harvest.

This idea of a "fixed" supply after harvest needs to be tempered by (1) the knowledge that inventories can be adjusted to account for price changes and changes in how and when to use the crop and (2) the knowledge that production around the world can adjust to production and price changes in other parts of the world. The northern and southern hemispheres have different production seasons, so a small harvest in one hemisphere does not mean 12 months of a smaller world supply. Higher prices due to the smaller harvest will provide an incentive for producers in the other hemisphere to increase production and thus the world supply within a few months.

Demand can also change as income changes. As income increases, people want more of some products and less of others. Demand for specific food products shows this change easily. A person whose income is very low may not be able to afford enough food to provide a good diet with proper energy and protein levels. As income increases, the person consumes more food. In other instances, when income is low, people tend to have a diet of grains for both protein and starches. While this diet can be sufficient and balanced nutritionally, people tend to buy more meat as their income increases. As income increases, they tend to buy more processed food requiring less preparation at home and will eat away from home more often. Also, as income increases, people also tend to eat more food, even beyond their immediate needs. This income effect is common for many products. The **income elasticity of demand** is a measure of how much the quantity demanded of a product or service responds to a change in consumers' income. It is computed as the percentage change in the quantity demanded divided by the percentage change in income.

Opportunity Cost

Opportunity cost is a concept used to specify a cost for using resources. It is very important in farm management but easily misunderstood.

When any resource is used, the income from using it in any other way is lost. The income from the best alternative use is called the opportunity cost of that resource because the farmer has given up the opportunity to earn that income. The "cost" of using the resource in the chosen use is its **opportunity cost** (that is, the income that it could have earned in the next best alternative). Although this may seem to be a vague and useless concept, it has real applications.

Labor, land, and capital resources can be used in several ways. Each alternative may generate a different income from those resources. For example, land could be used to produce several crops. Each of these crops would produce a certain income, but only one crop can be grown at a time. Therefore, the income from other crops is forgone. The income from the best alternative crop is the opportunity cost for the crop planted. Land could also be rented to another farmer. So the potential income from renting can also be the opportunity cost of the farmer using the land to grow a crop himself.

For resources that are not purchased for each production period—such as equity capital or owner's labor—the opportunity cost of that resource can be used to evaluate whether the chosen use is the best use of that resource. For a farmer, the opportunity cost of farming is the income that could be derived in the next best job, perhaps a job in town. For a farmer's equity capital, the next best alternative may be investment in the stock market or in savings accounts. As will be seen in Chapter 12, these opportunity costs of using the farmer's time, management skills, and money for farming can be used to evaluate the financial performance of the farm compared to alternative careers.

Opportunity costs are a factor in nearly all farm management decisions. The farm manager must not only ask, "Will this use of capital, labor, or land be profitable?" but must also ask, "Would this capital, labor, or land produce a higher income if it were used in another way?" Understanding the concept of opportunity cost can help answer both questions.

Total, Average, and Marginal Income and Costs

When analyzing income and expenses it is important to use the same units. Five different quantity relationship measures are listed below.

1. Total income or expense per farm (or enterprise). Total income and expense per farm are, as they say in literal English, the total of the particular item for the whole farm. Total crop sales per farm, total custom hire income per farm, total fuel cost per farm, total fertilizer cost per farm, or total feed cost per farm are examples. These figures are important to the calculation of whole-farm cash flow and income statements.

   The totals are interesting as a measure of the size of the business, but by themselves, they are not very useful in a detailed business analysis. For example, a farm may have spent $10,000 on fertilizer in the current year. But the farmer cannot determine whether enough, too little, or too much money was spent on fertilizer unless the farmer specifies the crops and the acreage of each, how the fertilizer was allocated between these crops, the types of soil involved, and several other items. Even where all farm costs are incurred by a single enterprise, the use of these figures is limited unless other measures are used that consider the size of the business.

2. Average income or expense per unit of land. Evaluating income and expenses on an average per acre, hectare, or other measure of land is more useful in business analysis than farm totals. Cost per hectare or per acre for individual items is particularly useful in analyzing the efficiency of the use of these items. Labor and machinery costs per acre, seedbed preparation costs per acre, weed control

costs per acre, and harvesting costs per acre are examples of useful measures in business analysis. Average net income or net return per acre or hectare is useful for comparing alternative crops.

3. Average cost or return per unit of production. Cost quoted on a per unit of production basis (per bushel of corn, per Dezzitonne of wheat, per ton of grapes, per cwt of pork produced, per MG of milk, etc.) are very useful in business analysis. These costs per unit of production are directly comparable to product prices. More effective marketing decisions can be made based on this information.

4. Marginal return or cost. The concept of margins is also important in farm decision making. Marginal returns and costs are used to choose the optimal level of production. Simply stated, the marginal return or cost is the additional return or cost, respectively, resulting from the production of an additional unit of output. The key to using this concept is the word "additional."

   A farmer may wish to decide, for example, whether to increase wheat production. The question is whether the added revenues will be greater than the added costs. The **marginal revenue** is the value of the additional production. **Marginal cost** is the additional cost of obtaining the additional production. It is the cost of the combination of additional fertilizer, pesticides, labor, and any other inputs needed to increase production. If the marginal cost of the additional inputs exceeds the marginal return from the additional production, the farmer should not increase production.

5. Marginal product and the value of the marginal product. **Marginal product** is the physical change in total product when input is increased. It is the increase in crop yield when more fertilizer is added or the increase in the quantity of milk when the amount of feed is increased. The value of the marginal product is the marginal product multiplied by the product price. These measures are different from marginal revenue which, as noted above, is the change in total revenue when total cost increases. Marginal product and the value of the marginal product are used to choose the economically optimal level of an input.

6. Marginal factor cost. Marginal factor cost, also called **marginal input cost**, is different from the marginal cost concept described earlier. The marginal factor cost is the cost of using an additional unit of a specific input, such as, the cost of applying an additional 25 pounds of fertilizer per acre or the cost of cultivating an additional time. The greatest application of the marginal factor cost concept is comparing it to the value of the marginal product to determine the amount of an input to use. For example, as more input (say, fertilizer) is added, at what level does the marginal factor cost become greater than the value of marginal production from that same unit of input? Or is the cost of cultivating greater or less than the additional yield obtained by decreasing the weed population by cultivating?

Variable versus Fixed Costs

The distinction between variable and fixed costs is important because of how each affects current decisions.[1]

Which costs are variable depends in large part on the planning horizon of the farm. The length of the planning horizon depends on the decision being made. In the long run, all inputs are variable, so all costs are variable. For example, if the decision is to build a new farmstead and expand the dairy herd, very few costs are fixed. In the short run, some costs will be fixed and some costs will be variable. For example, if the land and equipment are already owned and rented, many costs are fixed for the decision of what crops to plant.

---

[1] The distinction between fixed and variable is more applicable to costs than to income. Most farm income will vary with production, but very little income is fixed in the sense that a cost can be fixed. Thus, the discussion in this section concerns only costs.

Fixed costs are those that occur no matter what or how much is produced on a farm. Examples of fixed costs include taxes on land and buildings; interest on the investment in land, buildings, and machinery; and depreciation on buildings and machinery. Many costs, such as office expenses and supervisor's wages, are fixed costs in the sense that they will be incurred no matter what is produced. The operator's labor and family labor also may be considered fixed costs under certain circumstances; the cost of these items would be the same no matter how much is produced.

With a given set of fixed expenses, production increases will lower the fixed costs per unit of production. The expression, "spreading your fixed costs," comes from this lowering of cost per unit as production increases. For instance, harvesting more land with the same machine spreads the fixed ownership costs of equipment over more land. However, not all costs decline as acreage increases. Although the total fixed costs remain the same as the amount of land increases, equipment insurance and interest cost, for example, remain the same no matter how much land is harvested (unless the machinery is changed as size changes). That is why labor, fuel, and similar costs are called variable costs (since more fuel will be used to farm more land, for example).

Variable costs are those costs that are more directly associated with the volume of business. The costs of seed, fuel, repairs, fertilizer, herbicides, and so forth are examples of variable costs in crop production. Hired hourly labor, feed costs, veterinary expenses, repairs, and marketing expenses are examples of variable expenses of livestock production. Interest on operating loans is also a variable cost. These costs vary in total with the size of the farm business.

The level of some inputs and operations, such as weeding and cultivating, may not be changed as easily as the fertilizer level. However, these costs are still considered variable costs because they are specific to a certain enterprise and would not be incurred if that product was not produced.

Labor costs may be fixed or variable depending on how long the employment or work relationship is expected to be. The cost of a full-time, permanent employee is usually considered a fixed cost. In contrast, the cost of a temporary or seasonal worker is usually considered a variable cost. If labor is hired for a specific job especially if it is directly related to a product (e.g., crop weeding, plowing, hoof trimming), it should be considered a variable cost. Even though it is a non-cash expense (as discussed in a following section), unpaid family labor that works at the farm full-time is considered a fixed cost. Unpaid family labor that works occasionally is usually considered a variable cost, but that may vary with the person's commitment to the farm over time.

As noted earlier, the distinction between fixed and variable costs is important because of how each affects current decisions. By definition, fixed costs are fixed; they have to be paid no matter what happens or what is decided today or in the future. Although fixed costs are not affected by current decisions, a manager's decision to act (and thus incur a variable cost) or not to act may be influenced by fixed costs. Past investments can affect the response to and the value of the current decision to spend money.

For example, the decision to apply fertilizer after planting in the spring depends on the cost of the fertilizer and its application cost compared with the expected value of the crop response to the fertilizer. Expenses for the fertilizer that was applied in the previous fall and at planting should not be included in the spring decision because those expenses have to be paid regardless of what happens in the spring; they are now fixed costs. However, the presence of that previously applied fertilizer can affect the response to and the value of the spring fertilizer and thus the decision to apply that fertilizer. In another example, the past investment in feeding facilities greatly affects the decision to buy feeders this year, but the loan on the facilities has to be paid whether feeders are bought or not.

Many farmers try to cut their per-unit variable costs of production by replacing labor with machinery. These farmers may be substituting higher fixed costs (depreciation, interest, and property taxes on machinery) for lower variable labor costs. Decreasing variable costs while increasing fixed costs does not guarantee profits and may decrease a farmer's flexibility to change with changes in the economy.

All costs become fixed once they have been used or committed to use. These are sometimes called "sunk costs." Once seed is planted, fertilizer is applied, or gasoline is used in the tractor, they become fixed even though they were variable costs before they were used. The cost of the seed becoming a sunk cost as the seed is planted is a good visual picture of a "sunk cost." Since sunk costs are fixed costs, they do not affect current production decisions, as discussed earlier.

In some years, when it becomes obvious after planting that the future income from an enterprise will not cover total crop costs, an understanding of "sunk costs" will help the manager reduce losses. For example, a dry period during pollination can severely reduce yield to a point where the farmer will lose money on the crop. The farmer still has some variable costs, such as the harvesting expenses, which may or may not be incurred. The harvest decision will depend upon whether the potential value of the crop will exceed the variable harvest costs. If the potential value is less than the variable harvesting costs, the farmer should leave the crop in the field and not harvest it because doing so will increase the financial loss. If the gross income exceeds the variable harvesting costs, the farmer will reduce total losses by harvesting. Even though the final accounting may show a loss for the crop, the actual loss would have been higher if the crop had not been harvested. In decisions such as this one, any remaining variable costs become the key to the decision; variable costs already committed are now fixed or sunk costs.

Direct versus Overhead Costs (and Listed Costs)

The distinction between direct and overhead costs can be described in terms of the ease of assigning a cost to a certain crop or livestock enterprise. **Direct costs** are used directly in the production of a specific crop or livestock. Corn seed is used to grow corn, not soybeans, so, obviously, it is a direct cost for corn. Similarly, hog feed is for hogs, veterinary expenses for the dairy herd are for dairy, and so on. The fuel used to dry corn is obviously a cost of corn production. Although the fuel used for tractors and other machinery may come from the same fuel tank, we can use engineering data to estimate and then allocate how much fuel is needed to combine an acre of corn, for example, and how much is needed per hour to haul hog manure. Direct costs are most likely also variable costs.

Overhead costs are those costs that are hard to assign directly to a particular enterprise. Most fixed costs are overhead costs. The depreciation and interest costs for machinery used for both crops and livestock are harder to allocate to each of those enterprises, unless a detailed log is kept that shows when each machine is used and on what enterprise. We may still make an arbitrary allocation to the enterprises, but since we do not know for sure whether that allocation is exactly correct, we classify the cost as an overhead cost. A similar case can be described for the cost of a full-time employee who works on both crops and livestock. We cannot directly allocate the cost of this worker to the specific crops and livestock without detailed work records, so we make an arbitrary allocation and list the cost as an overhead cost in each budget.

Published budgets often refer to the total of all costs as "**listed costs**." While the budgets are very accurate, the authors of the published budgets know they may not contain all the costs that may occur on a specific farm since they are developed for a representative farm. The term "listed costs" is used to alert the user to that fact.

Cash versus Non-cash

The cash versus non-cash distinction is based on the nature and timing of a transaction. Income is "a value that is or should be received." Similarly, an expense or cost is "a charge that is or should be made." These definitions do not require that a cash transaction be involved in order for the income or expense to be listed in a budget. Examples of non-cash items include unpaid family labor, the value of farm products consumed at home and by employees, crops grown on the farm and fed to livestock, manure from the farm's livestock applied on crops, depreciation, and interest on equity. Although they do not affect the cash in your wallet or bank account today, these non-cash income and expenses may be important tomorrow or next year. Thus, both cash and non-cash items need to be estimated to make better decisions for the future and to prepare more accurate assessments of a farm's financial condition and performance.

For example, the feed raised by a farm and fed to the livestock on that farm is a non-cash expense for the livestock enterprise and a non-cash income for the crop enterprise. No cash is exchanged. The livestock enterprise does not buy the feed, and the crop enterprise does not sell the feed. However, to obtain an accurate assessment of the profitability of each enterprise, the non-cash value of the feed needs to be assigned as income to the crop enterprise and an expense to the livestock enterprise. If this is not done, the profit will be overstated for the livestock enterprise and understated for the crop enterprise.

The estimate of whole-farm profit will still be accurate if non-cash items are left out of both enterprises, but a manager will not have complete information to make decisions. If a farmer has a sufficient income so danger signs are not readily apparent, the farmer may not realize that more profit could be made from buying the feed in the market and using the land to produce another crop. A farmer may also realize that his or her skills are better used managing livestock, renting the land to another farmer, and buying feed from that farmer or the market. Without the estimates of non-cash transactions across enterprises within a business, the resulting management information and thus potential opportunities are lost.

In a real-life example, a California rancher estimated his cow/calf and hay budgets plus some alternative crop budgets. After considering this information, he realized, "I could raise more hay per acre by planting olive trees!" That statement may sound crazy, because olive trees do not produce hay and cows do not eat olives instead of hay. However, this rancher's budgets showed that, when the cows paid market prices for the hay he produced, hay was less profitable for the ranch than raising olives for cash and buying hay in the market. If he had not included the non-cash transactions of "selling" hay to the cows, he would not have seen the opportunity for increased profits and decreased risk by diversifying his income sources.

Buying land is another example of needing both cash and non-cash items for complete information. Today's land purchase involves the cash expenses of a down payment and loan fees today and the cash payments for interest and loan principal in future years. In those future years, the buyer plans and hopes to make a profit in two ways: first, by receiving sufficient cash income to pay all cash expenses (including principal and interest) plus some cash for family living, and second, by enjoying the appreciation in land values. The appreciation in value is a non-cash item until the land is sold. However, if this non-cash item is not included in budgets, a potentially profitable purchase may not be made. This non-cash appreciation also needs to be included in the market value of the asset in the buyer's financial statements (along with potential non-cash selling costs) to have a complete picture of the buyer's financial condition when the land is held and not sold.

Long-run versus Short-run

A manager's planning horizon affects how prices and quantities are chosen. The planning horizon relates to the length of time affected by the current decision. A manager who is deciding whether to sell steers today, tomorrow, or next week has a very short planning horizon for that decision. The same manager would have a longer-run horizon for a decision concerning the purchase of a neighbor's feedlot. Because of the different planning horizons, this manager might use two very different beef prices in developing the budgets involved with these analyses.

The length of the planning horizon affects not only values but also the process of choosing which prices and quantities to use in budgeting. For situations with longer horizons, the manager needs information that reflects a longer period, a broader geographical base, and a larger, more political economy.

A very short horizon dictates the use of current prices and quantities. That is, today's or next week's values may be used even if they are much higher or lower than what is normally expected. The very short-run decision is concerned with profitability in the short-run planning horizon.

The planning horizon for a farmer deciding which crops to grow next year is too long for him to rely on projections based only on today's prices. This manager needs to evaluate economic and environmental factors that may affect profitability next year.

Investment decisions require the longest planning horizons. Obviously, land and perennial crop decisions involve a longer commitment of capital than annual crop decisions. Machinery decisions require a longer planning horizon than fertilizer decisions. The longer the horizon is, the more information is needed to project prices and quantities into the future. For sizeable, long-term investments, a manager may need to evaluate historical data, long-run population trends, world climatic conditions, political conditions on both a regional and an international view, and other information (including the analysis and opinions of the appropriate experts).

In summary, the planning horizon affects the size and complexity of the information base that managers should use. As the planning horizon lengthens, the sources of information need to come from farther away in time, space, and markets.

Economic versus Accounting Values

An accounting value is based on actual transactions and a uniform set of rules called Generally Accepted Accounting Principles or GAAP. An economic value is based on its opportunity cost and not necessarily what was paid for the item. The distinction between economic and accounting values is made by considering three basic questions: How is the value determined? How is the value allocated between enterprises? Is the value cash or non-cash?

The method for determining value can vary with the situation or decision under consideration. For example, the financial cost of owning land should be estimated one way when we want to estimate the impact of existing loans on cash flow and another way when we want to compare the return from farming with the potential return from alternative investments. To evaluate the impact of existing loans, we would use the accounting cost of owning land that uses the actual interest rate on land loans. For comparing the returns from farming with potential returns in other investments, we would use the economic cost of owning land, which is the opportunity cost of the money tied up in the land. The money tied up in the land is both the actual loan and the equity in the land, including any market price appreciation. When land prices and interest rates change, the difference between economic and accounting values can be large and make a sizeable difference in how we interpret the information and, thus, the answer we develop.

The method of allocation can also cause a difference between economic and accounting values. In an economic sense, only part of the interest cost on land may be allocated to the crop. The rest could be allocated to a land investment enterprise. This allocation method recognizes that the value of land comes from two sources: farming and speculation. The accounting process may place the full cost of holding land on the crop because, until the land is sold, the crop is the only source of revenue. However, some accounting systems may be able to allocate land costs between farming and speculation.

The third distinction relates to the difference between cash and non-cash values discussed earlier. If the owner works on the farm but does not explicitly pay himself, his "pay" is a non-cash cost. An economic enterprise budget would include the owner's implicit pay because it is a cost of production. An accounting budget may not include the owner's pay as a cost. It might instead label the "bottom line" as the return to owner's labor, management, and risk. Including the owner's pay can make the analysis of the financial status of the farm or ranch more accurate, since the owner's labors would be a cash cost if they were done by someone else.

Planning Production

One major task for a farm manager is to plan production by allocating available resources between competing uses to meet the goals of the business. All problems of resource use involve one or more of three fundamental economic principles.

1. Increase the use of an input if the value of the added output (that is, income) is greater than the added cost. This principle involves the law of diminishing returns.
2. Substitute one input for another input if the cost of the substituted input is less than the cost of the replaced input and production level is maintained. This substitution can be a complete replacement or simply a change in the mix of inputs.
3. Substitute one product for another product if the value of the new product is greater than the value of the replaced product and the total cost is constant. This substitution can also be a complete replacement or a change in the mix of products.

These principles would be sufficient for planning if the manager had unlimited resources, no concern about time, and perfect knowledge. Since this is not true, three additional ideas must be introduced as aids to the decision-making process:

4. If resources are limited, use each unit of resource where it will give the greatest returns. This is the equimarginal principle, which says the optimal use of a limiting resource is found by allocating that resource across potential uses to equalize the return to the last unit in each in order to maximize total return. The goal would not be to maximize return from one use and then switch to another use.
5. When choices involve different time periods, compare the alternatives based on the present values of the resulting cash flows.
6. When risk and uncertainty cloud predictions, the potential variation in expected income and cash flow should be evaluated using different levels of prices, costs, and yields and changes in the expected behaviors of others.

In the rest of this section, the first four principles are discussed in more detail. The last two principles are discussed briefly and then explained in more detail in later chapters. The fifth principle is discussed as part of the investment analysis in Chapter 20, "Investment Analysis." The sixth principle is discussed in Chapter 23, "Risk Management."

How Much of Each Input Should Be Used?

If the goal is only profit maximization, each usage level of an input (such as fertilizer or feed) should be evaluated to figure out whether its cost is more than the income expected because of its use. For example, each increment of fertilizer use (say, 25 pounds) is evaluated for profitability. The optimal level is the highest fertilizer rate at which the cost of applying the last unit is less than the value of the resulting yield increase. An astute manager would not add the next increment past the optimal level because it would cost more than the value of the additional yield.

This approach to choosing the optimal input level can be seen in an example of wheat response to nitrogen fertilizer (Table 4.1). These data from Germany show the response of wheat to nitrogen levels of 0 to 220 kilogram per hectare (kg/ha) (or 0 to 196.5 lb/ac). The physical yield reaches a maximum yield of 73.64 dt/ha (or 109.7 bu/ac) with 140 kg of nitrogen. (Dezzitonne (dt) is a common yield measure in Germany.)

The optimal level of nitrogen should be chosen based on the value of the marginal product compared with the marginal input cost (that is, the value of the increased yield compared with the cost of the fertilizer that produces the increase). The process of calculating these values and costs is explained in the following paragraphs.

The marginal product is the difference in yield due to one fertilizer increment. In this example, the marginal product of the 10 kg of nitrogen from 90 to 100 kg is 1.46 dt of wheat. This is the difference between 71 dt (the yield with 100 kg of nitrogen) and 69.54 dt (the yield with 90 kg of nitrogen). The

Table 4.1   Wheat Response to Nitrogen Fertilizer, Germany

Nitrogen Applied kg/ha[*]	Wheat Yield dt/ha[*]	Marginal Product dt/ha	Value of Marginal Product €/ha	Marginal Factor Cost €/ha	Marginal Net Return €/ha
90	69.54				
		1.46	16.06	5	11.06
100	71.00				
		1.14	12.54	5	7.54
110	72.14				
		0.82	9.02	5	4.02
120	72.96				
		0.50	5.50	5	0.50
130	73.46				
		0.18	1.98	5	−3.02
140	73.64				
		−0.14	−1.54	5	−6.54
150	73.50				
		−0.46	−5.06	5	−10.06
160	73.04				

[*]1 dt = 1 Dezzitonne = 0.1 MG = 100 kg; 130 kg/ha = 116.1 lb/acre; and 73 dt/ha = 109 bu/acre. (1 bu wheat = 60 lb)
Source: Stephan Dabbert and Jurgen Braun, 2006, *Landwirtschaftliche Betriebslehre: Grundwissen Bachelor.* Stuttgart, Germany: Eugen Ulmer KG, pp. 32 and 35.

marginal products for the remaining increments are calculated in the same way. The highest level of nitrogen (160 kg) is too high from even a physical standpoint because the yield decreased due to the over application of nitrogen. The marginal product of increasing from 150 kg to 160 kg of nitrogen is negative.

The value of the marginal product will vary with the price chosen for the analysis. In this example, the price of 11.5 euro/dt or €/dt is used. The value of the marginal product is the price multiplied by the marginal product. With a price of 11.5 €/dt, the value of the marginal product from 90 to 100 kg of nitrogen is 16.06 €/ha (= 1.46 dt/ha * 11.5 €/dt). Values of the other marginal products are calculated in the same way.

The marginal factor cost is the price of the input multiplied by the input quantity for the increment. Using a price of 0.5 €/kg for nitrogen, the marginal factor cost of 10 kg of nitrogen is 5 €/ha. The application cost is a marginal cost for the first increment applied, but since it is a fixed cost regardless of the nitrogen level applied, it is not included in this analysis. Therefore, the marginal factor cost for each increment is 5 €/ha.

The value of the marginal product for the first increment in Table 4.1 (from 90 to 100 kg of nitrogen) is 16.06 €/ha compared with a marginal input cost of 5 €/ha, so it is profitable to increase the nitrogen level by this 10 kg. The value of the marginal product from the second increment (increasing to 110 kg) is 12.54 €/ha compared with a marginal input cost of 5 €/ha, so it is also profitable to increase the level by this 10 kg. We keep taking these steps for each 10-kg increment of nitrogen, but then we see the value of the marginal product for increasing from 130 to 140 kg/ha is only 1.98 €/ha compared with a marginal input cost of 5 €/ha, so it is not profitable to increase the level by this 10 kg. Since the previous 10-kg increment was profitable, we conclude that with the prices and costs used, the optimal level of nitrogen fertilizer is 130 kg/ha based on the data. This optimal level can be found by increasing the nitrogen rate to the next level as long as the marginal net return for that incremental step is positive.

The **law of diminishing returns** is an important concept in economics and very obvious in Table 4.1. The law of diminishing returns states that as one factor of production is increased while all other factors are held constant, the return from additional levels of the first factor will decrease or diminish. This can be seen in Table 4.1 as the value of the marginal product of 10 kg of nitrogen starts at 16.06 €/ha, declines continually, and eventually turns negative.

For space considerations, a subset of the data is shown in Table 4.1; the full set of data is shown in the graph in Figure 4.3. On the graph we again see the law of diminishing returns working, with the maximum physical yield increasing at a decreasing rate to approximately 140 kg/ha. By plotting and comparing the value of the marginal product and the marginal factor cost, we can see these two lines cross between 130 and 140 kg/ha. The optimal, profit maximizing level of nitrogen is thus 130 kg/ha.

What if the separate increments had not been evaluated? The maximum yield in the data is 73.64 dt/ha at 140 kg of nitrogen per ha compared to 42 dt with no nitrogen. If the maximum yield was chosen as a target, the value of the increase in the wheat yield would be 348.04 €/ha, which is greater than the increase in the input cost from 0 to 140 kg (70 €/ha). By that analysis, the nitrogen rate should be 140 kg. Although that level (140 kg) is profitable because total return is greater than total costs, it is not the optimal, profit-maximizing rate. This is true because, as we can see in the table, the marginal factor cost of increasing from 130 to 140 kg is greater than the value of the marginal product. The net return for using 140 kg of nitrogen is 278.04 €/ha compared to 281.06 €/ha using 130 kg. Although the difference of 3.02 €/ha is not great per hectare, if the farm has 200 hectares, the total for the farm is 604 €. If higher-yield targets were used without looking at the marginal steps of fertilizer use, profits would be reduced even more.

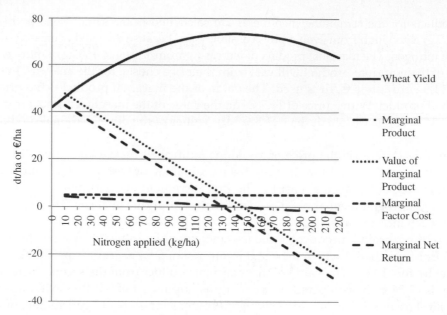

Figure 4.3   Wheat Yield Response to Applied Nitrogen, Germany

In this marginal analysis, we looked only at one hectare and chose the optimal level of 130 kg/ha while thinking we could purchase all the nitrogen we wanted. However, suppose our supply of nitrogen fertilizer was limited by either a physical inventory constraint or a financial constraint. Suppose we had 100 ha of wheat but only 10,000 kg of nitrogen, which is less than what is needed for the optimal level. We could apply 130 kg/ha to approximately 80 ha and nothing on the other 20 ha, but this would not maximize the total return to the 10,000 kg of nitrogen. As we noted earlier, the law of diminishing returns shows a decreasing value of marginal product as nitrogen increases. So putting nitrogen on some, but not all, hectares means some of the nitrogen could be producing more wheat if it was reallocated across all the land. If the nitrogen was applied at a rate of 100 kg/ha to each of the 100 ha, then every 10 kg of nitrogen would produce a value of marginal product of at least 16.06 €/ha, compared to giving some land more than 100 kg/ha and receiving less than 16.06 € from the amount above 100. This is an example of the **equimarginal principle** of allocating a scarce resource to equate the marginal return from all uses.

The equimarginal principle can also be used to allocate scarce capital for investments. The mix of investment in land, machinery, buildings, livestock, and labor costs should be done to equate the marginal return to capital in each use. For example, a farmer would not want to invest in machinery to the point of having a lower marginal return to the machinery investment than could have been obtained by investing in livestock.

For another example of choosing the economically optimal level of one input, let us consider the response of continuous corn to nitrogen fertilizer in Minnesota (Table 4.2). Using a corn price forecast of $3.00 per bushel and a nitrogen price of $0.35 per lb and the same steps used for the previous example, these data show an optimal rate of 160 lb of nitrogen per acre. Below that level, each

Table 4.2 Response of Continuous Corn to Nitrogen Fertilizer, Minnesota

Nitrogen Applied lb/ac*	Corn Yield bu/ac*	Marginal Product bu/ac	Value of Marginal Product $/ac	Marginal Factor Cost $/ac	Marginal Net Return $/ac
0	75				
		25	75	14	61
40	100				
		15	45	14	31
80	115				
		10	30	14	16
120	125				
		8	24	14	10
160	133				
		3	9	14	−5
200	136				

*1 lb = 454 g; 1 acre = 0.405 hectare; 1 bushel of corn = 56 lb.

additional step of 40 lbs of nitrogen has a positive marginal net return. However, the step from 160 to 200 lbs has a negative marginal net return even though the yield is estimated to increase.

The fertilization decision is dependent on many factors with some quite uncertain. As an example of the uncertainty of water supply, consider the impact of water availability on the optimal level of nitrogen (Example 4.2).

Example 4.2. Fertilizer Recommendations and Water Availability

In dryland farming (that is, without irrigation), a crop's response to fertilization is highly dependent on how much water is available in the soil at planting time and how much is received at critical points during the growing period. Water may be sufficient in most years so farmers are ready to plant, but the water availability in any one year can be highly uncertain in many areas of the world.

In a recent example for one wheat-growing region in Australia, researchers estimated the response to nitrogen under different conditions of soil water levels at planting and the amount of rainfall received during the growing season. Using prices from 2008, an expectation of 100% ROI (i.e., 100% recovery of fertilizer cost), and wheat yield response, they developed the following recommendations for nitrogen availability under different water availability conditions. The actual nitrogen to be applied each year would be the amount needed minus the estimated amount available in the soil. For example, if the soil moisture at planting was at the medium level and the forecast for rainfall was very good, the recommended level of available nitrogen is 155 kg/ha. If the soil test indicated that 60 kg/ha was available in the soil, 95 kg/ha should be applied. In contrast, if the forecast for rainfall was very poor, only 75 kg/ha of available is recommended and only 15 kg/ha should be applied.

(continued)

(continued)

Estimated Economically Optimal Levels of Available Nitrogen for Different Soil Moisture Levels at Sowing and Growing Season Rainfall

Soil Moisture at Sowing	Available Nitrogen/ha for 100% ROI according to Growing Season Rainfall		
	Very Poor	Average	Very Good
Very wet (222 mm/m soil)	60	85	135
Medium (124 mm/m soil)	75	105	155
Very dry (63 mm/m soil)	—	95	120

Source: R. J. Farquharson, B. Malcolm, and D. Chen, 2009, "How Much Is an Extra Kilogram of Nitrogen Worth? New Information for Fertiliser Decisions by Wheat Growers." Peer-reviewed paper at the 17th International Farm Management Congress, Illinois State University, Bloomington/Normal, Illinois, July 19–24, 2009, accessed on February 1, 2010, at http://www.ifmaonline.org/pdf/congress/09_Farquharson_etal.pdf.

When the decision involves two inputs, the decision process is similar but has a few more steps. As a first step when using the data in tabular format, the "temporary" best level of the first input is found when the second input is "fixed" at a low level. Then the first input is "fixed" temporarily at the "best" level just chosen and the "best" level of the second level is found. This process is repeated until neither input is increased again. This process can be visualized as working from the upper left corner to the lower right corner of a table showing yield response to, for example, both phosphate and nitrogen fertilization.

As an example of choosing the optimal levels of two inputs, let us consider the response of potatoes to nitrogen and phosphorus fertilizer in Germany (Table 4.3 and Figure 4.4). The applied nitrogen rate ranged from 0 to 1.5 dt/ha and the applied phosphorus rate ranged from 0 to 1.2 dt/ha. The maximum yield was 383.6 dt/ha (342.6 cwt/ac) at 1.4 dt/ha (125 lbs./ac) of nitrogen and 1.1 dt/ha (98.2 lb/ac) of phosphorus.

Table 4.3   The Yield Response of Potatoes to Nitrogen and Phosphorus Fertilizer, dt/ha,[*] Germany

Applied Nitrogen (N) (dt/ha)	Applied Phosphorus (P) (dt/ha)						
	0.5	0.6	0.7	0.8	0.9	1.0	1.1
0.9	347.7	351.4	354.2	356.2	357.3	357.6	357.0
1.0	356.2	360.0	362.9	365.0	366.2	366.6	366.1
1.1	362.8	366.7	369.8	371.9	373.3	373.7	373.3
1.2	367.5	371.5	374.7	376.9	378.4	378.9	378.6
1.3	370.3	374.4	377.6	380.0	381.5	382.2	382.0
1.4	371.2	375.4	378.7	381.2	382.8	383.6	383.5
1.5	370.1	374.4	377.8	380.4	382.2	383.0	383.0

[*]1 dt = 1 Dezzitonne = 0.1 MG = 100 kg; 1.0 dt/ha = 89.3 lb/acre; and 380 dt/ha = 339 cwt/acre. (1 cwt = 100 lb)
Source: Dr. Stephan Dabbert, Department of Farm Management, University of Hohenheim, Germany.
Accessed at https://www.uni-hohenheim.de/i410a/planung/folien3.pdf on September 22, 2009.

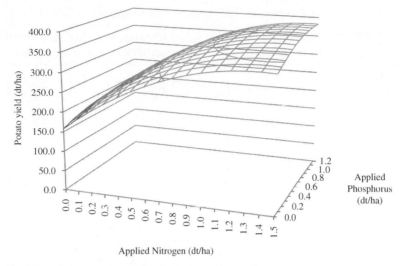

Figure 4.4 Potato Yield Response to Nitrogen and Phosphorus, Germany

As described above, choosing the optimal combination of nitrogen and phosphorus starts by finding the best level of phosphorus when nitrogen is "fixed" at the starting level. By looking at the graph, the starting level of 0.6 dt/ha was chosen as a reasonable place to start compared to the low levels without jumping past a potentially optimal level. We use the same procedures used earlier when only one input was being analyzed. Using a potato price of 7.5 €/dt and a nitrogen price of 0.7 €/kg, the best level of phosphorus (with nitrogen "fixed" at 0.6 dt/ha) is 1.4 dt/ha (Table 4.4). The value of the marginal product for the next increment of nitrogen is obviously less than the marginal factor cost since the yield decreases.

Now, with phosphorus "fixed" temporarily at 1.4 dt/ha, the "best" level of nitrogen is estimated using a potato price of 7.5 €/dt and a nitrogen price of 0.575 €/kg (Table 4.5). The row of yields with the phosphorus rate at 1.4 dt/ha is transposed into a column to fit the same format used in the earlier examples. This shows that with a phosphorus rate of 1.4 dt/ha, the best nitrogen rate is 0.9 dt/ha.

Table 4.4 Potato Yield Response to Nitrogen Fertilizer with Phosphorus "Fixed" at 0.6 dt/ha

Nitrogen Applied dt/ha	Potato Yield dt/ha	Marginal Product dt/ha	Value of Marginal Product €/ha	Marginal Input Costs €/ha	Marginal Net Return €/ha
0.9	351.4				
		8.6	64.5	7	57.5
1.0	360.0				
		6.7	50.2	7	43.2
1.1	366.7				
		4.8	36.0	7	29.0
1.2	371.5				
		2.9	21.7	7	14.7
1.3	374.4				
		1	7.5	7	0.5
1.4	375.4				
		−1	−7.5	7	−14.5
1.5	374.4				

Table 4.5 Potato Yield Response to Phosphorus (P) Fertilizer with Nitrogen (N) "Fixed" at 1.4 dt/ha

Phosphorus Applied dt/ha	Potato Yield dt/ha	Marginal Product dt/ha	Value of Marginal Product €/ha	Marginal Input Costs €/ha	Marginal Net Return €/ha
0.5	371.2				
		4.2	31.5	7	24.5
0.6	375.4				
		3.3	24.75	7	17.75
0.7	378.7				
		2.5	18.75	7	11.75
0.8	381.2				
		1.6	12	7	5
0.9	382.8				
		0.8	6	7	−1
1.0	383.6				
		−0.1	−0.75	7	−7.75
1.1	383.5				

At this point, we need to revisit the rate of nitrogen to decide whether it should be increased due to a better response at higher phosphorus levels. As shown in the original table, the estimated yield with 1.4 dt/ha of nitrogen and 0.9 dt/ha of phosphorus is 382.8 dt/ha (Table 4.3). The marginal product of changing from 1.4 to 1.5 dt/ha of nitrogen (with 0.9 dt/ha of phosphorus) is a yield loss of 0.6 dt/ha (382.8 minus 382.2). Thus, increasing nitrogen to 1.5 dt is not profitable.

The resulting recommendation is 1.4 dt/ha of nitrogen and 0.9 dt/ha of phosphate using the yield response data in Tables 4.4 and 4.5, a potato price of 7.5 €/dt, a nitrogen price of 0.7 €/kg, and a nitrogen price of 0.575 €/kg.

The analysis of the value of marginal product and marginal factor costs has wide applications. This method can be used for analyzing incremental levels of an input (such as fertilizer and feed) and it can be used to evaluate the use or non-use of such inputs as herbicides, cultivations, and so on. The basic approach is to estimate the biological or physical responses to inputs and then choose the appropriate prices and costs to apply to those data. The concept of marginal analysis is critical at several points in farm management: developing enterprise budgets, evaluating the current plans, or analyzing a potential new enterprise.

What Mix of Inputs Should Be Used?

More than one combination of inputs will often produce the same quantity of output. A common example is the mix of forage and concentrates for cattle feed. Another example is the different combinations of mechanical cultivation, herbicides, hand-hoeing, and other controls that will achieve the same level of weed control. A third example is the different methods of pruning: hand, mechanical, or both.

The optimal combination of inputs that produce the same output is the least-cost combination of those inputs. If the number of alternatives is not large, the simplest way to choose is to calculate the cost of each mix of inputs and select the lowest-cost mix. The lowest-cost mix will be the maximum profit combination if the output level does not change. If output levels do change, a partial budget can be used to include the changes in the value of the output and the changes in inputs.

Table 4.6 Combinations of Corn and Supplement Estimated to Produce a 40-lb Gain in a 40-lb Pig

Ration	Corn (lb/hd)	Supplement (lb/hd)	Cost of Corn	Cost of Supplement	Total Ration Cost
1	104	13	5.57	1.63	7.20
2	95	16	5.09	2.00	7.09
3	89	19	4.77	2.18	7.14
4	86	22	4.61	2.75	7.36

For a simple example of input substitution, suppose a farmer can estimate from his records that for the same level of weed control, one herbicide spray will substitute for four hours of hand-hoeing. If the total wage cost is $11 per hour, the hand-weeding would cost $44 per acre (4 hours per acre times $11 per hour). If the herbicide spray costs $27 per acre, that is the least-cost weed control method and without considering other factors would be the farmer's choice. Other factors that may affect this decision include potential changes in the weed population dynamics and environmental concerns.

As an example of choosing the optimal feed mix, let us consider four possible combinations of corn and supplement to feed a pig from 40 lb to 80 lb (Table 4.6). If we ignore potential time differences due to different protein levels, these different combinations of corn and supplement are estimated to produce the same 40-lb gain in a pig. Using feed costs of $3.00 per bushel for corn and $250 per ton for the supplement, the cost of each ration is calculated. The corn cost per pound is calculated by dividing the price per bushel by the standard weight of 56 pounds of corn per bushel. The supplement cost per pound is calculated by dividing the supplement price per ton by 2000 lb. The cost of each ration is the sum of the cost of corn plus the cost of the supplement. For the first ration, the cost of the corn is $5.57 and the supplement cost is $1.63, resulting in a total cost of $7.20 to feed the pig from 40 lb to 80 lb. This simple process is done for the other three rations. Although the differences are small, the second ration is the lowest-cost option at $7.09 and would be the choice if only the feed cost were considered.

Suppose the corn price increased to $4.00 per bushel and the supplement price increased to $350 per ton; the ration costs would change, but would the choice change? The total cost would be $9.70 for ration 1, $9.59 for 2, $9.68 for 3, and $9.99 for 4. Thus, in this case, ration 2 would still be the least-cost option even though the new prices make all the rations more expensive. The price of corn does not increase enough relative to the price of the supplement to cause a reason to change the ration to one with a higher level of supplement.

The choice of a ration may also be affected by the type of operation. In the previous example, the ration changed, but we assumed output did not because all rations were estimated to produce a 40-lb gain. However, animals gain faster with a ration higher in protein. If we consider the time of gain, these rations do not produce the same output. So managers concerned with the speed at which animals gain these 40 lb would need more information on the rate of gain and the potential for alternatives of the space. These managers could use a partial budget to analyze their choices.

Farm Size

How large should a farm be? This question should be answered in two directions: vertically and horizontally. The two directions come from considering the value chain, which is the process of making the final product starting with input suppliers and going through distributors, producers, processors, wholesalers, and retailers to the final consumer. When a river is used as the analogy for the value chain with primary production done at the beginning or upper end of the river and the final consumers at the end of the value chain river, the movement up and down the value chain is viewed as vertical movement. A firm that expands by producing more of a particular product at a specific point in the value chain is viewed as expanding horizontally since that movement is perpendicular to the vertical movement or flow of the product to the consumer.

Vertical Expansion

A farm can expand vertically by moving or integrating up- and downstream on the value chain. Deciding to market directly to consumers or to retailers is a vertical move downstream, closer to the consumer. Deciding to build specialized equipment on the farm instead of buying standard equipment from a machinery dealer is an example of moving upstream. Many livestock farms are already vertically integrated since they already produce the feed for their livestock. They do not concentrate only on the crops or livestock. Some livestock farmers have decided to specialize—that is, decrease their vertical integration by concentrating on livestock only and buying all their feed needs in the market. The choice to hire custom harvesters instead of owning the harvesting equipment is a question of vertical expansion, as is the question of hiring a full-time veterinarian on a livestock farm versus hiring veterinarian services as needed.

Vertical expansion (or contraction) is essentially a "make or buy" decision. A farmer must weigh the benefits of growing the feed within the farm business versus the benefits of buying feed in the market. What are the benefits of having a full-time veterinarian on staff for livestock versus paying for services as needed?

A dairy farm can evaluate the choice to concentrate on the milking herd only and buy replacement heifers or to include the raising of replacement heifers within the definition of the farm. The question is whether the farm should "make or buy" its replacement heifers. This question can be evaluated by estimating the costs of raising the calves and comparing this to the price of buying replacement heifers in the market. If the cost of raising calves on the farm is greater than the purchase price of replacement heifers in the market, then the farm should seriously consider not raising its own heifers.

This question can be altered slightly by considering the development of a relationship with a neighboring farmer who buys all the calves from the dairy farm, raises and breeds the heifers, and then sells the bred heifers back to the original dairy farm. This is still a make-or-buy question, but it is altered by the formation of a working relationship, perhaps with a written contract. The relationship decreases some uncertainty and concern for the dairy farm by knowing and controlling the genetics of the replacement heifers and the quality of the care given to the calves and heifers. The farmer raising the calves could benefit by having an established relationship and market for both inputs and outputs—that is, calves and heifers.

As a bad example of vertical expansion, consider the real-life case of the farmer who thought he had to control directly the quality and supply of feed for his dairy (Example 4.3).

Example 4.3. A Bad Example of Vertical Expansion

Several years ago, a farmer thought he had to control directly the quality and supply of feed for his dairy. He had to own the land and produce the hay himself. That was his rule, and he followed it as much as he could, although he did rent some land for feed production. During a period of rapid land price increase, he saw and heard of farmers losing rented land when someone else bought the land and stopped renting it to the original renter. The farmer became concerned when the owner of one farm he was renting decided to sell it. His immediate response was that he needed to buy the land in order to assure his supply of feed, especially hay. Without making the evaluation of "make or buy," this farmer bought the land at a very high price. But then in the early 1980s land prices dropped considerably. At the time of the visit with this farmer, his financial troubles were already great and his future on the farm was in question. If he had made even a simple calculation of the costs of producing his own hay versus buying it in the market, he would have very quickly seen that the interest costs alone on the land purchase were much greater per unit of hay than the price of hay in the market. He would have seen the wisdom in not buying the land. He could have traveled far and paid high prices in the market for hay and still had cheaper hay for his dairy than his chosen alternative of making his own. This farmer's assumption that remaining vertically integrated upstream into hay production was automatically better than purchasing hay nearly cost him his farm.

Source: Author's personal interview.

Besides making the budgetary estimate of whether it is better to make or buy, other factors need to be considered. The benefits of using the market include the following.

- Other firms may be able to achieve economies of scale and provide a lower input cost or better product price than can be obtained by keeping the production internal. As will be discussed in the next section, economies of scale occur when a firm can expand and achieve lower costs per unit of production and potentially better quality than possible at smaller sizes. This can be seen in the traveling harvest companies, especially in the wheat areas of the United States, which move north from Texas through Kansas to North Dakota as the wheat matures and is ready for harvest. These companies can buy larger combines, larger trucks, and spread these costs over more production. Repetition of the harvest process through the harvest season and year after year can allow these companies to learn the fine points of more efficient harvest and handling processes than the individual farms for which they harvest.
- Other firms are subject to the discipline of the market. The competition of the market will force firms to keep costs low or they will likely lose business to competitors. A wheat harvester who does not keep costs as low as competitors will soon find that farms will hire other harvesters. The market pressures the suppliers of services and products to innovate, to find new ways of producing and servicing. A farm that decides to do its own harvesting does not feel the same market pressure to keep harvest costs as low as possible (but they are still subject to the discipline of the market in the cost of wheat supplied to the market).
- By using the market, a farm can also avoid what is called internal slack. This is what happens when the internal operation has too much capacity, does not feel pressure to innovate, does not feel pressure to maintain high efficiency, and does not strive constantly to decrease costs. The difference between the higher cost of producing internally compared to cost of buying from the market is called internal slack.
- Another reason for buying from the market is to take advantage of innovation by others. If the machinery, for example, is owned by the farm, the tendency is to keep the well-maintained machine even though more efficient machines may be developed and available later.

By raising replacement heifers or gilts, a livestock farm may not be able to improve its genetic base as quickly as other farms and thus not achieve the productivity gains that other farms are achieving. The cost of the replacement female may seem lower in the short run, but the cost of lower productivity in the future may not be included. This potential increase in productivity could be estimated and built into the evaluation of whether to "make or buy" replacements.

- Buying in the market can also allow a farm to avoid the purchase of equipment and buildings. This avoidance or shifting of the financial burden of ownership to others allows the farm to (1) use the money on other investments that may have better returns to the farm and (2) avoid increasing debt relative to equity. The wheat farmer who hires the harvester instead of buying the harvesting equipment may be able to buy storage facilities and improve the return from marketing decisions.

Using the market also has costs that need to be considered. These include the following.

- Coordination of production with other firms can require more time and resources than making the product or service internally to the farm as well as with others in the value chain. If produced internally, control over the connections and communications can be done administratively, but if other firms are producing the product or service, this direct control is absent. As an example, the number and quality of replacement animals from an outside supplier may not meet the expectations of the livestock farmer. Thus, the productivity and efficiency of the farm may be harmed. The time and resources required for the initial contacts and selection of outside suppliers may be considerably greater than that needed to buy the equipment and perform the operation internally. Concerns about the reliability of the supplier may create a need for more contact and work to ensure arrival and completion of the task.

  Increased coordination costs are not always due to external firms. Internal operations may have been slowed or speeded up for many reasons, but the plans with an external supplier are based on a schedule developed before the slowing or speeding was even anticipated. If preliminary activities are slowed, the farm may incur additional costs trying to finish these activities so the farm is ready when the supplier arrives as initially scheduled. If the operation was performed internally, the equipment could be ready but waiting and the workers busy with other activities until the preliminary activities were finished in an orderly process without additional costs. If the preliminary activities were finished early before the hired supplier arrives, this may or may not be a problem depending on whether the potential delay in the next operation would create a quality or cost problem.

- The potential lack of timeliness when hiring others to make a product or perform a service is related to the coordination problem. However, lack of timeliness needs to be mentioned separately due to its potential for creating costs associated with loss of quantity and quality. This is especially true when working with perishable products such as fresh vegetables and fruit.

- For some farms, a cost of using the market may be the leakage of private information such as process ideas that help maintain competitive advantage. If the external supplier works with financial information, the private information may be decisions and plans to make purchases or sales of assets and thus disrupt the potential price. An example of this loss of private information involves a farmer who had a lumber supply firm build a few portable swine buildings to his specifications that were a new design. He was charged the lumber company's exact costs of producing these buildings. After a few months, the farmer asked for some more of these buildings and found that the lumber supply firm had offered the new design buildings to other farmers who were willing to pay more than just the cost of production. The farmer with the original design idea had to pay the higher cost because he had lost his private information.

- For livestock producers especially, the use of external suppliers increases the chance of disease entering the herd. Associated costs are the cleaning of facilities for people and equipment coming onto the site.
- Transaction costs are higher costs incurred due to participating in the market instead of performing the work internally. These costs can be either directly observable or subtle and hard to observe. Directly observable costs include, for example, the time and additional expense needed to negotiate contracts and coordinate schedules with a hired harvester rather than owning the machine yourself. Another example is the legal costs incurred for understanding the obligations, opportunities, and potential pitfalls associated with signing contracts. Transaction costs that may be hard to observe include a contractor (either supplier or buyer) working with competitors and charging them a lower cost because the first firm is covering more of the fixed costs of the contractor. The specifications of the contract may at first be advantageous, but the supplier may learn of a firm's private information and use that to its own advantage when working with other firms.

Horizontal Expansion

Horizontal expansion involves the questions of how large a farm should be in terms of the number of products and services and the amount of each product and service a farm should be producing. Answers to these two questions are dependent on what are called economies of scope and economies of scale.

Economies of scope occur when the costs of production decline as the variety of products and services increases. This situation takes place when total costs can be lowered by combining the production of different products within one firm compared to the total costs incurred by separate farms producing the same quantity of each product.

Economies of scale occur when the average cost per unit of production declines as the quantity of production increases. Thus, a farm will be more profitable at a larger size because the production cost per unit of product is lower and thus more money is received per unit (if the cost is below the market price).

However, costs per unit do not always continue to decline as production increases. At some size, costs can either start to increase or cease to decrease and level out at a certain cost per unit. We refer to diseconomies of scale when average costs increase. The size at which average costs start to increase is the optimal, low-cost size of the farm. To expand beyond this point increases the cost per unit and reduces profit. Farms that are smaller or larger suffer a competitive disadvantage due to higher costs associated with diseconomies of scale.

If average costs decline and then stabilize and not increase, the farm has a minimum efficient size to achieve minimum average costs but could continue to increase in size and still maintain low costs. Farms that are smaller suffer a disadvantage due to higher costs, but those that are larger have the same costs and remain competitive with all other farms equal to or larger than the minimum efficient size.

Economies of scale and scope come from several sources.

- Spreading of fixed costs. Fixed costs occur because some assets and their costs cannot be divided. The more a fixed asset, such as a building or machine, is used to produce product, the more units of production are available to help pay for the costs of that asset. For example, if more cows can be milked in a milking parlor, more milk is available to pay for that parlor and the lower the costs per unit of milk. Similarly, a crop planter that is used on more land will have lower costs for each unit of land.
- Marketing and purchasing economies. The cost of making a marketing or purchasing transaction is usually the same regardless of the quantity bought or sold. Costs of delivery may change, but the

costs in time for market research and negotiation as well as office expenses will likely remain the same regardless of the quantity. Thus, larger farms will be able to decrease costs per unit due to their larger sales volume.

- Increased productivity of variable inputs. Increased productivity of variable inputs can occur in at least two ways. As a farm grows, labor may become more specialized and thus workers may become more efficient in what they do. Instead of doing several tasks, a worker can focus on a smaller set of tasks and become more productive. For example, a farm that expands sufficiently may be able to have one person specialize in the office activities of selling, buying, and accounting. That person becomes more productive in those activities due to that specialization. Another person may be able to focus on the physical production activities of caring for the animals instead of also working in the office. This improvement in labor productivity may create both economies of scale and scope.

  Another source of productivity comes from the ability to use larger, more efficient machines. A tractor that has twice the horsepower of a smaller tractor does not use twice the fuel of the smaller tractor. In addition, the larger tractor will be able to pull larger implements, cover more land per hour, and thus increase labor productivity also.

- Inventories. Farms that need inventories may be able to decrease average inventory costs as farm size increases. The feed inventory of livestock farms is perhaps the best example for farms. Even though larger farms may have larger feed quantities in inventory, the total feed in inventory may be less per animal for larger farms.

- Physical properties of production. The physical properties of production can affect the average costs of production and create economies of scale. For example, storage capacity increases faster than the surface area of the storage facility. A grain bin that has a larger diameter and is taller than another grain bin will have a volume proportionately greater than the increase in diameter and height.

- Pecuniary economies. A large farm may be able to negotiate a better price just due to the size of the potential purchase or sale. This benefit come to farms who have already taken advantage of economies of scale and scope and reinforces those advantages.

Diseconomies of scale and scope may come from several sources.

- Rising labor costs. Larger farms will likely have more employees than small farms, and the cost of the owner may be paid as a wage instead of being a non-cash expense. They also may pay higher wages than smaller farms, so labor costs may rise for some farms and enterprises as they grow in size.

- Internal communication and coordination. A larger farm must take more time for communication and coordination. Even if the farm has a single operator with no employees, being larger requires more time for record keeping and information control to be sure all the necessary activities are done, done on time, and done properly. As employees and then supervisors are added, the time and thus cost of communication and coordination increases. The benefit of more employees can be achieved if this cost is kept to a minimum.

- Incentive and bureaucracy effects. Beyond problems of communication, large farms may have trouble motivating and monitoring workers. These workers may not see how they fit into the business; they may think they can avoid work if no one is watching, so productivity suffers. The manager of a larger farm needs to develop an incentive system along with a monitoring and measuring system to reward productive employees.

- Spreading of specialized resources. As a farm grows, some resources, such as the herd manager or the accountant and marketing person, may be stretched thin or spread over too many animals or land. This problem may occur in the initial stages of growth before a manager understands when and how to increase critical resources. At some point, the manager of a growing farm may realize that two persons are needed; one to do the marketing and one to do the accounting. Perhaps the accounting could be outsourced so that the internal person concentrates on marketing. Stretching may occur due to the "lumpiness" and cost of the critical resource, which means it can't be added in small enough units. So as a farm grows, the resource is stretched thin for a time and then the farm grows enough to be able to add another unit of the resource. For example, the milking parlor may work well until the herd becomes too big to send all the cows through and still maintain sanitation and maintenance procedures. Then the manager may decide that a new facility is needed. If the farm continues to grow, the pattern may repeat itself.

Economies of scale and scope are not always the main driving forces of increasing farm size. At times other factors or issues are the limiting growth. Consider the case of farm size in Russia (Example 4.4).

Example 4.4. Optimal Farm Size in Russia

Optimal farm size is usually thought of as largely determined by returns to scale. However, other factors may be more important in other geographical areas and in different times.

A study in Russia found that returns to scale was not as successful in explaining changes in the size of corporate farms near Moscow from 1996 to 2004. The ability to decrease transaction costs associated with obtaining access to markets was determined to be more important than returns to scale. The authors propose the development of business networks to reduce transaction costs by increasing knowledge of who to contact, where to market, and how to market products in developing markets. They also note that policy changes could also be made to decrease transaction costs and improve the access of all farmers to markets—milk markets specifically for the farms in this study.

Source: N. Svetlov and H. Hockmann, "Optimal Farm Size in Russian Agriculture." Contributed paper at the International Association of Agricultural Economics 2009 Conference, August 16–22, 2009, Beijing, China. Accessed on January 8, 2010, at http://purl.umn.edu/51667.

Markets and Market Structure

A **market** is a group of suppliers and buyers whose trading sets the price of a product. A farmer's market is the group of sellers and buyers in which the farm chooses to operate. The benefit of this general definition is that it requires a farmer to define his or her product(s) and the close substitutes for those product(s). By identifying a farm's products and the substitutes, a farmer can focus attention on the true competitors, suppliers, and buyers—that is, the farmer's market. By having a clear understanding of the market, a farmer can more easily identify and study the trends and factors that will indeed affect the farm, decisions, and success.

Identifying those products that are close substitutes to a specific product can be done by qualitative and quantitative methods. Qualitatively, products tend to be close substitutes when they (1) have the same or similar product performance characteristics, (2) have the same or similar occasions for use, and (3) are sold in the same geographic market. For example, a beef producer should realize that close substitutes for beef include pork and poultry. Nutritionally, all three of these products supply protein with the nine essential amino acids. They all are used as the main part of meals and are often the center of attention at festivities. They are almost always sold in the same geographical area. It is very easy to conclude that these are substitutes for each other.

Substitutes can also be identified by the cross-price elasticity of demand for two products. As described earlier in this chapter, the cross-price elasticity of demand between two products is the percentage change in the demand for one product because of a 1% change in the price of another product. The more sensitive demand is to price changes, the larger will be the elasticity. Products that are close substitutes of each other will be quite sensitive to each other's price and have a larger, positive cross-price elasticity.

Market Structure and Competition

Market structure refers to the number and size of firms within a market or industry. It affects the level of competition in an industry and how prices are determined within the market. There are four main forms of market structure: perfect competition, monopolistic competition, oligopoly, and monopoly.

Perfect competition.   An industry with many firms that each have a small percentage of the market is described as perfect competition. Farming is essentially a perfectly competitive industry (if we ignore the impacts of government subsidies and regulations). No one farm can affect the price; all farms can do is choose output levels and produce. In perfectly competitive markets, firms face infinitely elastic demand that is flat, and all firms face the same price. Even in a market with many sellers but not perfect competition, a firm will have trouble setting prices because customers have more freedom to change. Price-setting through the illegal strategy of collusion between sellers will not work for extended periods of time.

Monopolistic competition.   Monopolistic competition occurs when there are many sellers and each is slightly differentiated from the other. Firms may be able to set slightly different prices and change those prices without great reaction by other firms. However, if a firm in such a situation raises prices too high, the consumers may switch to other firms and other firms may enter the market. Either reaction causes profits to decrease and keeps prices low.

Oligopoly.   In an oligopoly, there are few firms due to natural or created barriers to entry. Those few firms believe their actions can influence market price and volume. In rural areas, gas stations and other input suppliers may have some oligopoly power due to being geographically separated from many competitors, but that power is minimized by communication and transportation abilities of buyers. At times, farmers may feel that they are subject to the power of oligopolies when dealing with their suppliers and buyers; however, that power may be more due to the larger size of the businesses (e.g., herbicide suppliers) compared to the smaller sizes of farms.

Monopoly.   In a monopoly, there are very few firms or perhaps even just one firm. Utility companies are prime examples. Utilities enjoy markets protected from entry by regulators, but their prices are regulated by public boards. Some monopolies exist for natural reasons such as owning the main resource(s) for the product(s) or being the only provider in a geographical area.

Table 4.7 Four Classes of Market Structure and the Intensity of Price Competition

Nature of Competition	Range of Herfindahls	Intensity of Price Competition
Perfect competition	Usually below 0.2	Fierce
Monopolistic competition	Usually below 0.2	May be fierce or light, depending on product differentiation
Oligopoly	0.1 to 0.6	May be fierce or light, depending on interfirm rivalry
Monopoly	0.6 and above	Usually light, unless threatened by entry

Source: Besanko, Dranove, and Shanley, 1996, p. 287.

Market concentration or market structure is often measured in two ways: N-firm concentration and Herfindahl indices. The N-firm concentration ratio is calculated as the combined market share of the N largest firms in the market. Market share is usually based on sales revenue. In public reports from the government, the number of firms, N, is usually four or eight. An industry consisting of five firms, each with a market share of 10% of the market, and 10 firms, each with a market share of 5%, would have a four-firm concentration ratio of 40% and an eight-firm ratio of 65%. Even though this example industry sounds concentrated, the next measure does not point strongly at concentration.

A Herfindahl index is the sum of the squared market shares of all the firms in the industry. (For the calculation, market shares are expressed as proportions; that is, a 15% share is written as 0.15 and is usually restricted to those firms with a market share of .01 or larger.) The Herfindahl index ranges between 0 and 1. A more concentrated industry will have an index closer to 1. For example, a true monopoly with one firm (and thus 100% of the market) has a Herfindahl index of 1^2 or 1. If there are two firms each with 50% of the market, the Herfindahl index is 0.5 (which is $0.5^2 + 0.5^2$). If one firm had a market share of 60% and the other firm had 40%, the Herfindahl index is 0.52 (which is $0.6^2 + 0.4^2$). The earlier example industry, which seemed concentrated when using the concentration ratio (with five firms each having a 10% market share and 10 firms with 5% each) has a Herfindahl index of 0.075, which points at perfect competition more than at monopoly or oligopoly.

Besanko, Dranove, and Shanley (1996) have identified the range of Herfindahl indices for the four types of industry and the resulting intensity of price competition (Table 4.7). Farming is obviously in perfect competition using this classification with the resulting intense or fierce price competition. Industries, such as agricultural chemicals, would be classified as facing monopolistic competition by this classification. The largest company may have some ability to set prices independently with no reaction from competitors or customers, but that ability disappears if it raises prices too much or loses its patent protections over time and competitors start making copies of its product.

This chapter provided a brief introduction to the principles of microeconomics as they apply to farming. It also explained the principles affecting farm size and how markets and market structure concepts can be used in strategic management.

Summary

- If resources are scarce or limited, people need to make tradeoffs in using them.
- Prices are determined by the value placed on a product by both sellers and buyers.

- Supply is determined by sellers, who see the market as providing a price that is at or above the value they place on their products.
- Demand is determined by buyers, who see the market as providing a price that is at or below the value they place on the product being offered for sale.
- The market price is the equilibrium price, determined by buyers and sellers as they find that price at which no more sellers want to sell their product and no more buyers want to buy the product.
- Elasticity refers to the responsiveness of demand and supply to changes in the price. More elastic demand means a greater change in quantity demanded when price changes.
- The opportunity cost of a resource is the income that could be received from the best alternative use of that resource.
- Total, average, and marginal income and costs provide different pieces of information for different kinds of decisions.
- Fixed costs are those that occur no matter what or how much is produced. Variable costs are those costs that will vary with the volume of business.
- Direct costs are those costs that are associated directly with production of a specific product or activity.
- Overhead costs are those costs that are hard to assign directly to a particular enterprise.
- Cash income and expenses involve an actual transfer of cash. Non-cash income and expenses do not involve a cash transfer.
- Long-run decisions need long-run information. Short-run decisions need short-run information.
- The distinction between economic and accounting values is important due to different questions being asked.
- The economically optimal level of input use is where the last increment of input use benefits the farm more than its cost but the next increment costs more than its benefit. That is, input use should be increased as long as the value of the marginal product is greater than the marginal input cost.
- Substitute one input for another if the cost of the substitute is less than the cost of the input being replaced (and output remains the same).
- Vertical expansion involves moving up or down the value chain. A livestock farm growing its own feed is vertically integrated back from the final consumer. A farmer selling directly to the consumer is vertically integrated toward the consumer.
- Horizontal expansion involves expanding either through greater size in terms of numbers of animals or amount of land or in terms of a greater number of separate products, such as more grains or adding custom hiring as a service to sell.
- Economies of scale and scope drive horizontal expansion.
- The four main forms of market structure are perfect competition, monopolistic competition, oligopoly, and monopoly.
- Perfect competition involves many producers and fierce price competition because no one has power over the price.
- Monopolistic competition may involve many firms but some, due to size, power, or product differentiation, have the power to affect their own price if they do not exercise that power too strongly.
- An oligopoly has few firms but may have fierce price competition depending on product differentiation.
- A monopoly has one or very few firms with light price competition unless the firm is threatened by potential entry of another firm or firms.

Review Questions

1. Identify two farm products that have more elastic demand than other products. Why do you think their demand is more elastic?
2. What is an opportunity cost? How is it used?
3. What does the term "marginal" mean? Why is it important in farm management?
4. What is the difference between fixed and variable costs? Why is the difference between fixed and variable costs so important?
5. Why is the distinction between cash and non-cash values important? Between long-run and short-run?
6. Given the fertilizer response data for corn following soybean shown below, a corn price forecast of $3.00 per bushel, and a nitrogen price of $0.35 per lb, what is the economically optimal nitrogen rate for corn after soybeans?

Nitrogen Applied	Corn Yield	Marginal (or Additional) Product	Value of Marginal Product	Marginal Input Costs	Marginal Net Return
lb/ac	bu/ac	bu/ac	$/ac	$/ac	$/ac
0	109				
40	134				
80	146				
120	153				
160	158				
200	158				

7. Consider a farm you are familiar with and describe how this farm could expand vertically. Provide examples of moving both up and down the value chain. What benefits and costs would this farm encounter in moving vertically?
8. Consider the same farm and describe how this farm could expand horizontally. How can this farm benefit from economies of scale and from economies of scope?
9. Considering the same farm again, describe the market(s) this farm is in.
10. How is this farm affected by the market structure and price competition in the farm's industry and in the industries of its suppliers and buyers?

Further Reading

Besanko, David, David Dranove, and Mark Shanley. 1996. *Economics of Strategy*. New York: John Wiley & Sons, 769 pp.

Mankiw, N. Gregory. 2004. *Principles of Economics*. 3rd ed. Mason, Ohio: South-Western Publishing.

5

Lessons from Macroeconomics

In this chapter:

- Basic concepts and terms
- Domestic issues
- International issues

Farmers may think of the larger economy as far removed from their daily decisions on the farm. However, changes in conditions at the national and international level can have large positive and negative effects on the financial performance and condition of a farm. A change in the economy can create opportunities and threats, whether they are due to legislation, central bank decisions, or a mood change among consumers. Understanding the elements of the larger economy can help farmers know what may be happening in the future or at least help them prepare their farm for changes that may occur.

Macroeconomics is the study of economy-wide issues, including economic growth, inflation, changes in employment and unemployment, trade with other countries and the balance of payments, monetary and fiscal economic policy, the role of central banks, and so on.

This chapter starts by explaining some basic concepts and terms of macroeconomics. Then we look at the domestic, national economy in the second section. The third section covers some pertinent issues of the global economy for farmers. The lessons and points in this chapter should help a farmer understand changes and trends in the national and global economies and the potential impact on his or her farm business.

Basic Macroeconomic Concepts and Terms

This section provides a short introduction to some basic concepts and terms used in discussions about economics and economies in the media. The goal of this section is to help a farmer (and any reader) better understand what is meant by these terms, how to interpret and monitor the health of an economy, and how this all relates to decisions on the farm.

National Income

How do we measure the health of an economy? There are many measures that cover a wide spectrum of views about an economy. Just as income is one measure of the health of a business, income is also one of the first measures of a healthy economy.

The **gross domestic product (GDP)** and **GDP per capita** are the most common measures we use to look at the income of an economy. GDP is the total measure and GDP per capita adjusts for population differences so we can compare the health of economies between countries.

GDP is the market value of all the final goods and services produced within a country within a certain time period. Market prices are used since they indicate what people are willing to pay for a product. Only final goods are counted, because counting raw materials and intermediate goods would create double counting or more and, thus, would be an overstatement of actual production in the economy. Also, only final, new products that are produced and sold are counted. The resale of used products is not included. Production within a country is counted regardless of whether the person or business is from that country or not. Similarly, if a citizen lives and works in another country, her income and spending will not be counted in her home country. Since income must equal expenditures in the national income accounts, GDP essentially measures both total income and total expenditures.

Other measures of income for an economy are not as accurate a measure as GDP is for indicating the health of an economy. **Gross national product (GNP)** includes the income produced by a country's citizens working in other countries as well as in their home country. National income is the total income earned by a country's residents in the production of goods and services; it does not include depreciation and indirect business taxes but does include business subsidies. Disposable personal income is the income that households have left after paying all their obligations to the government.

We also use GDP to measure economic growth. A growing GDP and especially growing GDP per capita indicate increasing income and better conditions in the same way as a higher salary indicates better conditions for an individual. As population grows, the economy needs to grow at least at the same rate in order to maintain the average income per person and thus maintain the country's standard of living (with other conditions remaining the same).

A nation desires economic growth as an indicator of improving lifestyle for the country's residents. A cynical view of growth is that it only benefits those already wealthy, but that view does not see the benefit of raising total GDP as a way of improving the distribution of income to the poor. A rising GDP means an increasing number of jobs and better paying jobs. Many of the new jobs will be taken by those who do not have a job now. Without economic growth, there is little chance of raising the income of the poor. However, a country also needs to work on distributing the jobs and income so that the poor—not just the current rich—will benefit.

Recession and Depression

A recession is a symptom of an unhealthy economy, a sign that something is not working (besides people). The economy, the people, the businesses, and the government try to "cure the illness." Just what is a recession? What is a depression? There are no fixed official definitions—only common usage.

A commonly held definition of a recession, especially in the media, is two consecutive quarters of decline in GDP. However, the definition is too simple and ignores people. The definition needs to include more than just GDP. Another common definition of a **recession** is "a period with significant decline in economic activity spread across the economy, lasting more than a few months, and normally visible in measures of real GDP, real income, employment, industrial production, and wholesale–retail sales." This is the definition used in the United States by the National Bureau of Economic Research (NBER), a private, nonprofit, nonpartisan research organization based in Cambridge, Massachusetts. A **jobless recovery** is an unofficial term used to describe an economy that is starting to grow again in terms of its GDP, but where the number of jobs and unemployment do not recover at the same rate.

A depression is usually thought of as a recession that lasts longer and cuts deeper into the economy. Although there is no hard line to say when a recession becomes a depression, one common, simple, but unofficial definition of a **depression** is a period in which the GDP drops 10% or more.

People, businesses, and governments worry about recessions and depressions because of the problems they cause in terms of high unemployment, lost revenue, and other slowness in the economy. A farm, and any business, should be wary of a recession for the drop in demand caused by job losses and lower consumer income and the subsequent decline in prices, sales, profits, and failed plans for the future. For an example of the current concerns and dilemmas in 2010, consider the situation in Example 5.1.

Example 5.1. The Long Tail of the Great Recession

"Last year it was the banks; this year it is countries," says *The Economist* (2010). The Great Recession, as it is now called, that started in 2008 continues to stretch into 2010 with worries that job growth won't come back until 2011.

The problem started in the financial sector. Governments stepped in to stabilize banks and other lenders with the argument that if the financial sector collapsed, the economies would be crippled. Now the deficits and debts of the governments, especially in the rich countries in Europe and the United States, are causing concerns.

One argument says governments should spend more in a recession to increase demand so businesses will hire more workers and, thus, increase private demand. However, that hasn't happened this time for a variety of reasons: lower than expected job growth, tight credit, low consumer confidence, and so on. All these have caused consumers to curtail spending and reduce their debt.

In 2010, governments are caught between the desire to spend more to stimulate their economies, the pressure to increases taxes to pay for the spending, and the worry that increasing taxes will hurt the recovery and throw the economy, the government, and the people back into hard times. Economic theory does not provide a clean picture of what decisions are needed and the timing of the moves.

So why should farmers worry about these events and decisions by governments?

They should worry because it will hit them personally and as a business. If the economy does not improve, consumers will buy less and demand lower prices. Consumers will not buy as much processed foods (or go out to eat as often) because of higher prices, lower incomes, and lower confidence about the future. However, since the food supply chain is set up for processed food and meals away from home, it cannot adjust quickly to increase the supply of less processed or unprocessed food. Thus, prices adjust down in stores and restaurants, which translate into lower prices at the farm gate.

Farmers are also interested in the timing of the recovery. Farmers who are poised to expand and move need to be sure the recovery is starting before major expansion plans are put into action. Starting too early will saddle a farm with fixed debt obligations while facing lower than expected demand and prices. Starting too late will take away any advantage of having moreproduction as prices move up. The decision to start implementation depends on the capacity of the farm to endure hard times and on the signals of job growth, consumer confidence, and GDP growth.

Source: "New Dangers for the World Economy," *The Economist*, February 11, 2010, accessed on February 11, 2010, at http://www.economist.com/opinion/displayStory.cfm?story_id=15498064&source=hptextfeature.

Unemployment

Unemployment literally means not having a job—but not having a job does not necessarily mean one is unemployed. Some people choose to work; others choose not to work. Retired people may be able to work, but do not need to have a job if retirement income is sufficient. Some people may be too sick to work. Some people may choose to live in ways to allow them to not have a job. Couples may choose to live on one income so the other spouse does not have a paying job.

Unemployment rate. When governments estimate the unemployment rate, they start with counting how many people are employed and how many are unemployed. A person is considered employed if he or she spent at least part of the previous week working at a paid job. A person is considered unemployed if laid off or actively looking for a job. The labor force is the total number of people employed plus the number unemployed. A person who is neither employed nor unemployed, such as a full-time student or a retiree, is not part of the labor force. The unemployment rate is the total unemployed expressed as a percentage of the labor force. A high and especially an increasing unemployment rate indicates the economy is not performing well enough to provide sufficient jobs for all who want one.

There are some problems with the unemployment rate, however. As people who want a job keep looking but are unsuccessful, they may become discouraged enough that they quit looking. When they quit looking, they are not considered unemployed and thus are dropped from the calculation. If enough job seekers quit looking, the unemployment rate may improve due to the lower number looking, not due to a rise in the number of jobs produced by the economy. Thus, especially during a recession, an apparent improvement in the unemployment rate needs to be evaluated in light of the change in the total number of jobs available. A more stable but infrequently used employment measure is the percentage of all adults who are employed.

The unemployment rate is never zero, even though zero unemployment sounds good. Unemployed people may be in between jobs, they may have just entered the job market after school, they may have just moved or be moving to a different area, or for several reasons they are temporarily looking but just not employed at the moment of counting. If an economy is growing, people who had not been looking before may decide to start looking and thus become counted as unemployed until they find a job or quit looking. The **natural rate of unemployment** is the normal rate of unemployment around which the actual rate fluctuates. Deviations from the natural rate of unemployment are caused by a shock to the economy, which causes it to slow down or grow faster than normal.

Inflation

Inflation is an increase in the overall level of prices in an economy. Since inflation causes many problems in economies, the goal of many governments and economic policymakers around the world is to keep inflation low.

Inflation is not a rise in individual prices, but an increase in all prices. An increase in prices caused by changes in supply and demand of a product is not inflation. For example, poor weather causing low production of wheat in the world causes wheat prices to increase, but this is the market striving to find a price to equate supply and demand; this is not inflation.

The inflation rate is calculated as the rate of change in the **consumer price index (CPI)** between two periods. The CPI is calculated as the cost to buy a fixed basket or set of products and services. The basket is described as the set of products and services bought by the typical consumer. The list of items in the basket is very long and covers everything we might find in a household, from food, clothing, and furniture to cars, cleaning services, and so on. The contents of the basket are fixed for extended periods but do change slightly as technology and products change over time. As prices of the items change, the total cost of the basket changes from one period to the next. To more easily see and compare the change in prices, a specific year (or consecutive years) is chosen as the base year, and that year's cost of the basket is converted to an index value of 100. The cost of the basket in other years or months is also converted to an index value relative to the base year. The inflation rate is the rate of change in the indices between periods. The "period" can be a year or a month. The change from one month to the next is converted to an annual percentage to make comparisons easier to understand.

Many ideas exist on what causes inflation, but the main cause is the increase in the supply of money in the economy. In economics, the **quantity theory of money** asserts that the quantity of money available determines the price level and that the growth rate in the quantity of money determines the inflation rate.

Some discussions center on the argument that governments face a tradeoff between controlling inflation or unemployment. In the short run at least, policymakers face a tradeoff between lowering inflation and lowering unemployment. In 1958, A.W. Phillips showed this relationship in Great Britain; subsequent research has shown this relationship to be true in other countries. In the long-run, the **natural rate hypothesis** argues that the unemployment rate eventually returns to its normal or natural rate regardless of the rate of inflation.

Stagflation is a term coined to describe a combination of stagnation (falling output) and inflation (rising prices). Policymakers do not have many tools to successfully control both of these problems at the same time. Fiscal policymakers could aim to increase the aggregate demand for goods and services through government spending to keep output from falling. However, this could keep prices up or even raise them. Monetary policymakers could lower the money supply in an effort to control rising prices, but that counters the fiscal policy aimed at increasing supply. Stagflation is not a pleasant time for the economy or for people.

Money Supply

What is the supply of money? We can obviously think of currency as a supply of money, but there are other sources of money. Two measures of the **money supply** are called M1 and M2. M1 is the total of currency plus demand deposits (that is, checking accounts and similar accounts), traveler's checks, and other checkable deposits. M2 is all of M1 plus savings deposits, small time deposits, money market mutual funds, and a few other minor categories. The **velocity of money** is the rate at which money changes hands.

Domestic Issues

Domestic macroeconomic issues involve concerns about the fluctuations in economic activity that we refer to as the business cycle. Business cycles have three phases: expansion, recession, and recovery. Expansion is the rather stable growth period when the economy is experiencing its normal, long-term trends in employment, output, and income. A market economy in this trend will eventually overheat with rising prices and interest rates, reach a peak, and turn down, causing what we call a recession. A recession involves falling employment, output, income, prices, and interest rates; it is felt by people in terms of rising unemployment. Eventually, the recession reaches its low point, turns around, and starts growing until it again reaches the expansion phase with its long-term trends in employment, output, and income.

Government macroeconomic policy strives to stabilize the business cycle and avoid the peaks and troughs. Governments have two basic tools for this stabilization effort: monetary policy and fiscal policy. A government also uses fiscal tools to encourage and discourage certain parts or industries of the economy, but this use of fiscal tools is not usually related to efforts to stabilize the business cycle. We will look at each of these policy tools in the following sections.

Monetary Policy

Monetary policy involves controlling the nation's money supply and setting certain interest rates and regulations of banks. The control of the money supply is the major form of countercyclical policy to stabilize the business cycle and the economy. Monetary policy is usually set by a country's central bank, such as the European Central Bank (ECB) and the U.S. Federal Reserve Bank, which are independent from the government's legislative and executive branches.

Monetary policy can be either expansionary or contractionary. Expansionary policy raises the money supply and thus lowers interest rates to stimulate the economy through increased borrowing and spending by businesses and citizens. Contractionary policy is the opposite: decreasing the money supply and thus raising interest rates. Expansionary policy creates a period of low interest rates or "easy money," and contractionary policy creates a period of high interest rates or "tight money."

The interest rate is essentially the price of money. And just like any other product or service, the interest rate or price of money is determined by the supply of and demand for money. The market for money adjusts the interest rate to bring the supply and demand into balance. As noted earlier, the central bank's main tool for stabilizing the economy is adjustments in the supply of money. Except for what is called the discount rate for short-term borrowing by certain banks, the central bank does not directly control the interest rate—even though the media often talks of it as having this power. Rather, the central bank increases or decreases the supply of money with the aim to affect the money market, which moves the rate up or down.

If the central bank wants to lower interest rates to encourage economic expansion, it needs to increase the money supply, which it does by buying securities from the open market. The bank pays for these securities by crediting those banks involved in the sale. With more money in their accounts, the banks lend more money, interest rates may fall through market forces, and spending hopefully increases.

If it wants to raise interest rates to slow economic expansion, the central bank sells government securities and collects payments from the participating banks by reducing the banks' reserve accounts. With less money in their reserve accounts, banks have less money to lend and market forces may raise interest rates, and spending may decrease.

The U.S. Federal Reserve Bank (commonly known as the Fed) also sets the discount rate, which is the interest rate that it charges eligible financial institutions for funds borrowed on a short-term basis. Changes in the discount rate may affect open market interest rates, but more important is its "announcement effect," which causes financial markets to respond to potential changes in monetary policy. If the discount rate is raised, even a little bit, the markets respond to it as an indication of the Fed moving toward a more restrictive policy; thus, interest rates go up, and borrowing and spending decrease. If the discount rate is lowered, even a little bit, the markets respond to it as an indication of the Fed moving toward a more expansive policy; thus, interest rates go down and borrowing and spending go up.

Central banks also regulate commercial banks and financial institutions. One of these regulations in the United States is the percentage of their deposits that must be set aside as reserves. These may be held either as cash on hand or as reserve account balances at a reserve bank. These reserve accounts are used by the institutions to satisfy reserve requirements and to process financial transactions through the Federal Reserve. Changing reserve requirements is rarely used as a monetary policy tool, but reserves do support the implementation of monetary policy.

Since there are different types of money, there are different interest rates. The interest rate on long-term loans will likely differ from the interest rate on short-term loans and savings accounts. Interest rates differ because of different demand levels for various kinds and uses of money. They differ because of different time periods for which businesses and people want to use the money and the different perceptions of the risks and inflation rates that will occur in these time periods. Businesses wanting to expand or buy new capital goods will want long-term rather than short-term money because the equipment and expansion will be used for many years. Businesses and people wanting to finance a purchase in the short term will demand a different type of loan—that is, a different type of money. These different interest rates are related as the market adjusts the different demands and supplies for money for different periods in order to bring the supply and demand of each type into balance.

Fiscal Policy

Fiscal macroeconomic policy is the use of taxation and government spending to stabilize the economy. During a recession, an expansionary fiscal policy could consist of lowering taxes, increasing government spending, or both. Increased government spending and decreased taxes will put more money in the economy and encourage people to spend more. This increase in spending encourages businesses to expand production and hire more workers, which in turn gives those new employees money to buy more. However, decreasing taxes, increasing spending, or both will increase the government's deficit, which together with more money in the economy could lead to higher inflation.

In an overheated expansion, a contractionary fiscal policy could consist of raising taxes, reducing government spending, or both. As a result, businesses and people spend less, credit may become tight, and businesses lay off workers, who now have less money to spend. Raising taxes and reducing government spending will reduce the government's budget deficit and, together with less money in the economy, may lead to lower inflation.

In both of these responses, we see the short-run tradeoff of inflation and unemployment. However, as noted earlier, the natural rate hypothesis argues that the unemployment rate has a normal or natural rate in the long run regardless of the rate of inflation, and that although fiscal policy can create a tradeoff in the short run, it does not last in the long run.

In previous attempts, the time lag between the actual fiscal policy decision and the resulting impact on the economy has been so long that the opposite of the desired effect occurred due to the economy recovering or slowing down on its own. Because of these unintended opposite effects, many argue that fiscal policy should not be used to fine-tune an economy. However, elected representatives and thus governments still do use fiscal policy in response to the public's concerns, especially during recessions.

Fiscal policy is also used to encourage or provide incentives for certain industries that a government considers to need help to either survive or to grow for the good of the whole economy. Both spending and changes in taxation policy to assist industries can help those industries and potentially the country. Agricultural examples of this help through fiscal policy include agriculture in general through direct subsidies and quota systems, textiles, and biofuels through subsidies. Other non-agricultural industries certainly strive for and obtain these benefits also. The policy argument is whether these industries are essential to the country, whether they would survive and prosper on their own without government support, and whether the money used for these industries has a greater public value if used for other purposes.

International Issues

International macroeconomic issues, especially for agriculture, revolve around currency exchange rates and trade. Let's take a brief look at each of these topics and how farmers can benefit from understanding the issues and discussions surrounding each topic.

Currency Exchange Rates

Exchange rates are essentially the price of one country's currency in terms of the currency of another country. For example, the exchange rate of the U.S. dollar to the EU's euro is the amount of U.S. dollars it would take to buy one euro. For most countries, their currencies can fluctuate with respect to other currencies; that is, the economic marketplace determines the value of each currency compared to other currencies. Other countries have set their currency value in terms of another country's currency; that country's currency does not trade in the market, but the fluctuations of the second country's currency does affect the first country's currency.

The importance of currency exchange rates to agriculture and farmers is in how fluctuations affect trade. The real exchange rate is the rate at which a person can trade the goods and services of one country for the goods and services of another country. The exchange rate can also be viewed as the value of one currency in terms of another currency. As the exchange rate or value of one's home currency, the U. S. dollar for example, declines, other countries find that currency less expensive to buy. When the U.S. dollar is less expensive, products in the United States are less expensive to buy for residents of other countries—even if U.S. residents do not see an immediate price change. The opposite effect also happens. When the U.S. dollar is less expensive, that means other currencies are more expensive for U.S. residents, so the products in those other countries are more expensive because they take more dollars to buy—again even though the residents in the other countries do not see an immediate price change.

Thus, news that the value of a farmer's home currency is declining should be interpreted by a farmer as good news that his or her exports will appear less expensive to buyers in other countries and exports will increase. The bad news is that the cost of imports from other countries will increase. A declining U.S. dollar or EU euro will be bad news for fertilizer suppliers in Africa and Canada who ship their products to the United States and Europe since farmers will see a higher price for fertilizer and thus lower use. Or, to maintain demand, the fertilizer producers will have to lower their local price to counteract the change in exchange rate. Similarly, the wheat producers in the EU or United States will see lower prices for their wheat if the exchange rates for their home currencies rise relative to other currencies.

An excellent example of the relationship between local agricultural prices and exchange rates occurred in September 2007, when the Fed cut its rate target. "The result was a decline in the value of the dollar relative to other currencies by about 2 percent on average. Very little other news that week directly affected agricultural commodity markets—no unexpected USDA reports, no abrupt weather changes, no policy changes, etc. Nonetheless, wheat cash prices rose by 1 percent, corn by 3.5 percent, soybeans by 6 percent, and cotton by 5.5 percent'' (Collins, 2007, pp. 2–3). If farmers had been aware of the Fed's actions early enough and understood the potential impact on prices, they could have reacted in the market to capture at least some of the higher prices for commodities. This connection between exchange rates and local prices is true for other countries as well.

Trade

Trade occurs between people and between countries because each side sees benefits from the trade. The "gains from trade" is the economists' phrase to describe this effect. Gains from trade occur because of differences in comparative advantage.

Comparative advantage means it is better for one country or person to produce a good or service and trade with another country or person who likely has the comparative advantage in a different product or service. Comparative advantage results from your having a lower opportunity cost to produce a product than another producer, which means that you should produce that product and trade for other products. The rancher in the previous chapter, who decided to grow olives and buy hay rather than grow his own hay, saw the opportunity cost of his resources and thus his comparative advantage in producing olives and decided he would benefit from "trading" for hay. This was his "gains from trade." Similar phenomena are true between countries and are why trade occurs.

However, we do not have open trade between countries. Just having comparative advantages and potential gains from trade does not mean trade will take place. Countries have restrictions on what they allow to be traded by placing tariffs or quotas on both imports and exports. Tariffs and quotas are placed on imports to protect local industries. Tariffs, quotas, and sometimes complete restriction on exports are used to raise money for other governmental functions and to keep locally produced goods within the country. This latter reason is common in several countries such as India for food security reasons in order to ensure a supply of food for their citizens. In other instances, governments provide direct subsidies to producers or exporters in order to increase exports and thus demand so that local prices and farm income rise. Further details on trade and trade restrictions and incentives are given in Chapter 6.

Trade policy, tariffs, and non-tariff restrictions have been contentious for centuries. The World Trade Organization (WTO) is the current international agency designed to facilitate the discussion between countries to lower trade barriers and to help resolve trade disputes. The issues are often almost intractable with extremely little progress on global changes. The largest recent actions in international trade have been the development of bilateral and regional trade agreements between smaller countries around the world. Examples of these agreements include the North American Free Trade Agreement (NAFTA), Mercosur (the Southern Common Market with 26 countries), and Association of Southeast Asian Nations (ASEAN).

In this chapter, the basic concepts and terms of macroeconomics have been explained for both national and international levels. By understanding these concepts and terms, a farmer can better understand and interpret events in the larger economy and anticipate how the events may affect his or her farm.

Summary

- Gross Domestic Product (GDP) is the market value of all the final goods and services produced within a country within a certain period.
- A rising GDP per capita is an indicator of rising income and a rising standard of living.

- A recession is a period with significant decline in economic activity spread across the economy, lasting more than a few months, and normally visible in measures of real GDP, real income, employment, industrial production, and wholesale–retail sales.
- The unemployment rate is the total number of unemployed expressed as a percent of the labor force.
- The natural rate of unemployment is the normal rate around which the actual rate fluctuates.
- Inflation is the increase in the overall level of prices.
- The Consumer Price Index (CPI) is based on the cost of a fixed basket or set of consumer goods.
- The money supply in an economy is more than just the currency in circulation. It is measured in two ways. M1 is the total of currency plus demand deposits (that is, checking accounts and similar accounts), traveler's checks, and other check-writable deposits. M2 is all of M1 plus savings deposits, small time deposits, money market mutual funds, and a few other minor categories.
- Monetary policy involves controlling the money supply to control the market interest rate and setting certain short-term interest rates.
- Fiscal policy is the use of taxation and government spending to stabilize the economy (and to provide incentives to a few industries identified as critical to the economy).
- The exchange rate is the value of one currency in terms of another currency. The real exchange rate is the rate at which a person can trade the goods and services of one country for the goods and services of another country.
- The gains from trade are the result of persons and countries producing what they have comparative advantage in and then trading for other goods and services.
- Trade restrictions constrain our ability to benefit from the gains from trade but are used by a country to protect its industries and improve food security.

Review Questions

1. What is the business cycle? What are its three phases?
2. What is GDP and GDP per capita? What do they tell us about a country?
3. Why is economic growth important?
4. What is a recession? Why are recessions feared?
5. In the United States, who decides whether a recession has "officially" occurred? What are the general conditions they use to describe a recession?
6. How is the unemployment rate calculated? Is the unemployment rate ever zero? What is the natural rate of unemployment?
7. What is inflation? How is the inflation rate calculated?
8. What is monetary policy? How can it be used to counter a recession?
9. What is fiscal policy? How can it be used to counter a recession?
10. What is an exchange rate? Is a strong currency good or bad for farmers?
11. What are gains from trade? Is trade good or bad for farmers?
12. How can understanding macroeconomics help a farmer make decisions on his or her farm?

Further Reading

Collins, Keith. 2007. Statement before the House of Representatives Committee on Agriculture, October 18, 2007, accessed on October 10, 2009 at http://www.usda.gov/documents/10-18-07Collins.pdf.

Mankiw, N. Gregory. 2004. *Principles of Economics*, 3rd ed. Mason, Ohio: South-Western Publishing.

6

Government Policies Affecting Farming around the World

In this chapter:

• Estimates of government support for farmers
• Policies in selected countries

Government policies affect farming in virtually every country in the world. Whether the impacts of these policies are negative or positive depends on your basic opinion on the value of government intervention, your geographical location relative to the country and policy in question, and whether you are a farmer or not.

Since world markets and the world economy can affect local farming, farmers need to understand the basics of policy tools in other countries. Then as news of debates and changes in policy in other countries is heard, farmers can quickly begin to understand whether and how much such a change will affect them and their farm and, if necessary, start adjusting their plans and decisions to take advantage of opportunities and to avoid or compensate for threats.

In the next section, estimates of producer support in selected countries are reported. The second section of this chapter contains a summary of major policies and their impact on farming. This chapter draws heavily on the summaries by the Organisation for Economic Cooperation and Development (2009a and 2009b), and the interested reader is referred to these publications for greater detail. There are many policies and even more details that could be discussed, but this discussion is limited primarily to income and price support policies, and other policies that affect production and trade more directly.

Estimates of Government Support for Farmers

The level of support for agriculture and farmers varies widely between countries. The Organisation for Economic Cooperation and Development (OECD) estimates the amount of support provided to farmers or producers by both governments and consumers from data collected from OECD member nations and other cooperating nations. The OECD defines the producer support estimate (PSE) as "the annual monetary value of gross transfers from consumers and taxpayers to agricultural producers, measured at the farm gate level, arising from policy measures that support agriculture, regardless of their nature, objectives or impacts on farm production or income. It includes market price support, budgetary payments and budget revenue foregone, i.e. gross transfers from consumers and taxpayers to agricultural producers arising from policy measures based on: current output, input use, area planted/animal numbers/receipts/incomes (current, non-current), and noncommodity criteria" (OECD, 2009b, p. 65). In order to compare the size of this support between countries and relative to the size of the agricultural industry in the country, the PSE is expressed as a percentage (%PSE) of gross farm receipts (with PSE included in the gross farm receipts). The 2006–08 average %PSE varies from 1% in New Zealand to 62% in Norway. The United States has an average of 9.5% and the European Union, 27% (Figure 6.1).

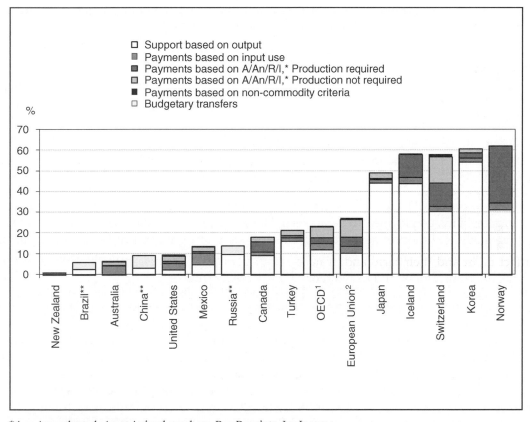

*A = Area planted, An = Animal numbers, R = Receipts, I = Income.
**Average of 2005–07.
1. The OECD total does not include the non-OECD EU member states.
2. Average of EU25 in 2006 and EU27 in 2007–08.

Figure 6.1 Producer Support Estimate by Country, 2006–08 (Percent of Gross Farm Receipts)
Sources: OECD 2009a and 2009b.

Policies in Selected Countries

This section briefly describes the main policies affecting farming directly to provide an overview of how different governments assist or hinder the farmers in their countries. The policies are not the only ones that affect farming, though. We do not summarize transportation policies, which can have a large impact on the ease of market access; nor do we discuss governmental support of agricultural research and development. What is covered are policies that directly affect farmers' income and management decisions through payments, subsidies, taxes, price controls, quotas, and so on. The summaries also include information on food programs that are available in some countries. The countries were selected on the basis of volume of agricultural production and geographical location, and to provide a cross section of the types of policies. The summaries that follow are truly summaries. Also, when reading about the goals and objectives, the reader is reminded that the effectiveness of the program depends on the events and conditions on the ground and the actual budgetary allocation by the country. The interested reader is referred to the OECD publications (2009a and 2009b), other information, and individual country reports for the full details.

Brazil

Brazil has an important but very dualistic agriculture. It has many commercial-size farms that produce mainly for the export market. There are many smaller family farms, which include domestic market-oriented farms and subsistence farms.

Although Brazil does support agriculture in several ways, its total support is quite low compared to gross farm receipts and especially low relative to other countries. Brazil's producer support (%PSE) averaged 5.8% for 2005–07, the most recent years that data were available. This compares to the EU average, 27.1% for 2006–08, and the U.S. average, 9.5% for 2006–08.

According to the OECD, the main policy objectives are to promote economic development, environmental sustainability, employment generation, and a more equitable income distribution, and to reduce regional inequalities. Producer support programs include direct government purchases at guaranteed prices and in auction systems. The guaranteed prices are quite low, so the programs are more for price stability than for increasing domestic prices. Twelve commodities have guaranteed minimum prices, including rice, maize, wheat, cotton, and jute. Each year before the production season, the government auction system offers sell option contracts, which have a fixed "execution" price and quantity. The government is required to buy if the holder of the option decides to exercise the option. These options have been offered on a regular basis for maize and less regularly for wheat, rice, sorghum, cotton, and coffee. A recent program essentially operates like a deficiency payment by paying the producer the difference between the guaranteed price and the price received at auction. This program has been mainly used with soybean and maize producers but has been extended to other crops as well.

Some small- and medium-scale producers are targeted by some programs by restricting the terms for receiving price supports and by having different price supports in different regions. To reduce the risk of borrowing money, a recent program gives family farms a guaranteed price in the event of a credit transaction amortization or liquidation. By reducing the risk of borrowing, the government hopes to increase production and income of family farms. However, the program has a limit (US$1,800 in 2006) per farm per crop. The government also makes direct purchases from family farms at market prices, although the amount is capped per farm (US$1,500 in 2006).

The Brazilian government also supports buyers of certain agricultural products. The most important of these programs supports buyers by paying them the difference between the minimum guaranteed price and the price the buyer is willing to pay as discovered by auctions run by the government. The smaller program pays a subsidy to livestock feeders and feed industries that buy government stocks and ship it to a specified region.

Producers also receive support through credit programs that direct credit to agriculture, controlled interest rates below market rates, and, recently, debt rescheduling. The national rural credit system (SNCR) provides credit at concessional interest rates for marketing and storage credit, working capital, and investment credit. The programs also now allow the purchase of used harvesting and tractor machinery and fund investments in farming and livestock integration to reduce environmental degradation. Due to concern about the relative level of debt and the percent (almost 30%) of borrowers who were in default on at least some of their debt in 2008, the government announced a program to reduce the additional levies charged on overdue debt, offer a discount of up to 45% for early repayment of current debt, offer a fixed discount of up to US$8,600 on current debt, extend repayment terms, and reduce interest rates on working and investment debt.

Since 1995, the National Programme for the Strengthening of Family Agriculture (PRONAF) has provided subsidized credit, training and extension, and promotion of value-added activities to small farmers. Starting in 2003, Brazil's Zero Hunger program includes support for family farming as part of combating hunger and poverty. A recent land reform program provides landless peasants with land confiscated, purchased, or reclaimed by the government, low-interest loans to buy land, and the funding of community and infrastructure projects.

The government also provides insurance programs for farmers. It assists family farms in borrowing capital for certain crops by guaranteeing full redemption of the liability in the event of a 30% or more drop in gross revenue caused by drought, flood, hail, wind, disease, or plague. Another program offers insurance to family farmers in arid areas who produce non-irrigated staple crops and cotton. Commercial farmers are provided a subsidy if they buy crop insurance from a specified list of companies.

The Brazilian government has created programs for protecting the environment. These include lines of credit for recovering soils that have been degraded and technical assistance to producers, training for technicians, and so on. Recently, the government formally established standards, certification, and other rules for organic products. There is now stronger enforcement of existing regulations for protecting the Amazon forest.

The government is also working to improve infrastructure by providing public money for highways, railways, irrigation projects, and port capacity. As with many countries, the government is also developing the biofuel market, including increased credit for building ethanol plants and modernizing sugar cane mills, incentives to encourage the purchase of flex-fuel vehicles, biofuel blending ratios for petrol and diesel, and efforts to increase trade and government involvement in the biofuel market.

Brazil has a fairly open import and export market. It is also very active at opening international trade and works with other nations to advocate for more open markets in the developed countries. It is a very active member of Mercosur, the Southern Common Market with 26 countries. Brazil has worked on the south–south dialogue on trade in the southern hemisphere and has bilateral agreements with several nations.

Canada

Canada's level of support for farmers is between the level of the United States and the European Union. In terms of %PSE, Canada averaged 18% for 2006–08 compared to the EU average of 27.1% and the U.S. average of 9.5%.

A new set of policies was finalized in March 2009 that replaced previous programs. There are four business risk management programs in this new set of policies:

• AgriInvest subsidizes farm savings. Participating farmers may deposit 1.5% of their allowable net sales into an account and receive a matching government contribution. Account balances are limited to 25% of sales for the current and two preceding years. Producers may use the funds to compensate for income variability or for on-farm investments, especially for risk mitigation. (Income variability is defined as margin declines of 15% or less, where margin is the difference between whole-farm gross revenue and expenses.)
• AgriStability insures profit margins when they decline 15% or more. It makes a payment to farmers whose margin is less than 85% of their five-year Olympic average. Farmers pay a premium that varies with the insured level.
• AgriInsurance provides insurance against natural perils. It covers losses to production and farm assets. Farmers pay a premium and receive a payment when they experience a loss. The program is closely related to AgriStability, so there are some linkages between the two programs.
• AgriRecovery provides ad hoc disaster assistance. The federal and provincial governments can use this program to move quicker in response to natural disasters.

Market price support is provided for dairy products, poultry, and eggs through tariffs, production quotas, and domestic price-setting organizations. The production quotas are tradable only within provinces. The Canadian Wheat Board (CWB) has statutory authority for the domestic and international marketing of wheat and barley in western Canada.

Other programs provide support for Canadian farmers. Governmental assistance is available for environmental improvements for those farmers who have completed an agri-environmental risk assessment. For biofuels, new programs are aimed at meeting the goals of 5% renewable content in gasoline by 2010 and 2% in diesel and heating fuel by 2012. Credit programs provide up to US$370,531 loans repayable in 18 months with the first US$92,632 interest free. Hog producers can receive a subsidy of 50% for vaccination costs up to US$1,853 per year under the Circovirus Inoculation Programme. Cost sharing is available for irrigation projects. Assistance is available for organic growers.

China

China's producer support (%PSE) averaged 9.2% for 2005–07, the most recent years that data were available. This compares to the EU average of 27.1% for 2006–08 and the U.S. average of 9.5% for 2006–08.

Market price support is provided through tariffs, tariff rate quotas (TRQ), and state trading. The government also provides minimum guaranteed prices for rice and wheat, which are supported by government purchases. Auctions are held when needed to slow the rise in prices.

The government also provides input subsidies for agricultural chemicals (especially fertilizers), improved seeds, and agricultural machinery. The high use (and overuse) of fertilizers due to the low price and encouragement to use fertilizers has increased production costs and surface and groundwater pollution. Due to a reduction in pig production in 2007, the government started a subsidy for reproductive sows that was US$14.50 per sow in 2008. Other livestock subsidies include payments for artificial insemination of dairy cows and payments for high-quality dairy cow heifers produced from registered purebred stock. Public expenditures for agricultural infrastructure are primarily for irrigation and drainage facilities.

Grain producers also received direct payments based on area sown to rice, wheat, and corn. The federal payment can and has been supplemented from local sources in some areas. OECD estimates that an average direct payment of US$25/ha was about 2.3% of wheat producers' gross revenues in 2007 (OECD, 2009a).

Other assistance for agriculture includes a decrease in taxes and fees paid by farmers with the federal government reimbursing local governments for the loss in revenue. The "Grain for Green" program reflects environmental concerns through its payments for returning farmland to forests on environmentally fragile land. The government has started some pilot programs for studying the subsidization of agricultural insurance.

European Union

The European Union's producer support (%PSE) averaged 27.1% for 2006–08 compared to the U.S. average of 9.5%. Even though the EU's %PSE is still higher than the U.S. average, both levels have decreased in recent years in large part to higher product prices.

The Common Agricultural Policy (CAP) has two main pillars. The first consists of Common Market Organizations (CMOs) and direct payments. The second pillar, Rural Development Regulation (RDR) of Agenda 2000, includes agro-environment programs, payments to less favored areas, and investment assistance.

Direct payments include the Single Payment Scheme (SPS) and the Single Area Payment Scheme (SAPS). The SPS started with the 2003 CAP reform and was adjusted in 2008. SPS replaced part of all of the subsidies that existed under the CMOs. Payments to farmers are based on historical amounts received in 2000–02. Most of the payments are to be phased out before 2013 as agreed in 2008. SAPS is a transitional scheme in place in 10 of the 12 member states that joined the EU since 2004. Under SAPS, each hectare receives the same payment rate (except for land that historically held sugar quotas or produced fruit and vegetables, which may have adjusted payments).

Intervention prices for cereals will be limited to wheat as the 2008 reforms are fully implemented. Public intervention for maize is gradually being phased out. There are no intervention prices for oilseeds and protein crops. Sugar is supported by production quotas and private storage, which is gradually replacing intervention. Tariffs, tariff rate quotas (TRQs), and export subsidies also support cereals and sugar when export prices fall below domestic prices. Fruits and vegetables are supported through producer organizations, minimum import prices, and ad valorem duties. Livestock prices are supported through intervention prices, basic prices, production quotas, import protection, tariffs, TRQs, and export subsidies; the mix of these support programs varies with the livestock product.

With the Health Check in 2008, several changes were made and will be instituted over time. Intervention is abolished for pig meat and set at zero for barley and sorghum. For wheat, butter, and skimmed milk powder, intervention purchases are allowed up to certain limits, but further intervention must be done by tender above those levels. Milk quotas are scheduled to decrease by 1% every year until they expire in April 2015. The requirement for arable farmers to leave 10% of their land fallow is abolished. Further decoupling of support will be done by integrating those payments that could be kept separate under previous reforms into the Single Payment Scheme; exceptions are made for suckler cow, goat, and sheep payments. Investment aid to young farmers is increased from €55,000 (US$80,411) to € 70,000 (US$102,342). Aid to farmers is linked to environmental, animal welfare, and food quality standards. Minimum payments are set at an EU average of € 100 (US$146) or a minimum size of 1 hectare; countries may adjust this minimum based on the national average farm size compared to the EU average. The energy crop premium is abolished. Other adjustments are made in the Health Check that affect implementation, extending SAPS, assistance to sectors with special problems, new EU countries, and unspent SPS money.

Common Market Organization (CMO) reforms have also been implemented in recent years. The main change in the CMO programs for fruits and vegetables and for wine is that some support measures are phased out or adjusted while the sectors become eligible for payments in SPS.

The Rural Development Regulation (RDR) programs aim at:

1. Improving the competitiveness of the agricultural and forestry sectors. These programs include farm modernization, setting up young farmers, early retirement, restructuring semi-substance farms, vocational training, producer groups, value-added products, and restoring production capability damaged by natural disasters.
2. Improving the environment and the countryside. These programs include agri-environmental and animal welfare payments, payments to farmers in areas with handicaps, payments for afforestation (that is, planting forests on new land), payments for protecting biodiversity in specific sites, and support to non-productive investments.
3. Improving the quality of life in rural areas and encouraging the diversification of the rural economy. These programs encourage the diversification into non-agricultural activities, tourism activities, the creation and development of micro-enterprises, rural services, and the conservation of rural heritage.

Current debates about future policy and the economics and politics of those debates in any country can be seen in the current debate in the EU as the commissioner of agriculture changes and the ravages of the 2008–2011 recession are felt (Example 6.1).

Example 6.1. Future Policy Directions

The political forces that shape agricultural policy around the world are very evident in Europe in early 2010 as the European Union changes its agricultural commissioner and engages in the debate over how to fund subsidies after 2013.

The outgoing commissioner, Mariann Fischer Boel, has spent her 5-year appointment striving to decrease the level of subsidies under the Common Agricultural Policy (CAP). Among the notable changes during her tenure are that she has made spending more transparent by prodding countries to disclose beneficiaries, reduced European sugar surpluses essentially by paying some companies to go out of business, and brought back the curvy cucumber and knobby carrot by eliminating historical market standards that dictated the shape of vegetables.

However, the debate over how and at what level to fund the CAP after 2013 is not settled, and the political climate does not point toward a likely reduction in levels. Farmers, especially French farmers who receive the most subsidies, are vigorously defending current funding levels and even pushing for more. The opposition says the subsidies are too much. The CAP consumes almost half of the EU budget. Other interests say farmers in new member states in the east should receive the same level of benefits as farmers in the west. The Times quotes Ms. Fischer Boel as saying this equality will not be achieved easily, "'If you want to reduce differences then there will be significant losers, and I doubt you would get political support.'"

Her likely successor supports current funding levels and thus is receiving support from farming organizations and from EU members. Cutting payments may be difficult, especially during the current recession when farmers are lobbying and protesting for more subsidies. The recession also creates concern on how to raise the funds to maintain CAP funding. "We have not been good enough," Ms. Fischer Boel said, "at explaining to consumers and to taxpayers why they have a CAP or what they get for their money. This will be one of the basic challenges we will face." The need to reform the CAP continues, she argues "because we need to modernize our agriculture."

Source: S. Castle and D. Carvajal, "Farm Subsidy Battles: A Fighter Looks Back," *New York Times*, February 1, 2010. Accessed on February 6, 2010, at http://www.nytimes.com/2010/02/02/world/europe/02farm.html.

Japan

Japan's level of support for farmers (%PSE) averaged 49% for 2006–08 compared to the EU average of 27.1% and the U.S. average of 9.5%.

Market price support is provided both through tariffs and tariff rate quotas (TRQs) and payments based on output. Tariff-rate quota systems are applied to major commodities such as rice, wheat, barley, and dairy products. These border protection measures are quite strong and are a major source of support for producers.

In the last decade Japan has moved away from price support to direct payments. The administered price for rice was abolished in 2004, and administered prices for wheat, barley, sugar beet, sugar cane, and starch potatoes were abolished in 2007. Administered prices remain for pork, beef, and calves, and they were raised in 2008 in response to higher feed prices. The government also supports manufactured milk through direct payments but with a maximum amount allowed per farm.

In 2007, Japan started three new direct payments for what are called core farmers to replace previous commodity-specific payments based on output. Direct payments are now targeted at farmers who manage at least 4 ha of land (or 10 ha in the Hokkaido area) and to local community units that manage more than 20 ha along with other conditions. If these minimums are not met, the local municipality could approve the farmer as a local core farmer and the farmer would become eligible for the payments.

Budgetary support is provided mainly toward infrastructure needs, such as irrigation and drainage facilities and the readjustment of agricultural land. Prefecture and local governments provide infrastructure and extension services.

Environmental programs include direct payments for environmentally friendly farming and reduction in fertilizer and pesticide usage. Direct payments are made to farmers in hilly and mountainous areas to prevent the abandonment of agricultural land and to maintain the multifunctional character of agriculture.

India

OECD was not able to calculate the level of support for agriculture in India due to the lack of participation in the agricultural policy review process by the government of India. However, based on recent evaluations by other analysts, OECD concluded that the level of assistance became higher than the level of other emerging economies in the early 2000s but below the OECD average for that period (OECD, 2009a, p. 95).

Food security remains the main agricultural policy objective for India and the main cause for heavy involvement in agriculture. The government has the authority to regulate and control production, distribution, and pricing of commodities listed as essential for consumers. The government regulates the markets and marketing of agricultural produce so that all trade between farmers and the initial buyers must go through a regulated market. Compared to previous policies, the 2007 National Policy for Farmers "suggests a greater focus on the economic well-being of farmers and rural development, rather than just on agricultural production" (OECD, 2009a, p. 99).

The Indian government sets minimum support prices on 26 essential commodities, including paddy (rice), maize, coarse cereals, pulses, cotton, wheat, barley, sugar cane, and several other crops. The minimum support price is set considering the cost of production (including the value of family labor and land rental). Government intervention occurs when market prices fall below the minimum support price. For other crops, the federal and state governments buy specific quantities at minimum intervention prices. The government also maintains buffer stocks, which are increased through domestic purchases and imports as needed or decreased by allowing exports when possible. The government also places high import tariffs on agricultural products (40.8% on average; OECD, 2009a, p. 99) and ad hoc export bans on some products while it offers export subsidies on others.

The Targeted Public Distribution System (TPDS) distributes subsidized food to India's poor. The government covers the difference between the minimum support prices for procurement, costs of operation, and the central issue prices (CIPs) for retail sales. Food also has a low value-added tax (VAT) compared to the VAT for other products.

The Indian government subsidizes fertilizers, water, electricity, and occasionally seeds. The largest share of these subsidies is for fertilizers. Fertilizer prices are controlled by the government, and fertilizer producers are compensated for the difference between the controlled price and the market price. Electricity producers are subsidized in a similar procedure. Water subsidies are the losses incurred by the government irrigation systems resulting from gross revenues being below operating costs. Small-scale crop producers can receive a 10% subsidy on crop insurance premiums.

Commercial banks, cooperatives, and regional banks are required to provide credit to farmers for input purchases at interest rates below the market rate. Other programs seek to provide credit through institutions instead of through private money lenders, which are still very common and charge high rates. A recent program is aimed at reducing the indebtedness of farmers through debt relief and waivers.

The government has also started programs to help specific commodities. For example, the National Horticultural Mission is designed to increase horticultural production through research, adoption of improved technologies, improved post-harvest management and marketing, export promotion, and adding value through processing.

The government also has a high priority for the improvement of rural infrastructure, which includes irrigation, rural roads, rural housing, rural drinking water, rural electrification, and rural telephone systems.

Russia

Russia maintains high border protection for key agricultural products and that is the source for most of the producer support. Budgetary support has been increasing in recent years. Russia's producer support (%PSE) averaged 13.9% for 2005–07, the most recent years that data were available, which is in between the EU average of 27.1% and the U.S. average of 9.5% for 2006–08.

Russia's federal Law on Development of Agriculture (2006) defines six objectives:

1. Improvement of competitiveness and quality of agricultural products
2. Sustainable rural development and improvement of the living standard for the rural population
3. Conservation and reproduction of natural resources used in agriculture
4. Formation of an efficiently functioning agricultural market and development of market infrastructure
5. Creation of a favorable investment climate in the agro-food sector
6. Support of agricultural input–output price parity

The State Program for Development of Agriculture (2008–12) works on the first three objectives and has five parts:

- Sustainable development of rural territories: improvements of rural settlements, infrastructure, and housing for rural people
- Creation of basic conditions for agricultural production: land conservation and development of farm services
- Development of priority sub-sectors of agriculture: support for breeding of pedigree animals, elite seed production, and development of specific activities such as production of flax, rapeseed, perennial plantations, sheep and horse breeding, and other activities
- Achieving financial sustainability of agriculture: interest rate subsidies on loans to agricultural producers and rural households. This is the largest part in terms of budget.
- Regulation of markets for agricultural food and fiber products and foodstuffs, including financing for grain interventions, development of standards for meat products, and monitoring of supply and disappearance for key commodities

In Russia's price and income support policy, direct payments amount to a small part of total support; they were 3% of PSE in 2006–07. Direct payments are provided for marketed meat, milk, eggs, and wool. About 74% of the payments were for milk in 2006–07, but poultry and pork producers received additional subsidies in 2008 due to higher feed prices.

Market interventions are based on minimum and maximum prices separately for milling wheat, feed wheat, rye, feed barley, and maize. When market prices fall below the minimum, the government either purchases grain in the market or provides loans against pledged grain. When the market price is below the minimum, the government may also restrict imports. When market prices rise above the maximum, the government releases grain into the market. When the market price is above the maximum, the government may also restrict exports.

Subsidies to interest rates on loans are one of the main support measures. All producers are eligible: agricultural organizations, small family-type farms, and households. The subsidy may be applied to producer cooperatives involved in agro-processing and in some cases to food processors. Short- and long-term loans are eligible. In Russia, the subsidy is transferred directly to the borrower and not the lender. The subsidy rate is defined in terms of the refinancing rate of the Central Bank of Russia (CBR) and varies by type of beneficiary. Agricultural organizations and food processors receive a subsidy of two-thirds of the CBR rate. If the loan is for the construction of livestock facilities or the purchase of agricultural machinery, regional governments are required to subsidize no less than the remaining one-third. For small farms and agricultural cooperatives, the subsidy is 95% of the CBR rate and regional governments are required to subsidize no less than the remaining 5%. The borrower is to cover the difference between the bank lending rate and the government-subsidized portion. Most of the subsidy has been received by agricultural organizations for construction of livestock facilities.

Russia also provides several direct subsidies for variable inputs and investment for purchasing mineral fertilizer, chemicals, and high-quality seeds, and for transporting seeds to areas with adverse climatic conditions for cultivations of feed crops. When fuel prices rose recently, a subsidy was provided for fuel used for planting. Livestock can receive subsidies for young pedigree livestock and artificial insemination. Subsidies for leasing agricultural machinery are also available. Recently, the government negotiated an agreement for Russian fertilizer producers to supply some fertilizer to domestic markets with a maximum price, and the government lifted the export tax on fertilizers.

United States

The United States producer support (%PSE) averaged 9.5% for 2006–08 compared to the EU average of 27.1%. The U.S. %PSE has decreased in recent years due to higher world prices for agricultural products.

In 1996, the United States separated support payments from current production and reduced production constraints on farmers. However, in 2002, the policy reverted to support more directly tied to current production due to financial stress in the farming sector following the 1996 policy. The main policy tools in the United States are direct payments (DP), counter-cyclical payments (CCP), and loan deficiency payments (LDPs) or marketing loans for maize and other grains, soybeans and other oilseeds, rice, cotton, peanuts, and pulse. DPs are based on payments per unit of the farm's historical yields and acreage. CCPs are based on current prices and historical production. Neither DP nor CCP require current production for a payment to be paid. LDPs are paid based on current production and prices. At current market prices, only the DPs are paid to farmers. Target prices set in the legislation are low relative to currently high market prices, so CCP and LDP payments will not be made until prices fall considerably.

Starting with the 2009 crop year, a new revenue support program, Average Crop Revenue Election (ACRE), was added as a choice for farmers. If they choose ACRE, they do not receive CCP, and their DP payment is decreased by 20% and the marketing loan rate is decreased by 30%. If they choose ACRE, all crops must be enrolled, but potential payments are made separately for each crop. An ACRE payment is made for a crop only if both (1) actual state revenue per acre is less than the state revenue guarantee per acre and (2) an individual farm's actual revenue per acre is less than the farm's benchmark revenue per acre. The state revenue guarantee and the individual farm benchmark revenue are based on moving averages of the state and farm yields and a two-year average of the national market price. Actual revenue is calculated using the national market price. If the two triggers are met, the ACRE payment is based on the per acre difference between the actual state revenue and the state revenue guarantee, the farm's historical crop acreage, and is adjusted for the farm's historical yield relative to the state historical yield of that crop.

Current legislation continues planting restrictions such that farmers cannot receive payments if they plant fruits and vegetables on land that was historically planted to crops covered by the commodity payments (except for processing vegetables with maximum acres in some states). Farmers receiving payments must comply with conservation requirements.

Payments are limited to a maximum amount per person, and a person becomes ineligible for any payments if personal income exceeds maximum levels. In the 2008 legislation, payments are limited to US$40,000 for DP and US$65,000 for CCP, including ACRE payments. There are no payment limits on marketing loan benefits and LDPs.

Dairy market price supports are now made through support for manufactured products instead of fluid milk. The Milk Income Loss Contract (MILC) payment continues and is based on the difference between a set price and the market price in the northeast United States and limited to a maximum amount of milk per farm.

A permanent whole-farm revenue disaster assistance program for crop producers replaces ad hoc disaster assistance. The Supplemental Revenue Assurance (SURE) program pays producers 60% of the difference between the disaster assistance program guarantee and total whole-farm revenue for all crops. Four other programs provide disaster assistance to livestock, forage, and orchard and nursery producers.

Other features of the 2008 U.S. policy include the following:

- Loan rates for sugar are raised gradually from US$397 per tonne in 2008 to US$413 per tonne by 2011.
- Credit policy continues to subsidize loans for beginning and socially disadvantaged farmers, increases lending limits per person to US$300,000, and extends the guarantee program for seller-financed land loans.
- Environmental programs for conservation and for conversion to organic practices are continued and adjusted.
- New funding for programs in marketing, research, education, food safety, and pest and disease management for specialty crops is added.
- Several programs are continued for infrastructure, economic development and health care in rural communities, including water, energy, and health programs, broadband Internet expansion, and loan guarantees to support value-added agricultural enterprises.
- Country of origin labeling (COOL) is now mandatory.
- Funding is expanded for federal purchases of bio-based products, construction and development of advanced biofuel refineries, biomass research and development, and biodiesel education.

Food assistance programs account for more than two-thirds of the budget for the 2008 legislation. The food stamp program is adjusted and renamed the Supplemental Nutrition Assistance Program (SNAP). The funding for other food assistance programs was increased.

In this chapter, the major policies affecting farming have been described briefly for a few example countries. By understanding the basic ideas, a farmer can better understand discussions and debates and be better able to estimate the impact of policy changes in another country on his or her own farm.

Summary

- Government policies affect farming in virtually every country in the world—sometimes positively, sometimes negatively.
- The producer support estimate (PSE) is "the annual monetary value of gross transfers from consumers and taxpayers to agricultural producers, measured at the farm gate level . . . It includes market price support, budgetary payments and budget revenue foregone . . . " (OECD).
- The %PSE is the PSE expressed as a percentage of gross farm receipts (with PSE included in the gross farm receipts).
- The 2006–08 average %PSE varies from 1% in New Zealand to 62% in Norway. The United States has an average of 9.5% and the European Union averages 27%.
- Policies vary in all the countries, from very heavy support of farm income through direct support of income and price for specific commodities to support not directly tied to commodities or current production.
- With varying degrees of success, almost all countries are striving to reduce support that affects the market.

Review Questions

1. What are PSE and %PSE? Why are they useful for comparing policies in different countries? Do you think they are the right measure for comparing policies?
2. Which countries have the lowest level %PSE? Which countries have the highest?
3. Describe the policies in generic terms of three of the countries described in this chapter. Generic terms include input price support, farm product price support, food price support, and similar terms.
4. Which generic type of policy is more supportive of agricultural production—that is, more supportive of farmers?
5. Which type of policy would you prefer as a farmer? Or would you prefer to have no policies like these in your country?
6. From the information in this chapter, what do you think are the differences in policies in those with a low %PSE and a high %PSE?
7. Policies change over time and different countries have different policies. What type of new or different policies do you know of in the world today?

Further Reading

Organisation for Economic Co-Operation and Development (OECD). 2009a. *Agricultural Policies in Emerging Economies 2009: Monitoring and Evaluation*. Paris: OECD Publishing, 191 pp.

Organisation for Economic Co-Operation and Development (OECD). 2009b. *Agricultural Policies in OECD Countries: Monitoring and Evaluation 2009*. Paris: OECD Publishing, 277 pp.

7

Strategic Management: Planning

In this chapter:

- Strategic management: planning, execution, and control
- Strategic planning: stakeholders, vision, mission, and objectives

Strategy is the pattern of actions used by a farmer (or any business or organization) to accomplish goals and objectives. Strategy consists of the moves and approaches crafted to strengthen the farm's position, satisfy customers, achieve performance targets, and accomplish what it wants to do in the long term. Having a strategy helps a farmer make reasoned, cohesive, and consistent choices among alternative courses of action in an uncertain world.

Developing a strategy consists of answering four questions. The questions look deceptively simple; but, since the world is complicated, answering them well requires considerable thought, work, and communication with the people involved in the farm. These four questions are:

What do we want to do?
What do we bring to the table?
Where should we put our efforts, and why?
What do we need to do to compete, survive, and meet our goals?

Answering these questions should not be seen as a one-time event. Strategy is not a big, complicated plan that never changes. Instead, it involves watching and answering these questions anew as the world changes. A farmer's actual strategy is made up of both planned actions and relatively quick reactions to changing circumstances.

Strategic Management

Strategic management consists of planning a strategy, implementing the chosen strategy, controlling the outcomes of the strategy implementation, and adjusting the chosen strategy over time as conditions change (Table 7.1). **Strategic planning** involves the identification of the vision, mission, values, and objectives of the farm; analysis of the external environment; analysis of the internal environment;

Table 7.1 The Elements of Strategic Management

Strategic Planning
    Identify stakeholders
    Develop vision, mission, objectives
    Analyze the external environment
    Analyze the internal environment
    Craft strategy
Strategy Execution
    Obtain and organize the farm resources
    Direct the resources
Strategic Control
    Measure and evaluate farm performance
    Monitor external events
    Take corrective actions as needed

and crafting the best strategy for the farm in its current environment. **Strategy execution** involves designing the organizational structures and procedures needed for the chosen strategy and obtaining and directing the resources needed to put it into action. **Strategic control** involves designing control systems, comparing actual results to goals and objectives, monitoring the business environment, and modifying the organizational structure, implementation plan, or even the chosen strategy as needed to meet goals and objectives. This chapter includes an overview of strategic management and the first two elements of strategic planning. External and internal analyses are explained in Chapter 8. Crafting strategy is covered in Chapter 9. Strategy execution and control are covered in Chapter 10.

The sports metaphor of choosing a "game plan" is often used when describing strategic management. In business, we often speak of "positioning the business." Good team players read the playing field before deciding what to do during the game. They know their own strengths and weaknesses. They see where their own team members are and know what their strengths and weaknesses are. Good team players see where the competitors are and know what their strengths and weaknesses are. They see where the ball is relative to the goal. And they see the opportunities and threats and move to the best position to help the team accomplish its goal. Wayne Gretzky, a former professional hockey player with the Los Angeles Kings and a member of the Hockey Hall of Fame, described his strategy for hockey in this way: "I don't skate to where the puck is. I skate to where the puck will be."

Using this sports metaphor, a farmer crafts a strategy by understanding the business environment, seeing where and what is happening, and looking for strengths and weaknesses in his or her own farm and in the competition. Then the farmer "moves" the farm to the best position to take advantage of opportunities, to protect the farm from threats, and to help accomplish goals and objectives. Successful strategic management will position the farm, not where the profits were or are, but where they will be in the future.

The sports metaphor continues for strategic management because strategy evolves as the game is played. In a game played outside, the weather, the fans, and the other team can cause the initial strategy to become ineffective and in need of change. The analogy continues to the business world. A farmer may go through a strategic management process only to find the world and the farm has changed or that the chosen strategy was not executed well. The chosen strategy isn't chosen only once—it is an evolving process.

Crafting a strategy can help keep a farmer, as manager, focused on what is truly important when making decisions (even day-to-day decisions) that will affect the success and survival of the business. Short-term opportunities (a good deal on machinery, for example) or threats ("sign now or lose this chance," for example) may create distractions and possibly decisions that do not fit the chosen strategy and may not contribute to the long-run goals of the farmer. When a long-run strategy has been developed, it can be used to evaluate potential opportunities and threats for their ability to contribute to the strategic goals of the farm.

Let us look more closely at the idea that crafting a strategy is not a one-time event. Short-term opportunities and threats should not be ignored completely. They may be a signal that the business environment has changed so a farm's strategy needs to change as well. Taking advantage of the unexpected availability of land at a low price during an economic downturn may signal the need to reevaluate a strategy that did not include land purchase. Paying attention to short-term events is part of scanning the business environment, as described later in this chapter. The idea that crafting strategy is a continuous process is described from a different view in Example 7.1.

Example 7.1. Intended versus Emergent Strategies

The elements of strategic management listed in Table 7.1 are one variation of the classical school of strategic management. The list looks like and is often taught as a linear process that a business, organization, or family goes through to develop and implement strategies they intend to implement.

However, there are other ways of thinking about strategy. These different schools of thought include the following:

1. The *resource-based school* focuses more on the internal organization of the firm and says the firm's resources determine its response to external opportunities and threats.
2. The *contingency school* can be seen when greater uncertainty requires the business to have contingency plans—that is, an adaptive strategy focusing on effective structure and how it might adapt to unforeseen changes.
3. The *learning school* starts with the idea that strategy is as much a state of mind within an organization as it is a set of actions. It includes the idea that strategies emerge as people come to learn about a situation and the capabilities of the firm.
4. The *emergence school* represents a rebellion against the classical school and its focus on planning, leadership, organization, and control. The emergence school looks at the complexity of management and argues that adaptive systems enable strategic thinking through innovation, learning, and emergence.

The classical school provides a useful framework for understanding the strategic management process. However, in a complex and uncertain environment the formal steps of the classical school can be too cumbersome and can slow business progress. The classical school develops *intended strategies*. The alternative schools recognize the need for and allow *emergent strategies* to

(continued)

(*continued*)

come out of a knowledgeable, adaptive management team as the people work and live in an uncertain world.

Source: Andrew Beijeman, A. N. M. Shadbolt, and D. Gray, "Strategy Recognition and Implementation by New Zealand Pastoral Farming Strategists," peer-reviewed paper at the 17th International Farm Management Congress, Illinois State University, Bloomington/Normal, Illinois, U.S., July 19–24, 2009, accessed on February 1, 2010, at http://www.ifmaonline.org/pdf/congress/09_Beijeman_etal.pdf.

The need for strategic management is as true for a one-person or one-family farm business as it is for a multi-partner, multi-employee farm. The sole farmer's focus can be diverted from long-term goals just as easily as or perhaps more easily than a multi-person management team. If the sole proprietor has taken the time to develop a strategy, he or she can use that strategy to guide his or her own day-to-day decisions. However, the sole proprietor does need to remember that strategy evolves as conditions change.

A disciplined strategic management process can provide several advantages compared to the potential results following decisions made on the basis of freewheeling improvisation, gut feeling, good deals, or drifting along. A good strategic management process will:

• Stimulate thinking about the future.
• Make farmers more alert to and anticipate the winds of change, new opportunities, and threatening developments.
• Provide clear statements of the farm's goals and objectives for both a single owner-operator farm and a farm with many employees.
• Help coordinate the numerous strategy-related decisions by managers and partners across the organization or as the sole proprietor performs different functions for the farm.
• Create a more proactive management posture and counteract tendencies for decisions to be reactive, defensive, or spur-of-the-moment.
• Encourage the allocation of resources, capital, and staff to areas that will support the chosen strategy and help attain strategic and financial objectives.
• Allow for the constant adjustment of the business model to produce sustained success in a changing environment.
• Help farmers become better decision makers.

Although every farm may not see every advantage, all farms can benefit from strategic thinking and management. Large farms can benefit from the focusing and communicating that strategic planning creates. Smaller farms with only one or a few stakeholders can benefit because they are doing so many tasks that focusing on strategy for part of their duties can give direction and focus to their other duties.

Following all the steps of strategic management will not guarantee success. But farms that do follow a strategic management process have a higher probability of success in meeting both strategic and financial objectives. Farms that have good intentions, work hard, and hope but do not look into the future or outside the farm have a lower probability of success.

Strategic Planning

Strategic planning involves five elements that will provide the answers to the questions posed at the beginning of this chapter.

- Identification of stakeholders and their values, philosophy, and ethics
- Development of the farm's vision and mission, clarifying values, and setting of objectives
- External analysis of the farm's competitive environment including the general economy and the industry to which the farm belongs (for example, dairy, wheat, fruit). The goal of external analysis is to understand the environment in which the farm operates and to identify opportunities for and threats to the farm.
- Internal analysis of the farm's operating environment. The goal of internal analysis is to understand how the farm is meeting the current vision and goals and to identify the farm's strengths and weaknesses. Internal analysis includes but is also broader than the financial results.
- Crafting of the strategy for the whole farm and a complementary strategy for each part of the farm (corn production, hogs, custom work, for example) and each management function (marketing and finance, for example). Crafting strategy is explained in Chapter 8.

Even though these elements of strategic planning are listed in a linear fashion, they are completed after many loops back and forward to other elements of the process. Each element needs to be done (and often redone or updated many times) before the final strategy is determined for the farm in its current situation.

In the rest of this chapter, we examine the first two steps in strategic planning that set the stage for external and internal analysis and for crafting strategies, which are examined in the next chapters.

Identification of Stakeholders

Every farm involves more than one person even if there is only one owner. **Stakeholders** are the people interested in the farm itself, the outcomes (e.g., profit, products, runoff), and the processes of farming. The farmer, the farm family, the partners, the creditors, the community—they all hold an interest, a stake in the farm. If these stakeholders are ignored or not included in strategy development, conflict will likely occur. Also, the farm will likely not operate as efficiently as possible and not obtain the goals envisioned by the farmer and the farm family. Thus, identifying the stakeholders in the farm is a critical step in strategic planning.

Stakeholder groups are people, businesses, and institutions that have some claim on the farm. Stakeholders can be divided into internal and external stakeholders. Internal stakeholders include the farmer, the farm family, partners, employees, other owners or stockholders, and, often, creditors. External stakeholders may include the farm's customers, suppliers, governments, unions, competitors, local communities, environmental advocacy groups, and the general public.

The farm owner/operator is an obvious internal stakeholder. On most farms, members of the farm family are also included as internal stakeholders. The family is very concerned and interested in what the farm does, how it is done, and its results. Because they feel so close to the farm, family members may want, and even demand, to be part of strategic planning even if they neither work on nor own part of the farm. Older and younger generations of a farm family may be, or consider themselves to be, stakeholders also. For some families and circumstances, the yet-to-be-born generation may also be considered as stakeholders in the farm.

If these potential stakeholders are not recognized and their connections are not dealt with in some manner, the farm may have trouble formulating and implementing a plan for the future. At the least, social friction in the immediate and extended family may result if the actual and perceived connections are not dealt with explicitly. This is not saying that all conflict will be avoided (people do have different opinions), but discussion between stakeholders can help avoid needless conflict and, hopefully, improve the business.

While a farm may have many stakeholders, not all of them need to be or even should be directly involved in the development of a strategic plan. The management team obviously needs to be involved. Depending on how the farm operates, family members may be involved closely or at least kept informed and involved in some general discussions. Other owners and stockholders may be involved, unless they are silent partners or elder owners, but even these owners should be kept aware of plans and changes to plans. External stakeholders such as lenders need to be kept informed of strategic plans, but will not be involved directly, because the farmer(s) want to make their own plans and lenders do not want to become too involved and thus liable for losses in a legal sense. Other external stakeholders need to be considered in planning but would rarely be involved directly.

Values, philosophies, and ethics can directly affect what a farm produces, the production methods it chooses to produce those products, and how it relates to its employees, customers, suppliers, and the community. Sharing a common set of values within a management team is also critical to the success of a farm. By identifying the internal stakeholders, they can discuss and identify their shared values, their philosophy of business, and their operating ethics for the farm. These values, philosophy, and ethics can be communicated to employees, suppliers, creditors, and others doing business with the farm to help it accomplish its vision and objectives.

The reason for discussing and developing a set of ethics for any business is to give people the tools for dealing with moral complexity and the ability to identify and consider the moral implications of their decisions. For example, knowing that all internal stakeholders believe in complete truthfulness will help keep a farmer or family member from making decisions that would violate that ethic even though it means giving up higher profits in a low-income year.

These values, philosophies, and ethics come from personal beliefs, social mores, religion, humanitarian relationships, environmental concerns, and so on. They also include beliefs in how hard a person should work, what time a person should start work, how many hours a day a person should work, how much leisure time is needed, the value of manual work compared to desk work, the need to be fully honest with others, and so on. These seemingly obvious values to some may be viewed differently by others. Differences over even small items like the time to start work in the morning can create problems or be the beginning of other problems within the management team.

Concern for the environment and farming's impact on it is another example of the role of values. Stakeholders on one farm may hold the value that using any chemically processed herbicides, insecticides, fertilizers, etc. is not good for the environment; those values will likely push the farm into using organic production methods and selling in the organic market. Another set of stakeholders on another farm may have a multiple set of values: to produce food as inexpensively as possible without harming the environment. This farm may use some chemicals but not others; it may also evaluate the topography of the land and decide to not farm land on steep slopes and close to lakes, rivers, and streams.

The discussion among internal stakeholders should include identifying the core values of the farm. The number of core values is usually small, no more than three to five, to ensure that they are the core values indeed. These core values drive or guide other values and decisions; they are not changed easily.

Core values are kept even if the market changes and penalizes the company for holding those values. If the penalties are large enough, the stakeholders will change the vision, mission, and operation (perhaps even sell the farm) to alleviate the penalties, but they will not change their core values.

The importance of shared values, philosophies, and ethics cannot be overestimated. If these are shared by internal stakeholders, the rest of strategic planning and even day-to-day management is greatly simplified and the probability of success is greatly enhanced. A unified team does not guarantee success, however; goals and objectives may still not be accomplished due to events outside the farm. If differences are not discussed and reconciled among the internal stakeholders, there is no question that conflict will occur and goals will not be accomplished.

Some people argue that businesses (including farms) should incorporate social responsibility or social criteria and goals into their decision-making process. Some have a very strict environmental ethic that cannot be violated regardless of the profit potential. Another group says that social responsibility is a sound financial investment for the business. Others argue that a business' only social responsibility is to use its resources wisely to increase profits and employ people as long as it obeys laws and engages in open and free competition without deception or fraud. The differing strategies that may result due to differing ethics can easily be seen. One farmer may choose to only consider organic production methods. Another group may be very careful in its use of processed inputs. Yet another may be willing to use any chemical input that is legally allowed for the crops and livestock on the farm. The farm's customers and their preferences need to be considered. Each person and farm needs to choose which ethic is to be followed.

Vision, Mission, Objectives, and the Balanced Scorecard

The next step in strategic planning is the explicit development and statement of the farm's vision, mission, and objectives. Spending the time and energy to develop written statements will result in the cohesiveness of the management team and the improvement of decisions and efficiency of the operation toward short- and long-term goals. The cohesiveness and improvement come from the discussion and thinking that are required to discover and agree on a common view of what they want the farm to be in the future, what the farm is striving to do now, and how progress toward the desired future can be measured.

In a sailing analogy, the vision is developed by looking through a telescope at the distant shore and the safe harbor. The mission is the task of the crew to analyze and use the wind and boat to avoid shoals and aim at the safe harbor seen through the telescope. The objectives are measurable points identified through evaluating the sun and stars and geographical sites to indicate progress toward the safe harbor.

Vision.   The vision is, as it sounds, a picture of what the internal stakeholders want the farm to look like in the future—say, 10 years or more. It includes the common values or reasons for the farm to exist. It explains how the business helps both internal and external stakeholders. It helps current management lead the business into the future. A vision should have stability to guide decisions through changing times. Taking the time and energy to develop a common vision will make sure all stakeholders are pointing toward the same goals and working to improve the farm's efficiency in reaching those goals.

A vision can be described as a dream based in reality. Developing a vision can start with each stakeholder answering a set of questions such as those listed below. At this stage, the answers can be a dream; reality can shape the final wording. For the process to work the best, each stakeholder should answer the questions in writing as individuals first. Then all the internal stakeholders should join the conversation to shape their individual ideas into a commonly held vision of the future.

The following questions are a guide to developing a vision, but they certainly are not the only questions that could be asked. Since most farms are close to the family, family dynamics are certainly part of the answers. The questions are to be answered in terms of how they picture the farm in 10 years or more.

- What do I want the farm to look like?
- What products and activities will the farm be involved in?
- How big will the farm be?
- Who will be involved as owners, managers, and employees?
- How will the older, middle, and younger generations be involved?
- Where will the farm be located?
- How will the farm be organized? What will be its legal structure? Who will be responsible for what?
- How will the farm be involved in the community?
- Who will be the customers of the farm?
- What will the farm be good at?
- What will be the public perception of the farm?
- Why does the farm exist?

After answering and discussing these questions (and others that will be thought of), write a short statement that explains what the farm will be producing, who will be involved, what the farm will be recognized for, and why the farm exists. The statement should be worded to be rather stable over time, so it should not include specific quantities, steps, or current-year references. However, the statement should not be so general that it can't serve as a guide to management for making decisions.

As an example of a vision, consider two partners in a crop farm with one dedicated employee, and all the families have young children. Their vision could read: "Long Prairie Farms will be the preferred producer and supplier of quality feed to local dairy and hog producers. We will work directly with our customers to meet their feed and waste management needs and be a respected, profitable, sustainable neighbor in the community. We will strive to provide continuity of the business by working with interested employees and children to become part of the management team and owners of an expanding business."

A second example involves a dairy farmer who now sells milk to a local processor. Both the farmer and processor have decided to start the process to become USDA certified organic. The farm's vision could read: "Sparkling River Farms will be the premier supplier of USDA certified organic milk to Sparkling River Creamery. We will be a profitable producer of feed and milk. We will follow the full spirit of the national organic standards. We will be respected and active members in our community and the larger dairy industry."

A third example is a farm that produces undifferentiated commodity crops for the general market. "We will be a profitable, sustainable, and expanding producer of commodity grains and vegetables demanded by our buyers. We will be low-cost leaders through our choice of technology, production practices, and science-based decisions. At the same time, we will protect the environment for use by others today and in the future. We will be the employer of choice based on management skills, respect for all, and livable wages."

Sometimes a vision seems to change, but perhaps the change is actually a clarification of the vision. One farm family had the vision of being a top hog-crop farm in their home community, caring for the land, and keeping the farm into the fourth generation. However, their son wanted to farm, but he did not want to raise hogs. From their discussion, the entire family realized the vision that focused their decisions did not really include hogs. Raising hogs was part of the mission for the second and third generations, but the stable vision of the family was being a top farm in their community, caring for the land, and farming into the fourth generation.

Mission.   A business mission deals more with the present and very near future, whereas a vision deals with the long term. A mission statement defines a farm's current business directions and goals and indicates what the farm is trying to do for its customers now. A mission statement flows from and is closely related to the vision. It states who is involved in the farm, what they do, and who they are doing it for.

In today's world, a farm's mission statement needs to define its business using a customer orientation rather than a product orientation. That is, a farm needs to view its business in terms of the customers it is producing for, not what products it is producing. Abell (1980) provides three questions to answer to help develop a customer orientation for a farm. These questions should be answered in the context of the answers to the questions listed above and the resulting vision statement. Abell's three questions are:

Which consumer or customer groups are being satisfied?
What needs are being satisfied?
How are customer needs being satisfied?

As part of the answer to the first question, a farmer needs to consider three kinds of customers: final consumers, processors of farm products, and consumers of intangible products from the farm.

The first group of customers are the final consumers of products produced on the farm or produced from products produced on the farm. This first group includes people who consume food, wear cotton or wool clothes, use biofuels, use agricultural products in construction, and so on. For example, (among many decisions) a dairy farmer needs to decide whether this farm's final consumers are those consumers who want to avoid rBST, the recombinant bovine growth hormone, or not. If this farmer's final consumers do want to avoid rBST, then that will affect many decisions on the farm. Similarly, a soybean producer needs to decide whether he or she is aiming to satisfy livestock producers who want a protein source, consumers who want soy products for human consumption, organic customers, specialty soybean customers, and so on.

The second group of customers is those that buy farm products and transform them into the products used by the final consumer (or the next step in the supply chain). These customers can be processors such as cereal producers, meat processors, sugar processors, cotton millers, dairies, processors, and other companies. This group also includes other farmers who buy grain and soybean meal to feed animals. A rice exporter will want different varieties depending on their international customer. Meat processors want a certain size of animal because their equipment is designed to handle that size and that size will provide the meat cuts their customers want. Cotton millers are concerned about the variety of cotton grown as well as how production practices affect the ultimate strength and appearance of the cloth wanted by the final consumer.

The third group of customers is those who consume a more intangible set of products produced by farmers. These intangible products include, but are not limited to, environmental quality, hunting access, rural landscapes, and so on. Except for the possibility of paying for hunting access, these consumers most likely do not pay farmers directly for these products. However, these consumers may stimulate the imposition of alternative policies and regulations that affect how a farmer can operate and what potential payments they may receive.

In terms of satisfying the needs of the chosen consumer group(s), do they want the lowest cost product, a certain set of product characteristics, or do they place a higher priority on something else such as dependable delivery of a consistent quality product? Are they consumers of only certified organic products, or do they want goods produced locally by family farmers? Cereal producers, such as General Mills, need specific wheat varieties that produce the cereal characteristics that their consumers want. A soybean crusher may need a certain type of soybean that produces oil with the baking characteristics needed by bakers who need to make products with certain characteristics that the retailer and ultimately final consumers want. A hunter wants to have a successful hunt. The public wants a clean, safe water supply. The list of demands and needs is long and will vary with the consumers, the geographical location, and the time.

Once the customers are chosen and their needs identified, each farmer has to choose production methods to be sure customer needs are being met. This often involves knowing how the entire food chain operates from the farm's input supplier through the local buyers, shippers, processors, wholesalers, retailers, and ultimately the consumer. Identity preservation is becoming increasingly important for meeting the needs of many customers and consumers who want characteristics such as a specific variety of grain, specific production methods, and so on.

For example, if a dairy farmer is aiming at those consumers who want rBST-free milk, several things need to happen to meet the needs of those consumers. The dairyman cannot use rBST of course, but then the milk processor needs to keep that milk separate from milk that may have been produced using rBST, and the retail label has to report that the milk comes from cows not treated with rBST. Finally, the milk has to be sold in stores where these consumers will shop.

Another way of understanding and developing a mission statement comes from a personal discussion with Bengt Göransson, a retired CEO in Sweden. He describes a mission statement as completing the following statement:

"We, [*the farm, farmer, and others involved*]
will [*plans and objectives*]
by [*the process*]
so that [*customer's needs being met*]."

Following this model, the mission for Long Prairie Farms (introduced in the first example of a vision statement) could read: "We at Long Prairie Farms will produce consistently high-quality maize, silage, rapeseed, barley, and soybeans by using the best technology and practices available to keep costs down without harming the environment, so that our customers, local hog and dairy producers, will have feed with proper protein and energy levels that has been stored safely and delivered in a timely manner."

From the second vision example, the mission statement for the organic conversion years could read: "We at Sparkling River Farms will convert our farm and production practices to produce USDA certified organic milk by following all standards described for certification so that the buyer of our milk, Sparkling River Creamery, can also become a USDA certified producer of organic dairy food products." Note that the vision statement did not mention the conversion to organic. The vision is a longer-term view and it saw the farm as organic. The current mission is to make the conversion.

From the third vision example, the mission statement for the commodity crop producer could read: "We will produce high-quality grains and vegetables by using the best technology and science so that we can deliver a low-cost, environmentally sensitive product to our customers."

For the farm that clarified visions, the new mission statement could read: "We will produce and deliver the best quality hay and load and remove dairy animal waste in a timely manner by knowing our customers' feed requirements, feed storage capacities, and manure pit capacities so that our dairy farm customers can concentrate their management time and energy on their milking herd."

Objectives. Key objectives need to be identified and communicated as part of the development of the vision and mission statements. The purpose of setting objectives is to convert managerial statements of business mission and company direction into specific, measurable performance targets. Measurable objectives can serve as yardsticks for tracking performance and progress toward the vision. Without measurement, the organization does not know how well it is performing and whether its long-term vision will be accomplished with the current strategy.

Key objectives need to include both financial and strategic objectives. If only one type is developed, the other type may not receive proper management attention and, thus, the vision may not be met.

Financial objectives focus on specific measures of financial position and performance: liquidity, solvency, profitability, repayment capacity, and financial efficiency. If a farm does not have an acceptable financial position and performance, that farm may not receive the resources (capital and land, for example) that it needs to meet other objectives and the farmer's vision for the farm. (Financial statements, analysis, and management are explained in Chapters 12, 13 and 14.)

Strategic objectives focus on activities that affect competitive position: entry into a new market, being a low-cost producer, recognition for quality, farm size, and so on. Strategic objectives are needed to encourage managerial efforts to strengthen a farm's overall business and competitive position.

Objectives need to be both long-term and short-term. While some objectives are needed to track progress toward the long-term vision, a business also needs to monitor its progress in smaller steps. Performance targets and objectives five or more years ahead cause managers to take actions now to meet those long-term objectives and to consider the impact of today's decisions on longer-term performance. Short-term objectives should be steps toward long-term objectives. They provide the ability to check progress so the strategy implementation, or the strategy itself, can be adjusted, if needed, to achieve the long-term objectives and vision.

Some commonly expressed goals make poor visions and missions, but they can be converted into good objectives. For example, stating the farm's mission as maximizing profit does not describe the business of the farm and probably places too much emphasis on money. However, obtaining a certain income level and its related standard of living is an obvious financial objective for many farmers. Similarly, reducing estimated phosphorus runoff to a certain level and achieving a specific corn yield are good examples of strategic objectives. However, achieving zero erosion or maximizing crop yields do not describe a farm's business or mission.

Objectives need to be challenging but reachable if they are to push a farm to achieve the vision set by the stakeholders. Thus, several points need to be considered when setting objectives.

- Objectives need to focus on important issues.
- Objectives need to be precise and measurable, not vague and indeterminate.
- Objectives need to specify a time period in which they are to be accomplished.

- Desired performance levels (e.g., profitability, productivity, efficiency, etc.) will have to reflect what the industry and competitive conditions realistically allow. Performance objectives have to meet industry minimums if the farm is to remain a viable business and, at the same time, not surpass realistic maximums for the industry.
- Objectives need to be set to ensure the farm will be a successful performer in terms of its overall vision and mission.
- Objectives need to reflect the potential capability of the farm.
- To improve future performance, objectives also need to require "stretch"—that is, some extra work and disciplined effort on the part of the farm and those working there.
- The challenge of trying to close the gap between actual and desired performance levels can help a farm improve its operations, be more inventive, feel some urgency in improving both its financial performance and its business position, and be more intentional and focused in its actions.

Balanced Scorecard. Values, vision, mission, and objectives should be connected and can be connected by using the balanced scorecard as described by Kaplan and Norton (). The balanced scorecard helps a manager see multiple goals and the need to achieve objectives in each. A farm needs to meet financial objectives, but they are not the only perspective with which to measure success. The balanced scorecard lists different perspectives on success and includes indicators or measures of success for each perspective. The balance in the scorecard comes from the need to monitor progress from all perspectives, to view them as equal in importance, to keep a balance in the progress on the perspectives, and to signal a need for corrective action if the balance is not kept. In their original work, Kaplan and Norton specified four perspectives: customer, internal business, innovation and learning, and financial. These four may fit large businesses well, but family businesses such as farms may need two more: natural resources and family, lifestyle, and community. These six perspectives are described below:

- Customer perspective: How do customers see us? In general, customers' concerns involve time, quality, performance and service, and cost. Customers of farms may express these as timely delivery, proper protein levels in grain and livestock, color, taste, cost per unit, and many others.
- Internal business perspective: What must we excel at? These measures should be based on what needs to be done to meet and exceed customer needs. Examples of internal measures for farms include productivity measures (such as yield), quality measures (such as minimum foreign matter in delivered grain or bacteria count in milk), and cost per unit measures.
- Innovation and learning perspective: Can we continue to improve and create value? Examples of these measures for farms include technology leadership (such as adoption of new profitable technology and biotechnology), focus on the most profitable products, and decreases in per unit costs.
- Financial perspective: How do we look to shareholders, that is, the owners of the farm? These include traditional financial measures of net farm income, sales growth, rates of return to assets (ROA) and to equity (ROE), and growth in business assets.
- Natural resource perspective: What is the condition of the natural resources we use? The long-run performance of a farm depends on the quality of the soil, water, and air we use. Measures can include those with direct effects (such as organic matter in the soil) and regulatory concerns (such as manure lagoon management measures).
- Family, lifestyle, and community perspective: How does the business affect family life? Farms and families are most often very closely intertwined. The quality of each affects the quality of the other. How is the farm seen by the community?

Table 7.2 Example of a (partial) Balanced Scorecard for the Gables' Farm Business

Strategic Objectives	Measures	Targets
Family, lifestyle, and community perspective		
Retirement accounts	Fund levels	$1,000,000
Participation in the community	Board membership	Office
Financial perspective		
Efficient use of assets	Average monthly sales	$260,000
Family living standard	Cash available each month	$7,000
Customer perspective		
Seen as preferred supplier	Feedback	Repeat business
Producer of quality products	Tests by buyer	
Internal business process perspective		
Milk production costs	Cost per 100 lb	$14.00/cwt
Milk produced per cow	Average daily production per cow	80 lb
Natural resources perspective		
Optimal use of pasture without degradation	Stocking rate	Carrying capacity
Grouse count	Birds in spring	>1 per 10 acres
Learning and growth perspective		
Improvement in marketing skills and knowledge	Take class	Complete
Increase in child's ownership in farm	% of land owned	55%

Objectives in each of these perspectives can have both lagging indicators and leading indicators. Most financial analysis measures are lagging indicators, since they show the results of past actions. What businesses also need, and what are more important in many ways, are leading indicators that point toward future performance. Leading indicators include capacity growth, customer feedback, knowledge and skills, soil and livestock quality, production and sales reports through the year, and so on.

An example of a balanced scorecard with these six perspectives for the Gables (introduced in Chapter 3) is shown in Table 7.2. This scorecard contains mostly leading indicators and would contain more objectives if fully developed.

Using a balanced scorecard provides the farm manager a very explicit management tool to measure progress toward the farm's vision while balancing all the different perspectives needed to achieve complete progress. As we will see in Chapter 10, the scorecard can be a major source of controlling the execution of the strategy chosen through the crafting process described in Chapter 9. The balanced scorecard has been used in farming in other countries. Shadbolt describes how she found the scorecard to be useful in New Zealand (Example 7.2).

Example 7.2. Using the Balanced Scorecard

In her studies of and work with farms and agribusinesses on farms, Shadbolt found the balanced scorecard (BSC) to be a useful tool for helping a business and family make progress toward their goals and vision—if it is used and implemented well. The advantage of the BSC is its ability to help management focus on multiple goals from multiple viewpoints. Key measures for each viewpoint are needed, but Shadbolt noted that too many measures can turn the

(continued)

(continued)

BSC into a monitoring system and reduce its ability to allow flexibility in strategy while still aiming the business toward goals. Thus, the BSC allows for "emergent" strategies as well as "intended" strategies. Shadbolt notes that the BSC (and all strategy tools) should be used to support managers but not to substitute for the manager's capabilities and experience.

In conclusion, Shadbolt describes the BSC as a useful framework to force "the perspectives of human resources (innovation, continuous improvement and learning), internal processes (turning inputs into outputs), the market (customer relationships, product and service criteria) and shareholders (profitability, return on assets, wealth, non-financial and ethical goals) to be managed simultaneously and the linkages between them to be determined."

Source: N. M. Shadbolt, "Strategic Management of Farm Businesses: The Role of Strategy Tools with Particular Reference to the Balanced Scorecard," peer-reviewed paper at the 16th International Farm Management Congress, UCC, Cork, Ireland, July 15–20, 2007. Accessed on February 8, 2010, at http://www.ifmaonline.org/pdf/congress/07Shadbolt.pdf.

Strategic management is a continuous process. Large companies have strategic planning departments that even have an annual schedule of reviewing, monitoring, and evaluating the different parts of the business and its environment. When the year is over, the process does not stop but restarts at the top of the list. There is some flexibility in this schedule due to the changing economy and business environment, but the basic idea of strategy as a continual process can always be seen.

For farmers (most of whom do not have a strategic planning department), the continual part of the strategic management process comes after the planning is done formally for a first time. After the initial development of a strategy, a farmer needs to scan the external environment, evaluate the impact of new conditions and events, and choose any needed corrective actions. Scanning the environment involves such activities as listening to both agricultural and general news, monitoring what the government and other institutions are doing, watching what their competitors are doing, reading magazines, and contacting others who are also watching and monitoring the farming environment. Evaluation of the potential impacts is done either on paper in a formal estimation of the impacts of events or using mental models of how the business and its environment interact. The mental models may be used to evaluate whether the potential problem or opportunity needs a formal analysis.

Summary

- Strategy is the pattern of actions used by a farmer to accomplish goals and objectives.
- Having a strategy helps a farmer make reasoned, cohesive, and consistent choices among alternative courses of action in an uncertain world.
- Actual strategy is a mixture of planned action and relative quick reactions to changing circumstances.
- Strategic management consists of planning a strategy, implementing the chosen strategy, controlling the outcomes of the strategy implementation, and adjusting the chosen strategy over time as conditions change.
- Strategic planning involves the identifying the stakeholders, selecting the vision, mission, values, and objectives of the farm; analyzing the external environment; analyzing the internal environment; and crafting the best strategy for the farm in its current environment.

- Strategy implementation involves designing the organizational structures and procedures needed for the chosen strategy and obtaining and directing the resources needed to put it into action.
- Strategic control involves designing control systems, comparing actual results to goals and objectives, monitoring the business environment, and modifying the organizational structure, implementation plan, or even the chosen strategy as needed to meet goals and objectives.
- The need for a disciplined strategic management process is as true for a one-person or one-family farm as it is for a multi-partner, multi-employee farm.
- Both strategic and financial objectives need to be specified.
- A balanced scorecard helps a manager see multiple goals and the need to achieve objectives in each.
- For farms, six different perspectives can be useful for the balanced scorecard. These are the customer; internal business; innovation and learning; financial; natural resource; and family, lifestyle, and community perspectives.

Review Questions

1. What is strategy?
2. Why is strategy sometimes called "management's game plan for the business"?
3. What is strategic management?
4. Why bother with strategic management? Just start working!
5. What is a company's vision? Its mission?
6. Why should a farm set objectives? Why both financial and strategic objectives?
7. Describe the balanced scorecard. Why can this be useful in farm management?
8. What are the six perspectives that can be useful in a balanced scorecard for farms?
9. What are lagging indicators in contrast to leading indicators?

Further Reading

Besanko, D., D. Dranove, D., and M. Shanley. 1996. *Economics of Strategy*. New York: John Wiley and Sons, 769 pp.

Dunn, B. H., R. N. Gates, J. Davis, and A. Arzeno. 2006. "Using the Balanced Scorecard for Ranch Planning and Management: Setting Strategy and Measuring Performance." EC922, South Dakota State University Extension Service, Brookings, South Dakota.

Gillespie, Andrew. 2007. *Foundations of Economics*. New York: Oxford University Press, 400 pp.

Hill, C.W.L., and G.R. Jones. 1998. *Strategic Management Theory: An Integrated Approach*. 4th ed. Boston: Houghton Mifflin.

Kaplan, R. S., and D. P. Norton. "The Balanced Scorecard—Measures that Drive Performance." *Harvard Business Review*, 1992 (January–February): 71–79.

Kaplan, R. S., and D. P. Norton. "Using the Balanced Scorecard as a Strategic Management System." Harvard Business Review, 1996 (January–February): 75–85.

Thompson, A. A., A. J. Strickland III, and J. E. Gamble. 2005. *Crafting and Executing Strategy: The Quest for Competitive Advantage: Concepts and Cases*. 14th ed. Boston: McGraw-Hill/Irwin, 1140 pp.

8

Strategic Management: External and Internal Analysis

In this chapter:

- External analysis of the competitive environment
- Internal analysis of the farm's operating environment

In 1624, John Donne wrote, "No man is an island, entire of itself; every man is a piece of the continent, a part of the main." Although Donne was writing about life and death, not business and strategic management, his point that everyone is connected applies extremely well to the issues in this chapter. No farm works in isolation from other farms and the business and physical environments. The prudent farm manager will look far and wide to see what is happening outside the farm, as well as look inside his or her farm for capabilities, strengths, weaknesses, and issues that need to be addressed.

In this chapter, we delve into one core of strategic planning—external and internal analysis. The previous chapter introduced strategic management planning; identification of stakeholders; and development of vision, mission, and objectives. The next two chapters cover crafting strategy and strategy execution and control.

External Analysis

An external analysis of the farm's competitive environment includes understanding the forces operating within both the general economy and the industry in which the farm belongs (e.g., dairy or corn). External analysis evaluates the environment in which the farm operates, outside of the farm itself. The process of external analysis can be seen as answering eight questions (Table 8.1). External analysis is a broader term and includes what is called industry analysis.

The Macro-Environment. The farm and its industry operate within a larger business environment. Conditions and trends in that environment are important to consider when crafting strategy for the

Table 8.1   Eight Key Questions for External Analysis

1. What are the conditions and trends in the macro-environment?
2. What are the industry's dominant economic traits?
3. What is competition like, and how strong is each of the competitive forces?
4. What is causing the industry's structure and business environment to change?
5. Which farms are in the strongest/weakest competitive positions?
6. What strategic moves are others likely to make next?
7. What are the key factors for competitive success?
8. Is the industry attractive and what are the prospects for above average profitability?

Source: Adapted from Thompson and Strickland, 2005.

farm. A common method used to study this large environment is PESTEL analysis of the macro-environment. PESTEL is an acronym for six factors: political, economic, social, technological, environmental, and legal.

Policy factors include changes that can affect the demand for products, the supply of inputs, and the availability of production processes. In general, the trend toward more open borders and hence freer trade (North America Free Trade Agreement (NAFTA) or the European Union, for example) should increase demand for farm products and the supply of farm labor. Political changes affecting that trend could cause changes in product demand and input supply. Policy can affect the education of the workforce, health, and the quality of roads, rails, and the electrical power grid. Greater concern over the environment may translate into stronger environmental legislation, which could result in decreased availability of some inputs, decreased potential to use some production methods, and, perhaps, larger penalties for not following recommended or regulated production methods. Changes in farm policy can affect potential income of farms, the regulations on what can be produced, and so on. Policy changes in one country can affect the international competitiveness of farms in another country.

Economic factors, including changes in the growth rate of the economy, interest rates, currency exchange rates, and inflation rates, are major determinants of the overall level of demand for an industry's products as well as the supply of inputs. By understanding how the macro-economy is changing, a farmer can better understand how these forces will affect the farm and what strategic changes may be needed.

Social factors, including the change over time in what is socially acceptable and desirable, create both threats and opportunities for an industry. The changing social environment can be seen in even a very short list of current debates within and about agriculture and farming: globalization, immigration, industrialization, organic versus conventional methods, animal welfare, and farm size. Debates on these issues could be seen as threats to farmers' freedom to choose production methods. Alternatively, they could be seen as opportunities to serve new and perhaps more profitable markets.

Changing demographics—that is, changing proportions of the population by age and ethnicity—is another social factor that can have major impacts on the industry. New opportunities can develop with these changes along with threats of decreased demand for current products. Some demographic changes are slow trends (an aging population, for example); however, they can affect the long-term profitability of major investments. Other trends, such as changes in the ethnicity of the farm labor force, can be rapid enough to affect investments and, perhaps, encourage a current farmer to learn a second language to better communicate with a new labor force.

Technological factors include changes that can easily make established products and processes obsolete but at the same time create new products and processes. Continuing to use the same production methods even though new technology has made them physically or economically obsolete will keep a farm from being competitive. Monitoring, evaluating, and updating technology appropriately will help keep a farm competitive.

Environmental factors include weather and climate change. Changes in temperature and rainfall patterns have tremendous impacts on agricultural production. Traditional production areas may suffer in terms of productivity and variability while other, new areas may improve their productivity and thus their economic attractiveness. The increasing concern for protecting the physical environment may produce major changes in where and how production and transportation take place.

Legal factors include new restrictions on how farms can operate. Concerns on immigration and the environment may create laws that limit the supply of labor and the methods of production. Concerns for worker safety may create new rules and reporting regulations. Increasing concerns regarding food safety and bioterrorism may also change the way farmers operate.

An extension of PESTEL is called LoNGPESTEL, which reminds a user to consider the Local, National, and Global aspects of the macro-environment, not just one of these.

Dominant Economic Traits.   The second step in external analysis draws our attention to the chosen industry or market. A farm's market is defined by its product(s) and its close substitutes. As described in Chapter 4, close substitutes are other products whose supply and demand conditions can affect your product's price. For example, beef, pork, chicken, and turkey are considered close substitutes of each other. A beef producer may consider himself to be in the beef industry, but that producer also needs to monitor the larger meat market, especially for pork, chicken, and turkey. Similarly, a producer of barley in northern Europe needs to monitor market conditions for wheat, rye, and other small grains. In the United States, the dominance of wheat for food and corn (or maize) for feed removes some of the closeness of substitutes, but the relationships are still present, just quantitatively smaller.

Identifying our product's close substitutes increases our awareness of the trends and conditions we need to monitor for other products. A sugar beet producer should realize he needs to study cane sugar and corn sweeteners. An apple producer needs to understand conditions and trends in fresh grapes, bananas, pears, and other fruits.

Another way to improve our understanding of an industry and where a farm fits in that industry is to draw the vertical chain of production for the final product sold to consumers. The chain starts with the raw inputs and shows the steps to supply the final product to the consumer.

A simple vertical chain for pork is shown in Figure 8.1. Producing pork for the consumer takes many steps as seen even in this simple chain; and many more could be listed within each of those shown. The chain starts with the raw inputs (including both hogs and feed) and shows the major phases of processing and handling. The chain also explicitly shows, in the list on the right, the support services that are needed throughout the chain.

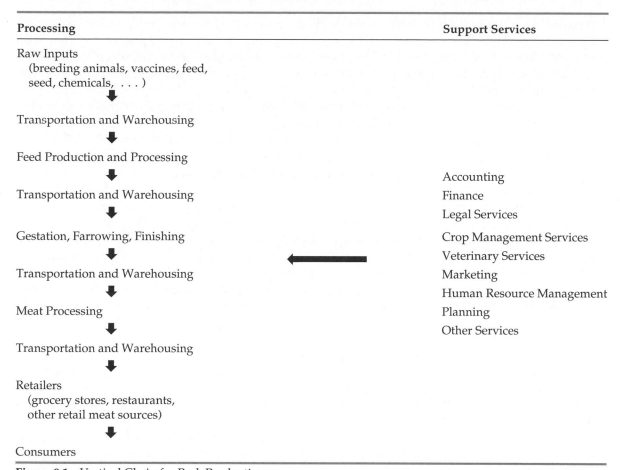

Figure 8.1   Vertical Chain for Pork Production

The benefit of drawing the vertical chain is the ability to see current and potentially new connections and to see points where efficiency (and thus profit) could be improved. Drawing the chain on paper also helps us improve our external analysis by seeing where other businesses and major players elsewhere could affect us in our part of the chain.

Once we have identified close substitutes and described the vertical chain, we can do a better job of understanding the many factors that describe an industry's economic traits. By considering the following list even for a familiar industry, a farmer will be in a better position to craft a strategy for his own farm.

- *Market size:* What is the total amount sold of the product? In a more detailed view, what is the amount sold of fluid milk, cheese, organic milk, ice cream, and other dairy products?

What is the amount sold of beef, pork, chicken, turkey, buffalo, and other meats? What are total sales in fresh carrots, processed carrots, and frozen carrots? Small markets do not tend to attract big or new competitors. Large markets, however, often draw the attention of farms interested in expanding. Larger markets will also attract larger suppliers and buyers who change the competition.

- *Scope of competitive rivalry:* Is it a local, regional, national, international, or global industry? How many producers, buyers, and sellers are involved? Where are the producers located geographically? How important (in quantitative terms) is each production area? Which areas are growing? Which are shrinking? The level of competition is discussed more in the next section.

- *Market growth rate and where the industry is in the growth cycle:* What stage is the industry in: early development, rapid growth and takeoff, early maturity and saturation, stagnant and aging, decline and decay? Fast growth breeds new entry; growth slowdown spawns increased rivalry and a shake-out of weak competitors. A corn grower may view the #2 yellow corn market as stagnant and perhaps aging due to slow growth, while the organic, blue corn market could be viewed as in the early development stage or moving into a rapid growth stage. The search for new consumer products by commodity groups is part of the response to stagnant markets. The intensity of competition within the hog industry could be because growth is stagnant or slow (compared to a high-growth industry) even though it is definitely not in decline or decay.

- *Prevalence of backward and forward integration:* Integration usually raises capital requirements and often creates competitive differences and cost differences among fully versus partially integrated firms. If an industry is highly integrated through either ownership or contractual relationships, the possibility of entry by new firms may be limited due to the inability to find an open market for their product.

- *Ease of entry and exit:* High barriers protect positions and profits of existing firms. Low barriers make existing firms vulnerable to entry of new competitors. Barriers can be in several forms and are discussed in more detail in the next section on competitive forces.

- *Pace of technological change:* The pace of change in both production processes and products can affect an industry. Rapid technological change increases risk. Investments in technology, facilities, and equipment may become obsolete before they wear out. Rapid product innovation shortens product life cycle and increases risk because of opportunities for leapfrogging—for example, when a farm with older technology skips a generation or two of technology to buy the newest available and thus jumps over other farms in terms of technology. Technology change may allow one region or country to grow at the expense of another.

- *Level of differentiation of the rival product(s)/service(s):* With standardized products, buyers have more power because of their ease in switching from seller to seller. With product(s)/service(s) that are highly differentiated or even weakly differentiated, the seller has more power. The same reasoning is present on the input side. If inputs are standard (fertilizer, for example), farmers can easily switch suppliers to find a better price and service.

- *Presence of economies of scale and scope:* Can farms realize scale economies in purchasing, manufacturing, transportation, marketing, or advertising? Economies of scale increase the volume and market share needed to be cost competitive. As discussed in Chapter 4, these economies may be present in farms as well as in the input and processing industries.

- *Capacity utilization levels:* High rates of capacity utilization are crucial to achieving low-cost production efficiency. Surplus capacity pushes prices and profit margins down; shortages pull them up. Are dairy facilities full or close to full? Do farmers have too much machinery capacity?
- *Impact of learning and experience:* If the industry has a strong learning or experience curve, average unit cost declines as cumulative output builds up (because the experience of "learning by doing" builds up). This is usually present in new industries, but may also be present when new technology is developed.
- *Capital requirements:* Large capital requirements make investment decisions critical and create a barrier to entry and exit. Timing of investment, entry, and exit becomes important.
- *Industry profitability:* Whether the industry profitability is above or below par will affect the pressure from new entrants or alleviate existing pressure due to firms exiting the market or industry. High-profit industries attract new entrants; depressed conditions encourage exits. In agricultural production, farm exits may not decrease the amounts of land in production due to the remaining farms becoming larger; so economies of scale are needed for the larger farms to improve their profitability.

Competitive Forces.   Farming is an industry that is often described as having perfect competition. That is, with so many farmers, none of them can control the price they receive for their products. However, farms are not the only part of the vertical chain, as discussed earlier and illustrated for the pork industry in Figure 8.1. Today's market places a farmer much closer to the consumer, which means a farmer needs to understand the industry and the competitive forces in which he or she operates. Farmers also need to understand the forces affecting the processors to which they sell their products and the forces affecting the suppliers of their inputs.

Michael Porter's "Five Forces Model" provides an excellent framework for analyzing industry competition. In his framework, Porter (2008) describes competition in an industry as a composite of five forces:

1. Threat of entry
2. Bargaining power of suppliers
3. Bargaining power of buyers
4. Substitute products and services
5. Rivalry among established farms

In his diagram of the forces, Porter puts rivalry in the center because the existing firms are affected by the other forces and the existing firms are, of course, the focus of our interest for setting strategy (Figure 8.2). The dominant force or forces will affect the profitability of the industry and drive the development of strategy to resist those forces.

Two other forces affecting competition in an industry have been identified.[1] These are:

6. Role of technology
7. Drivers of change

---

[1] Adapted from M. Boehlje and S. Hofing, 2005, "Managing and Monitoring a Growing Production Agriculture Firm: Part II." AAPEX, Centrex Consulting Group, LLC.

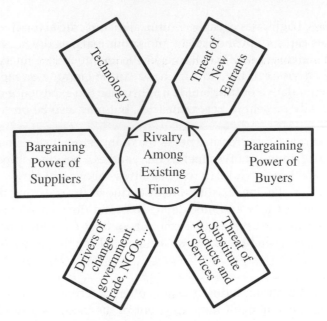

Figure 8.2 Porter's Five Competitive Forces Plus Two
Adapted from Porter (2008).

1. Threat of entry

For farmers, potential rivals and competitors may be just down the road, in another part of the nation, or across the ocean. Each of these three groups needs to be considered when evaluating the threat of entry by competitors.

If the risk of entry is low, farmers will have more bargaining power when negotiating both input and product prices. If the risk of entry is high, farmers will have less bargaining power. This competitive pressure also may show up at the processor level and affect farmers indirectly. If the risk of entry by potential competitors is high for a product buyer, that buyer's negotiating power is not as strong with its customers so it cannot obtain as favorable a price for its products, which translates into a lower price that the buyer can afford to pay the farmer for the raw product. For input suppliers, a similar story can be described, except the farmer could benefit from lower input prices due to the threat of new suppliers entering the market.

The level of the competitive pressures coming from the threat of entry by potential competitors depends on the height of barriers to entry. These barriers to entry are determined by several factors.

- The extent to which established companies have scale economies—that is, they are large enough to be able to spread fixed costs over more units and thus operate at lower costs per unit than a new entrant who would likely be smaller or forced to use more capital in order to build a larger operation. Economies of scale may also have a demand side effect. For example, the larger farmer with a good history has an advantage in renting more land than a new, smaller, unproven farmer.
- The extent to which established companies enjoy a market and/or cost advantage over potential entrants. An absolute cost advantage may occur due to a depreciated processing plant, established dealers, being farther down the learning curve, closer to markets, better geographical location, and so on.

- Higher capital requirements can be a barrier for new entrants. The capital requirements for building a cost-competitive livestock facility will stop many potential entrants. On the other side, a current farmer with land and machinery may have a low capital requirement to switch to a new crop.
- Established farms may have better access to distribution channels for both inputs and products. This is a larger barrier in specialty or niche markets than for commodity producers. For example, a farmer may have difficulty obtaining a new contract to produce vegetables under contract, while farmers with current contracts can usually keep them—if their performance is good. In another example, an established producer and long-time seller at the local farmers' market will likely have a better position for customer exposure in the market compared to a new farmer/seller at the market.
- The extent to which government regulation restricts entry. The most obvious government regulations creating barriers to entry are those that govern utilities, such as power and water companies. Because they have this entry protection, private utilities are usually monitored and controlled by the government. For farmers, government regulations affect how farms operate and thus create advantages to current farms due to knowing and understanding the bureaucratic system of rules, regulations, forms, and potential payments. Zoning regulations may allow current operations to continue but keep new entrants out of a geographical area.
- The extent to which established companies have brand loyalty. Brand loyalty builds barriers to entry by the unwillingness of consumers to switch from a brand they know to a new brand. While brand loyalty may not have a strong, direct effect on farms, the connection is stronger for those farms that are closer to the consumer (direct marketers, contractees, and members of cooperatives who sell directly, for example) compared to farms that produce commodities such as #2 yellow corn or hogs for the open market.

2. Bargaining power of suppliers

Suppliers can be viewed as a threat when they are able to force up the price a farmer must pay for inputs or to reduce the quality of goods supplied. More suppliers mean more competition among the suppliers. Fewer suppliers gives the suppliers greater power. If the number of suppliers in a local area is small, they may have more power even though the national number is higher. However, the Internet and better communication and delivery technology have taken away much of the pricing power of local suppliers.

With sellers, the competitive pressure grows out of their ability to exercise bargaining power and leverage when negotiating or setting prices for farmers' inputs. The recent mergers of input suppliers and consolidation of present and future input technologies (e.g., seed and pesticide as a single input) have increased the suppliers' bargaining power relative to the farmer and allow the suppliers to receive a higher price from the farmer and thus retain the profit potential of the inputs. Suppliers have power if:

- They are more concentrated than their buyers. This condition is very common in agriculture.
- They do not receive a high percentage of their revenues from one industry. If they sell to several industries, suppliers have more power to push for higher prices. Machinery manufacturers who sell to both agriculture and construction have more power in price-setting in both. Multinational fertilizer companies have this same power in playing one agricultural region or country against another.

- Farmers have high switching costs in changing suppliers. For example, once the machinery and equipment are purchased, farmers may be forced to pay higher prices for parts and repairs because the cost of switching to new machinery from a different manufacturer is too high.
- A supplier has differentiated its product from others. This often comes with company name recognition, as with John Deere and Pioneer.
- A supplier has a product with no substitutes, either through real differences or patent protection. In its early years, Roundup herbicide was an obvious example of this.
- Suppliers could indeed integrate forward into the industry if it seems too profitable.

3. Bargaining power of buyers

The number of product buyers has a very large impact on how the market works for farmers as producers. More buyers mean more competition among the buyers for the farmers' products and presumably fairer prices for farmers. Fewer buyers mean less competition and a higher chance of less than fair prices for farmers due to a shift in market power. The number of buyers needed to ensure a competitive market is a central question in the concentration debate, whether at a local, national, or international level. If producers cannot easily ship their products to other markets, a few local buyers can have considerable power even though the total number of buyers is large in the national and international markets.

Powerful buyers are the mirror image of powerful suppliers. Buyers can be viewed as a competitive threat when they force down prices or when they demand higher quality and better services. With buyers, the competitive pressure grows out of their ability to exercise bargaining power and leverage when negotiating or setting prices for farmers' products. This ability depends on the buyer(s)' size and power relative to that of the farmer(s). The recent mergers of buyers of agricultural products have increased the level of concern about the decline of bargaining power of farmers. The increasing use of contracts is another aspect of the buyer gaining bargaining power by controlling the amount of price information in the marketplace. In ways similar to suppliers, buyers have power if:

- There are few buyers or a few buying a large percentage of product in the market. This power is especially felt in agriculture, where farmers have high fixed costs in land, buildings, and machinery and thus feel pressure to keep these resources at capacity even if they are forced to accept low prices to sell their product.
- Products are standardized or undifferentiated, which is the most common situation in agriculture. Buyers can use the pressure of another farmer willing to sell at a lower price to force the first farmer to sell at the lower price.
- Buyers could indeed integrate backward into the industry—for example, when processors buy or build the facilities to produce the input they need rather than buy it from others. The poultry and other meat industries have experienced some of this.

As Porter points out, buyers are price sensitive and will bargain harder if:

- The product constitutes a major portion of its total costs.
- The industry's product has little effect on the quality of the buyer's product or on the buyer's other costs.

4. Substitute products

Substitute products limit the price that farmers can seek or ask for without losing customers to the substitute products. With substitute products, competitive pressure comes from the market attempts of outsiders to win buyers over to their products. The advertising campaigns of the pork, beef, and poultry industries are an obvious example of the competitive pressures due to substitute products: each industry feels forced to spend money advertising, and also cannot charge as much as it would like without pushing its customers into buying the other products.

5. Rivalry among established farms

Is the industry fragmented with many small farms or concentrated and dominated by a few large ones? As described in Chapter 4, industries can be grouped into four groups based on the level of competition: perfect competition, monopolistic competition, oligopoly, and monopoly. Most agricultural industries are described as perfect competition, although government regulation and intervention as well as the size and dominance of a few input suppliers and product buyers provide different flavors of perfect competition. For agricultural commodities, especially crops, most industries consist of many farms that are relatively small compared to the market size. This is true even if only farms with sales over $100,000 are counted. The poultry industry has experienced considerable concentration and has a few large producers relative to the size of the total market. The hog industry and now dairy industry are in the early stages of similar concentration.

Competitive rivalry is generated by the competitive forces created by jockeying for better market position and competitive advantage within an industry. The extent of this rivalry will affect how a farmer operates and how well a farmer can expect to achieve his or her financial and strategic goals. The extent of rivalry among established farmers depends on several factors, especially demand conditions and exit barriers.

Rivalry can vary depending on whether demand is growing with new customers, growing with existing customers, stagnant, or declining. When demand is growing with new customers (ethanol and biodiesel producers, for example), farmers have a much better chance of finding a market or contract for selling the product and finding a better price. However, if demand is increasing with existing customers or farmer groups, farmers may find it harder to locate a buyer because existing buyers and farmers have established relationships that are operating well. If demand is stagnant, farmers will have more trouble finding buyers as the buyers start to look for better and/or lower-cost producers. The extent of rivalry, and thus competitive pressure, is the greatest when demand is declining, because established farmers (those who have had contracts to produce canning vegetables, for example) vie for a shrinking supply of the market (production contracts from the processor, for example, as the consumption of canned vegetables decreases).

Higher exit barriers increase rivalry and competitive pressures. Exit barriers can keep the established farms from quitting; thus, they compete to remain or increase profitability and achieve other goals. These exit barriers can take several forms:

- Investments in specialized assets (e.g., a farrowing barn)
- High fixed costs of exit (e.g., removing a building or cleaning waste facilities)
- Emotional attachments to an industry
- Relationships between businesses (e.g., production contracts)
- Dependence on an industry

In farming, the question "Who are a farmer's competitors?" can have a complicated answer. Farmers do not always see their immediate neighbors as competitors. In a commodity market, immediate neighbors are not a farmer's direct competitors because they do not compete aggressively for market share (unless the local elevator is almost full during harvest). However, neighbors are competitors in commodities because they produce the same product. They also can be competitors in other markets. For example, farmers are obvious competitors in the land market and are well aware of who their competitors are. In another example, farmers know that other farmers (including their neighbors) want a chance to produce processing vegetables or corn for ethanol (that is, have a share of the market). This knowledge or perception of how many farmers want the chance or contract to produce and how much they want it will affect how hard a farmer negotiates a contract with the buyer. More competition will mean less ability to negotiate a more favorable contract; less competition means the farmer has more negotiating power. In some cases, producing corn for ethanol or soybeans for biodiesel, for example, may result in the competition for market share taking place in the form of competition for shares in the closed membership of the cooperative producing the ethanol, biodiesel, or other product. If competition for shares is high, the price of the share will be high. Farmers in other parts of the country and the world can easily be seen as competitors when they visibly try to take market share away from the local group of farmers.

When analyzing an industry, Porter warns that several factors, as he calls them, or characteristics of an industry, should be interpreted through the lens of the five forces and not by themselves. The industry growth rate, for example, is not always positively correlated with profitability. A high industry growth rate may lessen some competition due to the larger market, but suppliers may raise input prices due to a capacity constraint within their industry or due to their power to do so. Changes in the overall economy also need to be interpreted through the five forces. Recession and growth can have different effects that need to be traced through several areas to understand. Other factors that need to be interpreted through the forces include technology, innovation, government, and complements.

6. Role of technology

Technology can have a large impact in the production of and demand for a service or product of a firm. Advances in technology can be disruptive; they can be leaps that leave users of the old technology far behind. The expected lifespan or change in technology can put businesses on a treadmill of continually having to retool to keep up with their competitors. New technology can alter not only the efficiency and cost of the production process but also the actual products and services offered and demanded by others in the value chain. New supply chains may be created due to new technology in communication as well as products and services. The risk from technology change depends on the size of the role of technology in the industry.

7. Drivers of change

Drivers of change are forces imposing change on the industry. Examples of these drivers include changes in government policy, changes in international trade agreements, and other factors not included in the first six forces. The impact of these forces depends on the scope of the change and the speed at which change is anticipated or actually felt, as well as on the width and depth of the changes.

Porter's five (plus two) forces provide an excellent way to understand the forces affecting the structure and profit potential of an industry. These seven forces can also provide critical insights into changes in competitive pressures due to changes in the structure and the economic environment as discussed in the next section.

Changes in Industry Structure and Business Environment. Change is always occurring. Most of the time, change is gradual in small steps. At other times, it is drastic and sudden. In either case, Porter's five forces can be used to (1) identify the most important changes, (2) help understand the impact of change on the industry, and (3) help manager(s) of a specific farm see changes needed to maintain profitability or even survival.

The threat of new entrants will change if any of the entry barriers increase or decrease. For example, if new disease prevention techniques are developed that increase economies of size for livestock production, livestock facilities will expand, thus increasing the capital requirements and that barrier for new entrants. In the recent past, the introduction of Roundup herbicide and Roundup-resistant crops allowed farmers to replace labor intensive mechanical cultivation with herbicide control and thus increase their economies of scale, driving out current farmers and decreasing the number of new entrants.

Changes in the power of suppliers and buyers can quickly affect the profitability of farming. An obvious example is the new biotechnologies that have created mergers in the seed, herbicide, and insecticide industries. These fewer and larger companies have had greater power to set higher prices for farmers. Access to the Internet and other improvements in communication technology have decreased the power of local suppliers and buyers. Farmers can now quickly learn what prices are being charged and offered by others and use that knowledge to negotiate better prices. That positive impact for farmers was negative for many small suppliers and buyers in their own industries; those industries underwent change with the result of larger firms that sell to and buy from farmers.

The threat of substitutes can increase or decrease over time. At the consumer level, new convenience foods with chicken became substitutes for beef and pork and increased the demand for broilers at the producer level. Convenience foods with beef and pork were soon developed to counter the substitution effect partially at least. A decrease in shipping costs can increase the threat of the same product from a different region or country. The converse is also true. A food safety concern about a substitute can decrease its threat quickly, even though the effect may be short-term.

Rivalry within an industry usually intensifies as the industry matures. This is true for agricultural products, even though most are standardized commodities and thus already subject to competitive pressure. Farmers feel the increased rivalry, not in immediate confrontation with their neighbors, but in the continuing need to decrease their cost per unit as the other four forces exert their own pressure on farming.

The cause of change comes from many sources and directions. The groupings of potential sources below can serve as a beginning for identifying, monitoring, and evaluating sources of potential change.

- Changes in the long-term industry growth rate. Is the market expanding or declining? For example, per capita consumption of chicken and turkey is increasing while the per capita consumption of beef and pork has been more stable. The consumption of organic food products is the fastest increasing category in percentage terms, but it is still a small portion of total food sales.
- Changes in who buys the product: male or female, old or young, preferences of new ethnic groups.
- Changes in where and how the product is used: at home, away, or take-home; fast food or slow food.
- Product innovation: convenience foods, irradiated foods, emerging buyer preferences for differentiated and branded products.

- Technological change: biotechnology, mechanical, management, communication, processing, handling, shipping.
- Marketing innovation: direct buying by processors, increasing product specification by processors, Internet access.
- Entry or exit of major firms (and countries). In international grain trade, which countries will be buying or selling: China, Russia, the European Union? Mergers and acquisitions of companies can create changes in business strategy that cause them to leave or enter markets.
- Diffusion of technical knowledge to other companies and countries.
- Increasing globalization of the industry. Transportation improvements allowing more rapid and cheaper movement of products and thus closer alignment of local markets with world markets. NAFTA, WTO, and other trade agreements.
- Regulatory influences and government policy changes: new farm policies, new environmental regulations, changes in local zoning rules.
- Changing societal concerns, attitudes, and lifestyles: health concerns for less fat and less pesticide use; environmental concerns caused by chemical use, erosion; leisure versus work time.
- Changes in uncertainty and business risk in the industry and around the world.

Strong and Weak Competitive Positions.   What are the competitive characteristics that differentiate farms? What are the characteristics of the strongest? The weakest? Characteristics that are important to consider include at least these seven points: size, location, production methods, age of equipment and/or workforce, specialization, diversification, and vertical integration. A good evaluation of these positions requires good data on the financial performance of farms over time as well as an understanding of how the forces and changes identified in other parts of external analysis will affect different types of farms. At times, an individual farmer may not be able to see the whole industry and thus have a hard time grasping the complete picture of which firms are in the strongest and weakest positions. Then industry studies such as the one described in Example 8.1 can help our understanding.

Example 8.1. Strongest and Weakest Positions in the Industry

Identifying those farms that are in the strongest and weakest positions and the characteristics of each can be a daunting task. In some situations, observation of different farms can help in this identification. Statistical analysis is another useful tool for sorting out what is important and what is not. As an example, consider a recent study of the competitiveness of commercial milk producers in South Africa.

The statistical analysis done by these researchers showed that dairy herd size, the level of farm debt, production per cow, technological and policy changes over time, and the proportion of trading income to total milk income influence the long-term competitiveness of these milk producers as measured by their cost per unit of production. The study's authors conclude that relatively small and profitable milk producers should consider increasing herd size, as the importance of herd size in explaining competitiveness suggests that size economies exist. They also conclude that all milk producers should also consider utilizing more pasture and other forages to lower production costs and should select dairy cattle of superior genetic merit to improve milk yields. While some of these may seem obvious, the analysis does reinforce those notions.

Source: J. P. du Toit, G. F. Ortmann, and S. Ramroop, "Factors Influencing the Long-Term Competitiveness of Commercial Milk Producers in South Africa," peer-reviewed paper at the 17th International Farm Management Congress, Illinois State University, Bloomington/Normal, Illinois, U.S., July 19–24, 2009, accessed on January 30, 2010, at http://www.ifmaonline.org/pdf/congress/09_duToit_etal.pdf.

The Next Strategic Moves. Based on their competitive positions, what moves are competitors likely to make? Which companies, regions, or countries may change? What are the makers of substitute products doing, and what might they be changing? Will their potential changes make a large impact? This may seem like a game of chess in some ways, but a serious discussion of the strengths and weaknesses of the major players in the context of the future industry is critical to deciding how an individual farm should react and perform in the future.

Key Success Factors. Farmers could worry about many measures and conditions and spend valuable time and resources to improve them. But within each agricultural industry there are critical or key success factors (KSFs) that a farm must identify and keep at performance levels required by the industry. If this is done, other measures of success will follow. If the KSFs are not met, the farm will not perform adequately and its viability will be threatened.

A KSF can be identified as the word or phrase that would complete this sentence for a farmer: "If we _____, we will be successful." A dairy farmer found and worded one of his KSFs this way: "After visiting several new facilities, I knew we had to milk at least 120 cows per hour per worker in order for our expansion to be successful." Once the KSFs are identified, each farm needs to develop plans and procedures to monitor and improve them.

KSFs can be grouped in several ways:

- *Technology related:* science, production process, expertise in marketing, use of computers internally and externally
- *Manufacturing related:* scale economies, quality in production, labor skills and costs, flexibility versus costs
- *Distribution related:* local versus regional markets; networks of roads, railroads, barges, etc.; costs of distribution
- *Marketing related:* substitute products, competition for shelf space, customer desires and needs ("fat free," for example), direct marketing—meeting a customer's needs in quantity and quality
- *Skills related:* labor abilities, quality—getting it done correctly, expertise, management
- *Organizational capability:* ability to respond to changes, management, information systems
- *Other factors:* reputation, location, access to capital, etc.

Attractiveness and Profitability. This is an overall assessment of the industry's attractiveness or unattractiveness, special issues and problems, and its profit outlook. Attractiveness is a very subjective term. Each person or set of stakeholders needs to evaluate all the information obtained in the external analysis and decide whether he or she would like to work in the industry. Is it a good industry to be in or is it nasty? Information about the profit outlook can be found in reports available from USDA's Economic Research Service, the annual reports of the farm record associations available in many states, Federal Reserve reports, and many other sources of analyses and commentary on national and local economic trends.

In this section, we examined the procedures for external analysis. These procedures help a firm and manager evaluate and understand the whole industry in which a farm operates (or wants to operate). Understanding the whole industry is critical to developing strategies that will allow an individual farm to achieve its objectives and ultimately fulfill the stakeholders' vision of the farm in the future.

In the next section, we look inward and evaluate the condition and situation within the farm itself. This internal analysis is also critical for developing the correct strategies for an individual farm and its objectives and vision.

Internal Analysis

A full internal analysis will include consideration of the three main internal factors that shape an individual farm's strategy: (1) shared values and culture; (2) personal ambitions, philosophies, and ethical principles of the managers; and (3) the farm's strengths, weaknesses, opportunities, threats, and competitive capabilities. The importance of the stakeholders developing a set of shared values was discussed earlier in this chapter. Beyond the shared values, the managers themselves shape the strategies of the farm by their own ambitions, philosophies, and principles. The work culture created by the shared values and individual managers create a culture within the farm that affects which strategies are chosen, how they are carried out, and whether they will be successful within the industry as understood through the external analysis described in the previous section. How these first two internal factors are developed and woven together have a tremendous impact on the ability of the farm to take advantage of its strengths, opportunities, and capabilities and overcome its weaknesses and threats identified in the third phase of internal analysis.

The third phase of internal analysis is the evaluation of the farm's strengths, weaknesses, opportunities, threats, and competitive capabilities. A farm's strategy needs to be grounded in what it is good at doing, its strengths and competitive capabilities. Until they are defended against or overcome, weaknesses cannot be the basis for success. The third phase of internal analysis centers on five key questions (Table 8.2). The first step is to analyze the farm's financial condition and past performance needs and evaluate how well it is meeting the current vision, mission, and objectives. The next steps of internal analysis are identifying the farm's strengths, weaknesses, opportunities, and threats and comparing the farm to other farms in the industry. The last step in internal analysis is developing the list of strategic issues that need to be addressed when crafting strategy, which is the last step in strategic planning.

How Well Is the Present Strategy Working? This question can also be asked this way: How well is the farm achieving its financial and strategic objectives and progressing toward the stakeholder's vision for the farm? We start our answer by assessing the farm's current financial condition and

Table 8.2 Five Key Questions for Internal Analysis

1. How well is the present strategy working?
2. What are the farm's strengths, weaknesses, opportunities, and threats?
3. Are the farm's costs competitive with rivals?
4. How strong is the farm's competitive position?
5. What strategic issues need to be addressed?

Source: Adapted from Thompson and Strickland, 2005.

performance. Starting with financial data allows us to look at the "concrete" results of past strategic and operational decisions. As explained in Chapter 7, we are interested in the farm's profitability, solvency, liquidity, repayment capacity, and efficiency. Although profitability is often of foremost interest, a major part of this first question of internal analysis is our evaluation of the farm's success at balancing profit objectives with other financial and strategic objectives.

Another reason for starting with financial analysis is to find out whether the farm has a sustained competitive advantage—that is, whether its profit rate has been higher than the industry average for several years running. The profit rate is usually measured as either the rate of return on assets (ROA) or the rate of return on equity (ROE). Those farms with a higher rate are performing better financially than the industry. A major part of internal analysis is striving to understand why some farms have sustained competitive advantage and how that can be continued and replicated on other farms.

Hill and Jones identify four building blocks of competitive advantage: efficiency, quality, innovation, and customer responsiveness. These building blocks need to be worked on and developed and maintained in balance with each other. One building block—efficiency, for example—cannot be emphasized over the other three without a detrimental effect on profitability and thus competitive advantage.

Superior Efficiency: Efficiency involves using inputs in the most productive way possible. It is commonly measured by the cost of inputs required to produce a given output. Increasing efficiency obviously decreases costs. Other ratios can be used to measure and monitor efficiency: asset turnover, output or sales per worker, yields per acre, productivity per animal, and so on.

Superior Quality: Quality is defined as meeting and exceeding the customer's expectations. Quality products and services are reliable in the sense that they do the job for which they were designed. Superior quality means providing higher quality in terms of product design, production, reliability, and service. However, note that the customer defines quality, not the farmer. A fuller description of quality measurement, management, and control is in Chapter 6.

Providing higher quality (that is, doing a better job of meeting customer specifications) will do several things for a farm. It has been shown in many companies that higher quality will increase efficiency and lower costs, thus helping another building block of competitive advantage. Higher quality will also create a good reputation for the farm and, thus allow a farm to receive a higher price and/or increase the market for its products. With higher quality, less time is spent making defective products, fixing mistakes, and hauling away mistakes and scrap. Worker productivity improves, so costs decrease.

Superior Innovation: Innovation involves advances in products, production processes, marketing processes, management systems, organizational structures, strategies, and so on. It is anything new or novel about the way a farm operates and the products it produces. Innovation that creates a unique product may allow the farm to differentiate itself and receive a higher price. Innovation can also allow a farm to lower its costs below competitors and thus improve profitability.

Superior Customer Responsiveness: To be responsive, a farmer must know what the customer needs and how to satisfy those needs—whether the customer is the final consumer, a local elevator, the processor, or a neighbor. Customer responsiveness increases the value the customer receives, the price they are willing to pay, and the likelihood of repeat and new business. If a processor has been pleased with a farmer's performance, that processor will likely be interested in bringing new business to that farmer compared to one they are not satisfied with. The ability to customize products and services (such as specific varieties, special harvest windows, specific animal characteristics) to the unique needs of individual customers increases customer responsiveness and thus the ability to receive a higher price and/or increase market potential. Faster customer response time to a customer query (whether to rent more land or grow a certain product, for example) or for job completion (custom harvest, for example) is superior responsiveness. Superior responsiveness can improve both prices received and market share. Poor response is a major source of dissatisfaction and potential market loss.

What Are the Farm's Strengths, Weaknesses, Opportunities, and Threats?   The traditional **SWOT analysis** involves identifying and analyzing a farm's strengths, weaknesses, opportunities, and threats (Figure 8.3). A strength is something a business is good at doing or a characteristic that gives it an important capability. As discussed below, a core competency is something a company does especially well in comparison to its competitors. A weakness is something a company lacks, does poorly, or a condition that puts it at a disadvantage. Strengths and weaknesses are internal conditions for the farm.

Some strengths and weaknesses may be identified when performing an analysis of the farm's financial condition and performance. Other strengths and weaknesses may be identified by reviewing the functional areas of the farm: production, marketing, finance, and human resources. In each of the functional areas, both the tangible resources (such as land, buildings, livestock, equipment) and intangible resources (reputation, technological knowledge, marketing knowledge, for example) need to be evaluated as to whether any resources are obviously better or worse than the competitor's resources. Capabilities, such as the skills at organizing and directing resources or the ability of the farm's organizational structure to make use of those skills, should be compared to the competitor's capabilities. As described in the next section, benchmarking can show differences in prices, costs, and operational efficiencies and thus help explain differences in performance that are not explained by differences in resources between the farm and its competitors.

	Good	Bad
Internal to the farm	STRENGTHS	WEAKNESSES
External to the farm	OPPORTUNITIES	THREATS

Figure 8.3   SWOT Analysis

Those strengths that cannot be easily duplicated by another farm are candidates for core competencies. For example, a hog producer may have these strengths: lower feed costs per animal, better performance, and better worker productivity. The first two strengths might be easily duplicated by competitors. The third may be a core competency due to the manager's ability to attract, hold, train, and improve good workers and the difficulty for other managers to achieve the same level of people skills. While not ignoring other strengths (and weaknesses), core competencies should be maintained and used to build and sustain the success of the farm.

Opportunities and threats are, simply put, good and bad things that could be taken advantage of or could happen to a business. Opportunities and threats are external conditions in the marketplace and thus could be analyzed as part of the external analysis for the farm. However, they are examined here in an internal analysis in terms of what an individual farm can take advantage of or needs to be protected from because (1) not all industry opportunities and threats are available to or threatening an individual farm, and (2) an individual farm may face opportunities and threats that are unique to its situation. At times, whether an event or condition is a threat or opportunity depends on the situation of the firm and the other events in the external environment of the firm (Example 8.2). At other times, events unfold in the external environment where we know we may be facing a threat but we are not sure how much it will affect our own business (Example 8.3).

Example 8.2. Carbon: Opportunity or Threat?

Climate warming concerns have created the opportunity for some farmers to benefit economically by sequestering carbon through changes in production practices that create crop production, rangeland, and afforestation offsets. A recent study showed how the variance in the carbon price at the U.S. Chicago Climate Exchange has ranged between $2 to $5 per tonne, which provides a return ranging from $1 to 5 per acre. This return is uncertain in the future, with potential forces pushing it down and other potential forces pushing it up.

However, the concern over carbon is also a threat due to potential regulations. The livestock industry, especially dairy farmers, are especially aware of this threat. In both Europe and the United States, political debates involve whether and how farmers (and all carbon users) should be taxed and at what level. Ruminants such as dairy cows are mentioned as relatively sources of carbon and, some argue, should be assessed a tax. The dairy industry claims a tax would create economic calamity for many dairy farmers and so opposes such a tax.

At the same time, the dairy industry, governments, and processors are pursuing alternative management practices and other methods to decrease the carbon footprint of cattle. The *Financial Times* reports work being done by the International Dairy Federation, retailers such as Sainsbury, and processors such as Cadbury, who are working with farmers to spread research findings, knowledge of best practices, and simple changes in herd management that can decrease emissions in CO_2 gases.

For strategic management, the concern over carbon can be an opportunity to adjust practices and gain income in the carbon market. The carbon concern is also a threat that needs to be

(continued)

(*continued*)

considered when making decisions about direction, location, size, and production practices and facilities for dairies especially.

Sources: L. A. Ribera, B. A. McCarl, and J. Zenteno "Carbon Sequestration: a Potential Source of Income for Farmers, *Journal of the ASFMRA* (Denver, Colorado: American Society of Farm Managers and Rural Appraisers), vol. 72, no. 1, (June 2009), pp. 70–77. Accessed February 11, 2010, at http://portal.asfmra.org/userfiles/file/300_Ribera.pdf.

R. Tieman, "Livestock: Burping Cow Is Just Part of the Problem," *Financial Times*, January 26, 2010. Accessed on February 3, 2010, at http://www.ft.com/cms/s/0/bdde1dec-0a00-11df-8b23-00144feabdc0, dwp_uuid=1f25d038-0a1d-11df-8b23-00144feabdc0.html.

Example 8.3. The Threat of Losing Your Buyer

When economic forces push processors' profits, farmers need to be alert for who may make major strategic shifts. An example of this happened in early 2010 in Sioux City, Iowa.

The hog industry had been squeezed since 2008 by the sharp rise in feed costs and the drop in export demand due to the H1N1 flu scare that fell unfairly on pork exports from the United States Farmers sold sows and decreased production. The six hog processing plants in and within 100 miles (60 km) of Sioux City were having trouble finding enough hogs to keep their plants working at capacity.

There appeared to be excess capacity in hog processing. So which plant should close to balance capacity with supply? If the six plants were owned by the same company, the obvious decision would be to shut down the plant that is the costliest to operate. However, the six plants in this area were owned by five different companies.

Farmers could benefit from knowing which plant would close so they could make better marketing and expansion decisions. However, the companies would not invite farmers into their discussions.

Farmers can develop an understanding of which processing plant might close by considering (1) the age of each plant (when it was built and when it was last remodeled), (2) where the plants are located, (3) the local plant's age and condition compared to the other plants that each company has, and (4) estimates of the cost efficiency of each plant. A plant may not be the oldest and least efficient in the area, but if it is a company's least efficient plant, the company may decide to close it.

This latter case is what apparently happened in Sioux City in early 2010. One company announced it would be closing and described its plant as its oldest, least efficient, and costliest to renovate. Farmers will still have five processors bidding for their hogs, but those closer to the now closed plant will have higher transportation costs.

Source: D. Dreeszen, "As Pork Producers Lost Money, Morrell Closing Became 'Inevitable.'" *Sioux City Journal*, Iowa, February 1, 2010, posted January 30, 2010. Accessed on February 4, 2010, at http://siouxcityjournal.com/news/local/article_0332d485-8379-5729-a18b-b8a03e797717.html?mode=story

A SWOT analysis is not complete with the identification and listing of a farm's strengths, weaknesses, opportunities, and threats. Five additional questions still need to be addressed:

1. How should the strengths be used? Which should be used to improve the farm's situation?
2. Which weaknesses are critical to success? That is, which need to be improved and which can be ignored for now? From which weaknesses does the farm need to be protected?
3. Which opportunities can be taken advantage of?
4. Which threats are potentially destructive?
5. Can the use of or response to any of these be done together to gather synergism, efficiencies, and other benefits?

Are Costs Competitive? One of the major sources of competitive advantage for farms is having costs per unit be lower than those of competing farms. These competing farms may be next door neighbors or across an ocean. The question is whether the specific farm has lower costs of production and delivery than others producing the same product for the same market. Costs per unit need to be estimated and then compared to those of other farms. This comparison can be done with USDA costs of production survey data and with the farm record associations present in many states.

As will be described in more detail in Chapter 13, cost comparisons can be done in several ways. The first is a horizontal comparison across farms of the total costs per product unit (bushel, hundredweight, head, for example). A historical comparison shows how the costs have changed over time for both the specific farm and all farms. A vertical analysis will show the importance or size of the various cost categories and identify which areas show the largest potential for cost reduction. Vertical cost analysis leads into value chain analysis.

A value chain identifies the activities, functions, and business processes that have to be done in designing, producing, marketing, delivering, and supporting a product or service. Value chain analysis breaks down the whole process in detail so a manager can understand how costs are generated and how the process can be changed to improve efficiencies, increase quality, and decrease costs. A major goal of value chain analysis is to identify the farm's sources of competitive advantage (or disadvantage).

To perform a value chain analysis, costs need to be organized by activity rather than by broad category. That is, the list of costs in a whole-farm statement or on a Schedule F for tax purposes is not sufficient to perform a complete value chain analysis. For farm management, a good place to start value chain analysis is with enterprise budgets developed from the farm's own records. As will be described in Chapter 15, enterprise budgets will show the separate activities of, for example, tillage, planting, crop protection, harvest, storage, marketing, feeding, sanitation, housing, health, and transportation. Allocating whole-farm costs to separate activities can be difficult, but experience shows the information obtained is worth the effort. These activity-based costs can be compared to the potential value created by each activity to ascertain which activities need to be improved or changed to bring costs more in line with the value created.

The activity-based costs can also be used to compare the farm's cost structure and cost level to competing farms. This comparison can be done by using USDA survey data, but it should be noted that with survey data usually just an average is reported. For improvement to be made, comparisons need to be made with the best farms. These data are harder to come by but are available in the annual reports of farm record associations. Comparisons can also be done by benchmarking with other farms.

Benchmarking involves comparing costs and physical efficiencies of performing activities as well as the physical process of performing those activities. Through tours and private discussions, a farm can identify the best practices of other farms and then, after assuring that they are estimated using the same procedures, compare the costs of those best practices with its own practices. Advances in benchmarking in the UK and around the world, specifically process benchmarking, are described by Jack (Example 8.4).

Example 8.4. Process Benchmarking

Benchmarking in agriculture is comparatively sophisticated compared to non-agriculture industries. A common form of benchmarking is the gathering, summarizing, and reporting overall averages (and perhaps high and low subgroup averages) on production and performance by large groups. However, the farmers in these groups may not use and benefit from this benchmarking information as much as researchers, policymakers, lenders, and others in agricultural industries who work with farmers.

Another form of benchmarking may be much more useful to farmers. This is called process benchmarking, which is as it sounds. Farmers meet together to discuss specific processes being done on their farm to learn from each other how to improve these processes. The farmers involved realize that no one does everything perfectly, but some do certain processes better than others so all can learn from others' experiences.

Process benchmarking can be grouped into four types:

1. *Internal benchmarks* are found when a farm looks inside itself to see whether there are ideas for improvements from other parts of the business.
2. *Competitive (or external) benchmarks* result from looking outside the farm to see what can be learned and observed at other companies in the same industry.
3. *World-class benchmarks* extend the external comparison to companies in other industries that are known as the best in what they do.
4. *Activity-type benchmarks* focus on a small part or piece of a process and look across companies and industries in search for new ideas, approaches, and solutions.

Benchmarking, especially process benchmarking, aids adaptive and generative innovation by farm managers. Benchmarks can be extended beyond costs and other financial measures to look at process efficiencies and methods as well as non-financial measures [as discussed in relation to the balanced scorecard in other parts of this book]. Small group and one-to-one discussions can be used internationally to increase the knowledge and use of best practices.

Source: L. Jack, 2009, *Benchmarking in Food and Farming: Creating Sustainable Change* (Farnham, Surrey, England: Gower Publishing Limited), 132 pp.

Who would not only allow another farmer to come in and study the physical process but would also open his or her books to another farmer who is really a competitor? Farmers who allow this realize they need to continuously improve their own farm and can learn from others. The cooperating farms agree (1) to share data, (2) to produce it on a time schedule, and (3) not to share the data with anyone else outside of the group. Benchmarking sessions tend to be organized by management consultants, farm record associations, and accounting firms. These groups can organize the connections among small groups of farms and create comparable data if these are unavailable. Some private accounting firms are industry specific and supply benchmarking studies and information on best management practices to their clients, but not to the general public.

Strength of the Competitive Position. The ability of a farm to improve and/or maintain competitiveness depends not just on the farm's past record but also on the strength of the position the firm is in. That is, strengths and core competencies found in the SWOT analysis need to be strong in relation to the trends present in the industry. Also, the firm needs to be making the correct moves to position itself to take advantage of the trends in the industry. Upon reviewing both the internal analysis done to this point and the external analysis done on the industry, the farm can be evaluated for the signs of competitive strengths and weaknesses as exemplified in the lists below.

Signs of Competitive Strengths

- Important core competencies
- Distinctive strategies
- Cost advantages
- Good match of the farm's strategic product groups with the industry's growth areas
- Above average profit margins
- Taking advantage of cost economies
- Above average technological and innovational capability
- Creative, entrepreneurially alert management
- Capable of capitalizing on opportunities
- Possessing skills in key areas

Signs of Competitive Weaknesses

- Competitive disadvantages
- Losing ground compared to other farms
- Below average growth
- Short on financial resources
- Poor strategic product groups compared to industry growth
- Weak where best growth potential is
- High-cost producer
- Not able to take advantage of cost economies
- Poor quality of and/or missing skills in key areas

Strategic Issues to Be Addressed. At this point, the external and internal analyses are reviewed and put together to assess how well the farm is placed in the industry situation and what strategic issues or points need to be studied, improved, changed, and so on. This identification of issues is the beginning of crafting strategy, which is described in the next chapter.

Summary

- The answers to eight key questions provide a comprehensive external analysis.
- Porter's five forces describing competition are risk of entry by potential competitors, rivalry among established farms, bargaining power of buyers, bargaining power of suppliers, and substitute products. Two other forces affecting competition are the role of technology and drivers of change.
- Key success factors (KSFs) are measures and performance standards that must be met to be competitive. They are "key" because other results will follow if the KSFs are met.
- The answers to five key questions provide a comprehensive internal analysis.
- A farm has a sustained competitive advantage when its profit rate has been higher than the industry average for several years running.
- Four building blocks of competitive advantage are efficiency, quality, innovation, and customer responsiveness.
- SWOT analysis identifies a farm's strengths, weaknesses, opportunities, and threats.

Review Questions

1. What are the eight questions for external analysis?
2. If I have already done an external analysis, why should I do an internal analysis?
3. Describe Porter's five competitive forces and the two additional forces. How can a farmer use this information for crafting strategy?
4. What are key success factors (KSFs)?
5. What are some key success factors for a dairy farm? A hog farm? A crop farm?
6. Describe a farm and develop an elementary external analysis for that farm.
7. What are the five questions for internal analysis?
8. When we say a farm has a sustained competitive advantage, what do we mean?
9. What are the four building blocks of competitive advantage? Give an example of each.
10. Describe SWOT analysis. Discuss each part and give examples of each category.
11. Describe a farm and develop an elementary internal analysis for that farm.

Further Reading

Besanko, D., D. Dranove, and M. Shanley. 1996. *Economics of Strategy.* New York: John Wiley and Sons, 769 pp.

Gillespie, Andrew. 2007. *Foundations of Economics.* New York: Oxford University Press, 400 pp.

Hill, C. W. L., and G. R. Jones. 1998. *Strategic Management Theory: An Integrated Approach.* 4th ed. Boston: Houghton Mifflin.

Jack, L. 2009. *Benchmarking in Food and Farming: Creating Sustainable Change.* Farnham, Surrey, England: Gower Publishing Limited, 132 pp.

Porter, M. 2008. "The five competitive forces that shape strategy." *Harvard Business Review,* pp. 79–93.

Thompson, A. A., A. J. StricklandIII, and J. E. Gamble. 2005. *Crafting and Executing Strategy: The Quest for Competitive Advantage: Concepts and Cases.* 14th ed. Boston: McGraw-Hill/Irwin, 1,140 pp.

9

Crafting Strategy

In this chapter:

- Crafting competitive strategy
- Strategies for specific situations
- Tests for evaluating strategies
- Improving strategic planning
- Managing strategic risk

The previous two chapters introduced and described the first four elements of strategic planning: identification of stakeholders; development of vision, mission, and objectives; external analysis; and internal analysis. This chapter finishes our lesson in strategic planning by describing the process of crafting strategy. The next chapter explains the processes and procedures for successful execution and control of the chosen strategy.

In this, the fifth and last element of strategic planning, the process of developing or crafting a strategy is described for the overall business and for each part of the business. Some people call this determining the business model—that is, how the farm will make a profit and meet other goals too. The term "crafting strategy" is used to emphasize that this is an evolving process and involves interpreting the future. Crafting strategy is not a short, simple, or linear process, and neither is there a formula that will choose a strategy for a farm. Crafting strategy is a continual process because internal and external conditions change, and the strategy needs to be adjusted to cope with the changes. Using the information developed by the processes described in the previous chapters, several steps need to be taken and choices made in order to form a cohesive, solid strategy for a farm under current and expected conditions. The strategy is written, evaluated, and rewritten perhaps many times, as times and conditions change.

Crafting Competitive Strategy

Crafting strategy is the managerial process of deciding how to achieve the desired vision and objectives within the reality of the farm's physical and economic environment and how that environment may change in the future. Vision and objectives are the ends; strategy is the means. A well-crafted strategy provides direction for day-to-day activities by defining "our way of doing business."

A Framework for Crafting Strategy

An effective strategy reflects organizational resources and capabilities, the industry, and the competitive environment. Good strategies are based on the competitive advantages of a business—that is, those points at which a business has an edge over its competitors. As seen in the previous chapter, both external and internal factors shape strategy.

External factors that shape a farm's strategy include:

- Societal, political, regulatory, and community citizenship considerations. These are usually limiting factors, but if they are changing, they could be opportunities.
- Industry attractiveness; changing competitive conditions and requirements. A farm's strategy ought to be closely matched to these conditions and requirements.
- Specific market opportunities and threats. A well-conceived strategy aims at capturing a farm's best opportunities and defending against external threats to its well-being and future performance.

Internal factors that shape a farm's strategy include:

- Organizational strengths, weaknesses, and competitive capabilities. A farm's strategy ought to be grounded in what it is good at doing. It is perilous for success to depend on what it is not so good at doing.
- The personal ambitions, business philosophies, and ethical principles of managers. Managers stamp these on the strategies they craft.
- Shared values and culture. A farm's values and culture can dominate the kinds of strategic moves it considers or rejects. Values run deeper than strategy. The final strategy needs to flow from values and culture for the farm to be most effective in achieving its goals.

Crafting strategy essentially begins within internal analysis. As described in the previous chapter, the comparison of a farm's capabilities with the external conditions and requirements of the industry identifies strengths, weaknesses, opportunities, threats, and strategic issues that need to be addressed. This comparison helps identify what the farm needs to do in order to move toward its vision and to accomplish objectives. Out of this comparison, a farm can realize which one of four basic generic strategies needs to be the basis for the chosen strategy and which, if any, of several complementary strategies can be used to craft a strategy that best fits the farm's capabilities and external conditions. In the next sections, these generic and complementary strategies are explained in more detail.

Generic Strategies

In the early stages of crafting strategy, the first goal is to identify the generic strategy that best fits the external and internal situation of a farm. The final strategy that a farm chooses to follow will be an adjustment or fine tuning of this basic generic strategy. As a first step, let's look at four generic strategies that farmers can follow. These four strategies are:

- Low-cost leadership
- Differentiation
- Best-cost provider
- Focus or niche

Low-Cost Leadership. In this strategy, a farmer aims to develop a low-cost production position within the industry based on experience, size, and/or efficient operations. This strategy fits an industry with many buyers, whose power is a major force in the industry. (See the previous chapter for a detailed discussion of the seven forces.) Due to their size, the importance of the product to the buyers and their profit, or the ease of switching between farms, the buyers have considerable power over the product price. When the product is very standard and the industry has many producers, each producer has little power to negotiate a price.

Pursuing low-cost leadership is attractive when economies of scale and learning economies are potentially significant but other firms are not taking full advantage of them. Economies of scale help lower costs as a firm becomes larger. Learning economies help lower costs as a firm produces more of a product and over time and due to the quantity produced learns how to become more efficient and lower unit costs. Cost leadership also is the main strategy when the nature of the product limits opportunities for enhancing its perceived benefit to the customer. For example, pork is essentially always pork to a processor when it is buying from the farmer. The hog farmer has little chance to increase the value greatly for the processor even though the processor may be able to enhance value to the final consumer by the way it cuts, flavors, and markets the meat. Cost leadership is also needed when customers are price sensitive and not willing to pay a large premium for enhanced product quality, performance, or image. Cost leadership is again important for products when customers value a low price over the experience of using the product.

This situation describes the industry for many agricultural commodities. Thus, for most of agriculture, the only strategy available to producers is this low-cost strategy. Managers must make all decisions based on lowering costs of production to increase the probability of being below the offered market price. In a strictly low-cost strategy, product quality standards and customer's expectations have to be met but not exceeded if exceeding the standards causes costs to increase. The manager has to avoid all steps and operations that add cost with an insufficient increase in product quality.

Differentiation. A farm following this strategy strives to create unique perceptions about its product(s) among its consumers. A farm selling directly to the public will most likely strive to include such elements in its chosen strategy. The recent interest in identity preserved (IP) grains and meat are examples of farms striving to differentiate their products. A certified organic farmer is an example of following a broad differentiation strategy. That is, the farmer has decided to produce for a market that is smaller (certified organic beef, for example) compared to the larger commodity market (such as conventional beef). The producers of certified organic products have differentiated their products from the larger market for the potential benefit of higher product prices.

In Europe, product differentiation is also obtained through regulations that limit the geographical production areas for some products. For example, the name Parmesan cheese can only be applied to cheese produced by a certain process within the Parmigiano-Reggiano region of Italy. Producers in other areas can use the same process and make the same cheese, but unless they are in the Parmigiano-Reggiano area, they cannot use the name Parmigiano. Other products that have this regional designation or denominazione di origine controllata (DOC) include champagne and Danish ham. These regulations were developed to protect historical regional products in the European Union and differentiate those products from others in the market.

A differentiation strategy can be a viable choice if most customers are willing to pay a higher price for different attributes that improve the product's performance for the customer. Differentiation is also a viable choice when economies of scale and of learning are already being used by a firm.

Differentiation is a potential strategy when the product is an experience good rather than a search good—that is, customers are willing to pay more for the experience of using the product rather than just searching for certain physical attributes at the lowest cost.

Best-Cost Provider.   With this strategy, a farmer may be producing a commodity (milk, for example) but supplying it to a certain market at a reasonable cost and, at the same time, meeting other special characteristics (such as delivery, quantity, etc.) that a specific buyer wants. The farmer mentioned in the previous chapter who changed to produce alfalfa hay and remove animal waste from neighboring farms should be following a best-cost strategy. This could be done by understanding how often each customer needs animal waste hauled away, directly monitoring manure levels in the pits as a service so a customer does not need to do so, and monitoring each farm's supply of hay to anticipate delivery needs again as a service to the customer. These additional services can keep customers happy and thus serve as a barrier to entry for other potential providers—as long as, of course, the farmer keeps costs within a reasonable range and maintains a friendly relationship.

Even a farmer producing a commodity can follow a best-cost strategy if he cultivates a relationship with customers. An example is a Swedish hog producer who has established connections and a reputation with small-scale pork processors and restaurants. The farmer provides a dependable product quality and quantity with personal service in delivery. He now has the power to set a reasonable price that is higher than the main commodity market price because the buyers know him and the product they are getting. The product involves not only quantity and quality but also service from the seller. This farmer could be described as using aspects of a focused strategy (which is discussed next). The most appropriate description of his generic strategy is the best-cost strategy due to the service provided and the number of potential hog farmers who could compete against him.

Focus or Niche.   A farm with a focused strategy strives to serve a small but well-defined market niche. Examples of this include a supplier of organic vegetables to local markets and restaurants, a producer of rabbit or buffalo meat, a grower of organic blue corn for a food processor, and so on. While these farmers may also employ aspects of the differentiation and best-cost strategies, the focused or niche strategy fits best due to the small total market size and the resulting ability to defend against potential competitors. An example of the excitement and the realities of niche products can be seen in heritage turkeys (Example 9.1).

Example 9.1. Niche Markets Are Not Automatic Profits

Niche markets do not automatically generate large profits even though the product price may look high. Take the example of heritage turkeys.

Heritage turkeys are older breeds of birds that resemble their wild cousins. They almost disappeared as the industry switched to the conventional turkey breeds in today's supermarkets. According to an article in the *New York Times*, heritage turkeys sell for 10 to 20 times the price of conventional turkeys.

So why don't more farmers raise and sell heritage turkeys? Because it is the profit margin that makes products attractive, not the price.

A few consumers are willing to pay high prices for locally produced, free-range, organic heritage breeds. However, the heritage birds cost more to produce for several reasons: they grow slower, more labor is required per bird due to smaller flocks and the bird's longer life, longer life also means higher losses due to disease and predators, organic feed is higher priced than conventional feed, and processing needs to be done in specialized facilities that have higher costs since they are small. Marketing is also more specialized and costlier for the farmer than the conventional method of selling to a large processor.

Heritage turkeys are like many niche products. Profit can be made, but even with high prices compared to conventional products, specialized knowledge in production and marketing is required and costs are higher. Otherwise the products would be commodities, not niche products.

Source: William Neuman, "Heritage Turkeys Selling Briskly, Even at $10 a Pound," *New York Times*, November 26, 2009. Last accessed on January 30, 2010, at http://www.nytimes.com/2009/11/26/business/26turkeys.html.

As noted earlier, the first step in crafting strategy is to decide which of the four generic strategies is the best fit for the combination of the people involved, the industry or market that the farm is part of, and the internal situation of the farm. But this choice is not the end of crafting strategy. Other actions and plans need to be chosen to fill out or complement the generic strategy for the specific farm in its specific situation.

Complementary Strategic Actions

The overall strategy of a farm will involve more than the chosen generic competitive strategy. Other actions can be chosen to complement that basic competitive strategy. These potential complementary strategic actions include:

- Horizontal expansion (scale)
- Diversification (scope)
- Vertical integration (span)
- Innovation (speed)
- Prospecting
- Protecting
- Alliances and partnerships
- Functional strategies

Horizontal Expansion.   The usual view of expansion is for the farm to add land, animals, or both to the existing base. By doing so the farm is increasing in size due to expanding the production of current products; it is not adding new products. This is called "horizontal expansion" because the business is pictured expanding horizontally in the vertical chain of production (see Figure 7.1 for an example). Horizontal expansion takes advantage of economies of scale to increase income for the owners, to increase production to meet an increasing share of the market, and to serve as a barrier or threat of a barrier to potential entrants. If one of the goals of the farm is to bring the next generation into the business, horizontal expansion is one (but not the only) potential way to add business capacity and greater income potential. Horizontal expansion can be done by building new production capacity (building a new livestock facility, for example) or by buying existing capacity from other producers (such as from another farm).

Diversification.   Diversification is a traditional risk management strategy for stabilizing sales, and thus income, by selling a variety of products. Different products can have different cycles of good and poor production levels and high and low market prices. By producing a variety of products, the good and bad years of each product may be better balanced and the farm does not experience the extremes in sales that may occur with only one or two products.

Diversification is done in two ways. First, a farmer can diversify by expanding the list of products he or she produces and sells. These products may be new to the market or just new to the farmer. Completely new products may be developed by industry (e.g., genetically engineered crops) or developed by farmers themselves (e.g., vegetables that are new to a specific farmers market). A farmer may also diversify by starting to produce a product that is commonly produced but is just new to him or her.

The second method of diversification can take place in the production process. For example, diversification can be obtained by planting different varieties of the same crop that have different maturities or different levels of tolerance to diseases, pests, or drought. Different crop maturity lengths can spread the harvest and thus marketing period, which can be important for vegetable and fruit producers. A hog producer may diversify by farrowing pigs and then selling some as feeder pigs and feeding others to market weight.

Vertical Integration.   Livestock farms have been vertically integrated for centuries. That is, they have produced the milk, meat, eggs, and other livestock products and they have also produced the feed for the livestock. Direct marketing at local markets is an example of the producer moving forward in the product chain—that is, closer to the consumer. The benefits of vertical integration include better quality of inputs or product marketing, less dependence on suppliers or marketers, and ability to capture greater value now taken by other businesses.

Vertical integration is not automatically beneficial. Decreasing vertical integration is also common for livestock farms in recent decades. Many livestock farms have stopped producing feed in order to concentrate on the livestock. Some dairies have even contracted with other farms to raise heifer calves until they return to enter the milking herd. These farms saw an advantage in decreasing vertical integration to (1) better focus on the core product of the farm or (2) benefit from the advantages of economies of scale other farms can obtain.

The decision to vertically integrate or not is essentially the traditional ''make-or-buy'' decision. Whether to make the inputs or buy them depends on the industry structure and the farm's situation. The essential question is whether the farm can make the input cheaper or better than the price and quality available in the market. The answer to this question depends on economies of scale in input production, location of input producers, and transportation costs. For example, new technology may allow a hay producer to expand and produce at a lower cost per unit than an individual livestock feeder could do on its own. A similar story can be told about whether marketing services should be ''made'' internally or bought from external companies.

Outsourcing is the opposite of vertical integration. It involves the same questions as whether to vertically integrate and whether to make or buy. The livestock producer who decides to buy feed instead of growing it is outsourcing the production of feed; it is also de-integrating a formerly integrated farm. The farmer who decides to hire an accounting firm rather than keeping his own accounts is outsourcing rather than integrating the accounting function for his farm.

Whether we call it vertical integration, make or buy, or outsourcing, several questions need to be answered to evaluate the advantages and disadvantages of the choice.

- Is the product or service provided at lower cost inside the farm or by an outside business?
- Can the outside business provide a better quality product or service (with quality measured in many dimensions)?
- Does outside production allow the farm to concentrate on and improve its core process and product?
- Is the activity crucial to the core competency of the farm?
- How would external production increase or decrease risk exposure?
- How would internal production increase or decrease risk exposure?
- Does owning the productive capacity tie up financial resources too much, especially considering that external production may allow easier switching to new lower cost producers? That is, does internal production decrease the chance of being able to quickly adapt to new, significantly lower cost technology?

Prospecting.   Seeking or prospecting for new markets and buyers can complement the generic strategies of differentiation, best-cost, and focused or niche, but even a low-cost leader can seek better markets. In prospecting, a farmer emphasizes marketing effectiveness and market development.

Protecting.   Once a market position has been developed with a differentiation, best-cost, and focused or niche strategies, a farmer may adopt a protector attitude to maintain that market share. These actions may include improving the product quality and service to meet the buyers' current and evolving needs, lowering product price, signing a contract, and other actions that will discourage potential market entrants.

Alliances and Partnerships.   Many situations require new capabilities, connections, and knowledge for a farm to take advantage of opportunities or counter threats. In order to acquire these new skills and abilities, either quickly or at less expense, farms can form alliances or partnerships with other farms and/or with non-farm businesses. These may be informal, handshake agreements, or they may be formal written relationships. Although they may become merged businesses, these alliances and partnerships usually start as operating agreements without merger and may stay that way. The benefit is obtained, however, by having a much closer, interwoven relationship than the typical arms-length contract.

The reasons for forming alliances and partnerships include moving into new markets quicker and accessing new skills, knowledge, and technology. Alliances may be critical for moving into international markets through better supply locally; better connections and logistics for transportation and trade regulations; and better knowledge of the markets, consumers, and regulations in the other country.

The hog farmer who wishes to deal with smaller processors and restaurants may need more skills and knowledge of how those businesses operate and what they need. Once contacts are made by prospecting, alliances could be developed for supplying, processing, and selling the final product. Each business remains separate, but they communicate freely and frequently and have developed a working relationship that benefits all parties.

In general business, alliances often do not last for many years (Thompson, Strickland, and Gamble, 2005). Reasons include changing objectives, inability to continue working together, changing conditions, and other shifts in the businesses and the environment. The danger of an alliance or any relationship is the over-reliance on external skills that disappear leaving a business without a crucial piece. The answer to this problem is to learn the needed skills internally or, ultimately, to merge if the two businesses can indeed work together beneficially.

Functional Strategies.   While it is obvious that strategy needs to be developed for the whole farm, we also need to develop complementary strategies for each business function and enterprise within the farm. Business functions, as described in Chapter 2, include production, finance, marketing, and human resources. Enterprises, as will be described in Chapter 14, include profit centers, such as wheat, milk, hogs, and vegetable production, and cost centers, such as machinery and land.

The strategies for each of these functions and enterprises need to be consistent with and supportive of the strategy crafted for the whole farm. For example, although it may seem obvious, if the low-cost strategy for the farm requires the use of technology that needs highly trained and knowledgeable employees, the human resource function should pay an appropriate wage to hire that knowledge and skill, rather than pay low wages because that is the low-cost method. Similarly, if the farm has a best-cost strategy for supplying high-protein wheat to a local bakery, the wheat enterprise should be producing that high-protein wheat and not striving for the lowest cost regardless of protein level.

Strategies for Specific Situations

In some situations, specific strategies are needed that are not necessarily useful and indeed may be detrimental in other situations. These situations and strategies are discussed in this section.[1]

Emerging Markets and Industries.   An emerging market or industry is one in the formative stage. In agriculture, examples include biofuels and organic food products and some markets in developing countries. In emerging industries, information on how big the market may become is uncertain, as is information on which technologies may survive. In addition, technological information is often privately held, strong learning curves exist, many potential entrants exist, many consumers are first-time buyers, raw materials are often in short supply, and credit is also often more limited than the businesses would prefer. Potential strategies include being an early leader; improving product quality, perfecting technology, being ready to adopt or switch to the emerging dominant technology and product characteristics, forming alliances to gain access, understanding consumer needs quickly, and being ready to cut prices to increase the market and market share. Remember that latecomers may have deep pockets and the advantage of knowing the right technology, so be prepared for late entrants.

Maturing Industries.   A maturing industry is moving from rapid growth to significantly slower growth. In a mature market, sales are mostly repeat and replacement sales to existing customers. Growth comes from finding the few new buyers and from natural growth in the population. The industry changes to more competition for market share, buyers bargaining more, greater emphasis on cost and service, increased chance for adding excess capacity. Also, product innovation decreases, international competition increases, industry profitability declines, and consolidation occurs through mergers, acquisitions, and closures. Potential strategies include (1) dropping less profitable products; (2) improving the

---

[1] This section is based on the ideas in Thompson, Strickland, and Gamble (2005, pp. 203–229).

value chain to decrease costs, improve quality, increase capability to produce multiple products, and shorten design cycles; (3) drive down costs through negotiating input prices, cutting low-value activities, developing more economical product designs, and so on; (4) increasing sales to existing customers; (5) expanding horizontally; (6) expanding internationally; and (7) developing more flexible capabilities.

Stagnant or Declining Industries. In a stagnant or declining industry, demand is growing more slowly than the economy-wide average or is even declining. For many agricultural products, this is the situation that farmers face. However, strong farms can still have good results. A stagnant market demand does not necessarily make an industry unattractive. Different strategies are needed, however. Potential strategies include:

- Pursuing the fastest-growing segments of the market. Total sales may seem very stable, but the whole market may not be stagnant. For example, total food demand increases as population and income rise, but the demand for organic food products is growing very rapidly.
- Differentiating based on quality improvement and product innovation.
- Decreasing costs and becoming a low-cost leader. This is the obvious strategy for most farms. As long as the farm is alert and ready to change as needed, financial performance and goal achievement can still be attractive.

Fragmented Industries. A fragmented industry has many, perhaps thousands, of small producers with a complete absence of a dominant, or even close to dominant, player. Agriculture, especially crop production, is a fragmented industry. Market demand is large and geographically dispersed. Agriculture has relatively low entry barriers compared to other industries. Compared to other industries, economies of scale have not pushed crop production to extremely large farm sizes with very few producers. The market is becoming more global, which increases the number of competitors. Technology is improving to allow and perhaps even require producers to specialize. Potential strategies in a fragmented industry include:

- Constructing "formula" facilities, as is happening in livestock production and, to some extent, in crop production
- Being a low-cost producer
- Specializing by product type, such as only corn or maize, milk, hogs, or vegetables
- Specializing by customer type, such as low price, organic, local foods, or other characteristics
- Focusing on a limited geographical area

Weak and Crisis-Ridden Businesses. A farm (and any business) that has become competitively weak, or has had a crisis thrust upon it, has four general strategic options: an offensive turnaround strategy, a fortify-and-defend strategy, a fast-exit strategy, or an endgame or slow-exit strategy. For a turnaround strategy, four actions can be employed: (1) sell off assets to raise cash to pay down debt and save, potentially, parts of the business; (2) develop a new strategy for the business; (3) boost revenues through improved marketing; and (4) cut costs to the bare minimum levels needed in the short run. The fortify-and-defend strategy uses a slightly revised current strategy and then works very hard to preserve the farm. The fast-exit or liquidation strategy is to be pursued if the farm cannot be saved; it is sold to another farm intact, or sold in pieces. An end-game strategy is pursued when cash can be generated by the farm operating with a reduced operating budget and essentially no reinvestment, and the farm is eventually sold to maximize the cash received.

Tests for Evaluating Strategies

Alternative proposed strategies need to be compared using a set of tests, but before those tests are described and the strategies evaluated, each proposed strategy should be reviewed to determine whether it is written in a clear, concise fashion and is internally consistent. If it can't be understood or has conflicts between its parts, a proposed strategy needs to be either rejected or rewritten before it can be considered further.

To help choose which potential strategy may be the best for a farm to adopt and follow, several tests have been proposed to evaluate how each would help a farm attain its objectives and vision. Since each test evaluates alternative strategies from a different perspective, several tests should be used to provide a better overall evaluation and, hence, the choice of the most robust strategy. Seven tests that may be useful for farmers are:

Vision consistency
Goodness of fit
Building for the future
Performance
Importance
Feasibility
Resource
Confidence

Vision Consistency.   How well does the proposed strategy fit with the business and personal vision of the farmer and other stakeholders? If a strategy does not fit with the visions and ambitions of the people involved, the chances of success are low because enthusiasm and attention will be low, so the strategy should be rejected.

Goodness of Fit.   How well does the proposed strategy fit with the external analysis of the industry? How well does it fit the internal analysis of the farm? Even though an idea or strategy sounds great, if it does not fit both the external and internal conditions of the firm, it needs to be rejected.

Building for the Future.   How well does the proposed strategy help maintain and develop the building blocks of competitive advantage: superior efficiency, superior quality, superior innovation, and superior customer responsiveness? How well does it contribute to value creation, low-cost processes, and product differentiation? Does the proposed strategy contribute to building resources and capabilities for the future? If a strategy uses but does not build resources, it should receive a low score on this test. A low score may not require rejection, however. Consider a farmer with no heirs or partners who want to continue the farm business. This farmer may be very justified in following a strategy to use up depreciable assets (buildings and machinery, especially) at a rate correlated with his or her retirement plan.

Performance.   How well does the proposed strategy contribute to achieving the strategic and financial objectives of the farm? What are the predictions for income, rates of return, net worth growth, expansion in physical size, transition to the next generation, and so on? The score for performance should not be based solely on high income. The performance score should be based on a balanced view of the proposed strategy's contribution to the strategic objectives of the farm.

Importance.   Are important issues identified in the external and internal analyses addressed by the proposed strategy, or does it focus on trivial issues? Does the proposed strategy feel comfortable (or enjoyable) but fail to explain how opportunities will be taken advantage of and threats will be defended against? Does it explain how it will build on strengths as well as improve weaknesses, or does it talk about new buildings? For example, does the proposed strategy aim to have the best Holstein herd in the region or the most advanced use of precision farming technology but ignore the need to achieve, say, cost objectives required by the industry to remain profitable? If a proposed strategy does not address the important issues, it should be rejected as it is written. Perhaps the basic idea is sound, but it may need to be rewritten to explain, in terms of the external and internal analyses, why and how the strategy meets the important issues.

Feasibility.   Is the strategy amenable to programs that can effectively be implemented? Can it be broken down into programs and projects with measurable objectives? Can these smaller parts be accomplished? A well-written, grand strategy, which no one can figure out how to implement, is infeasible and should be rejected.

Resources.   Are resources available to implement the strategy? Can people be hired to do the work needed? Can financing be obtained?

Confidence.   How high is the confidence that the anticipated outcomes of the proposed strategy will occur? What is the risk that events will occur and change the expected results, especially in a negative direction?

These tests can be used to identify how different strategies perform or satisfy different objectives and, thus, help improve the final selection process. To use these tests, a farmer and his or her stakeholders give each proposed strategy a subjective score for each test chosen. Their scores come from their opinion of how each strategy would help the farm perform according to different tests. For example, how well does each strategy fit the vision of the stakeholders or fit the external analysis of the industry?

In most instances, the scores range from 1 to 5 with 5 being the highest score. That is, 5 indicates the best a given strategy can do in terms of a specific test. Once a score is estimated for each test, the scores are summed across all tests for each strategy. The strategy with the highest score is the apparent best strategy for the farm. However, since the scores are subjective, a farmer could also drop from consideration those strategies with the lowest scores and spend more time evaluating the remaining strategies before making a final decision.

As an example of scoring and evaluating strategies, suppose a dairy farm has developed four potential strategies. The proposed strategies (and the generic strategies involved) are producing low-cost milk (low-cost leadership), finding new markets for milk (prospector), merging with a neighbor (growth and cost leadership), and producing organic milk for an ice cream manufacturer (prospector and best-cost provider). After describing the strategies, estimating the financial performance of each strategy, and reviewing the farm's vision and objectives, the farmer and others involved gives each strategy a score of 1 to 5 for all the tests (Table 9.1).

Table 9.1   Example of Scoring Proposed Strategies

| Proposed Strategy | Score in Each Strategy Test (high = 5, low = 1) | | | | | | | | TOTAL SCORE |
	Vision Consistency	Goodness of Fit	Building for the Future	Performance	Importance	Feasibility	Resources	Confidence	
Low Cost	2	3	2	3	4	4	3	2	23
New Markets	4	3	3	4	2	2	2	3	23
Merger	3	4	5	3	4	4	3	4	27
Organic	4	3	4	4	3	3	3	3	27

In this example, two strategies are tied for the top score: merging with a neighbor and producing for the organic market. To choose between these two, the farmer and other stakeholders can evaluate the differences between the scores on individual tests, such as vision consistency, performance, or confidence. The two strategies could be evaluated in more detail to help the decision.

Also, remember that crafting strategy is a dynamic and cyclical process. In this example, the farmer should not feel constrained to the current list of strategies. Since two were tied with the top score, a new, combined strategy could be developed and considered. In this example, the farmer and the neighbor could develop and consider the combination of merging and producing for the organic market.

Since these are subjective scores, there is obvious concern that the person doing the evaluation could manipulate the scores in order to obtain the result they think is the best. These concerns can be minimized if the evaluator strives to score without following preconceived notions of the desired result. If a group is evaluating the proposed strategies, each member of the group could estimate scores independently and then discuss them as a group. These and other potential problems and solutions are described in the next section.

Improving Strategic Planning

Four problems or weaknesses that farmers (and any company or organization) may encounter with strategic planning are planning under uncertainty, ivory tower planning, planning for the present, and managers' biases (Hill and Jones, 1998). Let us discuss each of these and how they can be overcome plus three other ideas for improving strategic planning: devil's advocacy, dialectic inquiry, and using an advisory board.

Planning under Uncertainty

Problems due to uncertainty of the future show up in two ways. First, we think we can forecast the future accurately, so we do not incorporate risk and change into our plans. We choose a strategy, and as conditions change we may find that another strategy or an adaptation of the strategy would have been better, but it is too late for the business to recover. Second, we know we can't predict future events accurately, so many people do not think planning is worthwhile. The resultant strategy is, at best, reactive and profitable by chance. At worst, the farm is put at risk as conditions change.

The problems of blind faith in forecasting and rejection of planning both can be solved by understanding and using the techniques discussed in the next section, "Managing Strategic Risk." As explained there, one major technique for reducing the uncertainty of the impact of future events is using scenarios to develop pictures of possible futures.

Ivory Tower Planning

In a large farm, managers may not stay in touch with the rest of the farm and the marketplace. Thus, their planning easily could be unrealistic in terms of what the farm can do and what the market wants or how it will respond. This could also happen in a smaller farm, even in a one-person farm, if the manager does not look realistically at what he or she and the farm can do and what is happening in the market.

The solution may be easier in a single-person farm, but the solutions are the same in all sizes of farms. Managers and people involved need to talk to people in every part of the farm and should consider having a person outside the farm interview them and any employees about what is happening. Benchmarking could provide an objective comparison of the farm's productivity and financial measures with other farms in the area and industry. Obtaining and listening to others' evaluation of the market and the economic environment will help open one's own thinking to alternative views of the marketplace and what needs to be done in all aspects of farming.

Planning for the Present

A very common problem in crafting strategy is using the fit model alone. A manager crafts a strategy to fit the world and the farm as they see it, but don't incorporate any adaptations needed for the future. They study, analyze, present, discuss, list, and so on; it's all very structured and neat. They fit our existing resources into the current environment but don't spend enough time on developing new resources and capabilities. They also don't spend enough time on creation and/or exploitation of future opportunities.

The solution is to develop a strategic intent—that is, a bold ambition for the future. But strategic intent is more than unfettered ambition. Developing a strategic intent helps focus managers' and workers' attention on the vision of what we want the farm to be, motivates people by communicating the value of the target, leaves room for individuals and teams to adapt to changing circumstances, sustains enthusiasm over time by providing new operational definitions as circumstances change over time, and consistently guides resource allocations.

In practice, both fit and intent are used. That is, set an ambitious goal, go through the strategic planning process, continually monitor the external environment and internal performance, and be ready to change if necessary to keep moving toward the bold ambition.

Managers' Biases

Cognitive biases affect how we think and what we assume to be truth. As individuals, we all have cognitive biases; thinking we don't is a cognitive bias because it's not true. Cognitive biases and potential solutions to deal with them are listed in Table 9.2.

These cognitive biases are often easily seen in individuals. Groups can exhibit a problem called groupthink. When a group starts analyzing and making decisions without questioning their underlying assumptions of the situation, they are said to suffer from groupthink. This may be due to an overly influential member of the group or acceptance of one idea and then rationalization for accepting that one idea or plan.

Table 9.2 Cognitive Biases and Potential Solutions

Cognitive Bias	Potential Solution
Prior hypotheses or beliefs	Pay attention to evidence that refutes prior beliefs
Escalating commitment	Don't commit more if things aren't working
Reasoning by analogy (especially overly simple analogies of a complex situation)	Ask if the analogy really does make sense in the current situation
Representativeness of our knowledge (generalizing from a small sample or even one vivid anecdote)	Base decisions on large sample theory
Illusion of control	Accept the fact that we don't control everything

Devil's Advocacy

Devils' advocacy involves bringing up all the reasons that might make the proposed strategy unacceptable. This can be a very effective method of developing an improved, robust strategy to deal with different events in the future. Care needs to be taken that this is done in an objective way and, if one group member is doing this, that he or she is not painted as a negative person, which might taint his or her future with the group.

Dialectic Inquiry

Dialectic inquiry involves developing a plan (thesis) and a counter plan (antithesis) that represent possible but conflicting approaches to running the farm. The plan and counter plan are discussed and poked at to find weaknesses in assumptions, actions, and so on. Out of this discussion, a better plan should emerge—either a third strategy that is a combination of the first two or a strengthened plan or counter plan that develops from the discussion. To improve results, a management team of managers, partners, parent and child, or an advisory board can rotate their roles being the advocate for the plan and counter plan so alternative ideas and concerns are raised.

An individual farmer can benefit from dialectic inquiry by developing a plan and counter plan and then playing opposite roles poking and probing each strategy to find weaknesses and strengths. To aid in the role-playing, an individual farmer could do the simple, physical action of wearing different hats and changing seats when being the advocate of the plan and then the counter plan.

Using an Advisory Board

An advisory board consisting of persons interested in and knowledgeable about the farm but not directly involved in it is one way a farmer can benefit from others evaluating his or her plans and ideas. The advisory board is discussed more fully in Chapter 25, Business Organization. An advisory board can help an individual overcome many of the problems just discussed, although groupthink can still be a problem if it is not addressed directly.

Managing Strategic Risk

A farmer faces many sources of risk. Two broad classifications are operational risk and strategic risk. Operational risks include weather variability, price changes, accidents, health, fire, and financial risk due to higher debt. Strategic risks include policy and regulatory changes, technology changes,

Table 9.3 Examples of Strategic Risks

Source of Risk	Examples
Government policy	New policies that eliminate payments
Social	Farming is seen as the source of pollution
Technology	New technology creates obsolescence in previous technology, new products
Industry	Major buyer closes plant, bankruptcy of supplier or buyer, new demand sources
Macroeconomic	Interest rates change, economic growth or decline
Government regulation	New regulations limit practices such as fertilizer use or impose other restrictions
International	Changes in exchange rates, changes in import and export rules and tariffs, instability in oil markets that cause higher fuel prices
Relationships	Termination of contracts, divorce, death

Source: Adapted from Boehlje and Erickson, 2007.

changes in government policy, social attitudes toward farming, decisions by suppliers and buyers in the industry, cultural changes, changes in other countries, and so on (Table 9.3). Since it is important to crafting strategy, some points on managing strategic risk are discussed in this section; a more thorough discussion of risk management in general is in Chapter 22, Risk Management.

Identifying and Classifying Strategic Risks

The first step in managing strategic risk is identifying and listing the potential sources of strategic risk that could be encountered by a farmer. These sources are then given scores for (a) the probability of happening and (b) the potential impact on the business if they were to occur (Table 9.4) and placed on a graph to show relative importance and potential management reaction (Figure 9.1). Management reactions to the scorecarding and mapping of the strategic risks include avoiding the options with a high probability of a catastrophic impact, reducing the probability and/or impact of less risky options, sharing or transferring those options that have high potential impact but low probability of occurring, and retaining those options with smaller impacts even if they have a high probability of occurring. The example strategic risk of the buyer canceling the contract (#1) is given an illustrative score of 3 for the probability of happening and a score of 5 for the potential impact on the business. These scores place the risk on the border between "avoid" and "reduce." Although the position of this border in the graph is subjective, the risk's position does show a manager that this is one of the riskier options and should either be avoided completely or the risk should be reduced by, for example, renegotiating the terms of the contract to reduce the buyer's ability to cancel the

Table 9.4 Illustrative Score Card for Example Strategic Risks

#	Potential Risk	Probability of Happening[*]	Potential Impact on Business[**]
1	Buyer cancels contract	3	5
2	Government restricts fertilizer use	2	2
3	Oil-producing country is politically unstable	3	4
4	New technology creates obsolescence	5	3
5	Fire destroys livestock buildings	1	5

[*]1 = low probability, 5 = high probability
[**]1 = small potential impact, 5 = catastrophic impact.

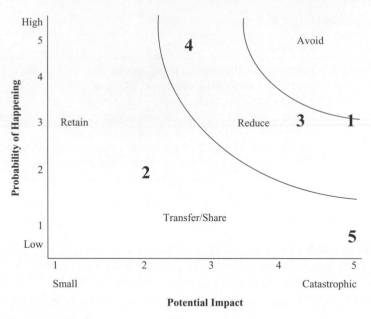

Figure 9.1　Mapping Strategic Risks
Source: Adapted from Boehlje, Gray, and Detre, 2005.

contract. The risk of fire (#5) can be transferred to an insurance company. The risk of fertilizer-use restrictions (#2) could be retained, for example.

The development of potential strategies can be guided by this scoring and mapping of strategic risks, but the final crafting and choice of strategy requires another method. Some of the methods and tools for managing risk in general, as discussed in Chapter 22, can be used for managing strategic risk. These include enterprise diversification, flexibility, and vertical integration. However, strategic risk is present because the future is not known with certainty and tools are not readily available. Thus, strategic risk is harder to predict and manage because of the lack of conventional tools for managing it. Thus, strategic risk needs to be managed by modifying the strategy itself.

Using Scenarios for Crafting Strategy

A major tool for piercing the veil of the unknown future and helping a manager develop robust strategies for it is the use of alternative scenarios or pictures of the future. These alternative scenarios are built around uncertainties in the future and the potential paths that the uncertainties may take. For instance, we do not know how rapidly the world economy may grow, but we can make estimates of ranges and from that we can estimate the impacts on overall demand for food and fuel and thus prices. We can also evaluate the dynamics of our industry and formulate different scenarios in which a farm's product buyers close, expand, or maintain plant capacity. The value of scenario planning lies in the expansion of people's thinking, the testing of alternative strategies, and the development of better strategies. The process of developing scenarios is described with an example in Chapter 22.

Scenarios are used to estimate the impact of each proposed strategy toward the farm's vision, goals, and objectives. Based on these results, a manager can use several methods to help decide which strategy best fits the farm and its situation. Methods for choosing a strategy are described below.

1. Bet on the most probable scenario. Decide which scenario is the most likely to happen or is happening and choose the strategy that positions the business in the best way for that picture of the future. If only one scenario is very likely to happen, this is the wisest and easiest choice.
2. Bet on the scenario and strategy that is the "best" for the business. This involves choosing a likely scenario and the strategy that is estimated to provide the best outcomes in terms of financial and strategic objectives in that scenario. However, choosing a strategy that is crafted for only one scenario may be expensive in terms of the opportunities given up by not following other strategies or because of business failure when the expected scenario doesn't happen.
3. Hedge on what will happen (i.e., keep a door open). Choose a strategy and make your plans on the likelihood that a specific scenario will occur but keep evaluating what is happening and be ready to change if needed.
4. Preserve flexibility (i.e., don't shut a door). If two (or more) scenarios are considered equally possible, craft a strategy that allows flexibility and ability to make adjustments to adapt to reality as the future unfolds.
5. Influence the outcome (affect what happens). If policy changes are needed, work with legislators to help make those changes. As an individual or as part of a larger group, use advertising and public relations to influence and change consumers' opinions and choices. A farmer can also talk to the people and businesses that make the crucial decisions affecting the farm and strive to convince them to make decisions that would be beneficial to the business. Managers can negotiate deals.

    (Please note that the idea of influencing outcomes is based on legal behavior. Some companies and persons have gotten into trouble by trying to influence outcomes in illegal ways such as price fixing, collusion, and other unlawful activities. Illegal behavior is not being encouraged here.)
6. Combine methods. For example, bet on the most probable, try to influence the outcome, but keep an eye on the future as it unfolds and be ready to move and change if necessary.

Concluding Thoughts

As we finish this chapter on crafting competitive strategy, here are some concluding thoughts on the overall process of crafting strategy.

Strategy should change and evolve as the business environment changes and evolves. However, if a strategy is rewritten or reworked too often, managers are probably guilty of erratic decision making and weak "strategizing." Large changes in plans and strategy can occur, especially in crisis situations, but if changes are made too often, confusion will reign within management and employees. Performance will suffer.

In reality, strategy involves both proactive and reactive actions. Proactive strategies are deliberate and intended actions resulting from the careful, purposeful evaluation of the business environment. A farm's strategy also includes adaptive, perhaps even knee-jerk reactions to unanticipated changes, new developments, unexpected events, and so on. Although proactive actions certainly sound the best, the rate of change in today's world means that staying with the planned strategy may be the wrong choice when new events occur and new information is obtained. Thus, well-reasoned reactive strategies can be just as valuable to the success of a farm as carefully planned proactive strategies. Having a solid understanding of the industry and the farm and a well-chosen strategy can provide a solid base from which to adapt and adjust strategy or to reject potential changes.

Farmers need to be entrepreneurial (i.e., creative, risk-taking, innovative) when crafting strategy, and they need to be able to do outside-in strategic thinking. Outside-in thinking can be understood best when contrasted against its mirror: inside-out thinking. A person, manager, company, or any organization that thinks inside-out is (or becomes) risk-averse, accepts currently acceptable performance, concentrates on current plans and operations to do them better, dismisses new trends because "they won't affect us," studies new trends to death, and so on. Inside-out strategies tend to be traditional approaches, acceptable to internal coalitions, philosophically comfortable to the current management, and safe in terms of not disturbing current conditions; they are not very forward thinking. Outside-in strategies look at what the industry and customers are asking for and make adjustments to the farm. Outside-in thinking leads to changes that allow the farm to survive in the long term.

Other factors can be considered in crafting strategies. These have obvious advantages and some disadvantages also.

- First mover advantage. If you are the first to ask about the purchase of land, for instance, you may be the one who gets to buy it. Being the first to say you are able to produce according to the proposed contract may provide you a chance to participate in a very beneficial venture. The obvious disadvantages are of moving too fast into uncharted waters. Success is not guaranteed to those who move first, or to those who wait. Success comes when the choices are evaluated and decisions made appropriately to the opportunity.
- Initial competitive position. By being the first or among the first, a business may have considerable advantage over other, later entries. For example, processors do not share new ideas and profitable ventures with all farmers. The first farmers who receive a chance to consider new, potentially beneficial contracts are those whom the processor already knows.
- Costs or resources required. A large initial investment and high operating costs create greater risks for the business. Smaller investments may allow a strategy to be followed with smaller rewards except that the financial cost is lower if conditions change enough to warrant a change in strategy.
- Risk. Several aspects of risk can affect the decision on which strategy to follow:
  - The timing of the resource commitment. Having to invest a large amount up front increases the risk of losing that investment.
  - The degree of inconsistency of strategies for alternate scenarios. If alternate scenarios require very different investments and operations, the cost of going with one can be great if another scenario is the one that develops in the future.
  - If the probabilities of different scenarios are very different, then the business can see which is the more likely. However, if the relative probabilities of occurrence are very close, the decision is more difficult.
  - If the cost of changing strategies to adapt to future scenarios is low, management has an easier time in crafting robust strategies. However, if the cost of changing is high, management needs to spend considerable time and thought evaluating potential scenarios and crafting strategies to deal with different futures.
- Competitor's expected choices. As a last note, management should also consider and monitor what competitors are doing. For farms this involves not only what close neighbors are doing, but also what producers in other regions and countries are doing. The producers of products with close

substitutes (such as pork, beef, poultry, and other meat producers) need to consider their competitors' choices or potential choices as they make their own.

Strategies can be modified and combined to develop a more robust strategy designed to make progress toward the farm's vision under several scenarios. However, a robust strategy may be very expensive due to the costs of maintaining options for the future, so financial goals may not be met. Also, developing a strategy of being ready to move as needed in all or several scenarios may seem robust, but the business may lose by ending up stuck in the middle!

As a final note on crafting strategy, these points from Thompson, Strickland, and Gamble (2005, pp. 229–230) can serve as useful guides (or "10 commandments," as they called them) for developing sound strategies.

1. Place top priority on crafting and executing strategic moves that enhance the farm's long-term competitive position. Short-term profits are nice, but short term. The best way to ensure long-term profitability is to strengthen long-term competitiveness and market position.
2. Be prompt in adapting to changing market conditions, unmet customer needs, buyer wishes for something better, emerging technological alternatives, and new initiatives of competitors.
3. Invest in creating a sustainable competitive advantage.
4. Avoid strategies capable of succeeding only in the most optimistic circumstances.
5. Don't underestimate the reactions and the commitment of rival firms, whether they are in another part of your country or across the border or ocean.
6. Consider that attacking competitive weakness is usually more profitable and less risky than attacking competitive strength.
7. Be judicious in cutting prices without an established cost advantage. Only a low-cost producer can win a long price war.
8. Strive to open up very meaningful gaps in quality or service or performance features when pursuing a differentiation strategy.
9. Avoid stuck-in-the-middle strategies that represent compromises between lower costs and greater differentiation and between broad and narrow market appeal.
10. Be aware that aggressive moves to wrest market share away from rivals often provoke retaliation in the form of a price war—to the detriment of everyone's profits.

In this chapter, the process of crafting strategies started by using external and internal analysis to choose which of the four generic strategies best fit the farm and then which of the seven complementary strategic actions could be used to adapt the generic strategy to the farm's specific situation. Strategies for specific situations were discussed. Several tests were also described that can be used to decide what strategy is the best for a farm. The chapter also looked at several pitfalls of strategic planning and how it can be improved. Included in the chapter was a discussion of strategic risk and some procedures that can be used to manage and control that risk. Some concluding thoughts on crafting strategy ended the chapter.

Summary

- Crafting strategy starts with choosing a basic generic strategy and then adapting it to a farm and its specific situation.

- The four generic strategies are low-cost leadership, differentiation, best-cost provider, and focus or niche.
- The seven complementary strategic actions are horizontal expansion, diversification, vertical integration, innovation, prospecting, protecting, and alliances and partnerships.
- Specific strategies are needed for specific situations: emerging markets and industries; maturing industries, stagnant or declining industries, fragmented industries, and weak or crisis-ridden businesses.
- Several tests are available to farmers for evaluating potential strategies. Eight example tests include vision consistency, goodness of fit, building for the future, performance, importance, feasibility, resource, and confidence.
- Four problems or weaknesses in strategic planning are planning under uncertainty, ivory tower planning, planning for the present, and managers' biases. Three other ideas for improving strategic planning are devil's advocacy, dialectic inquiry, and using an advisory board.
- Managing strategic risk involves understanding the probability and potential impact of the potential sources of strategic risk.
- Scenarios can be used to evaluate potential outcomes under alternative scenarios.
- Strategy should change and evolve as the business environment changes and evolves.
- Farmers need to be entrepreneurial (i.e., creative, risk-taking, innovative) when crafting strategy, and they need to be able to do outside-in strategic thinking.

Review Questions

1. Why strategy will be both proactive and reactive?
2. Describe the four generic competitive strategies. Which strategy must most farmers follow?
3. What are the complementary strategies that can be used to craft a strategy that best fits a specific farm?
4. What are the eight tests that can be used to evaluate potential strategies?
5. What are potential problems in crafting strategy, and how can the process of crafting strategy be improved?
6. How can a farmer manage risk and uncertainty when crafting strategy?
7. How can scenarios be useful for crafting strategy?
8. What are some other factors that can be considered in crafting strategies?

Further Reading

Boehlje, Michael, and Bruce Erickson. 2007. ''Assessing and Managing Strategic Risk in Agriculture.'' Top Farmer Crop Workshop Newsletter, accessed on June 6, 2008, at www.agecon.purdue.edu/topfarmer/newsletter/TCFW12-2007.pdf.

Boehlje, Michael, Allan W. Gray, and Joshua D. Detre. 2005. ''Strategy Development in a Turbulent Business Climate: Concepts and Methods.'' *International Food and Agribusiness Management Review*, 8(2): 21–40, accessed at http://purl.umn.edu/8158 on December 8, 2009.

Hill, C.W.L., and G.R. Jones. 1998. *Strategic Management Theory: An Integrated Approach*. 4th ed. Boston: Houghton Mifflin.

Schroeder, R. G. 2008. *Operations Management: Contemporary Concepts and Cases*. 4th ed. Boston: McGraw-Hill/Irwin, 528 pp.

Thompson, A. A., A. J. Strickland, III, and J. E. Gamble. 2005. *Crafting and Executing Strategy: The Quest for Competitive Advantage: Concepts and Cases*. 14th ed. Boston: McGraw-Hill/Irwin, 1,140 pp.

10

Strategy Execution and Control

In this chapter:

- Strategy execution
- Strategic control

Planning and plans are great, especially if done well—but if the plan is not executed, all the planning is for nothing. Also, the world is always changing, so a plan can become obsolete almost the day it is finalized. However, the question is not, "Why plan?" The questions that need to be asked are, "How can this plan or strategy be executed for the best possible probability of success?" and "How can we keep adjusting both the strategy and the execution to respond to the changes in the world?"

In this chapter, we address these two questions. The first major section looks at how to execute or implement the chosen strategy. The second discusses how to monitor both the success in achieving the strategic objectives set forth in the plan and the conditions in the economy and industry to see whether corrective actions need to be made in response.

Strategy Execution

Strategy execution is, in many ways, the most difficult part of strategic management. Execution involves designing the structure of the organization, obtaining and directing the needed resources, convincing people to change, and adapting the plan and execution to the changes that are inevitable. The difficulty of these tasks is compounded by the need to keep the overall vision in mind without getting immersed in and overwhelmed by the details of day-to-day operations. Execution is a hands-on job that includes the following activities (adapted and expanded from Thompson, Strickland, and Gamble, 2005):

- Building a capable organization with the competencies, capabilities, and resources needed to carry out the strategy successfully
- Obtaining and allocating resources to the activities critical to strategic success
- Establishing policies and procedures that support the execution of the chosen strategy
- Adopting best practices and programs for continuous improvement in how the value chain activities are performed

- Developing function area strategies, programs, and project plans designed to aim and move the farm along the chosen strategy
- Installing internal support systems that monitor performance and implementation of the chosen strategy, especially in terms of the measures listed on the balanced scorecard
- Tying rewards and incentives directly to the achievement of strategic and financial targets and to good strategy execution
- Creating a company culture and work climate that fits the chosen strategy
- Exerting the internal leadership needed to drive implementation forward and to keep improving the way the strategy is being executed

Building a Capable Organization

Successful strategy execution depends on having knowledgeable personnel, competitive capabilities, adequate resources, and good internal organization. Thompson, Strickland, and Gamble identify three types of organization-building activities: staffing, building core competencies and competitive capabilities, and structuring the organization and work effort.

Staffing the organization involves both building the management team and recruiting and retaining employees with the needed experience, skills, and capacity to deal with change and achieve progress toward objectives, goals, and ultimately, the vision of the firm. This intellectual capital, as it is often called, can be built deliberately through good recruitment and hiring processes, continuous training over a career, providing promising employees the opportunity to try new and challenging duties, encouraging creativity (with management's acceptance of the possibility of failure), creating an invigorating work environment, paying to retain good employees, coaching average performers to improve, and releasing poor performers. These points will be discussed in more detail in Chapter 23, Human Resource Management.

Building competencies and capabilities involves training and retraining yourself and your employees in new and old skills required for a new strategy, hiring new staff with needed skills, reassigning duties, redesigning jobs, and acquiring the necessary resources. The goal is to mould basic abilities into core competencies that provide competitive advantages for the farm.

Structuring the organization and work effort involves organizing value chain activities and business processes and deciding how much decision-making authority to give supervisors and employees. The structure of the organization refers to the organization chart: what is considered within the business, how the parts of the business are organized into work groups, who reports to whom, who is in charge of what and whom, and so on. One of the first decisions involving structure is the make-or-buy decision: which activities are kept internal to the farm and which are outsourced. Those that are kept internal and are also critical to strategic success are the activities that the structure is built around. The structure also needs to allow communication and coordination between different parts of the farm—between the livestock enterprise and the grain production enterprise, for example. The structure also needs to provide for proper collaboration with suppliers and strategic allies.

Obtaining and Allocating Resources

While it seems obvious, each strategy-critical piece of the business needs to be fully funded to ensure the highest probability of achieving strategic objectives. If not identified and dealt with explicitly, historical practices and customs could hinder the growth of critical parts of the business. For example, consider a dairy farm whose new strategy focuses on the milking herd and outsources grain production. This dairy farm needs to make sure the milking herd and its closely related activities are fully funded. The historical practice of replacing the crop tractor or harvester after a fixed number of years needs to be rethought to be sure the milking herd is funded; replacement of crop machinery is given second priority (even if the shift to outsourcing is gradual) in the new strategy and the replacement practice needs to reflect that change. This change in strategy for a dairy farm may also signal the need to hire another or more qualified person to manage the dairy herd and to decrease the number of employees or hours spent on crop production. This requires a shift in funding for personnel as well as new job descriptions and potential new hires, job reassignments, training, retraining, and possible release of current employees.

Policies and Procedures

A company's past and its habits were the number one barrier for executing a new strategy according to executives in a recent survey (Welbourne, 2005). Thus, whether the new strategy is a major change or a readjustment, managers need to set up new policies and procedures that reflect the change. Employees need to be trained in the new procedures. These actions are needed even if the farm is owned and run by one person. The manager needs to realize the need to change and then make sure the worker follows the new methods. For example, a grain farmer has decided to expand her marketing strategy to include the futures markets and insurance so she needs to set up policies and procedures to follow for pre-harvest marketing as well as post-harvest marketing. As manager, she needs to develop policies to be sure she, as marketer, follows the new procedures. As another example, a conventional grain farmer who decides to convert to organic production has to adopt a very different set of crop production policies and procedures plus instituting a new system to ensure that the new policies and procedures are followed and verifiable by an outside certification agency.

New policies and procedures can also help alter a work climate to better reflect a change in strategy. For example, consider a farm that formerly followed a low-cost strategy and pushed hard for the lowest input prices and lowest costs of operation. Suppose this farm now switches to a best-cost strategy as a provider to a small set of customers—say, grain to livestock farms or vegetables to stores. As the manager, this farmer needs to rewrite policies and procedures to reflect the change. For example, the farmer may need to stop arguing about prices or cutting operations that add value for the customer but not directly for the farmer. In essence, this farm needs to change policies and procedures because the value chain has changed. For example, product delivery may now need to be made in smaller, higher-cost quantities and at the customers' schedule rather than at the pleasure of the farmer.

However, policies and procedures do not need to be written for every activity. Setting some in place to show how to operate under the new strategy can be presented as models of how management expects employees to work. Of course, for these models to work, management needs to explain the bigger picture of the farm's strategy and not just the small details of the day's work schedule.

Best Practices and Programs for Continuous Improvement

Benchmarking is the term used to identify what other farms and businesses are doing compared to you and similar farms. The goal of benchmarking is to identify the best way of operating, producing, marketing, financing, and other business functions. The task is to then adapt the newly identified best practices to your farm and see that they are instituted. This may involve setting a new procedure as described in the previous section. Benchmarking can be done by talking with other farmers or going on tours both close to home and in other countries. As one farmer describes his learning experience, "I used to think I was a good hog producer, but then I visited Denmark and realized I could be a lot better." Being a member of a farm record system and comparing records is another form of benchmarking.

Commitment to continuous improvement can help a farm business survive in an ever changing world. As new technologies and new competitors come, the prudent manager will strive to always improve and not be complacent with current efficiencies, costs, and prices. The ideas, concepts, programs, processes, and procedures described in Chapter 17, Quality Management, show how to improve and continue to improve the business.

Function Area Strategies, Programs and Project Plans

To implement strategy well, each business function needs its own execution plans that are designed to support the overall farm strategy. Important activities for each function need to be identified that will facilitate that function's contribution to the overall strategy for the whole farm. The business function execution plan should contain specific steps, action items, responsible persons, target dates, measurable objectives, and needed resources. As an example, consider the strategy execution plan for financing the expansion of a crop farm shown in Table 10.1.

Another part of implementation is to identify programs and projects that are needed to achieve the vision and objectives identified as part of the planning process. These programs or projects are not the

Table 10.1 Example of a Functional Strategy for Financing a Crop Farm Expansion

Functional Area:	Finance
Specific strategic steps needed:	1. Negotiate land purchase by, and a land rent contract with, a local investor.
	2. Negotiate machinery loan.
	3. Consolidate and increase operating loan.
Reason/motivation for steps:	Investor with local connections is willing to buy land and rent to us if we can obtain financing for larger machinery line and operating needs.
Plan of action:	1. Negotiate and sign letters of agreement between current land owner, investor, and ourselves.
	2. Use letters of agreement to negotiate and obtain financing for machinery and operating capital needs specified in business plan.
	3. Talk to regional and local banks and machinery dealers.
	4. If financing terms meet goals stated in projections, finalize and sign financing agreements, and then sign contracts for land purchase and rental.
Responsible person(s):	Mary to negotiate with current land owner and investor. Mary and Bill to negotiate with potential creditors.
Measurable objectives:	Letters of agreement, needed level of financing in agreements, and contracts to purchase and rent.
Target dates:	Letters of agreement by August 1.
	Finalize financing and contracts by August 25.
Budget and resources needed:	$1,000 for attorney fees; 120 hours estimated by Mary and Bill; use of car and computer.

Table 10.2   Example of a Strategic Project Plan for Building a Swine Finishing Barn

Title of program or project:	Building a swine finishing barn
Reason/motivation:	Achieve new operating efficiencies and increase capacity
Plan of action:	Finalize contractor bid, obtain building permits, initiate and monitor building progress
Responsible person(s):	Tim
Measurable objectives:	Bid finalized, permits obtained, building started, pit poured, roof and walls, building finished and pigs in
Target dates:	Bid by April 1; permits by June 1; building started by July 1; pit poured by July 20; roof and walls by August 15, building finished and pigs in by September 15
Budget and resources needed:	$440,000 and 5 acres

whole strategy but pieces or steps needed to accomplish or move forward with the strategy. Examples of these programs or projects are building a new milking parlor, seeking new markets, leasing more cropland, and so on. These projects could be explicitly needed to achieve the stated goals of, respectively, a larger herd, diversified markets, and increased size. Under this method of implementation, the farmer (or management team) assigns a program leader (or specifies a certain amount of time by an individual farmer), sets specific measurable objectives with target dates, and allocates the needed human, physical, and financial resources to the program or project. As an example of a strategic project plan, consider the plan for building a new swine finishing barn as shown in Table 10.2.

As an example of a strategic program, consider a farmer's decision to become a certified organic producer and capture the organic price premium (Table 10.3). This farmer knows he has to educate himself on both production and marketing of organic products before he actually starts the 3-year certification process.

These last two examples of projects and programs can also be shown as Gantt charts, which are discussed in Chapter 18, Operations Management. This is done for the example of a strategic program to become certified organic (Table 10.3).

Internal Support Systems

Internal support systems are needed to monitor performance and implementation of the chosen strategy. As part of strategy execution and in preparation for strategic control (described in the next section), a farm's internal support system starts with the measures listed on the balanced scorecard. As described in Chapter 7, these measures should be indicators of progress and performance, not measures of past performance. Other measures and data should support the early observation of performance and progress toward accomplishments and indicators of improving efficiencies especially within those activities that are crucial to the strategy. Internal support systems should also include the monitoring of external conditions in order to evaluate the need to adjust strategy as the situation changes.

Rewards and Incentives

As will be discussed more in Chapter 24, Human Resource Management, the basic principle guiding the setting and awarding of incentives and rewards is the simple, old phrase, ''Reward what you want

Table 10.3   Example of a Strategic Program to Become Certified Organic

Title of program or project:	Organic certification and marketing
Reason/motivation:	Estimated budgets show better profits
Plan of action:	Educate, start production, negotiate markets
Responsible person(s):	Steve and Mike
Measurable objectives:	Attend classes, join association of organic producers, finalize budgets and production process, contracts
Target dates:	Join association, fall year 1
	Attend classes, fall and winter year 1 & 2
	Finalize plans and budget, December year 1
	Solidify market contacts, January year 2
	Production & control, years 2–4
	Attend association meetings, all years
	Become certified, year 4 (after 36 months of organic practices)
	Market certified organic products in year 4
Budget and resources needed:	$5,000 for 4 years of training and related expenses; 600 hours for extra planning

done." That is, if you want employees to help move the farm toward the specified goals, objectives, and ultimately the vision of the farm, reward them for making the decisions and performing well in ways that help achieve those goals and objectives. The rewards can be both monetary and non-monetary. They need to be the result of actions and results that are controllable by the employee. They can range from simple payments to perks, benefits, promotions, listening to employees and their ideas, sharing information on the farm's progress toward objectives (to instill company pride), caring for employees, and being aware of cultural differences. All of these can improve performance through rewarding specific results and instilling the desire to work effectively and efficiently to help the business because they have a personal interest in the business succeeding. On the other side of rewards, lack of rewards or punishment for poor performance or wrong decisions can serve as a stimulant for better performance. However, a balance is needed between these two types of stimulus.

Company Culture and Work Climate

The culture of a business is its internal work climate and personality as shaped by its values, beliefs, ethics, principles, traditions, behaviors, and operating style. It is taught to newcomers and perpetuated by stories, shared experiences, training of new employees, peer pressure, model behavior, leadership examples, and in many other ways. Culture is important to strategy execution in how it guides employee behavior and striving for critical results. If there is a change in strategy, culture may help or hinder the change. In Welbourne's (2005) survey of executives, culture was one of the top barriers to executing strategy behind the company past and habits (as noted earlier), economic climate, and budget. A culture deep in tradition may hinder the process of changing not only visible policies and procedures but also deeply ingrained behavior that guides decisions not set in policy. A culture that has the reputation of being adaptive to new situations will more easily move and accept a new strategy and thus a new way of operating. Changing a current business culture starts with identifying those aspects that do not support the chosen strategy, along with a lot of communication and modeling of how different behaviors will increase the probability of success. Replacing managers, policies, and procedures with new managers, policies, and procedures, for example, is a very strong, substantive signal that cultural changes are expected.

Exerting Internal Leadership

Even the best strategic plan needs leadership to be executed well. When variables were bundled into groups, Welbourne (2005) found that surveyed executives indicated leadership was a larger barrier than external factors and process to executing strategy for companies other than those changing both strategy and tactics. For this latter group, those executives indicated that external factors were the largest barrier, followed by leadership. In the groupings, leadership included senior management, company culture, the way people work together, the CEO, the company's past or habits, and policies. External factors included customers, the economy, and the organization's reputation in the external environment. Process included employees, technology, and middle management.

Leaders need to be aware of what is happening both through internal information systems and by "walking around" to visit with employees and seeing progress and results firsthand. They push and encourage employees to work toward strategic objectives; they work on keeping culture correctly aligned with strategy. Leaders need to encourage the development of best practices, benchmarking, and continual improvement of all aspects of the business. They make sure employees are well trained; they institute good hiring practices. They serve as role models for ethics, company culture, and social responsibility. Ultimately, the leaders are responsible for taking corrective actions when performance does not produce the results needed to achieve strategic objectives.

Strategic Control

Since the world changes, strategic planning and execution are not one-time exercises. Strategic control is needed to evaluate a farm's performance and results during and after execution of the chosen strategy. New developments and circumstances may call for corrective adjustments. The underlying situation may change, and execution may not go as planned. So each phase of strategic management requires frequent review and evaluation, and decisions need to be made whether to adjust direction, objectives, or execution plans. Strategic planning and execution are never finished. Evaluating performance, reviewing changes in the surrounding environment, and making adjustments are normal, constant, and necessary parts of the strategic management process.

Strategic control systems provide the ability to monitor, evaluate, and take corrective actions, as needed, to ensure that strategic objectives will be met. Control involves the following steps: choosing the key indicators that measure progress toward objectives (such as the balanced scorecard discussed next), establishing standards against which performance is to be evaluated, creating measurement systems for the key indicators, comparing actual performance to the established standards, evaluating the results, and taking corrective actions, as necessary.

A major part of the strategic control system can come from the balanced scorecard as described in Chapter 7, Strategic Management: Planning. As you may recall, the balanced scorecard consists of objectives for four or more different perspectives. The example in Chapter 7 included six perspectives: family, lifestyle, and community; financial; customer; internal business process; natural resources; and learning and growth. While this list of six is a good place to start, the final list of perspectives for an individual farm is chosen due to their importance for that specific farm. Financial objectives, such as net farm income, rates of return on assets (ROA) and on equity (ROE), and net worth, are really lagged measures; they indicate the consequences of past actions and choices. Of greater interest to a prudent, long-term manager and owner are leading objectives that are, as described in Chapter 7, to strive for because they are the drivers of future performance. That is, they are early indicators of how well the farm's financial and other objectives will be met in the future. As part of strategic control, the balanced scorecard with these leading objectives will quickly show whether progress is being made toward goals in each of the perspectives. Since all these perspectives were chosen for their importance to the farm, progress should be made in all of them.

Key indicators for strategic control should include more than a farm's specific balanced scorecard objectives. Key indicators can also be selected from the issues identified in the first step of strategic planning, evaluating the general macro-environment. Changes in the general economy, consumer preferences, political climates around the world, competitors' behavior, and many other elements should be checked on a regular basis if they were identified as critical to the development and crafting of the farm's chosen strategy.

Strategic control can also be described as having two basic parts: strategic product and strategic process (Molz, 1988). For strategic product, actual outcomes are compared with targeted outcomes projected in the strategy implementation program. Causes of deviations are evaluated and corrective actions taken as needed. For strategic process, a farmer needs to routinely reevaluate the assumptions and inputs used to develop the strategic plan and decide whether unanticipated deviations from expectations will alter the viability of the plan and the need to re-craft the chosen strategy.

Another view separates a strategic control system into five areas: (1) financial controls for rates of return, income levels, and so on; (2) output controls such as productivity measures, efficiency measures, and cost measures; (3) behavior controls, such as budgets and standardization of inputs and processes that can be used when it is difficult to monitor outputs; (4) values and norms embodied in organizational culture to ensure that employees will show the desired behaviors; (5) reward systems designed to recognize behavior and actions that contribute to achieving financial and strategic objectives (Hill and Jones, 1998).

This is the last chapter on strategic management, but it is not the end of strategic management, for it is a continuous process. In Chapters 7 and 8, the first phases of strategic planning were described: developing a strategic vision of the farm; setting strategic and financial objectives, performing an external analysis, and performing an internal analysis of the farm. In Chapter 9, the process of crafting strategy was described.

This current chapter covered the last two phases of strategic management. The first section described the process of executing or implementing the chosen strategy. The second described how to monitor the success in achieving the strategic objectives set forth in the plan and balanced scorecard, as well as the conditions in the economy and industry to evaluate whether corrective actions to the strategy and execution plan are needed in response to these changes.

Summary

- Successful execution of strategy involves:
  - Building a capable organization with the competencies, capabilities, and resources needed to carry out the strategy successfully.

- ○ Obtaining and allocating resources to the activities critical to strategic success.
- ○ Establishing policies and procedures that support the execution of the chosen strategy.
- ○ Adopting best practices and programs for continuous improvement in how the value chain activities are performed.
- ○ Developing function area strategies, programs, and project plans designed to aim and move the farm along the chosen strategy.
- ○ Installing internal support systems that monitor performance and implementation of the strategy, especially in terms of the measures listed on the balanced scorecard.
- ○ Tying rewards and incentives directly to the achievement of strategic and financial targets and to good strategy execution.
- ○ Creating a company culture and work climate that fits the chosen strategy.
- ○ Exerting the internal leadership needed to drive implementation forward and to keep improving the way the strategy is being executed.
- • Strategic control involves designing control systems, comparing actual results to financial and strategic objectives, monitoring the business environment, and modifying the organizational structure, execution plan, and even the chosen strategy as needed to meet goals and objectives.

Review Questions

1. What are the steps or parts of strategy execution?
2. What is intellectual capital, and why does it show up in a discussion of strategy execution?
3. Why are writing new policies and procedures critical to the execution of a new strategy?
4. Why are benchmarking and continuous improvement important for strategy execution?
5. How can functional strategies, strategic project plans, and strategic programs be used in strategy execution?
6. How are rewards, incentives, company culture, and internal leadership used in good strategy execution?
7. What is strategic control? Why is it needed?
8. How can the balanced scorecard be used in strategic control? Does the list of indicators on a farm's scorecard need to be expanded?

Further Reading

Hill, C. W. L., and G. R. Jones. 1998. *Strategic Management Theory: An Integrated Approach*. 4th ed. Boston: Houghton Mifflin.

Molz, R. 1988. *Steps to Strategic Management: A Guide for Entrepreneurs*. Plano, Texas: Wordware Publishing.

Thompson, A. A., A. J. Strickland III, and J. E. Gamble. 2005. *Crafting and Executing Strategy: The Quest for Competitive Advantage: Concepts and Cases*. 14th ed. Boston: McGraw-Hill/Irwin, 1,140 pp.

Welbourne, T. M. 2005. "Leaders Talk about Executing Strategy." Ross School of Business, University of Michigan. Accessed on June 16, 2009, at www.eepulse.com/documents/pdfs/Executing-Strategy.pdf.

11

Marketing Basics

In this chapter:

- The marketing mix
- Marketing plans for farmers
- Historical price patterns
- General price forecasting methods
- Marketing control

A primary concern of any business is: Will someone buy my product or service? The questions of whether there is a buyer and what price they are willing to pay are crucial to the success of the business and should be addressed quite early in the planning process. However, to find good answers, a farm manager also needs to answer other questions simultaneously in the planning process (such as production and operations, financing, staffing) so good cost estimates can be made to help develop the marketing plan. The simultaneity or iterative process is needed for developing good plans for other parts of the business.

The first section of this chapter reviews the traditional, basic elements of marketing: the marketing mix or the "Four Ps," now expanded to seven. The next section briefly reviews some of the main marketing and pricing options for farmers. The third section covers the components of a marketing plan. The rest of this chapter is a brief review of different historical price movements, general price forecasting methods, and, in the last section, the rudiments of setting up a marketing control system. The goal of this chapter is to introduce marketing terms, methods, and fundamentals to those not familiar with them. The goal is not to explain how to watch markets and make marketing decisions. Other texts (such as Usset, 2007, and Bokelmann et al., 2001), classes, and materials are much more appropriate for those decisions.

The Marketing Mix

Many farmers view marketing as pricing their product through all the options they have available or just monitoring the markets and hoping to catch a good price. General business thinks of that view as just pricing or even just peddling the product. In the economic climate of today and the future, farmers need to develop a larger view of marketing—a view that thinks beyond price. This move is necessitated by the increasing global market exposure, the narrowing of the profit margin per unit of product, and the closer working arrangements with buyers through contracts, networks, and the necessity of prospecting and protecting better markets.

In general business, the traditional phrase in marketing is the marketing mix or the "Four Ps": product, price, place, and promotion. The plan for marketing a product or service will include these four items, but the mix will vary for different products in different locations. A farmer producing pork in a large facility in Sweden has developed a marketing mix with the Four Ps—whether he knew the Four Ps or not (Example 11.1). Some people have added three more Ps: people, physical evidence, and process. Farmers dealing directly with consumers can benefit from understanding these parts of marketing. The Farmers Fresh Market Project is such a group of farmers (Example 11.2). However, farmers producing a very common commodity such as wheat or milk can also benefit from understanding all the parts of the marketing mix even though their price is essentially set by the market. This need for understanding the other aspects comes from the desire to find and keep a market or just obtain a slightly higher price than the general market. Let's look at each of these elements of the mix separately.

Example 11.1. The "Four Ps" of Marketing Directly

A Swedish farmer has developed a market for his hogs by working directly with a slaughterhouse and customers in Stockholm (which is about an hour away from the farm). He is a part owner (with three others) of a hog-finishing business that finishes 8–9,000 hogs each year. They buy feeder pigs weighing 28 kg and feed them to slaughter. They do not just sell to the market, but have developed their own marketing mix starting with the "Four Ps": product, price, place, and promotion.

The product is a 125-kg hog with known and consistent quality. Based on spot market prices in the week and days before, the farmer sets the meat price each Friday for the next week. For promotion, the prices are then posted and sent electronically to their regular customers—retail stores and restaurants. In regard to place, on Monday, orders are taken and the hogs shipped to a slaughterhouse on a private arrangement. On Wednesday, the meat is in Stockholm; by Friday and Saturday, the meat is all gone—eaten in the restaurants or purchased by consumers. And that Friday is also the start of the next week.

But the other three Ps are not forgotten: people, physical evidence, and process. This arrangement did not start overnight. Buyers were contacted and personal relationships were established. Physical evidence is shown in terms of the pork product both at the initial contact and every week when it is delivered. Quality and quantity problems, if any, would be quickly noted by the customers if they were not dealt with by the farmer. The process is the connection from producer through one slaughterhouse to the customers. The pricing system and notice is standardized. The delivery schedule is known and kept.

Source: Personal interview by author.

Example 11.2. The Farmers Fresh Market Project and the Internet

Farmers very close to the consumer need to pay attention to the Seven Ps of marketing.

One example of many around the world is The Farmers Fresh Market Project in North Carolina,

(*continued*)

(*continued*)

U.S. The project connects potential buyers of fresh food (restaurants, stores, and consumers) with producers of the fresh food. The product includes vegetables, fruit, meat, and farm-processed products such as jelly and jam. The price is initially set by the buyer and ultimately determined by the interaction between buyer and producer. The place is the innovation of this project; it is the Internet, where producers list their products and buyers can see pictures, descriptions, and prices. The Web site is also the place for ordering and paying, with delivery taking place at either the buyer's location or a central site for smaller orders. Promotion of the Market is done online as well as through press releases and news stories in local media. For the people part of the Seven Ps, since buyers and consumers of fresh foods often want to know where the food comes from and who produced it, the producers are identified and pictured on the Web site. Physical evidence includes the paperwork completed at order and delivery time and the pictures of the farms and farmers. The process involves the farmers posting the products available; the buyers choosing the products and paying by credit card; farmers delivering the ordered products to a central location on the delivery day; and the Project delivering either directly or to a central site "picked, packed, and shipped within 24 hours!"

Source: For more information, see the Project's Web site at www.farmersfreshmarket.org, last accessed on January 29, 2010.

Product

Most of the time, product is the tangible, physical item or the intangible service that is performed. However, the customer may see and want more than just the physical product. Thus, marketing must also talk about the three aspects of a product: the core, the actual product, and the augmented product. The core product is the benefit or value perceived by the customer; it is not physical. The wholesomeness and safety of the milk and its nutritional value is what the customer wants. A seller of Christmas trees told me that his business became much more profitable when he realized that he was selling the experience of the family going into the woods, selecting a tree, and enjoying some food afterward at his business; the tree was a simple thing taken home to remember the experience. The actual product is the Christmas tree standing in the home or the milk itself that can be seen in the glass and tasted as it is consumed. The augmented product is the non-physical part of the product, such as delivery, warranties, and other after-sales services. For a purebred livestock breeder, the animal may be the physical product; the core product includes the future production of quality animals; and the augmented product is the delivery of the animal to the seller and the readiness to replace the animal if it does not perform.

For some products, the producer needs to consider the idea of the product life cycle. The cycle consists of a product's introduction to the market, the growth in demand, the maturity of the demand, and the decline in demand. Most agricultural commodities are not affected by the cycle due to their use as raw materials for other products. However, some products from farms that are closer to the consumer may experience this cycle directly. Examples of such products include different types of wine, lean red meat from elk or buffalo, non-rBST milk, different vegetables, and so on. If a farm is very close to consumers, such as one selling directly through farmers markets or through grocers and restaurants, the farm will likely need to keep a mix of products in all stages of the life cycle in order to stabilize income over time.

Price

Setting the price is not an accounting process of determining the cost of production per unit. The basis of pricing should be the value to the customer. The cost of production is the bottom price you need; the customer's value per unit is the top price. If the market does not provide a price equal to or above your cost, you as producer need to seek ways to lower costs, raise value for the customer, or to evaluate whether to continue production.

The pricing strategy is also important. The product can be designed so the price can be set low to expand market share, or the product can be designed for a high-end market with the price set high to enjoy a wider margin between price and production costs. This choice is not just made at the option of the producer. The market, the buyers, and the competition need to be considered as well as the capabilities of the producers before the appropriate pricing strategy can be forged.

Although commodity producers may not have as much control over their price as they wish, they still have some options to take advantage of opportunities as they arise. The issues of price, value, and pricing strategy still are important. Commodity producers need to know their costs of production not because they can set that as their price, but to know when the market price will provide a profit to them.

Place

In marketing, "place" is thought of as getting the right products in the right quantity to the right place for the lowest possible cost without sacrificing customer service. The right products involve product development and production. The right quantity to the right place involves internal and external logistics. The right place can vary between the customer's place, a store, a distributor, and online. The lowest possible cost involves the distribution strategy and the efficiency and effectiveness of the entire distribution and logistics process. "Without sacrificing customer service" refers to making the transaction easy, not complicated, and not forcing the customers to go out of their way to obtain the product.

Promotion

Promotion is aimed at helping the potential customers realize a need and then convincing them your product is the best. This aim is not evil in itself, but people can misuse the process and sell products that customers do not need. The good side of this aim is the idea of finding solutions to customers' problems.

Promotion covers all aspects of marketing communication: advertising, selling, and sales. It includes the actual media advertising as well as publicity, training sales staff, training customers, and designing gimmicks and gifts to accompany the promotion and product. In the short term, promotion strategies aim to give potential customers reasons and incentives to buy the product. In the long term, promotion strategies aim to turn new customers into repeat buyers.

People

Promotion also involves people classified into four groups: staff, suppliers, customers, and competitors. Customer Relationship Management (CRM) is a large part of the people side of the marketing mix. Knowing your customers and letting them know you as well as your products is part of CRM. Understanding psychology and how people interact and relate to others is part of maintaining good customer relations. On the selling side, the seller wants the buyer to trust the seller and transfer that to trust of the product. The farmer selling at the farmers market wants customers to know that the products are wholesome, produced locally, and have been handled safely. On the input side, customer relationships take the form of keeping good suppliers part of the business. Farmers who rent land know they need to keep the landowner happy, which includes more than just a good rental rate. Care needs to be shown to the land and buildings, information on the crops and land needs to be provided in the way and frequency the owner wants, and extra efforts to help the owner may be appreciated, especially if they live on the property. Maintaining good relations with the feed supplier, for example, can increase the chances of better services during hard times.

Physical Evidence

Physical evidence is used for services, since a service is intangible. Physical evidence includes business cards, signs, business names and logos on vehicles, paperwork (letters, orders, invoices, etc.), brochures, and many more items. A farmer who does custom harvesting or other work can provide a business card, a work order form showing work to be performed, and an invoice showing work accomplished. If the customer is not located nearby, the physical evidence can include pictures of the work being done or accomplished. A letter to an absentee landowner describing current conditions and other information about the farm can help keep the owner satisfied and less likely to change tenants.

Process

Processes can take both internal and external forms. For the marketing mix, we are interested in those processes that focus on the customer. Process is closely tied to other elements of the marketing mix, but it involves the customer in more than just the selling of the product. For example, Disney works very hard to be sure the process of enjoying the Disney property is enjoyable for their customers, but they also make sure customers have a good experience making the reservations, arriving, enjoying the park, and returning home. Disney then asks for feedback on their experience. The time in the park is only part of the process even though it may be the main part of the product. Handling luggage may be part of the augmented product, but does the handling process add or detract value for the customer?

For a farmer, the process is seen in how easy it is for customers and potential customers to contact the farmer, whether deliveries are made at the time and manner requested, whether billings are made in a timely manner, whether post-sales problems are dealt with quickly, and so on. Similar points can be made for the suppliers and the process the farmer creates for them.

Understanding the concepts involved in the marketing mix is crucial for farmers. Those who produce commodities and consider themselves to be price takers, not price setters, still need to understand the concepts. Most individual farmers also do not need to spend too much time on promotion and advertising their own commodity; this expenditure would do little to improve the price. But some farmers do need to understand promotion and advertising—those closer to the consumer. The basic concepts of the marketing mix can be seen in good marketing plans for all farmers.

There is a reason this list of ''Seven Ps'' is called the marketing mix: every farmer mixes the components differently to create the best fit for his or her own farm. This is the topic of the next section.

Marketing Plans for Farmers

There are many pricing tools for farmers and there are many marketing methods. The basic, perhaps naïve, method is to produce, harvest, and then sell on the cash market. But farmers can also use forward contracts, production contracts, hedging and options in the futures market, and many other tools derived from the futures markets. All tools have their own unique mix of risk and reward. The best commodity marketers develop and follow a marketing plan that uses a mix of tools and that adjusts the mix to the market conditions each year or production cycle. The best marketers also realize that they will make mistakes and will seldom, if ever, obtain the top price. However, they do develop a plan to help them make marketing and pricing decisions that provide stability to income and a profit in most years. In this section, we step through the marketing mix and look at how it fits into a marketing plan for farmers. This process is used for both products and inputs.

Understand the Market

The first step is to understand the market. Ask some questions. What are the long, multi-year price trends? Does the price vary over the year in a fairly predictable pattern? Are there typical high and low price periods during the year? Is the price pattern different after poor, good, and normal production years? How does production in other countries affect the local market? How can the futures markets be used for pricing products? What tools of the futures markets are available in my area? How well does the local market follow the national market and the futures markets? What insurance options are available for the physical product and revenue? Where are the sellers and the buyers? How many and how big are they? The questions go on. The historical graphs in a later section of this chapter are examples of looking for these trends and patterns. Finding or developing similar graphs for your products and your local area is a large step toward understanding your market.

Understanding the market also involves watching the current market conditions. However, as Usset (2007) recommends in his book on marketing grain, we should listen to the market but not to market chatter. That is, listening to what the market does day to day or what the analysts say this week may provide entertainment and discussion points for the coffee shop or other gathering places, but the chatter may also provide bad advice that can destroy a good marketing plan. Usset says to listen to what the market says for the long term and make decisions based on that market voice, not the chatter. For grain producers, he recommends paying attention to what grain markets say through local basis and carrying charges.

Product: What and How Much Will Be Produced? What Are the Costs of Production?

Listing this production question as the first question for marketing points out the need to answer many questions simultaneously or, at least, in an iterative process. Before a farm manager can decide how to market products, he or she needs to know what products will be produced and how much of each. And, before that, a farm manager needs to know a likely price for each product and to estimate the costs of production. These issues are addressed in detail at several points in this text and will not be addressed here. Understanding the industry and the potential for products is discussed in Chapters 7–10, which cover strategic management. Calculating the costs of production is explained in Chapter 15, Enterprise Budgets. Choosing enterprises and the level of production is discussed in Chapter 16, Whole-Farm Planning.

Knowing the cost of production will help a farmer understand his or her competitive position in the market. By comparing historical market prices to the cost of production per unit, a farmer can decide whether the market will provide an acceptable profit potential for specific products. The expected cost of production per unit also serves as the breakeven or minimum desired price and as the initial point for setting price goals or targets. The market may not always provide a price above the breakeven price, but knowing the cost of production allows for better production and marketing planning than not knowing costs.

Product specification also involves choosing the form, grade, and quality to deliver and purchase. Buyers may want or be willing to buy different grades of the same product. For instance, the price of corn is based on certain standards on moisture, foreign matter, and so on, but corn does not have to meet those standards to be sold. Farmers have a choice of selling corn at higher moisture levels and paying the elevator to dry the corn or taking a cash discount and selling it upon delivery. Farmers could also dry the corn themselves before selling it. So the farmers' decision revolves around the current versus future price, the cost of drying and storing at the elevator, and the cost of drying and storing on the farm. Livestock feeders also have a choice of the weight at which to sell their animals. A cow-calf operator can decide whether to sell calves or keep them longer and sell yearlings. Crops need nitrogen, but farmers can choose whether to deliver that nitrogen in the form of anhydrous ammonia, urea, manure, or another form of nitrogen fertilizer.

Price: When to Price? How to Price?

Most agricultural products do not need to be physically delivered to be priced. With the increased understanding and increased opportunities to forward contract and use the futures market, pricing does not have to take place solely upon delivery or after storage. The promise to deliver is often sufficient to be able to obtain a price; usually this "promise" is in the form of a contract. So the timing question has expanded to whether to price the product before, upon, or after physical delivery of the product. Buying insurance for crops and livestock will increase a marketer's confidence that pricing before production will not create problems if production is not at the levels expected. A forward contract for milk or wheat, for example, is a contract that sets a price for those products and specifies delivery dates in the future. Delivering grain to the local elevator may involve satisfying a forward contract, selling some at that day's cash price, and putting some in storage to be sold on a future date. The timing question also involves whether to price the product before or after input purchases. After checking the costs of feeders and estimating her own feeding costs, a cattle feeder may decide to use the futures market to price the finished steers even before an agreement is made to buy feeders. Seed and fertilizer purchases are often priced and paid before delivery to take advantage of sales and price incentives.

Some producers of fruit and vegetable crops market directly to consumers through roadside stands and farmers markets. One option used by a few growers, especially organic growers, is community supported agriculture (CSA). A person buys a share in a CSA farm and then receives a share of the production that year. The CSA shareholder is not guaranteed specific quantities, only their share of the actual production obtained that year.

Selling a product at the cash price available in the market may be the easiest way to price a product, but the cash price is not always the best price. For some commodities, other pricing methods, such as forward contracts, hedging, futures options, and other contractual arrangements, may help a farmer improve on the cash price. These methods can be used for both selling products and buying inputs. We look closer at the first three methods in the rest of this section.

Forward contracts are contractual obligations for the farmer to deliver a specified volume of a product (grain, milk, or livestock, for example) at a certain time in the future and for the buyer to pay a specified price for that volume of product. Forward contracts specify the desired quality attributes of the product and any discounts and premiums that may occur if the actual product deviates from the specified levels. The price specified in a forward contract is fixed and will not change with changes in the market.

Hedging involves purchasing a futures contract to reduce the risk of adverse price movements for either products or inputs. A futures contract is a legal and binding contract to deliver or accept delivery of a particular commodity on or before a specified date in the future. These contracts are available at several locations around the world. The two most recognized in the United States are the Chicago Mercantile Exchange (CME) and the Chicago Board of Trade (now owned by CME). In Europe, futures contracts are traded at the Commodities Futures Exchange Hannover and the Euronext location in Paris. Trading is also done at locations in Asia.

Hedgers already hold what are called cash positions, in the form of cattle on feed, grain they are growing, stored grain, and so on. They enter the futures market to hold the opposite position. For example, when a hog feeder buys hogs, he sells a futures contract to deliver hogs at a future date. When the hogs have reached market weight, the hog feeder buys back the futures contract and sells the hogs in the cash market. The feeder receives the cash price plus the difference between the selling and buying prices on the futures contract (minus the cost of the hedging transactions). The difference between the local cash price and the futures prices is called the basis. The example hog feeder has hedged the price for his live hogs by trading the risk of fluctuations in the cash price for the smaller risk of fluctuations in his basis.

This same hog feeder may hedge his price for feed by using the futures market. In this case his cash position is that he needs feed in the future, so he buys a futures contract. When the feed is actually bought locally, the feeder sells the futures contract. Again, the feeder is hedging the cost of his feed by trading the risk of fluctuations in the cash market for the smaller risk of fluctuations in his basis.

Speculators do not have any cash position. They do not own livestock, grain, or any other commodity. They are gambling that they know in which direction the futures market will move and they position themselves to take advantage of that movement. Speculators provide liquidity to the futures market by being willing to speculate and take chances, thus providing more buyers and sellers to the marketplace. Unhedged producers are essentially speculators in the cash market.

A futures option is the right but not the obligation to buy or sell a futures contract at a specific price on or before a certain expiration date. Options can be used to protect a price for a product or input for a specific cost that is known at the time of the transaction. As with a futures contract, the opposite positions are taken in the cash and options markets. To protect his price, a hog feeder could buy a put option (that is, the right to sell hogs in the future). As the cash market moves, the value of the option adjusts. When the hogs are sold, the hog feeder would sell back the put option bought earlier. One advantage of options is that the buyers and sellers of options are not subject to the margin calls that buyers of futures contracts may receive if prices move against their position.

Usset (2007) argues for having both a pre-harvest marketing plan and a post-harvest marketing plan. For livestock producers, this translates to having a pre-production and post-production plan. Even though livestock and livestock products cannot be stored as grain can be, the needs and reasons for pre- and post plans are essentially the same.

In his analysis, Usset finds that having a pre-harvest plan beats waiting for the harvest price and not doing anything. Having price objectives, decision dates for the pre-harvest pricing, and the discipline to follow was a successful strategy in Usset's work. Having price objectives requires knowing costs of production. After harvest, the pricing question depends on market conditions each year. Usset recommends answering a series of questions about the market before making the decision. First, is the carrying charge large or small? That is, is the difference between the futures price at harvest and the futures prices in a few months large enough to pay for storage of the grain for those few months? Second, is the market price low or high compared to typical levels? Third, is the basis narrow or wide? Answering these questions will help a farmer decide whether the best option each year is to (1) sell at harvest, (2) store unpriced grain for a few months, (3) store and sell with a forward contract, or (4) store and sell with a futures contract or a hedge-to-arrive (HTA) contract.

Setting decision dates and default dates are critical for pricing products. Decision dates are those times when the current market price is compared to price goals or targets and a decision is made to price a portion of the product to be produced. Default dates are those times when historical price patterns say the good price period will soon be over and it is time to force the pricing of an unpriced product. Default dates keep a farmer from waiting too long for a better price when the market conditions are not allowing targets to be met that year. Both decision dates and default dates help a marketer "pull the trigger" as they aim for the best price possible. These dates also keep a marketer from making the mistake of aiming to find the highest price. The goal, Usset says, is to search for ways to "find the dime or dimes," that are almost always available if pricing is done wisely.

Place: Where to Price? When and How to Deliver?

Farmers have both decreased and increased opportunities for pricing. The number of local product buyers and input sellers has decreased in many areas. However, the ability to sell and buy regionally has increased. Some groups of farmers have even made international sales directly. Electronic markets are also more prevalent and will continue to increase in number. "Where to price?" is a geographical question. Should the farmer sell locally, regionally, nationally, or internationally? What type of business should be used—a cooperative or a private business?

To decide when and how to deliver, a farmer needs to know the potential transportation and storage costs. With these cost estimates, the farmer can then evaluate the price available locally versus regionally and analyze market information and trends to decide whether it would be best to market now or in the future. Estimating the costs of direct retail and marketing are needed to evaluate the benefits of these options.

Promotion: What Marketing-Related Services to Use?

This question concerns inputs mainly but also affects products. For example, who should deliver the input to the farm? Will the dealer apply the fertilizer or will the farmer? Does the fertilizer dealer do the soil testing or does an independent lab do it? When machinery is purchased, should a repair contract be purchased as part of the package? What is the tradeoff between paying points or fees to obtain a loan and the interest rate? What options are included for the buyer to ship product to market or to buy in bulk versus packaged?

People, Physical Evidence, Process

As noted and explained earlier, the marketing mix also needs to consider how the farmer will interact with people involved in buying and selling his or her products and inputs, how physical evidence can be used to document and improve communication and understanding, and how the process of marketing can be made easier for all involved. The reader is referred to the several examples mentioned earlier to better understand how to incorporate people, physical evidence, and process into the marketing mix.

Mistakes Will Be Made!

The prudent marketer knows that mistakes will be made. Fundamentally sound pricing decisions will likely not produce the highest price of the year. The market in the current year may not behave as in previous years. Unexpected market shocks may send the price in different directions, so that another person who does not have a plan benefits greatly. However, good fundamental marketing plans and decisions are still the best in the long run. Usset's recommendation is to look at unexpected (but missed) high prices as pricing opportunities for future years, not as a time to try to correct mistakes in the current year.

Even though we know mistakes will be made due to unforeseen events, Usset argues for eliminating five common mistakes to improve any marketing plan. These five common mistakes are:

- Reluctance toward pre-harvest or pre-production marketing even though seasonal price patterns show the possibility of favorable pricing opportunities before production. Insurance can help eliminate some of the uncertainty of not having the physical product to sell after production.
- Failure to understand and track local basis. Basis helps determine local prices and can help determine which pricing tool to use.
- Lack of an exit strategy. Set a rule either through price or time to get out of the market position before losses mount.
- Holding grain in storage too long. Prices usually decline as harvest approaches, so it is good to establish a default date.
- Misunderstanding carrying charges (that is, the value of storing or carrying grain into the future).

This discussion is obviously not the full set of information needed to understand markets and pricing options and tools. The reader interested in more information and details on these marketing and pricing tools is referred to Usset (2007) and many other agricultural marketing books and Web sites.

Historical Price Patterns

Many factors affect prices. Supply and demand forces affect how the marketplace behaves and where the market price is discovered. Since these forces change and move over time, we also see prices change and move over time. It is with these movements that we start to understand what determines changes in prices and how we can forecast prices. We start with systematic or regular price movements and look at irregular price movements or shocks.

Systematic Price Movements

A **trend** is a gradual and sustained increase or decrease in prices over many years. In the last 20–30 years, price trends have been associated with technical change, population growth, increases in international trade, and so on. Changes in consumer tastes and preferences (such as the increase in poultry consumption) can also create a price trend.

Recognition of long-term trends in prices and demand can help a manager make long-run plans and decisions. Profitability projections are different if the price trends are up, stable, or down. If price trends are up or stable, older, less efficient units may remain profitable. Downward price trends will force

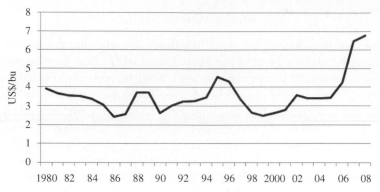

Figure 11.1   Marketing Year Price, All Wheat, United States, 1980–2008
Source: USDA and FAO.

those units out of production. However, expansion may still take place in the face of decreasing demand and lower prices, because new technologies may allow new units to be profitable at lower prices.

Except for the rapid increase in the last few years, the U.S. average price for all wheat does not exhibit any consistent price trend from 1980 to 2008 (Figure 11.1). The average price for rapeseed in Hamburg, Germany, does show a long-term trend upward even without considering the jump and then fall in recent years (Figure 11.2). Historical milk prices in Minnesota and Wisconsin, U.S., do not show a dramatic price trend, but they do show the increase in volatility when price controls were removed (Figure 11.3).

Cyclical movements are repeated patterns of increasing and decreasing prices over several years. These patterns are longer than one year and may be several years long. They are related to lags in production response to price changes and overreactions of producers to price chances.

Twenty years ago, cycles were obvious in hog and beef prices as producers would slowly build up their breeding herds in response to good prices and then slowly decrease them in response to poor prices. Together, producers would build the total breeding herd too large in response to good prices and cut their herds too much in response to poor prices. This slowness to respond and then the over-reaction to price-level changes caused prices to cycle up and down over several years. The beef price cycle was longer than the hog cycle due to the breeding cycle being longer for beef than for hogs. In

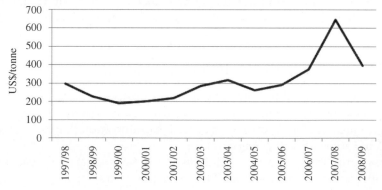

Figure 11.2   Average Price for Rapeseed, Hamburg, Germany, 1997–2009
Source: USDA and FAO.

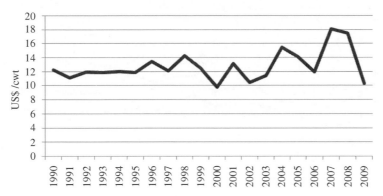

Figure 11.3 Average Annual Class III Milk Price, Minnesota–Wisconsin, 1990–2009
Source: USDA and FAO.

more recent years, these cycles have become less obvious for several factors, including the increasing size of production units that have more stable production levels.

Although cycles are not as obvious today as they once were, a contrarian investor or manager can benefit from knowledge of cycles. The contrarian acts in the opposite manner from the behavior causing the cycle. For example, as others are divesting and decreasing production due to a cyclical downturn in prices, a contrarian manager would be increasing production to be ready when the price turns up. However, the successful implementation of this strategy requires more knowledge than merely the hope that prices may rise. The underlying demand for the product (and any changes occurring) needs to be understood as well as the length of the production cycle and other forces causing the cyclical behavior in the market.

Boom and bust cycles are examples of severe price cycles. Often, the prices never recover from the bust; there is only one cycle. Rapid increases in profitability (or promises of profitability) need to be studied carefully to see whether they are sustainable or are without long-term support.

Seasonal movements are patterns of price changes within the year associated with seasonality in supply and/or demand. Weather and production patterns cause prices to move in similar patterns each year. In a normal weather year, crop prices are at their lowest point in the year at harvest. This can be seen in the average monthly prices for rapeseed at Hamburg, Germany for 2004–2008 (Figure 11.4).

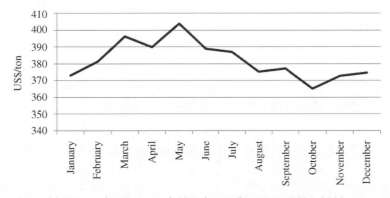

Figure 11.4 Average Monthly Prices for Rapeseed, Hamburg, Germany, 2004–2008
Source: FAO.

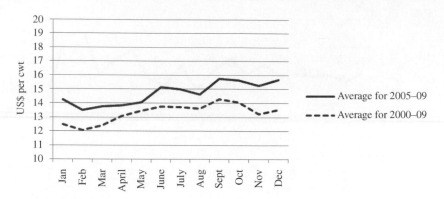

Figure 11.5   Average Monthly Class III Milk Price, Minnesota–Wisconsin, 2000–2009
Source: USDA and FAO.

Livestock prices can also show patterns through the year. Minnesota–Wisconsin milk prices show an obvious pattern of being lower during spring months and increasing through the summer into the fall months (Figure 11.5). Holiday demands for turkeys, hams, and the like create higher prices during parts of the year. For some products, such as Easter lilies and Christmas trees, the demand is so seasonal that, immediately after the holiday, demand disappears and price approaches zero.

   With storable products such as grains, farmers may be able to benefit from seasonal movements in prices. As just noted, harvest prices are typically the lowest of the year, but a few exceptions to this pattern do exist. In years following poor crops, prices tend to be high in the fall and decrease through the year. In years following poor crops, the futures market may provide a signal that the best pricing option is different from the plan used in normal production.

Irregular Price Movements (Shocks)

Irregular price movements result from "sudden and unforeseen" shocks to market supply or demand. Outlook information is especially important to monitor events that may be unusual and thus shocks to the market. Shocks can be local, regional, national, or global and have natural or human causes. Floods, winds, hailstorms, and other destructive storms are examples of weather changes that can cause sudden market shock. Since it develops slowly, a drought is not a sudden shock. However, since it is not expected to last from one year to the next, a drought in the United States is a shock to the market in that year. Political changes, both at home and abroad, can also cause market shocks and sudden price movements. Disruptions in the normal transportation flow of a product, such as a train wreck, labor strike, or damage to the locks, dams, or bridges can cause local and regional fluctuations in prices. Farmers can protect themselves from price shocks through crop insurance and general methods of price protection such as hedging.

General Price Forecasting Methods

Forecasting is the act of striving to see into the future without knowing all impacts and relationships. It is an uncertain science. Forecasting prices can be done by five general methods: commodity balance sheets, econometric models, time series analysis, charting, and historical price movements. Understanding these methods can help a manager understand basic market forces and mechanisms and be better able to formulate his or her own forecast.

Before starting forecasting, a farm manager needs to decide whether a specific price forecast or a forecast price direction is needed. The answer to this question will determine how much work and data are needed and which method should be used.

Commodity Balance Sheets.   Balance sheets are developed to show the "balance" of supply versus disappearance for a commodity. These sheets are developed for both the national and global levels. In a balance sheet for a country, supply of a commodity is estimated from (1) the commodity carried over from the previous year, (2) current year production, and (3) imports during the current year. The disappearance of a commodity is estimated from (1) domestic use, (2) exports during the year, and (3) ending stocks. At the global level, exports and imports are reported as a separate item called "trade" and are not included in the totals of supply and disappearance. Commodity balance sheets can be viewed as the global or national version of an individual farm's estimates of beginning inventory plus production plus purchases compared with estimates of on-farm uses (fed to livestock, for example), sales, and ending inventory.

As an example, in September 2009, USDA's World Agricultural Outlook Board forecasted that the total supply of wheat in the world would be 833 million metric tons for the marketing year starting September 1, 2009 (Table 11.1). This estimate is higher than the supply for the previous two marketing years. This total supply comes mostly from output or production (664 million metric tons) but also comes from the forecasted ending stocks or carryover (169 million metric tons) from the previous year. For the marketing year starting September 1, 2009, the total projected total use or disappearance is 646 million metric tons and the estimated ending stocks or carryover to the next marketing year is estimated to be 187 million metric tons, which is higher than the previous two years.

For crops, production estimates are made from surveys—first, of planting plans, and then of crop condition as the growing season progresses. For livestock, production estimates are made from surveys of animal inventories and productivity estimates. Domestic use is estimated from trends in consumption and population, the estimated impact of any price changes, and other information that can help in forecasting. Exports and imports are projected from past trends and from conditions in international markets. Beginning stocks are the ending stock or carryover from the past year. Ending stocks or carryover from the current year to the next year is calculated as a residual amount.

While large companies do their own forecasting, USDA's reports of production estimates are highly anticipated, and markets can make sudden shifts if the estimates are different from expected levels. The publication dates are known and well publicized, so watching for and reading the information contained in these balance sheets promptly can help a farmer adjust marketing decisions quickly if needed.

Analyzing balance sheets involves looking at the fundamentals of supply versus demand; in balance sheet terms, it is supply versus disappearance. When disappearance is greater than supply, ending stocks decrease and prices tend to increase. If ending stocks from the previous year are high and production and use are at normal levels, prices tend to decrease. Expressing the ending stocks as a percentage of production can be used as an indicator of the pressure on prices. An increasing percentage (as seen over time in wheat in Table 11.1) or a percentage higher than normal indicates pressure for prices to move down. A decreasing percentage as seen over time in coarse grains and milled rice or a percentage lower than normal indicates pressure for prices to move up. For coarse

Table 11.1 World Supply and Use for Grains[1]

Commodity	Output	Total Supply	Trade[2]	Total Use	Ending Stocks	Ending Stocks as % of Total Use
Total grains[3]			Million Metric Tons			
2007/08	2,122	2,464	276	2,100	363	17.3%
2008/09 (Est.)	2,227	2,591	274	2,144	447	20.8%
2009/10 (Proj.)						
August	2,184	2,629	263	2,180	449	20.6%
September	2,187	2,634	264	2,183	451	20.6%
Wheat						
2007/08	611	739	117	616	123	19.9%
2008/09 (Est.)	682	805	139	636	169	26.6%
2009/10 (Proj.)						
August	659	829	123	645	184	28.4%
September	664	833	123	646	187	28.9%
Coarse grains[4]						
2007/08	1,077	1,216	127	1,056	160	15.2%
2008/09 (Est.)	1,100	1,261	107	1,072	188	17.6%
2009/10 (Proj.)						
August	1,092	1,278	110	1,097	182	16.5%
September	1,090	1,278	112	1,099	179	16.3%
Rice milled						
2007/08	433	509	31	428	80	18.8%
2008/09 (Est.)	445	525	28	436	89	20.5%
2009/10 (Proj.)						
August	433	522	30	438	84	19.2%
September	434	523	29	438	85	19.4%

[1] Aggregate of local marketing years.
[2] Based on export estimate. See individual commodity tables for treatment of export/import imbalances.
[3] Wheat, coarse grains, and milled rice.
[4] Corn, sorghum, barley, oats, rye, millet, and mixed grains (for U.S., excludes millet and mixed grains).
Source: World Agricultural Outlook Board, USDA. 2009. World Agricultural Supply and Demand Estimates, WASDE 474, USDA, September 11, 2009, (as updated September 14, 2009), accessed on October 5, 2009 at http://usda.mannlib.cornell.edu/usda/current/wasde/wasde-09-11-2009.pdf. (Current reports are available at http://www.usda.gov/oce/commodity/wasde/.) Ending stocks as % of total use was calculated from data in table.

grains and milled rice, the percentage for the forecast for 2009/10 has dropped slightly compared for 2008/09 so we might expect prices to increase slightly. However, the percentage in 2009/10 is still higher than the percentage in 2007/08, so although prices may be pressured to rise in 2009/10 it may not be as high as it was in 2007/08.

Econometric models.   Econometric models of supply and demand help develop statistical estimates of changes in physical levels and prices. Econometric models are often used to estimate some components of the balance sheets. They are used to estimate the effects and cross-effects of changes in some factors underlying demand and supply for a specific commodity and its substitutes.

Time series analysis is a statistical approach to monitoring changes over time and finding any patterns in those changes. It does not have as strong an economic foundation as the balance sheet or econometric modeling. Thus, time series analysis, while useful for predicting price changes based on past data, cannot explain the underlying behavior of producers and consumers. It also cannot predict the impact of new market shocks because these new shocks have not been seen in earlier data.

Charting. Technical charting is the plotting of prices over time. It allows us to see patterns and trends. Especially in the futures markets, these graphical patterns are used as signals of future price changes. Since it does not have a strong foundation of economic reasoning behind its predictions, charting cannot predict the impact of new changes. However, because so many people understand and follow charting, the market is forced into following some "rules of charting." Thus, it can be useful to follow and understand charts especially for immediate marketing decisions.

Historical Price Movements. Simple statistics and graphs of historical price movements can provide an understanding of past market behavior and the impact of certain factors. As noted earlier, historical data shows U.S. wheat prices having rather high volatility but no clear trend (until recently perhaps); rapeseed prices in Hamburg, Germany, increasing in recent years; and the volatility of milk prices increasing in recent years as price controls were removed in the United States (Figures 11.1–11.3). Historical data also show the average rapeseed price in Hamburg to be at its lowest near harvest and higher in the spring near planting (Figure 11.4). This pattern of low crop prices at harvest is seen in U.S. crops as well. Monthly milk prices show a pattern of being lower in the spring than in the fall for both the recent 5-year average and 10-year average (Figure 11.5).

Simple statistics can also be useful to understand where a current price is in the historical range. For example, in Worthington, Minnesota, the weekly cash corn price was greater than $2.75 per bushel 22% of the time in the ten marketing years from 1998 to 2007 and 44% of the time in the five marketing years from 2003 to 2007 (Table 11.2). This frequency information tells an astute manager that if a cash price greater than $2.75 were to become available in this area, the manager may need to seriously consider selling corn. The fundamentals of the corn market may suggest that not all corn should be sold, but the uncertainties of the market and the certainty of obtaining a historically high price may cause at least

Table 11.2 Percent of Time Weekly Corn Prices Were at or above Specified Prices, Worthington, Minnesota, Marketing Years 1983–2007

US$/bu.	1983–2007 (25 years)	1998–2007 (10 years)	2003–2007 (5 years)
$3.00	13	19	38
$2.75	17	22	44
$2.50	22	24	47
$2.25	39	28	51
$2.00	59	41	60
$1.75	80	71	83
$1.50	93	93	96
$1.25	99	100	100
$1.00	100	100	100

Source: David Bau, *Farm Resource Guide 2009.* Unpublished report, University of Minnesota Extension, Worthington, Minnesota.

some corn to be sold. Recent market movements have altered these percentages, but the example of knowing what a high and low price is in relation to history is the point to learn and use in making marketing decisions. Similar information can be developed for other commodities and markets.

Marketing Control

Control is one of the four main management functions: planning, organizing, directing, and controlling. **Control** is the process of determining and implementing the necessary actions to make certain that plans are transferred into desired results. Through effective control, we are better able to achieve the goals and objectives established in a plan.

In marketing, control takes place in three steps: establishing standards, measuring performance, and, if needed, taking corrective actions. Standards are established during planning (especially during enterprise and whole-farm planning). Examples of marketing standards include expected production levels and prices, needed product-quality levels, timing of production, needed input quantities, and so on. Measuring marketing performance takes place in two ways: monitoring market conditions and recording actual performance by the farm.

Three kinds of corrective actions are used in market control:

1. Change the marketing plan if market conditions change. Forward contract more if prices move up, for example.
2. Change the implementation of the marketing plan. For example, change marketing location if prices improve at locations other than the original, selected location.
3. Change the goals and standards if market conditions change drastically. Raise the expected price for milk when market conditions improve, for example.

As in production control (covered in Chapter 19), marketing control also uses three types of control: preliminary, concurrent, and feedback. When used before crop or livestock production begins, hedging, forward contracting, and options are examples of preliminary control for obtaining expected prices. Concurrent control consists of monitoring current and expected market conditions and taking corrective actions, such as entering the options market to protect prices. Feedback control involves first, analyzing how marketing was done in the past production cycle and how well expectations were met and, second, deciding whether changes in the marketing plan are needed to better meet goals in the next production cycle.

Summary

- The marketing mix consists of four main parts, the Four Ps plus 3 "new" Ps: product, price, place, promotion, people, paper evidence, and process.
- Product can be a physical item or a service.
- Price is determined by the customer and depends on what is included in the product.
- Place is getting the right products in the right quantity to the right place for the lowest possible cost without sacrificing customer service.

- Promotion is aimed at helping the potential customers realize a need and then convincing them your product is the best.
- People include staff, suppliers, customers, and competitors.
- Physical evidence is used for services since a service can't be seen.
- Process involves making the process of finding your farm and your farm's product easily.
- Systematic price movements include trends, cycles, and seasonal patterns.
- A trend is a gradual and sustained increase or decrease in prices over many years.
- Cyclical movements are repeated patterns of increasing and decreasing prices over several years.
- Seasonal movements are patterns of price changes within the year associated with seasonality in supply and/or demand.
- Price shocks or irregular price movements result from sudden and unforeseen shocks to market supply and demand.
- Outlook information and other news needs to be monitored in order to see these unforeseen events as early as possible.
- Forecasting prices can be done by five general methods: balance sheet, econometric modeling, time series analysis, charting, and historical price movements.
- Marketing control consists of three phases: establishing standards, measuring performance, and, if needed, taking corrective actions.

Review Questions

1. Why is it wrong to say that a farmer only needs to worry about producing a good product?
2. What are the seven Ps that make up the marketing mix? How can a farmer use the marketing mix?
3. Compare and contrast the three systematic price movements: trend, cyclical, and seasonal.
4. How can a commodity balance sheet be used in price forecasting?
5. When we need to make decisions based on what prices we think will be in the future, why should we study historical prices?
6. Once the marketing plan has been developed, why should a farmer develop a marketing control plan?
7. How are marketing control standards set?
8. How are corrective actions developed for marketing control?

Further Reading

Bokelmann, Wolfgang, Norbert Hirschauer, and Martin Odening. 2001. ''Marketing.'' Chapter 5 in Martin Odening and Wolfgang Bokelmann. 2001. *Agrarmanagement. Landwirtschaft, Gartenbau (Agrarian Management: Agriculture, Horticulture;* written in German). Stuttgart: Verlag Eugen Ulmer, 372 pp.

Usset, Edward. 2007. ''Grain Marketing Is Simple: It's Just Not Easy.'' St. Paul, Minnesota: Center for Farm Financial Management, University of Minnesota.

12

Financial Statements: Balance Sheet, Income Statement, Statement of Owner's Equity, and Statement of Cash Flows

In this chapter:

- The need for financial information
- The four main financial statements: balance sheet, income statement, owner's equity, and statement of cash flows

How do we know what time it is? If a clock does not have any hands or digits, we cannot tell the time even, if the rest of the clock is running perfectly. If the clock has only one hand or set of digits, we still do not know what time it is. To know the correct time, we need both the hour and minute hands and digits on our clock and some "outside information" on whether it is day or night.

Similarly, we need some "hands" to tell what the "financial time" is on a farm. Even if the business is running well, we do not know how well without a set of financial statements. Also, as with our clock, if we do not know how to build, understand, and interpret the statements, we cannot analyze how well the farm is doing financially. We call this evaluating the financial position and performance of the farm.

In this chapter, we introduce the four main financial statements: balance sheet, income statement, statement of owner's equity, and statement of cash flows. We will look at how they are built and how to understand and interpret the information contained in them. The format of these statements follow the recommendations of the Farm Financial Standards Council (FFSC, 2008). Taken together, the balance sheet, income statement, statement of owner's equity, and statement of cash flows record the progress toward financial goals—both personal and business. In the next chapter, we use these four statements to look much more closely at financial analysis, which evaluates the farm's financial position and performance.

The Balance Sheet

The **balance sheet** (also commonly called the net worth statement) shows the assets and the liabilities of a business on a specific date. It also shows the owner's equity or net worth—that is, the value of the farm's assets minus its liabilities. Based on the information in the balance sheet, we can evaluate a farm's long-run ability to meet financial commitments from its assets—that is, we can assess the farm's solvency.

A balance sheet should be built or developed for three main reasons. First, in order to know the farm's balance between assets and liabilities on a regular basis, a balance sheet should be built at the beginning of each fiscal year. Second, before granting a loan, the lender will likely want to know a current valuation of the farm business. Third, the current owners and potential owners, partners, and other stakeholders will want to know the current status of assets versus liabilities when considering or making a major change in the business such as new investments, rentals, partners, and other changes.

There is a slight difference between the net worth statement and the balance sheet due to the accounting procedure used to develop the information. Decades ago, before computers and even before electronic calculators, accountants kept their handwritten tallies of income, expenses, assets, and liabilities in separate ledgers. Since values were entered twice, once in two different ledgers, the system was called double-entry accounting. When financial statements were prepared, the accountants would compare their hand-calculated total asset values with the sum of separately calculated totals of liabilities and equities. If the comparison showed that the totals were equal, the accounts were said to be "in balance." Hence, we still use the name "balance sheet" for the statement showing assets, liabilities, and equity (or net worth). Today, computers allow us to keep our entries, tallies, and totals differently, but the name "balance sheet" remains.

Structure of the Balance Sheet

The first and most obvious feature of a balance sheet is the separate listing of assets and liabilities, with assets on the left side and liabilities on the right (Table 12.1). An asset is an item owned or controlled by a person or business for holding wealth or producing income. An asset can be a tangible item, such as land, machinery, livestock, supplies, and cash, or it can be an intangible item such as a patent or knowledge. Most farms have only tangible assets. A liability includes debts but has a bigger meaning and can include other claims. A liability is any debt or claim against a person or business, such as a multi-year loan for land, machinery, and livestock; a loan for purchasing seed, fertilizer, or feeder livestock that will be paid back within one year; or a bill at a supplier that has not been paid. The owner's equity or net worth is shown at the bottom of the liability list on the right side. With double-entry accounting, owner's equity is taken from a set of accounts separate from the accounts for assets and liabilities. With single-entry accounting methods, owner's equity or net worth is calculated as the total asset value minus total liabilities. The balance sheet lives up to its name when we check to be sure the total of all assets on the left side equals or "balances" with the total of all liabilities plus equity or net worth on the right side.

Another obvious feature of a balance sheet is the two pairs of columns of numbers: two for assets and two for liabilities.[1] The two pairs of columns are a result of two ways of valuing assets. These two ways will be discussed in more detail later in this chapter, but a short summary here will explain the reason

---

[1] Some institutions and customs do not use the double-column balance sheet. Instead, they report information separately in two tables or in supplementary information.

Table 12.1 Example Balance Sheet Using FFSC's Format

FARM ASSETS			FARM LIABILITIES		
	Cost Basis	Market Value		Cost Basis	Market Value
Cash and checking account	5,000	5,000	Accounts payable	21,267	21,267
Hedging accounts	0	0	Notes due within one year	44,518	44,518
Accounts receivable	12,037	12,037	Current portion of term debt	37,090	37,090
Inventories: crops	229,274	229,274	Accrued interest	0	0
Inventories: market livestock	158,012	158,012	Current portion—deferred taxes	0	0
Prepaid expenses and supplies	59,154	59,154	Other accrued expenses	0	0
Other current assets	0	0	Other current liabilities	0	0
TOTAL CURRENT ASSETS	463,477	463,477	TOTAL CURRENT LIABILITIES	102,875	102,875
Breeding livestock	0	0	Non-current portion—notes payable	83,629	83,629
Machinery and equipment	94,621	322,992	Non-current portion—real estate debt	131,866	131,866
Real estate	406,570	665,570	Non-current portion—deferred taxes	xx	164,385
Buildings and improvements	199,423	281,742	Other non-current liabilities	0	0
Other assets	9,816	27,215			
TOTAL NON-CURRENT ASSETS	710,430	1,297,519	TOTAL NON-CURRENT LIABILITIES	215,495	379,880
			TOTAL BUSINESS LIABILITIES	318,370	482,755
			FARM BUSINESS EQUITY	855,537	1,278,241
			(Retained capital + valuation equity)		
TOTAL BUSINESS ASSETS	1,173,907	1,760,996	TOTAL BUSINESS LIABILITIES AND OWNER EQUITY	1,173,907	1,760,996
TOTAL PERSONAL ASSETS[a]	120,044	126,826	TOTAL PERSONAL LIABILITIES[a]	3,572	5,471
TOTAL ASSETS	1,293,951	1,887,822	TOTAL LIABILITIES	321,942	488,226
			TOTAL NET WORTH	972,009	1,399,596

[a]Since business and personal finances are closely related for many farm families, personal assets and liabilities are often listed on a farm's balance sheet, as they are for this example. They should not be comingled with business assets and liabilities but kept as separate line items.

for two columns. The traditional accounting method of valuing an asset is to start with its original basis or cost when purchased and then subtract any depreciation taken since it was purchased. This is called the cost basis method; it uses values that are easy to document and create little debate.

However, asset values do change over time in the market. The asset value determined by the cost basis value does not always provide an accurate estimate of what the asset could sell for in the market. This can easily be seen in land purchased several years ago. Except for a few periods, land prices have an upward trend. Thus, the cost basis value of land purchased earlier may be significantly lower than its current price. This situation happens with other assets too, but perhaps not in such an obvious way as with land, since land is usually owned longer than other assets. The opposite situation can also happen when market prices drop and the market value is less than the cost basis value. For example, when new technology becomes available, the market may drop the price of old machinery faster than the rate of depreciation so the market value is actually less than the cost basis value.

Since owners and managers need to know the cost basis value for some decisions and the market value for other decisions, the double-column balance sheet was developed. On the asset side of the balance sheet, the cost basis column shows the asset value as the original cost minus depreciation (or a related method) and the market value column shows an estimate of what the assets could be sold for in the market (after selling costs are subtracted) on the date the balance sheet was prepared. The cost basis value is quite reliable since it is based on known or "hard" numbers. The market value has to be viewed as a "softer" number because it is an estimate based on a subjective view of the market. (Asset valuation methods are discussed later in this chapter.)

The double columns of cost basis value and market value are also on the liability side of the balance sheet due to the potential taxes if assets were to be sold. If an asset is sold for a price greater than its cost basis, income results and, in the United States at least, the government says the capital gain is taxable. If an asset is sold for less than its cost basis, the farm incurs a loss and that loss can be used to decrease taxable income and thus taxes. Therefore, lines are included on the liability side for what are called deferred taxes, because they are not due now but are estimated to be due if assets are sold for the values listed in the market value column on the asset side. In the United States, current assets such as inventories, prepaid expenses, and supplies can create taxable income if they are sold at values greater than their cost; so deferred taxes are possible for current liabilities in both the cost basis and market value columns. For non-current assets, deferred taxes are not included in the cost basis column of liabilities because non-current assets are valued at cost and would not create taxable income if sold at those values. All other liabilities (loans, accounts payable, for example) are the same in the two columns.

In the example balance sheet, the total business asset value is $1,173,907 using a cost basis value and $1,760,996 using a market value. The difference is due to either market prices rising after an asset was purchased or the amount of depreciation taken being greater than the actual decline in market value. For land and buildings, the market price rise is likely the reason for the difference. For machinery, equipment, and livestock, a fast depreciation or write-down is the likely reason. For example, a large harvester that is expensed quickly for tax management reasons at the end of its first year will likely still have a high market value in its second year.

Since the market value of the assets is higher than the cost basis, the owner would be required (in the United States) to pay taxes on the difference in values if sold. Therefore, based on the owner's potential income level, an estimate of $164,385 in deferred taxes is listed as a liability in the market value column; other liabilities remain the same. In the example, total business liabilities are $318,370 under cost basis and $482,755 under market value.

Net worth or equity is the difference between total asset value and total liabilities. In the example, business net worth or equity is $855,537 using cost basis values and $1,278,241 using market values. The cost basis estimate can be interpreted as a solid, hard estimate, while the market value estimate has to be interpreted as a soft estimate due to the uncertainty of the real value of the assets in the market. The owner could use the cost basis estimate to convince a banker of the solid financial position of the business and the larger market value estimate to support the argument for a larger loan to expand the business. The market value net worth also shows progress toward financial goals such as increasing net worth or size of business. The market value net worth also can be used for decisions such as the timing and wisdom of retirement from active farming.

Looking further into the balance sheet, we see that the FFSC format divides the assets into current and non-current assets. Current assets are unrestricted cash and assets that will be converted into cash, consumed, or sold in the normal course of business within 12 months. Examples of current assets include cash, checking accounts, grain in storage, livestock held for sale, and accounts receivable. All other assets are classified as non-current assets because they have a useful life greater than one year, are usually not purchased for resale in the normal flow of business, and are used but not destroyed in the production of salable products or services.

Table 12.2 Example Personal Balance Sheet Using FFSC's Format

PERSONAL ASSETS	Cost Basis	Market Value	PERSONAL LIABILITIES	Cost Basis	Market Value
Cash and checking account	4,484	4,484	Current notes	3,572	3,572
Savings accounts	0	0	Accounts payable	0	0
Readily marketable securities	7,001	7,001	Accrued interest	0	0
Other current assets	5,900	5,900	Current portion of term debt	0	0
TOTAL CURRENT ASSETS	17,385	17,385	TOTAL CURRENT LIABILITIES	3,572	3,572
Retirement accounts	19,597	19,597	Non-current portion—notes payable	0	0
Cash value of life insurance	10,784	10,784	Non-current portion—real estate debt	0	0
Non-farm equipment	5,487	5,487	Non-current portion—deferred taxes	xx	1,899
Household goods	7,615	7,615	Other non-current liabilities	0	0
Non-farm real estate	36,023	40,562			
Other non-current assets	23,153	25,396			
TOTAL NON-CURRENT ASSETS	102,659	109,441	TOTAL NON-CURRENT LIABILITIES	0	1,899
TOTAL PERSONAL ASSETS	120,044	126,826	TOTAL PERSONAL LIABILITIES	3,572	5,471
			PERSONAL NET WORTH	116,472	121,355

Liabilities are claims on the assets of a business by outside entities (such as, banks and other lenders). Liabilities are classified in the same way as assets. If a debt is due within 12 months, it is a current liability. Operating notes is a common name for loans that are held less than 12 months and used to finance the current year's operations. Accounts payable, accrued interest, and government crop loans are current liabilities. Any loan payment due within the next 12 months is classified as a current liability even if the loan is a multi-year or term loan. The "current portion of term debt" of $37,090 is listed in the example balance sheets as a current debt. The remaining portion of that debt is included as the "Non-current portion—notes payable" ($83,629) and "Non-current portion—real estate debt" ($131,866).

As noted earlier, personal and business finances are closely related for many farm families. However, the manager should prepare separate balance sheets to make the line very obvious between farm business and personal assets and liabilities. Personal information should not be comingled with business information. This separation allows the owner and manager to keep a better distinction between business and family assets and liabilities and still see the entire financial position of the family. Bankers, partners, and other stakeholders will see this separation as a positive way to build trust between stakeholders. Personal net worth for the example farm was estimated to $116,472 on a cost basis and $121,355 on a market value basis (Table 12.2).

At times, total personal assets and liabilities are included at the bottom of the business balance sheet (as in Table 12.1). Adding the farm business and personal information together, the total net worth of this example farm owner is $972,009 on a cost basis and $1,399,596 on a market value basis.

Building a Balance Sheet

There are three main steps in building a balance sheet. First, a list or inventory of the farm's resources needs to be taken. Second, a value needs to be placed on each of those resources. Third, a record of the liabilities or claims against those assets needs to be developed.

Taking an Inventory. The inventory of resources is a list of all the farm assets on a given date. The inventory is a valuable piece of knowledge for a manager. Besides building a balance sheet, other reasons for having an up-to-date inventory include (a) providing a basis for determining the extent to which resources are available or lacking; (b) showing the condition of machinery, equipment, and improvements; and (c) providing information needed for the preparation of income tax statements, potential insurance claims, or rental agreements. An inventory can also be a larger management tool for planning, by including more than the usual list of physical and financial assets. These additional items include the available line of credit, managerial abilities, land and buildings that could be rented or purchased, and so on. The three main times for taking an inventory are the same as noted earlier for building a balance sheet: (1) at the beginning of each fiscal year, (2) when applying for a loan, and (3) when considering or making a major change in the business.

The job of preparing the inventory can be made easier if it is done in an orderly process. One such process is described in the following steps.

1. Start with the land:
   a. Proceed from field to field until the entire farm is covered.
   b. Identify the fields and building sites on a map.
   c. Note in each field:
      i. Size of the field, soil type, topography, condition
      ii. Crop planted, if any, and its stage, condition, expected yield
      iii. Improvements such as fences, tiles, irrigation systems, bridges, etc. Be sure these improvements are entered in the farm's depreciation schedule.
2. Buildings should be listed next after the land:
   a. Note the type of structure, size, use, and condition. Be sure these are entered in the farm's depreciation schedule.
   b. While at each building, record its contents: grain, hay, other feedstuffs, livestock, machinery, chemicals, and other supplies. Also, record the information noted below for each type of asset found in the building.
3. Livestock should be listed by kind, age, sex, weight, condition, and location. Breeding and working livestock should be entered in the depreciation schedule.
4. Machinery, equipment, implements, and tools should be identified by manufacturer, use, capacity or size, serial or identification number, condition, and location. These should be entered in the farm's depreciation schedule.
5. Operating inputs (seed, feed, fuel, fertilizer, spare parts, etc.) should be listed by type, kind, amount, condition, and location.
6. Harvested crops:
   a. From both on-farm and off-farm storage sites.
   b. Note the type, amount, condition, and location.
   c. If needed, note the weight of the units (60 bags of barley @ 80# each, for example).
7. Financial assets:
   a. Cash on hand and in liquid accounts
   b. Stocks, bonds
   c. Deferred patronage dividends
   d. Accounts receivable

    e. Available lines of credit
    f. Other financial assets
  8. Managerial knowledge, experience, skill, and ability.
  9. For many farms, family records are needed to provide complete information for analysis and planning. These records include:
    a. Personal expenses
    b. Off-farm income and expenditures
    c. Investments and other assets
    d. Farm products used by family
10. Availability of other resources that could be purchased, rented, or hired. This list should cover land, buildings, machinery, labor, custom work services, etc. This list is very useful in planning the operation and growth of a farm.

Asset Valuation. Since different asset valuation methods can result in very different asset values, the analyst has to know which methods were used in order to interpret the balance sheet information and, thus, interpret the true financial position of a farm. The biggest distinction between methods is the choice between using a cost-less-depreciation basis or a current market value basis. These are commonly called "cost basis" and "market value." The names are very literal. The cost basis value is the original basis of the asset minus any depreciation taken since it was purchased. The original basis is the cash paid for the asset adjusted for the cost basis of any assets traded as part of the purchase. The cost basis is also called the "book value." GAAP prefers the cost-less-depreciation method since the original cost and actual depreciation taken can be found in the farm's records. The market value is the value of the asset on the open market minus any selling commissions. The differences between cost basis and market basis values are typically larger for assets purchased several years before the preparation of the balance sheet. For example, the market value of land will be closer to the purchase price of land bought last year than to the purchase price of land bought 15 years ago.

    The basic methods of asset valuation are listed below. The list starts with methods for assets with a short economic life (such as supplies, feed, and fertilizer) and finishes with methods for assets with long economic lives (such as land and buildings). The recommended methods for valuing different types of assets are listed in Table 12.3.

Cost

This method uses the original purchase price as the current value of an asset such as feed, fuel, and fertilizer. Small tools such as hammers and wrenches may be valued using the cost method. If current market conditions have changed the prices considerably since the asset was purchased, the current price is a more accurate estimate of current market value. The value also may be adjusted for wear and damage if necessary.

    For the cost to be valid, specific information and identification of the asset is needed. This information could be found during the steps for taking an inventory described earlier in this chapter. Otherwise, an average price paid recently could be used for fuel or feed, for example.

    Alternatively, for supplies stored and replenished throughout the year, an inventory control system needs to be chosen. FIFO (first in, first out) assumes items purchased first are used first; thus, items purchased most recently are in inventory and the most recent prices are used to value the inventory. LIFO (last in, first out) assumes items purchased most recently are used first; thus, the

Table 12.3   Recommended Asset Valuation Methods by Asset Type

Asset Type	Recommended Valuation Method or Choice
Current assets to be sold within one year (slaughter cattle and hogs, grain, for example)	Expected selling price minus selling costs
Supplies (feed, fertilizer, machinery parts, for example)	Cost
Growing annual crops	a. If crop is not mature: incurred cash costs adjusted for any damage b. If crop is close to harvest: market value minus harvest and selling costs
Machinery, breeding livestock, and other intermediate assets	a. Cost basis: original basis or purchase price less any depreciation taken b. Market value: expected selling price minus selling costs.
Buildings, real estate improvements and other long-term depreciable assets	a. Cost basis: original basis or purchase price less any depreciation taken b. Market value: expected selling price minus selling costs. c. Replacement cost less a depreciation amount reflecting the age of the asset d. Replacement cost for equivalent function less depreciation
Farmland	a. Cost: original basis or purchase price b. Income capitalization c. Market value: expected selling price minus selling costs

inventory consists of items purchased earlier so earlier prices are used. In most situations, FIFO is the recommended method to keep values close to the current market conditions.

Net selling price
This method uses the current market price minus any costs of selling the asset. The current market price and any selling costs can be found or estimated by checking local markets and calculating transportation, commission, and other selling costs.

Purchase cost less depreciation
This method uses the original cost of the asset and subtracts the accumulated depreciation. This information is usually found in the business' depreciation schedule or list of assets such as machinery, equipment, breeding livestock, and buildings.

Replacement cost less depreciation
This method is similar to the previous method of purchase cost less depreciation. During periods of inflation or deflation, using the replacement cost will provide a more accurate estimate of owner equity. The information is not listed in the depreciation schedule, but similar methods should be used to estimate replacement cost less depreciation.

Replacement cost for equivalent function less depreciation

This method is useful when trying to estimate the value of assets (usually buildings) that have been renovated for new purposes. This method is needed when new production methods are developed that cause old methods and thus old buildings to be inefficient and obsolete. Rather than leave a building empty when its roof and walls are still solid, an owner may renovate the inside for new uses. The new uses may be for a new product or as only one part of a new design. For example, the old livestock barn that housed different types and ages of livestock may be renovated to be a calving and calf-raising center within a now larger dairy operation. Instead of building a new building, the owner chose renovation instead. This method of using the replacement cost for a new building allows the owner's equity in the renovated building to be estimated based on the productive value of the building.

Income capitalization

This method bases the value of an asset on its ability to produce future income for the owner. This method is usually used for land and buildings, which last for several years and produce income in each year. The name, "income capitalization," comes from the process that is called "capitalizing" future income into the asset value. (We will discuss the specific procedure in more detail in Chapter 20.)

Market value

This method bases the value of an asset on the value of similar assets that have sold in the market. For example, an unsold piece of land can be compared to recent sales of land nearby, and a value can be estimated after adjusting for differences in soil quality, location, and other characteristics. (We will discuss this method in more detail in Chapter 20.)

Liability information. A record of liabilities is needed to determine the financial position of the farm and its ability to obtain additional capital. Liability records include:

1. Loan information: date, form, purpose, amount, length, rate (and other specifications if it is a non-traditional loan)
2. Current portions of the principal and interest payments
3. Accounts payable
4. Unpaid, accrued interest
5. Delinquent principal and interest payments
6. Credit and debit card account information
7. Personal liabilities

The information obtained from these three steps (inventory, asset valuation, and liability records) is combined to build the balance sheet. The assets that were identified in the inventory are grouped into current and non-current assets and listed on the left side of the sheet. If needed, the non-current assets could be further categorized as intermediate and long-term assets. The value of each asset is written next to each asset. If the list of assets is long (as it often is), separate lists, or schedules as they are called, are kept by type (machinery, for example) and the subtotals are shown in the balance sheet. If the double-column balance sheet is being used, both the cost basis and market values are shown. If only one method of asset valuation is to be used, the balance sheet should be clearly identified as having only cost basis values or market values and only those values should be used.

Liabilities are also grouped into current and non-current liabilities (and, if needed, intermediate and long-term). The portion of non-current liabilities that are due in the next 12 months should be added to the current liabilities and, to avoid double counting, subtracted from the total amount of that liability. For example, next year's principal payment for a five-year machinery loan is a current liability and any remaining balance after next year is included as the "non-current portion."

If market values are being used in the balance sheet, any taxes that would be incurred, if the asset were indeed sold, need to be estimated and listed as deferred taxes.

Income Statement

The income statement shows the farm's income, the costs incurred to produce that income, and the resulting net farm income for a certain period of time. It is used to measure profitability and is also called the profit/loss statement or even the "P and L" in short. The income statement includes both cash and non-cash income and expenses and usually covers a period of one year. Since it includes depreciation and amortization of capital assets, the income statement does not include transactions such as machinery purchases or sales and loan principal payments or receipts.

U.S. farmers have a choice of two ways to keep their accounts, and their choice affects the income statement format and income calculations. The two choices are cash accounting and accrual accounting. With a cash accounting system, income and expenses are recorded when received or paid (or considered to be received or paid). The exception to this is the money paid for machinery, buildings, and other capital assets depreciated over a period of years. Although all income and expenses are considered and counted eventually, the cash system does not accurately measure income attributable to a specific year or production period because it does not include changes in inventory.

With an accrual accounting system, transactions are recorded as production occurs or expenses are committed—regardless of whether they are received or paid (or considered to be received or paid). The accrual accounting system does account for changes in inventory, and thus the accrual system more accurately measures income generated within one year. That makes the accrual system better for evaluating business results and plans, and it is the system used in the examples in this section.

Structure of the Income Statement

Using FFSC's gross revenue format,[2] the income statement has six main sections: revenues, operating expenses, financing expenses, other revenue and expenses, income tax expense, and extraordinary items after tax (Table 12.4). Inventory changes are separated into changes in crop inventories, market livestock inventories, base value of raised breeding livestock, other receivables, feed and supplies, prepaid expenses, and accounts payable. Inventory changes related to revenue are listed

---

[2] The FFSC also describes an alternative format that shows the Value of Farm Production (VFP). The differences between the two FFSC formats are in the treatment of items purchased and held for sale later—feeder cattle, for example. In the gross revenue format, the costs of these items are listed with all other operating costs. In the VFP format, the costs of these items are subtracted from gross revenue (before other costs are subtracted) to estimate the value added by the farm after accounting for purchase price of these items. The VFP format is preferred by people who want to see the contribution of a farm versus the sales of a farm. The FFSC recommends the Gross Revenue format in order to move agricultural financial reporting closer to GAAP standards, so the VFP format is not discussed in detail in this text.

Table 12.4   Example Income Statement Using FFSC's Gross Revenue Format

Revenues			
Crop revenues (cash)	221,206		
Increase/(Decrease) in crop inventories	15,157		
Total Crop Revenues		236,363	
Market livestock (cash)	213,121		
Livestock products	0		
Increase/(Decrease) in market livestock inventories	39,485		
Total Market Livestock Revenues		252,606	
Raised breeding livestock sales (cash)	0		
Increase/(Decrease) in base value of raised breeding livestock	0		
Total Breeding Livestock Revenues		0	
Crop insurance proceeds	0		
Government programs	52,111		
Increase/(Decrease) in other receivable	4,105		
Other farm income	77,023		
Total Other Operating Revenues		133,239	
Gross Revenues			**622,208**
Operating Expenses			
Operating expenses (cash)	332,778		
Cost of purchased feed (cash)	45,133		
Increase/(Decrease) in feed and supplies inventories	15,157		
Cost of feeder livestock purchased (cash)	12,303		
Increase/(Decrease) in prepaid expenses	(7,308)		
Increase/(Decrease) in accounts payable	(6,218)		
Depreciation expense	62,836		
Total Operating Expenses		439,524	
Operating Margin			**182,684**
Financing Expenses			
(Interest income)	0		
Interest, current loans (cash)	8,989		
Increase/(Decrease) in interest payable on current loans	0		
Interest, non-current loans (cash)	17,978		
Increase/(Decrease) in interest payable on non-current loans	0		
Total Financing Expenses		26,967	
Net Farm Income from Operations			**155,717**
Other Revenue and Expense			
Cash received from disposition of property, equipment, etc.	0		
Less: Net book value of farm assets sold	0		
Total Gain (Loss) on Sale of Assets		0	
Miscellaneous revenue (with accrual changes if any)	0		
Miscellaneous expense (with accrual changes if any)	0		
Net Miscellaneous Revenue and Expense		0	
Net Farm Income, Accrual Adjusted			**155,717**
Income Tax Expense			
Income tax expense (cash)	0		
Increase/(Decrease) in accrued income tax	0		
Income Tax Expense		0	
Net Income before Extraordinary Items			**155,717**
Extraordinary Items after tax		0	
Net Income, Accrual Adjusted			**155,717**

as part of revenue, and expenses related inventory change are listed as part of expenses. Depreciation is included as part of operating expenses. In FFSC's gross revenue format, gross revenue is $622,208 and operating expenses are $439,524.

Since the FFSC format lists interest and other financing costs in a separate category, the operating margin can be calculated. The operating margin is gross revenue minus operating expenses, which is the return from operating the farm before the impact of financing decisions. In the example, operating margin is $182,684.

Financing expenses include any interest income (listed as a negative expense), cash interest paid, and changes in interest payable. Cash interest paid and changes in interest payable are separated between current and non-current loans. In the example, the total financing expenses are $26,967.

After subtracting the financing expenses from the operating margin, net farm income from operations is $155,717. The example farm has no other revenue and expense so the net farm income, accrual adjusted, is also $155,717. Since this is an accrual measure (that is, adjusted for inventory changes), this is an accurate picture of how this farm performed in this particular year. Income tax expense and extraordinary items are zero for this farm.

Building an Income Statement

Building an income statement depends on the development of the farm's records of sales, expenses, and cash flow for the year and the inventory and balance sheet information. Cash income and expenses are taken from the farm's accounts. Inventory information is assembled as described in the steps earlier. Any purchases and sales of inventory items are included in the inventory section if they are not included in cash income and expenses. Depreciation information is assembled from the farm's depreciation schedule with purchases and sales taken from the farm's cash flow accounts if this information is not in the depreciation schedule. This information is listed in the appropriate sections of the income statement, and the calculations are made to find net farm income.

Statement of Owner Equity

The statement of owner's equity shows the allocation of the change in owner's equity between changes in contributed capital and retained earnings, market valuation of assets, change in non-current deferred taxes, and change in personal net worth. It explains how and why the owner's equity changed during the year. The statement is developed from the income statement and the balance sheet. The change in retained earnings was projected to be $87,701 since there were no capital contributions or distributions for the example farm (Table 12.5). The retained earnings came from the net income ($155,717) after the family living withdrawals ($68,016) are subtracted. The example farm gained $191,345, mostly from the market value appreciation of real estate and buildings. Market value appreciation is calculated from the changes in market value between the beginning and ending balance sheets adjusted for changes in cost basis. The total change in business owner equity for the example farm was a positive $328,973. The positive change in personal net worth of $1,882 completes the allocation of the change in owner equity between the beginning of the year and the end of the year.

Table 12.5 Example Statement of Owner Equity

	Subtotal	Total
Owner Equity, Beginning of Period (market value)		**1,068,741**
Changes in Contributed Capital and Retained Earnings:		
Net income/loss (business income statement)	155,717	
Withdrawals for family living	−68,016	
Capital contributions: debt forgiveness/gifts/inheritances	0	
Capital distributions: dividends/gifts/inheritances	0	
Total Change in Contributed Capital and Retained Earnings:	**87,701**	
Changes in Market Valuation (market value over cost basis) of:		
Breeding livestock	0	
Machinery and equipment	−13,228	
Farm real estate	148,900	
Buildings	42,044	
Other farm capital assets	13,629	
Total Change in Market Valuation	**191,345**	
Change in Non-current Portion of Deferred Taxes	**49,927**	
Total Change in Valuation Equity	**241,272**	
Total Change in Farm Business Owner Equity		**328,973**
Change in Value of Personal Assets (Market Value)	2,418	
Less: Increase in Personal Liabilities	536	
Personal Net Worth Change		**1,882**
Net Worth Ending of Period		**1,399,596**

Statement of Cash Flows

The statement of cash flows shows the sources and uses of cash in the business—that is, how cash entered and left the business. It shows what activities provided cash flow into and what activities used or caused cash to flow out of the business. The FFSC format has three main sections that show the net cash provided or used by (1) operating activities, (2) investing activities, and (3) financing activities with summary and loan balance information at the bottom (Table 12.6). For the example farm, operating activities provided $146,280 while investing activities used $58,298 and financing activities used $96,502. The three sections of the FFSC show very clearly where cash is provided or used. The summary at the bottom shows the beginning cash balance was $13,520 and the ending cash balance was $5,000.

This chapter introduced the four main financial statements: the balance sheet, the income statement, the statement of owner's equity, and the statement of cash flows. These four statements form the basis for evaluating the financial condition and performance, which is discussed in the next chapter.

Table 12.6 Example Statement of Farm Business Cash Flows Using FFSC Format

	Annual
Cash provided—production income	563,461
Cash used for feeder livestock, purchased feed, and other items for resale	57,436
Cash used for operating expenses	332,778
Cash used for interest	26,967
Net cash used for income and Social Security taxes	0
Net cash provided—other operating activities	0
Net cash provided—other miscellaneous revenue	0
Net cash provided/used by operating activities	146,280
Cash provided from disposition of breeding livestock	0
Cash provided from disposition of machinery and equipment	2,127
Cash provided from disposition of real estate and buildings	0
Cash provided from disposition of marketable securities	0
Cash used for acquisition of breeding livestock	0
Cash used for acquisition of machinery and equipment	37,167
Cash used for acquisition of real estate and buildings	9,908
Cash used for acquisition of marketable securities	13,350
Net cash provided/used by investing activities	−58,298
Cash provided by operating loans	11,146
Cash provided by term debt financing	0
Cash provided from capital contributions, gifts, inheritances	0
Cash used for principal payments on term debt	34,350
Cash used for principal on capital lease obligations	0
Cash used to repay operating and CCC loans	5,282
Owner withdrawals	68,016
Dividends and capital distributions	0
Net cash provided/used by financing activities	−96,502
Net increase (decrease) in cash/cash equivalents	−8,520
Cash/cash equivalents at beginning of year	13,520
Cash/cash equivalents at end of year	5,000
Beginning operating debt	59,921
Less repays	5,282
Plus borrowings	11,146
Equals ending (calculated)	65,785
Ending—actual	65,785

Summary

- Financial statements are needed to analyze financial position and performance.
- Financial position refers to the total resources controlled by a business compared to the claims against those resources.
- Financial performance refers to the results of decisions over time.

- The four main financial statements are balance sheet, income statement, statement of owner's equity, and statement of cash flows.
- The balance sheet shows the assets and liabilities on a specific date.
- The income statement shows the difference between the gross income and the costs incurred to produce that income.
- The statement of owner's equity shows the allocation of the change in owner's equity between changes in contributed capital and retained earnings, market valuation of assets, change in non-current deferred taxes, and change in personal net worth.
- The state of cash flows shows the sources and uses of cash in the business—how cash entered and left the business.

Review Questions

1. Describe the balance sheet in terms of its content, structure, and purpose.
2. Describe the income statement in terms of its content, structure, and purpose.
3. Describe the statement of owner's equity in terms of its content, structure, and purpose.
4. Describe the statement of cash flows in terms of its content, structure, and purpose.
5. What is the difference between current and non-current assets and liabilities?
6. What is the difference between market value and cost basis value?
7. Why are inventory changes included in an accrual income statement?
8. Identify the appropriate financial statement(s) for each of the following items and where on that statement the value should be placed. Some will be entered in more than one statement.

Hog sales, $45,000
Hired labor, $58,000
Corn sales, $155,000
Fertilizer expense, $235,000
Unpaid feed bill, $72,500
Depreciation, $133,000
New tractor, $185,000
New tractor loan, $145,000
Current portion of new tractor loan, $25,216
Non-current portion—deferred taxes, $30,000

Purchased feed, $95,000
Unpaid family labor, $25,000
Corn in storage, $125,000
Prepaid fertilizer expense, $75,000
Farm truck, book value, $25,500
Farm land loan payment, $229,000
New operating note from bank, $250,000
Cash sale of old tractor, $20,000

Further Reading

Barry, Peter J., Paul N. Ellinger, John A. Hopkin, and C. B. Baker. 2000. *Financial Management in Agriculture*. 6th ed. Danville, Illinois: Interstate Publishers, 678 pp.

Farm Financial Standards Council (FFSC). 2008. *Financial Guidelines for Agricultural Producers*. Menomonee Falls, Wisconsin: Farm Financial Standards Council.

13

Financial Analysis

In this chapter:

- Measures of financial position and performance
- Liquidity, solvency, profitability, repayment capacity, and financial efficiency
- Initial analysis, benchmarking, enterprise analysis
- Diagnostic analysis
- An example analysis

Let us consider and evaluate two farms. Farmer A produced 200,000 bushels of corn, and Farmer B produced 100,000 bushels of corn. Who is the better farmer?

Well, we have trouble answering that question because we don't know anything else about these farms. All we know is how big their total production was.

Now suppose we find that Farm A had 1,300 acres of corn and Farm B had 600 acres of corn. This additional information allows us to see each farm's total production relative to its resources—that is, land used for producing corn. We can calculate that Farm A's average yield was 154 bushels per acre and Farm B's was 167. We also hear that both farms had normal rainfall and no unusual pest problems. Now can we decide who is the better farmer?

Well, we could easily be tempted to say Farmer B was better, because his yield was higher. Farmer B produced less total corn and had fewer acres, but we don't know what else he did. We still don't know much about these farms.

Suppose we learn that farms in close proximity to Farm A with similar soil quality had an average corn yield of 145 bushels per acre and that farms close to Farm B with similar soil quality had an average corn yield of 175 bushels per acre. Who is the better farmer?

Now we might be more willing to say Farmer A is better because her corn yield is higher than her neighbors' average yield on similar soil quality. We can evaluate each farm's performance in terms of yield relative to the performance of others. We see that Farm A is performing better than the average, and Farm B is performing below the average of its comparable farms.

Farmer A has more acres, so we can think of her as having the bigger farm. Farmer B's farm has a higher yield, so his performance is higher by that measure. However, not until we know the average yields of others do we have some kind of benchmark or relative measure so we can begin to make an evaluation or comparison of these two farms.

We know and use many measures in our daily lives—both absolute measures and relative measures. For example, we see the total amount on our paycheck and estimate what we can and can't do with that amount of money. Converting that paycheck number to our pay per hour gives us another perspective and point of comparison to other jobs and our choice for leisure.

Similarly, we discuss the speed and fuel efficiency of cars without thinking too hard about the fact that both are relative measures. We know that a safe speed varies with road, traffic, and weather conditions. We know what good and poor fuel efficiency are and that "good and poor" vary with type of vehicle and whether we're in the city or on the highway. We discuss fuel prices without mentioning the volume that can be purchased at that price. We know all these pieces of information and many more in our daily lives because we have grown up with them and used them so often and for so long.

However, new discussions can move us into new areas where we don't have an immediate understanding of the terms and measures, and this is often the case with financial analysis. Remembering that we are comfortable with many terms, measures, and ratios in our daily lives because we have used them for years should give us the confidence that over time and through repeated use and discussion, we can also learn this new language called financial analysis.

If financial analysis is new to you, please read this chapter quickly the first time, looking for terms and ideas, but ignoring equations and numbers. Then reread it looking especially at the short list of measures (not all of them, just the short list). Note the good and poor ranges for the measures. Read the example financial analyzes to catch terms, phrases, and reasons. Work on the problems at the end. Reread the chapter again. We know about the car's speed and fuel efficiency only because we have used those terms many, many times. It will eventually be that way with financial analysis too; just start with little steps and keep going back to learn more.

In Chapter 12, we started with the idea that we don't know what time it is if our clock does not have any hands or digits. We compared that to a farmer not knowing what the "financial time" is on his or her farm if he or she has not prepared and analyzed the financial position and performance of the farm.

To start understanding "financial time," the previous chapter described how to build and understand the four main financial statements: balance sheet, income statement, statement of owner's equity, and statement of cash flows. These statements are essentially the hands of the clock, but the data in those statements need to be interpreted in order to understand the "financial time." Now we will find out how to read and understand the hands of the financial clock.

In this chapter, we introduce and describe the major financial measures for evaluating financial position and performance. Financial position refers to the total resources controlled by a business and the claims against those resources. In other words, financial position is the value of a firm's assets compared to its debts. Financial performance refers to the results of management decisions over time. In other words, financial performance looks at how well assets were used to produce net income to the owners and the size of that income compared to total asset value and owner's equity.

The purpose of financial analysis is to:

1. analyze the farm's position and performance and
2. find opportunities and problems.

This analysis helps a manager develop potential solutions to the problems identified and plans to take advantage of those opportunities. Financial analysis consists of evaluating the financial measures. Then the farm manager uses her or his knowledge of the farm, industry, and situation and his or her creativity and wisdom to develop the solutions and plans.

However, what we often see first are symptoms and not the actual problems or opportunities. For example, while low income is a big problem, it is not one that can be corrected directly. Low income is a symptom of problems elsewhere in the farm business—problems such as small size, high input costs, too much machinery, too many workers, improper animal nutrition, poor crop yields, poor marketing, bad weather, the wrong strategy, and so on. The first step is to find the symptoms. Then, as explained in the last section on diagnostic analysis, we explore and analyze the business in depth to find the problems that can be solved.

Several points need to be remembered in financial analysis. First, an initial analysis should be used to find areas that need more analysis. We should not try to analyze everything and every part of the business in the initial analysis. Second, calculating every possible measure and ratio will only confuse the analyst and the manager. In this chapter, the list of measures and ratios is kept short on purpose. In subsequent analyses, other measures and ratios may be calculated and used to help ferret out the problem whose symptom has been found in the first step of the analysis. Third, financial statements should be interpreted in the light of the history of a farm, the history of its environment, its current environment, its expected future, and its goals and objectives.

This chapter has three main sections. The first section describes the main measures of liquidity, solvency, profitability, repayment capacity, and financial efficiency. The second section describes the procedures for an initial analysis of a farm business (including benchmarking and enterprise analysis). The third section explains diagnostic analysis of problems and opportunities facing the farm business (including financial stress tests). The final section contains an example analysis of a farm with some performance issues.

Measures of Financial Position and Performance

A full assessment of financial position and performance involves evaluating five areas: liquidity, solvency, profitability, repayment capacity, and financial efficiency. Liquidity is the ability to pay debts due in the next 12 months measured at a certain point in time. Solvency is the ability to pay all debts if assets were to be sold at a certain point in time. Profitability is the ability to produce income over a certain time period. Repayment capacity is the ability to meet cash flow obligations over time. Financial efficiency indicates how well financial resources and expenses were used.

Although many measures and ratios could be calculated and analyzed, this section defines and explains the 21 measures recommended by the Farm Financial Standards Council (FFSC) plus the measure of net worth or equity (Table 13.1). These 22 measures are standard and used by many lenders and institutions; they do, however, contain some duplicate information. A shorter list of nine measures is identified in Table 13.1 and can provide a comprehensive view of the financial position and performance of a farm. For those new to financial analysis, understanding the short list of measures should be emphasized first.

The choice of which measures to use for financial analysis depends on the farmer's and creditor's preferences and local customs. Several measures provide the same information because they are merely a rearrangement of numbers. For instance, as will be discussed later, since net worth equals total assets minus total liabilities, the ratio of total liabilities to total assets provides a mirror of the information expressed by the ratio of net worth to total assets.

Both an absolute measure and a relative measure are needed to fully understand solvency, profitability, and repayment capacity. Absolute and relative measures show position and performance in

Table 13.1 Measures of Financial Position and Performance

LIQUIDITY
   Current Ratio (CR)[†]
   Working Capital (WC)
   Working Capital/Gross Revenues (WC/GR) Ratio[†]
SOLVENCY (market value basis)
   Net Worth (NW) or Equity[†]
   Debt/Asset (D/A) Ratio[†]
   Equity/Asset Ratio
   Debt/Equity Ratio
PROFITABILITY (cost basis)
   Net Farm Income (NFI)[†]
   Rate of Return on Assets (ROA)[†]
   Rate of return on Equity (ROE)[†]
   Operating Profit Margin Ratio[†]
   EBITDA (Earnings before interest, taxes, depreciation, and amortization)
REPAYMENT CAPACITY
   Capital Debt Repayment Capacity
   Capital Debt Repayment Margin
   Replacement Margin (RM)[†]
   Term Debt and Lease Coverage Ratio
   Replacement Margin Coverage Ratio (RMCR)[†]
FINANCIAL EFFICIENCY
   Asset Turnover Ratio (market value basis)
   Operating Expense Ratio
   Depreciation/Amortization Expense Ratio
   Interest Expense Ratio
   Net Farm Income from Operations Ratio

Source: Farm Financial Standards Council (2008) except for net worth, which it does not include in its list of 21 measures.
[†]These nine measures are in the short list for evaluating financial position and performance.

different ways. For example, net farm income provides an absolute measure of income that can be compared with the income needs of the farmer. The rate of return to assets (ROA) is a relative measure that shows how well assets or resources were used to generate income. A small set of assets may have been used very efficiently (i.e., with a high ROA), but the resulting income may be too low to feed the family. Alternatively, a high income may provide for a family very well, but the resources were not used efficiently as could be noted in a low ROA. Each of these two problems calls for a different kind of solution. The first problem, good efficiency but low income, calls for increasing the size of the business. The second problem, high income but poor efficiency, calls for management changes to increase efficiency.

The need for both absolute and relative measures is not as strong for liquidity. Two relative measures provide a very good initial evaluation of liquidity. However, an absolute measure is available for the complete picture. (Financial efficiency is only evaluated by relative measures.)

Table 13.2 Measures of Liquidity

	Vulnerable and Strong Levels
Current Ratio (CR)[†]	
The CR is the value of the current assets relative to the current liabilities. The CR shows the farm's ability to meet debt obligations in the next 12 months from current assets, if liquidated.	Although exact levels vary with the type of business, a CR of 1:1 or less is considered vulnerable while a CR of 2:1 is considered strong.
Working Capital (WC)	
Working capital is the money that a farmer has available for use in the current and near future for production. It is a theoretical measure left if all current assets were sold and all current debts were paid.	The amount of working capital needed by a business varies with the type of business, but generally, the higher the WC the better the financial condition of the business.
Working Capital/Gross Revenues (WC/GR) Ratio[†]	
WC/GR shows the size of working capital relative to the size of the business (as measured by gross revenues).	Which levels show vulnerability and strength vary with the type of business, but generally, the higher the ratio the better the financial condition of the business.

[†]These measures are in the short list for evaluating financial position and performance.

Measures of Liquidity

Liquidity is the ability of the firm to meet its financial obligations during the next 12 months. Three primary measures capture liquidity: current ratio, working capital, and the working capital to gross revenue ratio (Table 13.2). Of these three, the current ratio and the working capital to gross revenue ratio are on the short list of measures. Even though these are both relative measures, they are easily understood, whereas the absolute measure of working capital requires a greater understanding of the farm, the risks it faces, and its plans for the future.

The **current ratio** (CR) shows the farm's ability to meet current debt obligations from current assets in the next 12 months. CR is the value of the current assets relative to the current liabilities and is usually written in the form XX:1, but is commonly referred to by just XX in daily conversation. A higher CR indicates greater liquidity. Using FFSC's definition, the current ratio for the example farm in Table 12.1 is 4.5:1, or simply 4.5.

$$\text{Current ratio} = \frac{\text{total current farm assets}}{\text{total current farm liabilities}} = \frac{463,477}{102,875} = 4.5$$

Although interpreting the current ratio depends upon the type of business in which the farm is involved, a current ratio value equal to or greater than 2 generally is considered healthy for farms. This value shows that the farm could cover its current obligations and still have some current working capital. A value of less than 1 obviously should cause concern because it says that the farm could not cover its current obligations from current assets. If the CR is considered too low, the appropriate management response depends on the value of other financial measures and on the circumstances at the time. A value between 1 and 2 is of concern, but requires further analysis before actions are recommended.

A farm with a fairly stable flow of revenue and expenses, such as a dairy farm in many countries, can be considered in good financial condition with a lower CR than a farm with a highly variable flow of revenue, such as a producer of fresh vegetables. The producer of fresh vegetables can have a product price that varies greatly from one week to the next. So the vegetable producer needs a larger financial cushion, such as indicated by a higher CR in order to have the financial capacity to weather periods of low prices. Even though milk prices do vary over time, they do not vary as much or as rapidly as prices in a fresh vegetable market. Thus a dairy farm can be considered in good financial condition even though its CR is lower than the vegetable producer's.

Working capital is the money that a farmer could have available for use in the current and near future for production if all current assets were sold and current liabilities were paid. The FFSC calculates working capital by subtracting total current farm liabilities from total current farm assets. Although some definitions include intermediate assets and intermediate liabilities in the calculation of working capital, FFSC does not. This measure is called working capital because it is capital that is available for use (or work) in the near term within the business. The adequacy of the level of working capital needs to be evaluated on the basis of the size and type of business. Using FFSC's definition, working capital for the example farm is $360,602.

$$\text{Working capital} = \text{total current farm assets} - \text{total current farm liabilities}$$
$$= 463,477 - 102,875 = 360,602$$

The **working capital to gross revenue ratio** shows the amount of working capital relative to the size of the business as measured by the business' gross revenues. A higher ratio indicates greater liquidity. Using FFSC's definition, the working capital to gross revenue ratio is 0.58 or 58%.

$$\text{Working capital to gross revenue ratio} = \frac{\text{working capital}}{\text{gross revenues}} = \frac{360,602}{622,208} = 0.58 \text{ or } 58\%$$

Measures of Solvency

Solvency is the ability to pay all debts if assets were to be sold at a certain point in time. The major measures of solvency are net worth, debt/asset ratio, equity/asset ratio, and debt/equity ratio (Table 13.3). Of these four, net worth and the debt/asset ratio are on the short list of measures (Table 13.1). Net worth is the absolute measure of solvency and wealth. The three ratios are related by the definition of net worth, only one of these is needed, and the debt/asset ratio is the most widely used and understood relative measure of solvency.

Net worth (NW) or owner's **equity** of the farm is the difference between the value of total assets (TA) and total liabilities (TL). It is the absolute measure of the cushion between asset values and liabilities. This cushion can be used for increased borrowing and/or enduring a loss in asset value.

Net worth can be calculated using cost basis values or market values. For the example farm in Table 12.1, net worth using cost basis is $855,537 and net worth using market values is $1,278,241.

$$\text{NW} = \text{TA} - \text{TL}$$
$$\text{NW(cost basis)} = 1,173,907 - 318,370 = 855,537$$
$$\text{NW(market value)} = 1,760,996 - 482,755 = 1,278,241$$

The **debt/asset ratio** (D/A) measures the size of the farm's debt load compared with the total asset value. This ratio became popular during the agricultural financial crisis in the early 1980s. It is usually expressed as a percentage. The debt-to-asset ratio shows the extent to which the farm's assets are

Table 13.3   Measures of Solvency

	Vulnerable and Strong Levels
Net Worth (NW) or Equity[†]	
Net worth (NW) or equity is the money left if all assets were sold and all liabilities were paid including potential capital gains and other taxes. NW shows the wealth of the individual or the business.	A higher net worth is always considered to signal financial strength as well as capacity to expand and grow. Exact desired levels depend on the type of business as well as the preferences of the owners.
Debt/Asset (D/A) Ratio[*,†]	
The D/A ratio measures the size of the farm's debt load compared with the total asset value, and is calculated as total liabilities divided by total assets. D/A is often expressed as a percentage and can be interpreted as the percent of the business' total value owed to creditors.	The higher the D/A ratio is, the more vulnerable the business is. Exact levels vary by type of farm, but a general rule to start with is strength at or below 40% and potential vulnerability at 70% or above.
Equity/Asset (E/A) Ratio[*]	
The E/A ratio measures the amount of equity the owner's have in the business compared to the total asset value, calculated as total equity divided by total assets. It is often expressed as a percentage and can be interpreted as the percent of the business' value owned by the owners.	The higher the E/A ratio is, the stronger the business is. Exact levels vary by type of farm, but a general rule to start with is strength at or above 70% and potential vulnerability at 40% or below.
Debt/Equity (D/E) Ratio[*]	
The D/E ratio expresses the level to which debt is used in relation to owner's equity. The D/E ratio is calculated as total liabilities divided by total equity.	The higher the D/E ratio is, the more debt is being used relative to equity. Exact levels vary by type of farm, but a general rule to start with is strength at or below 43% and potential vulnerability at 150% or above.

[*]These three measures are mathematically related to each other since net worth (or equity) is defined as total assets minus total liabilities. The sum of the D/A and E/A ratios will always equal 1 (or 100%). The D/E ratio will equal one when D/A and E/A equal 50%. To understand the financial position of a firm, only one of these three measures needs to be known. All three provide the same information on the relative solvency of the business.
[†]These measures are on the short list for evaluating financial position and performance.

financed by debt capital versus equity capital. A lower value is preferred. A higher value shows that creditors have a larger share of farm assets and the farmer and, thus, any creditor faces a higher level of financial risk. Using the FFSC definition and market values, the debt/asset ratio for the example farm is 27%.

$$\mathrm{D/A} = \frac{\text{total farm liabilities}}{\text{total farm assets}} = \frac{482,755}{1,760,996} = 0.27 \text{ or } 27\%$$

The **equity/asset ratio** (E/A) is also recommended by the FFSC. The E/A ratio measures the extent to which the farm's assets are financed by equity capital versus debt capital. It is usually expressed as a percentage. A higher value shows that the farmer has a larger share of farm assets and that the farmer and, thus, any creditors face a lower level of financial risk. The E/A ratio is the opposite or mirror image of the D/A ratio. These two measures always add up to 100% because they describe how total farm assets are financed. Increases in the E/A ratio indicate that the financial position of the farm has improved due to a smaller proportion of assets being owed to creditors. Using the FFSC definition and market values, the equity/asset ratio for the example farm is 73%.

$$\text{Equity/asset ratio} = \frac{\text{total farm equity}}{\text{total farm assets}} = \frac{1,278,241}{1,760,996} = 0.73 \text{ or } 73\%$$

The **debt/equity ratio** (D/E) measures farm debt relative to farm net worth or owner's equity. It shows the debt held by a farm for every dollar of equity. Historically, the D/E ratio was called the leverage ratio. While the D/A ratio is used extensively in the press, the D/E or leverage ratio has historical importance and is still used by many people in financial institutions. Using the FFSC definition and market values, the debt/equity ratio for the example farm is 0.38.

$$\text{Debt/equity ratio} = \frac{\text{total farm liabilities}}{\text{total farm equity}} = \frac{482,755}{1,278,241} = 0.38$$

All three ratios, D/A, E/A, and D/E, measure financial position, but they are mathematically related to each other since net worth (or equity) is defined as total asset value minus total liabilities. The sum of the D/A and E/A ratios will always equal 1 (or 100%). The D/E ratio will equal 1 when both D/A and E/A equal 50%. To understand the financial position of a firm, only one measure needs to be known. All three provide the same information on the relative solvency of the business. The choice among the three depends upon personal preference and experience. However, the D/A is the most commonly used ratio.

Measures of Profitability

Profitability is the ability to produce income over a certain time period. The main measures of profitability are net farm income accrual adjusted (NFI), the rate of return to assets (ROA), the rate of return to equity (ROE), operating profit margin ratio, and earnings before interest, taxes, depreciation, and amortization, or EBITDA (Table 13.4). Of these five, NFI, ROA, and ROE are on the short list of measures. NFI is an absolute measure, and ROA and ROE are relative measures that provide two different views of profitability. With all of these five measures, a higher value is desired. The nonfarm and family information is excluded from these measures unless explicitly stated otherwise.

Net farm income from operations (NFI) is an absolute measure of profitability. NFI represents the returns to unpaid labor, management, and owner equity. The return to taking on risk could be stated explicitly, but is usually considered part of the return to management, equity, and labor. Following FFSC guidelines, NFI is accrual-adjusted—that is, adjusted for changes in inventory value between the beginning and ending of the year. With that adjustment for inventory changes, NFI provides an accurate picture of the profitability of a farm within a specific year. For the example farm, NFI is $155,717 (Table 12.4).

$$\begin{aligned} \text{NFI from operations} &= \text{gross revenues} - \text{total operating expenses} - \text{total financing expenses} \\ &= 622,208 - 439,524 - 26967 \\ &= 155,717 \end{aligned}$$

The **rate of return on farm assets** (ROA) is the first of three relative measures of profitability recommended by FFSC. ROA represents the average interest rate being earned on all investments in the business. If assets are valued at market value, the rate of return on assets can be looked at as the

Table 13.4   Measures of Profitability

	Vulnerable and Strong Levels
Rate of Return on Farm Assets (ROA)[†]	
ROA is a relative measure of profitability representing the average interest rate being earned on all investments in the business.	The higher the value, the more profitable the business.
Rate of Return on Farm Equity (ROE)[†]	
ROE is a relative measure of profitability representing the interest rate being earned on the farm's average net worth or equity.	The higher the value, the more profitable the business.
Operating Profit Margin (OPM) Ratio[†]	
OPM is a relative measure of profitability representing the financial operating efficiency of the business.	The higher the value, the more profitable the business.
Net Farm Income (NFI)[†]	
NFI is an absolute measure of profitability. It is an accrual measure— that is, it is adjusted for changes in inventory value. NFI represents the returns to unpaid labor, management, and owner equity.	The higher the value, the more profitable the business.
EBITDA (Earnings before Interest, Income Taxes, Depreciation, and Amortization)	
EBITDA measures earnings before interest, income taxes, depreciation, and taxes. It is viewed as an earnings estimate before the impact of financing decisions; taxes and tax management; and decisions affecting the age of capital assets held by the business.	The higher the value, the more profitable the business.

[†]These measures are on the short list for evaluating financial position and performance.

opportunity cost of farming versus alternate investments. If assets are valued at cost value, the rate of return on assets more closely represents the actual return on the average dollar invested in the farm. The market value calculation can also be used for comparison between farms; the cost basis value can be used for comparison over time for the same farm. ROA includes both equity capital and debt capital, so the interest paid on debts has to be added in the equation since it has already been subtracted in the calculation of NFI. To provide a better picture of the whole year, the average farm investment is used in the formula; the average is simply the beginning value of total assets plus the ending value of total assets, all divided by 2. (From the balance sheet at the beginning of the year, the market value of all assets is \$1,258,830.) Using the FFSC definition, ROA for the example farm is 7.6%.

$$\text{ROA} = \left(\frac{\text{NFI from operations} + \text{farm interest paid} - \text{owner withdrawals for unpaid labor and management}}{\text{average farm investment}} \right)$$

$$= \frac{155,717 + 26,967 - 68,016}{(1,258,830 + 1,760,996)/2} = 0.076 \text{ or } 7.6\%$$

The **rate of return on farm equity** (ROE) is the second relative measure of profitability recommended by the FFSC. ROE represents the interest rate being earned on the farm's average net worth. The farm's average net worth is the average of the net worth at the beginning of the year and at the end of the year. If assets are valued at market value, ROE can be compared with returns available if the assets were liquidated and invested in alternate investments. If assets are valued at cost value, ROE closely represents the actual return on the funds invested or retained in the business. Using FFSC's NFI from operations avoids any distortions that may result from the gain or loss from the sale of capital assets. This gain or loss is included in CFFM's NFI, so FFSC's NFI from operations is preferred for calculating ROE.

The example farmer withdrew $65,000 from the farm for his and his family's unpaid labor. The balance sheet at the beginning of the year shows the example farm's net worth is $798,146 (market value basis). Using FFSC's definition, ROE for the example farm is 8.4%.

$$\text{ROE} = \frac{\text{NFI from operations} - \text{owner withdrawals for unpaid labor and management}}{\text{average farm net worth}}$$
$$= \frac{155,717 - 68,016}{(798,146 + 1,278,241)/2} = 0.84 \text{ or } 8.4\%$$

While a higher ROE is preferred to a lower ROE, the ROE also should be compared with the opportunity cost of equity capital—that is, the rate of returns available in alternative investments, such as savings or stocks. ROE is essentially the same measure as general business' ROI, where I is the owner's or stockholder's equity investment.

Owner withdrawals are the funds withdrawn from the business for family living and other purposes. For calculating ROE and ROA, the maximum amount of owner withdrawals should be the value or opportunity cost of unpaid labor and management including both the value of unpaid family labor and the opportunity cost or value of the operator's labor and management. For partnerships and corporations that pay wages to the operator(s), this value can be calculated as the owners' withdrawals for unpaid labor and management. In sole proprietorships, this value can be estimated from local, non-farm labor rates and the time spent working on the farm. This value can and should change over time and is due to a farmer's abilities and the local job market. When comparing across farms, the same value of operators' labor and management is typically given to each farmer so that the farms will be compared on a consistent basis. When analyzing multiple operator farms, the value of operator labor and management is increased by the number of operators. The value of a part-time operator should be a proportion of that for a full-time operator; a common proportion is one-half of the typical value for an operator who also has a full-time, non-farm job. Similarly, instead of estimating the number of hours worked by family members, their value could be expressed as a proportion of a full-time operator. For example, a child who does some work during the school year and works full-time on the farm in the summer could be valued at one-fourth to one-third of a full-time operator.

If any part of the ROE equation is negative or close to zero, special care is needed when interpreting the calculated ROE. If equity is positive and ROE is negative, it can be interpreted as a very negative event. If a farm's equity is negative, ROE cannot be used very well for analysis and other measures may be more important to analyze than ROE. If equity is positive but very close to zero, ROE may be overinflated and comparison with other farms is impossible with ROE. In these cases of negative equity or low equity, the rate of return on assets (ROA) should be used for comparisons instead of ROE.

The ratio of ROE to ROA shows how well the farm used debt capital versus equity capital. If debt capital is used effectively, ROE will be greater than ROA, and the ROE/ROA ratio will be greater than 1. However, if debt capital is not used effectively, the interest and other finance charges will be greater than the net income from using the debt capital, and the ROE/ROA ratio will be less than 1. The ratio identifies potential problems by signaling when debt capital is not being used effectively.

For the example farm:

$$ROE \ / \ ROA = 8.4/7.6 = 1.1$$

Since the ratio is greater than 1, the farm has used debt capital well this year. The farm's debt capital contributed more than it cost in this year.

The **operating profit margin ratio** (OPM) is the FFSC's third relative measure of profitability. OPM is a measure of the operating efficiency of the business. It is usually written as a percentage. If expenses are held in line relative to the value of output produced, the farm will have a healthy net profit margin. A low net profit margin may be caused by low prices, high operating expenses, or inefficient production. Using the FFSC definition with gross revenue, OPM is calculated to be 18.4%.

$$OPM = \left(\frac{\begin{array}{c} \text{NFI from operations} + \text{farm interest paid} - \\ \text{owner withdrawals for unpaid labor and management} \end{array}}{\text{gross revenues}} \right)$$

$$= \frac{155,717 + 26,967 - 68,016}{622,208} = 0.184 \text{ or } 18.4\%$$

EBITDA (earnings before interest, income taxes, depreciation, and amortization) is a measure of earnings before those expenses. Thus, EBITDA measures earnings before management decisions affected financing and thus interest, tax levels and rules, and the speed at which assets are depreciated or amortized. Using FFSC's format (Table 12.4), EBITDA is calculated as:

$$\begin{aligned} EBITDA &= \text{NFI from operations} + \text{interest expense} + \text{depreciation/amortization expense} \\ &= 155,717 + 26,967 + 62,836 = 245,520 \end{aligned}$$

Measures of Repayment Capacity

Repayment capacity is the ability to meet cash flow obligations over time. There are several measures used to evaluate repayment capacity: capital debt repayment capacity, capital debt repayment margin, replacement margin, term debt and capital lease coverage ratio, and replacement margin coverage ratio (Table 13.5). Of these five, replacement margin and replacement margin coverage ratio are on the short list of measures.

The **capital debt repayment capacity** (CDRC) is an absolute measure of the farm's ability to generate funds needed for debt repayment and asset replacement. Using the FFSC definition, the capital debt repayment capacity for the example farm is $168,515.

Capital debt repayment capacity =	
+ NFI from operations	+ 155,717
+/− total miscellaneous revenue/expense	+ 0
+ total non-farm income	+ 0
+ depreciation/amortization expense	+ 62,836
− total income tax expense	+ 0
− total owner withdrawals	− 68,016
+ interest expense on term debt	+17,978
	168,515

Table 13.5 Measures of Repayment Capacity

	Vulnerable and Strong Levels
Capital Debt Repayment Capacity (CDRC)	
CDRC is an absolute measure of the total cash earnings available for debt repayment and capital asset replacement.	The higher the value, the more money is available for debt repayment and asset replacement and for business expansion.
Capital Debt Repayment Margin (CDRM)	
CDRM is CDRC minus total uses of repayment capacity. It is an absolute measure of the amount by which cash earnings exceed payments due.	The higher the value, the larger the monetary cushion is between cash available and cash requirements for term debt payments and for business expansion.
Replacement Margin (RM)[†]	
RM is CDRM minus the cash replacement allowance. It is the amount by which earnings available for debt repayment and replacement exceed payments due and cash replacement needs. It allows for the evaluation of the ability to acquire additional business assets and/or service additional debt and to evaluate the risk margin for capital replacement and debt service.	The higher the value, the higher the monetary cushion and, thus, cushion for acquiring additional business assets and/or service additional debt.
Term Debt and Capital Lease Coverage Ratio (TDCR)	
TDCR measures whether the business generated enough income to cover term debt repayments. It is CDRC divided by total principal and interest on term debt.	The greater the ratio is over 1:1, the greater the margin to cover scheduled payments. A ratio less than 1:1 indicates that the business did or does not generate sufficient cash to cover payments.
Replacement Margin Coverage Ratio (RMCR)[†]	
RMCR measures whether the business generated enough income to cover both scheduled term debt payments and estimated capital replacement needs.	The greater the ratio is over 1:1, the greater the margin to cover scheduled payments and estimated payments for replacement needs. A ratio less than 1:1 indicates that the business did or does not generate sufficient cash to cover these actual and estimated payments.

[†]These measures are in the short list for evaluating financial position and performance.

The **capital debt repayment margin** (CDRM) measures the ability of the farmer to generate funds to repay debts with maturity dates longer than one year and to replace business assets. CDRM is the CDRC minus total uses of repayment capacity. Using the FFSC definition, the capital debt repayment margin for the example farm is $116,187.

$$
\begin{array}{lr}
\text{Capital debt repayment margin} = & \\
+ \text{ capital debt repayment capacity} & + \, 168{,}515 \\
- \text{ total uses of repayment capacity} & - \, 52{,}328 \\
\hline
& 116{,}187 \\
\end{array}
$$

where
total uses of repayment capacity =

+ total principal and interest on term debt	+52,328
+ payment on unpaid operating debt from a prior period (loss carryover)	+0
+ total annual payments on personal liabilities (if not included in withdrawals)	+0
	52,328

and where
total principal and interest on term debt =

+ prior year current portion of long-term debt	+34,350
+ prior year current portion of capital leases	+0
+ interest expense on term debt	+17,978
	52,328

The **replacement margin** (RM) is an indicator of the farm's ability to generate funds necessary to repay debts with maturity dates longer than one year and to replace assets. The replacement margin is the capital debt repayment margin minus the replacement allowance and unfunded capital expenditures. Using the FFSC definition, the replacement margin for the example farm is $116,187.

Replacement margin =	
+ capital debt repayment margin	116,187
− replacement allowance/unfunded capital expenditures	0
	116,187

The **term debt and capital lease coverage ratio**, or term debt coverage ratio (**TDCR**) as it is sometimes called, measures whether the business generated (or is projected to generate) enough cash to cover term debt payments. Total term debt payments are the annual scheduled principal and interest payments on intermediate and long-term debt. Note that this ratio requires the scheduled payments; these may or may not be the same as the actual payments.

Since TDCR is a coverage ratio, it can be pictured visually as the funds available to cover the scheduled principal and interest payments. The "coverage" can also be seen in the equation below, which shows CDRC "covering" the total principal and interest payments on term debt.

TDCR is usually written as a percentage. A ratio greater than 100% indicates the business generated enough cash to pay all term debt payments. A ratio less than 100% indicates the business did not or will not generate sufficient cash to meet scheduled payments, and other sources of cash are needed. Using FFSC's definition and the term debt payment information from Tables 12.4 and 12.6, the term debt coverage ratio for the example farm is 3.22.

$$\text{Term debt coverage ratio (TDCR)} = \frac{\text{capital debt repayment capacity}}{\text{total principal and interest on term debt}} = \frac{168,515}{52,328} = 3.22$$

The **replacement margin coverage ratio** (RMCR) provides a measure of the farm's ability to cover all term debt and capital lease payments and recurring unfunded acquisitions. (For the formula below, "total uses of repayment capacity" is defined above in the description of CDRM.) Using the

FFSC definition, the replacement margin coverage ratio for the example farm is 3.22.

$$\text{Replacement margin coverage ratio} = \frac{\text{capital debt repayment capacity}}{\left(\begin{array}{c}\text{total uses of repayment capacity}\\ +\text{replacement allowance/unfunded capital expenditures}\end{array}\right)}$$
$$= \frac{168,515}{(52,328 + 0)} = 3.22$$

Measures of Financial Efficiency

Financial efficiency indicates how well financial resources and expenses were used. The major measures of financial efficiency are the asset turnover ratio, operating expense ratio, depreciation/amortization expense ratio, interest ratio, and the net farm income from operations ratio (Table 13.6). Other measures such as cost per unit of product can be useful for finding problems in the business.

The **asset turnover ratio** is a measure of how efficiently farm assets are being used to generate revenue. It measures how fast the assets of the farm are turned over annually. Typical asset turnover ratios in farming are between 40% and 50% with some variation between types of farms. For example, a dairy farm typically has a lower asset turnover ratio than a fresh vegetable farm because the

Table 13.6   Measures of Financial Efficiency

	Vulnerable and Strong Levels
Asset Turnover Ratio	
Asset turnover ratio measures how efficiently a farm uses assets to generate revenue. Assets are valued using the market value basis to make comparisons among farms more comparable. It measures how many times the total value of farm assets is "turned over" by the value of production from the farm.	The higher the ratio, the more efficient the farm is in using its assets.
Operating Expense Ratio*	
This ratio measures the proportion of gross revenues used to pay operating expenses.	The higher the ratio, the more gross revenues are being used to pay operating expenses.
Depreciation/Amortization Expense Ratio*	
This ratio measures the proportion of gross revenues used to pay depreciation/amortization expenses.	The higher the ratio, the more gross revenues are being used to pay depreciation and amortization expenses.
Interest Expense Ratio*	
This ratio measures the proportion of gross revenues used to pay interest expenses.	The higher the ratio, the more gross revenues are being used to pay interest expenses.
Net Farm Income from Operations Ratio*	
This ratio measures the proportion of gross revenues remaining available for net farm income.	The higher the ratio, the more gross revenues are being "saved" for net farm income.

*If these four ratios are measured correctly, they should sum to 1.0.

dairy farm has a more stable income flow and can operate with a thinner margin. The vegetable farm operates at a higher risk level so it requires a faster rate of asset payment. Most cash crop and crop-livestock farms have asset turnover ratios between these two levels. Using the FFSC definition, the asset turnover ratio for the example farm is 41%.

$$\text{Asset turnover ratio} = \frac{\text{gross revenue}}{\text{average total farm assets}} = \frac{622,208}{(1,258,830 + 1,760,996)/2} = 41\%$$

The value of production can be used in place of gross revenues when calculating the asset turnover ratio. However, as the FFSC points out, the analysis should consistently use either gross revenues or value of production to avoid misinterpretation. Multiplying the asset turnover ratio by the operating profit margin ratio should result in the rate of return on farm assets. If the value of production or gross revenue is not used consistently, this relationship will not exist.

This ratio can cause problems when comparing farms that have different mixes of owned and rented assets even though other measures of size are similar. Without adjusting the equation, the farms with more rented assets will have a falsely higher asset turnover rate because their value of assets owned is less than a farm that owns all of the assets it uses. So, although this is neither mentioned nor recommended by the FFSC, an analyst may find it appropriate to use the value of controlled assets (that is, both rented assets and owned farm assets) to provide a more accurate comparison between farms. Then the asset turnover ratio is defined as:

$$\text{Asset turnover ratio} = \frac{\text{value of production}}{\text{average total controlled assets}}$$

Four operational ratios define the distribution of gross revenues to cover total farm expenses and generate farm income. The sum of the operating expense ratio, the depreciation expense ratio, and the interest expense ratio equals the percent of gross revenues used to pay farm expenses. The amount remaining is net farm income from operations. (In all four of these ratios, the FFSC allows the use of the value of farm production rather than gross revenues if used consistently.)

The **operating expense ratio** shows the percent of the gross farm income used to pay operating expenses. FFSC's recommended definition of operating expense is on a pretax basis that includes inventory changes and depreciation/amortization expense but does not include interest expense. Using the FFSC definition, the operating expense ratio for the example farm is 61%.

$$\text{Operating expense ratio} = \frac{\left(\text{total farm operating expense} - \text{depreciation/amortization}\right)}{\text{gross revenues}}$$

$$= \frac{439,524 - 62,836}{622,208} = 61\%$$

The **depreciation/amortization expense ratio** shows the percent of the gross revenues used to cover depreciation/amortization. Using the FFSC definition, the depreciation expense ratio for the example farm is 10%.

$$\text{Depreciation/amortization expense ratio} = \frac{\text{depreciation/amortization expense}}{\text{gross revenues}} = \frac{62,936}{622,208} = 10\%$$

The **interest expense ratio** shows the percent of the gross revenues used for farm interest expenses. Using the FFSC definition, the interest expense ratio for the example farm is 4%.

$$\text{Interest expense ratio} = \frac{\text{total farm interest expense}}{\text{gross revenues}} = \frac{26,967}{622,208} = 4\%$$

The **net farm income from operations ratio** shows the percent of the gross revenues that remain after all expenses. Using the FFSC definition, the net farm income from operations ratio for the example farm is 25%.

$$\text{Net farm income from operations ratio} = \frac{\text{net farm income from operations}}{\text{gross revenues}} = \frac{155,717}{622,208} = 25\%$$

Cost measures show the efficiency with which costs are controlled relative to production levels. The total cost per unit (bushel, head, kilogram, metric ton, cwt., etc.) can be compared with that of other farmers and, if adjusted for inflation, with other years. The total costs per unit can be divided between direct operational costs per unit (i.e., variable) and overhead costs per unit (i.e., fixed). Feed costs per livestock production unit are especially important for livestock operations. Comparing the investment per acre, hectare, or livestock unit can explain differences between farms and changes over time. For more detailed analysis, the total investment could be divided into building investment (especially for livestock) and machinery investment (especially for crops). Cost measures can be used for (1) efficiency comparisons, (2) comparison of operational differences between farms (e.g., labor-intensive versus capital-intensive farms), (3) determination of whether a cash flow problem is due to a production problem or a marketing problem (or both) and (4) break-even and marketing analysis.

Initial Analysis

We have many ways to analyze the financial position of a farm. The procedure described in this section is for a first-time analysis of a farm and assumes no previous knowledge of the farm. This procedure is not the only one that will work. It is offered as a guide to be used as described or to help the development of the reader's own analysis procedures. This procedure is designed to find the areas that have problems or opportunities so that further analysis can better focus on those areas.

The steps to analyze the overall financial position and performance of a farm are:

1. Gain an overview of the farm
2. Identify the vision, goals, objectives, and standards of the farm
3. Check the accuracy of the records
4. Prepare the financial statements
5. Evaluate liquidity
6. Evaluate solvency
7. Evaluate profitability
8. Evaluate repayment capacity
9. Evaluate efficiencies
10. Examine marketing performance
11. Analyze livestock and crop enterprises
12. Analyze internally, historically, vertically, and comparatively
13. Evaluate managerial ability and personal characteristics

1. Gain an Overview of the Farm

What is the location of the farm and its major enterprises? How large is the farm? What is its history? What are the characteristics of the farm family or families: size, participation, interests, and so on? What are the management abilities and risk attitudes of the principals involved in the farm business?

One step that could be taken at this time, especially if the analyst has no experience with the farm, is to complete an inventory of the farm's resources. This step is also necessary if the financial statements are not available. The process of taking an inventory is described in Chapter 12.

2. Identify the Vision, Goals, Objectives, and Standards of the Farm

Vision, goals, objectives, and standards are compared against actual performance and plans. They tell us what the owners, operators, managers, and family members want to do and where they want to go. If we do not know the goals, objectives, and standards, we will not know how to evaluate or grade the performance and position of the farm.

Vision, goals, objectives, and standards are similar yet different. A vision is what the farmer and others involved in the business want the farm to be or become in the future. Goals are usually thought of as long-run targets, such as retirement by age 60 or the farm paid for in 10 years. Objectives are the specific items that a person wants to accomplish in a shorter time (say, a year). Objectives may be items like a dairy herd average of 30,000 pounds of milk per cow, a corn yield of 180 bushels per acre, or feed costs of $35 per feeder pig (given the assumptions and practices of a farm). Objectives are what we strive for in order to improve the farm's performance and position. Standards are very similar to objectives, but standards are usually more realistic in expectations. Standards are what we wish to be measured against because we feel that we need to attain these levels for short-term survival of the farm.

The development of goals, objectives, and standards should involve all the internal stakeholders of the farm: the operator(s), other partners and equity holders, and family members. Goals may come from dreams, wishes, and needs. Objectives and standards can be developed from:

- past performance
- comparable farms
- benchmarking with the best farms
- experiments and recommendations
- requirements by a bank, the government, or other institution
- dreams and expectations
- normal prices, yields, efficiencies

3. Check the Accuracy of the Records

To trust the results of the analysis, we must trust the initial information used for the analysis. Various consistency checks can be done to assess the accuracy of the records. These are explained in the appendix at the end of this chapter.

4. Prepare the Financial Statements

Once the records are deemed accurate (that is, accurate enough), the four main financial statements should be prepared. These are the:

- Balance sheet (or net worth statement)
- Income statement (or profit/loss statement)

- Statement of owner's equity
- Statement of cash flows

The balance sheet shows the balance between the value of the assets and the debt owed by the farm. The income statement shows net income left after expenses are paid. The statement of owner's equity shows the change in equity and the sources of that change. The statement of cash flows shows how and where cash comes into and goes out of the business. The development and interpretation of these statements are presented in Chapter 12.

5. Evaluate Liquidity

Liquidity is the ability of the firm to meet its financial obligations in the next 12 months. Liquidity is measured by the working capital and the current ratio. Sometimes these measures are referred to as measuring balance sheet liquidity because they require information from the balance sheet.

Using the information in the financial statements and the FFSC definitions, calculate the current ratio and the working capital. The actual current ratio and working capital to gross revenues ratio can be compared with accepted standards as shown in Table 13.7 for the example farm, but there is no standard for working capital since farms differ widely in size and type and thus the need for working capital is different. The example farm has a strong liquidity position.

6. Evaluate Solvency

Solvency evaluates the asset–liability balance at a particular point in time. It measures both the ability to repay all debts and the financial ability of the firm to withstand periods of poor profitability and, if measured with assets at market value, decreases in asset values. Solvency does not consider past or future profitability or liquidity. It only considers the farm's position on a certain date.

Using the information in the financial statements and the FFSC definitions, calculate the farm's net worth, debt-to-asset ratio, equity-to-asset ratio, and debt-to-equity ratio, and compare the actual results with accepted expectations as shown in Table 13.7 for the example farm. The example farm is in a strong solvency position.

7. Evaluate Profitability

Profitability is usually the first goal of farmers, so it is listed first in the analysis procedures. When analyzing profitability, we are concerned not only with the absolute amount of profit but also with the relative amount. Indirectly, it also measures the managerial ability of the farmer. We are interested in (1) whether the actual level of net farm income provides enough for family living and other commitments and (2) whether that net farm income is adequate compared with a farmer's equity capital investment, the unpaid operator and family labor used in business, and the contribution of management ability.

Using the information in the financial statements and the FFSC's definitions, calculate the net farm income, the rates of return to farm assets and to farm equity, and the operating profit margin. To gain a better understanding of this farm's financial condition and performance, compare the actual measures to widely accepted expectations by using a form as shown in Table 13.7 for the example farm. The example farm shows performance that is neither vulnerable nor strong. A more complete analysis would require information from other years.

Table 13.7 Evaluation Form for the Example Farm's Financial Position and Performance[*]

Category and Measure	Actual Results	Relative Rating of Actual Measure[**]			
		Vulnerable			Strong
Liquidity					
Current ratio[†]	4.5	1.0		2.0	✓
Working capital	$360,602				
Working capital to gross revenues[†]	58%	10%		25%	✓
Solvency (market)					
Net worth (equity)[†]	$1,278,241				
Debt/asset (D/A) ratio[†]	27%	70%		40%	✓
Equity/asset (E/A) ratio	73%	40%		70%	✓
Debt/equity (D/E) ratio	0.38	1.5		0.43	✓
Profitability (market)					
Net farm income[†]	$155,717				
Rate of return on assets (ROA)[†]	7.6%	4%	✓	8%	
Rate of return on equity (ROE)[†]	8.4%	3%	✓	10%	
Operating profit margin ratio[†]	18.4%	15%	✓	25%	
EBITDA	$245,520				
Repayment Capacity					
Capital debt repayment capacity	$168,515				
Capital debt repayment margin	$116,187				
Replacement margin[†]	$116,187				
Term debt coverage ratio	3.22	1.20		1.50	✓
Replacement margin coverage ratio[†]	3.22	1.10		1.40	✓
Financial Efficiency					
Asset turnover rate (market)	41%	20%		40%	✓
Operating expense ratio	61%	80%	✓	60%	
Depreciation expense ratio	10%	15%	✓	5%	
Interest expense ratio	4%	10%		5%	✓
Net farm income ratio	25%	10%		20%	✓

[*]These measures are taken from and defined by the Farm Financial Standards Council (2008). The scorecard and vulnerable and strong borders are based on Becker et al. (2009).

[**]While the borders between vulnerable and strong are not well-defined, these guidelines serve to help describe the farm relative to widely accepted expectations for financial condition and performance.

[†]These nine measures are included in the short list for evaluating financial position and performance.

At this point we can begin to see that the example farm is in fairly good shape. So we may be wondering what this farm should be doing with its income. Some ideas are offered in Example 13.1.

8. Evaluate Repayment Capacity

The ability to repay loans is critical to both the farmer and the creditor. The traditional measures of liquidity ignore a farm's cash inflow and outflow and thus are unable to predict adequately the future ability to service debt and other commitments. To look at a business's ability to generate cash

Example 13.1. What to Do in Good Times

Profits are good, but what should a farmer do with them? Throwing a party and taking a long vacation may sound like fun, but they do not add much to the long-term success of the business and help it progress toward the farm and family vision. Another set of ideas for using net farm income or profit are listed below.

First, use two-thirds of the profit to increase the earned net worth of the business. Pay down debt to manageable levels, especially if the debt-to-asset ratio is greater than 40%. Don't pay the land loan just to accomplish the goal of owning the land debt free; pay down the loans with the highest interest rates first. Earned net worth can also be increased by using profits to increase the size of the business or to increase production efficiencies.

Second, increase working capital by adding to the business savings account. Building this financial reserve decreases the risk of unforeseen problems and allows the farm to take advantage of unforeseen opportunities. Don't just pay cash for inputs; use cash to bargain for discounts.

Use some of the profits—say, 10%—to help achieve business, family, and personal goals and objectives. Consider starting or adding to a retirement fund beyond the wealth tied up in land and buildings. Diversification of assets is a good goal.

to meet obligations, using the term debt coverage ratio and capital replacement margin is suggested. Sometimes these measures are referred to as measuring cash flow liquidity because they require information from both the balance sheet and the cash flow statement.

Using the information in the financial statements and the FFSC definitions, calculate the term debt coverage ratio and the capital replacement margin. The actual term debt coverage ratio and the replacement margin coverage ratio can be compared with accepted standards as shown in Table 13.7 for the example farm, but there is no accepted standard for the absolute measures of liquidity since farms differ widely in size, type, and capitalization. The ratios show the example farm to be in a strong position for repayment capacity.

9. Evaluate Efficiencies

Financial measures of efficiency include the asset turnover rate, the distribution of gross income, and costs and investment per unit. Using the information in the financial statements, calculate the five financial measures of financial efficiency defined by the FFSC: asset turnover rate (market), operating expense ratio, depreciation expense ratio, interest expense ratio, and the net farm income ratio. The actual values for these five measures can be compared with standard expected values for these measures as shown in Table 13.7 for the example farm. Three of the efficiency measures are in the strong category for the example farm; depreciation expense ratio and interest expense ratio are in the middle range.

Physical measures of efficiency include crop yields, livestock production per animal, feed efficiency, calving and weaning rates, death loss, and output per labor hour. These and other measures are used to compare actual performance with the farm's internal standards and goals, the farm's historical performance trends, and the performance of comparable farms. When these physical measures are calculated and compared, the same rules and procedures should be used. For instance, the weaning rate (number of young weaned per adult female) can be altered drastically by different methods of counting the numbers of breeding adults. Sometimes, only the adults that have young are counted; in other places, those bred but never kept for birthing are counted also. The question is not really which way is right, but whether the same method is being used for all calculations.

10. Examine Marketing Performance

The prices that a farmer receives or pays can suggest marketing ability, market timing, storage, discounts and other factors. A farmer's marketing performance in economic terms can be measured by the price received rate and the price paid rate. Physical measures of marketing performance include storage and handling losses, insect and mold damage levels, and so on. The critical question when evaluating marketing performance is not whether the best price was obtained but whether the marketing plan needs to be changed.

When evaluating prices received, several items needed to be checked. Products marketed in a timely fashion will usually command a higher price. To be timely, a farmer needs to monitor the markets and watch for signals that suggest changes in market patterns and seasonal differences. Market strategies such as hedging, options, and contracting, need to be used to their best advantage rather than being always or never used. Also, inattentiveness to quality can cause price penalties at marketing time. Quality problems can be caused by many problems, such as improper ventilation in grain storage or feeding livestock to weights that receive price penalties (unless market movements suggest that prices are going up faster than the price penalty). A good indicator of marketing performance is the price received rate.

$$\text{Price received rate} = \frac{\text{farmer's average price}}{\text{average market price}} * 100\%$$

The farmer's average price is the weighted average of what the farmer actually received for his/her product. The average market price is calculated from market information for the general market area and marketing year where the farm is located.

The analysis of prices paid is done similarly to the analysis of prices received. Supplies purchased in a timely and orderly fashion should obtain more favorable prices for the farmer. The price paid rate is a good indicator of input purchasing ability.

$$\text{Price paid rate} = \frac{\text{farmer's average price}}{\text{average market price}} * 100\%$$

Any analysis of prices and marketing performance should be done with a good knowledge of the farmer's marketing plan. For instance, a farmer without input storage cannot take advantage of large purchase discounts or preseason sales; the farmer may have already decided that the cost of owning storage is greater than any potential price discounts. The same reasoning needs to be applied when analyzing prices received.

11. Analyze Livestock and Crop Enterprises

So far the analysis has focused on the whole-farm level without explicitly considering the parts of the business—that is, its crop and livestock enterprises. At this point in the analysis, the enterprises need to be analyzed individually. Enterprises need to be evaluated to discover problems and opportunities hidden at the whole-farm level and to answer questions generated during previous analysis, such as why prices or yields are low. Enterprise analysis can also help answer questions such as: Should I stop growing crops and specialize in dairy?

The basic questions to be answered in enterprise analysis are:

- Is each enterprise being operated efficiently from an economic view? Does it produce the correct products? Does it produce them with the proper mix of inputs? Is it the proper size?
- Is the mix of enterprises appropriate for this farm, its management, and its economic environment? Is each enterprise the correct size? What is the strategic position, or desired position, of the farm?

Enterprise analysis is very similar to whole-farm analysis, but is limited to one enterprise. However, the process of getting enterprise information can be involved. The steps for developing enterprise budgets from whole-farm information are discussed in the Chapter 14 in the section, "Developing Enterprise Budgets from Whole-Farm Records."

Enterprises can be analyzed in three ways.

a. Gross margins (or contribution to overhead expenses):

The gross margin (gross income minus variable expenses) is used for short-run analysis. On a per unit basis (e.g., per acre or per dollar invested), gross margins can be used to decide what product and how much of each product to produce. Gross margin analysis ignores fixed and sunk costs in the short run.

b. Allocation of direct and indirect expenses and income:

This type of enterprise analysis includes both variable and fixed costs to estimate the enterprise's contribution to whole-farm profit. The allocation of indirect expenses can be an arbitrary process, but to evaluate the enterprises on a longer-run basis, the allocation needs to be done.

c. Allocate assets and liabilities to enterprises:

This level of analysis involves more arbitrary decisions on what assets and liabilities belong to each enterprise. With this allocation, a financial analysis can be done for each enterprise including profitability, solvency, liquidity, financial stress, and efficiency analysis. While some people argue that this type of analysis cannot be done because enterprises do not own assets or take on debt by themselves, how else can long-run decisions be made concerning starting and quitting major enterprises?

12. Analyze Internally, Historically, Vertically and Horizontally

Once the measures and ratios are calculated, there needs to be some point of comparison for analyzing the numbers. Four methods of comparison are internal, historical, vertical, and horizontal.

Internal.   The vision, goals, objectives, and standards are the first point of comparison. Are they being met? Is there sufficient income to meet the family's needs and run the business? Does the business perform at expected levels? Are the performance standards (such as crop yields, weaning rates, or debt repayment) being met or exceeded?

Historical.   How has the business performed over time? What are the trends for the same farm business? Are the trends meeting plans and objectives? Is this year better or worse than previous years?

Vertical.   Vertical analysis gets its name from its comparison of a column of numbers—say, income and expense items—and calculating each item as a percentage of the total income or expenses. The farmer or analyst then can quickly see which item(s) dominates the other income or expense items. This provides information on which items need attention because they are a large component of the total. Vertical analysis can be used when comparing with other farms to see how the mix of income and expense items differ or are the same.

Horizontal.   How does the business compare with other farms? One group of other farms should be similar in size and type to compare performance and efficiency. Another group of farms could be different to show the effect of different resource allocation and enterprise and strategy selection. These other farms should have their financial analysis done with similar methods so that comparisons are possible.

   In horizontal comparisons, conclusions need to be made carefully due to differences in the percentage of land owned versus rented, the level of debt, the amount of paid and unpaid interest, and the allocation of direct and indirect costs. These differences can give misleading information about the performance of one farm versus another. The amount of land rented will create differences in ROE and ROA between farms that are otherwise very similar. Owned farm land will increase the asset value of a farm compared to renting, so ROA and ROE for the farm owning more land will be lower than for the farm that rents more. One solution is to recalculate the financial ratios using rental costs instead of land ownership costs; this recalculation will put the farms on a more equitable basis. Farms that have lower debt levels will have lower interest payments; to make comparisons more accurate they can be made using the net farm income from operations (and thus before financing expenses). The allocation of direct and especially indirect costs between enterprises is a subjective process, so care should be taken to understand how these costs are allocated and to use the same methods.

13. Evaluate Managerial Ability and Personal Characteristics

Although evaluating people is a difficult and subjective process, a financial analysis is not complete until it is done. Without this managerial evaluation, the probability of success cannot be determined. Factors that need to be considered are: skills, knowledge, experience, capacity (to learn and to work), honesty, integrity, risk attitudes, goals, and drive. Other factors also may be evaluated depending on the geographic location, type of farm, and purpose of the financial analysis.

Final Points for the Initial Analysis

Remember that one primary purpose of analysis is to identify those portions of the business that need further study for improvement or cessation. After completing a financial analysis of a farm, the decisions to be made include these options:

1. Continue the farm business largely as it is.
2. Make adjustments or changes in the business that will result in a higher net farm income in the future or that will solve other problems. This decision requires a more thorough analysis of the business as discussed in the next section.
3. Liquidate the business, invest the capital elsewhere, and seek off-farm work.

When problems or symptoms of problems (or opportunities) are discovered in the initial analysis or are known to exist, the source of the problems needs to be found. Usually the source can be found with a more thorough analysis of the business, but having a diagnostic structure to follow can be helpful in the search for a solution. This diagnostic structure or system is described in the last section of this chapter.

Diagnostic Analysis

If a problem or symptom of one becomes evident or was evident before the analysis started (e.g., inability to meet debt obligations), a diagnosis of the problem and its solution is needed. This process is similar to that used by a medical doctor or a veterinarian who, when confronted with symptoms, diagnoses the disease and determines the best course of treatment.

Problem diagnosis and solution discovery start with the question: What is the problem or, rather, what is the symptom of the problem? Problems and their symptoms are usually tied to the lack of performance toward goals and objectives. Goals and objectives are found on the balanced scorecard and include farm income, wealth or equity growth, leisure, high yields, high milk production, and many other measures. Problems and symptoms can include low income, insufficient money to cover debt payments, and no time for vacation. The problem can also be competing goals. Farmers and their families may need to decide which goals have higher priorities than other goals. Priorities may also change as different levels of goals are attained; for example, income may be quite important until a certain level is reached at which point, vacation time becomes more important than higher income.

Once a problem or symptom is found, a structured diagnosis procedure follows a set of steps similar to those identified below. The procedures follow the discovery of an earnings or income problem. For other problems such as lack of wealth accumulation or lack of vacation time, similar procedures for finding solutions could be followed.

1. Is there an earnings problem?
   a. Compare these measures: net farm income (NFI) and the rates of return on equity and assets (ROE and ROA). Net farm income is what is used to support the family living expenses as well as other personal needs such as retirement funds. The rates of return show how efficiently resources are used.
      i. If NFI is lower than the goals of the farm but ROE and ROA are at reasonable or strong levels, the problem may be size of the business.
      ii. If NFI meets goals but ROE and ROA are lower than expectations and benchmarks, the problem is within the operation and organization of the business.
2. Is the problem absolute or relative?

a. It is absolute if there is just not enough money or cash inflow to meet expenses, debt obligations, family living, and other commitments.

b. It is relative if there are enough money and cash inflow, but earnings do not meet internal goals and standards or other farms have better earnings.

c. It might be both absolute and relative.

d. An absolute problem suggests an immediate cash flow problem, whereas a relative problem does not.

e. Both relative and absolute earning problems can be either permanent or temporary, and either organizational or operational.

3. Is the problem temporary or permanent? Both can be serious.

a. A temporary problem is caused by an event that is not controlled by the farmer and not expected again. Temporary problems can be caused by events such as drought, flood, market collapse, or illness of the operator. If a problem is temporary, its solution can be developed knowing that it will not likely occur again. However, the short-run problems caused by temporary problems still can be very serious and dangerous to business survival.

b. A permanent problem is due to a situation that can be expected to occur again. The situation may not last forever, but it is expected to last for more than one or two years.

  i. Has a structural change occurred? This may not be a sudden change but instead a realization that a change has occurred or is occurring. Examples are closing of slaughter plants at nearby locations, new processing plants built near the farm, changes in consumer demand (e.g., decreasing red meat consumption), and the entry of other countries into the world trade market.

  ii. Is it a management problem? A possibility is mismanagement of the farm's resources. If these problems persist, severe financial damage could result. Such problems could occur in many areas of the business: organization, operation, marketing, finance, personnel, timeliness, etc.

c. The distinction between permanent and temporary problems may be found by comparing current prices, yields, inputs, etc., with their normal values. These normal values come from historical data for the farm and for local area and national trends. With these norms, the current year can be put in perspective concerning trends, changes, and other geographical areas. If a farm's current year figures differ from its own norms, the problem is most likely temporary (unless it is the beginning of a permanent change). If the current year figures and the norms differ from the local or national norms, the problem is most likely permanent.

4. Is it an operational or organizational problem?

a. A very common and tested way of evaluating the operational or organizational question comes from what is called the DuPont model (because it was developed at the DuPont company in the 1920s). The answer to this question comes from the mathematical relationship found in the calculation of the rate of return of assets (ROA). Mathematically, ROA is the operating profit margin (OPM) multiplied by the asset turnover rate (ATR) (Figure 13.1). Both measures have to be estimated in terms of either market value or cost basis. (This is the initial step in the DuPont model. Further steps and details can be found in Barnard and Boehlje (1998) and Barry at al. (2000).)

  i. If the OPM is low compared to standards and the ATR is reasonable, the low ROA is probably due to operational problems, and that area of the business should be checked first. The

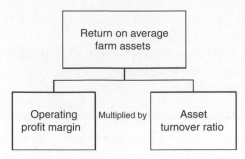

Figure 13.1   DuPont Financial Analysis Model, Initial Step

other financial efficiency measures and enterprise efficiencies are places to start for comparing the farm's results with standards and benchmarks.

ii. If the ATR is low compared to standards and the OPM is reasonable, the low ROA is probably due to organizational and size problems.

b. Operational problems are due to inefficient use of resources.

i. What are the practices followed in carrying out the production, marketing, and financial plans? Are they specified correctly and done in a timely manner?

ii. What are the production costs and efficiencies? How do the actual results compare with standards, benchmarks, expected values, normal values, and comparable farms?

iii. Can costs be decreased through more efficient use of resources or through better purchasing methods?

iv. Each enterprise and other phase of the business (e.g., financial management) needs to be analyzed separately. The basic question is whether each enterprise or phase is performing well and as expected or improvement is needed.

v. Other areas to re-evaluate for operational problems:

1) Production costs
2) Rents
3) Purchasing practices
4) Capital spending plans
5) Financing costs
6) Employment levels (both too much and too little)
7) Inventory levels
8) Make-or-buy decisions
9) Cost control procedures

c. Organizational problems are due to poor choice of enterprises, poor allocation of resources, insufficient size, or lack of resources. If the enterprises met their standards and norms as described in the previous section on operational problems and there is still a problem, it is an organizational problem.

i. To solve this problem, there are a few options:

1) select a different enterprise combination
2) move resources from one enterprise to another
3) add more resources (land, labor, and capital)
4) move resources from farming to other investments and uses

ii. To analyze the enterprise combination, calculate the enterprise budgets and analyze them for gross margins, profit contribution, asset requirements, and debt load. Analyze alternative mixes of current and new enterprises to find a mix that increases earnings or solves other problems. If alternative enterprise mixes do not solve the problem, the problem is most likely one of size.

iii. Size problems.

    1) Is the farming unit large enough to take advantage of modern technology? Is it large enough to produce enough sales to provide sufficient income? Is the farm using current technology but just not large enough? How, where, and when can it be expanded? What are the options for owning, renting, leasing, or hiring more resources, and would they help solve the problem?

    2) Is the farm too large given its management level or is one area too large (e.g., acreage) compared with another area (e.g., labor and machinery resources)? What are the alternatives to solve these problems? Decreasing the size of the farm may help solve problems if the smaller resource base can be managed more efficiently and still meet other objectives. Adding labor resources to an understaffed farm may be all that is needed to improve a farm that has expanded faster in land and livestock than in labor supply.

iv. Other areas to increase revenues from existing assets:

    1) Increase production through current assets (e.g., cows milked per hour, land covered per day)

    2) Reconsider the crop and product mix for the farm

    3) Improve the marketing program

    4) Improve crop yields and livestock productivity

    5) Explore custom work availability

    6) Consider non-farm jobs

v. Other options for nonperforming or underperforming assets:

    1) Sell excess capacity (e.g., too much machinery)

    2) Sell assets that have a market value higher than the current income capitalization value (e.g, nonproductive land for hunting or vacation homes)

    3) Share assets such as machinery sharing

    4) Rent or lease versus own assets

5. If the options considered so far have not solved the problem(s), a manager must consider the option of putting the resources into other uses. This includes other employment for the operator. Although this drastic option may not meet the goal of being a farmer, it may help meet such goals as living standards and leisure time.

An Example Analysis

The example farm we have been using is doing quite well. In Table 13.7, we see that all of the financial measures are in the strong category except for the profitability measures, which are in between vulnerable and strong. ROA and ROE are closer to the strong range, while the operating profit margin ratio is closer to the vulnerable range. Although the ROA is close to 8%, it is not in the strong range, and the farmer should be concerned about what is holding it back. Since the asset turnover rate is strong but the operating profit margin ratio is closer to the vulnerable range, the financial analysis using DuPont model tells us that the problem causing the less than desired ROA lies in the operation of the farm—either with low revenue or with high costs. These areas can be explored in more depth in enterprise analysis, comparison of average prices received, and in comparison of cost and productivity measures against benchmarks from other farms.

For another example, let us consider the case of I. B. Porly's farm. The farm's financial measures are shown in Table 13.8. The I.B. Porly dairy farm is not doing as well as our first example farm. As

Table 13.8 Evaluation Form for the I. B. Porly Farm's Financial Position and Performance[*]

Category and Measure	Actual Results	Relative Rating of Actual Measure[**]			
		Vulnerable			Strong
Liquidity					
Current ratio[†]	1.6		1.0	✓	2.0
Working capital	$110,877				
Working capital to gross revenues[†]	14%		10%	✓	30%
Solvency (market)					
Net worth (equity)[†]	$1,043,346				
Debt/asset (D/A) ratio[†]	46%		70%	✓	40%
Equity/asset (E/A) ratio	54%		40%	✓	70%
Debt/equity (D/E) ratio	0.86		1.5	✓	0.43
Profitability (market)					
Net farm income[†]	$98,575				
Rate of return on assets (ROA)[†]	3.8%	✓	4%		8%
Rate of return on equity (ROE)[†]	2.2%	✓	3%		10%
Operating profit margin ratio[†]	8.7%	✓	15%		25%
EBITDA	$190,840				
Repayment Capacity					
Capital debt repayment capacity	$136,309				
Capital debt repayment margin	$ −48,820				
Replacement margin[†]	$ −48,820				
Term debt coverage ratio	1.25		1.20	✓	1.50
Replacement margin coverage ratio[†]	0.74	✓	1.10		1.40
Financial Efficiency					
Asset turnover rate (market)	43%		20%		40% ✓
Operating expense ratio	75.6%		80%	✓	60%
Depreciation expense ratio	5.5%		20%		10% ✓
Interest expense ratio	6.3%		20%		10% ✓
Net farm income ratio	12.6%		10%	✓	20%

[*]These measures are taken from and defined by the Farm Financial Standards Council (2008). The scorecard and vulnerable and strong borders are based on Becker et al. (2009).

[**]Although the borders between vulnerable and strong are not well-defined, these guidelines serve to help describe the farm relative to widely accepted expectations for financial condition and performance.

[†]These nine measures are included in the short list for evaluating financial position and performance.

another example of how a farm's financial information can be interpreted, read the following letter sent to Mr. Porly from Max M. Purses, his banker. It focuses on the short list of measures instead of trying to explain every possible measure. The letter also compares the farm's position and perform- ance to other farms in the area.

Dear Mr. Porly:

After assembling the income statement and ending balance sheet for your farm and calculating the standard measures of financial performance and position, I find your farm to be in a stable but not strong position in regard to your liquidity and solvency. However, your low profitability, especially as shown in your ROE, creates concerns for the vulnerability of your business even though your NFI is quite high. Your repayment capacity is also quite low and is a reason for concern. The underlying factors need to be evaluated in order to find the problems and conditions that can be improved. In the rest of this memo, I describe in more detail the measures that support these conclusions.

LIQUIDITY: Your current ratio is 1.6 and your working capital to gross revenue is 14%. These are not vulnerable, but neither are they strong. They are just below the averages for dairy farms, dairy and crop farms, and for all farms.

SOLVENCY: Your net worth (market value) is $1,043,346 and your debt-to-asset ratio is 46%. These show a fairly strong financial position and do not raise immediate concerns about your farm. Your net worth is much higher than that of other farms, and your debt/asset ratio is very similar to the averages for dairy farms, dairy and crop farms, and for all farms.

PROFITABILITY: Your NFI is $98,575, ROA(market) = 3.8%, and ROE(market) is 2.2%. Your net farm income is very good this past year; it is higher than the average dairy farms and just less than the average for all farms. However, your ROA and ROE are lower than those of other dairy farms, and they are far below the averages for all farms. The fact that your ROE is lower than your ROA is a concern.

REPAYMENT CAPACITY: Your replacement margin is negative, $ –48,820, and your replacement margin coverage ratio is less than 1! These create large concerns for me as your banker. The ratio is lower than that of other dairies and all other farms.

Since your ROA is lower than it should be and lower than other farms, I looked at the operating profit margin and your asset turnover rate. These two measures are related to ROA and tell us whether the problems are due to inefficient use of assets or in inefficient operation of the farm. Your asset turnover rate (market) is 43%, which is almost in the strong range and higher than the averages. So I do not think the generation of sales is a problem.

However, your operating profit margin is only 9%. It is well below the averages for your area and puts your farm in the vulnerable area for that measure. Looking a bit further, I see the operating expense ratio is 76%, which is similar to other dairies and slightly higher than the overall averages. However, since the operating expense ratio is closer to the vulnerable range than to the strong range, it points toward the need to evaluate your expenses. This evaluation needs to look at the prices you pay for inputs, the efficien- cies of using inputs (such as feed cost per cwt of milk produced), and the production practices you are using.

Thank you for this opportunity to help you understand the financial position and performance of your farm. If you have any questions about this analysis or about how to improve your farm, please contact me. I am ready to help.

Sincerely,

Max M. Purses

As can be seen in the letter, the banker has used the analysis together with the relationship between asset turnover rate and the operating profit margin to target the area of the farm needing attention. A more thorough analysis of the operating costs will, hopefully, point out the problems that can be solved. Some ideas and next steps for farms that do not have good financial position and performance are listed in Example 13.2.

Example 13.2. What to Do in Hard Times

Some years do not produce a profit, or profit is greatly reduced. If there is a small amount of profit, the first goals should be to maintain working capital and then to pay debt.

If the net farm income is negative, consider the list of possible actions below. This list is quite long and could be even longer. Each situation will be different, but the list below can serve as a starting point and idea generator.

- Talk with partners, family, and employees about the situation and potential plans.
- Develop or update a cash flow budget for the farm and share it with your lenders. Show them where you have made changes to cope with the hard times.
- Decrease cash outflow wisely. Cut costs where possible without drastically affecting income.
- Increase cash inflow where possible. Increase efforts to market well and increase productivity.
- Ask employees for ideas.
- Take on new debt only if it provides an immediate improvement in cash flow.
- Stop all investment and replacement of equipment and other capital assets. Repair if possible instead of replace.
- Reevaluate family expenses. Consider off-farm work by all family members.
- Make decisions that will have a positive impact in the future, not just today.
- Spend money when needed to feed animals, do necessary field operations, milk the cows, and so on.
- Don't spend when not needed. Eliminate waste and increase efficiency, especially where it can be done quickly, cheaply, and have an immediate effect. Check for feed waste, nonproductive fuel use, low or nonproductive use of labor, and so on.
- Keep low inventories. Buy supplies as needed.
- Sell nonproductive or seldom-used assets. Consider selling assets, such as timber from a woodlot, that are not part of your normal business, but check with your tax advisor about tax implications before the sale.
- Get enough rest and sleep so your judgment, processing, and managerial skills are not decreased. Seek counseling before problems become too much.

This list could keep going. The main points are to plan the operation and cash flow of the farm, spend money very wisely, save money wherever possible, and take care of yourself and others to maintain management and operation effectiveness and safety.

Financial analysis is an important part of managing any business. It provides critical information on how well the farm is progressing toward goals and objectives. Financial analysis can also help find the problems that can be solved so that progress toward goals can be resumed. Diagnostic analysis is just as critical as the initial understanding of the ratios.

This chapter covers a lot of territory—territory that can be rough for anyone new to financial analysis. If you are new to the subject, go through the summary points below, look at the questions, and then go back through the chapter, pausing on some of the areas that were especially new or hard. Concentrate on those measures that are on the short list, and don't aim to understand all measures.

Summary

- To assess financial position and performance adequately, profitability, solvency, liquidity, repayment capacity, and financial efficiency need to be assessed.
- Both absolute and relative measures are needed.
- Profitability can be evaluated by net farm income (NFI), rate of return on farm equity (ROE), and rate of return on farm assets (ROA).
- Liquidity can be evaluated by the current ratio (CR) and working capital/gross revenue ratio (WC/GR).
- Solvency can be evaluated by net worth (or equity) (NW) and the debt/asset (DA) ratio.
- Repayment capacity can be evaluated by the capital replacement margin (CRM) and the term debt and capital lease coverage ratio (TDCR).
- Financial efficiency is measured by the asset turnover ratio, four operational ratios (the operating expense ratio, depreciation expense ratio, interest expense ratio, and net farm income from operations ratio), and cost measures appropriate to the farm.
- An initial analysis is performed to gain an understanding of the farm and to find areas that have problems or opportunities so that further analysis can better focus on those areas.
- Diagnostic analysis is used once a problem or symptom of a problem becomes evident.

Review Questions

1. Why do we need both absolute measures and relative measures?
2. Describe and define liquidity, solvency, profitability, and repayment capacity.
3. For each of the measure below, (i) what does the measure show or mean, (ii) what is the equation for the measure, (iii) what are the strong and vulnerable ranges for the measure, and (iv) if the measure is in the bad range, what are some potential corrective actions?
   a. Current ratio (CR)
   b. Working capital/gross revenue ratio (WC/GR)
   c. Net worth (NW) or equity
   d. Debt/asset (DA) ratio
   e. Net farm income (NFI)
   f. Rate of return on assets (ROA)

   g. Rate of return on equity (ROE)
   h. Operating profit margin
   i. Replacement margin (RM)
   j. Replacement margin coverage ratio (RMCR)

4. Using the data shown in the table below, what are the total assets and net worth for this farm?

Assets (market values)	Jan. 1	Liabilities	Jan. 1
Cash and checking accounts	$ −2,173	Accounts payable	$ 0
Feed and grain in storage	42,028	Current farm loans	19,000
Market livestock	46,346	Intermediate farm liabilities	75,149
Breeding livestock	78,400	Long-term farm liabilities	231,703
Accounts receivable	0		
Supplies and prepaid expenses	0		
Machinery, equipment, and buildings	54,469		
Land and buildings	227,168		

5. Last year, another farm had a net farm income of $41,015, an average total asset value of $487,924 and an average total debt of $326,772.
   a. If she did not farm, the owner of that farm thinks she could get an off-farm job that pays $20,000 per year. Using these figures, calculate the rate of return on equity (ROE) for this farm.
   b. Suppose she could get 7% on her equity. Subtract 7% of the equity from her NFI to estimate the residual return to her labor and management.
   c. If $20,000 and 7% were her goals, did she achieve her goals?
6. Define and contrast an initial analysis and a diagnostic analysis.
7. Use the financial measures listed below for the Joe and Mary Harcom farm, and write a letter discussing the farm's financial position and performance as if you were the Harcom's lender or advisor.

LIQUIDITY (ending)
Current ratio = 4.90
Working capital to gross revenues = 70%

SOLVENCY (market and ending value)
Farm net worth = $6,776,878
Farm debt to asset ratio = 12%

PROFITABILITY
Net farm income (from operations) = $647,120
Rate of return on farm assets (market) = 6.8%
Rate of return on farm equity (market) = 6.9%
Operating profit margin = 40.5%

REPAYMENT CAPACITY (cash)
Repayment margin = $495,285
Replacement margin coverage ratio = 322%

EFFICIENCY
Asset turnover ratio (market) = 16.8%

Further Reading

Barnard, F. L., and M. Boehlje. 2004. "Using Farm Financial Standards Council Recommendations in the Profitability Linkage Model: The ROA Dilemma." *Journal of the ASFMRA*, 67(1): 7–11.

Barnard, F. L., and M. Boehlje. 1998. "The Financial Troubleshooting of Farm Businesses: A Diagnostic and Evaluation System (DES)." *Journal of the ASFMRA*, 62(1): 6–14.

Barry, PeterJ., Paul N. Ellinger, John A. Hopkin, and C. B. Baker. 2000. *Financial Management in Agriculture*. 6th ed. Danville, Illinois: Interstate Publishers, 678 pp.

Becker K., D. Kauppila, G. Rogers, R. Parsons, D. Nordquist, and R. Craven. 2009. "Farm Finance Scorecard." Center for Farm Financial Management, University of Minnesota, St. Paul. Online at http://www.cffm.umn.edu/Publications/pubs/FarmMgtTopics/FarmFinanceScorecard.pdf.

Boehlje, Michael, Craig Dobbins, Alan Miller, Dawn Miller, and Freddie Barnard. 1999. "Farm Management for the 21st Century: Measuring and Analyzing Farm Financial Performance." Department of Agricultural Economics, Purdue Cooperative Extension Service Publication Number 712. Purdue University, West Lafayette, Indiana.

Farm Financial Standards Council (FFSC). 2008. "Financial Guidelines for Agricultural Producers." Menomonee Falls, Wisconsin: Farm Financial Standards Council.

Appendix

Checking Record Accuracy

Several methods exist to check the accuracy of a set of records besides the visual impression of a neat, precise set of records kept in a timely and orderly manner. These methods or procedures are outlined below.

1. Does cash in equal cash out? Does all the cash spent, saved, or otherwise used account for all the sources of cash? A record of personal and non-farm expenses and income is needed to make this check accurately on farms that do not keep separate personal and business checking accounts.
2. Liabilities check:
   a. Ending debt = beginning debt − principal payments + new debt − debt forgiveness
   b. If accounts payable (A/P) are included, add: + beginning A/P − ending A/P to the equation.
   c. Partners and corporations may cause discrepancies if individuals hold some debt and it is not recorded properly in the accounts.
3. Income/net worth check:
   a. Does the change in net worth balance with the money left after expenses, debt servicing, family living, etc.?
   b. For farms that do not have separate business and personal accounts, non-farm income, expenses and investments need to be included in this calculation.
4. Livestock head count by month:
   a. Ending count = beginning count + purchases + transfers in − sales − deaths + births − transfers out
   b. This needs to be done each month, not only at the end of the year.
   c. The monthly check helps maintain schedules, record sales and purchases, and keeps the manager on top of the operation. It may also help in the crop/feed check.
5. Production records for both crop and livestock:
   a. Does the reported production check with the acreage or number of breeding livestock?
   b. Do the yields and production levels seem reasonable?
   c. These records may force recall of other production and resources, such as storage, sales, and other land/animals.
6. Crop/feed check:

a. Do the crop production estimates balance with feed fed, crops bought, crops sold, and crops stored?

b. The quality of this check depends upon quality of the estimates of crop production, feed fed, and storage amounts.

c. The crop/feed check may never balance completely due to having to use estimates, but the process of working through the check may stimulate memories and records to provide better records.

7. Average sales price and weight or yield:

a. Does the calculated average yield seem reasonable compared with the reported market average price?

$$\text{Calculated average price} = \frac{\text{total sales \$}}{\text{total prod wt. or volume sold}}$$

b. Estimate total production by using the market average price and the actual farm sales. How well does this backwards estimate compare with the actual production?

$$\text{Estimated total production} = \frac{\text{total sales}}{\text{market ave. price}}$$

c. Estimate average yield or production per animal from total farm sales, average market prices, and the number of acres or animals. How well do these estimates compare with actual yields and productivity?

$$\text{Estimated yield} = \frac{\text{total sales}}{\text{market ave. price} * \text{acres}}$$

$$\text{Estimated production} = \frac{\text{total sales}}{\text{market ave. price} * \text{head}}$$

d. These backwards estimates are useful for discovering missing information or other mistakes. Since market averages are used, some small deviations between the estimates and the actual numbers will exist. These small deviations are to be expected; we are interested in finding large deviations that suggest major problems.

14

Financial Management

In this chapter:

- Sources and uses of capital
- Time value of money
- Calculating loan payments
- Estimating the cost of credit
- Cash flow management
- Financial control

Financial management is the process of obtaining, using, and controlling the use of capital—both cash and credit. It uses some of the same tools as financial analysis. However, unlike financial analysis, which usually looks back at performance in the past, financial management works mostly on planning and managing current and future conditions. In this chapter, we look at alternative sources of capital, estimating the costs of credit, the steps for projecting a cash flow, and developing and using financial control systems.

Sources and Uses of Capital

Capital—that is, money—is a major input for today's farmer. Capital is needed to own the resources for farming, such as land, buildings, machinery, and other capital assets that are not used up during production. Capital is also needed to pay for operating expenses such as fertilizer, feed, market animals, and other current assets that must be replaced for each production cycle.

Capital comes in two basic forms: equity capital and debt capital. Equity capital is the money of the owner(s), partners, and other investors. It is the cash and other financial resources they own directly. Equity capital can be used for any purpose in the business: to buy capital assets, pay operating expenses, make loan payments, and so on. Equity owners expect a return on their money, much like expecting interest on a savings account or shareholders expecting a dividend from the stocks they own. However, equity capital on a farm is a residual claimant on income—that is, paid after other expenses and claims are paid. Debt capital is a liability or other financial obligation on which interest and perhaps other fees have to be paid. Credit is debt capital. Debt capital has to be paid before equity capital receives a return.

The return to debt capital is fixed by the terms of the loan or other financial contract. Except for bankruptcy or default by the owner, debt capital has to be paid whether the business has a good or poor year. The owners of equity capital can enjoy the higher returns during high income years but also incur the risk of very low returns or even loss of equity during poor years.

Owner-operator equity is the largest source of capital for U.S. farmers. This equity comes from savings or reinvestment from farm business income, decreased family consumption, gifts and inheritances, off-farm jobs, other investment income, and other sources. When asset markets, such as land markets, are appreciating, equity can come from increases in the value of the farm's assets, but if land prices fall, for example, equity can also shrink quickly.

Outside equity is another source of equity capital for farmers. Non-farm partners and other investors may be willing to invest in farms and thus increase the capital base for the operator of the farm. While the increased size may be of benefit to the owner-operator, this investment does not directly increase the farmer's equity, and the farmer is also obligated to share farm income with the outside investors. Usually, outside investors are more likely to be involved in owning real estate and other capital assets than in supplying operating capital for the farm.

The use of credit (that is, taking on debt) is the second largest source of capital for U.S. farmers. Debt or loans are used for real estate, machinery, and other assets as well as for operating expenses. Sources of loans include commercial banks, government credit sources, insurance companies, machinery manufacturers, merchants, dealer credit, and individuals.

Taking on debt is a risky venture and is avoided by some people. Debt creates future fixed financial obligations and commits a farm's financial resources to a fixed set of assets. However, debt can also help provide resources to improve farm income, wealth, and progress toward goals in several ways as listed below.

Debt can help a farmer:

- Create and maintain an adequate business size—to take advantage of economies of size, for example
- Increase the efficiency of the farm business—to change production systems or methods to improve process and product quality by reducing costs, improving timeliness, and so on
- Adjust the business to changing economic conditions—to purchase new technology, adapt to new markets, for example
- Meet seasonal and annual fluctuations in income and expenditures—to allow for purchasing sufficient resources (such as fertilizer and seed at planting) before products are sold (at harvest, for example)
- Protect the business against adverse conditions—to allow for payment of expenses and other obligations when revenue falls short due to adverse weather, disease, price fluctuations, for example
- Provide continuity of the farm business—such as from one generation to the next.

Leasing and contracting are methods for obtaining the use of capital assets without needing to use equity capital or take on the debt required to purchase those assets. However, leases and contracts are financial instruments and thus create financial obligations for the farm. Through leasing and contracting, a farmer can increase the capital base of the farm. Since they are usually shorter in duration than ownership, leases and contracts can preserve flexibility for adapting a farm to changing conditions in the future. Leasing and contracting do increase the risk of losing control of those specific assets if the leases or contracts are not renewed, but they reduce the risk involved in increasing debt in order to purchase the asset.

The Time Value of Money

One basic concept used in investment analysis is the time value of money. Some people want to spend or invest more money than they currently have, and they are willing to pay others a price to get that money. These "other people" apparently have sufficient money to meet immediate concerns and are willing to be paid not to spend all the money they currently have. In this view, money is a commodity and the market involves time. The time value or price of money is expressed as an interest rate usually expressed as a percentage per year. The price of money is determined in much the same way as any standardized product; the price is determined in the market by the balancing of the demand for money by people willing to pay to use someone else's money and the supply of money by people who are willing to let others use their money.

The time value of money is used in one of four ways: compounding, discounting, the present value of an annuity, and amortization (or capital recovery). These are described in the following sections. Understanding discounting and amortizing is critical to understanding and performing investment analysis, which is covered in Chapter 20.

Compounding

Compounding is the simple process of adding interest to a beginning amount. Compounding is what occurs in a savings account; after each period (perhaps daily), the interest to be paid is calculated based on the beginning balance and the interest rate and added to the saving account to calculate the value at the end of the period. This is called compounding because in the second and later periods, interest will accrue to both the initial amount and the interest earned in the early periods. We know the present value and the interest rate, but we do not know the future value.

For example, what is $500 worth after three years at 7% per year? To answer this, we calculate the interest earned in the first year on the initial $500, then the interest earned in the second year on the initial $500 plus the interest earned in the first year, and then the interest earned during the third year on the initial $500 plus the interest earned in both the first and second years. This is compounding because we earn interest in subsequent years on the interest earned in previous years.

In this example, we deposit $500 in the account today (which is usually referred to as year 0 in financial language). During the first year, we earn 7% interest on the initial $500. The first year's interest is $35, which is calculated by multiplying $500 by 0.07. Thus, the total value in the bank at the end of the first year is $535 as shown in Table 14.1.

During the second year, we earn 7% interest on $535, the value at the beginning of the second year. The interest for the second year is calculated to be $37.45, and the total value is $572.45 at the end of the second

Table 14.1   Example of Compounding $500 for Three Years at 7% Interest

Year	Value at the Beginning of Year	Interest Earned During the Year	Value at the End of the Year
0	—	—	$500.00
1	$500.00	$500 * .07 = $35.00	$500 + $35 = $535.00
2	$535.00	$535 * .07 = $37.45	$535 + $37.45 = $572.45
3	$572.45	$572.45 * .07 = $40.07	$572.45 + $40.07 = $612.52

year. During the third year, we earn 7% interest on the beginning value of $572.45. The interest earned during the third year is calculated to be $40.07, and the total value is $612.52 at the end of the third year.

Instead of having to prepare a table like Table 14.1 for every compounding problem, the future value can be calculated using the same ideas expressed mathematically. By looking at the process in the table above, we can see that the future value of $500 at 7% can also be calculated by multiplying $500 by 1.07 three times, as in the following equation. Note that 1.07 is equal to 1 plus the interest rate written in decimal form.

$$\$500 * 1.07 * 1.07 * 1.07 = \$612.52$$

We could also write this mathematical relationship using 1.07 raised to the power of 3 since $500 is multiplied by 1.07 three times.

$$\$500 * [(1.07)^3] = \$612.52$$

Written in a general form for any compounding problem, the future value (FV) of a present value (PV) after n periods at a certain interest rate, i, by substituting the actual values for PV, n and i into the following equation.

$$FV_{(n, i)} = PV * [(1 + i)^n]$$

In most applications, instead of calculating the expression $[(1 + i)^n]$ for each problem, the calculation of the future value is simplified by using a table of compounding factors (cf) calculated for many pairs of interest rates and different periods. The compounding factors (cf) are substituted into the equation for the future (FV) as shown below.

$$cf = [(1 + i)^n]$$
$$FV_{(n, i)} = PV * cf$$

For the example used above, the compounding factor for 7% and three periods is calculated as 1 plus the interest rate raised to the third power: $(1 + .07)^3 = 1.07 * 1.07 * 1.07 = 1.2250$. The future value is the present value multiplied by the calculated compounding factor:

$$FV_{(3, .07)} = 500 * 1.2250 = 612.50$$

Thus, the future value of $500 that earns 7% for three years is $612.50 using the compounding factor of 1.2250. The difference of two cents (between $612.52 in the table above and $612.50) is due to rounding when the compounding factor for 7% and three years (i.e., 1.2250) is used rather than multiplying $500 by 1.07 three times.

The compounding factors (i.e., $(1 + i)^n$) for several interest rates and periods are listed in Appendix Table I. For the example, the compounding factor for 7% and three years (i.e., 1.2250) is found at the intersection of the column for 7% and the row for three periods.

Discounting

When we know a future value but do not know its present value, we work backwards to estimate the present value by subtracting the interest that could have accrued over time from year 0 to the year in which we know the future value. We discount the future value to estimate a present value. Since we know we can earn interest over time but we do not know the future perfectly, we purposely use the verb "discounting." Due to this uncertainty, the term discount rate is used instead of interest rate when we are calculating future values.

Discounting can be thought of as the opposite of compounding, the opposite of accruing money in a savings account. For instance, we may know how much we have to pay in the future, and by discounting that future amount, we can estimate how much we need to invest today to have that future amount. For example, we may know what the future balloon payment on our loan will be and want to know what we need to put into a savings account now to make the future balloon payment.

Discounting is used in investment analysis to compare today's investment with the future income from that investment. We estimate the future income and then convert that into a present value. Those future incomes are not compared directly to the initial investment because they are in the future; so we discount them in both the financial and English meanings of "discount" because they are expected in future years and they are less certain than the price of the initial investment.

In discounting, the present value (PV) of a known future value (FV) received in n periods at a given interest rate, i, is calculated by multiplying the future value by the present value factor (pvf) for the appropriate interest rate and period. When discounting, the interest rate is referred to as the discount rate and is chosen based on the nominal real interest rate adjusted for inflation and risk. The choice of a discount rate is discussed in Chapter 20, Investment Analysis. The following equation is used to discount a future value and calculate the present value.

$$PV_{(n, i)} = FV * [1/(1 + i)^n] = FV * pvf$$

For example, how much should we pay for an investment that will pay us $800 in four years when we could invest the money in another investment that earns 12%? The present value factor for 12% and four years is calculated as 1 divided by the quantity 1 plus the interest rate raised to the fourth power: $(1/(1 + .12)^4) = 1/(1.12 \times 1.12 \times 1.12 \times 1.12) = 1/1.5735 = 0.6355$. Thus, the present value of an investment that would pay $800 at the end of four years is $508.40 at 12% interest. If we could earn 12% on our money in another investment, we should not pay more than $508.40 for that investment, which will pay us $800 in four years.

$$PV = \$800 * 0.6355 = 508.40$$

The present value factors (pvf) for several discount rates and periods are listed in Appendix Table II. For example, the discount rate for 12% and four years (i.e., 0.6355) is found at the intersection of the column for 12% and the row for four periods.

As a check on this discounting process, suppose we invested $508.40 in an account that earned 12%. Let us use compounding to find what we would have at the end of four years. At the end of the first year, we would have earned 12% on our original $508.40 for a total of $569.41 as shown in Table 14.2.

Table 14.2 Compounding Check of the Discounting Example: $508.40 for Four Years at 12% Interest

Year	Value at the Beginning of Year	Interest Earned During the Year	Value at the End of the Year
0	—	—	$508.40
1	$508.40	$508.40 * .12 = $61.01	$508.40 + $61.01 = $569.41
2	$569.41	$569.41 * .12 = $68.33	$569.41 + $68.33 = $637.74
3	$637.74	$637.74 * .12 = $76.53	$637.74 + $76.53 = $714.27
4	$714.27	$714.27 * .12 = $85.71	$714.27 + $85.71 = $799.98

During the second year, the amount increases to $637.74; the third year, to $714.27. During the fourth year, the amount increases to $799.98. (The difference of two cents between $799.98 and $800 is due to rounding of the present value factor instead of using the full equation and raising 1.12 to the power of 4.)

Present Value of an Annuity

In some investment problems, the investment needs to be compared with an annuity to be received in the future—that is, the same amount per period for several periods. For example, a land lease with a fixed cash payment for several years is an annuity to the owner. In this type of problem, we are estimating the present value (PV_A) of an n period annuity (A) at a given interest rate, i. To calculate this present value, the annuity is multiplied by the present value annuity factor (pvf_A).

$$PV_{A\,(n,\,i)} = A * [(1 - (1 + i)^{-n})/i] = A * pvf_A$$

For example, suppose a person expected to receive $150 in each of the next three years and could receive 12% in an alternative investment. The present value annuity factor (pvf_A) is:

$$pvf_{A(3,\,.12)} = (1/(1 + .12)^{-3})/.12 = 2.4018$$

and the present value of the annuity in this example is:

$$PV_{A(3,\,.12)} = 150 * 2.4018 = \$360.27$$

If the person could receive an interest rate of 12%, he would be indifferent between receiving $360.27 now and $150 in each of the next three years.

The present value factors for annuities (pvf_A) for several discount rates and periods are listed in Appendix Table III. For example, the present value factor for an annuity for 12% and three years (i.e., 2.4018) is found at the intersection of the column for 12% and the row for three periods.

Income capitalization for land value estimation. Estimating the value of land held in perpetuity is a special case of the present value of an annuity. If we own the land in perpetuity, the number of periods is infinite and the formula shown above for the present value of an annuity simplifies to the income capitalization formula shown below.

$$PV = R/i$$

where PV is the cash income value of the land, R is the estimated average annual return to the land, and i is now called the real income capitalization rate. As will be discussed in Chapter 21, when estimating the value of land using the income capitalization method, the term real income capitalization rate (or cap rate) is used instead of discount rate. The process of choosing the real cap rate is discussed in Chapter 21. For example, if cash rent was $85 per acre and taxes, insurance, depreciation, and other expenses amounted to $23 per acre, the net return to the land could be described as an annuity of $62 per acre for perpetuity. (Note that interest and principal are not included in those figures.) With a real income capitalization rate of 5%, the land would have a value of $1,240 per acre using the income capitalization method: 1,240 = 62/.05. This method of valuing land is discussed more in the Chapter 21, Land Purchase and Rental, along with several points of concern and caution surrounding this simple formula and the complex process of valuing and buying land.

Amortization or Capital Recovery

As discussed later in this chapter, loans that last longer than one year and have annual payments, or loans that have multiple payments per year, have their loan principal amortized over the length of the loan. In this situation, we know the loan principal, the interest rate, the length of the loan, and the number of payments per year. We want to calculate the periodic payment necessary to pay back the loan and the interest due. This periodic payment is also known as the principal and interest (PI) payment. The PI is calculated by the following formula.

$$PI_{(n, i)} = \text{loan principal} * \text{amortization factor}_{(n, i)}$$

where PI is the periodic principal and interest payment, the loan principal is the face value of the loan, n is the number of periods (that is, number of years times the number of payments per year), and i is the interest rate specified in the terms of the loan. For this calculation, the interest rate and the periods should be in the same units such as years and the annual interest rate or months and the monthly interest rate. The amortization factors can be found in Appendix Table IV for the specified loan terms or by using the following formula.

$$\text{Amortization factor}_{(n, i)} = [i/(1 - (1 + i)^{-n})]$$

As an example, suppose a farmer needs a loan of \$250,000 to expand his operation and could obtain financing from the local bank with these terms: annual payments, 20 years, 8.5 % interest, 1% loan origination fee, and a \$250 appraisal fee. Under these terms, each equal annual principal and interest (PI) payment is:

$$PI_{(20, .085)} = \$250,000 * .1057 = \$26,425$$

where the amortization factor$_{(20, .085)}$ = $.085/(1 - (1 + .085)^{-20})$ = 0.1057. This amortization factor can be estimated using the amortization factors for 8% and 9% in the row for the 20th period in Appendix Table IV. Since 8.5% is the average of 8% and 9%, its amortization factor is the average of the factors for 8% and 9%.

For some questions, we need to estimate the future annuity that is equivalent to a present total amount. For example, instead of calculating depreciation and interest payments for a depreciable asset (such as a tractor or building), the initial cost of that capital asset can be amortized over its useful life; this is called capital recovery. (The IRS has specific rules on how and when this method can be used for tax purposes. What is described here is how to use it for management planning, not tax preparation.) With capital recovery, we estimate the annual capital costs of an asset as the n period annuity ($A_{(n,i)}$) that is equivalent to its present value (i.e., the construction cost or purchase price) at a given interest rate.

$$A_{(n, i)} = PV * crf$$
$$crf = PV * [i/(1 - (1 + i)^{-n})]$$

For example, the annual capital recovery costs (ACRC) for a tractor that costs \$80,000 are estimated to be \$15,896 using a 9% discount rate and a useful life of seven years.

$$crf = .09/(1 - (1 + .09)^{-7}) = 0.1987$$
$$ACRC = \$80,000 * 0.1987 = \$15,896$$

The amortization or capital recovery factors (crf) can be found in Appendix Table IV.

Calculating Loan Payments

As noted in the previous section, using credit can provide several benefits to a farmer, but the loans and their associated interest do need to be paid according to the terms of the loan. For simple loans such as operating notes taken out and paid back within one year, the payment is a simple calculation of the loan principal multiplied by the stated interest rate. For example, suppose a farmer borrowed $50,000 at 10% to pay for feeder pigs purchased in April. Then, six months later, in October the pigs reached market weight and were sold and he paid the lender for the loan and the accrued interest. If the farmer had kept the loan for a full year, he would have owed the full 10% of the $50,000 as interest. But since he paid the loan back after six months or half of a year, the total interest charge was $2,500, which is $50,000 multiplied by 10% and then multiplied by 0.5 since the loan was only for half a year. The payment in October for this farmer is $52,500.

For loans that have multiple payments per year or last longer than one year with annual payments, the original loan principal is amortized (that is, spread out) over the length of the loan and interest is included in the periodic payment. As shown above, the principal and interest (PI) payment is calculated by the following formula.

$$PI_{(n, i)} = \text{loan principal} * \text{amortization factor}_{(n, i)}$$

where PI is the periodic principal and interest payment, loan principal is the initial or face value of the loan, n is the number of periods (that is, number of years times the number of payments per year), and i is the interest rate specified in the terms of the loan. The amortization factors can be found in Appendix Table IV for the specified loan terms or by using the following formula.

$$\text{Amortization factor}_{(n,i)} = [i/(1 - (1 + i)^{-n})]$$

As an example, suppose a farmer wants to buy a truck that costs $24,000. The lender says the farmer must pay at least 25% of the cost as an initial payment or "down payment," and the lender will then finance 75% of the cost at an annual 9% interest rate for three years with monthly payments and a $100 loan fee. Under these terms, the farmer pays 25% or $6,000 down and the loan is $18,000, which has to be paid back in 36 equal monthly payments over three years. Since the payments will be monthly, the annual rate of 9% is converted to an estimated monthly rate of 0.75% by dividing 9% by 12. The monthly amortization factor is calculated by inserting the monthly rate of 0.0075 and 36 periods into the equation, as shown here:

$$\text{Amortization factor}_{(36, .0075)} = .0075/(1 - (1 + 0.0075)^{-36}) = 0.0318$$

Thus, each monthly payment is the loan amount (or principal) multiplied by the amortization factor:

$$PI_{(36, .0075)} = \$18,000 * 0.0318 = \$572.40$$

In an earlier example, a farmer needs a loan of $250,000 to expand his operation and could obtain financing from the local bank with these terms: annual payments, 20 years, 8.5% interest, 1% loan origination fee, and a $250 appraisal fee. Under these terms, each annual principal and interest payment is calculated to be $26,425.

Suppose this farmer finds he could also obtain financing from an insurance company at these terms: annual payments, 20 years, 7% interest, 2.5% loan origination fee, and no other costs. The interest rate is lower, but the fee is higher. Under these terms, each annual principal and interest payment is:

$$PI_{(20,\ .07)} = \$250,000 * 0.0944 = \$23,600$$

where the amortization factor$_{(20,.07)}$ = $.07/(1-(1+0.07)^{-20})$ = 0.0944. This amortization factor also can be found in Appendix Table IV at the intersection of the row for the 20th period and 7%.

This farmer is now faced with a decision whether to (1) take a loan with a lower interest rate and thus a lower annual payment but a higher fee or (2) accept a higher interest rate with a lower fee. This question is addressed in the next section.

Estimating the Cost of Credit

Due to the many different sources of credit that can be used by farmers and the very different terms that those sources may use, the true cost of the alternatives can be difficult to see immediately. To evaluate alternative loan sources with different terms, we calculate the effective actual percentage rate (APR). This can be done in two ways. First, the true effective interest rate can be estimated using the procedures for estimating the internal rate of return (IRR) shown in Chapter 20, Investment Analysis, where this procedure is explained in detail. In the second method, the APR is approximated by slightly rewriting the PI formula above, solving for the amortization factor, and using the table of amortization factors in Appendix IV to estimate the effective APR. This is a fairly straightforward method for calculating, yet many farmers do not make the calculation, don't know what the different costs are, and don't change banks—as a recent survey of farmers in Germany found (Example 14.1).

Example 14.1. The Reluctance to Switch Banks

Many farmers work with only one bank or lending agency that they have worked with for many years. Consequently, they do not change banks even if another bank offers a higher interest rate on savings and a lower interest rate on loans. This "reluctance to switch" could be due to the farmer's actual and perceived transaction costs. The transaction costs are due to the cost in time and money of searching for another loan and bank and the time and money of applying at another bank. Farmers may also perceive the value or advantage of staying with their current bank in anticipation of better terms in the future and a preferential treatment of a long-time customer during potential hard times to come.

However, a survey of North German farmers showed that they underestimated the monetary disadvantages caused by the higher interest rates for loans from their current bank. They do not switch banks even if their individually perceived transaction costs are already "covered" by the lower interest rates of the alternative loan offer. They may have incomplete information about the other bank. They may also not have the proper tools or assistance to analyze alternative loans.

One can extend the results of this study to conclude that the prudent student will realize the value of learning the tools of financial analysis, the tools for comparing alternative loans, and the realization that avoiding the costs of high interest rates will lead to a better financial position of the farm. That financial position—rather than the longevity of the business relation-ship—will indeed be the better tool to obtain better loan terms in the future.

Source: O. Musshoff, N. Hirschauer, and H. Wassmuss, "The Role of Bounded Rationality in Farm Financ-ing Decisions: First Empirical Evidence." Contributed paper at the International Association of Agricul-tural Economists 2009 Conference, August 16–22, Beijing, China. Accessed on January 8, 2010, at http://purl.umn.edu/51545.

The PI formula is rewritten by replacing the "loan principal" with the "net amount borrowed" and referring to the amortization factor as "estimated."

$$\text{Periodic loan payment} = \text{net amount borrowed} * \text{estimated amortization factor}_{(n,i)}$$

The net amount borrowed is the original or stated loan amount minus any non-interest charges and fees such as loan points, origination and other signing fees, appraisal fees, stock purchases, and so on. The borrower either does not receive the full loan or has to pay the fees from other sources. Either way, the borrower is left with the net amount borrowed as his or her additional money available to be used.

Solving the previous formula for the amortization factor$_{(n,i)}$, we see it equal to:

$$\text{Estimated amortization factor}_{(n,i)} = \frac{\text{periodic loan payment}}{\text{net amount borrowed}}$$

This estimated amortization factor is used in the amortization tables (Appendix IV) to estimate the interest rate related to the number of periods for the loan being analyzed. If the loan requires more than one payment per year, than the resulting interest rate estimated from the table is multiplied by the number of payments per year to estimate the annual rate.

As an example, let us look again at the two loans the farmer was considering in the last section. This farmer needs a loan of $250,000 to expand his operation. The local bank was willing to provide a loan with these terms: annual payments, 20 years, 8.5% interest, 1% loan origination fee, and a $250 appraisal fee. Under these terms, as we saw in the last section, each annual principal and interest payment is:

$$\text{PI}_{(20, .085)} = \$250,000 * .1057 = \$26,425$$

This farmer could also obtain financing from an insurance company at these terms: annual pay-ments, 20 years, 7% interest, 2.5% loan origination fee, and no other costs. Under these terms, as we saw in the previous section, each annual principal and interest payment is:

$$\text{PI}_{(20, .07)} = \$250,000 * .0944 = \$23,600$$

To decide whether he should accept a loan with a lower interest rate but higher fees or one with a higher interest rate and lower fees, this farmer can estimate the effective APR to compare the two options.

The local bank will require the farmer to pay a 1% loan origination fee ($2,500) plus a $250 appraisal fee. Thus, the net amount borrowed is $250,000 minus $2,750, or $247,250. Coupling this net amount with the annual payment of $26,425, the estimated amortization factor is calculated to be

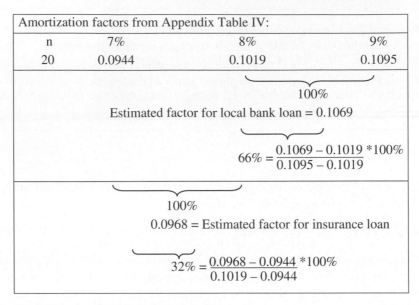

Amortization factors from Appendix Table IV:

n	7%	8%	9%
20	0.0944	0.1019	0.1095

100%

Estimated factor for local bank loan = 0.1069

$$66\% = \frac{0.1069 - 0.1019}{0.1095 - 0.1019} *100\%$$

100%

0.0968 = Estimated factor for insurance loan

$$32\% = \frac{0.0968 - 0.0944}{0.1019 - 0.0944} *100\%$$

Figure 14.1   Example Estimation of APR by Interpolation

0.1069 for this loan:

$$0.1069 = \frac{26,425}{247,250}$$

Looking at the row for 20 years in Appendix Table IV, we see this estimated factor, 0.1069, lies between the factors for 8% and 9%. A more accurate estimate of the effective APR can be estimated by linear interpolation. For example, the factor 0.1069 is 66% of the way from 0.1019 (the factor for 8%) to 0.1095 (the factor for 9%), so the effective APR is 66% of the way from 8% to 9% or 8.66% (Figure 14.1). So the true effective APR for the local bank loan is slightly higher than the 8.5% listed in the terms.

The insurance company will require the farmer to pay a 2.5% loan origination fee ($6,250), but there are no other fees. Thus, the net amount borrowed is $250,000 minus $6,250, or $243,750. Coupling this net amount with the annual payment of $23,600, the estimated amortization factor is calculated to be 0.0968 for this loan (23600/243750). Looking at the row for 20 years in Appendix Table IV, we see this estimated factor, 0.0968, lies between the factors for 7% and 8%. Again using linear interpolation, the factor 0.0968 is 32% of the way from 0.0944 (the factor for 7%) to 0.1019 (the factor for 8%), so the effective APR is 32% of the way from 7% to 8% or 7.32% (Figure 14.1). So the true effective APR for the loan from the insurance company is slightly higher than the 7% listed in the terms. We also see, as expected, that the larger fee gives a larger increase in the APR for this loan.

Based on the effective APRs, the loan from the insurance company is a lower-cost loan even though it has a higher fee associated with it. However, the final choice between these two loans also has to take into consideration the availability of funds to pay the higher fee when the loan is received versus the benefits of lower annual payments. In this example, the difference in fees, ($6,250 − $2,750 = $3,500), would be paid back within two years of lower payments, so paying the higher fee is probably worth its cost. In other situations, this decision may need the preparation of a cash flow for the potential expansion and an analysis of the impact on the farmer's balance sheet.

Cash Flow Management

Cash flow management is critical to all farms. Financially strapped farms need to watch their cash flow. Even profitable and growing farms can experience periods of tight cash flow. Farm growth and wise use of cash reserves depend on knowing when cash will flow into the farm and when cash needs to flow out to cover expenses, loan payments, and living expenses, for example. The cash flow statement is the main tool of cash flow management.

The cash flow statement shows the annual flow and timing of cash in and out of a business. It has four major sections: sources of cash, uses of cash, a flow of funds summary, and the loan balances. As its name implies, the cash flow statement contains any and only cash transactions. It does not include non-cash items such as depreciation or farm-produced feed, for example. However, some items not found on an income statement, such as receipt of loans and loan payments, are found in a cash flow statement because they are part of the flow of cash though they are not part of the expenses and incomes for an income statement. An example of a cash flow statement is shown in Table 14.3.

Projected versus Actual Cash Flow

A projected cash flow statement or budget for a future period is used by a manager for two main purposes: planning for the future and adjusting plans according to actual results.

1. Projecting future cash flows allows a farmer to adjust the timing of sales, expenses, loan receipts, and loan payments before production starts. Planning and arranging for new borrowing can decrease potential business disruption if cash is not available and provide the opportunity to obtain better loan terms.
2. Comparing projected to actual cash flows allows a farmer to fine-tune the timing of sales, expenses, loan receipts, and loan payments as production is taking place and to change plans and expectations during the current production period. This process of comparing is explained later in the chapter under "Financial Control."

A projected cash flow statement is called a cash flow budget in common usage. This change in the name is probably because the projection shows our expectations of the amounts we have budgeted for spending and receiving—that is, the cash going out and the cash coming in.

Cash flow budgets for planning are prepared on a monthly or quarterly basis. The projected quarterly cash flow statement for the example farm in this chapter is shown in Table 14.3.

Building a Cash Flow Statement

Projecting a cash flow budget requires a great deal of information and effort but, in return, it provides very crucial information to the farmer. To ensure an accurate statement, an orderly process such as the steps listed below need to be followed. This process was introduced in Chapter 10 and is described in much more detail in the following example. Let us follow the projection made by the example Iowa farmers, Dave and Sue Sanderson, for their dairy farm. The result of their work is shown in Table 14.3.

1. Develop the crop and livestock production plan for the whole farm. The Sandersons have a total of 770 crop acres on their farm. They own 310 crop acres and rent an additional 460 acres. They

Table 14.3   Projected Cash Flow Budget for Sandersons' Dairy Farm

CASH RECEIPTS	Jan.–Mar.	Apr.–Jun.	Jul.–Sept.	Oct.–Dec.	Annual
Milk sales	248,000	244,000	239,000	235,000	966,000
Calf sales	5,500	5,800	5,500	5,110	21,910
Corn sales	0	1,400	0	0	1,400
Soybean sales	19,000	0	0	22,350	41,350
Alfalfa sales	1,250	0	0	0	1,250
Government payments	4,239	556	0	4,830	9,625
Other farm income	0	0	0	0	0
Miscellaneous	0	0	0	0	0
Cull cows	20,000	19,000	18,500	18,940	76,440
Machinery	0	0	0	0	0
New term debt	0	95,000	0	0	95,000
Total cash receipts	297,989	365,756	263,000	286,230	1,212,975
CASH OUTFLOW					
Operating expenses					
Seed	11,950	0	0	7,160	19,110
Fertilizer	20,000	3,250	0	14,800	38,050
Crop chemicals	0	12,500	0	4,250	16,750
Crop insurance	2,860	0	0	0	2,860
Drying fuel	0	0	0	5,700	5,700
Crop miscellaneous	600	2,200	700	800	4,300
Machinery expenses	2,200	8,700	2,000	4,700	17,600
Purchased feed	82,600	65,200	72,300	35,800	255,900
Veterinary	10,325	10,325	10,325	10,325	41,300
Livestock supplies	14,875	14,875	14,875	14,875	59,500
Breeding fees	4,375	4,375	4,375	4,375	17,500
Fuel, utilities, repairs	14,000	14,000	14,000	14,000	56,000
DHIA and accounting	2,625	2,625	2,625	2,625	10,500
Hired labor	43,000	52,000	47,000	52,000	194,000
Land rent	33,350	0	0	33,350	66,700
Real estate taxes	14,319	0	0	14,319	28,638
Farm insurance	5,900	3,300	1,100	5,300	15,600
Trucking and marketing	6,000	2,000	5,000	10,000	23,000
Miscellaneous	4,500	4,500	4,500	4,500	18,000
Capital purchases					
Breeding livestock	0	0	0	0	0
Machinery	0	127,500	0	0	127,500
Buildings and improvements	0	0	0	0	0
Other assets	0	0	0	0	0
Proprietor withdrawals	15,000	15,000	15,000	15,000	60,000
Term loan payments	0	0	0	0	0
Principal	44,023	14,532	0	14,023	72,578
Interest	39,061	5,850	0	13,563	58,474
Total cash outflow	371,563	362,732	193,800	281,465	1,209,560

(*continued*)

(continued)

FLOW OF FUNDS SUMMARY	Jan.–Mar.	Apr.–Jun.	Jul.–Sept.	Oct.–Dec.	Annual
Beginning cash balance	36,500	5,000	5,000	33,665	36,500
Total cash receipts	297,989	365,756	263,000	286,230	1,212,975
Total cash outflow	371,563	362,732	193,800	281,465	1,209,560
Cash difference	−37,074	8,024	74,200	38,431	39,915
Borrowing this period	42,074	0	0	0	42,074
Payment on operating loans					
Principal	0	2,261	39,813	0	42,074
Interest	0	763	722	0	1,484
Ending cash balance	5,000	5,000	33,665	38,431	38,431
LOAN BALANCES AT END OF PERIOD					
Term debt	791,310	871,778	871,778	857,755	857,755
Operating debt	42,074	39,813	0	0	0

Beginning loan balances:			
Term debt	835,334	Operating loan interest rate:	7.25%
Operating debt	0	Desired minimum balance:	5,000

also have a 350 acres of cow dairy and facilities about 12 years old. They have the equipment for corn, corn silage, soybeans, and alfalfa. Based on their estimates of feed requirements and of costs and returns, they decide to grow 250 acres of corn for grain, 135 acres of corn silage, 175 acres of soybeans, and 210 acres of alfalfa. With a three-year rotation, they plan to have 70 of those 210 alfalfa acres in an establishment year using an herbicide treatment, not an oat cover crop.

2. Estimate the crop production levels and livestock feed requirements. This involves both the quantities produced and needed and the timing of those quantities. End of year inventories may need to be maintained for feed until the next year's crop production is harvested.

For their dairy herd, the Sandersons estimate they will need 39,550 bushels of corn, 2,800 tons of corn silage, and 2,100 tons of alfalfa hay. They expect to have enough production of corn and corn silage to meet all their feed needs, but they estimate they will need to buy 1,100 tons of alfalfa hay in the winter besides their own production. They also estimate how much of last year's corn and hay they will have in storage and be able to sell.

3. Estimate cash receipts from livestock and crops. Based on these production and feed estimates and projected market prices, they estimate the amount of each product they will sell next year. For example, they think they will sell $966,000 in milk and $11,350 in soybeans next year. Since they plan to feed most, but not all, of the corn they grow, their estimated corn sales for next year are only $1,400.

4. Estimate other income such as interest, government payments, and insurance payments. This category would include non-farm income if that is to be included in the farm cash flow.

For example, the Sandersons estimate that the total government program payments they will receive are $9,625. This total includes part of the payments based on this year but paid next year and the part of next year's payments that will be paid next year.

5. Estimate cash operating expenses.   These would include both variable expenses such as purchased feed, fertilizer, and labor and fixed expenses such as real estate taxes, insurance payments, and loan payments.

From their records, published budgets, county offices, insurance agents, and so on, the Sandersons estimate their expenses for the crops and dairy to be $19,110 for seed next year, $38,550 for fertilizer, $225,900 for purchased feed, $23,000 for trucking, and so on.

6. If included with the farm, estimate personal and non-farm cash expenses.   This category includes either family living expenses directly or withdrawals for family living.

Together the Sandersons estimate they will work about 3,000 hours in labor time plus more time in management. Based on their living expense records, they want to pay themselves $60,000 for their own labor and management. This is entered as a total withdrawal and not itemized.

7. Estimate the purchases and sales of capital assets such as machinery, breeding livestock, buildings, land, and ownership in other businesses.   The value of the cull cows expected to be sold is estimated as part of the enterprise budget for dairy. They plan to buy a new combine in June using $32,500 in cash, a $95,000 loan, and their two-year-old combine as a trade-in. The loan is entered in the cash receipts section. The $32,500 cannot be seen directly but is part of the $127,500 capital purchase in the cash outflow section. They do not plan to make any other capital purchases or sales next year.

8. Calculate the scheduled principal and interest payments on current loans and capital leases. The Sandersons have four term loans. To be sure, they check with their creditors to verify their calculations of next year's principal and interest payments. For example, their real estate payment is due in December with $14,023 in principal and $13,563 in interest. The loan for their dairy facilities is due in February. One of their machinery loans is due in March; the other is due in June. These four term loans will have a combined balance due at the beginning of next year of $835,334. They will not carry any operating loan into next year. They can obtain an operating loan at an annual rate of 7.25% with a credit line of $100,000 without having to check with their banker.

9. Estimate the beginning balances of all cash accounts such as checking, saving, and marketing accounts.   Determine the desired minimum cash balance needed to carry from one period to the next.

After checking their current balances and estimating what they will receive and spend for the rest of this year, they estimate that they will start next year with a cash balance of $36,500. The Sandersons decide they would like a minimum cash balance of $5,000 at the end of each quarter to cushion unexpected fluctuations in the cash flow.

10. Enter this information into the cash flow format and complete the flow of funds summary.   As part of the flow of funds summary, project the timing of new debt and potential payments on new debt. Estimate the ending loan balances for each period in the cash flow statement.

All of the information on cash receipts, cash outflows, their beginning cash balance, and their beginning loan balances are entered into the quarterly cash flow statement as shown in Table 14.3. Since this is a projection, they do not know the precise amount and timing of each actual receipt and expenditure; totals are divided among the four quarters based on when the Sandersons think they may occur. Fertilizer expenses, for example, usually occur in the late winter and early spring except for fall-applied fertilizers and any prepayments made in late fall for next year. Seasonal patterns in prices are reflected in some differences. The timing of some amounts is known quite well—real estate taxes, principal and interest payments, for example—so these can be entered in the specific quarter. The timing of other amounts, such as veterinary expenses, cannot be determined very well and are simply divided evenly between the quarters.

As a first step in completing the flow of funds summary, the Sandersons estimate the cash difference for each quarter. For example, they start with a cash balance of $36,500, add total projected cash receipts of $297,989, subtract total projected cash outflows of $371,563, and find a negative cash difference of $37,074 in the first quarter.

Since the cash difference is negative, they know they need to borrow to maintain their desired minimum balance of $5,000 at the end of the quarter. They do not need to borrow to pay any operating interest since they are not bringing an operating debt into the year. So they estimate they will need to borrow $42,074 to cover the negative cash difference and to have $5,000 left at the end of the quarter.

In the second quarter, the cash difference is $8,024. Since this is greater than the desired minimum balance ($5,000) plus the interest on the operating loan from the first quarter, they will not need to borrow any more. The operating interest of $763 is estimated by multiplying the operating loan balance at the end of the first quarter ($42,074) by the annual interest rate of 7.25% and dividing by 4 since the cash flow is quarterly. To avoid paying interest when they do not need to, the Sandersons estimate they will be able to pay $2,261 in principal on the operating loan they took out at the end of the first quarter. This $2,261 is estimated by subtracting the interest payment of $763 and the minimum balance of $5,000 from the cash difference of $8,024.

In the third quarter, the cash difference is large enough to pay off the remaining operating debt and have an ending balance greater than the minimum.

Loan balances are calculated by adding new borrowings to the beginning balances and subtracting any principal payments. For example, the beginning total term debt of $835,334 is decreased by a principal payment of $44,023 in the first quarter so the balance at the end of the first quarter is $791,310. In the second quarter, the term debt is increased by a loan of $95,000 listed in cash receipts and decreased by a principal payment of $14,532. So the term debt balance at the end of the second quarter is $871,778. The operating balance starts at $0, increases to $42,074 when that amount is borrowed in the first quarter, and decreases to $39,813 and then to $0 as it is paid off.

With this projected budget, the Sandersons can see when their cash is expected to flow in and out. They can also see that their ending cash balance will have a slight increase by the end of the year: from $36,500 to $38,431. The direction is right, but the quantity is not large, especially when the only additional capital purchase is for a new combine. However, they know they can probably meet their desired level of pay ($60,000).

Other uses of the projection are outlined in the next section. These other uses include trying to see whether the loan payments due in the first part of the year could be rescheduled to the end of the year and avoid the $1,484 in operating interest costs shown in this projection.

Uses of a Cash Flow Budget

As just noted, the main use of a projected cash flow is to project the amount and timing of both new borrowing and loan repayments through the year. With the projected cash flow, partners, family members, and financial advisors can offer better advice to the farmer. The projected cash flow budget can also be used for many other uses, such as those listed below.

- Evaluate changes in the timing of product sales to coincide with cash needs and thus reduce borrowing needs.
- Consider changes in the timing of expenditures and scheduled debt repayments to reduce borrowing needs.
- Develop a borrowing and debt repayment schedule that fits the project cash flow. This could reduce interest expenses and allow for a more orderly process of arranging for financing needs.
- Assess the value of potential discounts for cash payments for inputs obtained by rearranging the timing of cash inflows and outflows instead of borrowing.
- Calculate potential tax impacts of alternative decisions and decide to take advantage of or avoid those impacts.
- Obtain a better balance of short-term and long-term debt by observing the impact of alternative debt structure plans on the projected cash flow.
- Observe the interdependence of farm, non-farm, and personal cash flows, take advantage of synergies, and avoid potential conflicts.
- Estimate the sensitivity of the initial plan to unexpected changes in prices, crop yields, animal productivities, and so on to determine whether adjustments are needed to develop a more robust plan.
- Monitor and control the financial side of the farm, as described in the next section.

Financial Control

Control is one of the four main management functions: planning, organizing, directing, and controlling. Control is the process of determining and implementing the necessary actions to make certain that plans translate into desired results. Through effective control, we are better able to achieve the goals and objectives that have been established.

Financial control takes place in three parts: establishing standards, measuring performance, and taking corrective actions, if needed. Standards are established during planning (especially during enterprise and whole-farm planning as discussed in later chapters). Examples of financial standards include expected interest rates, needed borrowings, and timing of borrowing needs. Measuring financial performance takes place in two ways: monitoring financial conditions and recording actual performance. The three kinds of corrective actions are:

1. Rules to change the plan if conditions change (repair instead of replace a tractor if interest rates and machinery prices increase, for example)
2. Rules to change the implementation of the financial plan (such as to change how much equity capital is used if new sources are found)

3. Change the goals and standards (change the expected interest rate as bank policies change, for example)

The three types of control (preliminary, concurrent, and feedback) are used in finance also. For example, a projected cash flow statement can show the expected size and timing of needed operating loans, so preliminary control can take place by negotiating for credit and interest rates before the need is immediate. Monitoring of the actual cash flow through the year is one example of concurrent control that allows early detection of deviations from expectations and implementation of needed corrective actions. Year-end financial analysis of actual performance provides feedback information to plan for the future.

Financial control revolves around the three financial statements: the cash flow statement, the income statement, and the net worth statement. For concurrent control, the cash flow statement is the most useful statement. For feedback control, all three financial statements are useful.

The projected cash flow budget is compared with the actual cash flow to develop the cash flow deviation report. This report shows the source, direction, and size of deviations from the budget or plan. It is used to monitor and control the cash flow of the business and as an early warning system for changes in the plans for profitability, liquidity, and solvency. The cash flow deviation report may not show the problem to be corrected, but it can show where to look. Whereas a cash flow statement contains all the cash transactions for a firm during a period, a cash flow deviation report shows only the deviations between planned and actual cash flow that violate previously set minimums for deviations in absolute amounts and in percentage changes. This is the "management by exception" method where only those items that deviate by a certain amount or percentage—say, $2,000 or 10%—are listed in the report because they are exceptions. They deviate enough that they need some management attention.

Cash Flow Deviations Report Example

As an example, let us consider again the Sandersons' dairy. For their cash flow deviations report, they set deviation minimums of $1000 and 10%. An abbreviated example for the second quarter and the six months from January through June is shown in Table 14.4.

The first item they see is good news: milk sales are going up. As of July 1, sales are up 11.3% for the second quarter and 6.1% for the year to date. Their records confirm what they had been noticing: milk production is close to the planned amounts and the actual milk price has been higher than the price used to project the cash flow. While the deviation is less than 10% year to date, the amount ($29,948) is large enough to check on its effect on cash flow, credit needs, and the ability to alter plans in a favorable way.

Table 14.4 Cash Flow Deviation Report for the Sandersons' Dairy

| | Second Quarter | | | | Year to Date | | | |
| | | | Deviation | | | | Deviation | |
	Budget	Actual	$	%	Budget	Actual	$	%
Milk sales	244,000	271,583	27,583	11.3	492,000	521,948	29,948	6.1%
Crop chemicals	12,500	1,633	−10,867	−86.9	12,500	10,763	−1,737	−13.9%
Crop misc.	2,200	2,483	283	12.9	2,800	3,024	224	8.0%
Purchased feed	65,200	38,760	−26,440	−40.6	147,800	216,865	69,065	46.7%

At first glance, the second item in the deviation report, crop chemicals, is startling. The actual amount spent in the second quarter is $10,867 or 86.9% lower than planned. Then they note that the year-to-date actual expenditure is closer to the budget. The deviation for this item may be due to a sale on herbicides in January that had not been anticipated. So the physical amount of herbicide used is close to the plan, but due to the timing of the sale, the expenditure is both lower and earlier.

The third item, miscellaneous crop expenses, is an example of the deviation violating one minimum, 10%, but not violating the absolute minimum ($1,000). Although even small differences can be important, deviations such as these could be ignored (in favor of larger problems to correct or opportunities to explore) after considering the sources of the deviations.

The fourth item, purchased feed, is much lower in the second quarter than planned: down 40.6%. However, the Sandersons were reading crop reports and saw lower hay production estimates pointing to increases in hay prices. So they decided to buy more hay than planned and to buy it earlier in the first quarter rather than in the second quarter. The year-to-date deviation shows an increase compared with the plan, which supports the story of buying more and buying earlier. The deviation may mean that other parts of the cash flow need attention. For instance, a larger operating loan may have been needed in the first quarter to pay for the increased hay purchases in that quarter, but the milk price increases that caused the increases in milk sales may have offset that need. Further evaluation of the full cash flow statement would answer these overall questions.

Deviations should be evaluated for their sources, for needed adjustments in production and marketing plans, and for impacts on the financial plan (borrowing more or less, for example). Rather than poring over two full cash flow statements (projected and actual), a manager can use a cash flow deviation report to survey the deviations quickly, identify problems or opportunities, and move onto other management issues. The year-to-date section is necessary so that a month or quarter is not evaluated in isolation from other months. Timing of sales and purchase may be altered from the plan to take advantage of better prices. This can cause major deviations in one month but they are not a deviation in a longer view. It may be good to be able to look ahead too, in case a sale has been made earlier or a purchase has been delayed.

In each overall category (or set of rows) in a cash flow statement, the question asked by management varies slightly but in general terms it is still: What caused the deviation? As an example, let us look at the following categories.

Receipts and Expenditures.   If there is a deviation, a manager needs to evaluate how large the difference is and whether the deviation merits any more investigation to learn what may have caused the difference.

Borrowings and Loan Payments.   Evaluate these with the focus on the ending cash balance for the whole farm. If the ending cash balance is too low, the farm may need to borrow more or make some adjustments elsewhere in the business. These adjustments may include selling earlier than planned, delaying expenditures until the cash is available, or decreasing expenditures. If the ending cash balance is higher than desired, the farmer could evaluate the options of borrowing less, paying more on current loan balances, or building cash reserves for poor cash flow years.

Cash Difference.   If this deviates too far from expected levels, the deviations may be from the receipts and expenditures for that period or a carryover from another period.

Beginning and Ending Cash Balances.   If other deviations do not "net out," the manager may need to check with the banker about borrowing more money or prepaying some loans. Deviations in the ending cash balance may need special action whether the causes are differences in receipts or expenditures.

In all cases, the manager needs to decide whether the deviations are due to timing, mistakes, price, unplanned purchases, quantity, unplanned sales, or other events. The appropriate actions will vary with individual farms.

This chapter discussed the sources and uses of capital. It then presented the concepts of the time value of money and how that helps us understand and calculate loan payments and estimate the cost of credit. The chapter presented the details of the cash flow statement and the process of building that statement. The last section discussed financial control, how to understand a cash flow deviation report, and how to respond to major deviations.

Summary

- Financial management is the process of obtaining, using, and controlling the use of capital.
- Capital comes in two forms: equity capital and debt capital.
- Equity capital is the money of the owners, partners, and other investors.
- Debt capital is a liability or other financial obligation on which interest and other fees have to be paid.
- Owner-operator equity is the largest source of capital for U.S. farmers.
- Taking on debt increases risk but can also improve farm income, wealth, and progress toward other goals.
- Leasing and contracting allow a farmer to obtain the use of capital assets without using equity or debt capital, but they are financial obligations.
- Principal and interest payments are calculated by multiplying the loan principal by an amortization factor. The amortization factor is based on the loan's interest rate, the number of payments per year, and the number of years of the loan.
- Since different loans can have different interest rates, fees, and other terms, the effective actual percentage rate (APR) can be calculated and used to compare the cost of alternative sources of credit.
- Cash flow management is critical for both financially strapped and profitable farms.
- The four major sections of a cash flow statement are sources of cash, uses of cash, flow of funds summary, and loan balances.
- A projected cash flow statement is used for planning for the future and adjusting plans according to actual results.
- Cash flow budgets are projected in a series of steps, starting with estimating the physical quantities and timing of production and inputs and selecting appropriate prices and costs.
- Financial control involves establishing standards, measuring performance, and taking corrective actions, as needed, to ensure that plans translate into desired results.
- Preliminary, concurrent, and feedback controls are used in financial control.
- Actual cash flows can be compared to a projected cash flow budget to develop a cash flow deviation report. This report can be used to identify those categories deviating from the plan by more preset levels and thus needing management attention.

Review Questions

1. Why are farmers interested in increasing their risk by borrowing capital?
2. How can the alternative sources of credit be compared for their true or actual cost of borrowing?
3. What is the annual principal and interest payment for a loan of $250,000 with these terms: annual payments, 20 years, 7.5% interest, a 2% loan origination fee, and a $200 appraisal fee?
4. What is the effective actual percentage rate or APR for the loan in the previous question?
5. What are the four major sections of a cash flow statement?
6. What are the steps for projecting a cash flow budget?
7. Complete the quarterly flow of funds summary below by filling the correct numbers in the boxes. The beginning operating loan balance of $58,000 paid in January, but more may need to be borrowed in that quarter. The beginning term debt is $125,000; more is borrowed in September,and a payment is made in December. The balance at the end of each quarter reflects these changes.The desired minimum balance is $5,000 at the end of each quarter.

Flow of Funds Summary	Jan.–Mar.	Apr.–Jun.	Jul.–Sept.	Oct.–Dec.	Annual
Beginning cash balance	10,180				10,180
Total cash receipts	256,563	61,688	216,000	335,803	870,054
Total cash outflow	244,985	217,553	332,648	159,603	954,789
Cash difference					
Borrowing this period					
Payment on operating loans					
Principal	58,000				
Interest	1,015	740	3,480	5,582	10,817
Ending cash balance					

8. How can a projected cash flow be used by farmers to improve their cash flow management and their profitability?
9. How can the projected and actual cash flow statements be used in financial control?
10. Describe "management by exception" and how it can be used by farmers.

Further Reading

Barry, Peter J., Paul N. Ellinger, John A. Hopkin, and C. B. Baker. 2000. *Financial Management in Agriculture*. 6th ed. Danville, Illinois: Interstate Publishers, 678 pp.

15

Enterprise Budgets: Uses and Development

In this chapter:

- Purpose of enterprise budgets
- Organization of a typical enterprise budget
- Developing enterprise budgets from whole-farm records and by economic engineering
- Estimating annual costs of durable assets such as machinery, land, and buildings

Management is a dynamic process that needs information. An enterprise budget is a critical, basic piece of that information. It is the building block for many decisions made by a farm manager. An enterprise budget shows the expected receipts, costs, and profits from a certain part of the business such as wheat or hogs. In large general businesses, these parts may be called product divisions; in farm management, the tradition is to call them enterprises. A manager can use the information in an enterprise budget to improve the profitability of each part of the business and to choose which enterprises are best for the profitability of the whole farm.

In farm management, a profit center is an enterprise that is expected to generate revenue and thus profit for the farm. Examples of profit centers include crop production, the dairy milking herd, hogs, and custom hire work done for others. A cost center is an enterprise that is expected to incur costs but provides services used by other enterprises on the farm. Examples of cost centers include land ownership and management, building services, and machinery services. A farmer will view and manage profit centers differently from cost centers, but enterprise budgets are needed for both.

In the rest of this chapter, we discuss the purpose of enterprise budgets; organization of a typical enterprise budget; developing enterprise budgets from whole farm records and by economic engineering; estimating annual costs of durable inputs: machinery, buildings, breeding livestock, and perennial crops; and adjusting enterprise budgets for changes in productivity, competition, and industry structure.

Purpose of Enterprise Budgets

An enterprise budget is a projection used for planning the future. It is not a historical accounting. An enterprise budget shows the projected receipts, costs, and net returns to be expected if specific methods and inputs are used to produce a specified amount of a product or products. It is based on the economic and technological relationships between inputs and outputs. An enterprise budget provides information that can be used to support a variety of management tasks such as:

1. Estimating the economic and financial feasibility of alternative production technologies and management practices
2. Uncovering costs that may have been overlooked
3. Selecting the best crop and livestock enterprise combinations for a farm (see Example 15.1)
4. Refining organizational and operating structures
5. Developing production and marketing plans
6. Developing and organizing information useful to lending agencies when the farm is applying for loans
7. Making investment decisions
8. Comparing the projected and actual results of implementing a plan.

Whereas an enterprise budget provides bottom-line information about a part of a farm business, such as "growing corn," or "dairy operations," or "whatever we are doing with the west field," budget calculations are based on smaller standard units of measurement, not the present size of the enterprise. For example, most crops are described on a per acre or hectare basis, and livestock budgets are usually estimated on a per head basis. Sometimes a unit may be too small to be practical (e.g., one chicken), so the budget unit should be a larger unit. The "smallest rational unit" depends upon the enterprise being analyzed, the conditions surrounding that enterprise, and what is typically used in publically available enterprise budgets. Rather than using the present size of the enter-

---

Example 15.1. Budgets to Compare Traditional Crops to Energy Crops

Enterprise budgets are crucial to comparing the profitability of traditional grain crops to the potential of growing energy crops. In a recent study, enterprise budgets for the costs and returns expected for traditional food and feed crops (corn grain, soybeans, spring wheat, sugar beets, and alfalfa hay) as well as potential energy crops (grassland crops, hybrid poplar trees, willow trees, and corn stover) were estimated for 2010 in Minnesota, United States.

These enterprise budgets can help a farmer choose crops based on profitability. They can also, as in this case, show how much subsidy or increase in price is needed for energy crops to be competitive with traditional crops. The net returns per acre show the profitability of each crop on an annualized basis. Sugar beets are estimated to be more profitable than any crop but require a contract or ownership share in a processor. Alfalfa is next in profitability, followed by soybeans and corn (especially if corn stover is included). The annualized negative returns for prairie, poplar, and willow point to the need for subsidy or higher prices paid by energy processors before many farmers will be willing to plant these crops.

Estimated Net Returns, Minnesota, 2010

Crop	Net return ($ per acre)
Corn	18
Soybeans	43
Wheat	(70)
Sugar beets	130
Corn silage	(3)
Perennial: Alfalfa—direct seeded (4 yr)	87
Perennial: Alfalfa—cover crop (4 yr)	68
Perennial: Switchgrass (10 yr)	4
Perennial: Prairie (20 yr)	(46)
Perennial: Poplar (17 yr)	(52)
Perennial: Willow (20 yr)	(93)
Corn stover (harvested after corn grain)	29

Source: W. F. Lazarus and A. Goodkind, 2009, ''Minnesota Crop Cost and Return Guide for 2010,'' Department of Applied Economics, University of Minnesota, St. Paul. Accessed on February 13, 2010, at http://www.apec.umn.edu/faculty/wlazarus/documents/cropbud.pdf

prise (e.g., 200 acres or 200 sows), the smallest rational unit (e.g., one acre or one litter) is used to describe enterprise budgets for three reasons.

1. The amounts and values are expressed in constant and understandable terms (e.g., pounds per acre, pounds per head).
2. The constant unit makes it very easy to compare different sizes of current and potential enterprises.
3. The smallest rational units are usually the units used by the USDA, extension, credit sources, and other agencies that develop representative budgets. By using these standard budget units, the manager can easily compare his or her estimates with other sources of information.

The development of enterprise budgets also requires a view of the future. To grow or only to remain viable, a manager has to be as efficient as the industry requires to remain competitive. Since change will always be with us, this knowledge is extremely critical for any business planning to expand or just stay in business. The critical benchmark that should be used in budgets is not today's productivity and efficiency requirements, but what will be required in, say, 10 to 15 years when the buildings and equipment (and investment) are still capable of production. Also, the critical benchmark is not the average but the competitive edge.

A simple estimate of future productivity can be made by extending past trends. This can be done by estimating the annual percentage change and subsequent progression of future percentages. It can also be done by graphical extrapolation of past trends.

Care must be taken, however, to project a benchmark productivity level required to be competitive. Projecting the average productivity will not provide a good benchmark. Future producers are not among the average producers today. In the strategic analysis of the industry, the best producers must be identified and benchmarks developed based on their abilities. For example, average milk production per cow has been increasing for many years. We could take that data; it is easily available; and we could quickly make a projection into the future. However, that past data contains many farms in the average that are not expected to be competitive in the future: farms with smaller herds, older equipment, less productive management techniques. Thus, planning to compete against today's projected averages will be planning to compete against producers who will not be in business tomorrow. Data must be obtained that shows the productivity of today's top producers because they will be tomorrow's competitors.

This analysis of productivity and efficiency trends needs to be done for different regions of the country (and the world) to be sure we understand which regions, farms, and technologies will have competitive advantages in the future. With this knowledge we can better understand the forces shaping structural change and their impact on our decisions. This is part of external analysis within strategic management described in Chapter 8.

Organization of an Enterprise Budget

An enterprise budget is organized with several major sections including the title, receipts, operating costs, returns over operating costs, ownership costs, net return, cost per unit, footnotes, and seasonal distribution of inputs. As examples of enterprise budgets, we will use the projected enterprise budget for growing spring wheat in southwest Texas (Table 15.1) and for a dairy enterprise in Kansas (Table 15.2).

Title

While calling the title a section of the enterprise seems extremely detail oriented, the title is important because it can and should contain a lot of information for a user of the budget. The title should name the crop or livestock enterprise and date the budget was estimated as well as the budget unit, location, size, irrigated or non-irrigated, and other major descriptions of the enterprise. From its title, we know the example crop budget is for one acre of non-irrigated spring wheat to be grown in southwest Texas in 2008. From this description we expect the yield and input needs to be based on the climate and yield potential for spring wheat in southwest Texas. In the dairy enterprise budget, we note that the estimated budget is for one milk cow in a 600-cow herd projected for 2009 in Kansas.

Receipts

In the section on receipts, all expected sources should be listed. The main product is usually listed first with secondary products listed after that. List all products, including cash sales of all products in the market as well as non-cash products sold or considered sold to other parts of the farm or bartered to other farms. Prices for the products are obtained from the market or its value as an input

Table 15.1　An Example Enterprise Budget for One Acre of Spring Wheat, Non-irrigated, Southwest Texas, 2008

	Unit	Price	Quantity	Total
INCOME				
Wheat, spring	bu	4.5	35	157.50
Government payment				13.00
Crop insurance indemnity payment				0.00
TOTAL INCOME				170.50
OPERATING COSTS				
Seed	lb	0.34	70	23.80
Crop insurance	acre	5.04	1	5.04
Nitrogen, dry	lb	0.5	60	30.00
Phosphate	lb	0.4	30	12.00
Custom harvest per acre	acre	14	1	14.00
Custom harvest per bu	bu	0.14	35	4.90
Custom haul wheat	bu	0.15	35	5.25
Diesel fuel	gal	2.8	1.57	4.40
Gasoline	gal	3	0.46	1.38
Repairs and maintenance	acre	3.98	1	3.98
Land rent	acre	20	1	20.00
Interest on oper. capital	6 mo.	8.0%	124.75	4.99
TOTAL OPERATING COSTS				129.74
RETURN OVER OPERATING COSTS				40.76
OWNERSHIP AND FIXED COSTS				
Machinery and equipment				7.62
TOTAL OWNERSHIP AND FIXED COSTS				7.62
Operator labor	hour	10	0.31	3.10
Operator management	wheat sales	5.0%	157.50	7.88
TOTAL COSTS				148.33
NET RETURN to management and risk				22.17
TOTAL COSTS per bushel				4.24
Cost per bushel (net of government payment)				3.87

Source: Adapted from Extension Agricultural Economics, 2007, ''Spring Wheat, Dryland, Projected Costs and Returns per acre for 2008,'' Department of Agricultural Economics, Texas A & M University, College Station, Texas, accessed on June 30, 2009, at http://agecoext.tamu.edu/fileadmin/user_upload/Documents/Budgets/District/10/2008/swd.pdf.

Table 15.2 An Example Enterprise Budget for One Cow in a 600 Lactating Cow Herd, Kansas, 2009

RECEIPTS PER COW:	Per cow	Per cwt
Milk sales, 25,000 lb @ $17.57/cwt	4,393	17.57
Volume premium	125	0.50
Government payment (MILC)	0	0.00
Calves sold: 95% × $246/head	234	0.93
Cull cows sold: 1,350 lb × 27.5% × $57.90/cwt	215	0.86
Manure credit	126	0.51
GROSS RECEIPTS	5,093	20.37
OPERATING COSTS		
Feed	2,036	8.15
Labor	403	1.61
Veterinary, drugs, and supplies	140	0.56
Somatotropin (rbST)	83	0.33
Utilities and water	125	0.50
Fuel, oil, and auto expense	67	0.27
Milk hauling and promotion cost	250	1.00
Building and equipment repairs	135	0.54
Heifer replacement cost: 32% × $1,950/head	624	2.50
Semen A.I. services and supplies	53	0.21
Interest on 1/2 operating costs @ 8.0%	128	0.51
TOTAL OPERATING COSTS	4,044	16.18
RETURN OVER OPERATING COSTS	1,049	4.19
OWNERSHIP AND FIXED COSTS		
Interest on herd	156	0.62
Insurance on herd	20	0.08
Professional fees (legal, accounting, etc.)	17	0.07
Depreciation on buildings and equipment	272	1.09
Interest on land, buildings, and equipment	244	0.98
Insurance and taxes on land, buildings, and equipment	85	0.34
Miscellaneous	26	0.10
TOTAL OWNERSHIP AND FIXED COSTS	820	3.28
TOTAL COSTS PER COW	4,864	19.46
RETURNS OVER TOTAL COST	229	0.91
Break-even milk price (net of other receipts)		16.66

Source: Adapted from Kevin Dhuyvetter, John Smith, Michael Brouk, and Joseph Harner III, 2008, ''Dairy Enterprise—600 Lactating Cows (Freestall),'' Farm Management Guide MF-2441, Department of Agricultural Economics, Kansas State University, October 2008.

in another part of the business. The main products (wheat, milk, or market livestock, for example) usually have prices determined by the market. If the product is not sold but is used as feed for livestock on the same farm, the market price of the feed can be used to value it as a receipt for crop production. (As noted in the next section, the market price can be used to value the feed as an input cost for the livestock.) The value of pasture can be estimated from the rent typically paid for pastures in the area (if that is known) or from the value of the forage that does not have to be purchased. Grazing on land after harvest does have value for livestock even if no cash payments are made. The value of the grazing can be estimated by the value of the forage that does not have to be purchased in the market or by the rates paid for grazing in the market. Any payments from the government tied to the enterprise should be listed also. Enterprise budgets usually are projections of future receipts (and costs), so the yields, prices, and other receipts should be viewed that way also, as projections and not guaranteed, actual numbers.

In the enterprise budget for spring wheat, the expected yield is 35 bushels per acre valued at a cash price of $4.50 per bushel for total receipts from wheat sales totaling $157.50 per acre. The main product is the 35 bushels of wheat, but the farm also expects to receive a government payment of $13 per acre. Crop insurance indemnity payments are an important source of revenue if yields (and revenue, if that is covered) suffer. In a planning budget, revenue from crop insurance should not be included if yields and prices are at normal levels. Expected total receipts are thus $170.50 per acre. This is a fairly straightforward estimation and listing of receipts since crop production involves planting seed, caring for the crop, and harvesting, a fairly straightforward process.

The receipts for the dairy enterprise budget are not as easy to understand without knowing the biology and process of the dairy operation. Notice that the receipts are not just milk and one calf per cow. This is a realistic budget showing the receipts for an average cow in the herd. From the notes in the receipts section of this enterprise budget, we know the average milk cow in this herd is expected to produce 250 cwt or 25,000 lb of milk, 0.95 calves, and 0.275 cull cows per year. Milk is valued at $17.57 per cwt and the farm receives a volume premium due to producing enough milk for one large truck to come to the farm and return to the processor. The base price is high enough that no government payments are received. A manure credit is listed as a receipt but this is a non-cash value. Total receipts are estimated to be $5,093 per average cow.

Operating Costs

Operating costs are, as the name implies, those costs incurred to operate the enterprise—that is, to produce the products from crop and livestock enterprises. Operating costs are different from ownership costs, which are described in the next section. Most operating costs are also variable costs as described in Chapter 4, Lessons from Microeconomics. Both operating costs and variable costs are incurred due to the production of a product; they will be zero if the farm decides not to produce the particular product. Fertilizer costs will be incurred only if a crop is grown that needs nutrients applied. Labor costs are considered an operating cost, especially if the labor is hired specifically for the production of a certain crop or livestock. For example, the cost of labor hired to hand-weed would be an operating cost since it would not be hired if that crop was not produced. Seasonal labor hired for a specific operation, such as harvest, could easily be considered an operating cost. At other times, labor may be considered a fixed cost if the worker is a permanent full-time employee and would be listed as a fixed cost in the next section of the budget.

In the spring wheat enterprise budget, operating costs consist of $23.80 per acre for seed, $30 for nitrogen, $12 for phosphate, $14 per acre plus $0.14 per bushel for custom harvesting, and so on. Fuel costs for operating machinery are listed as operating costs. (The ownership costs of these assets are included in the ownership section.) Land rent of $20 is included as an operating cost in this example. (If this is a long-term lease (or used as a proxy for ownership), the rent could be included as a fixed cost. Even though a farmer may have sufficient cash reserves to pay for all expenses, an interest charge is added to the budget to reflect the opportunity cost of having the money tied up for production of wheat. The operating interest cost of $4.99 for wheat was estimated by adding all the other operating costs together ($124.75 in this example) times the interest rate of 8% and adjusted for having the loan for only 6 months instead of 12 (124.75 * 0.08 * 6/12 = 4.99). With the operating interest cost added in, the total operating costs for growing spring wheat were estimated to be $129.74 per acre for this set of assumptions about input use and operations.

Operating costs for the dairy enterprise budget were estimated by the authors of the budget based on the biology and engineering estimates and estimated costs for feed, machinery, and labor. Feed costs are estimated as $5.99 per day for lactating and $2.18 per day for dry cows with an average feed efficiency of 1.55 pounds of milk per pound of dry-matter feed. Labor is based on 7.5 full-time persons paid $38,000 per year for both salary and benefits. Veterinary and related costs are based on average costs. Somatotropin is administered at 75% of the labeled rate for this herd. Fuel, oil, and auto expenses are based on the dairy's share of farm expenses plus the costs of feed and manure handling. Milk hauling and promotion costs are estimated to be $1 per cwt. Other costs are estimated based on records of similar farms. The total operating costs were estimated to be $4,044 per cow.

The section on operating costs shows those costs that would not be incurred if the product was not produced. These are the costs that would not have to be paid if, for example, the land was not rented and the crop not grown, or the pigs sold and not fed to market weight.

Return over Operating Costs

The return over operating costs shows the potential contribution of the enterprise to paying ownership and fixed costs, labor and management opportunity costs, and a return to risk. It is estimated by subtracting the total of operating costs from the total receipts. In some areas, the return over operating costs is called the gross margin or contribution margin. For spring wheat, the return over operating costs is estimated to be $40.76 per acre, which is calculated as the total receipts ($170.50) minus the total operating costs ($129.74). For the dairy operation, the return over operating costs is estimated to be $1,049 per cow. This is calculated by subtracting the operating costs ($4,044) from the estimated total receipts ($5,093). The return over operating costs can be used for short-run decisions such as choosing which crops to grow next year or whether to buy feeder cattle to raise to market weight.

Ownership and Fixed Costs

Ownership costs are those costs associated with owning a durable asset that will be used in more than one year or production cycle. Land, machinery, livestock, and perennial crops are examples of durable assets that are used as inputs to produce a product but are not used up completely during production. These assets may suffer some damages or be worn out, but the asset is not used in the way feed or seed is used once in the production cycle. Ownership costs are usually fixed and will have to be paid or incurred regardless of whether production takes place or not. Labor may be considered a fixed cost if the employee is a full-time, essentially permanent employee who will be paid regardless of whether a specific product is produced or not.

For spring wheat the ownership and fixed costs total $7.62 per acre. This includes machinery and equipment depreciation, interest, insurance, housing, and property taxes as appropriate. (Remember that the fuel and repair costs for machinery were listed as operating costs.)

For the dairy enterprise, fixed costs included the depreciation, taxes, insurance, and interest on building structures, equipment, and livestock as appropriate. Ownership and fixed costs are estimated to total $820 per cow.

Operator Labor and Management

Since most farmers are self-employed, they are the management and thus are responsible for making sure they have included the values of both their labor and management as a cost. If the cost of their labor and management has not been included earlier as an operating cost or fixed cost, it should be included here. If operator labor was included as part of the labor costs listed earlier for machinery operation or livestock care, it should not be included here to avoid double-counting. If the labor charge listed earlier in a budget does not include management, a charge for management should be included in this section. If labor and management costs are not included here or earlier, the net return calculated below should be interpreted as the net return to labor, management, and risk.

In the spring wheat example, the operator labor is estimated to be 0.31 hours per acre based on the operations done and engineering estimates of time requirements. Since this example has no hired labor listed as either operating or fixed costs, this operator labor is assumed to be the owner's labor. It is a non-cash cost, but it is still given a cost of $10 per hour in this example. A management charge of 5% of the wheat sales is also listed as a cost. The 5% is a common, but not fixed or statistically determined, value; it is only an estimate.

For the Kansas dairy example, all labor is included as an operating cost. Some of that may be the owner's labor. The enterprise budget does not include a specific line item for management, so we assume that a portion of the return over total cost is intended to be a return to management and risk.

Total Costs

The total cost is the sum of operating costs; ownership and fixed costs; and the charge for operator labor and management. For the spring wheat enterprise, the total listed costs are $148.34 per acre. For the dairy enterprise, the total listed cost is $4,864 per cow.

Net Return

The net return is the difference between the total receipts and the total costs. If a charge for operator labor and management is included in the costs above, the net return can be considered as economic profit (or loss) or the return for taking on risk. If these costs are not included, the net return needs to be interpreted as the net return to labor, management, risk, and profit.

Since charges for operator labor and management ($3.10 + $7.85) are listed as expenses in the spring wheat enterprise budget, the resulting net return is $22.16 per acre. If the net return was negative after including the charge for labor and management, the receipts are not large enough to pay all expenses including the desired pay for labor and management. The farmer should question whether the crop is being produced in the most optimal way or whether other uses may provide a better return to these resources. However, some costs are opportunity costs (operator labor and management, for example) and some costs in the budget (such as depreciation) are not cash costs, so the farmer may not experience a negative cash flow even though a projected budget estimates a negative return.

For the dairy enterprise, the net return is estimated to be $229 per cow, which is calculated by subtracting the total listed costs of $4,864 from the total receipts of $5,093.

Costs per Unit of Production

One of the first uses of the enterprise budget is the calculation of costs per unit. This is usually done for the main product after adjusting appropriately for other revenue generated by the enterprise.

For the spring wheat enterprise, the main product is wheat. However, the enterprise is also estimated to receive a government payment of $13 per acre. Before subtracting this government payment, the farmer should consider whether the payment depends on the amount of wheat produced. If none of the payment depends on wheat produced, it should not be subtracted because it will be received anyway; it is not due to producing wheat. Without subtracting the government payment, the total cost per bushel is calculated to be $4.24 per bushel ($148.33 per acre divided by 35 bushels per acre). If the farmer receives more than $4.24 in the market, the farm has a positive profit. If receiving the government payment is dependent on producing wheat, the $13 is subtracted from $148.33 and the resulting cost per bushel is $3.87. This cost of $4.24 or $3.87 per bushel is an estimate of the price the farmer needs in the market to pay all costs including the charge for unpaid labor and management.

For the dairy enterprise, milk is the main product, but the dairy also receives revenue from the volume premium ($125), sales of calves ($234), sale of cull cows ($215), and the manure credit ($126). These revenues will vary with milk production. Thus, to have a better estimate of the breakdown costs and price needed in the market, the revenue from these other sources is subtracted from the total costs of $4,864 and then divided by the milk production of 250 cwt per cow to estimate the net cost of production to be $16.66 per cwt of milk in this example. Thus, after adjusting for the other revenue sources, this example farm need $16.66 per cwt to pay all costs. A market price above $16.66 would generate positive profit. A market price below $16.66 would result in a loss.

Enterprise Budget Development

So far we have described the basic format of enterprise budgets along with some budget terms and concepts. Now we will build upon that information and explain how enterprise budgets are developed using farm records, economic logic, and your knowledge of agriculture.

Enterprise budgets can be developed from either whole-farm records or economic engineering. In the first method, whole-farm receipts and expenses are divided and allocated to each enterprise.

Enterprise budgets developed from whole-farm records show historically how each enterprise contributed to the whole-farm performance. They also can be used to evaluate performance in comparison to the historical enterprise budgets of other farms available through farm record associations and other public reports. With some updating, these budgets can be used to forecast performance under future conditions. The second method, economic engineering, starts by listing all the inputs, labor, operations, equipment, buildings, and land needed to produce a product. Economic engineering is needed when a farmer has no experience with an enterprise, wants to expand, or wants to create a benchmark to compare actual performance. After a few comments about sources of data, the steps involved in both methods are described in the following sections.

Sources of Data

Good data are needed to develop good budgets. Without good data, the information in budgets will be incomplete or inaccurate. If the information is not good, any decisions based on that information may be wrong. Wrong decisions can result in problems for the business, including the loss of profits.

The GIGO principle is valid for budgeting and all analyses: if you put garbage in, you will get garbage out. Budgeting involves the input of large amounts of data to produce detailed and accurate budgets. Much of this data must be specific to an individual farm (such as machinery and equipment use, irrigation use and efficiency). Other data (such as yields, input rates, prices) may be more effective if they are farm specific, but more general sources can be used. In this section, several sources of farm and ranch data are discussed.

Many sources of information and data exist for budgeting. Income tax records and historical records for individual farms and ranches provide very localized information on yields, production, weather, fertilizer use, and so on. National, state, and local government units collect and distribute price, production, and acreage data for the major crops. Recommendations for fertilizer rates, seeding rates, chemical rates, and such are available from the manufacturers, dealers, government and university research and extension units, and other groups. Some farmers hire independent consultants to recommend the right rates for inputs; this is done especially for pesticides and other chemicals that are often more strictly regulated than other inputs. In Chapter 4, we discussed the economic principles for making input and product decisions.

Labor requirements, wage rates, and benefits can be determined from several sources. The "going rate" (that is, the most common wage) in the local area is the usual source. If they work in the area, labor contractors will provide workers for a specific job—weeding a crop, for example—charge the farmer one total fee, and then pay the workers individually. Union contracts may set wage rates, benefits, hours, and other conditions for some workers. Labor productivity estimates can be obtained from the farm's records as well as from government, university, and private sources.

Developing Enterprise Budgets from Whole-Farm Records

When enterprise budgets are developed for the first time, many managers will start with records for the whole farm. Although whole-farm records may be accurate, all of the costs and returns are not easily identified with specific enterprises. Whole-farm costs and returns can be allocated to individual enterprises by using the following steps.

1. Determine the costs of separate items for the whole farm. If your whole-farm records are in good order, they should show expense figures by individual item (i.e., seed corn, fertilizer for soybeans, feed for the dairy calves, etc.). If these records are not up to date or individual items are not specified, the data must be gathered and organized before costs can be allocated to specific enterprises.
2. Identify the enterprises on the farm. Most farms grow more than one crop and/or raise more than one category of livestock. If only one crop is grown, allocation is very easy. If the farm business involves more than one crop or livestock enterprise, these enterprises have to be identified and listed. At this time, the farmer should decide whether to separate some enterprises into its parts. For example, the dairy herd could be divided into two sub-enterprises: the milking herd and all other dairy cattle, such as calves and replacement heifers. The farrow-to-finish hog enterprise could be split into feeder pig production and hog finishing. Corn production could be split into different land types or different tenure arrangements. These divisions are done to have a better idea of how each part of the business is performing. The divisions can be made even though all of the activity takes place on the same farm.
3. Classify the costs as direct or indirect. The costs on the farm can be classified as either direct or indirect costs. Direct costs are those costs that can be attributed to a specific enterprise. Examples of direct costs are fertilizer applied to wheat and feed fed to dairy cows. Indirect costs are those costs that cannot be associated with a specific enterprise. These would include, for example, costs for a truck used for several crops (or general farm duties), and fencing used for several types of livestock.
4. Allocate the direct costs and returns. Direct costs and returns are easily allocated to enterprises because they are used or produced by that enterprise directly. Corn harvesting costs are allocated to corn. Weed control for wheat is allocated to wheat. Veterinary expenses for dairy cows are allocated to dairy.
5. Determine the best way to allocate indirect costs. Indirect costs can be allocated to enterprises by determining how they are related to those enterprises. Three main methods are used to allocate indirect costs:
   a. On the basis of use. Machinery-use hours can be used to allocate fuel, repairs, and other machine costs to the appropriate enterprise. Factors such as total crop acreage, total herd value, and number of head may be used as the basis for allocating costs such as insurance or erosion control to the various enterprises that benefit from them. General farm liability insurance may be allocated to crops based on an average cost per acre.
   b. On the share of gross income. Office expenses (e.g., telephone, an accountant) may be related to the farm's total expected income. Thus, an enterprise's contribution to total gross income for the farm may be the best basis for allocating those costs. For example, office expenses can be allocated between enterprises based on each enterprise's share of total expected gross income.
   c. On the share of variable costs. Some costs may be allocated based on that enterprise's share of total variable costs for the whole farm. For example, an employee may spend more time on those enterprises that have the largest costs. Thus, the employee's salary should be allocated based on each enterprise's share in total variable costs, rather than on gross income. The share in costs more accurately reflects each enterprise's share of the employee's salary.
   d. With a combination. Choosing among the three main methods is an arbitrary decision. The goal is to obtain accurate enterprise budgets for analysis and planning. Sometimes, a combination of the three methods will provide the most accurate allocation between enterprises.

6. Calculate the percentage of total use, gross income, and variable costs for each enterprise.
  a. Shares of total use (e.g., machinery hours) are calculated by:
      i. determining the actual (or expected) use for each enterprise;
      ii. calculating the total use for the whole farm; and
      iii. calculating each enterprise's share in the total use.
  b. Shares of gross income are calculated by:
      i. determining the actual (or expected) acreage, production, and price for each enterprise;
      ii. calculating the gross income for each enterprise; and
      iii. calculating each enterprise's share in the gross income for the whole farm.
  c. Shares of variable costs are calculated by:
      i. determining the actual (or expected) variable costs for each enterprise;
      ii. calculating the total variable costs for the whole farm; and
      iii. calculating each enterprise's share in the total variable costs.
7. Allocate the indirect costs. The whole-farm indirect costs are allocated to the enterprises by multiplying the total whole-farm cost by each enterprise's shares of use, gross income, or variable costs.
8. Calculate the costs per unit. The per unit cost in each enterprise is calculated by dividing the enterprise's share of the total costs by the number of units of that enterprise (e.g., the number of corn acres or cows in the milking herd).

As an example of allocating indirect, whole-farm costs, consider how a dairy-corn-alfalfa farm could allocate general office expenses ($15,436) and an employee's salary and benefits ($24,878).

Since most of the office expenses are used for marketing or for those enterprises that have the higher gross income, the farmer decides these expenses should be allocated based on gross income shares. From her records, the farmer takes the gross income for each enterprise, estimates the shares of total, and allocates the office expenses based on those shares (Table 15.3). The allocated office expenses are $154.36 per dairy cow, $20.58 per acre for corn, and $18.52 per acre for alfalfa. These costs can be used in the respective enterprise budgets.

Although the employee's time is also related to the potential income, the farmer has decided that the share in operating costs is a more accurate method to allocate the employee's salary and benefits between the enterprises. From her records, the farmer totals the operating costs for each enterprise, estimates the shares of the total, and allocates the costs based on those shares (Table 15.4). The allocated costs are $252.33 per dairy cow, $34.55 per acre for corn, and $19.90 per acre for alfalfa. These costs can be used to itemize the employee's salary and benefits in the respective enterprise budgets.

As an example of developing an enterprise budget from whole-farm records, let us follow Ron Purcell as he estimates a soybean enterprise budget from his whole-farm information. He grows corn and soybeans only and has no livestock. Mr. Purcell has 870 tillable acres. Last year he had 420 acres of corn and 450 acres of soybeans. His corn yield was 151 bushels, which he sold for an average of $3.80 per bushel. His soybean yield was 46 bushels, which he sold for $8.25. He also received an average of $21.50 per corn acre and $20.20 per soybean acre from the government. Knowing he would need the information later, he calculated each crop's percentage share of the farm's gross income. This is shown in Table 15.5.

From his records, Mr. Purcell easily divided his seed, fertilizer, chemical, and crop insurance expenses between corn and soybean (Table 15.6). For repairs and fuel and oil, he considered the total hours of machinery operations required for each crop and decided to allocate 54% to corn and 46% to

Table 15.3 Example of Allocation of General Office Expenses Based on Enterprise's Share of Gross Income

Enterprise	Size	Total Gross Income	Enterprise's Share of Gross Income	Enterprise's Share of General Office Expenses	General Office Expenses per unit
Dairy	70 cows	$126,300	70%	$10,805	$154.36/cow
Corn	180 acres	43,560	24	3,705	20.58/acre
Alfalfa	50 acres	11,000	6	926	18.52/acre
Whole Farm:		180,860	100	15,436	

Table 15.4 Example of Allocation of employee's Salary and Benefits Based on Enterprise's Share of Operating Costs

Enterprise	Size	Total Operating Costs	Enterprise's Share of Operating Costs	Enterprise's Share of Employee's Salary & Benefits	Employee's Salary and Benefits per unit
Dairy	70 cows	$73,640	71%	$17,663	$252.33/cow
Corn	180 acres	25,560	25	6,220	34.55/acre
Alfalfa	50 acres	4,000	4	995	19.90/acre
Whole Farm:		$103,200	100	$24,878	

Table 15.5 Ron Purcell's Gross Income Shares by Crop

	Corn	Soybean
Acres	420	450
Yield	151 bu	46 bu
Price per bushel	$3.80	$8.25
Other income per acre	21.50	20.20
Gross income per acre	595.30	399.70
Total gross income for the crop	$250,026	$179,865
Total gross income for the farm	$429,891	
Crop's share of total gross income	58.2%	41.8%

Table 15.6 Ron Purcell's Allocation of Direct Expenses

Direct Expense Item	Whole-Farm Total	Corn Expenses		Soybean Expenses	
		Farm Total	Per Acre	Farm Total	Per Acre
Seed	47,868	31,290	74.5	16,578	36.84
Fertilizer	52,197	48,867	116.35	3,330	7.4
Chemicals	23,516	10,164	24.2	13,352	29.67
Crop insurance	22,736	10,878	25.9	11,858	26.35
Drying fuel	11,697	11,697	27.85	0	0
Fuel and oil	24,102	13,015	30.99	11,087	24.64
Repairs	26,803	14,474	34.46	12,329	27.40
Miscellaneous	13,156	8,551	20.36	4,604	10.23
Operating interest	9,552	6,409	15.26	3,143	6.98
Total direct expenses	231,626	155,345	369.87	76,280	169.51

Table 15.7 Ron Purcell's Allocation of Overhead Expenses

Overhead Expense Item	Whole-Farm Total	Corn Expenses		Soybean Expenses	
		Farm Total	Per Acre	Farm Total	Per Acre
Hired labor	5,464	3,180	7.57	2,284	5.08
Term interest	6,031	3,510	8.36	2,521	5.60
Opportunity interest on land			163.50		163.50
Machinery depreciation	27,067	14,616	34.80	12,451	27.67
Real estate taxes	14,268	6,888	16.40	7,380	16.40
Farm insurance	4,220	2,456	5.85	1,764	3.92
Utilities	2,259	1,315	3.13	944	2.10
Miscellaneous	9,041	5,262	12.53	3,779	8.40
Total overhead expenses	68,349	37,226	252.13	31,123	232.66

soybeans. So he wrote $11,087 of the fuel and oil and $12,329 of the repairs in the soybean column. After looking at the list of miscellaneous expenses, he estimated 35% (or $4,604) of those expenses were due to soybeans. He decided to split his operating interest between corn and soybeans on the basis of each crop's share of all other direct expenses. Since soybeans' share of all the other direct expenses was 32.9%, he wrote that percentage or $3,143 in the soybean column. When he was done allocating the totals, he divided each column of total crop expenses by each crop's acreage (420 for corn and 450 for soybeans) to calculate his direct costs per acre.

Mr. Purcell realized that the costs in his records that he could not easily allocate directly to either corn or soybeans were his overhead costs. He decided to allocate 46% of the machinery depreciation to soybeans as he did for the direct machinery expenses. Purcell also realized that the real estate taxes should be allocated on an average per acre basis. He decided to allocate the rest of his overhead costs to each crop by using each crop's share of gross income. Once he made the allocation of the totals to each crop, Mr. Purcell again calculated the per acre costs (Table 15.7).

Mr. Purcell also realizes that his records only contain his cash expenses. He does not pay himself for his own labor and management or for his equity in the farm. To obtain the most accurate estimate of his soybean costs, he decides to estimate these too. In return for his labor and management, Mr. Purcell wants to earn about $45,000 from his farm for family living expenses. Since his crops are the only source of income, he divides the $45,000 by his tillable acres (870) to calculate his labor and management cost as $51.72 per acre. He bought his land many years ago and has steadily paid off his debt. He also has a mix of new and used machinery. His balance sheet shows he has $3,270 in equity capital per acre. This equity is the total for land, buildings, and machinery. He would like to receive a 5% return on this equity from farming and hopes to receive more when he retires and sells the land. He calculates his desired return to equity from farming as 5% of $3,270 or $163.50 per acre.

Now Mr. Purcell develops his soybean enterprise budget by putting his estimates of his receipts and costs per acre into one report (Table 15.8). Since this budget comes from whole-farm records, he does not have any specific quantity information except his yield. Mr. Purcell estimates his total listed costs are $462.85 per acre and $9.62 per bushel (after accounting for the government payment). Based on his yield and price information, he has a negative net return or loss of $63.15 per acre.

Table 15.8   Mr. Purcell's Soybean Enterprise Budget from Whole-Farm Records

	Unit	Price	Quantity	Total
GROSS RECEIPTS				
Soybeans	bu.	$8.25	46	$379.50
Government payment				20.20
TOTAL RECEIPTS				399.70
DIRECT EXPENSES				
Seed				$36.84
Fertilizer				7.40
Chemicals				29.67
Crop insurance				26.35
Fuel and oil				24.64
Repairs				27.40
Miscellaneous				10.23
Operating interest				6.98
TOTAL OPERATING COSTS				169.51
RETURN OVER OPERATING COSTS				230.19
OWNERSHIP AND FIXED COSTS				
Hired labor				$5.08
Interest on machinery				5.60
Opportunity interest on equity				163.50
Machinery depreciation				27.67
Real estate taxes				16.40
Farm insurance				3.92
Utilities				2.10
Miscellaneous				8.40
TOTAL OWNERSHIP AND FIXED COSTS				232.66
Operator labor and management				51.72
TOTAL COSTS				462.85
NET RETURN				63.15
TOTAL COSTS per bushel				10.06
Cost per bushel (net of government transition payment)				9.62

So while Mr. Purcell appears to be doing well with a positive net return after paying all cash costs, he does not have sufficient income to meet his non-cash expenses for labor, management, and equity capital. This may be due to lower than normal prices and yields, higher than normal expenses, unrealistic expectations, a changed business environment, or a combination of these factors. Mr. Purcell will now have to spend some time considering these numbers and conditions and decide how to continue.

Developing Enterprise Budgets from Economic Engineering Studies

When a farmer has no experience in a particular enterprise or with a new set of technology, an enterprise budget can be developed from engineering data from manufacturers, university reports, and other sources. The steps in this process are:

1. Prepare a process map. In an economic engineering study, the first step in developing an enterprise budget is to list all the products, operations, and resources associated with that enterprise. (This list is also called a process map and is described in more detail in Chapter 18.) Products include the obvious ones such as wheat, tomatoes, and beef, and not-so-obvious products such as stubble for grazing and manure for fertilizer. Operations and resources include everything done for or because of that enterprise. For crops, operations include tillage, planting, irrigating, spraying, harvesting, marketing, management, and so on. For livestock, operations and resources include land, buildings, feeding, veterinary costs, trucking, management, and such.

The object of this step is to write down a reminder of every receipt and expense. The most logical way to ensure that this list is complete is to start at the beginning and think of everything that happens through the production period. Breaking this list into major stages may be helpful. Crop production might be divided into tillage, planting, growing, harvesting, and marketing. Stages in a livestock business might be feeding, calving, moving, and marketing.

2. Identify specific resources to be used. The next step in the enterprise budget development process is to identify the specific resources to be used for each activity listed in the first step. Which plow will be used? Which tractor will be used to pull that plow, and who will drive it? What kind of fertilizer will be applied as a plow-down fertilizer? What kind of insecticide will be applied? What medicines and veterinary services will be needed? Which trucks will be used to haul the cows to the range, and who will drive the trucks? Farm operations need to be defined to link resources (e.g., tractor, range seeder, driver, seed, and fertilizer) in one operation. The object of this step is to identify the specific names of all of the resources used in the enterprises; finding the quantities, prices, and costs is done later.

3. Specify input use levels. When all the operations and resources have been listed, the next step is detailing specific physical information about those resources. How much fertilizer will be applied in the fall? How many seeds will be planted per acre? How much hay and concentrate do the cattle eat? How fast will the trucks go, and how much fuel do they use per hour? The object of this step is to quantify your estimates of resource use. (The economic principles used in these resource and input decisions are discussed in Chapter 4.)

4. Select prices and costs. The next step is to search for prices and costs. Selecting prices and costs is a critical step to obtaining correct answers to the questions being asked. Some estimates may merely involve a review of your records, or calls to dealers and brokers. This seems easy, but even this information must be selected carefully. A budget being prepared to help decide what to plant this year may require very different prices from a budget being prepared to help decide whether to buy land or construct buildings. The difference goes back to the distinction between short run and long run discussed in Chapter 4. Planting decisions for the current year need price forecasts for the current year. Building and investment decisions need a longer outlook of where prices will be rather than where they are at the time of building. The sources of price and cost information should be noted so the final budget can be more clearly understood and interpreted.

Other costs, such as machinery and building costs, may be harder to estimate. For machinery and building costs, an average value based on farm records or published reports may be sufficient. In other situations, the annual costs of machinery and buildings also can be estimated using standard engineering and economic formulas and the machine's or building's list price, purchase price, annual use, and useful life. Computer programs are available to estimate these costs for a specific farm and situation.

Annual machinery costs are divided between ownership costs and operating costs. Ownership costs are fixed once the machine is purchased. They include depreciation, interest, housing, insurance, and taxes. An alternative to calculating depreciation and interest separately is the annualized capital recovery cost, which incorporates both the original cost and a charge for having money tied up in the machine—much like calculating the annual loan payment. If the machine is leased, the lease payment is used in place of the capital recovery or depreciation and interest costs. Operating costs vary with the use of the machine, and include fuel, lubrication, repairs, maintenance, labor, and custom services. Different methods are used to calculate each category of costs. An example of calculating machinery costs is shown later in this chapter.

The annual costs of building services can be remembered by the acronym DIRTI: depreciation, interest, repairs, taxes, and insurance. An example for calculating building costs is included later in this chapter.

5. Assemble reports.　　The last step in the budget development process is to calculate receipts and expenses and then assemble reports. Luckily, computer programs can eliminate much of the drudgery of the calculations and report preparations.

As an example of developing an enterprise budget using the economic engineering method, let us follow Richard and Louise Vansickle as they estimate the returns for buying and feeding medium no. 1 yearling steers. They have farmed and fed cattle for many years in northern Iowa so they have many records from past years. However, they also know that cattle and feed prices can vary greatly from year to year and the condition and weight of the cattle can vary too. So they always estimate what their costs and returns will be for each group of yearlings before they buy them and bring them to their farm.

As they start their calculations, the market for 850 lb yearlings is near $80 per cwt in Sioux Falls, South Dakota. They anticipate they could sell them in about six months weighing 1,350 lb. Based on the current future prices and expected basis, their expected cash price at market time is $68 per cwt. They expect a 0.5% death loss.

Based on past experience and their expectations of feeding this group for six months, they estimate the feed they will need for one yearling is 60 bushels of corn, 270 lb of hay, 0.8 ton of corn silage, and 150 lb of supplement. Prices for these feedstuffs can be locked in at $2.20 per bushel for corn, $90 per ton for hay, and $350 per ton for supplement. They grow their own corn silage and think they could sell it for $15 per ton.

They estimate their other costs by updating their previous expenses based on current conditions. Veterinary and medical costs are estimated to be $15 per head; utilities and other operating costs, $3 per head; hired labor costs, $9 per head; and transportation and marketing costs, $8 per head.

Table 15.9 The Vansickles' Projected Enterprise Budget for Feeding Yearlings from 850 lb to 1,350 lb

				Total
GROSS RECEIPTS				
Fed cattle	13.5 cwt/head	$68/cwt	0.95 head	$872.10
TOTAL RECEIPTS				872.10
DIRECT EXPENSES				
Yearling	850 lbs/head	$80/cwt.	1 head	$680.00
Corn grain		$2.20/bu.	60 bu.	132.00
Hay		$90/ton	270 lb	12.15
Corn silage		$18/ton	0.8 tons	12.00
Supplement		$350/ton	150 lb	26.25
Vet and medical				15.00
Other operating costs				3.00
Hired labor				9.00
Transportation and marketing				8.00
Operating interest (6.5% on yearling and half of other direct costs held for 6 mo)				25.63
TOTAL DIRECT COSTS				923.03
RETURN OVER DIRECT COSTS				−50.93
OVERHEAD COSTS				
Facilities depreciation and interest				$27.00
The Vansickles' labor, management, and risk				10.00
TOTAL OVERHEAD COSTS				37.00
TOTAL COSTS				960.03
NET RETURN				−87.93

They estimate their interest rate will be 6.5% for operating loans. They would borrow the cost of the yearlings for six months and estimate that they would carry the rest of the operating costs for three months.

For fixed costs, they have their facilities and their own labor. They have estimated the depreciation and interest on their 15-year-old facilities to be about $0.15 per day. For the estimated six-month feeding period, depreciation and interest are expected to be $27 per head. They would like to earn a minimum of $10 per head for their labor, management, and risk.

After preparing these individual estimates of costs and revenues, the Vansickles compile the data in a standard enterprise budget format for feeding yearlings (Table 15.9). Based on their calculations, they estimate they would lose $87.93 per head after paying for the yearlings and all their variable and fixed costs. If they ignored their fixed costs for facilities and did not pay themselves, they would still lose $50.93 per head. If they did not buy the feeders they would lose the $27 per head for facilities depreciation and interest. They could use their time (that is, the $10 per head) in other enterprises. Based on these estimates, they decide this group is not worth buying.

Computerized enterprise budget generators are available to simplify the process of estimating budgets. Two examples of these include the Mississippi State Budget Generator (Laughlin and Spurlock, 2008) and Missouri's Crop Budget Generator (FAPRI, 2009). Worksheet programs such as

Excel© can be used to assist in the development of enterprise budgets but do not always have the supporting data that the generators have. Three good examples of using spreadsheets for estimating crop budgets, machinery costs, and machinery repair costs are by William Lazarus at Minnesota (see Lazarus, 2010).

Estimating Annual Costs of Durable Assets

In this section we estimate the annual costs of durable assets. Durable assets include machinery, equipment, buildings, breeding livestock, and perennial crops. Estimating the annual costs of these assets is more involved than for inputs such as fertilizer or feed. Durable assets last longer than one production cycle and thus their initial purchase price and associated ownership costs need to be calculated in different ways than the cost of inputs such as seed and feed that are used up during production. In this section, we describe these procedures for each type of durable assets.

Estimating Annual Machinery Costs

Annual machinery costs are composed of two parts: ownership costs and operating costs. Ownership costs include depreciation, interest, taxes, insurance, and housing. Operating costs include fuel, oil, repairs, and labor.

The procedures, equations, and data for estimating machinery costs are explained in a handbook from the American Agricultural Economics Association (AAEA, 2000) and in two publications from the American Society of Agricultural Engineers (ASAE, 1998, 2001). Lazarus and Selley (2002) provide a very good description of the procedures and issues encountered when estimating machinery costs. Fortunately, we do not have to go through these procedures every time. Cost estimates are available for typical situations through extension publications (e.g., Lazarus and Smale, 2010). Also, computer programs and spreadsheets that have the equations and data embedded in them are often available through extension services (e.g., Lazarus, 2010).

The interest expense for machinery is used to estimate the opportunity cost of capital invested in the machine. Choosing the interest rate is critical to having correct estimates. The interest rate should reflect the life of the machine or building—shorter term rates for machinery and longer term rates for buildings. The chosen rate should be the real interest rate   that is, the common, nominal interest rate adjusted for inflation. The real interest rate is calculated as

$$i = \frac{(1 + r)}{(1 + r)} - 1$$

where i = real interest rate, r = nominal interest rate, and f = inflation rate. All three are expressed as proportions between 0 and 1.

This formula comes from the relationship that the nominal rate reflects both the real rate and the inflation rate. It is a multiplicative relationship, not additive. For example, an asset's value should increase by both the real rate and the inflation rate—that is,

$$(1 + r) = (1 + i) \times (1 + f) = (1 + i + f + if)$$

Table 15.10 Price, Use, and Life for Example Tractor and Grain Drill

	130 HP Tractor	30-ft Grain Drill
List price	$76,200	$34,600
Purchase price	70,000	30,000
Annual use	450 hr	80 hr
Useful life	10 yr	10 yr

The real interest rate is often approximated as the difference between the nominal rate and the inflation rate:

$$i = r - f$$

but this approximation is inaccurate by the magnitude of the product of the real and inflation rates (as seen in the previous equation). If the real rate and the inflation rate are low, the inaccuracy may be inconsequential, but if the rates are high, the inaccuracy may affect the calculations enough to cause wrong decisions to be made. Since the calculation for the real rate (i) is very simple, a prudent manager would use that at all times to avoid inaccurate calculations.

To increase our understanding of how machinery costs are estimated, let us consider a planting operation that uses a 130 HP tractor and a 30-ft grain drill. We start with the basic price and use information as listed in Table 15.10.

Depreciation and interest can be estimated by two methods. The traditional method estimates them separately. An alternative method is the capital recovery method, which estimates them together.

As a first step, the ending salvage value and the average annual investment are calculated since they are used in subsequent calculations. The salvage value (SV) = list price × remaining value pct. (RV%). The RV% comes from estimates made by comparing list prices to published prices for used machines. They are available on the web from ASAE (1998, 2001). For the tractor, the RV% after 10 years is estimated to be 37.1%, and the tractor is estimated to be worth $28,270 after 10 years:

$$SV\ (tractor) = 76,200 \times 0.371 = \$28,270$$

For the grain drill, the RV% after 10 years is estimated to be 40.5%, and the grain drill is estimated to be worth $14,013 after 10 years:

$$SV\ (grain\ drill) = 34,600 \times 0.405 = \$14,013$$

The average annual investment = (purchase price + salvage value)/2. For the tractor, the average investment over 10 years is:

$$(70,000 + 28,270)/2 = \$49,135$$

For the grain drill, the average investment is:

$$(30,000 + 14,013)/2 = \$22,007$$

When using the traditional method of estimating depreciation and interest, average annual depreciation is calculated as:

$$\text{Annual depreciation} = \frac{\text{purchase price} - \text{salvage value}}{\text{useful life in years}}$$

For the tractor, the average annual depreciation is $4,173 for the tractor and $1,599 for the grain drill:

$$\text{Annual tractor depreciation} = \frac{\$70,000 - 28,270}{10} = \$4,173$$

$$\text{Annual grain mill depreciation} = \frac{\$30,000 - 14,013}{10} = \$1,599$$

The average annual interest charge under the traditional method is estimated as the average annual investment multiplied by the real interest rate. In this example, the chosen real interest rate is 6%:

$$\text{Annual tractor interest charge} = 49,135^*.06 = \$2,948$$
$$\text{Annual grain mill interest charge} = 22,007^*.06 = \$1,320$$

These calculations result in a total charge for depreciation and interest of $7,121 (= 4,173 + 2,948) for the tractor and $2,919 (= 1,599 + 1,320) for the grain drill.

These traditional estimates of depreciation and interest are simple to calculate and understand, but they do not reflect the reality of how machinery values change over the life of the machine. Except for a potential decrease in value when a machine is taken from the dealer, the value of a machine declines slowly in the first years of use and then rapidly in later years. The average annual depreciation ignores this rate of change and so does the average annual interest charge.

An alternate method of estimating depreciation and interest is to amortize the cost of the machine over its useful life. This alternative method is called the annual capital recovery charge (ACRC). The ACRC includes (1) the allocation or amortization of the purchase price (minus any salvage value) and (2) an interest charge on the salvage value of the machine. The formula for calculating ACRC is:

$$\text{ACRC} = (\text{purchase price} - \text{SV}) \times \text{CRF} + (\text{SV} \times \text{interest rate})$$

The capital recovery factor (CRF) is an annuity factor equal to: $\{i/[1 - (1 + i)^{-n}]\}$. These CRFs can be found in Appendix Table IV of this book. The CRF for the real interest rate of 6% in this example and 10 years is 0.1359.

$$\begin{aligned}\text{Tractor ACRC} &= [(70,000 - 28,270) \times 0.1359] + [28,270 \times 0.06] \\ &= 5,671 + 1,696 \\ &= \$7,367 \text{ per year}\end{aligned}$$

$$\begin{aligned}\text{Grain drill ACRC} &= [(30,000 - 14,013) \times 0.1359] + [14,013 \times 0.06] \\ &= 2,173 + 841 \\ &= \$3,014 \text{ per year}\end{aligned}$$

The ACRC is higher than the traditional method of estimating depreciation and interest: $7,367 versus $7,121 for the tractor and $3,014 versus $2,919 for the grain mill. Since the ACRC reflects the actual change in asset value more closely, the ACRC estimates are entered into Table 15.11 and are used to estimate ownership costs.

Table 15.11   Estimated Ownership Costs for Example Tractor and Grain Drill

	Tractor	Drill
Annual capital recovery cost (ACRC)	7,367	3,014
Taxes, insurance, and housing (TIH)	1,376	616
Total ownership costs per year	$8,743	$3,630
Estimated annual usage	450 hr	80 hr
Ownership cost per hour	$19.43	$45.38

Taxes, Insurance, and Housing (TIH) costs are often expressed as percentages of the average investment. Some states and countries do tax personal property such as farm machinery, others do not. For this example the tax percentage is set at 0%. The insurance cost often ranges from 0.6% to 1.0% of the average value; 0.8% is used in this example. The housing cost often ranges from 0.5% to 3.0% of the average value; 2.0% is used in this example. For this planting example, the total TIH is 2.8%, which is the sum of T = 0.0%, I = 0.8%, and H = 2.0%.

$$\text{Tractor TIH costs} = 49{,}135 \times 0.028 = \$1{,}376 \text{ per year}$$
$$\text{Grain drill TIH costs} = 22{,}007 \times 0.028 = \$616 \text{ per year}$$

Total ownership costs per year are the sum of ACRC and TIH. For the tractor, the total ownership cost is $8,743 per year (= 7,367 + 1, 376). For the grain drill, the total ownership cost is $3,630 per year (= 3,014 + 616). Dividing the annual ownership cost by the estimated annual usage provides the estimate of the total ownership cost per hour as $19.43 for the tractor and $45.38 for the grain drill. For the two together, the ownership cost for planting is estimated to be $64.81/hour ($19.43 + $45.38).

Operating Costs.   The fuel cost per hour = gallons per hour × price per gallon. The consumption rate (gal/hr) can come from either performance records or engineering equations and is based on engine size (ASAE, 1998, 2001). For fuel use calculations, engine size is expressed as the horsepower measured at the power take off or, simply, PTO HP. (Remember that PTO HP is different from draw bar HP and engine HP.) For example:

$$\text{gal/hr} = a \times \text{PTO HP}$$
$$\text{For gasoline}: a = 0.06$$
$$\text{For diesel fuel}: a = 0.044$$
$$\text{For LP}: a = 0.072$$

Machinery lubrication cost is usually estimated to be 10% to 15% of the fuel cost.

For the planting example, the 130 HP tractor, which uses diesel fuel, has a fuel consumption and cost and lubrication cost of:

$$\text{Fuel use}: 130 \text{ HP} \times 0.044 = 5.7 \text{ gal/hour}$$
$$\text{Fuel cost}: 5.7 \times \$.90/\text{gal} = \$5.13/\text{hour}$$
$$\text{Lubrication cost} = 5.13 \times 15\% = \$0.77 \text{ per hour}$$

The grain drill requires no fuel, so how should lubrication costs be estimated? The easiest way is to increase the % of tractor fuel, which is why 15% is used in this example.

Machinery repair and maintenance cost estimates are based on estimates of the accumulated repair and maintenance costs (RMC) over the life of the machine. The engineering equation is:

$$RMC = \text{list price} \times RMC\%$$

The machine type and the total use (in hours) determine the RMC%. Estimates of RMC% for different machines have been developed from economic engineering data and are available on the Web from ASAE (1998). The RMC is calculated by dividing RMC by the total hours of use:

$$RMC \text{ per hour} = \frac{RMC}{\text{total hours of use over useful life}}$$

For the planting example, the tractor is expected to have a useful life of 10 years, estimated use of 450 hours per year, total hours over its life of 4,500 hours, and from ASAE (1998), a RMC% of 14.2% of the tractor's list price. The total accumulated repair cost (over the useful life of the tractor) is estimated to be:

$$RMC(\text{tractor}) = \$76,200 \times 14.2\% = \$10,820$$

And the average repair cost per hour is estimated to be:

$$\$10,820/4,500 \text{ hours} = \$2.40 \text{ per hour}$$

The grain drill is expected to have a useful life of 10 years, estimated use of 80 hours per year, total hours over its life of 800 hours, and thus a RMC% of 20.0% of the grain drill's list price. Thus, the drill's total accumulated repair cost (over its useful life) is estimated to be:

$$RMC (\text{grain drill}) = \$34,600 \times 20.0\% = \$6,920$$

And the average repair cost per hour is estimated to be:

$$\$6,920/800 \text{ hours} = \$8.65 \text{ per hour}$$

The machine operating costs per hour are estimated to be $8.30 for the tractor; this includes $5.13 for fuel, $0.77 for oil and lubrication, and $2.40 for repairs and maintenance. For the grain drill, there are no fuel, oil, or lubrication costs, so the cost per hour is the $8.65 for repairs. Thus, the total machine operating costs are $16.95 per hour for the planting operation.

For many decisions the costs per hour need to be converted into costs per acre. This can be done by using engineering estimates of machine capacity measured in acres per hour.

$$\begin{aligned} \text{Acres per hour} &= SWE/8.25 \\ &= [(\text{speed in mph}) \times (\text{width in feet}) \times \text{efficiency}]/8.25 \end{aligned}$$

The coefficient 8.25 converts the English units of speed and width into machine capacity as measured in acres per hour. Performance data for machine and operation efficiencies are estimated from engineering data and are available on the Web from ASAE (1998).

In many calculations, hours per acre is easier to use than acres per hour:

$$\text{Hours per acre} = \frac{1}{\text{Acres per hour}}$$

and machine cost per acre = cost per hour × hours per acre.

For the planting example:

$$\text{Acres per hour} = (5\,\text{MPH} \times 30\,\text{ft} \times 0.70)/8.25 = 12.73\,\text{ac/hr}$$
$$\text{Hours per acre} = 1/12.73 = 0.079$$

The machinery ownership costs per acre are \$5.11 (= \$64.79 × 0.079) and the machinery operating costs are \$1.34 (= \$16.95 × 0.079).

Labor cost is usually budgeted as an operating cost even though the labor may be full-time and thus fixed. The labor required depends on the machinery time adjusted for other work required by the machine and operation:

$$\text{Labor hours/acre} = \text{machine hours/acre} \times \text{adjustment factor}$$

The adjustment factor varies from 1.0 to 1.2 depending on how much preparation time and infield maintenance time are required by the machinery and the operation plus an allowance for operator comfort. An adjustment factor of 1.2 is used the most.

For the planting example,

$$\text{Labor hours per acre} = 0.079 \times 1.2 = 0.095\,\text{hours/acre}$$

The labor cost per acre is simply the labor hours per acre multiplied by the wage per hour. For the planting example, the labor cost is

$$0.095\,\text{hours per acre} \times \$8.00\,\text{per hour} = \$0.76\,\text{per acre}$$

In summary, the estimated machinery costs for this planting operation are as listed in Table 15.12. The total cost of planting is \$7.22 per acre, which is the sum of the ownership costs (\$5.12), operating costs (\$1.34), and labor costs (\$0.76).

Estimating Annual Costs of Buildings

Annual costs of buildings consist of depreciation, interest, repairs, taxes, and interest. They are often referred to by the acronym DIRTI, which reflects the first letter of each cost component. The calcula-

Table 15.12 Estimated Total Cost per Acre for Example Planting Operation

Machine	Ownership Costs	Operating Costs
Tractor	\$19.43/hour	\$8.30/hour
Grain drill	45.38/hour	8.65/hour
Total costs	64.81/hour	16.95/hour
Machine hours	.079 hr/acre	.079 hr/acre
Machinery cost	\$5.12/acre	\$1.34/acre
Labor cost per acre		\$0.76/acre
Total cost per acre	\$7.22/acre	

tions for buildings are similar to those for machinery. However, since salvage value is normally zero for buildings, the calculation can be simplified by writing the formula as a multiplicative relationship of purchase price. For example, average investment is usually calculated as

$$\text{Average investment} = (\text{purchase price} + \text{SV})/2$$

Since $\text{SV} = 0$ for most buildings, we can drop SV from the equation. Also, to write the equation as a multiplicative relationship, we do not divide by 2, we multiply by $(1/2)$. Thus for most buildings,

$$\text{Average investment} = \text{purchase price} * (1/2)$$

As with machinery, the depreciation and interest costs of buildings can be estimated separately in a traditional way or as one charge using the ACRC method.

Using the traditional method, the depreciation of a building with an expected life of 25 years is estimated as a multiplicative relationship:

$$\text{Depreciation} = \text{purchase price} * (1/25)$$
$$= \text{purchase price} * 0.04$$

The traditional interest cost is the average investment multiplied by the real interest rate. Using the formula for average investment and a real interest rate of 6%, we estimate the interest cost as:

$$\text{Interest cost} = \text{purchase price} * (1/2) * 0.06$$
$$= \text{purchase price} * 0.03$$

The total cost for depreciation and interest estimated in the traditional way is 7% ($= (0.04 + 0.03) * 100\%$) of the purchase price. This is a lower percentage than the ACRC using the same real interest rate of 6%. In the Appendix table of capital recovery factors, the CRF% for 6% and 25 years is 7.82% ($= 0.0782 * 100\%$). Since ACRC is a more accurate reflection of declining asset values, 7.82% is used in the example below.

Building repair and maintenance varies with the type of building and the amount of use. Estimates of these expenses are not as available as they are for machinery. Boehlje and Eidman suggest a range of 1.0 to 3.5% of the original cost. They suggest a rate of 2% for normal use with higher rates for buildings used continuously. A higher percentage may be appropriate for newer buildings that include more computerized controls. For this example, we will estimate building repairs and maintenance to be 2% of purchase price.

Taxes and insurance rates will vary across regions and countries. For this example, we use a tax rate of 1.5% of average investment and an insurance rate of 0.6% of the average investment. To write these as a percentage of the purchase price, these percentages are divided by 2 since the salvage value is zero and average investment is thus $^1/_2$ of the purchase price or original building cost.

As an example of calculating a building cost, consider a building with a purchase price of $130,000 and a salvage value of $0 after a useful life of 25 years. Using the assumptions and calculations described above, the cost categories can be expressed as a percent of purchase price (Table 15.13). Thus, for this example building, the average annual cost for building services is $14,131 = $130,000 × 0.1087.

Table 15.13 Annual Cost of Building Services as a Percent of the Purchase Price

	Percent of Purchase Price
Annual capital recovery charge (ACRC)	7.82%
Repairs and maintenance	2.0%
Taxes (1.5%)	0.75%
Insurance (0.6%)	0.3%
Total	10.87%

In this chapter we covered enterprise budgets, a crucial building block for management decisions. We looked at the purpose of enterprise budgets and the need to have them estimated for the future, not the past. We learned about two ways to develop enterprise budgets: from whole-farm records and by economic engineering. And we have learned how to estimate annual costs of machinery and buildings.

Summary

- Budgeting provides economic information for a variety of management tasks and decisions.
- A budget is a projection of income and expenses used for planning the future.
- An enterprise is a common name for a part of the farm business.
- An enterprise budget is a statement of expected receipts, costs, and net returns for a specific enterprise.
- Enterprise budgets can be developed in two ways: from whole-farm records and by economic engineering.

Review Questions

1. How can enterprise budgets be used in farm management?
2. How should the appropriate unit or size for an enterprise budget be chosen?
3. Why should an enterprise budget include a charge for labor and management for a family farm with no hired workers?
4. What are the two ways an enterprise budget can be developed? Briefly describe each.
5. When would economic engineering be needed instead of whole farm records for estimating enterprise budgets?
6. Using the following information, use economic engineering to develop an enterprise budget for corn following soybeans in the Northern Corn Belt in the United States. The expected yield is 150 bushels of corn per acre and the expected price is $3.30 per bushel. The expected government payment is $25 per acre. The corn is estimated to need 140 lb of nitrogen at a price of $0.28 per lb; 50 lb of P_2O_5 at a net price of $.42 per lb; 58 lb of K_2O at $0.54 per lb; and 480 lb of lime at $18/ton. Seed costs are expected to be $95 per acre. Pesticides are expected to cost $38 per acre. Diesel fuel use is estimated to be 7.5 gallons with a price of $2.70 per gallon. Machinery repairs are

estimated to be $20 per acre; hauling, $12; and miscellaneous expenses, $19 per acre. Cash rent is projected to be $225 per acre. Interest on operating expenses (including cash rent) is 6.5% per year, and the operating loan on expenses is expected to be an average of 8 months long. Over-head costs are estimated to be $76 per acre for machinery depreciation and interest, $10 per acre for drying and handling equipment, and $45 per acre for family and hired labor.

7. Which of the following are ownership costs for machinery?
   a. Capital recovery
   b. Housing
   c. Insurance
   d. Taxes
   e. All of the above.

8. Which of the following are not operating costs for machinery?
   a. Fuel
   b. Lubrication
   c. Repairs and maintenance
   d. Labor
   e. Interest on the loan
   f. All these are operating costs.

Further Reading

American Agricultural Economics Association (AAEA). 2000. *Commodity Costs and Returns Estimation Handbook: A Report of the AAEA Task Force on Commodity Costs and Returns.* Ames, Iowa: Author.

American Society of Agricultural Engineers. 1998. "Agricultural Machinery Management Data," ASAE D497.4 January 1998, available at http://asae.frymulti.com/request2.asp?JID=2&AID=2524&CID=s2000&v=&i=&T=2, accessed December 17, 2002.

American Society of Agricultural Engineers. 2001. "Agricultural Machinery Management," ASAE EP496.2 DEC01, available at http://asae.frymulti.com/request2.asp?JID=2&AID=2523&CID=s2000&T=2, accessed December 17, 2002.

Boehlje, Michael D., and Vernon R. Eidman. 1984. *Farm Management.* New York: John Wiley and Sons.

FAPRI. 2009. "Crop Budget Generator." Accessed at www.fapri.missouri.edu on October 29, 2009.

Laughlin, David H., and Stan R. Spurlock, 2008. "User's Guide for the Mississippi State Budget Generator." Accessed at www.agecon.msstate.edu/what/farm/generator on October 29, 2009.

Lazarus, William F. 2010. MACHDATA.XLS, University of Minnesota, Department of Applied Economics, Saint Paul. Accessed on June 28, 2010, at www.apec.umn.edu/faculty/wlazarus/tools.html.

Lazarus, William F., and Andrew Smale. 2010. "Machinery Cost Estimates,"St. Paul: University of Minnesota, Minnesota Extension Service, June 2010. Available at: http://www.apec.umn.edu/faculty/wlazarus/documents/machdata.pdf, accessed June 28, 2010.

Lazarus, William F., and Roger A. Selley. 2002. *"Suggested Procedures for Estimating Farm Machinery Costs."*St. Paul: University of Minnesota, Department of Applied Economics [Staff Paper P02-16]. Electronically available only at: http://purl.umn.edu/14072, accessed June 28, 2010.

16

Partial Budgets

In this chapter:

- Partial budget analysis procedures
- Partial budget examples
- Limitations of a partial budget

A powerful but simple tool for a manager is the partial budget. Many decisions involve a question of whether a change in the original plan is worthwhile. The whole business or enterprise does not change, only parts of the operation change. Small incremental changes are more common when running a farm than large complex shifts. The partial budget is designed for addressing these smaller, incremental questions in a simple straightforward format.

These changes may be quite small, such as whether to feed livestock to a heavier weight or sell them now. The change can also seem rather large, such as the initial look at whether a dairy farmer should drop the dairy herd and concentrate on crop production. While this last decision is a strategic redirection of the farm that involves and needs more detailed work, managers like to have a quick look at whether a change is worth pursuing further and spending precious management time on the detailed analysis.

Evaluating only the changes is what sets the partial budget apart from the enterprise budget and the whole-farm budget. As discussed in the previous chapter, the enterprise budget is set up to help plan the organization of an individual enterprise. As will be discussed in the next chapter, the whole-farm budget is set up to help plan the organization of the entire farm business. The partial budget is a budgeting shortcut and, thus, a time-saver.

This chapter describes the procedures of partial budget analysis and examines some examples of using partial budgets. The last section discusses the limitations of partial budget analysis.

Partial Budget Analysis Procedures

In partial budget analysis, only changes are considered. The current plan is described, and the change is described in contrast to the current plan. The name, "partial budget," tells us that the whole budget and whole farm are not included here. The partial budget is used for estimating the effects of changes in the net income of the business, and only changes are included.

The change can be one of four types. Two are positive changes to net income; two are negative changes. Positive effects or changes include additional revenue and reduced expenses. Negative effects or changes include reduced revenue and additional expenses.

Additional revenue include additional revenue from higher yields due to improved fertility testing, sales of livestock held to a heaver weight, sales from an enterprise that has increased in size, sales from new enterprises added to the farm, revenue from custom work or hiring from the farm, and many other examples.

Reduced expenses include reduced machinery and labor costs due to a shift to chemical weed control, reduced electrical costs due to the installation of more efficient lights and motors, decreased expenditures from an enterprise not produced, machinery expenses not incurred due to hiring out the work to others, and many other examples.

Reduced revenue includes sales from an enterprise decreased in size or dropped from the farm, lower yields due to a change in production practices, sales of livestock held to be sold at a heavier weight, and many more.

Additional expenses include the cost of feeding livestock to a heavier weight, costs for additional or more detailed soil fertility testing, the cost of hiring custom work done by others, costs of additional machinery operations, and other examples.

Estimating and Valuing Changes

The first step in partial budget analysis (after describing the change, of course) is to identify those changes that are a result ONLY of the change in the business. For example, price decreases or increases due to fluctuations in the larger market should not be included as an effect of a potential change. However, if the production change is estimated to improve product quality that results in a higher price, this increase in the price should be included. In a similar manner, change in crop yield or animal productivity due to weather or other environmental changes should not be included, but estimated yield and productivity changes due to a management change need to be valued and included. Examples of management changes that can affect productivity include a different fertilizer plan, different weed control methods, improved feed and feeding, and increased efficiency in operations.

Additional revenue is revenue that is not now being received but would be if the potential change was actually put into practice. Additional revenue includes increased enterprise and farm size, increased production from current enterprises, production from new enterprises, improved prices due to new markets or improved marketing, higher crop yields, and higher animal productivity. These changes can be estimated and valued from past history, experimental evidence, company information, public university and government sources, and other trusted sources.

Reduced expenses are current expenses that would not be incurred if the potential change were actually put into practice. Reduced expenses include the expenses of an enterprise that would be dropped from the farm, inputs that would not be used, and lower prices for inputs. Reduced expenses can be either fixed or variable expenses. For example, the partial budget analyzing whether to own a specific machine, such as a harvester, or continue hiring the harvesting operation done by someone else requires the calculation of both ownership and operating expenses for the purchase option.

Reduced revenue is revenue that would be lost if the change were instituted. It is essentially the reverse or opposite of additional income. It includes decreased size, decreased production, dropping of current enterprises, lower prices due to new markets, lower crop yields, and lower animal productivity. Why, an alert reader may be wondering, would anyone consider making a change to lower prices, yields, or productivity? It may happen if a manager is wondering whether some production practices or procedures are indeed profitable. These changes can be estimated and valued using the same sources as other changes.

Additional expenses are new expenses that would be incurred if the potential change were actually put into practice. They are essentially the opposite or reverse of reduced expenses. Additional expenses include the expenses of an enterprise that would be added to the farm, new inputs that would be used, and higher prices for inputs. Additional expenses can also be either fixed or variable.

Care should be taken when estimating changes in both revenue and costs due to economies and diseconomies of scale and scope as described as Chapter 4, Lessons from Microeconomics. For example, increasing the size of the beef or dairy herd by 20% may increase some expenses by 20% but others such as labor and office expenses will not increase by 20%. Also, dropping or adding an enterprise may affect the costs of other enterprises. For example, increasing the amount of cropland will increase seed and fertilizer expenses proportionately but the fixed costs of machinery may not increase as much, especially if the farm had more than sufficient machinery capacity before the expansion.

Opportunity costs also need to be considered. As you may recall, an opportunity cost is the value of an input in its best alternative use. This is especially important for farm labor. If an enterprise is being added or increased in size, what is the opportunity cost of the increased labor requirement? In other words, what is not done so the labor can be used in the new or increased enterprise? If the additional labor needed previously worked off the farm or in another activity on the same farm, what is the value of the job being given up? That off-farm or other job that would be lost needs to be counted as reduced revenue to calculate an accurate estimate of the impact of the change on net income. In the opposite example, if an enterprise is dropped from the farm, the opportunity cost of the labor needs to be counted as additional revenue due to the potential change.

Incorporating Uncertainty

Even though utmost care is taken to estimate the values for each of the four types of change, a manager knows that these values are not known with certainty. The values used in the initial analysis should be the most likely values: the most likely price, the most likely yield change, and so on. After the initial analysis, the impact of different prices, yields, productivities, and so on can be estimated for their impact on the change in net income. For some variables, such as crop yields, we may easily pick rational low, median, and high values. For other variables, such as prices in the future, we may need to estimate the impact of a 5%, 10% or 20% change. However, these choices need to be based on reality too; it would be a mistake to reject or accept a change due to the impact of an arbitrary 20% variation when that magnitude of change rarely occurs. Scenarios or pictures of the future could be developed to analyze the impact of uncertainty; this process is described in Chapter 22, Risk Management.

Partial Budget Format

The four types of changes are organized in the partial budget with a format to show clearly what has changed and the net effect of the change from the current plan. The basic form starts with the date of estimation and the name of the person who prepared the estimation (Table 16.1). To clearly show what is changing, both the current plan and the change are described next, along with the unit of the budget (e.g., one acre or hectare, one animal, or whole farm). In some situations, estimating the impact of a potential change on the whole farm may be more accurate and easier than making the estimate on a per land or animal unit. While it may not seem important at the time, this information can help in understanding and following up on questions if the analysis and decision are reviewed at a later date.

The main part of the partial budget format contains the four types of changes. To simplify the organization in computerized spreadsheets, the four types of changes are listed vertically with a subtotal for the positive changes and a subtotal for the negative changes. Putting this vertical

Table 16.1   Partial Budget Format

Date of estimation:	Prepared by:
Current plan:	
Change in plan:	
Unit:	

POSITIVE EFFECTS:

1. ADDITIONAL REVENUE

2. REDUCED EXPENSES

	Total Positive Effects =

NEGATIVE EFFECTS:

3. REDUCED REVENUE

4. ADDITIONAL EXPENSES

	Total Negative Effects =

NET EFFECT = Positive Effects minus Negative Effects =

NOTES:

DECISION:

form in a spreadsheet allows for easy expansion of each section as needed. The net effect of the change is shown at the bottom after the positive and negative subtotals. To finish the analysis and the form, any notes related to how changes were estimated should be written at the bottom along with any assumptions about the situation and the change. The final note to be made is the decision made after the partial budget analysis was done: Was the change made or not? Having all this written and filed in the year's operation file can be helpful during reviews and subsequent decisions.

Partial Budget Examples

To show the usefulness and versatility of partial budget analysis, four examples are shown in this section. The examples are whether to substitute one input for another input; whether to change from hiring crop machinery operations to owning the machinery; whether to change the mix of crops grown on the farm; and whether to consider a change in strategic direction.

Substitute One Input for Another Input?

As an example of how to adjust a current plan by substituting one input for another input and evaluating the impact, consider the farmer who is growing soybeans and considering the substitution of a second mechanical cultivation for the post-plant herbicide application. By not applying the post-plant herbicide, the farmer is estimated to save $16.19 (Table 16.2). However, the potential yield loss of 4 bushels per acre valued at $5.25 per bushel and the cost of the additional cultivation ($4.01) is estimated to create a total negative effect of 25.01. So the net effect of this potential change is a loss of $8.82 per acre. If the farmer considers only the income effect, the change is not an improvement but a potential detriment to farm income. So the farmer does not make the change.

Change from Hiring Crop Machinery Operations to Owning the Machinery?

As an example of how to adjust a current plan by changing ownership of machinery, consider the farmer who is considering owning grain drill to plant 1,000 acres of wheat instead of hiring a custom operator. The farmer benefits from this change by not hiring the custom operator. The farmer now pays $7.50 per acre for the custom operator, so $7,500 is entered as a reduced expense in the partial budget (Table 16.3). Since the farmer already owns a tractor that can be used for planting wheat, he will not have any additional ownership expenses for the tractor. However, he does need to buy a grain drill. Using the costs estimated in Chapter 15, the farmer estimates the annual capital recovery cost (ACRC) for the grain drill to be $3,014. (As the reader may recall from Chapter 15, the ACRC includes both the depreciation and interest charge.) The annual costs of taxes, insurance, and housing (TIH) for the grain drill are estimated to be $616. The costs for fuel and lubrication are estimated to be $5.90 per hour; tractor repairs, $2.40 per hour; grain drill repairs, $8.65 per hour; and labor, $8.00 per hour. The drill is estimated to plant 12.73 acres per hour. Labor time is increased by 20% to reflect the additional time for labor to prepare the machine and to maintain and fill the grain drill. These additional costs of operating

Table 16.2   Partial Budget Analysis of a Substitution of One Input for Another Input

Date of estimation: January   Prepared by: Ann Young
Current plan: weed control using post plant herbicide

Change in plan: drop herbicide and add second cultivation

Unit: 1 acre

POSITIVE EFFECTS:

1. ADDITIONAL REVENUE
   None

2. REDUCED EXPENSES
   No post-plant herbicide application; cost of materials and application = $16.19

Total Positive Effects = $16.19

NEGATIVE EFFECTS:

3. REDUCED REVENUE
   Decreased corn yield: 4 bushels @ 5.25 = $21

4. ADDITIONAL EXPENSES
   Cost of second cultivation = $4.01

Total Negative Effects = $25.01

NET EFFECT = Positive Effects minus Negative Effects =

$ −8.82 per acre

NOTES: With this estimated yield loss and these cost changes, it is not worthwhile to drop the post-plant herbicide in favor of a second cultivation.

DECISION: Don't change. Continue with chemical weed control.

the grain drill (if owned) total $5,715 for the 1,000 acres. The net effect is a positive $1,785. So the farmer is inclined to buy a grain drill and plant his own wheat. Other factors need to be considered before a final decision can be made. These other factors include timeliness and availability of the custom operator, quality of custom operation, other uses of the equipment, value of the owner's labor in other uses, impact on the balance sheet, and so on.

Table 16.3 Partial Budget Analysis of a Machinery Ownership versus Hiring a Custom Operator

Date of estimation: July   Prepared by: William Henry

Current plan: Hire a custom operator to seed the wheat

Change in plan: Own the tractor and grain drill for planting wheat

Unit: 1,000 acres

POSITIVE EFFECTS:

1. ADDITIONAL REVENUE
   None

2. REDUCED EXPENSES
   Annual cost of hiring custom seeding for 1,000 acres @ $7.50/acre = $7,500

> Total Positive Effects = $7,500

NEGATIVE EFFECTS:

3. REDUCED REVENUE
   None

4. ADDITIONAL EXPENSES

Annual capital recovery costs (ACRC) for grain drill	$3,014
Taxes, insurance, and housing (TIH)	616
Operating expenses for 1000 acres at 12.73 acres per hour:	
Tractor fuel and lubrication at $5.90 per hour:	463
Tractor repairs at $2.40 per hour:	189
Grain drill repairs at $8.65 per hour:	679
Labor cost at $8.00 per hour with an additional 20%:	754

> Total Negative Effects = $5,715

NET EFFECT = Positive Effects minus Negative Effects =

> $1,785

NOTES: The costs of owning the grain drill are less than the costs of hiring the job done.

DECISION: Make the change. Buy the drill.

Change the Mix of Crops Grown on the Farm?

Our example farmers, the Gables, currently grow corn for silage on 191 acres for their dairy herd. However, they do have a contract for 155 acres of sweet corn that they could sign. After considering this initial cropping plan, the Gables decide to change it. They decide to do a partial budget analysis of changing the cropping plan by dropping corn silage and growing sweet corn and corn for grain instead.

For the Gables, the increase in revenue comes from 36 acres of corn grain and 155 acres of sweet corn from the 191 acres that would have been corn silage. Expenses decrease because they would not grow 191 acres of corn silage. Since the corn silage was being fed, there is no decrease in revenue. Expenses increase due to growing 36 acres of corn grain and 155 acres of sweet corn and having to buy sufficient corn silage in the market to replace the corn silage that won't be grown. The impact of these changes is estimated using their cost and revenue information (see Table 17.1) and assembling them into the partial budget format (Table 16.4). The total positive effects of the change are $200,013. The total negative effects are $162,690. This creates a net effect of $37,323 for the farm. Based on the partial budget analysis, the Gables decide to make the change to sweet corn and more corn grain.

Table 16.4 Partial Budget Analysis of Changing the Cropping Mix

Date of estimation: October	Prepared by: Jake Gable

Current plan: Grow corn silage for the dairy herd

Change in plan: Quit growing corn silage, buying corn silage
in the market, and grow sweet corn and corn for grain

Unit: 191 acres

POSITIVE EFFECTS:

1. ADDITIONAL REVENUE
   Sale of corn grain from 36 acres at 182 bu. per acre and $3.85 per bu. = $25,225
   Sweet corn receipts from 155 acres at 7.5 tons per acre and $94 per ton = 109,275

2. REDUCED EXPENSES
   Not growing 191 acres of corn silage with variable costs of $343 per acre = $65,513

> Total Positive Effects = $200,013

NEGATIVE EFFECTS:

3. REDUCED REVENUE
   None

4. ADDITIONAL EXPENSES

  Growing 36 acres of corn for grain with variable costs of $360 per acre = $12,960
  Growing 155 acres of sweet corn with variable costs of $202 per acre = $31,310

  Purchasing corn silage in the market:
    191 acres with a yield of 20 tons per acre at $31 per ton = $118,420

Total Negative Effects = $162,690

NET EFFECT = Positive Effects minus Negative Effects =

$37,323

NOTES: Due to changing from growing corn silage to sweet corn and corn for grain and buying the needed corn silage in the marketplace, net farm income would increase by $38,198.

DECISION: Switch. Net farm income increases significantly.

Consider a Change in Strategic Direction?

Another example is the initial analysis of a potential strategic change of dropping the milking herd and concentrating on crop production and other activities. This is a large change that requires considerable thought and analysis before the final decision is made. However, a quick analysis is often done to decide whether the idea is worth the work and time of completing the detailed analysis. This initial ''back-of-the-envelope'' analysis can be done using a partial budget.

  In the partial budget framework, additional revenue would come from the crops that could be sold instead of fed (Table 16.5). For this quick analysis, the farmer didn't consider other crops but only the feed that could now be sold. Reduced expenses would come from all the other dairy expenses such as other feed expenses, veterinary expenses, fuel, and so on. Reduced revenue would be the milk, calves, cull cows, and replacement heifers that are normally would be sold but would not be available if the dairy enterprise were sold. In this quick analysis, there are no additional expenses included. Base on these estimates, the positive effects of this potential change are estimated to be worth $2,540.15, the negative effects are $3,821.55, and the net effect is $−1,281.41 per cow. Based on these estimates, the farmer decided to keep milking and not to pursue any further analysis of this potential change.

Limitations of Partial Budget Analysis

Partial budget analysis is extremely flexible, but it does have limitations. The first and most obvious limitation is that it can only evaluate one alternative at a time. Although it would not be hard to do, analysis of more than one alternative would require multiple partial budgets. Another limitation is that only one set of values can be analyzed unless sensitivity is done. The partial budget is essentially limited to annual analyzed. Changes that take place over multiple years (such as planting trees, new buildings) can be hard to fit into the simple partial budget framework. Multiple years could be

Table 16.5   A Partial Budget Format as an Initial Analysis of a Strategy Change

Date of estimation: April   Prepared by: Henry Smith
Current plan: Milk 75 cows

Change in plan: Sell dairy herd, continue to grow and sell crops without feeding to livestock

Unit: One cow

POSITIVE EFFECTS:

1. ADDITIONAL REVENUE

Corn equivalents	$3.80 per bu × 104 bu	= $ 395.20
Corn Silage	$34.00 per ton × 8 tons	= 272.00
Hay equivalents	$125.00 per ton × 6.1 tons	= 762.50

2. REDUCED EXPENSES

Other feed expenses		= $1,755.00
Veterinary and health		= 98.00
Fuel, utilities and repairs		= 150.00
DHIA and accounting		= 28.00
Breeding fees		= 40.00
Bedding, supplies, and miscellaneous		= 160.00
Hauling	$0.29 per cwt of milk	= 58.00
Interest on variable costs	9% for 3 months	= 12.02
Interest, insurance on herd		= 239.00

> Total Positive Effects = $2,540.15

NEGATIVE EFFECTS:

3. REDUCED REVENUE

Milk sales	$17.00 per cwt × 200 cwt	= 3,400.00
Cull cow	0.36 head × $0.30 per lb × 1350 lb	= 145.80
Dairy calf	$125.00 per head × 0.51 head	= 63.75
Replacement heifer	$400.00 per head × 0.18 head	= 72.00
Lower labor revenue in off-farm job, loss of	$2.00 per hr × 70 hr	= 140.00

4. ADDITIONAL EXPENSES
     None

> Total Negative Effects = $3,821.55

NET EFFECT = Positive Effects minus Negative Effects =

> $ −1,281.41

NOTES: Based on 75 cows milking 20,000 lb per cow

DECISION: Keep milking, don't pursue further analysis of this change.

evaluated using annual averages, but these ignore many variables and details. A full investment analysis is needed instead of a partial budget analysis; see Chapter 20.

Some decisions, even though they look simple, need to have risk considered explicitly rather than just looking at one set of numbers as in standard partial budget analysis. To overcome these limitations, the uncertainty of prices, yields, productivity, and costs can be handled by adding the use of payoff and regret matrices and scenarios to encompass the range of potential outcomes; see Chapter 22.

Summary

- The partial budget is a simple but powerful tool for managers.
- A partial budget considers only the changes that would take place if a management plan were changed.
- The changes included in a partial budget are additional revenue, reduced expenses, reduced revenue, and additional expenses.
- Uncertainty can be included by expanding the use of payoff matrices and scenarios.

Review Questions

1. Why are only changes used in partial budget analysis?
2. What are the four types of changes included in a partial budget?
3. Consider a farmer who plans to sell a group of hogs this week but wonders whether feeding them another week before selling them would be more profitable. During this week, the hogs are expected to gain 7 pounds, going from 250 pounds to 257 pounds. The price for both weights is expected to be $55/cwt (100 lb) for both weeks, but next week's price is uncertain. The change in the plan would mean that a 250 lb hog will not be sold this week, and the interest that could have been received on that hog's value for one week is lost. In your calculations, use an annual rate of 8%. The farmer does not estimate any reduced expenses for this change. Additional expenses due to the change are additional feed, labor, and other costs, and the chance of some hogs dying during the next week. Additional feed expenses are for corn (28 lb at $0.07/lb), soybean meal (4 lb at $0.15/lb), and distillers dried grain (2 lb at $0.06/lb). Labor and other costs for one week are estimated to be $0.35. The potential death loss is estimated to be 0.1% of the value of the hog not sold this week. Using the partial budget format below, what is the net effect of the potential change? What do you think this farmer should do?

Date of estimation:

Current plan: Sell pigs now

Prepared by:

Change in plan: Feed pigs for one more week. The pigs will gain 7 pounds and go from 250 pounds to 257 pounds.

Unit: One hog

POSITIVE EFFECTS:

1. ADDITIONAL REVENUE

2. REDUCED EXPENSES

Total Positive Effects = $

NEGATIVE EFFECTS:

3. REDUCED REVENUE

4. ADDITIONAL EXPENSES

Total Negative Effects = $

NET EFFECT = Positive Effects minus Negative Effects =

NOTES:

DECISION:

4. An input supplier is pushing a farmer to change his traditional corn production practices to strive for higher yields. The supplier is saying that the plan needs additional major nutrients as well as micro-nutrients plus changes in other practices. Rather than evaluate each suggested change by itself, the whole package of changes can be evaluated in a partial budget framework. The estimated changes in yield, operations, and costs for converting from corn following soybean with common practices to continuous corn with high input practices are listed below.

    The corn yield is expected to increase from 181.9 to 191.5 bushels per acre if all the changes below are done. The expected corn price is $3.30 per bushel.

    Fall tillage is changed from using a chisel plow with a disk in front (costing $9.82 per acre) to using a moldboard plow (costing $16.13 per acre).

    No manure was applied under the previous plan, but the change would add a fall manure application (costing $12 per acre). The following nutrient amounts from manure are estimated but they are not paid:

    N: 207.6 lb/acre valued at 0.35/lb
    P: 193.2 lb/acre valued at 0.37/lb
    K: 174 lb/acre valued at 0.23/lb

    In the spring, fertilizer is already applied but additional amounts are now applied. Since the operation is already done, the application cost is not included in the cost of the change of practices. The following additional amounts of fertilizer are applied in the spring:

    | Nitrogen | 10 lb/acre at $0.35/lb |
    | Phosphorus | 2 lb/acre at 0.37/lb |

Potassium	25 lb/acre at 0.23/lb
Sulfur	12.5 lb/acre at 0.20/lb
Zinc	4 lb/acre at 1.13/lb

The change to strive for higher yields also requires some additional costs at planting. These additional costs are:

Seed	4,000 more seeds per acre at $1.50 per 1,000 seeds
Insecticide	$18/acre
Nitrogen	10 lb/acre at $0.35/lb
Phosphorus	34 lb/acre at $0.37/lb

In June, additional nitrogen is added as part of the change in practices. The custom application costs $9.50/acre and the additional nitrogen is 40 lb/acre, costing $0.35/lb.

Since the farmer would have a higher yield, the costs of drying and trucking would also increase. Drying the additional yield is estimated to cost $0.208/bu. and the additional trucking would cost $0.065/bu.

Since costs increase, the farmer will incur additional interest costs due to borrowing more money to finance production. This interest cost is calculated on the basis of the increase in all other costs financed with an annual interest rate of 7.0% for six months.

Using the partial budget format below, what is the net effect of the potential change? What do you think this farmer should do?

Date of estimation: Prepared by:

Current plan: Grow corn in a corn-soybean rotation using common production practices

Change in plan: Change practices and input levels to strive for a higher yield

Unit: One acre

POSITIVE EFFECTS:

1. ADDITIONAL REVENUE

2. REDUCED EXPENSES

Total Positive Effects = $

NEGATIVE EFFECTS:

3. REDUCED REVENUE

Total Positive Effects = $

4. ADDITIONAL EXPENSES

Total Negative Effects = $

NET EFFECT = Positive Effects minus Negative Effects =

NOTES:

DECISION:

17

Whole-Farm Planning

In this chapter:

- The whole-farm plan from the strategic vision and chosen strategy
- Plan development: enterprise selection, partial budget, whole-farm budget, and projected cash flow budget
- Preparation of pro forma financial statements
- Progress on the farm's balanced scorecard

In this chapter, we show how the strategy developed using the strategic management procedures in Chapters 7 and 8 are transformed into a whole-farm plan with detailed financial plans. This process is done in step with the implementation plans developed in Chapter 9. After the ''big picture'' analysis and planning done in those earlier chapters, the work that needs to be done and is described in this chapter will seem like a tremendous amount of detail. However, this is a necessary step in the process to show to internal and external stakeholders (especially lenders) that the strategic plan will contribute to the success of the farm business.

In the next section, we work through the process of developing the whole-farm plan for the first year. We first look at how to select the enterprises. Even if the strategic plan has a very narrow list of enterprises, the current situation of the farm may mean that the process of moving to the new strategic plan will not be a single step but a series of steps over a few years. We will also show how a partial budget can be useful for adjusting an initial plan, and how to develop a whole-farm budget and an input supply management plan. Once these pieces of the plan are developed in detail, we will use the information to project a whole-farm cash flow and then the performance financial statements for the first year. We will also discuss how to compare progress for the chosen strategy and strategic goals using the balanced scorecard.

We will work through this process using the Gables farm. It is currently a crop and dairy farm, and the Gables have chosen a strategy to expand and become more focused on the dairy enterprise and decrease the emphasis on crop production. However, they have also decided to use a more market-oriented approach for deciding where and how to obtain the feed for their animals. That is, they used to grow all their feed but now as they focus on and expand the dairy they realize that they may not be able to produce the needed feed as cheaply as they can buy from other producers. Plus they realize that the time reallocated from crop production to managing the dairy will allow them to focus on improving the productivity and efficiency of the dairy.

Whole-Farm Planning

The Gables currently farm 1,250 tillable acres and have a milking herd of 600 cows. They own 775 of the tillable acres and rent the rest. Their strategic plan is first to improve their herd average for milk per cow from 20,000 to 25,000 lb per cow and then to expand to 800 cows within five years and possibly more in the future. They have been producing all the corn grain and corn silage for their cows. They have also grown soybeans and wheat almost every year. They have had contracts to grow sweet corn and peas for a processing company. The first step they need to do is to choose which crops they will grow. The process for enterprise selection is described next.

Enterprise Selection

The optimal combination of products is the combination that best meets the farmer's objectives as defined in their strategy and shown in their balanced scorecard. Usually that is first measured as the combination that yields the highest return to the resources used in production. As discussed in Chapter 4, profitable supplementary and complementary products are chosen and expanded until they become competitive with other products. An example of crop choice in the United Kingdom includes energy crops and shows whether they can compete with traditional uses (Example 17.1).

When evaluating the choices between competitive products, the decision becomes a process of resource allocation between potential products. Several methods are available for choosing the best mix of crops, livestock, and other products. Some methods for making decisions are not very good: trial and error or the coffee shop, for example. Mathematical techniques (such as linear programming, see Appendix 17.1) are very useful but require high initial costs in terms of learning the technique, understanding the results, and data acquisition. The alternative of using gross margins for choosing crop enterprises is a simple, useful method with a pragmatic, structured procedure.

Gross Margin Analysis. Gross margin analysis is especially useful for choosing which crops to grow in the next growing season when the constraining factors are few in number and relatively simple. More complicated situations may require more sophisticated analysis tools such as linear programming (see Appendix 17.1). These complications may include having several fields with different yield potentials, the need to buy new machinery, the need to consider planting and harvesting schedules, and the need to evaluate the profitability of hiring temporary labor. Whether and how to allocate labor and other resources between livestock and crop production is another complication that may require more sophisticated decision tools.

The gross margin (GM) for an enterprise is defined as that enterprise's gross income (GI) minus its variable costs (VC):

$$GM = GI - VC$$

Example 17.1. Economic Viability of Energy Crops

Production of crops for alternative sources of energy is very new and very exciting for many, but not necessarily an easy choice for farmers. Using enterprise budgets and comparing crop choice, Jones in the United Kingdom tested the economic viability of energy crops compared to alternative land uses. His results showed energy crops to be competitive against alternative land uses (set aside and grazing livestock) and even against arable crops, if the arable work was undertaken by contractors. "However further analysis showed that even under these circumstances the viability of energy crops was reliant on support from public funds to compensate for market failure. It was barely viable without an establishment grant and could only be justified as an alternative to set-aside if all subsidy support was withdrawn."

Similar studies show that energy crops require government subsidies either directly or through support of the processors who produce the alternative energy. Consequently, farmers need to evaluate the level of government support and the stability and longevity of that support before making new investments for the production of energy crops.

Source: J. V. H. Jones, "Testing the Economic Viability of Energy Crop Production in Competition with Alternative Land Uses." Peer-reviewed paper at the 17th International Farm Management Congress, Illinois State University, Bloomington/Normal, Illinois, U.S., July 19–24, 2009, accessed on February 1, 2010, at http://www.ifmaonline.org/pdf/congress/09_Jones.pdf.

In the enterprise budgets in Chapter 15, the return over operating costs is also the gross margin if the list of operating costs includes only variable costs. For example, land rent is included as an operating cost in Table 15.1; however, it is not a variable cost like fertilizer or seed, so it should not be included in the list of variable costs used to calculate the gross margin for gross margin analysis.

The steps for gross margin analysis are listed below.

1. If livestock are part of the farm and, correctly or incorrectly, viewed as the most profitable enterprise, their feed requirements are often determined and feed crops are chosen as the first step. This step of selecting crops for livestock feed first was done historically but is not done as often now—as the Gables have decided in our example.
2. After meeting feed requirements or if that step was skipped, the next step is to select the crop with the largest GM/acre. The acreage of this crop is increased up to the total farm acreage limit or to another limit (e.g., crop rotation rules for disease and pest management, a production contract, or other institutional limit).
3. Next, select the crop with the second largest GM/acre. Increase the acreage of this crop up to the acreage limit or another limit as described above.
4. Continue selecting crops in this manner until the total farm acreage limit is reached.
5. As a test, the process in steps 1 through 4 can be repeated using the gross margin per hour instead of per acre. If these results are different from the crop mix chosen using gross margins per acre, evaluate the two plans in terms of the total gross margin for the farm. If the two crop mixes are

vastly different, this may indicate that the situation is too complex for the simple gross margin analysis. The farmer may need to use a more complex method, such as linear programming.

As noted in step 1, farmers with livestock often choose the crops needed to produce the feed requirements of the livestock. If any land is not used to meet the feed requirements, the crop selection for that acreage would follow the steps listed above. However, this livestock-first approach assumes livestock are the most profitable and ignores the opportunities provided by more profitable, non-feed crops. If livestock are expected to pay the market price for feed and there are no differences in quality, skipping the first step listed above will provide the profit-maximizing mix of crops for the farm. If the crop mix chosen by these steps does not produce the feed needed by the livestock, another crop must be more profitable. That is, the advantage of producing one's own feed is less than the advantage of producing more profitable crops and purchasing the required feed. As a California rancher once told me, "I found I could grow more hay by raising olives on that land." With the profit from the olives, he could buy more hay per acre than he could grow per acre.

As an example of using gross margins, let us consider the Gables farm. The Gables produce milk (and thus calves and cull cows) and historically they have produced corn grain, corn silage, soybeans, spring wheat, sweet corn, and peas. They have 1,250 tillable crop acres and 600 lactating dairy cows. Using their records and making some adjustments for next year, the Gables have estimated the gross margins for the crops on their farm (Table 17.1). Since they plan to improve their milk per cow yield and eventually expand, they have adapted the enterprise budget for their dairy shown in Table 15.2.

They maintain a rotation of 50% non-legumes and 50% legumes. If wheat or peas are planted, wheat would be counted on the corn side of the 50-50 mix, and peas would be counted with soybeans. Since they have 1,250 tillable acres, they plan to plant a total of 625 acres of non-legumes (corn, corn silage, sweet corn, and wheat) and a total of 625 acres of legumes (soybeans and peas). For next year, they could have contracts for 225 acres of peas and 155 acres of sweet corn, but they have not signed them yet.

In past years, they first decided how many acres of corn for grain and for silage they needed to grow. Their records indicate they need 6.35 tons of corn silage per cow and 124 bushels of corn grain. Using the yields in Table 17.1, they estimate they need 191 acres of corn silage and 409 acres of corn grain. So their first step is to allocate those acres. These acres are corn, so 600 acres of the available non-legume acreage is used.

After meeting their feed requirements, the Gables start using the estimated gross margins to choose the next crop. Evaluating the gross margins in Table 17.1, the Gables first choose to increase the pea acreage up to the contractual limit of 225 acres since that has the largest gross margin per acre ($516). Now, even though sweet corn has the second highest gross margin ($503), they realize they cannot plant sweet corn because the processor will not reduce the contract limit of 155 acres and they have only 25 acres left before their self-imposed rotation limit becomes constraining.

Corn for grain has the third highest gross margin ($365). The acreage of corn is also limited by the 50-50 rotation rule and the earlier decision to meet feed requirements by planting corn for grain and for silage. They decide to plant another 25 acres of corn for grain, which will increase the non-legume acreage to the limit of 625 acres.

Table 17.1   Estimated Gross Margins for the Gables' Farm

	Corn	Soybeans	Spring Wheat	Corn Silage	Sweet Corn	Peas
Unit	bu.	bu.	bu.	ton	ton	lb
Yield	182	48	55	20	7.5	3500
Price ($/bu., ton, or lb)	3.85	9.65	7.8	31	94	0.17
Other income ($/acre)*	24	21	69	0	0	0
Gross income ($/acre)	725	484	498	620	705	595
Variable Costs ($/acre)						
Seed	74	35	30	69	0**	0**
Fertilizer	116	8	48	67	108	19
Crop chemicals	34	28	14	31	30	17
Crop insurance	27	28	12	24	14	8
Drying expense	26	0	0	0	0	0
Fuel and oil	31	24	20	47	15	10
Repairs	33	27	26	47	20	14
Other crop expenses***	19	22	24	58	15	11
Total variable costs	360	172	174	343	202	79
Gross margin ($/acre)	365	312	324	277	503	516
Rank by gross margin	3	5	4	6	2	1
Total hours required/acre	2.4	2	1.7	4.5	1.5	1.4
Planting hours	1.2	0.9	0.9	1.2	1.3	1.2
Growing hours	0.3	0.3	0	0.4	0.1	0.1
Harvesting hours	0.9	0.8	0.8	2.9	0.1	0.1

*Other income includes government payments, straw sales, etc.

**Seed costs were paid by the processing company for sweet corn and peas.

***For simplicity, several expenses are grouped together; in a full analysis these would be listed separately.

Spring wheat actually has the fourth highest gross margin ($324 per acre), but since wheat is a non-legume, the Gables realize they cannot plant any wheat without violating their rotation rule. So they now consider soybeans.

Soybeans have the fifth highest gross margin ($312). Because they do not want to plant more than 50% of their 1,250 tillable acres to soybeans and peas, they limit their soybean acreage to 400 acres since they already have decided to sign the pea contract and will plant 225 acres of peas. These two crops will total 625 acres which is the rotation limit for legumes.

This initial cropping plan uses all of their 1,250 tillable acres. Under this plan, they will plant 434 acres of corn for grain, 191 acres of corn for silage, 400 acres of soybeans, and 225 acres of peas under contract.

Partial Budget Analysis.   After considering this initial cropping plan, the Gables decide they want to change it. In their strategic plan, the Gables want to focus more on their dairy operation, but they also want to use a market approach to decide where and how to obtain the feed for their animals.

After looking at the initial cropping plan, they realize that their first step of growing feed for the dairy caused them to choose corn silage when it had the lowest gross margin per acre. They also realize that choosing crops to raise the feed for the dairy first did not reflect their desire to look at decisions from a market view. To reinforce their desire to change the way they make decisions, they decide to do a partial budget analysis of changing the cropping plan by dropping corn silage and growing sweet corn and corn for grain instead.

As a first step in the reevaluation of their gross margin analysis, the Gables look again at the GMs (Table 17.1). Since they are considering not growing corn silage, they need to look at the other non-legume crops to be sure they keep their rotation of 50% legume and 50% non-legume crops. They quickly see that sweet corn has the highest GM and corn for grain has the second highest GM of the non-legumes. Since it has the highest GM, sweet corn is put in the plan first, up to the contract limit of 155 acres. Since the initial plan had 191 acres of corn silage, the 155 acres of sweet corn leaves 36 acres (= 191 – 155). These 36 acres are in addition to the 434 acres of corn for grain in the initial plan.

As shown in their partial budget (see Table 16.4), the Gables have increased revenue from 155 acres of sweet corn and 36 acres of corn for grain. Their expenses would decrease due to not growing 191 acres of corn silage. They do not expect any decrease in revenue since the corn silage was fed, not sold. However, their expenses would increase due to growing 155 acres of sweet corn and 36 acres of corn for grain. They would also have to buy silage for the dairy herd to replace the silage they are not growing. The partial budget shows that total positive effects of the change are $200,888, total negative effects are $162,690, so there is a positive net effect of $38,198 for the farm. From the partial budget analysis, the Gables decide to make the change.

The final crop mix plan for the first year is thus 470 acres of corn for grain, 400 acres of soybeans, 155 acres of sweet corn, and 225 acres of peas.

Whole-Farm Budget. After the cropping and livestock plan is developed, the next step is to estimate the whole-farm budget. This step is both simple and detailed: (1) multiplication of the livestock revenue and operating expenses per head by the chosen number of animals, (2) multiplication of the crop revenue and operating expenses per acre by the chosen number of acres per crop, and (3) estimation of whole-farm expenses from previous records and known costs.

Although they are aiming for 25,000 lb of milk per cow, the Gables know they won't achieve that immediately. So they estimate their average annualized milk production to increase gradually from 20,000 to 22,200 by the end of the year. On an annualized average, they plan their production to be 20,000 lb per cow in January and February; 20,500 in March; 21,000 in April and May; 21,500 in June and July; 22,000 in August and September; and 22,500 in October, November, and December. Thus, they estimate their total whole-farm milk sales to be $2,257,745 and their volume premium to be $64,250 (Table 17.2). For calf sales, they multiply the estimate of $234 per cow by 600 cows to estimate the whole-farm total of $140,400. The same method is used for the cull cow sales.

Their whole-farm crop sales are estimated in a similar fashion except for the corn grain, which is kept for feeding the milking herd and is subtracted from the total production before corn grain sales are calculated. To explain in more detail: total corn grain production is estimated by multiplying the predicted yield, 182 bushels, by the planned 470 acres, but then the grain to be fed is subtracted. The corn to be fed is estimated by multiplying the 124 bushels needed per cow by the 600 cows in the

Table 17.2   Gables' Whole-Farm Budget for Their Dairy and Crop Farm

Gross Receipts	Whole Farm
Milk	$2,257,745
Volume premium	64,250
Calf sales	140,400
Cull cow sales	129,000
Manure credit	75,600
Corn grain	42,889
Soybeans	185,280
Sweet corn	109,275
Peas	133,875
Other crop income	19,680
Total Gross Receipts	3,157,994
Operating Costs	
Seed	$48,780
Fertilizer	78,735
Crop chemicals	35,655
Crop insurance	27,860
Crop drying expense	12,220
Machinery repairs	32,560
Other crop expenses	22,530
Purchased feed	935,160
Veterinary, drugs, and supplies	84,000
Somatotropin (rbST)	49,800
Milk hauling and promotion cost	150,000
Building and equipment repairs	81,000
Semen A.I. services and supplies	31,800
Utilities	75,000
Fuel, oil, and auto expense	68,945
Labor	241,800
Land rent	71,250
Interest on operating costs	76,800
Total Operating Costs	2,123,895
Ownership and Overhead Costs	
Professional fees	$10,200
Depreciation on buildings and equipment	196,579
Opportunity interest on land, buildings, and equipment	153,740
Insurance and taxes on land, buildings, and equipment	51,000
Opportunity interest on herd	67,200
Insurance on herd	12,000
Miscellaneous	45,757
Total Ownership and Overhead Costs	536,476
Owner Labor and Management	100,000
Total Listed Expenses	2,760,371
Net Return	$397,623

herd. After the corn to be fed is subtracted from the estimated production, the difference is multiplied by the expected price of $3.85 per bushel, and the whole-farm sales in corn grain are estimated to be $42,889. The whole-farm sales of other crops are estimated more simply since they are not used for feed. Total soybean sales of $185,280 are estimated as 400 acres multiplied by 48 bushels per acre and $9.65 per bushel.

Whole-farm operating expenses are estimated in a similar fashion. Expenses per head and per acre are multiplied by the appropriate number of head or acres. A subtotal is calculated by category for items such as fuel and oil, which are used for both crops and livestock.

Whole-farm overhead and fixed expenses are estimated or projected from historical farm record information or projected from market information. Items such as professional fees and miscellaneous expenses would be based on past expenses with an adjustment for inflation if needed. Depreciation can be estimated from asset records. Insurance costs can be estimated from past records or found by checking with insurance companies. Opportunity interest is the cost of owning capital assets based on the market value of the assets and the interest rate that the farmer could receive if the value was invested in the marketplace rather than in farm assets.

Owner labor and management is based on what the owner wants as a return for working on the farm and should be based on what the farmer could be earning in another occupation. The Gables plan to have two family members working on the farm and have estimated both could earn $50,000 off the farm, and thus have entered a cost estimate of $100,000 for the total owner labor and management.

In summary, the total revenues for the whole farm are estimated to be $3,157,994. The total listed expenses are estimated to be $2,760,371. The resulting net return is estimated to be $397,623 for the whole farm. These estimates are preliminary budget estimates designed to allow for a quick projection of whether the plans for the farm will result in positive returns or whether further adjustments are needed to attain profitability, especially at the desired level. The next step in whole-farm planning is the preparation of the projected cash flow budget, the subject of the next section.

Preparation of the Projected Whole-Farm Cash Flow Budget

The projected whole-farm cash flow budget is a planning tool that shows cash inflows and outflows on a monthly basis. The manager can evaluate when operating loans are needed and when they can be paid back. The timing of product sales and expenses, especially major capital purchases, can be evaluated and changed prior to the event in order to have a more orderly cash flow and to lower interest costs by lowering the need to borrow money. This projected cash flow budget is structured and used very differently from the statement of cash flows described in Chapter 12. The statement of cash flows is a report of the annual sources and uses of cash that actually did move into and out of the business.

The format of the projected cash flow budget is fairly standard but is not fixed across the industry. In addition, the level of detail and the exact line items within each category can vary with the type of farm and the needs of the farmer and the stakeholders. These main categories are included in most projected cash flow budgets: beginning cash balance, cash receipts, total cash available, cash outflow (operating expenses, other outflows, and scheduled debt payments), net cash position, new borrowings and savings withdrawals, repayment of operating loans and savings deposits, and ending balances.

The Gables start with their cash and loan balances on January 1. These are not projected but are the actual balances reported in the balance sheet at the end of the past year and thus the beginning of the year to be projected. For the Gables, these balances include cash of $10,000, savings of $199,780, and a total remaining unpaid principal balance of $1,101,768 on all their non-current loans. They do not have any balances in their operating loan, credit line, or accrued interest on any operating loan entries. While $126,788 of the principal of their non-current loans will be due within the next 12 months, they do not have any current scheduled debt, such as a six-month loan with monthly payments for a large repair bill.

They decide they want to keep a minimum balance of $10,000 as cash in their business checking account and $10,000 in their business savings account at the end of each month. (They also have personal checking and savings accounts, but since they are personal, they are not included in the business analysis.)

As we will see, the Gables will first transfer from their business savings back into their cash flow in order to cover expenses and maintain a cash balance of $10,000. If they do not have sufficient funds in savings, they will borrow an operating loan to maintain a $10,000 balance. If they have more than $10,000 in cash, the bank terms on their operating loan say they must first pay any accrued interest on operating loans. If sufficient funds are still available, they will then pay any principal on operating loans and transfer any remaining funds in cash over $10,000 into savings. While the interest rate for savings is low, it is greater than the zero interest earned on their checking account.

On the basis of their whole-farm plan and resulting budget and following the procedures described in Chapter 14, the Gables enter their projected revenues and expenses into the projected cash flow budget (Table 17.3). Only cash items are entered; thus the value of the manure added to the whole-farm budget revenue is not included and the value of the corn fed is not included in the projected cash flow. The expenses of manure application and corn production are included since these are cash outflows. The Gables project that their milk sales will gradually increase as they improve productivity; they use the same growth projections used for the whole-farm budget. Some revenues and expenses (such as calf sales and veterinary expenses) are simply divided evenly across the months since they do not have a more exact way of estimating when they will occur. Other revenues and expenses (such as crop sales, government payments, and seed purchases) are distributed through the year as they think they will occur. Scheduled debt payments are taken from loan information, with the principal and interest payments entered in separate lines in the months when they are scheduled to be paid.

After entering all the information into the cash flow projection, the Gables estimate that their net cash position (line E in Table 17.3) is a positive $48,347 for January. This is the difference between the total cash available and the total cash outflow. The total cash available for January is $270,483, which is the sum of the beginning cash balance of $10,000 and the total cash receipts of $260,483. The total cash outflow for January is $222,136. Since they have no beginning balances of accrued interest and operating loans, the Gables transfer $38,347 into savings leaving the desired balance of $10,000 in cash.

In February, the Gables see a different story. The net cash position is projected to be a negative $140,763 primarily due to the loan payments due in February. However, they have sufficient funds in savings and simply transfer $150,763 back into their cash account to cover expenses and maintain the $10,000 balance in cash. The non-current loan principal balance decreases by the principal paid in February.

Table 17.3 Projected Monthly Cash Flow Budget for Gables' Farm

	January	February	March	April	May	June
A. Beginning cash balance	10,000	10,000	10,000	10,000	10,000	10,000
CASH RECEIPTS						
Milk	175,700	175,700	180,093	184,485	184,485	188,878
Volume premium	5,000	5,000	5,125	5,250	5,250	5,375
Calf sales	11,700	11,700	11,700	11,700	11,700	11,700
Cull cow sales	10,750	10,750	10,750	10,750	10,750	10,750
Corn grain	12,000	0	0	0	30,000	0
Soybeans	45,000	0	0	35,000	45,000	0
Sweet corn	0	0	0	0	0	0
Peas	0	0	0	0	0	0
Government payments	0	8,000	0	0	0	3,500
Other farm income	0	0	0	0	0	0
Withdrawals from futures accounts	0	0	0	0	0	0
Sales of capital assets	0	0	0	0	0	0
Nonfarm income	0	0	0	0	0	0
Interest earned on savings	333	397	147	17	17	106
B. Total cash receipts	260,483	211,547	207,815	247,202	287,202	220,309
C. Total cash available (A + B)	270,483	221,547	217,815	257,202	297,202	230,309

CASH OUTFLOW

Operating Expenses	January	February	March	April	May	June
Seed	24,390		24,390			
Fertilizer	19,684		39,367			
Crop chemicals	8,914			26,741		
Crop insurance			27,860			
Crop drying expense						
Machinery repairs		3,500	5,000	3,000	3,200	2,400
Other crop expenses		5,530	1,500	1,500	3,000	3,000
Purchased feed	68,104	68,104	68,104	68,104	68,104	68,104
Veterinary, drugs, and supplies	7,000	7,000	7,000	7,000	7,000	7,000
Somatotropin (rbST)	4,147	4,147	4,147	4,147	4,147	4,147
Milk hauling and promotion cost	12,500	12,500	12,500	12,500	12,500	12,500
Building and equipment repairs	6,750	6,750	6,750	6,750	6,750	6,750
Semen A.I. services and supplies	2,625	2,625	2,625	2,625	2,625	2,625
Utilities	6,275	6,275	6,275	6,275	6,275	6,275
Fuel, oil, and auto expense	5,750	5,750	5,750	5,750	5,750	5,750
Labor	20,127	20,127	20,127	20,127	20,127	20,127
Land rent			71,250			
Professional fees	850	850	850	850	850	850
Insurance and taxes on land, bldgs, and equip.		14,656	21,985			

(*continued*)

Table 17.3   (*continued*)

	January	February	March	April	May	June
Insurance on herd		5,850				
Other operating expenses	3,820	3,820	3,820	3,820	3,820	3,820
Other outflows						
Deposits to futures accounts	0	0	0	0	0	0
Capital asset purchases	0	0	0	0	0	0
Heifer replacements	23,200	23,200	23,200	23,200	23,200	23,200
Machinery	0	0	0	0	0	0
Family living	8,000	8,000	8,000	8,000	8,000	8,000
Income taxes	0	0	30,000	0	0	30,000
Scheduled debt payments						
Current debt, principal payments	0	0	0	0	0	0
Current debt, interest payments	0	0	0	0	0	0
Non-current debt, principal payments	0	108,972	0	0	0	0
Non-current debt, interest payments	0	54,654	0	0	0	0
D. Total cash outflow	222,136	362,310	390,500	200,389	175,348	204,548
E. Net cash position (C−D)	48,347	−140,763	−172,685	56,813	121,854	25,761
NEW BORROWINGS AND SAVINGS WITHDRAWALS						
Current scheduled debt borrowed (+)	0	0	0	0	0	0
Non-current debt borrowed (+)	0	0	0	0	0	0
Borrowed from operating loan or credit line	0	0	104,444	0	0	0
Withdrawals from business savings (+)	0	150,763	78,241	17	0	0
F. Total new borrowings and savings withdrawals	0	150,763	182,685	17	0	0
REPAYMENT OF OPERATING LOAN AND SAVINGS DEPOSITS						
Interest payment on operating loan	0	0	0	609	340	0
Principal payment on operating loan	0	0	0	46,221	58,223	0
Transfers to business savings (−)	38,347	0	0	0	53,291	15,761
G. Repayment of operating loan and savings deposits	38,347	0	0	46,830	111,854	15,761

BALANCES AT END OF PERIOD	Beg. Jan 1 Balances:						
H. Ending cash balance (E + F − G)	10,000	10,000	10,000	10,000	10,000	10,000	10,000
Business savings	199780	238,460	88,094	10,000	10,000	63,308	79,175
Operating loan or credit line	0	0	0	104,444	58,223	0	0
Accrued interest on operating loan	0	0	0	0	0	0	0
Current scheduled debt	0	0	0	0	0	0	0
All non-current debt	1,101,768	1,101,768	992,796	992,796	992,796	992,796	992,796
Interest rate on operating loan:	7.00%						
Interest rate on savings:	2.00%						

Table 17.3   *(continued)*

	July	August	September	October	November	December	ANNUAL
A. Beginning cash balance	10,000	10,000	10,000	10,000	10,000	10,000	10,000
CASH RECEIPTS							
Milk	188,878	193,270	193,270	197,663	197,663	197,663	2,257,748
Volume premium	5,375	5,500	5,500	5,625	5,625	5,625	64,250
Calf sales	11,700	11,700	11,700	11,700	11,700	11,700	140,400
Cull cow sales	10,750	10,750	10,750	10,750	10,750	10,750	129,000
Corn grain	0	0	0	0	0	0	42,000
Soybeans	0	25,000	0	0	18,500	0	168,500
Sweet corn	0	0	0	109,275	0	0	109,275
Peas	133,875	0	0	0	0	0	133,875
Government payments	0	0	0	8,180	0	0	19,680
Other farm income	0	0	0	0	0	0	0
Withdrawals from futures accounts	0	0	0	0	0	0	0
Capital sales	0	0	0	0	0	0	0
Nonfarm income	0	0	0	0	0	0	0
Interests earned on savings	132	431	540	571	622	615	3,928
B. Total cash receipts	350,710	246,651	221,760	343,764	244,860	226,353	3,068,656
C. Total cash available (A + B)	360,710	256,651	231,760	353,764	254,860	236,353	3,078,656

CASH OUTFLOW							
Operating Expenses	July	August	September	October	November	December	ANNUAL
Seed							48,780
Fertilizer					19,684		78,735
Crop chemicals							35,655
Crop insurance							27,860
Crop drying expense					12,220		12,220
Machinery repairs	2,400	3,560	2,000	3,000	2,000	2,500	32,560
Other crop expenses		3,000	2,500	1,500	1,000		22,530
Purchased feed	68,104	68,104	68,104	186,214	68,104	68,104	935,358
Veterinary, drugs, and supplies	7,000	7,000	7,000	7,000	7,000	7,000	84,000
Somatotropin (rbST)	4,147	4,147	4,147	4,147	4,147	4,147	49,764
Milk hauling and promotion cost	12,500	12,500	12,500	12,500	12,500	12,500	150,000
Building and equipment repairs	6,750	6,750	6,750	6,750	6,750	6,750	81,000
Semen A.I. services and supplies	2,625	2,625	2,625	2,625	2,625	2,625	31,500
Utilities	6,275	6,275	6,275	6,275	6,275	6,275	75,300
Fuel, oil, and auto expense	5,750	5,750	5,750	5,750	5,750	5,750	69,000
Labor	20,127	20,127	20,127	20,127	20,127	20,127	241,524
Land rent							71,250
Professional fees	850	850	850	850	850	850	10,200
Insurance and taxes on land, bldgs, and equip.				21,985			58,626
Insurance on herd		5,850					11,700
Miscellaneous	3,820	3,820	3,820	3,820	3,820	3,820	45,840

(continued)

Table 17.3   (*continued*)

	July	August	September	October	November	December	ANNUAL
Other Outflows							
Deposits to futures accounts	0	0	0	0	0	0	0
Capital asset purchases	0	0	0	0	0	0	0
Heifer replacements	23,200	23,200	23,200	23,200	23,200	23,200	278,400
Machinery	0	0	0	0	0	0	0
Family living	8,000	8,000	8,000	8,000	8,000	12,000	100,000
Income taxes	0	0	30,000	0	0	30,000	120,000
Scheduled debt payments							
Current debt, principal payments	0	0	0	0	0	0	0
Current debt, interest payments	0	0	0	0	0	0	0
Non-current debt, principal payments	0	0	0	0	17,816	0	126,788
Non-current debt, interest payments	0	0	0	0	27,948	0	82,602
D. Total cash outflow	171,548	181,558	203,648	313,743	249,816	205,648	2,881,192
E. Net cash position (C − D)	189,162	75,093	28,112	40,021	5,044	30,705	197,464
NEW BORROWINGS AND SAVINGS WITHDRAWALS							
Current scheduled debt borrowed (+)	0	0	0	0	0	0	0
Non-current debt borrowed (+)	0	0	0	0	0	0	0
Borrowed from operating loan or credit line	0	0	0	0	0	0	104,444
Withdrawals from business savings (+)	0	0	0	0	4,956	5,113	239,090
F. Total new borrowings and savings withdrawals	0	0	0	0	4,956	5,113	343,534
REPAYMENT OF OPERATING LOAN AND SAVINGS DEPOSITS							
Interest payment on operating loan	0	0	0	0	0	0	949
Principal payment on operating loan	0	0	0	0	0	0	104,444
Transfers to business savings (−)	179,162	65,093	18,112	30,021	0	25,818	425,605
G. Repayment of operating loan and savings deposits	179,162	65,093	18,112	30,021	0	25,818	530,998
BALANCES AT END OF PERIOD							
H. Ending cash balance (E + F − G)	10,000	10,000	10,000	10,000	10,000	10,000	10,000
Business savings	258,469	323,993	342,645	373,237	368,903	390,223	390,223
Operating loan or credit line	0	0	0	0	0	0	0
Accrued interest on op. loan	0	0	0	0	0	0	0
Current scheduled debt	0	0	0	0	0	0	0
All non-current debt	992,796	992,796	992,796	992,796	974,980	992,796	992,796

In March they have a different story again. Due to many expenses, their net cash balance is a negative $172,685, and they do not have sufficient funds in savings to pay all expenses and maintain balances. They withdraw as much as possible from savings but leave a balance of $10,000. They still need to borrow $104,444 in an operating note to cover their cash outflow.

In April, their net cash position is again positive at $56,813. This is insufficient to pay the whole operating loan. The Gables first pay the accrued interest of $609 and then as much as possible on the principal and still maintain the minimum balance.

In May, the Gables have enough cash to pay all accrued interest and operating loan principal and transfer some funds to their savings account. This process of balancing inflow, outflows, and minimum balances continues for the rest of the year in the projected cash flow budget. With an increase in the milk produced and lower crop expenses, the balance in savings increases to $390,223 from $199,780 at the beginning of the year. Thus, the Gables are pleased with the increase in savings as part of their plan to expand the dairy herd in the future.

Pro Forma Financial Statements

The whole-farm budget and projected cash flow budget, as developed in the previous sections, show the Gables can anticipate a positive net return if the plans are carried out as intended. To gain an idea of whether progress is being made in the right direction and in the right magnitude for the financial goals set in the strategic plan and listed in the balance scorecard, the main financial statements need to be projected so that the resulting financial measures can be estimated. These projections are usually referred to as pro forma statements to differentiate them from the formal statements developed by accountants at the end of the year based on actual transactions and actual changes in values. Although these pro forma financial statements follow the format very closely, we should remember that they are projections and not actual results.

Preparing the pro forma statements is a more detailed process than developing the whole-farm budget, but the information allows for the estimation of the financial ratios and measures needed for a more detailed analysis of whether the implementation of the strategic plan is going to be carried out correctly or if changes are needed. Projecting the pro forma statements and assessing the impact of the plan before the year actually unfolds can help a manager see whether changes are needed to meet goals, as well as see potential problems and ways to avoid or mitigate them.

In the following sections, each of the four financial statements described in Chapter 12 are projected based on the beginning actual balance sheet, estimated whole-farm budget, projected cash flow budget, and the estimated results from implementing the plan for the next year. We start with the pro forma income statement, since that will show how the farm operation is projected to do in terms of production, revenue, and costs. The pro forma income statement will show how the year is projected to impact the ending pro forma balance sheet, pro forma statement of owner equity, and pro forma statement of cash flows.

Preparation of the Pro Forma Income Statement

After the details of projecting the cash flow budget, the preparation of the pro forma income statement is much simpler. Most of the estimates come straight from the cash flow budget. Crop revenues on the income statement ($453,650) are a simple sum of the sales of corn ($42,000) and soybeans ($168,500) and the income from the contract acres of sweet corn ($109,275) and peas ($133,875) (Table 17.4). The increase in crop inventories ($26,888) is the change in total value from the beginning to the end of the year; these inventory values come from the beginning and ending balance sheet. (The preparation of the ending balance sheet is discussed in the next section.) Market livestock is the total sales of dairy calves. The income from livestock products is the sum of milk sold and volume

Table 17.4 Gables' Pro Forma Income Statement Using FFSC's Gross Revenue Format

Revenues			
Crop revenues (cash)	453,650		
Increase/(Decrease) in crop inventories	26,888		
Increase/(Decrease) in crop accounts receivable	0		
Total Crop Revenues		480,538	
Market livestock (cash)	140,400		
Livestock products (cash)	2,321,998		
Increase/(Decrease) in market livestock inventories	0		
Increase/(Decrease) in livestock accounts receivable	6,947		
Total Market Livestock Revenues		2,469,345	
Raised breeding livestock sales (cash)	0		
Increase/(Decrease) in base value of purchased breeding livestock	−274,457		
Purchased breeding livestock sales (cash)	129,000		
Cost basis of purchased breeding livestock sales	0		
Total Breeding Livestock Revenues		**−145,457**	
Crop insurance proceeds	0		
Government programs	19,680		
Increase/(Decrease) in other receivables	0		
Other operating income	0		
Total Other Operating Revenues		19,680	
Gross Revenues			**2,824,106**
Operating Expenses			
Operating expenses (cash)	1,238,044		
Cost of purchased feed (cash)	935,358		
Increase/(Decrease) in feed and supplies inventories	−49,441		
Cost of feeder livestock purchased (cash)	0		
Increase/(Decrease) in prepaid expenses	0		
Increase/(Decrease) in accounts payable	−13,725		
Increase/(Decrease) in other current assets	−259		
Depreciation expense (book depreciation)	111,857		
Total Operating Expenses		2,221,834	
Operating Margin			**602,272**
Financing Expenses			
(Interest income)	−3,928		
Interest, current loans (cash)	949		
Increase/(Decrease) in interest payable on current oans	0		
Interest, non-current loans (cash)	82,602		

Increase/(Decrease) in interest payable on non-current loans	0		
Total Financing Expenses		79,623	
Net Farm Income from Operations			522,649

Other Revenue and Expenses

Cash received from disposition of property, equipment, etc.	0		
Less: net book value of farm assets sold	0		
Total gain (loss) on sale of assets		0	
Miscellaneous revenue (with accrual changes if any)	0		
Miscellaneous expense (with accrual changes if any)	0		
Net miscellaneous revenue and expense		0	
Net Farm Income, Accrual Adjusted			522,649

Income tax expense			
Income tax expense (cash) less tax on extraordinary items	120,000		
Increase/(Decrease) in accrued income tax	0		
Income tax expense		0	
Net Income before Extraordinary Items			402,649

Extraordinary items after tax		0	
Net Income, Accrual Adjusted			402,649

premium. Since the milk cows are purchased, the breeding livestock revenues are from the changes in value and the sales of cull cows. The total gross revenue is $2,824,106.

Projected expenses are calculated in much the same way. Cash expenses are taken from the cash flow budget. Changes in inventories, prepaid expenses, depreciation, and other items come from the change in total values from the beginning to the end of the year as listed on the beginning and ending balance sheets. The total operating expenses are projected to be $2,221,834. Total gross revenue minus total operating expenses show a projected operating margin of $602,272.

Financing expenses come from the cash flow budget and include the estimated interest earned on savings since savings is part of the financing plan for the farm. Because this is listed as a financing expense, the interest earned is listed as a negative number, resulting in a total net financing expense of $79,623.

The net farm income from operations is then estimated as $522,649 by subtracting the net financing expense from the operating margin. Since there are no other revenue and expenses, the net farm income (accrual adjusted) is also $522,649. After the income tax of $120,000 is subtracted, the net income (accrual adjusted) for the Gables is $402,649.

Preparation of the Pro Forma Ending Balance Sheet

The pro forma ending balance sheet is developed in much the same way as any balance sheet, except that the estimates of value are based on projections (Table 17.5). The cash balance ($10,000) and savings balance ($290,223) come from the cash flow budget. The values of inventories are projected based on what was on the beginning balance sheet adjusted by what is estimated to be used and

Table 17.5   The Gables' Pro Forma Ending Balance Sheet

ASSETS			Estimated tax rate for deferred taxes = LIABILITIES		28%
Current Assets	Cost	Market	**Current Liabilities**	Cost	Market
Cash	10,000	10,000	Accounts payable	73,202	73,202
Savings and short-term deposits	390,223	390,223	Notes payable within one year	0	0
Marketable securities	0	0	Current portion of non-current debt	135,618	135,618
Accounts receivable	63,525	63,525	Accrued interest, current loans	0	0
Market livestock inventories	45,000	45,000	Accrued interest, non-current loans	0	0
Crop inventories	201,843	201,843	Income taxes payable	0	0
Feed inventories	327,298	327,298			
Supply inventories	62,476	62,476			
Prepaid expenses	0	0			
Investment in growing crops	0	0	Current portion—deferred taxes	xx	0
Other current assets	6,812	6,812	Other current liabilities	0	0
TOTAL CURRENT ASSETS	**1,107,177**	**1,107,177**	**TOTAL CURRENT LIABILITIES**	**208,820**	**208,820**
NON-CURRENT ASSETS			**NON-CURRENT LIABILITIES**		
Machinery and equipment	502,578	839,314	Non-current portion of non-real estate debt	0	0
Breeding livestock	523,360	582,790	Non-current portion of real estate debt	947,677	947,677
Investments in cooperatives	0	0			
Real estate: land	1,625,000	2,889,994			
Real estate: buildings and improvements	1,046,190	1,645,702	Non-current portion—deferred taxes	xx	638,901
Other non-current assets	59588	80,705	Other non-current liabilities	0	0
TOTAL NON-CURRENT ASSETS	**3,756,716**	**6,038,505**	**TOTAL NON-CURRENT LIABILITIES**	**947,677**	**1,586,578**
			TOTAL BUSINESS LIABILITIES	**1,156,497**	**1,795,398**
			FARM BUSINESS EQUITY	**3,707,396**	**5,350,284**
TOTAL BUSINESS ASSETS	**4,863,893**	**7,145,682**	**TOTAL BUSINESS LIABILITIES AND OWNER EQUITY**	**4,863,893**	**7,145,682**
TOTAL PERSONAL ASSETS[a]	0	0	TOTAL PERSONAL LIABILITIES[a]	0	0
TOTAL ASSETS	4,863,893	7,145,682	TOTAL LIABILITIES	1,156,497	1,795,398
			TOTAL NET WORTH	3,707,396	5,350,284

[a]Since business and personal finances are closely related for many farm families, personal assets and liabilities are often listed on a farm's balance sheet, as they are for this example. They should not be comingled with business assets and liabilities but kept as separate line items or not shown on the business statement at all.

purchased during the year. The value of non-current assets is estimated based on the farm's depreciation records and estimates of what the market values of machinery, livestock, and other assets are at the end of the year. Liabilities are taken from the financial records of accounts payable and loan schedules. Deferred taxes are projected using a marginal tax rate of 28%. The projected ending total net worth is $3,707,396 (cost basis) and $5,350,284 (market basis).

Preparation of the Pro Forma Statement of Owner Equity

The pro forma statement of owner equity is developed from the pro forma income statement and pro forma ending balance sheet. From this projection, the Gables see that their total change in retained earnings is projected to be $302,649 since they have no contributed capital (Table 17.6). This comes from their net farm income ($522,649) after the family living withdrawals ($100,000) and income tax payments ($120,000) are subtracted. They anticipate $500,087 from a positive change in valuation equity, which is calculated from the changes in market value between the beginning and ending balance sheets adjusted for changes in the cost basis. The resulting total projected change in business owner equity for the Gables is a positive $802,736.

Table 17.6   The Gables' Pro Forma Statement of Owner Equity

	Subtotal	Total
Owner Equity, Beginning of Period (market value)		**4,547,548**
Changes in contributed capital and retained earnings:		
Net income/loss (business income statement)	522,649	
Withdrawals for family living	−220,000	
Capital contributions: debt forgiveness/gifts/inheritances	0	
Capital distributions: dividends/gifts/inheritances	0	
Total change in contributed capital and retained earnings:	**302,649**	
Changes in market valuation (market value over cost basis) of:		
Machinery and equipment	133,480	
Breeding livestock	1,255	
Investments in cooperatives	0	
Farm real estate	293,414	
Buildings	261,146	
Other noncurrent assets	5,270	
Total change in market valuation	**694,565**	
Change in non-current portion of deferred taxes	194,478	
Total change in valuation equity	**500,087**	
Total Change in Farm Business Owner Equity		**802,736**
Change in value of personal assets (market value)	0	
Less: increase in personal liabilities	0	
Personal Net Worth Change		**0**
Net Worth, Ending of Period		**5,350,284**

Preparation of the Pro Forma Statement of Cash Flows

The pro forma statement of cash flows shows the projected accounting of where cash flows into and out of the farm business during the next year (Table 17.7). The information comes completely from the projected cash flow budget. The statement shows that the net cash provided by operating activities is a positive $591,703, while the net cash flow from investing is a negative $464,915. The operating note needed early in the cash flow budget was paid off during the year. Non-current principal debt of $126,788 was paid during the year. Thus, as planned, the ending cash balance was $10,000, which is the same as the beginning balance.

Table 17.7 The Gables' Pro Forma Statement of Cash Flows

	Subtotal	Total
Cash Flows from Operating Activities		
Inflows		
Cash received from operations	3,064,728	
Cash received from interest (cash)	3,928	
Cash received from net nonfarm income	0	
Total Cash Inflows from Operating Activities		**3,068,656**
Outflows		
Cash paid for feeder livestock, purchased feed, and other items for resale	935,358	
Cash paid for operating expenses	1,238,044	
Cash paid for interest	83,551	
Cash paid for income and Social Security taxes	120,000	
Cash withdrawals for family living	100,000	
Total Cash Outflows from Operating Activities		**−2,476,953**
Net Cash Provided by Operating Activities		**591,703**
Cash Flows from Investing Activities		
Inflows		
Cash received from sale of machinery and equipment	0	
Cash received from sale of real estate and buildings	0	
Cash received from sale of breeding livestock	0	
Cash received from withdrawals from savings	239,090	
Cash received from sale of marketable securities	0	
Total Cash Inflows from Investing Activities		**239,090**
Outflows		
Cash paid to purchase machinery and equipment	0	
Cash paid to purchase real estate and buildings	0	
Cash paid to purchase breeding livestock	278,400	
Cash paid for deposits to savings accounts	425,605	
Cash paid to purchase marketable securities	0	
Total Cash Outflows from Investing Activities		**−704,005**
Net Cash Flows Provided by Investing Activities		**−464,915**

Cash Flows from Financing Activities
  Inflows

Proceeds from operating loans & short-term notes	104,444	
Proceeds from noncurrent debt financing	0	
Cash received from capital contributions	0	
Total Cash Inflows from Financing Activities		**104,444**

  Outflows

Cash repayment of operating & short-term notes	104,444	
Cash repayment of noncurrent debt scheduled	126,788	
Cash repayment of noncurrent debt unscheduled	0	
Cash repayment of capital leases	0	
Cash payments of dividends and other capital distributions	0	
Total Cash Outflows from Financing Activities		**−231,232**
Net Cash Flows Provided by Financing Activities		**−126,788**
Net Increase (Decrease) in Cash Flows		**0**
Beginning of Year Cash Balance		**10,000**
End of Year Cash Balance		**10,000**

Although this equality between ending and beginning cash balances may seem odd, remember that the Gables maintained a minimum cash balance of $10,000 while they were moving cash to and from the business savings account and borrowing operating notes as needed. The details in the statement show total withdrawals from savings of $239,090 compared to total additions to savings of $425,605. So the Gables do enjoy an increase in cash even though the pro forma statement of cash flows shows no change in the cash balance.

Measuring Against the Balanced Scorecard

While the Gables like what they see in their pro forma financial statements, they have already indicated they are interested in more than just financial numbers. So they turn to their balanced scorecard and the measures they put on it (Table 17.8). Since their son and his family have joined the family business, they are pleased to see progress both in terms of involvement in family and community activities and attainment of the family living withdrawals of $100,000 they had as a target for the two families. They had set this goal hoping they could increase their business savings in preparation for having the cash available for a planned expansion in a few years; they now see they will be able to exceed their target. They have not yet attained their targets of milk produced per cow and feed cost per 100 lb of milk, but they have made progress on both measures compared to previous years. With more attention to the dairy, they hope to see improved results in future years.

The steps the Gables went through to project the results for next year could be repeated in future years. Since they have plans to expand the herd and to build new facilities, they do need to look farther to see what progress they can attain on the measures in their scorecard. They would need to estimate the cost of the new facilities and start planning how they can bring the herd up to the productivity needed. These goals could be added to their scorecard to start tracking their annual progress on these long-term goals.

Table 17.8 The Gables' projected balanced scorecard

Strategic Objectives	Measures	Targets	Projected Results
Family, Lifestyle, and Community Perspective			
Welcome son and family back to farm	Participating	Yes	Yes
Participate in the community	Board membership	Office	Member
Financial Perspective			
Efficient use of assets	ROA (market)	9%	7.5%
Positive contribution from operations	Retained earnings	$250,000	$302,649
Increase in business savings account balance	Ending minus beginning	$100,000	$190,443
Family living withdrawals (total for 2 families)	Withdrawals	$100,000	$100,000
Customer Perspective			
Seen as preferred supplier	Feedback	Repeat business	Yes
Producer of quality products	Tests by buyer	Yes	Yes
Internal Business Process Perspective			
Milk productivity	Milk produced per cow	25,000 lb	22,500 lb
Low-cost milk producer	Cost per 100 lb	$14.50	$16.66
Natural Resources Perspective			
Proper management of manure lagoon	No leaks, smells	Success	Success
Learning and Growth Perspective			
Improve marketing skills and knowledge	Take class	Complete	1 of 2 people

Summary

- Whole-farm plans come from the vision and strategy.
- Enterprises can be competitive with each other, supplementary, or complementary.
- Gross margins can be used to select the best mix of enterprises for a farm.
- The gross margin equals gross income minus variable costs.
- The partial budget is used for estimating the effects of changes in the business and includes only those items that are affected by the change.
- The whole-farm budget can be developed based on the strategic plan, enterprise budgets, and other information such as loan schedules and previous financial records.
- The projected cash flow budget can be developed from the whole-farm budget and increased attention to the timing of revenue and expenses.
- The pro forma financial statements can be prepared to project the impacts of implementing the chosen strategic plan on the measures selected for the balanced scorecard.

Review Questions

1. What are gross margins? How can they be used to choose enterprises?
2. Based on the projected budgets available from extension, a farmer has developed the following estimates of yields, prices, and costs for six crops. The farm has 620 tillable crop acres. The farmer does not plant more than 50% of his farm to one crop. Given just this information, what is the best crop mix for this farm?

	Spring Wheat	Durum Wheat	Malting Barley	Corn	Soybeans	Lentils
Yield	28 bu.	28 bu.	50	64 bu.	22 bu.	1,150 lb
Price ($ per bu. or lb)	3.10	3.36	2.16	2.00	4.70	.10
Other Income ($/ac.)*	9	9	12	12	3	0
Variable Costs ($/ac.)	51	52	50	90	63	52
Fixed Costs ($/ac.)	56	56	58	73	58	55

*Other income includes government payments, straw sales, etc.

3. Describe the projected cash flow budget. How can it be projected? How it can be used?
4. Describe the projected whole-farm budget. How can it be projected? How it can be used?
5. What does the "pro forma" mean when placed at the beginning of the name of a financial statement?
6. What is the difference between the end-of-year financial statements and pro forma financial statements? How are each of the pro forma statements estimated? Why are they useful to a farmer?
7. How can the balanced scorecard be used in whole-farm planning?

Further Reading

Barry, Peter J., Paul N. Ellinger, John A. Hopkin, and C. B. Baker. 2000. *Financial Management in Agriculture*. 6th ed. Danville, Illinois: Interstate Publishers, 678 pp.

Beneke, R. R., and R. Winterboer. 1973. *Linear Programming Applications to Agriculture*. Ames: Iowa State University Press, 244 pp.

Boehlje, M. D., and V. R. Eidman. 1984. *Farm Management*. New York: Wiley, 806 pp.

Farm Financial Standards Council (FFSC). 2008. *Financial Guidelines for Agricultural Producers*. Menomonee Falls, Wisconsin: Farm Financial Standards Council.

McCarl, B. A. and T. H. Spreen. 2007. *Applied Mathematical Programming using Algebraic Systems*. Available on the Web at http://agecon2.tamu.edu/people/faculty/mccarl-bruce/books.htm.

Pannell, D. J. 1997. *Introduction to Practical Linear Programming*. New York: Wiley-Interscience, 332 pp.

Ragsdale, C. 2011. *Spreadsheet Modeling and Decision Analysis*. 6th ed. Florence, Kentucky: South-Western College Publishing, 864 pp.

Appendix 17.1

An Introduction to Linear Programming for Whole-Farm Planning

This appendix is a short introduction to the use of linear programming (LP) for whole-farm planning. LP is a very useful tool, but to use it well, it does require some high initial costs in terms of learning the technique, understanding the results, and data acquisition. This appendix shows an example using the Gables' farm and explains how LP could be used for other management situations and questions.

LP allows a farmer to identify the best combination of enterprises that will maximize income without exceeding resource constraints (such as land and labor) and other limits placed on the choice. (LP can also be used in ration formulation to minimize costs while still meeting all nutritional requirements for the livestock.) LP can handle more complicated situations involving, for example, fields with different crop yields, building and machinery capacity constraints, labor schedules, and other constraints. Unlike the separate answers found first with gross margin analysis and then with input supply management discussed earlier in the chapter, LP can find the optimal combination of enterprises and input supply needs as well as labor requirements, and the potential for other enterprises—all in one step. The LP also shows how sensitive the answer is to changes in prices, costs, and resource constraints.

As an example, let us consider the Gables' farm. They have the equipment and knowledge to grow several crops and manage a dairy herd of 600 cows. As described earlier, they have decided to focus more on the dairy and to use a market-based decision process for choosing the source of feed. Specifically, they were willing to consider buying feed instead of raising all the feed they needed. They supply some of the labor required but know they need to hire more.

Building an LP model

As a first step, the information needed for the LP analysis is assembled and presented in a table. The potential enterprises can be seen as columns and the constraints on what they can do on are shown in the rows (Table 17.A1). The center of the table contains the coefficients that show the resource

Table 17.A1 Linear Programming Tableau for Gables Example Farm

	1	2	3	4	5	6	7	8	9	10	11	12
	Corn production (acre)	Soybean production (acre)	Spring wheat production (acre)	Corn silage production (acre)	Sweet corn production (acre)	Pea production (acre)	Grass production (acre)	Sell corn (bu)	Sell soybean (bu)	Sell spring wheat (bu)	Sell grass for energy (ton)	Buy corn (bu)
Row	Constraints											
1	Objective function	−336	−151	−105	−343	503	516	−84.96	3.85	9.65	7.8	60	−3.9
	CONSTRAINTS												
2	Land (acre)	1	1	1	1	1	1	1					
3	Rotation constraint (acre)	1	−1	1	1	1	−1	1					
4	Sweet corn contract (acre)					1							
5	Pea contract (acre)						1						
6	Planting labor (hour)	1.2	0.9	0.9	1.2	1.3	1.2	0.9					
7	Growing labor (hour)	0.3	0.3	0	0.4	0.1	0.1	0					
8	Harvesting labor (hour)	0.9	0.8	0.8	2.9	0.1	0.1	1.02					
9	Rest of year labor (hour)												
10	Corn balance (bu)	−182							1				−1
11	Soybean balance (bu)		−48							1			
12	Spring wheat balance (bu)			−55							1		
13	Corn silage balance (bu)				−20								
14	Grass balance (ton)							−1.7				1	
15	Milk balance (cwt)												
16	Cow space limit (cow)												
17	Fixed costs ($)												

(continued)

Table 17.A1 (*continued*)

	13	14	15	16	17	18	19	20	21	22
Row	Constraints	Buy corn silage (bu)	Dairy production (cow)	Sell milk (cwt)	Hire Labor Planting (hour)	Hire Labor Growing (hour)	Hire Labor Harvesting (hour)	Hire labor rest of year (hour)	Fixed costs ($)	Constraint type	Constraint level
1	Objective function	−31	−2204.9	17.57	−10	−10	−10	−10	−1		
	CONSTRAINTS										
2	Land (acre)									<=	1,250
3	Rotation constraint (acre)									=	0
4	Sweet corn									<=	155
5	Pea contract (acre)									<=	225
6	Planting labor (hour)		4.73		−1					<=	960
7	Growing labor (hour)		12.615			−1				<=	1,920
8	Harvesting labor (hour)		6.3083				−1			<=	1,280
9	Rest of year labor (hour)		17.347					−1		<=	2,400
10	Corn balance (bu)		124							<=	0
11	Soybean balance (bu)									<=	0
12	Spring wheat balance (bu)									<=	0
13	Corn silage balance (bu)	−1	6.35							<=	0
14	Grass balance (ton)									<=	0
15	Milk balance (cwt)		−214.17	1						<=	0
16	Cow space limit (cow)		1							<=	600
17	Fixed costs ($)								1	>=	677,497

requirements, production of each enterprise (or activity in LP terminology). Let us look at each of these parts separately.

The production of corn, soybean, wheat, corn silage, sweet corn, and peas are seen in columns 1 through 6. They have heard about the possibility to produce grass and sell it to an alternative and decided to add this enterprise to the LP model in column 7. The next columns are selling activities for corn, soybean, spring wheat, and grass. By separating the selling activities from production, the LP can tell us more information on the sensitivity of the answers (or solutions) to production costs and prices. Since the Gables are ready to consider purchasing, rather than raising the corn and corn silage for their dairy herd, the next two activities (columns 12 and 13) allow the LP model to choose to buy those two crops. Dairy production is described in column 14 with selling milk in column 15. The Gables are also concerned about the need for labor so the next four activities (columns 16–19) allow for the hiring of labor as needed during the three crop seasons and the rest of the year. The last column is there to force the model to "pay" fixed costs that are not included in the production and buying activities. By including this last activity, the LP analysis will provide a better estimate of the income that will available for the Gables to use for loan payments, income taxes, family living, and savings.

This estimate of income comes from the values in row 1 and the final activity levels the LP chooses for each of the production enterprises and the selling of the products. Row 1 is labeled as the "objective function" in LP terminology since it can used for income, costs, and other measures according to the question being asked. In this example, the Gables want to know which activities will maximize their net income so the objective function is developed for that purpose.

The numbers in the objective (that is, row 1) are the costs of production for corn, soybeans, and so on (columns 1–7), the selling prices for the products (columns 8–11), the buying prices for two products (columns 12–13), the cost of producing milk and then selling milk (columns 14–15), the cost of hiring labor (columns 16–19), and the cost of "paying" fixed costs (column 20). Note that the cost of buying a product (corn at $3.90 per bushel, for example) is slightly higher than the selling price ($3.85 for corn); if the selling price were higher than the buying price, the LP would "run in circles" trying to buy and sell and there would be no solution. Costs are listed as negative values; and sales or income are positive in the objective function (row 1).

To keep this example simple, the production costs for crops in this row are decreased by the value of government payments and straw, if applicable, and for dairy by the value of calves and cull cows that are sold. These could have been included as separate activities if the detail was needed. Since the cost of hired labor will be paid if the LP model decides to use it, the cost of labor is not included as a production cost for crops or dairy. Also, since the Gables' land and their own labor are listed as constraints, those costs are not included in the production costs; a share of the estimated income in the answer will be seen as a payment for these resources.

The constraints are shown in the remaining rows. The Gables have 1,250 acres available. This is seen at the right hand side (RHS) of row 2. Each crop production activity requires 1 acre so a 1 is shown in row 2 for columns 1–7. The LP can choose different levels of each crops but the total cannot exceed the constraint, 1,250 in this example. Row 3 is the mathematical representation of the rotation constraint that the Gables want a 50–50 balance between legumes and non-legumes. Thus, a 1 is entered for any corn, wheat, and grass and a −1 is entered for soybean and pea production. Since the RHS of row 3 is constrained to equal 0, the LP model will have to add one acre of a legume for each acre of a non-legume. The contractual limits of sweet corn and pea production are shown in rows 4 and 5. A 1 is entered in row 4 for sweet corn and row 5 for peas, and the constraints of 155 acres for sweet corn and 225 for peas are placed at the RHS of the row for each crop.

Seasonal labor requirements for each crop and the dairy are entered in the respective rows 6–9. The seasonal availability of labor from the Gables is shown in the RHS for each row. The ability to hire labor in each season is shown by the −1 entered at the intersection of that season's labor balance row and labor hiring column. A separate row and column is needed for each season in order to keep the requirements separate and to allow the identification of how much labor needs to be hired in each season.

Crop yields are shown in the respective columns in rows 10–14. These are called "balance rows" because the production or supply is being balanced with the sales or uses. The balance row can be pictured as a bin in which production supplies a product and selling or other uses takes the product out. By tradition, the production or purchase is shown as a negative and the sale or use is a positive. For example, an acre of corn has a yield of 182 bushels so −182 is entered in the corn balance row (row 10). Selling a bushel of corn requires a bushel, so 1 is entered in the corn balance row for the selling corn activity. Dairy requires 124 bushels per cow so 124 is entered in the corn balance row for the dairy activity. Since the Gables are willing to buy corn if the market indicates they should, the corn buying activity has a −1 entered in the corn balance row; it is a negative to indicate that it is a supply of corn. The other crops are treated in a similar fashion except for sweet corn and peas.

Since sweet corn and peas would be under contract if the farmer signs the contract and the processor will harvest and take ownership the product, the farmer will not sell the product directly. Thus there is no need for sweet corn or pea balance rows. These crops have positive values in the objective function (row 1).

Similar to the crops, the dairy enterprise produces milk so the annual production per cow is entered in the milk balance row. So we see a −214.17 at the intersection of the milk balance row (row 15) and the dairy production column (column 14). Normally, we see milk production in the United States expressed in terms of pounds per cow, but since milk is sold in cwt (100 lb), the conversion is made at this point. The milk selling activity requires a cwt of milk so 1 is entered in that column of the milk balance row.

The Gables have space for 600 cows in their barn, so the dairy production activity is constrained to the level. This is accomplished by placing a 1 in dairy constraint row (row 16) for the dairy activity (column 14). The production is constrained by the 600 entered in the RHS of row 16.

As described earlier, to force the LP to "pay" the fixed costs so the net income will appear more reasonable, the fixed cost payment activity (column 20) has a 1 in the fixed cost constraint (row 17). The fixed costs to be paid ($677,497) is entered as the RHS in row 17.

Most of the constraints are maximum constraints such as a maximum total of land available. So the use of land, for example, has to be less than or equal to the maximum constraint. Other constraints, the corn balance row, for example, require any corn sold or fed to be produced or bought. So the constraint forces the production or purchase to take place before it can be fed or sold. The rotation constraint (row 3) is an equality constraint to force the legume acreage to equal the nonlegume acreage. The fixed cost constraint (row 17) is a minimum constraint to force the LP model to pay all of the fixed costs.

Solving the LP Model

There are several computer programs available to solve LP models. The Purdue Top Farmer Crop Workshop includes their B-21 linear programming analysis of the participant's farm plan.[1] Major spreadsheet programs (such as Microsoft's Excel©) have an algorithm available for LP analysis. Each program has a slightly different format and system for presenting the information and then mathematically solving the problem.

Interpreting the LP Solution

The Gables' LP model (that is, Table 17.A1) is solved to maximize the net income described in the objective function (row 1). The results are summarized in Table 17.A2.

The LP solution estimates that the value of the objective function (that is the Gables' net income) is $138,015. Based on the way the LP model was developed, this provides the Gables with an estimate of the money available for paying other costs not included in the model, paying their living expenses, and for their savings.

For the activities, the final value is the value of the variable in the optimal solution. Those activities which have a zero final value "did not enter the solution" in LP terminology. This solution for the Gables includes 470 acres of corn, 400 of soybeans, 155 of sweet corn, 225 acres of peas, and 600 dairy cows. As we saw in the partial budget analysis earlier in this chapter, the LP chose to buy 3,810 tons of corn silage rather than produce it. The LP analysis also did not choose to produce spring wheat or grass. The LP estimates corn sales to be 11,140 bushels; soybean sales to be 19,200; and milk sales to be 128,502 cwt (100 lb). The Gables also see they will need to hire 3,274 hours of labor during planting; 5,948 during growing; 3,286 during harvesting; and 8,008 during the rest of the year for a total of 20,516 hours.

The sensitivity analysis shows some interesting information. The "reduced cost" is the increase in the objective function value (net income in this example) for every unit increase in the activity. The reduced cost is calculated only for those activities that do not enter the solution. A negative value signals a decrease in net income if the activity were to be forced into the solution. The reduced cost is valid only for small increases in the activity.

The "reduced cost" shows that if an acre of spring wheat was forced into the plan, net income would decrease by $33.70. An acre of corn silage would decrease net income by $108.70. An acre of grass would create a loss of $342.86 showing the Gables that producing grass for alternative energy production is not a viable option with these yields, costs and prices.

The two columns, allowable increase and allowable decrease, define the range of the cost coefficients in the objective function for which the current solution (that is, those activities in the solution) will not change. For example, the results shows that the price of grass would have to increase to $261.68 before it would be produced. The $261.68 is the sum of the original price ($60) and the allowable increase ($201.68). The LP solution shows that the milk price could decrease by $2.21 per cwt (from $17.57) before the dairy activity level would change. The solution also shows with a very large allowable increase (4.17E+14) before a change in the solution; realistically, this large value just says that dairy production will stay in the solution for the Gable farm as milk price increases to very high levels. Other allowable increases and decreases can be interpreted similarly.

---

[1] More information on the Purdue Top Farmer Crop Workshop and the linear programming algorithm is available at www.agecon.purdue.edu.

For constraints, the "shadow price" is an extremely useful estimate. It is called "shadow price" because it doesn't come from the market but from what the LP calculates is the value of that constraint based on what could be produced and sold if it was increased.

For the Gables, the shadow price of land is calculated to be $316.45 which is what the estimate of net income would increase if another acre of land was available. That is, if the Gables could rent another acre, their income would rise by $316.45 (before any rent was paid). However, this estimate is valid only for relatively small changes in the constraint. The shadow prices of the contracts are $147.30 for sweet corn and $209.80 for peas, that is, the income would increase by these amounts if they could

Table 17.A2 Linear Programming Solution for Gables Example Farm

Part A. Objective function

Name	Final Value
Objective function (net income for the Gables)	138,015.39

Part B. Activity levels

Name	Final Value	Reduced Cost	Objective Coefficient	Allowable Increase	Allowable Decrease
Corn production (acre)	470	0	−336	147.3	33.7
Soybean production (acre)	400	0	−151	209.8	632.9
Spring wheat production (acre)	–	−33.70	−105	33.7	1E+30
Corn silage production (acre)	–	−108.70	−343	108.7	1E+30
Sweet corn production (acre)	155	0	503	1E+30	147.3
Solution pea production (acre)	225	0	516	1E+30	209.8
Grass production (acre)	–	−342.86	−84.96	342.86	1E+30
Sell corn (bu)	11,140	0	3.85	0.05	0.19
Sell soybean (bu)	19,200	0	9.65	4.37	9.65
Sell spring wheat (bu)	–	0	7.8	0.61	7.8
Sell grass for energy (ton)	0	0	60	201.68	60
Buy corn (bu)	–	−0.05	−3.9	0.05	1E+30
Buy corn silage (bu)	3,810	0	−31	31	5.44
Dairy producton (cow)	600	0	−2,205	1E+30	474
Sell milk (cwt)	128,502	0	17.57	4.17E+14	2.21
Hire labor planting (hour)	3,274	0	−10	10	100
Hire labor growing (hour)	5,948	0	−10	10	38
Hire labor harvesting (hour)	3,286	0	−10	10	75
Hire labor rest of year (hour)	8,008	0	−10	10	27
Pay fixed costs ($)	677,497	0	−1	1	1E+30

Table 17.A2 (*continued*)

Part C. Constraints

Name	Final Value	Shadow Price	Constraint R.H. Side	Allowable Increase	Allowable Decrease
Land (acre)	1,250	316.45	1250	3,620	122
Rotation constraint (acre)	0	24.25	0	800	0
Sweet corn contract (acre)	155	147.3	155	61	0
Pea contract (acre)	225	209.8	225	400	225
Planting labor (hour)	960	10	960	3,274	1E+30
Growing labor (hour)	1,920	10	1920	5,948	1E+30
Harvesting labor (hour)	1,280	10	1280	3,286	1E+30
Rest of year labor (hour)	2,400	10	2400	8,008	1E+30
Corn balance (bu)	0	3.85	0	1E+30	11,140
Soybean balance (bu)	0	9.65	0	1E+30	19,200
Spring wheat balance (bu)	0	7.8	0	1E+30	0
Corn silage balance (bu)	0	31	0	3,810	1E+30
Grass balance (ton)	0	60	0	1E+30	0
Milk balance (cwt)	0	17.57	0	1E+30	128,502
Cow space limit (cow)	600	473.86	600	90	405
Fixed costs ($)	677,497	−1	677,497	1E+30	677,497

increase the contract limit. The shadow prices for labor and the crops are the prices of those inputs and products. The LP estimates that net income could increase by $473.86 if another space for a dairy cow could be found. The allowable increases and decreases define or show the range of the constraint in which the shadow price is valid. The extremely high values written in scientific form (1E+30, for example) essentially say that the shadow price is valid to extremely high or low levels.

At this point, the Gables could change prices and constraints to see whether and how the solution would change or not change. However, by looking at the sensitivity report on activities and constraints, the Gables can see that the chosen activities and the level of those activities are quite stable in terms of changes in prices and constraints. So they can start planning for input purchases, product sales, and contracts for labor based on these results.

This stability is valid only in the sense of defining the plan of crops and dairy for the Gables. The uncertainty of what the market will provide for prices and what the weather will do for yields is still present. The Gables still need to prepare a risk management plan to manage these risks. The stability of the LP solution only tells them that a small change in expected prices or costs will not create large changes in what their plan should be.

This brief introduction is designed to show what LP can do for a manager. There are many books, classes, and electronic sources that can be used to deepen your understanding of the capabilities of LP and how to build an LP model for our own use. For a short list, the reader is referred to Ragsdale (2011), McCarl and Spreen (2007), and Pannell (1997). Two older books that are still good practical sources for understanding and techniques applied to farm management are Beneke and Winterboer (1973), and Chapter 10 in Boehlje and Eidman (1984).

18

Operations Management for the Farm

In this chapter:

- Process mapping
- Improving the process
- Scheduling operations: sequencing, dispatching
- Project scheduling
- Input supply and inventory management
- Lean management

The global market has become very close to the local farmer. As buyers have more access and willingness to acquire products from anywhere in the world due to improved and improving transportation, communication, and financial systems, the local market becomes increasingly competitive. A competitive market requires producers to become more efficient by lowering production costs per unit through higher production levels with the same level of inputs, stable production with fewer inputs, or a combination of higher production and fewer inputs. The need to become more efficient requires new management tools for the farm manager. Knowing these tools is essential for success and even survival. This is true for managers of any size farm.

This chapter explains several techniques and tools from general business management. We start with process mapping, which helps the manager and stakeholders understand the farm. Next we look at five general ways to improve production and operations processes. We then review two methods for improving the scheduling of operations and projects: Gantt charts and dispatching rules. We continue with tools for input supply and inventory management. We end the chapter by considering the ideas and concepts found in lean management.

Process Mapping

A **process map** is a depiction of a process for accomplishing a task. By mapping the processes on a farm, we can understand how each part works, how the parts are linked together and thus affect each other, and how the farm is linked to its economic, political, and physical environment. With this understanding, a farmer can make better decisions in today's risky, complex world.

Since a map usually refers to a geographical map, many people may picture a process map as a geographical mapping of physical movements. But a process map isn't necessarily a physical map. Instead, it may be a list of the movements made, materials required, and equipment used. A process map may show the flows of both materials and information. In general business, process mapping is seen in several ways: assembly drawings, assembly charts, parts diagrams, routing sheets, flow diagrams, and physical layouts, to name a few. A flow diagram for computer programming is a process map. In farming, the process can be a production process, such as crop production or livestock; a service process, such as custom work; or an internal process, such as paying bills or gathering market information.

Although drawing or describing these maps can seem simple, they are a very good way for management to understand its own business. This is true, perhaps especially true, for current management to see the business with "fresh eyes."

A process map can be used to understand the process for any level of a business. A farmer, in the role of general manager, sees one level of the processes involved in a business and needs to consider the problems or opportunities at that level. As a worker, a farmer sees the business from a different perspective and, so needs a different map to see the problems and opportunities at that level.

A process map for a whole farm will show the inputs and outputs of the business and how it is organized. As an example, consider a farm that grows corn and soybeans for both sale and feed, produces feeder pigs to finish or to sell, and does some custom field work. The internal organization of the business is shown by the smaller boxes inside the large box (Figure 18.1). Each of these smaller boxes represents an activity center of the farm: corn production, finish feeder pigs, livestock marketing, and so on. Since the other activity centers require their services, labor, machinery, and building services are organized as a separate center. The internal flow of materials, services, and information is shown by the lines within the process map of this level. This amount of detail may be sufficient for a farmer interested in improving his or her data collection and reporting within the business and the economic efficiency of production and marketing decisions.

The external boundary of the farm is drawn as the large box. The environment is everything outside of that box. The inputs are listed on the left and the outputs on the right. Both controllable inputs (such as land, fertilizer, feed, and capital) and uncontrollable inputs (such as market prices

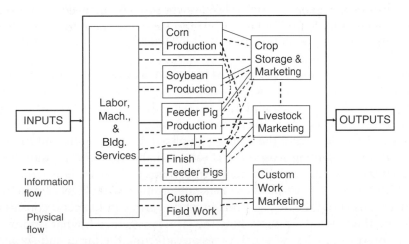

Figure 18.1 Process Map of a Whole Crop-Livestock Farm

and weather) are listed to provide a complete picture of what affects a farm. Similarly, both good outputs (such as crops, pigs, and income) and bad outputs (such as runoff) are listed to provide a complete picture of what the farm produces. Ignoring uncontrollable inputs and bad outputs can lead to bad decisions on the farm.

Farmers already use this simple view of their farm as a mental model when considering new products. To decide whether a new product is even feasible to consider in detail, a farmer considers the quantity and quality of the resources available and the potential products and by-products. He or she evaluates whether the new product and process fits into their view of the farm—that is, their process map of the whole farm. For example, when considering whether to sign a contract to finish hogs, a crop farmer does not need to consider the minute details of growing corn but does consider whether the capital and labor supplies are sufficient, the building location would be susceptible to runoff problems, and so on. In another example, a farmer may view the farm from this simple perspective when considering the impact of governmental and institutional requirements for reporting labor use, income and expenses, and chemical use. More complicated decisions and situations require more detailed maps of the farm and its environment.

Enterprise budgets (discussed in Chapter 15) are process maps. They describe the inputs and operations needed to produce a crop (Figure 15.1) or raise livestock (Figure 15.2). However, an enterprise budget does not include all the steps needed to produce a crop or raise livestock. For example, a more descriptive list of steps, inputs, and equipment needed to produce soybeans is shown in the more detailed process map (Figure 18.2). It shows how the farmer sees the production of soybeans, starting with finalizing the rental agreement for the land, working through planting and harvesting, and ending with selling the crop.

As another example, a process map of a cattle feeding operation shows time and equipment requirements, feed ingredient requirements, storage locations, retrieval processes, and mixing and feeding instructions (Table 18.1). Each step is identified by its type of activity, the time required, distance traveled, and the equipment and materials needed.

In this cattle feeding example, a farmer can evaluate each step to see whether that step is actually needed or can be modified or eliminated to increase efficiency. A farmer can see where the time requirements are the greatest or where the delays are longest and evaluate whether the process can be changed to decrease time requirements. In this example, the farmer may ask why loading and grinding takes so long, why the operator must wait for the auger before loading, or why the whole feeding process takes over an hour.

Another example map shows the steps involved in reloading a corn planter during the planting operation (Table 18.2). This job of reloading the planter is a very specific job; thus, the map is very focused. This map does not cover the whole planting process but only the process of just reloading the planter once the day's planting has begun. As in the previous example, the farmer may not realize how long the reloading takes (i.e., 33 minutes) until the map is completed. Evaluating this information and alternative procedures before the planting season could save valuable time during the planting season if it results in equipment investments or modifications of the steps to decrease time requirements.

The type of decision that a farmer needs to make determines what level of process map to use. A farmer making decisions about the future direction of the farm would spend considerable time looking at or considering the whole-farm map: how the farm is organized, what resources are available, what products are produced, what external forces are affecting the farm, and so on. For these decisions, a farmer would spend very little time worrying about process maps such as the feeding or

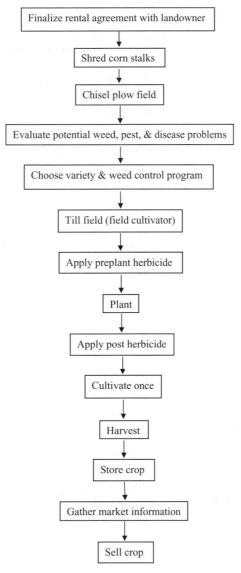

Figure 18.2   A Process Map for Producing Soybeans (following Corn)

planting examples. However, if feeding or planting efficiency needs to be improved (due to those same external forces, for example), a prudent manager would spend considerable time looking for steps that can be eliminated, steps that could be merged or improved through investment or re-design, and so on. A farmer who is planning to expand his hog operation is probably evaluating at least two levels of maps. The whole-farm map shows how the different units would work together (hog and crop production, for example). The same hog farmer would study other maps of the expansion in more detail—such as how pigs, feed, and animal waste would flow through the buildings and farm in both space and time.

Table 18.1   A Process Map for Feeding Cattle

Step	Description	Activity Type*	Time	Distance	Equipment/Materials
1	Pick up feed order	O	2 min.		
2	Inspect order for correctness	I	1		
3	Walk to machine shed	T	3	100 ft	
4	Attach mixer to tractor	O	5		95 HP tractor & mixer
5	Drive to feed shed	T	2	150 ft	Tractor & mixer
6	Load vitamin mix	O	8		4 bags premix
7	Drive to corn bin	T	3	150 ft	
8	Wait for auger	D	5		Auger
9	Inspect corn	I	1		
10	Load and grind corn	O	20		2.5 tons corn & auger
11	Inspect feed	I	1		
12	Drive to feedlot	T	2	300 ft	Tractor & mixer
13	Unload in bunker	O	3	100 ft	Tractor & mixer
14	Clean mixer	O	1		Tractor & mixer
15	Drive to machine shed	T	2	600 ft	Tractor & mixer
16	Park mixer and tractor	S	4		Tractor & mixer
17	Walk to office	T	2	100 ft	
18	Complete work order report	O	3		

*Activities are classified into five types:
O = Operation, the actual work being done
T = Transport, moving the worker, the input, or the product
I = Inspection, checking the work in progress or at the end of the process
D = Delay, any down time for any reason
S = Store, storing the product or work in progress

Table 18.2   A Process Map for Reloading the Corn Planter

Step	Description	Activity Type*	Time	Distance	Equipment/Materials
1	Stop at end of field	O	0 min.		
2	Inspect supplies on planter	I	1		Planter
3	Walk to supply truck	T	3	100 ft	
4	Drive to planter	T	1	100 ft	Truck
5	Check seed variety	I	1		
6	Load seed	O	13		Seed corn
7	Load fertilizer	O	8		Starter fertilizer
8	Check equipment	I	4		Tractor & planter
9	Move supply truck	S	2	15 ft	Truck
10	Start planting	O	0		Planter & tractor

*Activities are classified into five types:
O = Operation, the actual work being done
T = Transport, moving the worker, the input, or the product
I = Inspection, checking the work in progress or at the end of the process
D = Delay, any down time for any reason
S = Store, storing the product or work in progress

Farmers have many reasons for mapping a process. If a new process such as no-till crop production is being considered, the farmer needs to understand how it will affect other parts of the business. Process maps (written, verbal, or both) can be used to train a new employee. An expanding farm needs to evaluate new ideas for information gathering, machinery storage and use, communication between people, and so on. Process maps can help a farmer find potential efficiencies to counter the continual cost–price squeeze. This use is discussed more in the next section, "Improving the Current Process."

As with any management technique, the value of the potential information needs to be compared with the cost of obtaining the information. When developing process maps, the cost (in both time and money) is greatest for new maps, but the benefits of mapping and thus understanding new processes can be great. The greatest benefits may come from mapping complex systems that cannot be grasped easily, although for these systems it would cost more to prepare the maps.

Farm managers might be tempted to say, "I understand what needs to be done. Why bother to draw a map?" (This is especially tempting to say shortly after starting to map a process.) However, two points should be remembered. The first is how much information people say they learn when they develop a map. The second is how complicated farming is now and is expected to become. By learning to draw and understand the concepts of a simple map, this mental model of process mapping will be easier and more useful when complicated situations develop. At that point, the choice of putting the map on paper can be made on the basis of the number of people involved and the amount of detail needed to be understood.

Improving the Current Process

As conditions, technology, institutions, and markets change, the pressure to improve and cope with these changes is very high. Keeping abreast of the changes and finding ideas that will improve a process are demanding tasks. In this section, we look at different ways to consider adjusting the current process and how to evaluate whether the ideas will result in an improvement or not.

Ideas for improvement are not found in easy lists. They come from knowing the system and what it can do or could be doing. Ideas also come from a general willingness to ask questions about the process: Why is it done a certain way? How is this input used? Who is responsible for doing certain activities? What is to be done at certain points? When should this step be done? and so on. Ideas show up as process maps are being developed and discussed. Attending extension and dealer meetings, joining marketing and managing clubs, reading articles and reports, and just talking with neighbors are traditional ways of hearing about new ideas and their potential use.

Ideas for improvement can be found in five general areas: reducing input use, substituting inputs, increasing productivity, expanding, and reorganizing.

Reducing Input Use

No farmer will knowingly spend more money for inputs than is needed. But when new technologies come along, new knowledge is developed, and institutions change, the traditional production methods may become inefficient in their use of inputs. Examples of reducing input use include reducing pesticide application rates and the number of applications, reducing the number of tillage passes, changing to no-till equipment, and decreasing the level of antibiotics in feeds. Banding herbicides instead of broadcast application has been shown to decrease costs in many areas and crops.

Herbicide costs can also be reduced by using weed maps and scouting information so herbicides are applied only where and when needed. Investing in feeders and systems that reduce feed waste is another traditional method for reducing input use and cost.

An example of changing technology and knowledge is the development of new tillage equipment and how to use it. A study by West, Vyn, and Steinhardt at Purdue University found that a combination one-pass tillage tool produced corn and soybean yields that were statistically the same as the traditional tillage with a chisel plow in the fall and secondary tillage in the spring. Their study also showed that using the combination tillage tool in the fall, not using any spring tillage, and planting into a stale seedbed produced corn yields that were no different from systems that used spring tillage. These results can be used by farmers in similar geographical areas (and tested by others) to reduce operating costs by decreasing the number of tillage operations and to reduce ownership costs by decreasing the amount of equipment needed.

Sharing machinery ownership is another way that can decrease input use not by reducing the number of operations but by decreasing the amount of money tied up in owning a machine. Owning a combine with a neighbor is a very quick way to cut investment costs. Of course, multiple ownership requires more management time for communication about how costs will be allocated between owners and how the owners will determine scheduling priority.

Substituting One Input for Another

Examples of substituting one input for another include replacing labor and management for purchased inputs (or vice versa), using custom services instead of owned machinery, using manure for commercial fertilizer, and changing the type of tillage equipment.

As an example of how to adjust a current plan by substituting one input for another and evaluating the impact, consider the process for soybean production shown in Figure 18.2. Suppose this farmer is considering the substitution of a second mechanical cultivation for the post-plant herbicide application. This is shown on the right-hand side of Figure 18.3. This potential change was evaluated using partial budget analysis (see Table 16.2). By not applying the post-plant herbicide, the farmer is estimated to save $16.19. But the potential yield loss of 4 bushels per acre valued at $5.25 per bushel and the cost of the additional cultivation ($4.01) is estimated to create a total negative effect of $25.01, so the net effect of this potential change is a loss of $8.82 per acre. If the farmer considers only the income effect, the potential change is not an improvement but has a negative impact on farm income, and the farmer will decide against the change.

Another example of substitution is the choice of whether to own equipment or to hire a custom operator. The substitution is a change in who owns the machine—it is not necessarily a change in the physical operation. Owning a machine obviously obligates a farmer to both operating and fixed ownership costs. However, when a farmer hires a custom operator, the total cost is an operating cost for the farmer. Also, owning a machine entails having an asset and possibly a loan on the farmer's balance sheet. Hiring a custom operator does not affect the farmer's balance sheet directly.

Using standard engineering cost relationships and equations, the costs of owning and operating a 30-ft grain drill and a 75 HP tractor were estimated in Chapter 15. The partial budget analysis in Chapter 16 (see Table 16.3) compares the cost of hiring the planting done by a custom operator versus buying a grain drill and the farmer planting the wheat himself. The farmer now pays $7.50 per acre for the custom operator, so not hiring the operator would reduce his expenses by $7,500. Since

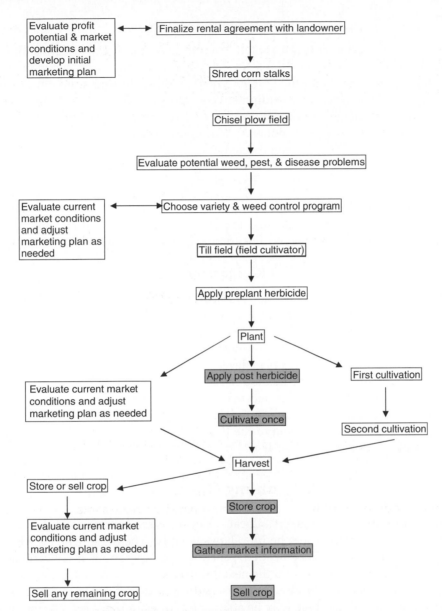

Figure 18.3 A Revised Process Map for Producing Soybeans (following Corn)

the farmer already owns a tractor that can be used for planting the wheat, he will not have any additional ownership expenses for the tractor. But he does need to buy a grain drill. The additional costs of owning and operating the grain drill total $5,715 for the 1,000 acres. The net effect is a positive $1,785. So the farmer is inclined to buy a grain drill and plant his own wheat. Other factors need to be considered before a final decision could be made, including timeliness and availability of the custom operator, quality of custom operation, other uses of the equipment, value of the owner's labor in other uses, impact on the balance sheet, and so on.

Improving Productivity

Examples of improving productivity are applying herbicides at the optimal plant and weed development stages (as well as optimal time of day), changing livestock rations for faster and/or better feed efficiency, buying better genetics for the breeding herd, and monitoring animal heat stages for optimal breeding periods. Hiring seasonal equipment operators can improve machine productivity by increasing the hours that tillage equipment is used per day and thus over the entire season. As will be discussed in Chapter 24, providing monetary incentives to employees for improved performance and efficiency is another way to improve productivity.

Expanding

Examples of expanding include buying or renting more land in order to spread the fixed costs of machinery, labor, and management; adding new building capacity; and adding new crops to the cropping plan. Hiring labor to allow more time for management will also allow a farm to expand.

Reorganizing

Examples of reorganizing the business include rescheduling tasks to fully utilize labor and machinery, hiring more labor to more fully utilize machinery, rescheduling the marketing process, and reassigning labor and management resources to better utilize talents and abilities. An example of reorganizing the marketing function for soybeans is shown on the left side of Figure 18.3. In this potential process improvement, market evaluation and market plan development are started very early and continue through the production process compared to the method in the old process map (Figure 18.2), in which the soybeans were produced first and then market information was gathered and pricing decisions were made.

Combinations of these four methods may also be used. Any expansion will also entail improvements in productivity and reorganization of the business. Methods for quantitative analysis of current and potential practices are explained in Chapter 19, Quality Management.

Scheduling Operations

Scheduling is an allocation decision—it allocates the resources already available due to earlier investment and hiring decisions. The schedule shows what is to be done, when it will be done, who will do it, and what equipment will be needed. Scheduling of operations is concerned with the next few months or weeks and even today and the next few hours.

Scheduling has three distinct objectives: cost, schedule, and performance. These are competing objectives. Often only two of the three may be attainable. For example, a crop farmer may be able to plant the crops and apply herbicides according to the optimal schedule and thus produce a crop and yield expected, but to do this, the farmer has to spend more for machinery and labor than the original budget allowed. Or the objectives of cost control and schedule may be attained but weed control due to poor application rates and uniformity.

Two scheduling techniques can be useful for farming: sequencing and dispatching. **Sequencing** is a procedure for scheduling people, jobs, equipment, and other resources over several weeks or months. **Dispatching** rules can help a manager decide which jobs have the highest priority and should be done first on a certain day or afternoon, for example.

Sequencing

Sequencing is concerned with the exact order of operations for processing several jobs. The value of sequencing is the ability to plan and forecast the needs for resources and the location and timing of how those resources are going to be used before they are actually used. Ensuring the proper scheduling of equipment will allow operations to be done on time, inputs to be applied at the proper time, and resources to be used in the most efficient manner. Sequencing can show when additional capacity is needed. For example, when weather and other uncertainties affect the amount of time available for field work, the amount (and thus cost) of machinery needed to produce a crop on time can be compared to the cost of not planting or harvesting on time. This is part of balancing the competing objectives of cost and schedule. Sequencing allows the planning of workloads and working hours to improve the use of hired labor, lower the labor cost per unit of product, and, perhaps, lower labor turnover by more even workloads between workers and over time.

Developed by Henry L. Gantt in 1917, the **Gantt chart** is the common tool for representing sequences of operations. In Gantt charts, time is listed across the top, and scarce resources, jobs, or both are listed down the side. The sequence of activities for individual jobs is marked on time lines for each job. The jobs being done by each resource at each point in time are shown on time lines for each resource.

As an example, let us consider a Gantt chart for one week of planting (Figure 18.4). From this chart we can tell when a field will be planted and by whom. Waiting times and project completion times are easily visualized. The risk of a rain day is included by marking one day, Friday in this example, as "R" to indicate a day as unavailable for field work. For example, the north field will be planted starting on Monday and be finished by midday on Wednesday. The Johnson farm will be started on Wednesday and finished on Saturday. We can also tell an employee what field he or she should be planting and when. For example, Alan will be planting on the Watson farm starting on Tuesday and finishing on Thursday. Then Alan will start at the home farm on Saturday after the potential rain day on Friday.

Of course, nature, breakdowns, and accidents may change this plan, but developing a plan allows us to see where there are potential scheduling problems and to correct those problems before they

	Sun.	Mon.	Tues.	Wed.	Thurs.	Fri.	Sat.
FIELD:							
North	X	┌─(Frances)─	─	─┐			
Johnson	X			┌─(Frances)─	─┐	R	┌─(F)─┐
Watson	X	R	┌─(Alan)─	─	─┐	R	
Home							┌─(A)─┐
DRIVER:							
Frances	X	┌─(North)─	─	─┐ ┌─(Johnson)─	─┐	R	┌─(J)─┐
Alan	X	R	┌─(Watson)─	─	─	R	┌(H)─┐

Symbols:

┌	Start of an activity
┐	End of an activity
┌─┐	Allowed activity time
■	Actual work progress (if the chart is used for charting actual progress)
X	Time set aside for nonproductive activities, such as, repairs, routine maintenance, material outages, days-off, etc.
M	Moving time
R	Day set aside for potential rainfall

Figure 18.4 Gantt Chart for One Week of Planting

Table 18.3 Mr. Johns' Soybean Harvest Commitment

Farm	Days Needed	Estimated Maturity Date
Own: Home	6	September 15
Own: Smith	9	September 20
Custom: Johnson	10	September 16
Custom: Watson	2	September 25
Total days =	27	

become real. Even though we don't know when rain may come, we know it will and field work will be affected. By finding the historical pattern of rainy days for certain weeks, we can build potential delays into the schedule and be better prepared for completing work on time.

The easiest way to compare alternative ways to schedule the same list of jobs is by comparing the total time required to complete all the work. The preferred plan is the one that completes all the work in the shortest time—provided that all work meets or exceeds specified quality standards. For the four fields to be planted in Figure 18.4, the total time required is 6 days. In this simple example, it may be hard to come up with a better plan.

As another example of sequencing, let us consider how Robert Johns schedules his soybean harvest season in northern Indiana. Mr. Johns grows soybeans on his own land plus custom combines soybeans for two neighbors (Table 18.3). He has estimated the work will take a total of 27 days. He has two combines and one full-time employee; he also can hire a part-time combine driver. By planning his harvest season early in August, Mr. Johns is able to (1) predict whether he can finish soybean harvesting by October 1, (2) know whether he has time to take on more custom work, and (3) decide whether it will be possible for him or his employees to have some time off between soybean and corn harvest.

On his own land, Mr. Johns needs to have a driver available to haul the grain to either his on-farm storage or to the elevator in town; this driver can be either the farmer or his full-time employee. The part-time employee will drive the combine only since the farmer and the full-time employee are familiar with the grain handling system, and they do not plan to train the part-time employee in that system.

To keep his clients happy, Mr. Johns has decided that custom work has a priority when custom fields are ready. However, he and his clients have agreed that at least one combine, but not necessarily both, will be in the customer's field if it is ready for harvest. He has also agreed that the driver will be either himself or his full-time employee, not the part-time employee. The contracting farmer will arrange for hauling the grain to storage.

Historical weather data show that, in 7 years out of 10, he can expect to lose one day per week due to bad weather for field work during the harvest season. Mr. Johns, his employees, and his neighbors also do not care to work on Sundays unless it is an extremely difficult harvest season. He also estimates (on the high side) that it will probably take $1/2$ day of potential harvest time to move between his fields and his neighbor's farms, but it will not take any harvest time to change fields on his own land. Moving could take place on a rainy day but not Sundays. Let us suppose that September 13 is a Sunday this year and that the poor weather days during the soybean harvest season will be September 21 and 24 and October 5. Poor weather days affect all farms.

The first step in developing a schedule is to decide what jobs and resources will be listed in the Gantt chart. In this scheduling plan, Mr. Johns wants to know when fields will be harvested, which combines will be used in each field, and which person will be driving the combine or hauling grain. So he wants to list the four fields: Home, Smith, Johnson, and Watson; the new and the old combines;

the job of hauling grain; and the farmer and the two employees. This listing can be seen in the Gantt chart (Figure 18.5).

The second step is to place any potential rain days on the schedule as well as days on which work cannot be done. This farmer has decided to not work on Sundays and has guessed which days may be rain days based on historical records.

September	Sun. 13	Mon. 14	Tues. 15	Wed. 16	Thurs. 17	Fri. 18	Sat. 19
FIELD:							
Home	X		┌── (Part-time, & Full for ½ day)──────────5½				
Smith	X						
Johnson	X		/M	┌── (Full-time)──────────4			
Watson	X						
COMBINE:							
Old	X		┌── (Home, Part-time)────────────				
New	X		┌(H)─ /M ┌── (Johnson, Full-time)────────				
HAULING:							
At home:	X		┌── (Farmer)────────────────				
DRIVER:							
Farmer	X		┌──(Hauling at Home)────────────				
Full-time	X		┌(H) /M ┌──(Johnson, New)────────				
Part-time	X		┌──(Home, Old)──────────────				

September	Sun. 20	Mon. 21	Tues. 22	Wed. 23	Thurs. 24	Fri. 25	Sat. 26
FIELD:							
Home	X	R	┌(P)6┐		R		
Smith	X	R	┌──(P)──1½		R		
Johnson	X	R	┌─(Full-time)──6		R	┌─ (Full-time)──8	
Watson	X	R			R/M	┌──(Farmer)──2┐	
COMBINE:							
Old	X	R	┌(H, P)┐ ┌(S, P)──		R/M	┌─(Watson, Fa)─┐	
New	X	R	┌─(Johnson, F)──		R	┌─(Johnson, Full)─	
HAULING:							
At home:	X	R	┌(F, H)┐ ┌(F, S)──		R		
DRIVER:							
Farmer	X	R	┌(H, h)┐ ┌(S, h)──		R/M	┌─(Watson, O)──	
Full-time	X	R	┌─(Johnson, N)──		R	┌─(Johnson, N)──	
Part-time	X	R	┌(H, O)┐ ┌(S, O)──				

Figure 18.5   Gantt Chart for Mr. Johns' Soybean Harvesting Schedule

(continued)

	Sun.	Mon.	Tues.	Wed.	Thurs.	Fri.	Sat.
September	27	28	29	30	Oct. 1	2	3

FIELD:

Home	X
Smith	X	M/ ┌──(Part-time, 4½ & Full-time, 3)──────────9┐
Johnson	X	┌(Full-time)─10┐ M/
Watson	X

COMBINE:

| Old | X | M/ ┌──(Part-time, Smith)──────────┐ |
| New | X | ┌(Full, Johnson)┐ M/ ┌(F, Smith)──────┐ |

HAULING:

| At home: | X | ┌──(Farmer)──────────────┐ |

DRIVER:

Farmer	X	┌──(Hauling at home)──────────┐
Full-time	X	┌(Johnson)───10┐ M ┌(Smith, New)─────┐
Part-time	X	┌──(Smith, Old)──────────┐

*Note: X = day scheduled for not working, R = rain day, M = ½ day for moving, Fa = Farmer, Full = Full-time, P = Part-time, H = Home, S = Smith, J = Johnson, W = Watson, O = Old, N = New, h = hauling

In this example, the third step is to schedule the custom fields on the Gantt chart since they are a contractual obligation. They require at least one combine and driver in the field if it is ready for harvest. His own fields have second priority.

The fourth step is to place this farmer's own fields on the Gantt chart where possible. This shows that harvest on the Smith place will not start on the estimated day of maturity. The priority of custom work and the earlier maturity of the soybeans on the Home place means his soybeans on the Smith farm will be the last to be harvested.

Most of the time, the full-time employee is scheduled for the new combine and often on custom fields. This allows the farmer to be on the other combine for custom work or at home hauling grain as well as managing the part-time employee and anything else that may come up. This plan is changed only in the last few days. On the 25th and 26th, both the full-time employee and the farmer are custom combining on different farms. On the 28th, the farmer moves the old combine home and the part-time employee start harvesting on the Smith farm again. When the full-time employee finishes, he comes home and also harvests on the Smith farm. The farmer resumes hauling grain. The part-time employee would work through October 2, but not on October 3. The full-time employee would finish the $1/2$ day of soybean harvest on the Smith farm on October 3.

This chart shows that, if weather is as expected and no major problems occur, Mr. Johns can harvest all his soybeans before corn harvest is expected to start on October 9, but he won't finish by October 1. It also shows that a part-time employee is needed for 10 days in September, and two in October.

There are 15 days available for field work between the start of harvest (September 15) and the finish of soybean harvest (October 3). With two combines, there are 30 combine days available (15 * 2 = 30). From Figure 18.5, Mr. Johns estimated he needed 27 days to harvest all four fields, but on the calendar he used 30 days, so his efficiency in the use of the two combines is 90% (= 27/30 * 100%). The three days of slack (30 minus 27) can be viewed as a cushion for unexpected mechanical delays and additional rain delays. The three Sundays (and thus six combine days) can also be viewed as an additional cushion for unexpected delays.

Dispatching Rules

Although a manager may wish to have all activities planned well ahead of time, a manager also knows that reality does not always fit nicely into plans. So even though sequencing and its Gantt charts are very useful for planning—say, a few months ahead or even longer—we still need a system to help decide which tasks need to be done this week, today, or this afternoon.

Such a system is called dispatching. As its name implies, dispatching comes from the work of a dispatcher—say, a manager of a mobile repair business or the dispatcher for a taxi company. Their job is to quickly assess which jobs need to be done and what their characteristics are. Then using a standard set of dispatching rules, the manager selects the order in which jobs will be done and who will perform each job. Some common dispatching rules are listed below. Each of them have their own logic and objective.

FCFS—First Come, First Serve. Who or what shows up first is served or worked on first. This is a very common rule. We see it being used on us as customers in stores, restaurants, banks, and so on. Most of us consider it to be very fair in those situations.

SPT—Shortest Processing Time. The first task to be started is the one requiring the shortest processing time before being finished. Since this can lead to some long jobs never being started because shorter ones keep showing up, an adjusted version of SPT is often used. "SPT with truncation" uses the basic SPT of shortest processing time and includes a maximum waiting time. When a task has been waiting more than the maximum time, the task is started even if shorter tasks are also waiting.

EDD—Earliest Due Date. The task that needs to be done the soonest is the first one to be started. Under this rule, a task may have a short processing time, but it will be done after other tasks that have earlier due dates.

LS—Least Slack Time per Operation. This rule compares the processing time needed with the amount of time before the task needs to be done. Slack time is an absolute measure of time. It is calculated as the time left before the due date minus the remaining processing time. In some instances LS is standardized by dividing by the number of operations remaining for each job. This standardization provides a rough accounting for the time it can take to start, finish, and wait for different aspects of the same job.

MINCR—Minimum Critical Ratio. This rule also compares the remaining processing time with the time to due date but does so in a relative sense. The critical ratio is calculated by dividing the time to due date by the remaining processing time.

ESD—Earliest Start Date. The task that can be or has to be started the soonest is the one that is started first. This rule does not consider remaining processing time, due date, or economic importance of any rule. It just starts the task that has the earliest start date listed.

RANDOM—Random Selection from among Jobs. This rule essentially has no rule. The manager or worker just starts a job whether it is the first one thought of, the closest, or the easiest. This rule uses no objective standard by which to rank jobs, so it will contribute to the objectives of the farm only at random.

Economic Importance. The dispatching rules just described do tend to ignore the economic importance of a task or job. The economic importance of a task includes its impact on the business: how important is it that the task be done, and will the business suffer a major setback if it is not done? A manager may also trade off the direct benefits of accomplishing a task versus the potential regret of not doing the task soon. A task can also be evaluated for its ability to help the farm maximize profits, minimize costs, decrease risk, or meet other goals.

Many farmers may find the most beneficial dispatching rules to be SPT, EDD, and economic importance, especially when used together. However, each dispatching rule helps accomplish its own specific objective. Different situations and businesses may need a different set of rules because they have different goals. A study at Hughes Aircraft indicated in manufacturing that SPT was the best for efficiency and flow rate while LS was the best for meeting due dates. The study found that FCFS and ESD did worse than RANDOM for most criteria.

As an example of using dispatching rules, suppose it is October 22 and let us consider how Dennis Bjerke decides what tasks he should do tomorrow, October 23. Bjerke has made a list of jobs that need to be done or could be done tomorrow. He is willing to work 14–15 hours tomorrow since it is the middle of the harvest season (Table 18.4).

As a first step in setting the priorities of what to do, the jobs are ranked in terms of the processing time and due date. The shortest processing time is ranked 1. Bjerke estimates two jobs will take $1/2$

Table 18.4 Mr. Bjerke's List of Jobs to Do and His Application of Dispatching Rules

| | Dispatching Rules: | | | | | |
| | SPT | | EDD | | | Final |
Jobs to Do:	Processing Time (hours)	Rank	Due Date	Rank	Economic Importance*	Priority Rank
Go to government office to discuss government programs for farmers	2	7	10/24	1	A	2
Change oil in tractor	1	3	10/28	8	B	8
Go to coffee shop	2	7	n/a	10	C	Don't go
Talk with hired harvester about grain left in field	$1/2$	1	10/25	3	B	4
Pay bills	1	3	10/24	1	B	1
Talk to workers about conflict between them	1	3	10/25	3	A	5
Clean out combine cab	$1/2$	1	11/1	9	C	9
Lawyer says finish business plan or it is too late	3	9	10/26	6	A	6
Finish harvesting soybeans	5	10	10/25	3	A	3
Weld reinforcement on wagon	1	3	10/27	7	B	7

*A signifies that this job is very important economically.
B signifies that this job has some economic importance.
C signifies that this job has little or no economic importance.

hour, so they are tied and both ranked 1. He estimates four jobs will take 1 hour; these four are tied and 3 in rank. The other jobs are ranked in a similar fashion, up to finishing soybean harvest as 10 since he estimates it is the longest job to complete.

The job with the earliest due date is ranked 1. Two jobs have a due date of tomorrow, so they are both ranked 1. Three jobs are due the day after tomorrow and are ranked 3. The rest of the jobs are ranked similarly.

The final ranking is a result of subjectively balancing processing time, due dates, and economic importance. Paying bills is ranked 1 because their due date is tomorrow. (Paying bills also is something that could possibly be done before going to the government office.) Because of its economic importance and early due date, going to the government office is ranked 2. After these two tasks are done, Mr. Bjerke decides he should finish the soybean harvest because he has ranked it an A in economic importance.

Talking to the hired harvester about adjusting the harvester to avoid grain loss in the field would only take half an hour, so Bjerke decides to do that before the end of "normal" working hours. Then, Bjerke decides to talk to the workers about their conflict before the problem becomes bigger. As probably the final task for the day, Bjerke decides he needs to work on the business plan due to its importance to the farm and the need to finish it within two days.

These first six jobs will take an estimated $12^{1}/_{2}$ hours and have the highest final priority because of their importance to the farm and the proximity of the due date. Since Bjerke is willing to work long days during harvest season, he ranks the next two jobs in descending priority: weld reinforcement on a wagon and replace the fan belt on the combine. If time permits, he may take time to clean out the combine cab.

Even though he would enjoy hearing what is happening, Bjerke decides that going to the coffee shop is something he just cannot afford to do because of the time it takes, its lack of economic importance, and the lack of a due date.

Project Scheduling

In the previous section, we talked about scheduling operations. Operations are rather simple compared to managing and scheduling a bigger project with many steps, such as building a bridge or ship. What differentiates a project from other work is that the project is often stationary and all workers and materials have to come to the work site. In that view, growing a crop is a project, because the field is stationary and all workers, machines, and inputs have to be brought to the field. Other examples of projects on farms include the construction of livestock facilities, flower production for a specific holiday, and conversion to and certification in organic production.

Some activities or jobs may seem like projects, such as receiving and caring for feeders, but these activities are often linear in the sense that one activity or job is started and finished before the next activity is started. Growing one crop in one field is usually a set of linear activities. These linear sets of activities can be managed in other ways, such as fail-safe plans, which are discussed in Chapter 19, Quality Management and Control. But when we speak of projects we are usually picturing rather large, complicated sets of jobs and activities that are related in more complicated fashion than a linear set of activities.

In general, a project is a set of related jobs or activities directed toward some major product or output and requiring a significant period of time to perform. The activities are not linear; some activities are on one path toward the final product, other activities are on other paths. These paths with activities may be separate from the main group and then join other paths to accomplish a joint

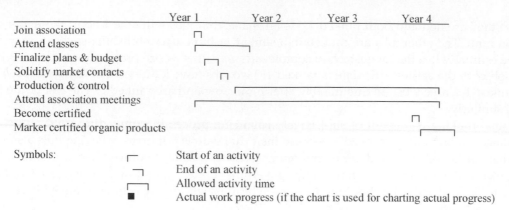

Figure 18.6   Simple Gantt Chart for Becoming a Certified Organic Producer

activity. Some jobs or activities have time precedence over others—that is, they need to be done first before the next steps can be done.

The activities of a project can be scheduled using a Gantt chart as described in the previous section. The Gantt chart will show when activities will take place, including when one starts and ends compared to other activities. The program for becoming certified as an organic producer described in Chapter 10 (see Table 10.3 can be organized as the activities in a Gantt chart (Figure 18.6). We see a simplified list of the steps: from joining the organic growers association in the fall of the first year through becoming a certified organic producer (after 36 months of organic practices) in the fall of year 4 and then being able to market certified organic products starting near the end of year 4.

In another example, a simplified process of building a new dairy facility is shown as a Gantt chart in Figure 18.7. The activities shown include construction, starting with site preparation and then the construction of the buildings and other facilities. Because the profitability of the new facility depends on utilizing it as soon as possible, construction is scheduled to allow the herd to be built up and delivered so that the first milking will start as soon as possible after construction is done. Thus,

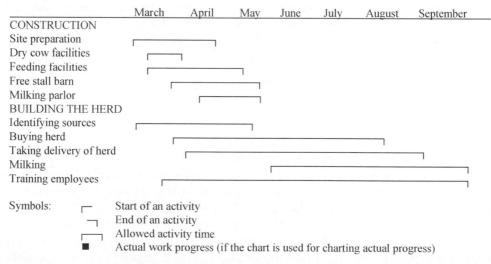

Figure 18.7   Simple Gantt Chart for Constructing Dairy Facilities and Building the Milking Herd

construction starts with the dry cow facilities and feeding facilities, moves to the free stall barn for the lactating herd, and ends with the milking parlor. The cow herd is not left until all construction is done—identifying sources of the herd begins at the same time as site preparation starts. Buying and taking delivery of the first cows starts as soon as the dry cow facilities and feeding facilities allow cows to be delivered, housed, and fed. Obviously these are not lactating cows yet because the parlor is not yet finished when the first cows arrive, but to allow for training of employees and a slower start to using the facilities, pregnant or cows ready to be bred arrive first. Also note that buying and delivering the herd continues even after the milking parlor is finished. Again, this is to allow for more training and gaining of experience before the facilities are at full capacity.

Input Supply Management

Most often, farmers do not worry about whether input supplies will be available. The input supply industry has developed an excellent ability to have available or very quickly deliver most inputs the day they are ordered or the next day. Strong examples of these inputs include feed, fuel, medicines, veterinary services, many implement parts, and minor repairs. Often even major items, such as tractors or combines, are available if the dealer has not had unanticipated sales. Other inputs are not set up for such a rapid delivery system, such as feeder livestock purchased directly from the grower. Also, suppliers do not always have enough supply to meet large orders, and they are much more willing to provide discounts if large orders are placed early so the suppliers can do more planning in their business.

Farmers can still, however, benefit from anticipating and planning for input needs. They can also incur costs for not planning. An obvious example of a benefit to planning is the discount price usually given to early seed orders. Other examples, which don't involve such direct monetary benefits, are the assured quality level in feeder stock and the reduction in stress in knowing that the credit line has already been secured. For small, inexpensive items, such as screws, nails, lubricants, and similar items, having a supply on the farm has an obvious benefit compared to having to order and obtain the part every time it is needed. An example of the cost of not planning is the higher cost incurred for feed if prices rise and a farmer did not purchase or secure the price of future needs. Another example is the cost of not planning and securing the commitment of custom operators early in the year.

Input supply management is part of what general business calls inventory management. **Input supply management** is a dependent demand inventory system that uses a requirements philosophy. That is, inputs are needed because the farmer wants to produce a product or service for sale. The need for the inputs (feed, seed, land, and so on) is dependent on the demand for the farmer's final product (milk, wheat, animals). The farmer orders a supply of inputs only because the product is demanded. The farmer does not order inputs just because his supply is low.

Dependent demand and its replenishment philosophy are the opposite of what retail stores face. Retail stores and other places that sell to the final consumer face independent demand, which is not in their control. They use a replenishment philosophy for their inventory management—that is, they don't wait for the consumer to walk in and ask for a box of a certain cereal. They replenish their inventory of that cereal when it becomes low; they anticipate future but uncertain demand by consumers, so they want to keep a supply to meet that demand.

Farmers anticipate that their products will be demanded and bought when they plan their production. They know the capacity of their livestock facilities and the amount of land they will farm, so they can estimate the amount of inputs that will be required to complete their plans successfully.

The input supply management system aims to meet these requirements. For example, crop seed is ordered to meet the amount of seed required to grow the size of the fields planned. Seed is not ordered just because the amount of seed in inventory is low.

Most farmers already operate with this requirement philosophy for input inventory management—whether they know the name for it or not. However, an understanding of the difference between requirement and replenishment philosophy can help understand which tools from general business can help improve efficiency and profitability on the farm.

ABC Inventory Planning

One of the first issues in input supply management is to decide which items need the most attention of the time-constrained manager. A very simple technique, named ABC inventory planning, can be used to sort the items in terms of which need more management time and which need less time. In this technique, inventory items are classified into three groups on the basis of annual monetary volume or total annual cost (not physical quantity but monetary volume). More attention is given to those inventory items with a high monetary volume than to those with a low volume. These are labeled simply A, B, or C.

A: High monetary volume items—say, 15% of the total number of items
B: Moderate monetary volume items—say, the next 35%
C: Low monetary volume items, the last 50%

For a rigorous classification, a farmer would need to take all the different inputs she uses, calculate the annual expenses for each, rank them by percentage of the total input costs, and decide which are in the top 15%, middle 35%, and lower 50%. An alternative and easier method would be to look at which expenses are already listed separately in the farmer's income statement; these are probably the A items. The B and C items are most likely grouped together as "supplies" or "miscellaneous expenses" on the income statement. The farmer can use this as a starting point and move items between categories as experience is gained and needs change.

For a dairy farmer, feed and replacement heifers are obvious A items; C items would likely be parts such as filters, cleaning supplies, screws, and so on. For a crop farmer, A items likely include seed, fertilizer, fuel, and similar items; C items would include small parts such as screws, bolts and nuts, oil filters, and lubricants.

Before we look at the methods for dealing with A items, let us look quickly at two common and simple techniques for dealing with the B and especially C items: one-bin and two-bin systems. Once set up, these techniques require little management time but can still deliver the supply of inputs when needed. These ideas are already used by many farmers and businesses. While they may seem obvious, knowing when to use these techniques can save management time for more important issues.

One-Bin System. In a one-bin system, the supply in the one bin is reviewed on a fixed schedule—say, every week or month—and inventory is brought up to a certain level. This "certain level" can be calculated using records of input use over time or it can be based on experience of how fast the input is used. A farmer can also realize that more needs to be ordered when the input is used faster than normal due to a particular event, such as unanticipated building repairs because of weather damage.

Two-Bin System. In the two-bin system, the first bin (or box or bottle) is used as the source of the input while a reserve is held in the second bin. When the first bin is emptied, the second bin is emptied into the first and an order is placed. When the order is received, it is placed in the first bin except for the reserve, which is placed in the second bin. The size of the reserve can be calculated from records of the input use or from experience of how fast the input is used and how long it will take to receive the new supply. For small, low-priced items, such as commonly used screws, nails, filters, and medicines, the two bins could be two boxes, containers, or bottles of the item. One box is open and used as needed. When that box is emptied, the second box is opened and an order is placed for another box.

Input Requirements Planning

For A inputs, farmers can utilize what is called materials requirements planning (MRP) in general business. In MRP, inputs are "pulled" or ordered due to the demand for production. The order is not placed until the need is known and planned. Crop production is an obvious example of how this can work. In the whole-farm planning process, the farmer determines the number of acres of each crop. From the enterprise budgets of each crop, the farmer knows the amounts of each major input—seed, for example—needed per acre and can calculate the total amount needed for the farm that year. The farmer will not buy more than needed just to replenish inventory for the next year; only the amount required is ordered.

As an example, let us consider the seed required for growing wheat in southwest Texas. The enterprise budget for wheat in Figure 15.1 shows a requirement of 70 lb of seed per acre. If the farm plans to have 1,000 acres of wheat, the total seed requirement is 70,000 lb (70 * 1,000). The farmer then knows he has to order 70,000 lb of wheat from the seed dealer (or from his supply of seed kept from the previous year). At this point, further planning would be needed if different varieties of wheat were to be planted. However, the process of determining the amount needed of each variety is the same: the amount of seed required per acre multiplied by the number of acres planned for each variety.

For another example of planning for a sufficient labor supply, let us return to the Gables and their whole-farm plan in the previous chapter. Although labor is not material inputs, the same techniques can help compare the amount of labor needed with their own supply of labor and estimate any additional labor that would be needed.

Mr. Gable and Jake, his son, are each willing to work 60 hours per week in a normal week and 80 hours per week in the busy planting and harvesting seasons. During the 6-week planting season, they each are willing to work 480 hours (6 * 80) (Table 18.5). During the 16-week growing season, they each are available 960 hours. During the 8-week harvest season, they each are available 640 hours (8 * 80). If they each take 2 weeks of vacation during the winter, they each are available for an additional 1,200 hours in the remaining 20 weeks between the end of harvest and beginning of planting. In total, Mr. Gable and Jake are willing to work 6,560 hours during the entire year.

This supply of labor needs to be compared to the estimated labor needed to grow the crops chosen and take care of the dairy cows. Using the hours shown in Table 17.1, the Gables need a total of 2,476 hours for their 1,250 acres of crops: 1,396 during planting, 300 during the growing season, and 782 hours during harvest. They estimate they will need 41 hours per lactating cow per year for the whole dairy enterprise. With 600 lactating cows, the total estimate is 24,600 hours. In total they estimate a need for 27,076 hours for crop and dairy production during the year.

Table 18.5 Estimation and Comparison of Gables' Labor Supply and Requirements

	Planting Season	Growing Season	Harvest Season	Rest of the Year	ANNUAL TOTAL
LABOR HOURS AVAILABLE					
Mr. Gable	480	960	640	1,200	3,280
Jake Gable	480	960	640	1,200	3,280
Total hours available	960	1,920	1,280	2,400	6,560
LABOR REQUIREMENTS FOR CROPS					
Corn for grain	564	141	423	0	1,128
Soybeans	360	120	320	0	800
Sweet corn	202	16	16	0	234
Peas	270	23	23	0	316
Total labor required for crops	1,396	300	782	0	2,478
LABOR REQUIRMENTS FOR DAIRY	2,838	7,569	3,785	10,408	24,600
TOTAL LABOR HOURS NEEDED	4,234	7,869	4,567	10,408	27,078
Additional labor hours needed	3,274	5,949	3,287	8,008	20,518

Compared to their willingness to supply 6,560 hours, they obviously need to hire labor. Based on these estimates, they need to hire an additional 20,518 hours during the year. Jake Gable plans to work with the dairy full time; an additional nine workers who each work just over an average of 45 hours per week would supply the labor needed for the dairy. If Mr. Gable spends his entire time available on crops during the planting and harvesting season, he would still need an additional 916 hours for the crops during planting and 141 hours during harvest. This need works out to an additional need for 153 hours per week during planting and 18 hours per week during harvest. At this stage of planning, Gable decides he needs to hire three more workers who would work 50 hours per week during planting (or some combination of part-time workers who would contribute roughly 150 hours per week). Only one part-time worker for crops appears to be needed during the harvest season. Further details on staffing are discussed more in Chapter 24.

Economic Order Quantity (EOQ)

For some farms, especially larger ones, some of the A inputs are used in sizable amounts throughout the whole year. The annual amount required may be large enough that it would obviously not be ordered and delivered at one time. For these inputs, such as feed and fuel, the concept of economic order quantity (EOQ) can be useful for these farms. The EOQ concept is usually associated with products that have independent demand and a replenishment philosophy (such as in a retail store), but the method can also be used for determining the optimal size and frequency of orders for inputs that are required due to production (in contrast to replenishing product due to sales in a retail store).

The basic EOQ calculation is based on the need to minimize the total cost of holding inventory. These costs include (1) the cost of the item; (2) the cost of ordering, including typing, calling, transportation, handling, and so on; and (3) the cost of holding (or carrying) the item including storage facilities, handling, insurance, pilferage, spoilage, depreciation, the opportunity cost of capital, and similar costs. The cost of holding the input is expressed as a percentage since it includes the opportunity cost of capital tied up in the inventory.

The total annual cost of inventory for one item is the sum of the annual purchase cost of the item, the annual cost of ordering, and the annual carrying cost of the inventory.

$$TC = DC + (D/Q)S + iCQ/2$$

where D = quantity required per year, C = cost or price per unit, Q = lot size (physical quantity), S = cost per order placed, and i = holding or carrying rate (annual percentage rate).

To find the order quantity that will minimize the total inventory cost, the equation above is solved to minimize TC with the resulting economic order quantity calculated as:

$$EOQ = \sqrt{\{(2SD)/(iC)\}}$$

As an example, suppose a hog farmer raises 3,000 feeder pigs to market weight each year. The farm mills its own feed and buys all the corn since it does not raise any. The demand for corn is estimated to be 9 bushels per pig. The price of corn is forecast to be $3.00 per bushel. The cost of ordering is estimated to be $25 per order to pay for ordering time and receiving time to ensure the grain is placed in the correct bin. The holding or carrying cost is estimated to be 30% of the inventory value per year. So the variables are defined as:

D = 27,000 bushels/year = 9 bushels/pig * 3,000 pigs/year
S = $25 per order
i = 30% (or 0.30)
C = $3.00 per bushel

Using this information, the EOQ is calculated to be:

$$EOQ = \sqrt{\{(2 * 25 * 27,000)/(0.3 * 3.00)\}} = 1,225 \text{ bushels}$$

The EOQ says the corn should be ordered in lots of 1,225 bushels in order to minimize the total cost of inventory. If all these conditions remained the same, the corn would be ordered approximately 22 times per year (= 27,000/1,225) or about every 17 days (= 365/22). The annual cost of ordering and carrying inventory would be:

$$(D/Q)S + iCQ/2 = (27,000/1,225) * 25 + 0.3 * \$3.00 * 1225/2 = \$1,102$$

If the corn was ordered in equal amounts each week throughout the year, the amount ordered each week would be about 519 bushels and the annual cost of ordering and carrying inventory would be:

$$(27,000/519) * 25 + 0.3 * \$3.00 * 519/2 = \$1,534$$

Thus for this corn for hog feed example, the farmer would save \$432 per year by ordering a larger quantity of corn fewer times per year. Since the holding cost is not changed, this estimate assumes the farmer already has the capacity to store the larger quantity when delivered.

In another example, suppose a farmer has 2,000 acres of wheat to harvest. Her fuel requirements are 1.5 gallons of diesel per acre. The price of diesel is forecast to be \$2.25 per bushel. The cost of ordering is estimated \$10 per order. The holding or carrying cost is estimated to be 15% of the inventory value per year. So the variables are defined as:

D = 3,000 gallons/year = 1.5 gallons/acre * 2,000 acres/year
S = \$10 per order
i = 15% (or 0.15)
C = \$2.25 per gallon

Using this information, the EOQ is calculated to be:

$$EOQ = \sqrt{\{(2 * 10 * 3,000)/(0.15 * 2.25)\}} = 422 \text{ gallons}$$

The EOQ says the fuel should be ordered in lots of 422 gallons in order to minimize the total cost of inventory. The cost of ordering and carrying inventory for the harvest season would be:

$$(3,000/422) * 10 + 0.15 * \$2.25 * 422/2 = \$142$$

If the farmer has a fuel tank that could hold 500 gallons and she decided to order 450 gallons whenever the tank was observed to have less than 50 gallons remaining, the cost of ordering and carrying inventory for the harvest season would be:

$$(3,000/450) * 10 + 0.15 * \$2.25 * 450/2 = \$143$$

In this example, the savings obtained by ordering a specific quantity (422 gallons) from the EOQ calculation would save very little for this farmer compared to watching the amount of fuel remaining and ordering a fixed amount of fuel each time. The estimate of the EOQ can serve as a guide for the size of tank needed for the farm.

While EOQ is simple to understand and use, it has several restrictive assumptions. These assumptions can be disadvantages for businesses closer to the consumer but not so much for farmers ordering production inputs. Even with these weaknesses, EOQ is a good place to start estimating optimal order size and frequency and comparing the estimate to current practices. EOQ assumes that the demand or requirement is constant, uniform, recurring, and known. For inputs used within a production season, this assumption is not especially troubling. It is more of a problem for a retail store that does not know for sure whether customers will buy its products.

EOQ also assumes that lead time is constant and known. For most farm inputs, the delivery time from a local supplier is known. Only in unusual situations may the availability of an input, such as a specific seed variety, and thus delivery be uncertain.

The price or cost per unit is assumed to be constant when using EOQ. The formula for EOQ does not account for price discounts for large orders. Within one production season, the price of an input is generally known and constant. When exceptions to this are found (fertilizer in 2008–2010, for example), the price uncertainty affects the decision to use the input more than the inventory question. Potential price discounts for larger orders may cause the most trouble in using EOQ, but there are ways to deal with price discounts. First, more complex formulas are available for dealing with price discounts. Second, if there is a simple rule for receiving price discounts, the EOQ could be calculated using the different prices to determine the impact of the discounts.

The inventory holding cost is based on an average inventory throughout the year in the EOQ formula. This assumption is based on a product or input that is held and used year-round, such as products in a retail store or feed on a livestock farm. For inputs such as fuel on a crop farm that is used in larger quantities during the planting and harvest seasons but is not held or used in large quantities during other parts of the year, the holding cost can be adjusted to reflect the shorter holding period (as was shown in the fuel example above).

Two remaining assumptions of EOQ are not very restrictive for farming, especially when analyzing orders within one production season. EOQ assumes ordering or setup costs are constant. For a retail store that sets up an inventory management system designed to last for several years, this can create problems over time. For farmers who are not handling so many input items in inventory, the costs of ordering are easier to estimate each year. EOQ also assumes that all demands or requirements will be satisfied. This assumption is not a problem for farmers ordering inputs. Farmers do not want to run out of fuel, feed, and many other inputs critical to production, so requirements will be satisfied.

Continuous and Periodic Review Inventory Systems

Two variations of inventory systems can be useful to farmers for managing input inventories. The first is the continuous review or fixed-order quantity system, which calls for ordering a fixed quantity whenever the remaining level in inventory reaches a specific point. The specific level for reordering is determined based on how much will be used before the order is received plus a safety stock for variations in input used. The farmer in the example above who orders fuel whenever the remaining amount is less than 50 gallons is using a continuous review system. The 50 gallons is estimated to be sufficient to fuel normal operations until the next order is received and to cover uncertain amounts that are not anticipated. In this example, the farmer may use 50 gallons for most of the year but increase that level during heavy harvest weeks when the cost of running out would be very high. With a continuous review system, or Q-system as it is sometimes called, the time between orders varies but the quantity ordered is fixed.

In a periodic review or fixed-time period inventory system or P-system as it is sometimes called, inventory is counted only at particular times and the size of the order varies. Compared to the Q-system, the P-system does not have a reorder point but rather a target inventory. A livestock farmer who checks the amount of grain and other feeds each week or every second week and then orders the quantity needed to increase inventory up to a certain level is using a periodic review or P-system.

The P-system requires a larger safety stock since inventory is not being reviewed continuously and there is a longer time when input use could vary from the expected level.

In this section on input supply and inventory management, several methods have been presented and explained that can help farmers monitor and control their supply and costs of inputs. As competition pushes farmers to control every cost, even ones that are not obvious such as inventory costs can be a source of cost savings. The tools have ranged from the simple ABC method of inventory planning and one-bin and two-bin systems to more complex methods of estimating input requirements and the concept of EOQ. These tools can be used by both large and small farms. Large farms may obtain larger savings, but if smaller farms want to compete, they too need to evaluate how they control and pay for inventories.

Lean Management

A common but unstated theme in this chapter has been the elimination of waste on the farm. We're not talking animal waste here; we're talking unnecessary costs. From understanding the farm through process maps to improving processes through scheduling and input supply and inventory management, the basic idea has been to streamline operations, eliminate waste, and improve the efficiency of the farm. Farmers have sought to do this ever since our ancestors first tilled the soil. In this last section, we look at the relatively new concept of lean management to learn what it may add to the farm manager's set of tools.

General business has gone through this process as well for many years. General business efforts and ideas have, for several reasons, progressed faster and have been recorded to a greater extent than those for farm management. For many years till today, the tools of materials requirements planning (MRP) have helped manufacturing push inputs through and thus products out of their plants. This focus on pushing products out the door changed over time for many leading manufacturers and became a focus on waiting for product demand to pull the products out of the plant. It is a subtle change in language but one that changed the way many companies operate. Toyota and its engineer, Taiichi Ohno, are credited with bringing the system of just-in-time (JIT) manufacturing and lean manufacturing into full force in the world. Now many companies in many countries strive to adopt and follow the principles of lean manufacturing.

Although the systems of JIT and lean manufacturing started in assembly line production systems, the concepts in those techniques and in how they have been adapted to lean management can be useful for farms and farm managers. Let us now take some time to look at these concepts and think about how they can be used to improve a farm's chances for success and survival.

The basic goal of lean management is to eliminate waste in everything and every step of the business process. Waste is defined as anything and any cost that does not add value for the customer. Eliminating waste is done through reengineering the business, empowering workers, and connecting with suppliers and buyers with the goal of streamlining production and communication in the supply chain, eliminating waste in and between businesses in the supply chain, and delivering the most value to the customer.

Lean management starts with the process map discussed at the beginning of this chapter and expands it to include the whole supply chain. The biggest change that lean management instills in strategic management as well as production management is to look at the process map and supply chain from the perspective of the customer and evaluate what adds and doesn't add to the value the customer perceives in the final product. What doesn't add value for the customer is identified as waste, and management's goal is to eliminate that waste. Waste can be unnecessary steps, unnecessary inputs, more quality than the customer wants, and so on. As listed by Womack and Jones (2009), the seven wastes identified in the Toyota Production System (TPS) were

- Transportation—moving products and inputs that are not actually required to perform processing
- Inventory—covering all components of inventory not being processed at the moment: raw materials, inputs, work-in-progress, and finished product
- Motion—people and equipment moving more than is required to perform processing
- Waiting—people, equipment, materials, work-in-progress waiting for the next step
- Overproduction—producing ahead of demand or orders for product
- Overprocessing—processing required not to produce a product but due to a poor tool or product design creating excess activity
- Defects—bad products as well as the costs of inspecting and fixing defects

Two other wastes that have been identified by others include the production of goods and services that do not meet customer specifications and the waste of unused human talent (Womack and Jones, Bicheno and Holweg, 2009).

In this chapter, we covered several tools that will help farmers improve the operations of their farm and thus their chances for success and survival in a global market. Process maps help managers understand their farm and its operations through new eyes to see steps that could be improved and others that could be eliminated. Several methods and ways for improving farm processes were discussed. Scheduling tools for operations and projects were described to help improve a farmer's ability to get work done in a timely, cost-effective, and high-quality manner. Managing input supply and inventories are critical steps to cost control as markets squeeze margins. A common theme through all these tools is the need and desire to cut costs to maintain and improve farm income. This effort to decrease costs comes together in the last discussion on lean management, which is an overall management strategy and approach that aims to understand the value chain and what adds to the value customers perceive and then drive out all waste from the system. These are new tools for many farmers, but a new era of increased global connections and increasing competition calls for new management tools.

Summary Points

- A process map is a description of a method or process of accomplishing a task.
- Process maps can help a farmer to understand how the farm and its processes fit together and to see potential areas for improvement.
- Five general areas for improving processes are reducing input use, substituting inputs, increasing productivity, expanding the process, and reorganizing the process.
- Scheduling is an allocation decision.
- The schedule shows what is to be done, when it will be done, who will do it, and what equipment will be needed.

- Scheduling has three distinct, competing objectives: cost, schedule, and performance.
- Two scheduling techniques can be useful for farming: sequencing and dispatching.
- Sequencing is a procedure for scheduling people, jobs, equipment, and other resources over several weeks or months. Gantt charts are used for sequencing.
- Dispatching rules help a manager decide which jobs have the highest priority and should be done first on a certain day or the next.
- The most beneficial dispatching rules for farmers are SPT, EDD, and economic importance.
- The benefits of inventory management include taking advantage of price discounts, anticipating inputs needs, and more orderly and timely delivery of inputs.
- The goal of lean management is to eliminate waste. Waste is defined as anything and any cost that does not add value for the customer.

Review Questions

1. What is a process map? Why develop a process map?
2. How can a process map be useful to a farm manager?
3. Develop a process map for an enterprise or operation on a farm.
4. What are the five general areas in which a farmer can find ideas for improving current processes?
5. Why is the following statement false? The same design for a livestock building can minimize production costs and maximize flexibility for adapting to future changes.
6. How can operations be scheduled using sequencing (with Gantt charts)? In what situations would schedule planning be important for improving the operation of a farm?
7. Describe the main dispatching rules, and how they can be used by farmers.
8. How can enterprise budgets and the chosen enterprise mix be used for input supply management? How could using them be beneficial to a farmer? When are they needed?
9. Describe the main inventory management systems that could be used by a farmer. When would one method be more appropriate than another?
10. What is lean management? How can lean management principles be useful for improving the operation of a farm?

Further Reading

Bicheno, John, and Matthias Holweg. 2008. *The Lean Toolbox*. 4th ed. Buckingham, England, United Kingdom: Picsie Books, 308 pp.

Ohno, Taiichi. 1988. *Toyota Production System*. Cambridge, Massachusetts: Productivity Press, 152 pp.

Schroeder, R. G. 2008. *Operations Management: Contemporary Concepts and Cases*. 4th ed. Boston: McGraw-Hill/Irwin, 528 pp.

West, Terry D., Tony J. Vyn, and Gary C. Steinhardt. 2002. "Feasibility of One-Pass Tillage Systems for Corn and Soybeans." AGRY 02-01, Agronomy Dept., Purdue University, West Lafayette, Indiana.

Womack, James P., and Daniel T. Jones. 2003. *Lean Thinking*. 2nd ed. New York: Free Press, 396 pp.

19

Quality Management and Control

In this chapter:

- Defining quality; product and process quality
- Costs of quality
- Quality management, lessons from the quality pioneers, total quality management (TQM), ISO 9000 standards, hazard analysis and critical control point (HACCP)
- Process control and improvement: preliminary, concurrent, and feedback control; developing process control systems; tools for process control and improvement

Quality has not been talked about very explicitly in farm management. However, it is very important for all farmers, especially when we consider both product quality and process quality.

We have established product quality standards, such as government grades for livestock and eggs; standards for moisture, foreign material, and other characteristics in grains; government inspections in processing plants; and federal and international certification regulations for organic certification. We have required or encouraged the use of procedures to reduce pesticide spills, bruised meat, safe operation of equipment, and so on. But we have not talked extensively about how farmers can improve the quality of their own processes and, thus, their success.

Managing and controlling quality on the farm will become more important in the future, whether a farmer produces commodities such as wheat or beef or sells directly to the consumer. The pressures and changes that are taking place now in the food and agriculture industry require farmers to look at quality from a new perspective—beyond just product quality to process quality and the needs and expectations of the consumer. Let us look at quality concerns for both the commodity producer and the producer who sells directly or almost directly to the consumer.

Commodity producers may think they are far from the consumer, but the consumers' expectations of quality are important because commodity buyers are very aware of and concerned about consumers' definitions of quality. Consumers' concerns include taste, look, and size characteristics. They are also increasingly concerned about the production process, as seen in environmental regulations and in the increasing demand for organic and local food. Whether producers like it or not, or whether they agree with it, animal welfare concerns are affecting how animals can be treated. Some countries already have animal welfare regulations, and some companies already will buy only from farmers who can document how they treat their animals.

These concerns about the production process will likely force farmers to record and report more information about their farms and how they produce their crops and care for their animals. Such concerns include animal treatment, water quality, soil runoff, chemical storage and use, and greenhouse gas emissions. The reporting process may require farmers to use methods such as ISO 9000 and HACCP, which are discussed in this chapter.

Another very important reason commodity producers should pay attention to quality management and control is for the internal cost control and increased efficiency that this can provide. In today's very competitive market, producers need to seek ways to improve processes and cut waste in the continual effort to lower the cost per unit. The procedures described in this chapter can help identify ways to improve internal processes, monitor production for correct implementation, and control the production process to more closely attain the productivity and efficiency needed to compete and better ensure success.

Farmers who sell directly to consumers or are very close to them in the supply chain have obvious needs to be concerned about quality. Consumers can be very quick to move to another supplier if their specifications for the product and process are not met. The concepts and procedures described in this chapter can help these farmers achieve high-quality products and better processes.

For both types of farmers, production contracts are becoming very common and are another reason for farmers to understand and use quality management and control procedures. Contracts can have many specifications that need to be met or the farmer will not be paid or may not be offered a contract again. The skills needed are introduced and described in this chapter.

This chapter focuses on quality management and quality control. **Quality management** involves a holistic view of the entire farm. Quality management aims to develop a philosophy of improving quality in all functions: marketing, production, finance, and personnel. It develops policies and procedures to instill a commitment to quality throughout the farm. Quality management covers all aspects of the business: the initial product choice and design, input purchases, choice of production processes, production and marketing of the product or service, and the warranty, repair, or replacement service after delivery to the customer. Producing quality is the responsibility of all management and labor personnel and is accomplished only by the application of proper management and control in all phases and levels of the business. A few of the buzz words heard in businesses today are total quality management (TQM), zero defects, and continuous improvement.

Quality control refers to controlling the already selected production process for the products already chosen and designed. Two major parts of quality control discussed in this chapter are process control and process improvement. **Process control** consists of the procedures to monitor production for compliance with the original plan and development of corrective actions designed to bring the process back into compliance. **Process improvement** includes a set of tools used to understand the current process better and to look for potential ways to improve both the process and the product.

This chapter starts by defining quality and the costs of quality. It then addresses quality management, process control, and process improvement.

Quality Defined

Quality is commonly defined as "meeting or exceeding customer requirements." This definition points to the first and most important lesson in quality management: *The customer, not the producer, defines quality.*

Farmers (and manufacturers, professors, and hamburger flippers) may want to define quality, because they "know" what quality is! But whether we like it or not, the customer is the one who decides whether a product is what they need or want. Quality is defined in terms of both **product quality** and **process quality.** The person who wants a sliced roast beef sandwich will not be swayed by the arguments that a ground beef sandwich has the same nutritional value. A person who wants certified organic milk from cows not treated with the rBST hormone will not be won over to "regular" milk by the argument (and fact in this case) that all milk has natural BST.

The phrase "fitness for use" can also help us understand that quality is related to value received by the customer and to customer satisfaction. In both "value received" and "satisfaction," we see that it is the customer and not the producer who defines quality.

A customer defines or describes quality using several dimensions, including design, performance, reliability, durability, service, reputation, conformance, safety, and so on. Price is included in some lists of quality dimensions. In one sense, price does not affect the performance of a product or service. Yet in another sense, price can affect a customer's ability to meet cost and profit goals, and thus, it does affect the customer's view of a product and its "fitness for use."

Product Quality

To understand better what customers are looking for, their dimensions of quality can be defined in four ways or into four determinants of product quality: quality of design, quality of conformance, the "abilities," and service after delivery. In other words, a customer is looking for how well the product or service is designed, how well it meets the design specifications, how available it is, and how well it is taken care of by the producer after sale and delivery.

Quality of design is determined before production takes place. How well does the product design meet the customers' needs and wants? For farmers, design quality has been present for a long time in the price breaks defined by factors such as grain moisture standards, market animal weights, milk fat levels, and grain protein levels. For a farmer, quality of design involves product specifications such as crop variety choice, the weight and type of the finished animal, milk fat percentage, and grain protein percentage. Design quality also involves the choice of production methods to meet food quality and safety concerns, desire for organically produced foods, and animal welfare concerns. Design quality is a common part of agricultural production contracts: choice of crop varieties, planting dates, delivery dates, and so on. Design quality is also important in a service product such as hired or custom harvesting when harvesting even a little early or late can have adverse effects on the quantity and quality of the customer's crop.

Quality of conformance is about how well the production process has produced the product or service to the design specifications. Was the protein percentage in the soybeans high enough? Was the animal weight within the specified range? Was the grain delivered on time at the proper moisture levels? Was the crop fertilized correctly? Were the proper crop protection methods used? Were chemical labels followed? Were organic practices followed? Was the machinery calibrated and set correctly? Were the animals fed the correct rations to produce the fat levels requested? Were animals with the right genetics used? Were sick animals treated appropriately? Was the crop harvested at the optimal time? These are examples of questions that need to be answered to achieve quality of conformance.

The **"abilities"** are reliability, maintainability, and availability. All these have a time element that reflects the continued satisfaction of the customer.

Reliability is the length of time that a product can be used before it fails to provide the service it was designed to produce. A machine can fail due to mechanical failure or being out of service for regular maintenance. A product can fail when it decays or falls out of specified quality ranges. Milk can spoil if not cooled to certain temperatures. Grain can be considered to have failed if insect damage has exceeded minimum levels during storage. Reliability can also be described as the probability that a product will function for a specified period without failure. Reliability can be described in terms of the average or mean time between failures or to failure (MTBF). For a machine, MTBF is the average time before breakdown or maintenance. For fruit and vegetables, MTBF could be described as the average time from harvest to spoilage with or without proper post-harvest storage. For food products, reliability can be viewed as shelf life in a grocery store and at home. The customers' definition of reliability differs by product, and the producer must be aware of their definition.

Maintainability is the restoration of a product to service once it has failed. For a machine, maintainability is the time required for regular service and maintenance or the time required for repair after failure. From a customer's view it could also be viewed as the time required to replace a product that has failed (spoiled, for example). Maintainability can be measured as the mean time to repair or replace (MTTR).

A product is available if it is in an operational state and not out of service for repairs or maintenance. For a machine, availability can be expressed as the percentage of time that it is operating or ready for work compared to the total of operating, ready, and out-of-service time. Thus, availability can be quantified as MTBF/(MTBF + MTTR) * 100%.

For agricultural products, availability can be the length of time that a product is at optimal quality. Examples of this are the length of time before the product fails (milk becomes too warm or sugar levels in grapes falls too low, for example) or insect damage exceeds the minimum level for stored grain. Availability can also be viewed as the time that the product is available to the consumer in a certain price range. Seasonality of production may affect availability. A local grocery store may be willing to buy produce locally if local producers can grow and supply it during a certain time period at a consistent and sufficient quantity and quality.

Service after delivery, the fourth dimension of product quality, is the warranty, repair, and replacement after the product has been sold. In farming, service examples include the replacement of breeding animals if they do not perform as expected, the hiring of replacement custom operators if other circumstances do not allow a contract to be fulfilled, and the buyback or replacement of the product that does not meet the expectations of the customer.

In summary, product quality includes quality of design, quality of conformance, the "abilities," and service after delivery. Product quality is only concerned with the product and says nothing about how efficient or how wasteful the production process is or isn't.

Process Quality

Process quality is concerned about efficiency, productivity, and cost control. It looks for how to improve the processes of production, marketing, financing, and all other processes on the farm. Process quality is the twin sibling of product quality and the best friend of lean management (discussed at the end of the previous chapter.) The quality pioneers introduced in a later section switched from product quality to process quality because they realized the solutions to quality problems lie in correcting the process, not just throwing out the bad product at the end of the process.

Process quality has external and internal components. Whereas product quality judges whether the final product meets customer expectations, this external concern drives a manager to ensure that processes are designed correctly so the product will meet those expectations. Internally, process quality is concerned with the efficiency of any process on the farm. The internal view of process quality involves physical and economic measures of efficiency and productivity. Process quality is the main topic of this chapter in the later sections on quality management and process control and improvement.

Next we discuss the costs of poor product quality and poor process quality.

Costs of Quality

The **costs of quality** include both the costs of meeting customers' requirements and the costs of NOT meeting them. The costs of quality consist of control costs and failure costs. Some of these, such as higher costs for better sanitation, are obvious and easily seen and measured. Other costs of quality, such as lost sales or lost contracts, cannot be seen so easily. As the reader will come to understand by the end of this chapter, the title of this section could easily have been "The benefits of quality and the costs of poor quality."

Control costs are the costs of removing defects by prevention or by appraisal or inspection. An example of cost prevention is choosing and following procedures that have higher costs but provide higher quality (e.g., higher sanitation procedures in the milking parlor, taking the time to test the accuracy of the sprayer). Another example of prevention costs is maintaining and operating equipment to meet higher standards, not just to get a job done (for example, operating a grain dryer to provide a lower percentage of burnt kernels, not just dry grain). Examples of appraisal or inspection costs include checking for correct seed placement in the soil, testing for correct nutrient levels in feedstuffs, monitoring the moisture level of grain in storage, sorting and selling livestock only within desired market weight ranges, and testing for chemical residues.

Failure costs are the costs of the product failing to meet specified quality standards. Failure costs can be divided into internal and external costs. *Internal failure costs* occur during production. Examples of internal costs include scrap material, rework, quality downgrading, and downtime. Animal disease that causes poor productivity and even death is an obvious example of the cost of internal failures on farms. Equipment breakdowns, repair costs, and lost timeliness due to poor maintenance or replacement are other examples. *External failure costs* occur after production and shipment. Examples of these include returned goods, price penalties, and warranty charges. Bruised meat caused by rough handling of the animals and then being rejected by the processor is an external failure cost. Products rejected due to chemical residues found after they left the farm are an example of external failures. One external failure cost that may be hard to measure is receiving a lower price due to lower quality and the resulting lack of or lower consumer demand. Lost contracts and lack of repeat sales are also external costs of poor quality, but they too are hard to measure.

The **total cost of quality** is the sum of control costs and failure costs—that is, the sum of prevention costs, appraisal costs, internal failure costs, and external failure costs. The manager should strive to lower the total cost of quality. External failure costs may be higher than the internal costs of prevention. Seeing the internal costs of prevention as an expense is very easy, but the manager must evaluate those costs against the harder to see losses of external failure.

The **benefits of quality** include an enhanced reputation, increased business, greater customer loyalty, and fewer production and service problems. All of these benefits mean the business will have higher efficiency and productivity, fewer complaints, and higher profits. The benefits of quality may also include lower production costs per unit sold, because even though some expenditures may increase in order to improve process quality, those improvements create less waste, a greater focus on what the customer wants, and a redesign of all the processes on the farm. These combine to lower the total costs of the higher quality products. In general business, the companies who have won the national Baldrige quality award have better financial performance than companies that have not won the award.

Quality Management

Every worker is responsible for quality, whether the worker is the owner, manager, tractor driver, milker, or manure handler. Every aspect of a farm needs to be scrutinized for quality. The concern for quality has to be present at all levels including top management, product and process design, input purchasing, production and operations, storage and shipping, marketing and sales, and customer service. Even on a one-person farm, the operator has to consider the benefits of meeting quality expectations versus the consequences of low quality in all decisions and operations. This all-encompassing need to pay attention to quality is why we start talking about quality management.

In this section, we first look at the ideas of a select group of people—the quality pioneers—who started talking about quality management early, left lasting contributions to quality management, and whose ideas are still relevant for farmers today. Then we briefly consider three approaches for improving quality that we hear about often and affect farmers now and even more in the future. First, we look at the overall concept of total quality management (TQM) and how it can be used by farmers. Second, we consider how farmers can use the ISO standards from the International Organization for Standards to improve the consistency of conforming to product design and to ensure customers that the product advertised will be the product provided. The third approach we study briefly is Hazard Analysis and Critical Control Point (HACCP), which is used more and more in the food industry.

Lessons from the Quality Pioneers

A small group of people has made a tremendous impact on how business views and improves quality. The most famous of this group include these five quality pioneers: Deming, Juran, Feigenbaum, Crosby, and Ishikawa. Let us look at the ideas and points that made each pioneer famous and how they can be used by farmers.

W. Edwards Deming. Deming is the best-known name of this elite group. One of his main messages was that the cause of inefficiency and poor quality is the system, not the workers. Deming felt that management was responsible for correcting the system. He expressed his "requirements for a business whose management plans to remain competitive in providing goods and services that will have a market" in 14 management principles (Table 19.1). The key elements of his 14 points are constancy of purpose, continual improvement, and profound knowledge. By profound knowledge, Deming meant understanding (1) the system and the impact of everyone in the system, (2) the causes of variation, (3) the need to learn from theory, and (4) the importance of psychology and how to motivate workers to contribute their collective efforts to a common goal.

Two points can be seen in this definition. First, all systems (administration, design, production, sales, etc.) must be stable in a statistical sense (i.e., a constant variance around a constant average). Second, continuous improvement is needed to reduce variation and better meet the customer's needs. To reduce variation, Deming saw the need to distinguish between special causes of variation (i.e., correctable or

Table 19.1 Deming's 14 Principles for Quality Management

1. Create constancy of purpose toward improvement of product and service with a plan to become competitive and to stay in business. Decide to whom top management is responsible.
2. Adopt the new philosophy. We are in a new economic age. We can no longer live with commonly accepted levels of delays, mistakes, defective materials, and defective workmanship.
3. Cease dependence on mass inspection. Require, instead, statistical evidence that quality is built in. (Prevent defects rather than detect defects.)
4. End the practice of awarding business on the basis of price tag. Instead, depend on meaningful measures of quality along with price. Eliminate suppliers that cannot qualify with statistical evidence of quality.
5. Find problems. It is management's job to work continually on the system (design, incoming materials, composition of material, maintenance, improvement of machine, training, supervision, retraining).
6. Institute modern methods of training on the job.
7. The responsibility of foremen must be changed from sheer numbers to quality . . . [which] will automatically improve productivity. Management must prepare to take immediate action on reports from foremen concerning barriers such as inherent defects, machines not maintained, poor tools, and fuzzy operational definitions.
8. Drive out fear, so that everyone may work effectively for the company.
9. Break down barriers between departments. People in research, design, sales, and production must work as a team to foresee problems of production that may be encountered with various materials and specifications.
10. Eliminate numerical goals, posters, and slogans for the work force, asking for new levels of productivity without providing methods.
11. Eliminate work standards that prescribe numerical quotas.
12. Remove barriers that stand between the hourly-rated? worker and his right to pride of workmanship.
13. Institute a vigorous program of education and retraining.
14. Create a structure in top management that will push every day on the above 13 points.

Source: W. Edwards Deming, "Quality, Productivity, and Competitive Position," Cambridge, Massachusetts: MIT, Center for Advanced Engineering Study, 1982, pp. 16–17, as quoted in Stevenson, 2002, p. 403.

assignable causes) and common causes of variation (i.e., random or uncontrollable). Deming promoted the PDCA wheel (Plan, Do, Check, Act) as a way to plan for continuous improvement through planning, doing, checking results, and acting on those results (Figure 19.1).

Briefly, Deming wants top management to (1) look at the long-run not short-run profits, (2) cease dependence on mass inspection of products, and (3) stress prevention of defects. However, Deming is also a strong advocate of quantitative, statistical tests to find sources of variation. He started working in statistical quality control but saw that more was needed than simple acceptance or rejection of the final product. He saw that the systems needed change, starting with top management.

Joseph M. Juran. Juran described quality as "fitness for use" as defined by the customer. Juran saw quality management as a trilogy of quality planning, quality control, and quality improvement. Quality planning is needed to develop processes that can meet quality standards. Quality control is needed to know when corrective actions are needed to bring the process back into control. Quality improvement is needed to help find better ways of doing things. Juran showed the potential for increased profits if the costs of poor quality could be reduced.

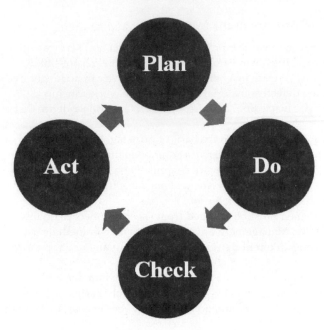

Figure 19.1   Deming's Plan, Do, Check, Act Wheel

Armand Feigenbaum.   Feigenbaum used the "cost of nonconformance" to obtain management's commitment to quality. He also saw that by improving the system in one part of a business, other areas also enjoyed improvements. With this understanding of systems, Feigenbaum encouraged (1) cross-functional work (that is, teams of people from production, finance, sales, and other parts of a business) and (2) the development of environments in which workers could learn from each other's successes. Feigenbaum argued that improving human factors were more important to improved quality than technological factors. He also believed that it is the customer who defines quality and that controlling quality at the source is important, not controlling at the end of the system.

Philip B. Crosby.   Crosby coined the phrases: "zero defects" and "do it right the first time." He argued against the idea of acceptable levels of mistakes and defects. Like the other quality pioneers, Crosby was convinced that quality improvement must start with top management's commitment to, support of, persistency toward, and communication for good quality. He argued that "quality is free" because the costs of poor quality are much greater than the costs of improving quality.

Kaoru Ishikawa.   Ishikawa followed both Deming and Juran but also provided the quality tools of the cause-and-effect diagram and quality circles. Cause-and-effect diagrams (also called fishbone diagrams) helped solve problems by helping identify potential causes. (Examples of cause-and-effect diagrams are shown later in this chapter.) Quality circles involve workers in quality improvement. Ishikawa was the first to talk about the internal customer—that is, the next person in the process. By providing internal customers with better quality inputs for their part of the process, the overall quality of the final product is improved. This description of the system allows workers to see potential ways to improve the part of the operation that is in their control. The crop farmer may be his own next internal customer if he also feeds livestock. For most farmers, the next person is the elevator or processor. By improving the quality of the product supplied to them, farmers can help improve the quality of the products supplied to the final consumer.

In summary, here are 12 points to remember from the quality pioneers and what they mean to a farmer.

1. Quality is defined by the customer. Farmers need to listen to customers. They are the ones who define a quality product.
2. Quality improvement must start with management's commitment. If a manager does not have quality as a top concern, neither will his or her employees.
3. Problems in the system, not the workers, cause inefficiency and poor quality. Employees will respond to how a farm is organized, how buildings are designed, how incentives are described, and so on. If these systems and structures are not designed well, employees will not work well.
4. Continual improvement is needed. Due to constant change in the world and our ability to learn how to do things better, we need to keep changing our products, processes, systems, and ourselves.
5. Prevent defects; do not just throw them out. Preventing problems by changing methods is usually more profitable and provides a better product for the consumer.
6. Quality planning, quality control, and quality improvement must go together. A manager needs to work on the whole package to make the best progress toward higher quality products and processes.
7. Improving human factors is more important than improving technological factors. Simply buying new machines and switching to new inputs will not make large improvements in product and process quality if workers do not fully understand how to use either the new or old technologies and systems.
8. Do it right the first time. It is better to take the time to plan and learn how a job needs to be done before it is started than to start the job and waste time and inputs, ruin products, and/or destroy customer faith.
9. Quality is free. The expenses for improving processes and products will be more than paid back through improved efficiencies and other benefits received because of the improvements.
10. Cause-and-effect diagrams can help us see potential solutions. Understanding all the possible factors affecting the desired outcome can help a manager see potential areas for improvement. Cause-and-effect diagrams are especially useful for helping managers see more than the "usual suspects" when trying to solve problems.
11. Quality circles involve workers in improving the business. Listening to workers and customers is beneficial in many ways: workers are closer to the work and know how it can be improved, workers feel respected when management asks them for information, customers can provide a better understanding of what they want, costs go down, and efficiencies go up. An example of quality circles are the knowledge circles being used in the Dutch fishing industry (Example 19.1).
12. Helping internal customers perform better will help the whole business. Whether one person or several are involved, the whole farm can see improvements when each person looks for ways to help the next perform his or her task easier and better. For example, how can the mechanic help the planter plant? How can the corn producer provide a better feed to the hog feeder? How can the worker provide better records to the financial analyst?

These quality pioneers led the way in convincing management that improving the quality of the process meant better product quality and better profits. In the next three sections, we look at three

---

Example 19.1. Knowledge Circles in the Netherlands

Knowledge circles are (study) groups of fishermen who have common challenges, questions, or problems and together are looking for solutions. For example, due to high oil prices, some knowledge circles are focusing on saving fuel; others are involved in alternative fish marketing or looking for new and cost-reducing techniques.

The aim of the knowledge circles is to find solutions that balance three main goals: reducing costs, increasing revenues, and reducing ecological impacts. Finding solutions is often easier if knowledge is accessed and shared among fishermen, between fishermen and researchers, and between fishermen and other stakeholders in the chain and in society. The goal of the knowledge circles is to tap into the industry's large (experiential) knowledge of fish stocks, fishing techniques, fish quality, ecology, etc., and to combine that knowledge with the knowledge from research institutions.

Members work with researchers and other organizations, and they receive logistical support and sharing of knowledge from government agencies. However, knowledge circles are groups of and for fishermen, who are looking for solutions together. They are not research projects led by researchers, nor are they government programs. The ownership of the challenge, question, or problem lies with the circles. Solutions are shared with other fishermen and the public.

More information on knowledge circles can be found on the Web site: www.kenniskringvisserij.wur.nl, last accessed on February 11, 2010. The Web site is written in Dutch, but an online translator (such as www.google.com/language_tools) can help.

---

current manifestations of quality management that can be useful for farmers to know: total quality management (TQM), ISO 9000 Standards, and Hazard Analysis and Critical Control Point (HACCP)

Total Quality Management (TQM) for Farmers

Total quality management (TQM) is a management philosophy that strives to involve everyone in a continual effort to improve quality and achieve customer satisfaction. Three points or terms should be noted in this description of TQM: *everyone*, *continual*, and *customer satisfaction*. Everyone should be involved in improving quality on a farm: from the owners and managers to the part-time workers. A farm practicing TQM to its fullest extent will even involve suppliers in the quest for quality improvement. TQM also involves a continual process of checking all aspects of the farm that affect quality: inputs, processes, and products. TQM also has customer satisfaction as its primary goal, which means, as discussed earlier, meeting or exceeding customer expectations.

For farmers, TQM involves the following steps.

1. Finding out what the customers want.

   For commodities such as #2 yellow corn, this could start with checking the standards for moisture, foreign material, and so on. This could also mean talking with the elevator about their preferences for delivery method and timing. For specialty products, such as high oil corn or contract vegetables, this step starts with checking the terms of the contract.

For services such as hired or custom harvesting, this step involves talking with current and potential customers and understanding what they want, including product quality at harvest, speed of work, timeliness, daily start and end times, product left in the field, and cleanup afterward.

2. Design a product or service that will meet or exceed what customers want.

   Most farmers will not participate in all the details of product design if they produce basic raw commodities (e.g., milk, pork, corn) that have long-established specifications as part of their product description. However, farmers do control the product that leaves their farm. For example, they choose the moisture percentage to which they will dry their grain, the temperature of the milk in the bulk cooler, the weight at which hogs are sold, the genetic potential of their livestock, the plant stage at which hay is cut and baled, and so on. Farmers do need to consider what their customers want.

3. Design processes that will facilitate doing the job right the first time.

   Designing, or choosing how to produce a product, should involve more than picking the steps, inputs, equipment, and workers needed. Designing the process should also look at the risks and uncertainties of production and include steps, procedures, and other aspects to ensure that the desired product will be produced with as little physical and economic waste as possible.

   Process design and product design need to be done simultaneously although they are listed as two steps here. For example, in producing #2 yellow corn, the decision of what the delivered moisture level should be is a joint process-product decision. The market defines a certain moisture level for pricing, but if the cost of on-farm drying is too great compared with the benefit, corn can be delivered at a higher moisture level and dried by the local elevator.

4. Keep track of results and use them to improve the system.

   Keeping the books for quality management involves more than financial data. Livestock and field records can be used to identify both good and poor producers, to spot areas that need improvement, and to eliminate waste.

5. Strive to have suppliers and processors adopt the ideas of TQM.

   Improving quality on the farm needs to eventually involve improving the quality of inputs used on the farm and discussing the standards requested by the buyers of the products. For example, after improving the feeding equipment and processes on a hog farm, the next step is to be sure that purchased feedstuffs are delivered at the farmer's chosen nutrient levels. This may involve more specific definitions of nutrient requirements, testing or requiring testing for nutrient levels in feedstuffs, and discussion with suppliers about the nutritional needs. It may also involve farmers serving on boards of directors for suppliers and processors.

Besides the five steps listed above, TQM includes other ideas and concepts that are crucial to its use by farmers. These ideas and concepts are listed below.

Continuous Improvement.   Always look for ways to improve the process and results of the farm, never be satisfied with the status quo, and do not accepting ''normal'' mistake levels.

Competitive Benchmarking.   Competitive benchmarking compares the processes and results of your own operation with the competition. This may involve visiting other farms, joining farm business associations, reading government and popular media reports that present the performance levels of other farms, and so on. At times, this benchmarking may not always be done with farms in the same business. For example, feed grain producers may learn how to maintain identity preservation in a commodity environment by visiting rice and bean farmers and their processors.

Employee Empowerment.   Give employees the responsibility for quality improvement and the authority to make changes. Doing so allows access to the employees' intimate knowledge of the process they are using and motivates them to be more involved in the success of the farm.

Team Approach.   Teams can provide synergies, better understanding of problems and potential solutions, and increased motivation and cooperation. Independent farmers can benefit from discussions with family members and from professional discussions with neighbors and others close to their business.

Data-Based Decisions.   Instead of relying on opinions and ideas of what may be the causes of problems and potential problems, TQM stresses the need to gather and understand the data relevant to a situation before decisions are made.

Knowledge of Quality Management Tools.   Understanding the basic tools of quality management will help farmers better understand and analyze their production processes, know what aspects need to be improved first and how to improve them, and know how to keep a process under control to produce the desired product.

Supplier Quality.   At some point, the on-farm processes are at a level of quality where suppliers need to become involved in understanding the farmer's needs and the implications for input quality in order to improve the results of the total system.

Quality at the Source.   Quality at the source is a philosophy that makes every worker responsible for the quality of his or her own work.

Adopting the five steps and other ideas of TQM can be critical to helping a farmer improve business profits. But adopting TQM is voluntary. The next two quality management systems (ISO 9000 and HACCP) may be required or effectively required in the future.

ISO 9000 Standards

Since 1947, the International Organization for Standards (ISO, the acronym in French) has promoted worldwide standards to improve operating efficiency, improve productivity, and reduce costs. Most of the ISO standards have been highly specific for a particular product, material, or process. Engineers have used ISO standards to ensure that a certain kind of bolt, for example, is the same everywhere in the world.

In 1987, the ISO deviated from this engineering specificity to develop the **ISO 9000 standards** for quality management. The ISO 9000 standards are not specific product, material, and process standards. They are generic management system standards to be used by businesses to describe the quality standards of their product, their production processes, and their monitoring and recording systems so customers can be assured they will receive the product they order. Farmers involved closely with international trade, especially with niche products such as organic, non-hormone, and other non-commodity products, will likely need to follow ISO 9000 or a closely related system.

A *management system* is what an organization, company, or business forms to manage its processes, activities, services, and so on. The ISO 9000 standards, thus, are a set of guidelines on how to set up and operate a management system to ensure and verify to customers that its products conform to the customer's requirements. ISO 9000 standards are not concerned with a customer's specific requirements; the standards are to be used by an organization to show a customer how it is ensuring that the customer's requirements are being met.

The ISO 9000 family is as follows:

- ISO 9000:2000, Quality Management Systems—Fundamentals and vocabulary. These establish a starting point for understanding the standards and define fundamental terms and definitions.
- ISO 9001:2000, Quality Management Systems—Requirements. This is the requirement standard used to assess an organization's ability to meet customer and applicable regulatory requirements and address customer satisfaction. This is now the only standard in the ISO 9000 family against which third-party certification can be carried out.
- ISO 9004:2000, Quality Management Systems—Guidelines for Performance Improvements. This standard provides guidance for continual improvement of an organization's quality management system to benefit all parties through sustained customer satisfaction.

The ISO 9000 family of standards, and specifically the ISO 9001:2000 standards, focus on assuring the quality of the process being used in the organization. This quality assurance system must include procedures, policies, and training. Extensive documentation is required that includes a quality manual, process flow charts, operator instructions, inspection and testing methods, job descriptions, and organization charts. To be certified, an organization must review, refine, and map functions such as process control, inspection, purchasing, and training. ISO registrars look for a well-documented quality system, completed training, and whether the actual process being used conforms to the process described in the documentation. The organization must be re-registered every three years.

Once it is registered as ISO 9000 certified, an organization can advertise and promote its products as being made consistently in the same way. It can show current and potential customers the standard processes and inputs used in the production of its products. The ISO 9000 family is especially important for companies involved in international trade, particularly in Europe, but certification can also be important for domestic customers.

As rigorous and time consuming as becoming certified sounds, ISO 9001:2000 standards do not address all aspects of quality. Product design is not addressed. An organization may be ISO 9001:2000–certified and follow the process flawlessly but be producing a product that nobody wants to buy. These standards also do not address organization leadership, strategic planning, customer satisfaction, continuous improvement, and business results.

Farmers can benefit from ISO 9000 certification in two ways. First, developing the ISO guidelines can help farmers see and take advantage of new ideas for decreasing costs and increasing profits by changing their process of production and service. Second, ISO certification can be a marketing advantage to show far-flung buyers that a farmer's production and identity preservation processes are designed to ensure that the resulting product will conform to the customer's required product characteristics.

Certification in the ISO standards allows potential buyers to understand and trust that they are buying the product described. Developing the processes and becoming ISO certified can allow farmers to produce products that meet the increasing concerns of food quality, food safety, and identity preservation. These concerns are present both domestically and internationally.

ISO certification is not a theoretical idea for farmers. In September 2000, a group of Iowa farmers became the first U.S. farmers to be ISO 9000–certified in grain production (Swoboda, 2001). Their local grain elevator also had to become ISO 9000–certified so the farmers could receive the full bene-fits of their certification. Their aim was to improve their competitive advantage in the export market. They needed to provide a higher-valued product to their international customers. The higher value came from being able to certify and document to their customers that their grain was produced in the certain way the customers wanted using certain identifiable inputs and was kept separate from contaminants (including non-certified grain). This is just one example of how being ISO 9000–certi-fied can provide benefits to a farmer.

ISO certification may be highly needed, especially by those farmers in international trade of spe-cialty or niche products, but being involved in those products is still voluntary. The next quality management system (HACCP) or a very similar system may become required for products close to consumers (such as meat and milk) as food safety concerns and scares continue to increase.

Hazard Analysis and Critical Control Point (HACCP)

Hazard Analysis and Critical Control Point or HACCP (pronounced "hassip") started 30 years ago to ensure safe foods for astronauts. Now it is a food safety program that does and will affect almost all farmers because it is used by both of the U.S. agencies that monitor and regulate the U.S. food system. The Food Safety and Inspection Service (FSIS) of the USDA inspects and regulates all feder-ally inspected meat and poultry processing plants. The Food and Drug Administration (FDA) inspects and regulates the rest of the U.S. food system.

In brief, the goal of HACCP is to design systems to monitor and reduce contamination through preven-tive and corrective measures instituted at each stage of the food production process where food safety hazards could occur (FSIS, 1999). It strives to do this by applying science-based controls through the entire system from raw materials to finished products. This goal is in contrast to the traditional system of spot-checks of manufacturing conditions and random sampling of final products to ensure safe food.

In 1996, USDA published a final rule on Pathogen Reduction; Hazard Analysis and Critical Control Point (HACCP) Systems (PR/HACCP) that "requires meat and poultry plants under Federal inspection to take responsibility for, among other things, reducing the contamination of meat and poultry products with disease-causing (pathogenic) bacteria" (FSIS, 1999, p. 3). FDA now applies HACCP to seafood and juice and intends to eventually use it for much of the U.S. food supply (FDA, 2009).

HACCP involves seven principles:

1. Analyze hazards. Potential hazards associated with a food are identified, and the measures that can be used to control them are identified. Potential hazards include biological (bacterial, parasiti-cal, or viral), chemical (toxins, drugs, cleaners, etc.), and physical (glass, metal, etc.). These haz-ards may be in the raw material or introduced at points in the processing and transportation process. Since farmers deliver raw materials, they are not immune from HACCP.
2. Identify critical control points. These are points at which a potential hazard (identified in the first principle or step) can be controlled or eliminated. Examples of these critical points include grind-ing, mixing, cooking, cooling, metal detection, and so on. The entire production process for a spe-cific food is evaluated, starting with its raw ingredients and continuing through processing, storage, and transportation to consumption by the consumer. Delivery of raw products is usually a critical control point for potential entry of hazards. Upon delivery, the temperature of milk is measured as an indicator of safety, health of animals is checked, and grain is inspected for mold.

3. Establish preventive measures with critical limits for each control point. These are exact, specific measures with both upper and lower limits that cannot be exceeded. Examples include cooking temperatures, cool down time, equipment washing temperatures, and dimensions of metal fragments. Specific milk temperatures or time above critical temperature are identified, as are maximum mold infection levels.

4. Establish procedures to monitor the critical control points. Monitoring procedures are done routinely, either by an employee or by mechanical means, to measure the process at a given critical control point and create a record for future use. These procedures describe, for example, how cooking time and temperatures are to be monitored or how mixing of ingredients is to be monitored. Raw products could be evaluated before being unloaded. Records of how and where raw products have been transported and stored may be required. Analytical tests are identified that will provide an accurate measurement of the potential hazard.

5. Establish corrective actions. HACCP requires that corrective actions be identified for those occasions when monitoring shows that a critical limit has been violated. Examples include intercepting affected food, reprocessing, disposing of adulterated food, cleaning equipment, rejecting contaminated raw material, changing procedures, retraining of employees, and so on. FSIS describes four points that their regulators will be checking: (1) identification of the cause of the deviation, (2) verification that the system will be in control after the corrective action is taken, (3) measures taken to prevent recurrence of the deviation, and (4) steps taken to ensure that no adulterated product enters the food chain.

6. Establish recordkeeping procedures. These are needed to document the HACCP system, including records of hazards, control methods, monitoring records, and corrective actions taken.

7. Establish verification procedures. Verification involves testing the system to be sure it is working as intended. This involves checking testing equipment such as thermometers and other analytical equipment as well as observing that monitoring is taking place as intended, corrective actions are being taken when needed, and records are being kept as designed.

In this section, we looked at the early quality pioneers and the lessons we can learn from them. We also looked at three quality management systems (TQM, ISO 9000, and HACCP) and how they are used by farmers.

Process Control and Improvement

In the first part of this chapter, we saw how farmers could benefit from the ideas developed by the quality pioneers and could become involved in overall quality management programs such as TQM, ISO 9001:2000, and HACCP. However, even though a farmer may develop a great TQM system and be certified in the most rigorous ISO 9001:2000 program, uncertainty and risk still creep in and create problems due to products not meeting customer expectations and processes being out of control. In this section we will look at how farmers can monitor and control their farm processes to be sure that all are working as they were designed to do. These ideas can be beneficial to a farm's success even without being in a rigorous program such as TQM, ISO, or HACCP.

A process control system consists of three simple parts: standards, measurement, and corrective actions. (1) Standards or expected performance levels come from the plans developed as part of strategic planning and short-term planning. These standards come from benchmarking (which is explained later), industry reports, and public information on performance. (2) The second part of a process control system is deciding how, when, where, and which results should be measured. These measurements show whether the process is operating according to the standards expected in the plans. (3) If the system is not in compliance, corrective actions are needed to correct the situation. Corrective actions are usually specified before common problems occur, or they may be the result of problem-solving sessions held when new problems occur.

Three types of control are available for the manager to keep a process in control: preliminary control, concurrent control, and feedback control.

Preliminary controls are anticipatory actions that take place before problems are noticed. Preliminary control is closely related to planning. An example of preliminary control is the use of pre-emergence herbicides even though no weed problems are seen or may even occur. Another example is the development of fail-safe plans to be sure all steps are done at a crucial point in a process, such as caring for newborn pigs or calves.

Concurrent control occurs during the production process. Two examples on farms are disease treatment for livestock and plant tissue testing to determine the plant's fertilizer needs.

Feedback control starts after production has occurred. Changes in disease control and sanitation methods for the next production period are examples of actions taken in response to feedback received about disease outbreaks or minimum sanitation levels being violated. Taking classes to understand new marketing options better is an example of actions taken due to feedback about missed pricing opportunities. Feedback control uses many of the same tools used in process improvement (which are discussed later in this chapter). For example, feedback control often starts with problems that were noted on trend charts or check sheets (also discussed later). Cause-and-effect diagrams (also discussed later) can be used to identify the causes of the problems and, thus, potential solutions and ways to improve the process.

The next section describes the procedures for developing process control systems, which can be a crucial part of concurrent control.

Developing Process Control Systems

Process control is the inspection of the product or service while it is being produced. It is the process of determining and implementing the necessary actions to make certain that plans are transferred into desired results. Through effective control, we are better able to achieve the goals and objectives that have been established. The number of critical points, and thus the detail and formality of the control system, depends upon the benefits versus costs of inspection, operator differences and needs, and the relative importance of the enterprise to the whole farm.

To develop a process control system, a manager needs to evaluate the system or operation and determine the opportunities for control that exist. This can be done in five steps that are similar to the steps for a HACCP system but simpler in the amount of documentation and verification. These five steps are meant for an internal process control system, not one meant for verification to external customers.

1. Identify critical points where inspection and testing are needed and can be done.

    These critical points can be at any place or time in the process. Process maps, which were described in Chapter 18, can be extremely useful. The critical success factors identified in strategic planning (Chapter 7) can be the critical points themselves or used to identify the critical points. These critical points may be to ensure that incoming raw materials or purchased services meet specifications, to test work in process or the service while it is being delivered, or to inspect the finished product or service. This step should result in a list of critical points in order of importance. Sometimes what seem to be obvious critical points and measures may not be right on the mark for improving the farm (Example 19.2).

Example 19.2. Choosing the Right Process Quality Indicators

At times, a manager may be achieving certain production goals but missing the larger picture of what is important. The best goal isn't necessarily the highest production efficiency. An example of this problem was evident in an interview with a Scottish pig producer.

''We had always been good at meeting targets and our primary focus was always on meeting targets like pigs weaned a sow a year.'' However, he says he didn't realize what they were missing in income because they were focused on the wrong indicator. For his farm, this revelation came due to the seemingly unrelated purchase of a new accounting software package and the resulting advice from the consultant.

What changed was the realization that ''what matters are kilos through the door,'' or sales output. While pigs per sow was still an important goal, the biggest limitation for sales and farm income was pigs weaned per week. The pens were not always full to capacity. To overcome this empty space problem, the farmer started paying more attention to breeding and farrowing enough sows to keep the finishing barn full and sales at capacity even after some sows were dropped because they were not pregnant.

The consultant estimated the sales impact in this way: ''When there are 30 crates in a room, but only 29 are filled every week, that is a total of 52 crates not filled a year. When we take an average of 10 pigs a litter, that's 520 piglets a year. When they finished at 80 kg deadweight, that means the farm is missing out on producing 41,600 kg a year. And at a price of 140 p/kg that amounts to £58,000 [US$90,700] a year, or £1,120 a week that could have been made by filling that extra one pig space'' [from that one room].

Source: S. Trickett, ''Conventional Targets Could Leave Pig Farmers Missing Out. *Farmers Weekly Interactive*, January 5, 2010. Accessed on January 6, 2010, at http://www.fwi.co.uk/Articles/2010/01/05/119363/Conventional-targets-could-leave-pig-farmers-missing.htm.

An interesting, educational, and related novel on production constraints is by E. M. Goldratt and J. Cox, 2004, *The Goal: A Process of Ongoing Improvement*. 3rd rev. ed. Great Barrington, Massachusetts: North River Press.

---

2. Choose the measurement plan and sensor to be used at each inspection point.

The measurement plan includes deciding the measure units, how performance will be measured, what sensors will be used, and what the recording system will be. The measurement plan should include some discussion of the reliability of alternative measurement methods.

Measurement is done either by variables or by attributes. Testing by variables uses a continuous scale for such factors as length, height, weight, time, and dimensions. Acceptance is based on how close the product or service meets these actual measurements. Testing by attributes uses a discrete scale by counting the number of defective items or defects per unit. These are qualitative or discrete measurements (good or bad, broken or not). Acceptance is based on the percentage of items that meet the standards.

The measurement plan also needs to specify how much inspection to use: 100% of the production or a sample of the production. If the testing destroys the product (protein tests in feedstuffs, for example), a sample is the obvious choice. If the product is not destroyed, the choice revolves around the cost of the testing process, the underlying variability of the measure, the need for information, and the need of the customer for conformance to the design.

Another part of developing the measurement plan is to decide whether the workers or someone else should do the inspection. By having the workers inspect their own work, they can see problems directly. Since they are closer to the process, they can quickly offer ideas for improving the process and the resulting quality. The traditional method of having someone else inspect the work may be needed if a third-party inspection is required or if worker inspection needs to be verified as accurate.

3. Set the monitoring schedule.

Another part of the measurement is deciding how often to measure performance. The frequency depends on how critical it is for the system to be in control. Frequency also depends on whether the critical point is a "one-time" concern, such as soil temperature for planting, or a potentially recurring problem, such as bacteria in milk.

4. Specify standards and "in-control" range.

Standards need to be quantitative in both physical and monetary terms. Even if qualitative attributes are used to measure quality, standards need to be defined in quantitative terms (e.g., percent acceptable). They need to be measurable and recorded as part of the plan. Standards can be developed from historical records for the farm, records from other farms, information from suppliers, and private and public budgets.

5. Establish corrective actions to bring the system back into control.

The final part of a process control system is the establishment of corrective actions to be taken if the measurements show the process to be out of control. These corrective actions take one of three forms: change the plan, change the implementation of the plan, or change the goals or standards by which production is evaluated.

As examples, consider the illustrative components of a process control for soybeans (Table 19.2) and for a beef finishing operation (Table 19.3). These examples are only illustrative of how a process control system could be developed and not meant to be the entire system that a farmer may need to control his or her own process.

Table 19.2 Illustrative Components of a Soybean Production Control System

Critical Point	Sensor	Monitoring Schedule	Control Standards	Corrective Actions
Soil conditions for planting	Visual, feel	Daily during planting season	Dry enough	Wait for soil to dry
			Proper soil texture	Till to break up clods or level seed bed
Seed placement: distance and depth	Tape measure	Test before planting begins and then once a day	$3/4$–$1\,1/4$" between seeds and $1\,1/2$–2" deep	Adjust planter to attain proper distance and depth

Seeding rate	Planter monitor	Continuous	Lights flashing in expected pattern for desired population & the same for each row	Inspect planter for plugs, broken parts, and incorrect settings
Planting speed	Acres per day	Daily	65–75 acres per day	If weather is not the problem, check for correct speed and other problems
Weed population	Visual	Daily during May and June	Weed count below thresholds for treatment	Apply post-emergence herbicide
Grain moisture at harvest	Moisture tester	Daily shortly before harvest begins	Moisture at or below critical level	Wait for soybeans to dry before harvesting
Harvest wastage	Visual count	Daily	Number of soybeans on ground behind combine below critical level	Inspect combine for proper settings Verify proper speed of combine

Table 19.3 Illustrative Components of a Beef Finishing Control System

Critical Point	Sensor	Monitoring Schedule	Control Standards	Corrective Actions
Feeding silage: 12 lb/day	Scale	Mondays	11.5 to 12.5 lb/head/day	Adjust amount delivered to desired level
Average daily gain	Scale	Every other Monday	1.5 to 1.7 lb/day	Inspect animal health, feed quality; calibrate scale
Water	Visual	Daily	Waterers clean and working, fresh water available	Clean waterers, fix waterers and supply lines
Clean lot and sleeping area	Visual and smell	Daily	No excessive manure buildups	Clean when manure reaches excessive level
Animal health	Auditory and visual	Daily	No coughing, no slowness, no down animals, no sores, etc.	Inspect closer, call the vet

Tools for Process Improvement

Process control, as discussed in the previous section, is concerned with making sure the process (growing wheat or hogs, for example) works as planned or that corrections are made during the process. Process improvement looks at a process in a different way—it is concerned with making a process better. A process does not have to be broken for improvement to be possible.

We may be meeting or even exceeding customer expectations and the standards we have developed. Nevertheless, we sense we could do better. By understanding and using the tools listed below, we can see possible ways to improve both averages and variability of critical measures, such as physical performance, cost of production, marketing results, and profitability.

Team Building and Group Interaction

Team-building and group interaction tools can improve how a group (of even two) can learn more about each other to improve trust, communication, and thus quality. Morning meetings can be more than just assigning the day's duties. Employee dinners can build loyalty. Normally, team building and group interaction are done internal to the business, but not always. As mentioned earlier, quality circles are groups of workers or, say, neighboring farmers who meet to discuss ways to improve products and processes. Management clubs and marketing groups are external groups that can be very useful for identifying new and improved processes and for comparing results.

Specific Process and Technology Tools

A specific process and technology tool is anything specific that helps improve process output. An example of this idea is buying specialized equipment to improve crop yields such as a planter designed just for corn and a drill designed just for soybeans.

Process Maps

Process maps involve describing the process and asking, "Why this way?" As described in Chapter 18, process maps can increase our understanding of our current process and make us see obvious areas to improve and potential areas that require further questioning.

Benchmarking

Benchmarking is the process of measuring a farm's performance on a key customer requirement against the best in the industry (or even wider than a specific industry). By benchmarking, a farmer can establish standards against which performance is judged and can identify models for learning how to improve. When benchmarking, we have four basic questions to answer: (1) What farm or group of farms does it best? (That is, meets or exceed customers' expectations best.) (2) How do they do it? (3) How do we do it now? (4) How can we change to match or exceed the best?

Check Sheets

Check sheets are forms that merely require a check to be made in the appropriate column or spot to show the frequency of certain events that relate to quality or process characteristics. They can be

Table 19.4 Check Sheet for Baby Pig Deaths

Cause of death	Week of: *April 3–9*	Total Deaths
Stillborn	√√√√√√	*7*
Diarrhea	√√√√√√√√√√√√√√√√√√√	*19*
Laid on	√√√	*3*
Unknown	√√√√√	*5*
	Total	*34*
Comments: *Need to use more intensive cleaning methods after this farrowing. Check with veterinarian for better ways to treat diarrhea.*		*Initials: KW*

Table 19.5 Check Sheet for Corn Header Plugging

Row (from left as seen by combine driver)	Week of: *October 15–17*	Total Plugs
1	√√	*2*
2	√	*1*
3		*0*
4		*0*
5	√√√√√	*6*
6	√√	*2*
7	√	*1*
8	√√	*2*
	Total	*14*
Comments: *The right chain in row 5 seems looser than the others. What else could be wrong?*		Initials: *KD*

used to show many things, such as the frequencies of error or problem sources, the variation of time required to do the same job, and productivity differences. No statistics are used with this tool. Examples of check sheets include causes of baby pig deaths (Table 19.4) and frequency of corn header plugging by row (Table 19.5). Check sheets can help pinpoint causes and sources of problems. Having a written record helps focus resources on the problem rather than missing or trying to recall information. The written record is especially useful when multiple workers operate the machinery or work with the livestock. For example, if multiple operators are harvesting, combining that information with the information on the corn header plugging may point to a mechanical problem or an operator problem.

Pareto Analysis and Charts

Pareto analysis (and Pareto charts) organize the frequencies of causes from most to least frequent and thus show which problem or source to try to solve first. The data for these can come from a check sheet—pig deaths, for example (Figure 19.2).

Cause-and-Effect (CE) Diagrams

In process control, if measurement and inspection find that a process is out of control (i.e., a problem is present), the process is stopped and an assignable cause is searched for. Assignable causes are specific factors or things that can be identified as the cause of a problem and thus are controllable.

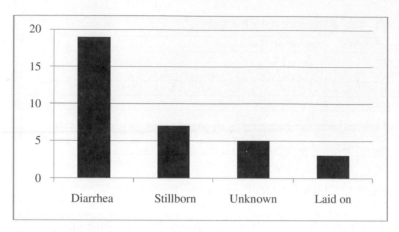

Figure 19.2   Pareto Chart of Causes of Baby Pig Deaths, April 3–9

Assignable causes are different from common causes, which are random fluctuations and not controllable. For example, if the seed monitor indicates a problem in one row, planting should stop, the assignable cause searched for, and the problem solved. Searching for an assignable cause can be done with the help of cause-and-effect (CE) diagrams or fishbone charts as they are sometimes called. Some causes, such as minor movements of the planter, may be deemed random and uncontrollable even though they can cause actual seed placement to differ slightly from planned placement.

CE diagrams are drawn with the problem or opportunity on the right and potential causes to the left along the spine of the diagram. When developing a CE diagram, any potential cause can be listed. For organization and readability, the causes should be grouped into major categories. For farming, five main categories to start with are workers, material, inspection, tools, and weather. Categories can be added and deleted as appropriate for the business and situation being analyzed.

In agriculture, finding the assignable cause could lead to one of many potential changes. Labor may need training, rotation to another team, rest, or a vacation. A machine may need fixing, adjusting, tuning, or replacing. The inputs or raw material may need to be replaced, reordered, or found from a new supplier. Animals may need to be treated for illnesses or even replaced. Even the inspection process may need adjustment in its frequency, standards, or methods. For farmers, weather may be the assignable cause of a problem. Here, since we cannot change the weather, the change would be an adjustment to the current weather conditions or in the production process. For example, when applying chemicals, choosing a different pressure and nozzle may be needed to compensate for different weather conditions. Adjusting the livestock ration mix for different seasons during the year to maintain the daily gain at the desired level is another example.

A first example of a CE diagram is diagnosis of an earnings problem (Figure 19.3). If the return to labor and management is lower than desired, a farmer would sort through the potential causes until the current cause(s) are found and corrected. The major categories of causes are listed as workers, equipment, enterprises, weather, inspection, marketing, and resources. Some possible problem areas shown in the diagram are workers who have poor training, a wrong mix of enterprises, and being undercapitalized.

In another example, the potential causes of seeding rate and placement problems are drawn as a CE diagram (Figure 19.4). The planter is a tool that may cause problems due to improper calibration

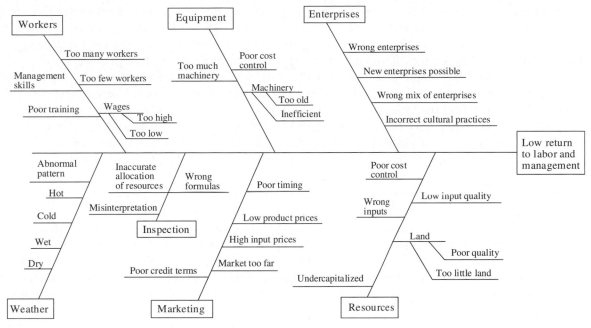

Figure 19.3 Cause-and-Effect Diagram to Diagnose an Earnings Problem

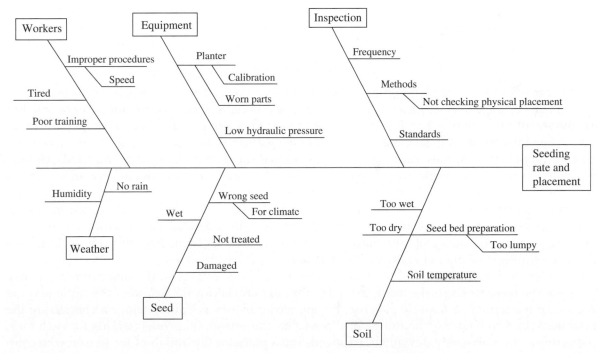

Figure 19.4 Cause-and-Effect Diagram for Seeding Rate and Placement Problems

or worn parts. The soil may be too wet or dry, or perhaps it was not prepared properly. The seed itself may be too wet or damaged; it may be the wrong seed. The workers may be poorly trained in operation of the planter or in inspection procedures. They may be tired and thus not watching the process properly. With some equipment and material, high humidity can cause problems.

At times, an obvious, major cause needs to be solved first. If no obvious causes can be seen quickly, potential causes can be ranked by frequency of occurrence, if known or inferred, or evaluated one by one to find the true cause of the problem (or opportunity for improvement). A check sheet, as described earlier, may be useful for choosing which causes should be addressed first.

While it may seem too obvious or too time consuming to draw a CE diagram when a farmer encounters a problem, the CE diagram is a useful concept to learn for three reasons. First, a CE diagram can be used to step back from an incorrect fixation on a potential solution, to review the symptoms of a problem, and to find the true problem elsewhere in the diagram. By having this CE model in their mental toolkit, farmers may not even have to draw the physical diagram.

The second reason for using a CE diagram is the increasing complexity of the systems that farmers manage. Complex systems require a better working knowledge of the systems to diagnose symptoms and problems. Farmers have to deal with several complex systems, even if specializing in just one or two products. For example, the concepts involved with sustainable agriculture are complex, and the concept of the CE diagram may help a farmer find alternatives to chemical practices.

The third reason for learning the concepts in a CE diagram is that it can be helpful in reducing variability. This is part of process improvement discussed in the next section. Reducing variability generally requires problem solving or changes in the design of the product or process itself; thus, a CE diagram can be extremely beneficial. Reducing variability can mean lower costs, higher quality, higher prices, or any combination of these improvements.

Fail-Safe Plans

A **fail-safe plan** is a process and product design tool that looks for ways to eliminate the possibility of problems or mistakes occurring. Fail-safe plans are especially useful for preliminary control, but can be useful for concurrent and feedback control as well. They are best used on those parts of an operation that are crucial to successful completion of the process and the business. One example is a task list that includes spaces for the worker's initials and the date the task was completed. Another example is a form that checks for completeness and consistency in the activities performed. However, fail-safe plans are not always lists on paper. Two non-paper examples are tying red flags on equipment parts that need repair, and designing the supply truck to be sure all needed materials, parts, and tools have a space and are included for the planting operation. A seed monitor mounted on the tractor is a fail-safe tool for planting because it provides an immediate signal if seeds are not being fed through the planter at the appropriate rate.

Consider the jobs that need to be done to care for feeder yearlings in the first hours after they arrive in the feedlot. The tasks that need to be done are crucial for the health of the cattle and the success of the farmer. A fail-safe plan for arriving feeder livestock would include a checklist of the tasks that need to be done, the timing of those tasks, the expectations or standards for each task, corrective actions needed if deviations are noted, and a place for the initials of the person who completed the task and when (Table 19.6).

Table 19.6 Illustrative Fail-Safe Plan for the First 36 Hours after Receiving Feeder Yearlings

Item to be Monitored	Method	Schedule	Control Standard	Corrective Actions, if Needed		Done by:		
						Initials	Day	Time
Initial health	Visual, auditorial	On arrival and at 8-hour intervals	Walking properly, active, no coughing	Call vet	On arrival 8 hours 16 hours 24 hours 36 hours			
Water	Visual, float	Before arrival, at arrival, and at 2-hour intervals	Fresh water is available, waterer operating properly	Repair and replace parts as needed to restore water supply	Before On arrival 2 hours 4 hours (and so on)			
Old hay only for first 24 hours	Visual	Before and on arrival	No feed in bunks except old hay	Clean bunks and replace with hay	Before On arrival			
Vet inspection	Visual	Within 6 hours	Healthy, active	Administer care as needed	Within 6 hours			
Feed silage	Visual	After 24 hours	Fresh silage	Feed if not done, repair equipment as needed	After 24 hours			

Trend or Run Charts

A **trend** or **run chart** is simply a running plot of measured quality characteristics: stored grain moisture, acres per day, pigs born per litter, milk per cow per day, bacteria or somatic cell counts, prices, basis movement, and so on. They are good, bad, or neutral characteristics that the manager has decided to watch for trends that may suggest the need for corrective actions. We are not deciding whether the process is in control; we are just watching how the process is working and seeing whether anything needs attention. Two examples of trend or run charts are stored grain temperatures (Figure 19.5) and market prices (Figure 19.6).

Trend charts are one source of data for data-based decisions rather than just trying to remember what something looked like before or how the measurement has changed over time. Trend charts can also be especially useful for a multi-person situation.

Experiments and Trials

Experiments and trials are used when the sources of problems are unknown or not obvious, or to test new ideas. Designing and using experiments in a controlled environment can help us understand how a process works; how, where, when, and why problems can occur; and how improvements could be made. On-farm experiments can be used to develop farm-specific data rather than using information from experiments that may have been done in different soil and climate environments. Farmers are using the tools of precision agriculture to take ideas from public and private tests and design experiments on new crops, new varieties, different fertilizer levels, for example, and then collect and interpret the data from their own farm.

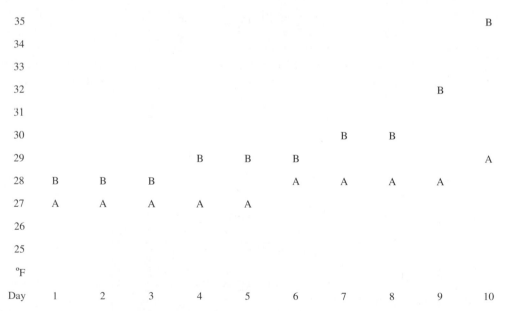

Figure 19.5   Trend Chart of the Temperature of Shelled Corn in Two Bins (A and B)

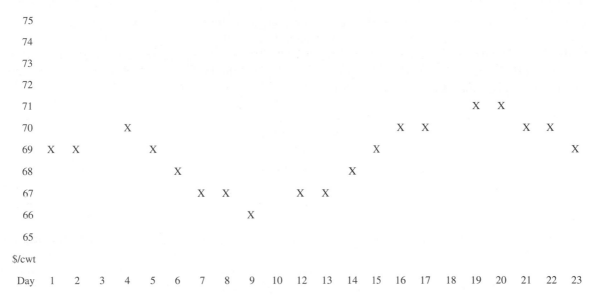

Figure 19.6 Trend Chart of the Price of Market Cattle

Scatter Diagram and Correlations

Scatter diagrams and correlations are statistical tools used to help decide whether events, things, and conditions are related. Data from experiments and check lists can be used to check correlations and potential cause-and-effect relationships. Simple plots of pairs of data can show whether one event or result is related to another event. For example, a feed mill could record feed moisture, ambient humidity levels, and feed flow problems and plot the conditions and events to see whether moisture levels are causing the flow problem. Correlation is a statistical measure of two events' interrelatedness.

These 11 tools for process improvement form the core of how a farmer can analyze his or her business, look for and find ways to improve how the farm operates, and ultimately improve the profitability and survivability of the farm. In today's competitive global market, continuous improvement is required, and these are the tools needed.

Concluding Comments

In this chapter we covered briefly many points, ideas, and tools for improving both a farm's products and processes. We considered the definitions of quality, the contributions of the quality pioneers, different management systems for quality, and several steps for improving quality on the farm.

These concepts and tools for quality management and control can be developed into a complete, detailed quality management system and described in a separate quality manual. For most farmers, incorporating the basic requirements and description of a quality management system into the farm's business plan would be sufficient for the farmer and stakeholders to understand what is planned and how the quality program will be implemented. By including these points in the business plan, the farmer will benefit by taking the time and attention to put the quality management system in writing. External stakeholders will be able to understand the farm's basic approach to quality; who has the responsibility for quality; who will be following quality procedures and when; how quality will be maintained and improved throughout the farm; and what records will be kept by whom to verify that procedures were followed.

Summary

- Quality management involves a holistic view of the entire farm and aims to develop a philosophy of improving quality in all functions.
- Quality control refers to controlling already selected processes for the products already chosen and designed.
- Process control consists of the procedures to monitor production for compliance with the original plan and development of corrective actions designed to bring the process back into compliance.
- Process improvement includes a set of tools used to understand the current process better and to look for potential ways to improve both the process and the product.
- Quality is meeting or exceeding customer requirements.
- The customer, not the producer, defines quality.
- Quality has many dimensions depending upon the customer. Price may be a determinant of quality for some customers.
- Product quality can be defined in four dimensions: quality of design, quality of conformance, the "abilities," and service after delivery.
- Process quality has external and internal dimensions. Externally, process quality ensures that the product will be made so that it conforms to what the customer wants. Internally, process quality is concerned with the efficiency of the production process.
- The costs of quality include control costs (prevention and appraisal) and failure costs (internal and external).
- The "quality pioneers" have provided new views on quality and many tools for improving quality.
- Total quality management (TQM) is a management philosophy that strives to involve everyone in a continual effort to improve quality and achieve customer satisfaction.
- TQM involves a set of steps and several ideas and concepts: continuous improvement, competitive benchmarking, employee empowerment, team approach, data-based decisions, knowledge of quality management tools, supplier quality, and quality at the source.
- The ISO 9000 family of standards is concerned with ensuring consistent application of a business' chosen production process.
- A process control system consists of three parts: standards, measurement, and corrective actions.
- Preliminary controls are anticipatory actions that take place before problems are detected.
- Concurrent control occurs during the production process as problems are detected.
- Feedback control evaluates production and makes recommended changes after production is finished.
- Process control systems can be developed by following a series of five steps.
- A fail-safe plan is a process and product design tool that looks for ways to eliminate the possibility of problems or mistakes occurring.

- Check sheets are forms that merely require a check to be made in the appropriate column or spot to show the frequency of certain events that relate to quality or process characteristics.
- A trend or run chart is a running plot of measured quality characteristics.
- Cause-and-effect (CE) diagrams show the factors that affect a desired result and are used to search for assignable causes of detected problems.
- Benchmarking is the process of measuring performance against the best in the industry.
- On-farm experiments and trials can be used to develop local data to help solve problems and improve processes.

Review Questions

1. What makes quality management different from quality control?
2. What is product quality? Who defines product quality?
3. For one of these products, describe how the farmer could define quality in terms of design, conformance, the abilities, and field service: (A) high oil corn for a food processor, (B) pork under contract for a specific processor, (C) apples for the fresh market, (D) horse boarding stable, (E) milk for a cheese processor, or (F) a product you are more interested in.
    a. Quality of design
    b. Quality of conformance
    c. Abilities: Name one item for each
        i. Availability
        ii. Reliability
        iii. Maintainability
    d. Field service
4. How is product quality different from process quality?
5. How can quality management be incorporated into the management of a farm?
6. What do you think are the three most important lessons from the "quality pioneers"?
7. How can a farmer use Deming's PDCA wheel?
8. How can a process map be useful in quality control and management?
9. What are the three types of process control?
10. What are the five steps in developing an enterprise control system?
11. Describe a corrective action.
12. Develop a concurrent process control system for a farm of your choice.
    a. Choose a type of farm (e.g., crop, dairy, horse) and a specific process on that farm (e.g., weed control, feeding).
       Type:
       Process:
    b. Describe how a farm of this type could use the ideas of preliminary, concurrent, and feedback control.
    c. Complete the following chart for a concurrent process control system for a specific process you chose. Specify 3 or 4 critical points within the process and complete the chart.

Critical Points	Type of Measurement	Sensor	Monitoring Schedule	Standards	Corrective Actions

13. How could a farmer benefit from benchmarking?
14. Develop a check sheet for potential sources of problems and errors for a specific operation on a farm of your choice.
15. What is a cause-and-effect (CE) diagram and how can it be used in farm management?
16. Develop a fail-safe plan that could be used by a farmer for a specific operation of your choice.
    a. Choose a type of farm (e.g., crop, dairy, horse) and a specific process on that farm (e.g., weed control, feeding) that would benefit from a fail-safe plan.
       Type:
       Process:
    b. Describe a fail-safe plan for making sure the process you chose is done correctly.
    c. If appropriate to the process you chose, describe what a kit or toolbox could look like to ensure that a worker would have everything he or she needed before starting the process.
    d. How can a farmer be sure that the tasks are done in this process?
17. During wheat harvest, Paula Whitney was concerned about the amount of grain coming out of the combine rather than going into the hopper. Over the past three days, Ms. Whitney has taken 10 measurements of how much wheat is coming out as waste and not going into the hopper. The measurements for the kernel loss are in kernels per square foot: 18, 21, 19, 23, 24, 21, 24, 27, 29, and 28.
    a. Prepare a trend chart that shows the kernel count measurements.

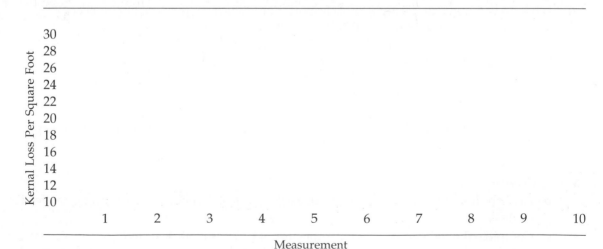

b. Based on what this trend chart shows, is the kernel count moving randomly or in a specific direction that is a cause for concern?

c. Draw a CE diagram to help Ms. Whitney identify different factors that affect the kernel count. Start with "kernel count" on the right. Group the factors into workers, materials or inputs, inspection, equipment or tools, and weather.

18.   Why would a farmer decide to perform an on-farm experiment or trial?

Further Reading

Brown, Mark. 2007. *Baldrige Award Winning Quality, 16 Edition: How to Interpret the Baldrige Criteria for Performance*. 16th ed. Milwaukee, Wisconsin: ASQ Quality Press.

Crosby, Philip B. 1979. *Quality Is Free*. New York: McGraw-Hill.

Deming, W. Edwards. 1986. *Out of the Crisis*. Cambridge, Massachusetts: MIT Press.

FDA, 2009. "Hazard Analysis and Critical Control Points (HACCP)." http://www.fda.gov/Food/FoodSafety/HazardAnalysisCriticalControlPointsHACCP/default.htm, accessed December 20, 2009.

Feigenbaum, A.V. 2004. *Total Quality Control*. 4th ed. New York: McGraw-Hill Professional.

Food Safety and Inspection Service (FSIS), USDA. 1999. "Guidebook for the Preparation of HACCP Plans." HACCP-1, September 1999.

Goldratt, E. M., and J. Cox. 2004. *The Goal: A Process of Ongoing Improvement*. 3rd rev. ed. Great Barrington, Massachusetts: North River Press.

Ishikawa, Kaoru. 1986. *Guide to Quality Control*. English ed. Tokyo: Asian Productivity Organization.

Juran, J. M. 2006. *Juran on Quality by Design: The New Steps for Planning Quality into Goods and Service*. Rev. ed. New York: Free Press.

Juran, J. M., and A. B. Godfrey, eds. 1999. *Juran's Quality Handbook*. 5th ed. New York: McGraw-Hill.

Mizuno, S., ed. 1988. *Management for Quality Improvement: The 7 New Tools*. Cambridge, Massachusetts: Productivity Press.

Ohno, Taiichi. 1988. *Toyota Production System*. Cambridge, Massachusetts: Productivity Press, 152 pp.

Schroeder, R. G. 2008. *Operations Management: Contemporary Concepts and Cases*. 4th edition. Boston: McGraw-Hill/Irwin, 528 pp. (especially Chapter 8, Managing Quality, and 9, Quality Control and Improvement).

Stevenson, W. J. 2002. *Operations Management*. 7th ed. Boston: McGraw-Hill/Irwin.

Swoboda, R. 2001. (February). "ISO 9002: What can it do for you?" *Wallaces Farmer*, 12–13.

20

Investment Analysis

In this chapter:

- Investment analysis (also known as capital budgeting)
- Investment examples
- Investment under uncertainty

Machinery, breeding livestock, buildings, land, and other capital assets are just as critical to farming as are seed, feed, and labor, but they are acquired, controlled, and used in different ways. Inputs, such as seed, fertilizer, and feed, are purchased and used up in one production cycle. They cannot be recovered. Labor and other services are hired or "rented" for a certain time period only (per hour, per job, or per year, for instance). In contrast, capital assets (machinery, breeding livestock, buildings, and land) can be purchased, leased, or rented for more than one production cycle. They are not used up completely during that time. Thus, the decision to use and how to use capital assets is more complicated than the decision to use other inputs. An interesting example of how investment analysis is used to determine the best ways to manage dairy cows (a multi-year asset) is called "Ecownomics" (Example 20.1).

Example 20.1. "Ecownomics"

"Ecownomics," as *The Economist* magazine calls it, is the analysis of the value of dairy cows as affected by milk price, milk production, disease, general health, and other factors on the farm. The author points out that the poem, "Farmer in the Dell," doesn't include a line about estimating the net present value of a dairy cow, but that calculation can show a farmer the value of maintaining a cow in good health and feeding her adequately. "'Cows have a built-in health-care system. It's very difficult to get high yields out of a cow if you don't take care of her. And perhaps it is easier to take care of her if you know exactly what it will cost you if you do not."

So studying the financial calculations of net present value is just as important a part of good dairying as knowing the proper nutrition for the "annuities—sorry, the cows—themselves."

Source: "Ecownomics: A Veterinarian's Case for Efficient Milk Production," *The Economist*, January 5, 2010, accessed on January 31, 2010, at http://www.economist.com/business-education/displayStory.cfm?story_id=15207866.

In this chapter, the decision to use or acquire capital assets such as machinery and buildings is analyzed first as an ownership question, which is as an investment or capital budgeting problem. Then the investment or ownership option is compared with leasing and renting. In the rest of the chapter, the process of investment analysis or capital budgeting is explained and shown through examples. Two machinery investment examples are presented: investing in a combine for custom work and leasing versus owning a tractor. An investment in a cattle feedlot is analyzed as an example. Planting a perennial crop, grapes in this example, is also analyzed. The chapter ends with a brief discussion of how to adjust investment analysis to account for risk and uncertainty.

Investment Analysis (Capital Budgeting)

The decision to invest in machinery, breeding livestock, buildings, land, and other capital assets requires an analysis process that is different from that used to buy seed, fertilizer, feed, and other operating inputs. If we buy seed or feed, we usually expect to receive the results of that purchase within a few months; we may do some budgeting to project whether the purchase will be worthwhile, but the budgeting is a simple, straightforward process. A capital asset, however, is bought once, and the income from that asset occurs for several years (in perpetuity for land). To decide whether we want to buy the capital asset, we make an *investment analysis*, or, in other words, we do *capital budgeting*. Both terms refer to the same process of determining whether an asset is a profitable or wise investment. Investment analysis involves multi-year budgeting, discounting of future benefits and costs to estimate a net present value of those future benefits and costs, and comparing the net present value with the initial investment in the asset.

Investment analysis can be described as a series of six steps.

1. Identify investment alternatives.

   At this initial point, all reasonable or seemingly reasonable alternatives are selected for an initial consideration. A first check is a determination of whether the potential investments fit with the strategy identified and described in the business plan. (See Chapters 3, 7, 8 and 9.) Some alternatives are dropped from consideration immediately for strategic, personal, and a host of other reasons. Some alternatives are rejected after a quick, "back of the envelope" calculation shows they are very likely not profitable and thus not worth considering further. Depending on the manager and the situation, only one alternative or just a very few alternatives may be analyzed in depth. Other alternatives that survived the first scrutiny may be kept as backups in case the first choices are ultimately rejected.

2. Estimate receipts and costs in each year.

   The initial investment needs to be calculated plus the revenues and expenses in each year of the planning horizon. The terminal or salvage value at the end of the asset's useful life (or analysis period) is also needed. The initial investment may be simply the purchase price for the machine or animal, or the construction costs for a building. The initial investment for a perennial crop may be followed by several years of costs for establishment without any receipts until production starts. Revenue and expenses for each year are estimated essentially as an enterprise budget for each year. Occasionally, as when buying bare land, the expected revenue and expenses may be the same in each year. With other investments, such as buildings, machines, or fruit trees, for example, the annual revenue and expenses (and the potential tax impacts) will change over time.

The planning horizon also needs to be chosen. This limits the number of years used in the investment analysis. Often the planning horizon is the useful life of the machine, animal, or building. Other assets, such as vines, trees, and/or improvements to land, can be productive for many years. As we will see in this chapter, the discounting of future values means that net revenue very far into the future may not have a noticeable impact on an investment decision. For these assets, the planning horizon will be the number of years needed to make a decision in the first year.

3. Evaluate economic profitability.

An investment is economically profitable if it returns a reasonable profit on the initial investment. The common methods for ranking alternative investments are the simple rate of return, payback period, net present value, and internal rate of return (including the modified rate of return). Although the payback period is not a true measure of economic profitability, it is included in this list because it is very commonly used to rank alternative investments.

4. Evaluate financial feasibility.

Financial feasibility is the investment's own ability to generate sufficient cash flow to cover any debt incurred to make the investment. An investment may be economically profitable but still be financially infeasible because of cash flow problems. For example, a lender may require a very quick payback of a loan, but the asset is expected to last longer, so the asset cannot pay its own loan back, but future net revenue makes it a profitable investment. Also, planting young apple trees may require outside capital during their development years before they start bearing fruit. Similarly, building a new livestock facility may require outside financing until the animals, equipment, and people bring the operation into the desired ranges of efficiency and productivity.

5. Conduct a sensitivity analysis.

After the initial determination of economic profitability and financial feasibility, the evaluation should be done again after changing the initial set of assumptions about productivity, prices, costs, interest rates, and other variables. This sensitivity or scenario analysis should determine the importance of different variables that affect the receipts and costs, for example. Both profitability and feasibility should be reevaluated with these new assumptions.

6. Select investment(s).

As with any managerial decision, the information from investment analysis and capital budgeting needs to be evaluated, along with any other pertinent information, and a choice made. If investment alternatives such as the stock market were not considered earlier, they should be evaluated at this point. Although this was done when they were initially selected for analysis, the alternatives again need to be compared with the chosen business strategy. As the alternatives were examined and evaluated more closely, new information may have been found that may change the evaluation of how well one alternative fits the chosen strategy compared with alternatives.

Implementation of the investment choice will vary with the magnitude or importance of the investment. The investment in a new, improved tractor may be viewed as an important but relatively minor investment left to the crop and livestock production aspects of the business. In contrast, the decision to build a new, larger dairy facility will likely be such a major, complex investment that all stakeholders need to be involved and the processes for strategy execution and control (described in Chapter 10) need to be used to ensure proper implementation of the investment.

Choosing the Discount Rate

The discount rate has a large impact on investment analysis and should be chosen carefully. In this text, investments are evaluated using an after-tax return to assets, so the discount rate needs to reflect that choice.[1]

The appropriate discount rate for after-tax return to assets is the weighted average of the cost of debt and equity:

$$i_a = (i_d)(1 - t)(D/A) + (i_e)(E/A)$$

where i_a is the weighted average cost of capital, i_d is the interest rate on debt, t is the income tax rate, D/A is the debt to asset ratio, i_e is the cost of equity capital, and E/A is the equity to asset ratio. If the farm has more than one loan, the interest rate on debt should be the weighted average of the loans. For example, if the farm has two loans, $200,000 at 8% and $100,000 at 9%, the weighted cost of debt is 8 * (200,000/300,000) + 9 * (100,000/300,000) or 8.3%. The cost of equity is the opportunity cost of equity—that is, the highest rate of return it could be earning in another investment with similar risk. To continue the example, suppose the best alternative use of equity capital would provide a return of 15%; then the cost of equity is 15%. Also, suppose the tax rate is 30%, the debt to asset ratio is 0.40, and the equity to asset ratio is 0.60. The average weighted cost of capital is thus:

$$i_a = (0.083)(1 - 0.3)(0.4) + (0.15)(0.6) = 0.10$$

In this example, the average weighted cost of capital is 10.0%.

Measuring Economic Profitability

Economic profitability can be measured in five ways: (1) simple rate of return, (2) payback period, (3) net present value (NPV), (4) internal rate of return (IRR), and (5) modified rate of return (MIRR). **Payback period** is the number of years required to recover the initial cost of the investment. It can be estimated with either discounted or undiscounted future after-tax net returns. **Net present value (NPV)** is the sum of the present values of future after-tax net cash flows minus the initial investment. **Internal rate of return (IRR)** is the discount rate that sets the net present value of the investment to zero. The **modified internal rate of return (MIRR)** corrects for an assumption used in the calculation of IRR (as will be explained later in this section).

For an example of calculating these measures, let us consider an investment with an initial outlay of $50,000. For now, we will assume no tax obligation, no risk, no inflation, and no terminal or salvage value. This simple asset has a life of five years, with the following estimates of annual net revenue:

Year	Net Revenue ($)
1	8,000
2	12,000
3	17,000
4	22,000
5	27,000

---

[1] Investments can also be analyzed in terms of their return to equity, but that approach is not discussed here. See Barry et al. (2000) for this method.

Simple Rate of Return (SRR).   The **simple rate of return** is the average annual net return divided by either the initial investment or the average investment.

$$\text{SRR} = \frac{\text{average annual net return}}{\text{initial or average investment}}$$

The average annual net return is the sum of the net return from each year of the planning horizon divided by the number of years. In our simple example, the sum of the net returns is $86,000 over the five years, and after subtracting $50,000 for depreciation in this example, the average annual net return is $7,200 (= 36,000/5). The average investment is the initial investment plus any terminal or salvage value divided by 2. For our example, which has no terminal value, the average investment is $25,000 (= (50,000 + 0)/2). The SRR using the initial investment is 14.4% (= 7,200/50,000 * 100%). The SRR using the average investment is 28.8% (= 7,200/25,000 * 100%).

Although SRR is simple, as its name says, it does have problems and may cause incorrect decisions. The biggest problem is its ignorance of the timing of cash flow. If a second investment had the same net revenue estimates as our example, but in reverse order (that is, $27,000 in year 1 and $8,000 in year 5), SRR would be the same for each investment so SRR says there is no difference in the two examples. However, the second example would be preferred if we consider the opportunity to receive the higher revenues earlier in the life of the investment.

SRR is shown and explained here only because it is often used and referred to in everyday discussions. But SRR is not recommended as the measure to use for choosing investments.

Payback period.   The payback period is the number of years required to recover the initial cost of the investment. It is simple to calculate and has a high emphasis on liquidity. The payback period is not a measure of economic profitability but is explained here due to its frequent usage for comparing investments.

Investments are chosen if the payback period is less than or equal to some established maximum. A maximum of four or five years is very common in general business. If investment funds are limited, investments are chosen according to the shortest payback periods.

The payback period is calculated in the following steps.

1. Sum the annual net cash flows until the cumulative sum will exceed the initial outlay if the next year's net cash flow is added to the sum. The net cash flows can be either undiscounted or discounted, with the most common method using undiscounted values.
2. Estimate the portion of the next period's net cash flow necessary to recover the initial investment exactly.
3. The payback period is the number of years of net cash flow needed to pay back the initial investment—that is, the number of years found in step 1 and the fraction of a year estimated in step 2.

For our simple example, described above, the sum of the undiscounted net revenue in the first three years totals, $37,000 (Table 20.1). To recoup the initial investment of $50,000, only $13,000 of the next year's undiscounted net revenue of $22,000 is needed. Thus, the

$$\text{undiscounted payback period} = 3 + 13,000/22,000 = 3.6 \text{ years}$$

The undiscounted payback period is the most common expression of payback period and is being used if a person just says "payback period." It has two major deficiencies, however. First, it ignores

Table 20.1 Estimation of Discounted and Undiscounted Payback Periods

Year	Future Value (FV) of the Undiscounted Net Revenue	Accumulated Sum of Undiscounted FV	Present Value (PV) of FV (at i = .08)	Accumulated Sum of PV
1	8,000	8,000	7,407	7,407
2	12,000	20,000	7,428	17,695
3	17,000	37,000	13,495	31,190
4	22,000	$13,000 of the $22,000 is needed to pay back the initial $50,000	16,171	47,361
5	27,000		18,376	$2,639 of the $18,376 is needed to pay back the initial $50,000

any revenue after the initial investment is recovered. For example, while one investment might take longer to pay back the initial amount than a second investment, the second investment would seem to be preferred. However, the first investment may continue to produce significant revenue after the initial investment is paid back, whereas the revenue from the second investment may decline. Thus, the first investment may be better, but evaluating by the payback period alone would miss that extra revenue. The second deficiency of the undiscounted payback period is that it ignores the time value of money. Two investments with different patterns of revenue over time may be incorrectly ranked using only the undiscounted payback period.

The second deficiency of the payback period can be overcome by using discounted net returns. In this alternative estimation of the payback period, the future net returns are discounted back to a present value and the length of time required to pay back the initial investment is estimated using the present values of the future revenues. The discounted payback period will always be longer than the undiscounted payback period because the discounted future returns are used and they are smaller because they are discounted. Using a discount rate of 8% in the example, the

$$\text{discounted payback period} = 4 + 2{,}639/18{,}376 = 4.1 \text{ years}$$

Even though the discounted payback period does account for the time value of money, it still has the deficiency of ignoring net revenue after the initial investment is paid back.

Net Present Value (NPV). The net present value (NPV) is the sum of the present values of future net cash flows minus the initial investment. The net present value measure accurately considers the timing of cash flows. It is the preferred measure of economic profitability for investment decisions. With the net present value measure of investment profitability, the criterion is to accept any investment if NPV > 0 when it is evaluated at the weighted cost of capital. If capital is limited, the choice is made by comparing different combinations of potential investments for the highest total NPV. Mathematically,

$$\text{NPV} = \sum_{t=0}^{n} [1/(1+r)^t] Y_t = Y_0 + Y_1 [1/(1+r)^1] + \ldots Y_n [1/(1+r)^n]$$

where NPV = net present value, r = the discount rate, and Y_t = estimated net revenue in period t. The initial investment can be either included as Y_0 (as a negative amount) in the formula above or, as shown in the table below, subtracted explicitly from the sum of present values.

Table 20.2 Estimation of Net Present Value

Year	Net Revenue	Discount Factor*	Present Value
1	8,000	0.9259	7,407
2	12,000	0.8573	10,288
3	17,000	0.7938	13,495
4	22,000	0.7350	16,171
5	26,000	0.6806	17,695
	Sum of the present values of the net revenues		65,056
	Minus the initial investment of		−50,000
	Net present value (NPV) at 8%		15,056

*The discount factors are taken from the 8% column in Appendix Table II.

In the example, with a discount rate of 8%, the present value of the net revenues is $65,056 (Table 20.2). After the initial investment of $50,000 is subtracted, the net present value is $15,056.

Internal Rate of Return (IRR).   The internal rate of return (IRR) is the discount rate that sets the net present value of the investment to zero.

$$IRR = r^*, \text{where NPV} = \sum_{t=0}^{n} Y_t[1/(1+r^*)^t] = 0$$

With IRR, the decision criterion is to make any investment with an IRR greater than the cost of capital for the farm. For example, suppose a farm's weighted cost of borrowed and equity capital is 12%; the decision criterion is that all investments with an IRR greater than 12% should be made. If capital is limited, the IRR provides a quick measure of which investments provide the best relative returns. The NPV and IRR measures should give the same order in the ranking of investments.

IRR can be estimated in three ways. First, it can be done by trial and error—that is, calculating and recalculating the NPV at different discount rates until the one is found for which NPV = 0. The second method is graphical. Two estimates of NPV at different discount rates are placed on a graph and a line drawn through them and across the discount rate axis. For more accurate estimations of IRR, one estimate of the NPV should be positive and one negative. The point at which the line crosses the discount rate axis is where the NPV = 0 and is, thus, the IRR. The third method is to use a function on a computer spreadsheet or financial calculator.

For the investment example, NPV is calculated for a few discount rates between 8% and 18% (Table 20.3). From the results of this trial-and-error approach, we estimate that the IRR is approximately 17% since the NPV is –183 at 17%.

For IRR to be estimated graphically, NPV is placed on the vertical axis and r on the horizontal axis as shown in Figure 20.1. Two pairs of r and NPV are plotted—for example, (0.16 and 1,235) and (0.18 and –1,543)—and a line is drawn through the horizontal axis connecting these pairs. In the example

Table 20.3 Estimated NPV of the Example Investment at Various Discount Rates

Discount rate (r):	8%	12%	16%	17%	18%
Estimated NPV:	15,056	7,544	1,235	−183	−1,543

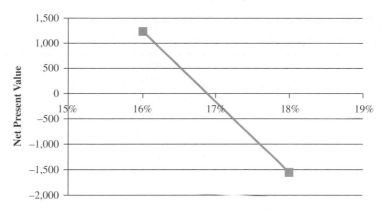

Figure 20.1 Graphical Estimation of IRR

investment, 16% and 18% are chosen because they are close but not too close and provide a positive NPV and a negative NPV and, thus, a more accurate slope for the line. The IRR is the point where the line crosses the horizontal axis since NPV is zero at that point. In the example graph, the line crosses at approximately r = 17% so the IRR is approximately 17%.

IRR can also be calculated using a hand calculator or a spreadsheet program. These typically use a trial-and-error approach by starting at a low discount rate and gradually increasing the discount rate until NPV is equal to zero. Using a spreadsheet formula, IRR is estimated to be 16.9%.

Modified Internal Rate of Return (MIRR). The IRR is the preferred measure for many people. It is an easy to understand rate of return that can be used to compare alternative investments. However, buried in its calculations is the potentially incorrect assumption that the earnings from an investment can be reinvested and earn the same rate of return as the original investment. The NPV does not have this problem because it uses the cost of capital as the rate of return for investment earnings. The NPV assumption is more realistic, so NPV is perceived as a more accurate measure than IRR. However, people still find a rate of return easier to understand and use than the NPV.

To overcome the problematic assumption on the rate of return on earnings and still have a rate of return measure to use, a modified internal rate of return (MIRR) was developed (McDaniel, McCarty, and Jessell, 1988). Following Barry et al. (2000), MIRR is calculated in three steps. First, the present value of all negative cash outflows (PV_{CO}) is estimated using the cost of capital as the discount rate. The initial investment (INV) is a negative cash outflow, and negative cash outflows may occur in other years as well during the establishment years for a perennial crop, for example. The present value of negative cash flows (PV_{CO}) is calculated using the following equation:

$$PV_{CO} = -INV + \sum_{n=0}^{N} \frac{-P_n}{(1+i)^n}$$

where P_n is the cash flow in period n, N is the number of periods, and i is the cost of capital.

In the second step, the cost of capital is used as the compounding rate to find the future value (FV_{CI}) of all positive or zero cash inflows:

$$FV_{CI} = \sum_{n=0}^{N} P_n(1+i)^{N-n}$$

In the third step, we solve for the discount rate (i_m) that equates the present value of the cash outflows (PV_{CO}) to the future value of the cash inflows (FV_{CI}). That is, we solve for i_m in the following equation:

$$PV_{CO} = \frac{FV_{CI}}{(1 + i_m)^N}$$

or

$$i_m = \left(\frac{FV_{CI}}{PV_{CO}}\right)^{1/N} - 1$$

The i_m is the estimate of MIRR.

In our simple example, the only negative cash outflow is the initial investment of $50,000, so:

$$PV_{CO} = 50,000$$

Using a cost of capital of 5%, the future value of the five cash inflows is:

$$FV_{CI} = 8,000(1.05)^4 + 12,000(1.05)^3 + 17,000(1.05)^2 + 22,000(1.05) + 26,000$$
$$= 91,458$$

MIRR is found by solving the following for i_m:

$$50,000 = \frac{91,458}{(1 + i_m)^5}$$

or

$$MIRR = i_m = \left(\frac{91,458}{50,000}\right)^{1/5} - 1 = 0.128 \text{ or } 12.8\%$$

For an example of comparing investments and to see the impact of a terminal value, suppose a farmer had $20,000 to invest in two alternatives: A and B. Investment A is estimated to provide a net cash return of $6,000 per year for 5 years but to have no salvage or terminal value. Investment B is estimated to provide $5,000 per year for 5 years and to have a terminal value of $8,000 at the end of the fifth year. (All values are received at the end of the year.)

Using the methods just described, the NPV of investment A is estimated to be $3,956, MIRR to be 10.6%, IRR to be 15.2%, the undiscounted payback period to be 3.3 years, and the discounted payback period to be 4.0 years (Table 20.4). For investment B, the NPV is estimated to be $5,409, MIRR to be 12.2%, IRR to be 16.3%, the undiscounted payback period to be 4.0 years, and the discounted payback period to be 5.0 years (Table 20.5).

This investment analysis shows that investment B is preferred when using the measures of NPV, MIRR, and IRR since they are higher for B compared with A. The higher annual net cash revenues for A do provide a shorter payback period for A. However, since NPV, MIRR, and IRR are considered better measures, investment B is still preferred.

In this section, we looked at five different measures for evaluating economic profitability: SRR, payback period, NPV, IRR, and MIRR. SRR and payback period pose significant problems because they do not account for the timing of cash flows, so they should not be used as the sole measures. MIRR corrects one assumption of IRR. However, when comparing different-size investments, MIRR and NPV may provide different rankings. NPV is the better indicator of the impact on the wealth of the farm and is recommended as the primary measure to use for ranking.

Table 20.4   Investment Analysis of Example Investment A

Year	Net Cash Revenues	PVF at 8%	Present Value of Net Cash Revenues	Accumulated Undiscounted Net Cash Revenues	Accumulated Present Value of Net Cash Revenues
1	6,000	0.9259	5,556	6,000	5,556
2	6,000	0.8573	5,144	12,000	10,700
3	6,000	0.7938	4,763	18,000	15,463
4	6,000	0.7350	4,410	24,000	19,873
5 + SV*	6,000	0.6806	4,083	30,000	23,956

Sum of present value of net cash revenue	23,956
Minus the initial cost (year 0)	−20,000
Net present value	3,956
Modified internal rate of return	10.6%
Internal rate of return	15.2%
Undiscounted payback period	3.3 years
Discounted payback period	4.0 years

*SV = salvage value of 0 for investment A.

Table 20.5   Investment Analysis of Example Investment B

Year	Net Cash Revenues	PVF at 8%	Present Value of Net Cash Revenues	Accumulated Undiscounted Net Cash Revenues	Accumulated Present Value of Net Cash Revenues
1	5,000	0.9259	4,630	5,000	4,630
2	5,000	0.8573	4,287	10,000	8,916
3	5,000	0.7938	3,969	15,000	12,885
4	5,000	0.7350	3,675	20,000	16,561
5 + SV*	13,000	0.6806	8,848	25,000	25,409

Sum of present value of net cash revenue	25,409
Minus the initial cost (year 0)	−20,000
Net present value	5,409
Modified internal rate of return	12.2%
Internal rate of return	16.3%
Undiscounted payback period	4.0 years
Discounted payback period	5 years**

*SV = salvage value of $8,000 for investment B.
**The discounted payback period is set at an even 5 years since the discounted salvage value is needed to reach $20,000 and that is not received until the end of year 5.

Investment Examples

In this section, we look at several investment examples to show how capital budgeting tools can be used to answer different types of questions. The examples are more complex, with the addition of tax considerations in the examples of a combine purchase, the choice between buying or leasing a tractor, building a new cattle feedlot, and establishing a vineyard.

Combine Investment

Suppose a farmer is considering the purchase of a combine to use for custom work. The initial purchase price of the combine is $329,000: $233,000 for the combine power unit, $68,000 for the 12-row, 30" corn head, and $28,000 for the soybean head. The combine is expected to last 8 years with a salvage value of $79,289 after 8 years. Based on expected usage of 1,485 acres of soybeans and 1,527 acres of corn, the direct operating costs per acre are estimated to be $13.44 for soybeans and $13.67 for corn. Labor expenses per acre are estimated to be $2.54 for soybeans and $2.47 for corn. By estimating the housing and insurance as 3% of the initial purchase price, total costs per acre (excluding depreciation and interest costs) are $19.27 for soybeans and $19.43 for corn. These costs are expected to increase at the rate of 2% per year.

Since he has done custom work for several years, this farmer thinks he could sign enough contracts to harvest 3,000 acres (1,500 each of corn and soybeans) starting in the first year. The local custom harvest market also provides $35 per acre for custom harvesting soybeans and $37 for corn. These custom rates are expected to increase at the rate of 2% per year. He has chosen a discount rate of 8%. By including a charge of $9 per hour for his labor, the annual net cash flow can be viewed as the return to the investment in the combine and not as a mixture of return to labor and investment.

For this example, U.S. tax laws are used to estimate the tax impact on the value of the investment. The marginal tax rate is set at 28%; that is, the farmer already has enough income so any income from this investment will be taxed at 28%. He has chosen to use the $17,500 left of his expensing option for this combine. The rest of the purchase price will be depreciated in the United States using the accelerated cost recovery system (ACRS) for a seven-year property with beginning and ending half-year convention. The tax due in each year is 28% of cash income minus cash expense minus the ACRS depreciation for that year. The expensing option is subtracted in the first year only. As can be seen in the results, depreciation and expenses are higher than income in the first two years, so the tax impact is negative. That is, the loss from custom harvesting in the first two years decreases the farmer's tax bill. In subsequent years, income is positive and taxes must be paid.

Using this information and these numbers, the annual net cash flow and its present value are estimated (Table 20.6). Cash income is the number of acres harvested multiplied by the appropriate custom rate, increased by 2% each year. Cash expense is the number of acres harvested multiplied by the appropriate total operating cost, increased by 2% each year. Taxes are calculated by subtracting cash expenses and depreciation from cash income and then multiplying by the marginal tax rate, 28%. The annual net cash flow (ANCF) is the cash income minus the cash expense and taxes plus the salvage value. The present value factor (pvf) is based on the discount rate of 8%. The present value of ANCF is the multiple of ANCF and pvf.

Based on these calculations, the investment in a combine for custom work has a net present value (NPV) of $2,689 at 8%, the modified internal rate of return (MIRR) is 6.8%, and the internal rate of return (IRR) of 8.2%. The payback periods are 6.5 years (undiscounted) and 8.0 years when the cash flow is discounted.

This investment is profitable, but is it financially feasible? Suppose the farmer could obtain a loan for 75% of the purchase price (that is, a loan of $246,750) and the bank offered loan terms of 8% for 5 years. Using the amortization formula, the annual payment is calculated to be $61,800, which is greater than the

Table 20.6 Present Value Analysis of a Combine Purchase

Year	Cash Income	Cash Expense	Taxes	Estimated Salvage Value	Annual Net Cash Flow (ANCF)	Present Value Factor	Present Value of ANCF
1	108,000	58,050	−255		50,205	0.9259	46,486
2	110,160	59,211	−2,419		53,368	0.8573	45,755
3	112,363	60,395	1,442		50,526	0.7938	40,109
4	114,610	61,603	4,158		48,850	0.7350	35,906
5	116,903	62,835	4,454		49,613	0.6806	33,766
6	119,241	64,092	4,757		50,392	0.6302	31,755
7	121,626	65,374	5,066		51,186	0.5835	29,866
8	124,058	66,681	10,719	79,289	125,947	0.5403	68,045

Sum of present value of annual net cash flows − 331,689

Initial cost of investment = 329,000

INVESTMENT CRITERIA:

Net present value of investment = NPV = 2,689

Modified internal rate of return = MIRR = 6.8%

Internal rate of return = IRR = 8.2%

Payback period (undiscounted) = 6.5 years

Discounted payback period = 8.0 years

ANCF in any of the first 5 years. Before declaring the investment not financially feasible, however, the tax savings due to the deductibility of the interest payments needs to be accounted for.

The tax savings are calculated from this farmer's marginal tax rate and the interest portion of each year's loan payment. The interest portion is calculated from the loan balance at the beginning of the year. After adjusting the loan payment to the after-tax payment, we can see that these loan terms (8% and 5 years) result in a deficit in all of the first 5 years (Table 20.7). The combine cannot pay for itself. If the farmer could negotiate a loan length of just one more year to 6 years, the combine purchase would be financially feasible even if the interest rate stayed at 9%. Another option is for the farmer to

Table 20.7 Financial Feasibility of the Combine Purchase

Year	Annual Net Cash Flow (ANCF)	Loan Payment	Interest Payment	Principal Payment	Tax savings from Interest Deductibility	After-Tax Payment Schedule	Surplus (+) or Deficit (-)
1	50,205	61,800	19,740	42,060	5,527	56,273	−6,068
2	53,368	61,800	16,375	45,425	4,585	57,215	−3,847
3	50,526	61,800	12,741	49,059	3,568	58,233	−7,706
4	48,850	61,800	8,816	52,984	2,469	59,332	−10,482
5	49,613	61,800	4,578	57,222	1,282	60,518	−10,905
6	50,392				0	0	50,392
7	51,186				0	0	51,186
8	125,947				0	0	125,947

leave the combine financing as originally planned and fund the combine purchase from other sources of capital. This latter option would be appropriate if the alternative uses of that capital cannot earn a better rate of return than the IRR of the combine investment, which is 8.2% in this example.

Investment analysis is needed to evaluate the investment in multi-year energy crops as evaluated for Germany (Example 20.2).

Example 20.2. Investing in Woody Energy Crops in Germany

One alternative energy crop often discussed is growing woody biomass. Since this involves a multi-year commitment of the land, the decision involves investment analysis to account for the time value of money. A recent study in Germany evaluated the alternative of short rotation coppice (SRC). (A coppice is a small grove or thicket of small trees or shrubs.) The German alternative used willow and poplar cultivars and compared profitability with a typical crop rotation.

Estimates of the net present value (NPV) for the crop rotation and the SRC varied widely under different price assumptions. The study found the NPV for SRC could be equal to or higher than the NPV for the crop rotation, but high market prices caused the NPV to be considerably higher for the crop rotation. The economic breakeven life for the SRC was estimated to be 8 years. If market prices rise sufficiently during these 8 years and cause the crop rotation to be more profitable, the SRC would tie the land up in a less profitable option. Thus, the authors conclude, while there are environmental reasons to plant an SRC, the economic considerations and uncertainties require a close evaluation before final planting decisions are made.

Source: H. Zeller, A. M. Häring, and N. Utke, "Investing in Short Rotation Coppice—Alternative Energy Crop or an Albatross around the Neck?" Peer-reviewed paper at the 17th International Farm Management Congress, Illinois State University, Bloomington/Normal, Illinois, U.S., July 19–24, 2009, accessed on February 1, 2010, at http://www.ifmaonline.org/pdf/congress/09_Zeller_etal.pdf.

Machinery Purchase versus Lease

Suppose a farmer has a choice of either purchasing or leasing a tractor. If purchased, the tractor would cost $71,000; would have annual cash operating expenses of $9,000; and would have a salvage value of $23,000 after 8 years. The terms of the loan were 20% down, 7% interest rate, 5 years, and one payment per year. Leasing would require an initial payment of $10,000, lease payments of $11,500 at the end of each year (including the first year), and the same operating expenses of $9,000 per year. The leased tractor has no terminal value for the farmer. For this farmer, let us say the marginal tax rate is 28%.

For this problem, the question is which alternative has the lowest cost. The farmer has already determined that a tractor is needed and that the same level of tractor services can be found by either purchasing or leasing; neither alternative will increase production or sales. Thus, the question is simplified to which alternative provides the lowest cost for the same tractor services. Including production and sales would be redundant and only add complexity in this problem. (In the previous example, the combine purchase was being considered to create income; thus, custom work income had to be included in the analysis.)

The information above is used to calculate the present value of the after-tax costs over the life of the tractor for purchasing and for leasing. The cash outlay is the initial payment (in year 0 for calculation purposes) and the costs associated with either owning or leasing the tractor in years 1 through

8. Tax benefits come from being able to deduct those expenses and thus decrease taxable income. For this problem, 7% is the cost of capital for this farmer and is used as the discount rate.

In this example, purchasing is the cheaper option. The total present value of the after-tax costs of purchasing the tractor are estimated to be $83,825 over the 8 years and the total present value of the after-tax costs of leasing are estimated to be $95,336 (Tables 20.8 and 20.9).

Although estimating the present value of the after-tax cash outlay for purchasing versus leasing provides crucial information for the decision, a farmer will likely consider the advantages and disadvantages of each option before a final decision is made. The impact of adding debt to the balance sheet needs to be considered and whether the lenders are willing to supply that credit. The terminal or salvage of the tractor after 8 years may be an advantage of purchasing, but how certain is that value? Also, that tractor will be 8 years old with 8-year-old technology and 8 years of use. If major repairs are not incurred during that time, might they occur shortly? The hours of use allowed in the lease contract need to be compared to the estimated actual hours of use and how the actual may vary and potentially affect any penalties for greater usage.

Table 20.8 Present Value of the Costs of Purchasing a Tractor

Year	Cash Outlay	Salvage Value	Tax Savings	After-Tax Cash Outlay	PVF at 7.0%	PV of After-Tax Cash Outlay
0	$14,200		$4,200	$10,000	1.0000	$10,000
1	22,853		5,313	17,540	0.9346	16,393
2	22,853		6,439	16,414	0.8734	14,336
3	22,853		5,589	17,264	0.8163	14,092
4	22,853		4,932	17,921	0.7629	13,672
5	22,853		4,695	18,158	0.7130	12,947
6	9,000		4,441	4,559	0.6663	3,038
7	9,000		4,441	4,559	0.6227	2,839
8	9,000	16,000	−999	−6,001	0.5820	−3,493
Present value of the after-tax cash outlay for purchasing						$83,825

Table 20.9 Present Value of the Costs of Leasing a Tractor

Year	Cash Outlay	Salvage Value	Tax Savings	After-Tax Cash Outlay	PVF at 7.0%	PV of After-Tax Cash Outlay
0	$10,000		$2,800	$7,200	1.0000	$7,200
1	20,500		5,740	14,760	0.9346	13,794
2	20,500		5,740	14,760	0.8734	12,892
3	20,500		5,740	14,760	0.8163	12,049
4	20,500		5,740	14,760	0.7629	11,260
5	20,500		5,740	14,760	0.7130	10,524
6	20,500		5,740	14,760	0.6663	9,835
7	20,500		5,740	14,760	0.6227	9,192
8	20,500	0	5,740	14,760	0.5820	8,590
Present value of the after-tax cash outlay for leasing						$95,336

Building a New Cattle Feedlot

For a livestock example and as a base for the uncertainty analysis at the end of this chapter, consider a young person who wants to start farming on the home farm and has proposed the idea of building a new cattle feedlot and building. After some research, she finds the low cost bid for the building and site is $265,000 with a capacity of 300 head. The building and equipment are assumed to last for 16 years with no salvage value at that time. For her initial investment analysis, she uses a market price of $85 per cwt for the market weight cattle. By starting with 330 young feeders and selling in groups as the cattle reach market weight, she estimates she could sell 1,520 lb per space. Total annual expenses per animal space are estimated to be $1,153 for feed, veterinary expenses, interest, death loss, and purchasing the cattle. For this initial analysis, these expenses are not increased annually. The marginal tax rate is 28% and the discount rate is 7%. Depreciation is calculated using ACRS for 15 year assets with the half-year convention; no expensing is taken.

Based on these estimates of revenue and expenses, the net present value is estimated to be $64,295 using a 7% discount rate (Table 20.10). The MIRR is estimated to be 7.3% and the IRR is estimated to

Table 20.10   Net Present Value of Building a Cattle Feedlot

Year	Cash Income	Cash Expense	Taxes	Annual Net Cash Flow (ANCF)	Present Value Factor (7%)	Present Value of ANCF
1	387,600	345,900	7,966	33,734	0.9346	31,527
2	387,600	345,900	4,627	37,073	0.8734	32,381
3	387,600	345,900	5,332	36,368	0.8163	29,687
4	387,600	345,900	5,963	35,737	0.7629	27,264
5	387,600	345,900	6,534	35,166	0.7130	25,073
6	387,600	345,900	7,053	34,647	0.6663	23,087
7	387,600	345,900	7,298	34,402	0.6227	21,424
8	387,600	345,900	7,298	34,402	0.5820	20,022
9	387,600	345,900	7,291	34,409	0.5439	18,716
10	387,600	345,900	7,298	34,402	0.5083	17,488
11	387,600	345,900	7,291	34,409	0.4751	16,348
12	387,600	345,900	7,298	34,402	0.4440	15,275
13	387,600	345,900	7,291	34,409	0.4150	14,279
14	387,600	345,900	7,298	34,402	0.3878	13,342
15	387,600	345,900	7,291	34,409	0.3624	12,471
16	387,600	345,900	9,487	32,213	0.3387	10,912

Sum of present value of annual net cash flows = 329,295

Initial cost of investment = 265,000

INVESTMENT CRITERIA:

Net present value of investment = NPV = 64,295

Modified internal rate of return = MIRR = 7.3%

Internal rate of return = IRR = 10.5%

Payback period (undiscounted) = 7.5 years

Discounted payback period = 11.1 years

be 10.5%. The payback period is 7.5 years. The financial feasibility was done as in previous examples (but not reported here) and shows that this feedlot could pay for its own loan without outside funds, assuming these prices and expenses were to hold.

Perennial Crop Establishment

Perennial crops such as trees, bushes, and vines usually involve a period of years before production starts and especially before the annual value of production exceeds the annual costs. A producer may have to endure several years of negative cash flow before positive cash flows are obtained. Other than the longer period of negative cash flow, investment analysis of the decision to invest in establishing a perennial crop follows the same procedures as the investment examples shown earlier in this chapter.

As an example, let us consider the McNalleys, who are looking for ways to increase and diversify the sources of their family income. Land is expensive and not widely available for sale in their area. They have decided that their neighbors are too close to consider building a hog confinement facility. At a meeting, they heard about how the grape and wine business is expanding even in their cold climate, and wineries are looking for more grapes. From the information at this meeting and with some more work on their part, they estimated the initial investment would total $8,120 per acre: $700 for site preparation; $1,200 for the vines; $220 for planting the vines; $3,200 for the trellis, wires, and posts; and $2,800 for the land. They decide to evaluate the vineyard based on 25 years even though the vines will live longer.

For the McNalleys' grapes, production will not start until the third year, and then it is estimated to be only 3,000 lb per acre. Production is estimated to be 6,000 lb in year 4 and then a relatively constant 7,000 lb each in years 5 through 25. They hear that the price for grapes can vary from $0.50 to $1.25 per lb, so they decide to use a somewhat conservative price of $0.75 per lb.

In addition to the initial investment costs, they estimate their operating costs to be $1,450 in year 1; $1,150 in year 2; $2,500 in year 3; $2,250 in year 4; $1,950 each in years 5 through 8; and $1,800 each in years 9 through 25. Their marginal tax rate is 28%. A negative tax impact means the losses from establishing the vineyard decreases the tax due on their other income. A positive tax means the vineyard is generating positive income and thus taxes are due.

Using a discount rate of 7%, the McNalleys calculate the annual present value for years 1 through 25, the net present value (NPV) of this investment, the modified internal rate of return (MIRR), the internal rate of return (IRR), the (undiscounted) payback period, and the discounted payback period (Table 20.11).

Using this same information, they also estimate the financial feasibility of planting the vineyard. Their bank is willing to loan 90% of the initial investment at 8% with annual payments for 10 years. Since the loan is for 10 years, only the first 10 years are analyzed. The feasibility analysis shows that the vineyard cannot pay for itself during the three establishment years (Table 20.12). The deficit in the first three years is made up in the next years as production starts and increases. However, the vineyard would have to be subsidized in those first three years from other capital sources.

Investment analysis is also useful for analyzing alternative production methods for multi-year assets. The analysis of alternative planting densities for tart cherry trees in Michigan is shown in Example 20.3.

Table 20.11 Investment Analysis of Planting a Vineyard in a Cold Climate

Year	Grape Yield (lb/acre)	Cash Income	Cash Expense	Tax Impact	Annual Net Cash Flow (ANCF)	Present Value Factor	Present Value of ANCF
1	0	0	1,450	−411	−1,039	0.9346	−971
2	0	0	1,150	−383	−767	0.8734	−670
3	3,000	2,250	2,500	−307	57	0.8163	47
4	6,000	4,500	2,250	205	2,045	0.7629	1,560
5	7,000	5,250	1,950	398	2,902	0.7130	2,069
6	7,000	5,250	1,950	398	2,902	0.6663	1,934
7	7,000	5,250	1,950	398	2,902	0.6227	1,807
8	7,000	5,250	1,950	398	2,902	0.5820	1,689
9	7,000	5,250	1,800	401	3,049	0.5439	1,658
10	7,000	5,250	1,800	401	3,049	0.5083	1,550
11	7,000	5,250	1,800	401	3,049	0.4751	1,449
12	7,000	5,250	1,800	401	3,049	0.4440	1,354
13	7,000	5,250	1,800	401	3,049	0.4150	1,265
14	7,000	5,250	1,800	401	3,049	0.3878	1,182
15	7,000	5,250	1,800	401	3,049	0.3624	1,105
16	7,000	5,250	1,800	401	3,049	0.3387	1,033
17	7,000	5,250	1,800	401	3,049	0.3166	965
18	7,000	5,250	1,800	401	3,049	0.2959	902
19	7,000	5,250	1,800	401	3,049	0.2765	843
20	7,000	5,250	1,800	401	3,049	0.2584	788
21	7,000	5,250	1,800	448	3,002	0.2415	725
22	7,000	5,250	1,800	496	2,954	0.2257	667
23	7,000	5,250	1,800	496	2,954	0.2109	623
24	7,000	5,250	1,800	496	2,954	0.1971	582
25	7,000)	5,250	1,800	496	2,954	0.1842	544

Sum of present value of annual net cash flows = 24,701
Initial cost of investment = 8,120

INVESTMENT CRITERIA:

Net present value of investment = NPV = 16,581
Modified internal rate of return = MIRR = 14.3%
Internal rate of return = IRR = 17.7%
Payback period (undiscounted) = 6.7 years
Discounted payback period = 8.4 years

Table 20.12 Estimated Financial Feasibility of Planting a Vineyard in a Cold Climate

Year	Annual Net Cash Flow (ANCF)	Loan Payment	Interest Payment	Principal Payment	Tax Savings from Interest Deductibility	After-Tax Loan Payment Schedule	Surplus (+) or Deficit (−)
1	−1,039	1,089	585	504	164	925	−1,964
2	−767	1,089	544	545	152	936	−1,703
3	57	1,089	501	588	140	949	−892
4	2,045	1,089	454	635	127	962	1,083
5	2,902	1,089	403	686	113	976	1,926
6	2,902	1,089	348	741	97	991	1,911
7	2,902	1,089	289	800	81	1,008	1,894
8	2,902	1,089	225	864	63	1,026	1,876
9	3,049	1,089	156	933	44	1,045	2,004
10	3,049	1,092	81	1,011	23	1,069	1,980

Example 20.3. Alternative Planting Densities, Yields, and Profitability of Tart Cherry Trees

Perennial crops such as fruit trees have a long life, so even simple production questions can involve many years. Investment analysis is needed to answer these questions. An example is the question of how densely to plant tart cherry trees. The density affects the both the total yield and the growth and decline of that yield over time. Since the growth and decline are at different rates over time for different densities, the income pattern is different, so capital budgeting is needed to more accurately compare the present value of future income flows.

A recent example analyzing production decisions for perennials is the planting density analysis done by Me-Nsope (2009). In this work, she developed the yield estimates for different densities for each year from planting through 25 years. The costs of planting, developing, and maintaining were estimated. The net present value (NPV) was estimated for eight densities, from 100 to 170 trees per acre. As shown in the table below, the planting density of 160 trees per acre had the highest NPV, using a discount rate of 10% and a tart cherry fruit price of $0.30 per pound. The discount rate of 10% was chosen based on a comparison of rates of return and risk for the prevalent cropping system in the geographical area (corn and soybeans, in this example). The price of $0.30 per pound was the 23-year average price.

Predicted Net Present Value (NPV) with Alternative Planting Densities

Planting Density (trees per acre)	NPV at 10% (US$ per acre)
100	4,560
110	6,090
120	7,230
130	8,050
140	8,320
150	8,270
160	8,500
170	7,660

Source: N. Me-Nsope, 2009, "Tart Cherry Yield and Economic Response to Alternative Planting Densities," Plan B paper, Department of Agricultural Economics, Michigan State University, East Lansing, Michigan. Accessed on January 19, 2010, at http://purl.umn.edu/54502.

Investment Analysis Under Uncertainty

In all the examples so far, the prices, expenses, production levels, discount rates, and all other parts of the investment decision have been used without mention of whether those values or levels will be attained in actuality. Even if we think the values are the "most likely" values, we also know that reality may look different once it arrives. This is especially true for investments when we are deciding to purchase, build, or establish an asset that will last for many years.

To improve our investment decision making, we need to evaluate the investment under more conditions than the most likely values. We'll discuss how to make risky decisions more in Chapter 22, Risk Management, but a few points are appropriate here before we close this chapter.

One of the main decisions in investment analysis is what discount rate to use. As its name implies, the discount rate is used to discount future values to a present value. In the analysis of the vineyard, we used a discount rate of 7%. If we think there is a chance that the future may not allow us to achieve the returns that we have planned, we can increase the discount rate as a way of saying, "I have less trust in the income farther in the future than I do closer to today." For example, if we use a discount rate of 10%, the net present value of the vineyard is $9,387 per acre down from $16,581 at 7%. The change from 7% to 10% for the discount represents a rather large increase of uncertainty about the future, but the vineyard still has a positive net present value.

Another main question is the price of the product in the future. In their planning, the McNalleys found that the grape price ranged from $0.50 to $1.25 per lb. In their initial analysis, they used a price of $0.75, and now they decide to check the impact of $0.50. With this lower price, the net present value is estimated to be only $358 per acre and the IRR is estimated to be 7.3%.

Many other variables could be changed and the analysis redone, but this could turn into a set of numbers without any organization as to why they were chosen. This situation could lead to management confusion and paralysis and possibly incorrect decisions. Instead of just changing variables, a better way to evaluate the impact of uncertainty is to develop and use scenarios as described in Chapter 22, Risk Management.

As an example of using scenarios, let us again consider the young farmer who proposed a new cattle feedlot and building with space for 300 head. Her base scenario is the one described earlier, and she has developed four other scenarios or pictures of the future. The conditions, NPV, and MIRR for each of her scenarios are shown in Table 20.13.

Now what had looked like a potential investment in the base scenario looks riskier when other scenarios of the future are used to calculate NPV and MIRR. The NPV was $64,295 in the base scenario, but ranged from −240,244 up to 374,447. MIRR ranged from −11.6 to 11.9%. As will be

Table 20.13 NPV and MIRR for a Feedlot Investment under Different Scenarios of the Future

Scenario	NPV	MIRR
Base: price = $85/cwt; costs = $1,153; no cost inflation; discount rate = 7%	64,295	7.3%
Increasing costs: costs increase by 1% per year; all other factors remain the same as in base	−85,168	3.0%
Pessimistic: price = $80/cwt; costs increase by 1% per year; all other factors remain the same as in base	−240,244	−11.6%
Optimistic: price = $95/cwt; all other factors remain the same as in base	374,447	11.9%
Optimistic, but!: $95/cwt; costs increase by 2% per year; all other factors remain the same as in base	62,352	6.9%

shown in Chapter 22, the probabilities of each scenario could be estimated and used to estimate the expected NPV and MIRR. The farmer could also reevaluate the feedlot to see whether a different size, production system, or marketing method could provide a better result.

The choice of production method for perennial crops needs to be made before the results are known, perhaps years into the future. The impact of uncertain factors can be evaluated within investment analysis by calculating the rates of return under different levels of price and yield, for example. The tart cherry example from Michigan is picked up again to show it can be done (Example 20.4).

Example 20.4. Uncertainty in Choosing a Planting Density for Tart Cherry Trees

As described in Example 20.3, net present value (NPV) can be used to help choose the optimal planting density for tart cherry trees. However, uncertainty of fruit prices and the future can cause a farmer to question whether the density chosen based on one price and one discount rate is a robust choice when faced with uncertain prices and other uncertainties in the future. In her work, Me-Nsope (2009) also evaluated the choice using higher discount rates of 12% and 15% to reflect greater risk and uncertainty of the future. To reflect variation in product price, additional tart cherry fruit prices of 15 and 50 cents per pound were used. Using the same procedures but with these different discount rates and prices, Me-Nsope estimated the NPV for the alternative planting densities. While the actual estimates of the NPV change with different discount rates and tart cherry prices, what can be seen in the tables below is that since the planting density of 160 trees per acre has the highest NPV for all prices and discount rates, the planting density of 160 can be viewed as a robust recommendation. While the NPV for 160 trees is the same as the NPV for 140 trees when the price is $0.15, the density of 160 trees remains as the recommended density since the NPV for 160 trees is higher than for 140 trees at the other prices.

Variation in Predicted NPV with Alternative Discount Rates and Alternative Planting Densities (US$ per acre with cherry price = $0.30)

Planting Density (trees per acre)	NPV at 10%	NPV at 12%	NPV at 15%
100	4,560	2,667	776
110	6,090	3,922	1,681
120	7,230	4,784	2,327
130	8,050	5,412	2,780
140	8,320	5,647	2,973
150	8,270	5,647	2,973
160	8,500	5,882	3,167
170	7,660	5,255	2,715

(continued)

(*continued*)

Variation in Predicted NPV with Alternative Tart Cherry Prices and Alternative Planting Densities (US$ per acre with discount rate = 10%)

Planting Density (trees per acre)	Cherry Price = US$0.15/lb	Cherry Price = US$0.30/lb	Cherry Price = US$0.50/lb
100	−1,338	4,560	10,196
110	−338	6,090	12,549
120	380	7,230	14,275
130	887	8,050	15,608
140	1,014	8,320	16,000
150	915	8,270	16,000
160	1,014	8,500	16,392
170	366	7,660	15,137

Source: Adapted from N. Me-Nsope, 2009, "Tart Cherry Yield and Economic Response to Alternative Planting Densities," Plan B paper, Department of Agricultural Economics, Michigan State University, East Lansing, Michigan. Accessed on January 19, 2010, at http://purl.umn.edu/54502.

This chapter introduced the basics of investment analysis and then provided several examples. The last section considered some ideas about dealing with future uncertainties.

Summary

- Investment analysis (or capital budgeting) is needed because capital assets such as machinery, buildings, and land last longer than one year and the benefits and costs occur in more than one year.
- Investments need to be analyzed for both economic profitability and financial feasibility.
- Economic profitability of an investment is measured by the simple rate of return (SRR), payback period, net present value (NPV), internal rate of return (IRR), and modified internal rate of return (MIRR).
- Payback period is the number of years required to recover the initial cost of the investment. It can be estimated with either discounted or undiscounted future after-tax net returns.
- Net present value (NPV) is the sum of the present values of future after-tax net cash flows minus the initial investment.
- Internal rate of return (IRR) is the discount rate that sets the net present value of the investment to zero.
- Modified internal rate of return (MIRR) is similar to IRR but corrects for the incorrect assumption that all returns to the investment can be reinvested at the same rate of return as the original investment.

• Investment analysis can be used to compare ownership with leasing of capital assets.
• Scenarios can be a useful way to organize and thus analyze uncertainty in an investment decision.

Review Questions

1. What is the difference between "regular" budgeting (as in Chapter 15) and investment analysis or capital budgeting?
2. What is the difference between the interest rate earned on a savings account and the discount rate used in investment decisions?
3. Compare and contrast economic profitability and financial feasibility in investments. Why are both needed in investment analysis?
4. Why is the timing of receipts and expenses critical in the analysis of an investment?
5. Define the payback period used in investment analysis. Why is the discounted payback period preferred to the (undiscounted) payback period? What is the main disadvantage or problem with the payback period, whether it is discounted or not?
6. Define the net present value (NPV) of an investment. How is NPV calculated?
7. Define the internal rate of return (IRR) of an investment. How can IRR be calculated?
8. Describe the modified internal rate of return (MIRR). How is MIRR calculated?
9. Given the investment example with the after-tax net cash flows listed below, calculate the net present value (NPV) using a discount rate of 10%, modified internal rate of return (MIRR), internal rate of return (IRR), and (undiscounted) payback period.

Year	After-Tax Annual Net Cash Flow ($)
1	−43,300
2	12,680
3	34,000
4	49,200
5	65,600
6	62,400

10. How can uncertainty be included in investment analysis and decisions?

Further Reading

Barry, Peter J., Paul N. Ellinger, John A. Hopkin, and C. B. Baker. 2000. *Financial Management in Agriculture*. 6th ed. Danville, Illinois: Interstate Publishers, 678 pp.

McDaniel, W. R., D. E. McCarty, and K. A. Jessell. 1988. "Discounted Cash Flow with Explicit Reinvestment Rates: Tutorial and Extension." *The Financial Review*, 23(3): 369–385.

21

Land Ownership and Use

In this chapter:

- Purchasing land
- Leasing land

Land is a critical asset for farming. Unlike machinery, buildings, breeding livestock, and other depreciable assets, land is not expected to wear out (aside from the problems caused by erosion or contamination). Income from land is expected to accrue to the owner in perpetuity—that is, forever.

Compared to the investment analysis described in the previous chapter, a different method is needed to evaluate potential land investment and control. In the next section, we look at how to estimate the value of land to be purchased and the maximum rational bid for land. Trends in land values are always of interest to farmers, landowners, and others close to the land. The factors underlying land value are discussed in Example 21.1.

Example 21.1. Non-farm Demand for Farmland

The two basic sources of farmland value are farm income and non-farm sources. Farm income from producing crops and livestock is the main source of farmland value. The fluctuations in prices, yields, government subsidies, costs, and other factors affect the income from the farm. But farm income is not the only factor that affects farmland values. Non-farm sources of farmland value include the demand for rural residences, recreation (such as hunting, fishing, wildlife watching), urban expansion, and investment alternatives (compared to the stock market, for example).

In a recent article, these non-farm sources are discussed in light of the recession that started in 2008. The recession has slowed down house construction both in the city and in rural areas. Fewer developers are buying land in anticipation of future construction. Fewer potential buyers are willing to start commuting a longer distance in an uncertain economy. Current rural residents may be moving or wanting to move closer to their city jobs, thus softening demand for rural residences. The recession has also decreased the demand for farmland purchased for recreation. When the economy was strong, wealthy outdoor enthusiasts were buying farmland to gain or guarantee their access to hunting, fishing, and recreational sites. For now that wealth-generated demand has dried up. Farmland is also seen as an alternative to investing in stocks and bonds. While the recession has dampened the interest in stocks and bonds and farmland values have not fallen, investors' wealth has decreased due to the decline in stock values. Investors do not have the capacity to move funds from stocks to farmland, so that source of demand has decreased.

Will the world and national economies improve and once again add strength to the farmland market? Any good economist will say, "Well, that depends." There are many answers to the question, and all of them have caveats and qualifiers. Timing is the biggest question. As economies improve, non-farm demand will increase, but it may not manifest itself in the same way as it did a few years ago. Demand for urban expansion will come back in different forms as people and companies adjust to higher energy costs, causing future expansion to have higher densities. However, communication technology will increase the ability to have businesses farther from current urban centers, so urban expansion demand may occur as expansion in rural areas. Recreational demand will be slower to come back as people adjust their priorities in a new economy. As the stock market improves, capital may move out of the farmland market to stocks, thus decreasing the demand for farmland. These are some of the non-farm issues that anyone involved in the farmland market will be watching.

For now the basic source of farmland value remains farm income. Although farm income is not as high as in 2008, it has not fallen as much as other parts of the economy. An increasing world population will demand more food, fiber, and energy, which will gradually work its way through to higher demand for farmland.

Source: J. Henderson, "Will High Farmland Values Hold?" *The Main Street Economist*, Federal Reserve Bank of Kansas City, Vol. IV, issue VI (June 2009), last accessed on February 10, 2010, at http://www.kc.frb.org/RegionalAffairs/MainStreet/MSE_0609.pdf.

The use of land also can be obtained by leasing or renting. The second section of this chapter explains the rental options commonly used by farmers, how to compare a tenant's costs with a landowner's costs, and how this information can be used for negotiating a rental agreement.

Purchasing Land

The value of land comes from several sources. The income the land can produce and the appreciation in land market values are the two sources of value that we consider in this section. Land value also comes from factors such as natural resources, recreation, hunting, open-space interest, water quality impacts, an alternative investment, and historical considerations.

Land value can be estimated by either the market value or income capitalization method. With the market value approach, the value of land is determined by comparing it with similar pieces of land that have sold recently. With the income capitalization method, the estimated income per year is assumed to last into perpetuity, and a simple formula is used to capitalize that income into a present value of the land. These methods are described below.

These two methods, market value and income capitalization, provide potential buyers and current owners with estimates of what they think a specific piece of land may be worth to them. They need to compare their estimated values with what the land market is asking and decide whether to buy or sell.

Market Valuation

Market valuation involves comparing the land of interest with the sales of comparable pieces of land. The best comparable sales are close to the land of interest and similar in land quality, buildings, proximity to markets, access to roads, and other factors that affect economic returns. However, even the best comparable sales will not be identical, so adjustments in the value need to be made. A first step in estimating market value would be to estimate the value of the bare land by subtracting the value of any buildings from the total value of the sale. Then the quality of the land (soil type, topography, drainage, crop yield potential, etc.) can be assessed and used to adjust the price of the bare land. The value of any buildings on the land of interest needs to be appraised and added to the total value of the bare land. Adjustments are also made for differences in the size of the parcels, proximity to the buyer's current operation, and other factors that affect economic returns.

Income Capitalization

Using the income capitalization method, land value is calculated from the expected annual return to land and the real income capitalization or cap rate. As discussed briefly in Chapter 14, Financial Management, the income capitalization formula is:

$$PV = R/i$$

where PV = the present value of the future stream of net returns, R = the annual net returns to land, and i = the real cap rate. This is usually done on a per acre basis but could also be used for a whole farm or an individual building.

Annual net returns are after-tax estimates from enterprise budgets and projected yields, prices, and costs. Since these obviously will vary in the future, a sensitivity analysis is necessary to evaluate the variability of the land price and the importance of different factors.

The real capitalization or cap rate is the nominal interest adjusted for the anticipated inflation rate. Rather than estimating future inflation ourselves, the apparent real cap rate can be estimated from recent land sales and the income capitalization formula. By rearranging the capitalization formula, we can estimate what the land market says the apparent real cap rate is in terms of the estimated annual return (R) and the actual sale price (PV):

$$i = \frac{R}{PV}$$

For an actual sale, the apparent real cap rate can be found by dividing the estimated return for the land by the actual sales price. This is an estimate of what the land market is using as the real cap rate. Since different sales will result in different estimates of the real cap rate, the real cap rate chosen for current analyses should be representative of those estimated. Sales used for this estimation should be recent, close to the land under consideration, and similar in productivity.

The example of income capitalization in Chapter 14 was of a landowner who received $85 in cash rent per acre, paid $23 in taxes, insurance, depreciation, and other expenses (but not including any interest and principal for the land), and received a net return from the land of $62 per acre. With an income capitalization rate of 5%, the land would be valued at $1,240 per acre:

$$PV = 62/.05 = 1,240$$

For another example, consider a farm couple, the Robinsons, who are considering buying the farm they have been renting for the past six years. The current owners have offered to sell the farm to them privately for $2,500 per acre. They have become very familiar with its yield history and are confident their future net returns would be similar to those they have had in the past. They have had the 300 acres in a 50-50 corn-soybean rotation and expect to continue that rotation in the future. The Robinsons want to average $18,000 or $60 per acre from their crops for living expenses. (They also have some other farm-related business activities for additional income.)

For the six years the Robinsons have rented this farm, their average net cash returns (before paying cash rent and themselves) have been $127 per corn acre and $138 per soybean acre. With an average government payment of $41 per acre, their average net cash return has been $174 per acre for the 50-50 corn-soybean rotation. To estimate the resulting land value, they must first subtract their estimated real estate tax ($11 per acre), general insurance ($5 per acre), and a charge for their labor and management ($60 per acre). This results in an estimated net return after all these expenses of $98 per acre (i.e., 174 − 11 − 5 − 60 = 98).

Using a real cap (or capitalization) rate of 5%, the value of the land using the income capitalization method is estimated to be $1,960 per acre (i.e., 98/.05 = 1,960). Based on this income capitalization value of $1,960 per acre, the offer price of $2,500 is too high. The Robinsons do not think they could afford to pay that price and still cover all the costs plus their desired living expense.

If the current owners were to say that $2,500 per acre was a firm asking price (say, due to local land market conditions) and the Robinsons still wanted to buy the farm, they have several possibilities to consider that might allow them to raise the estimated value under the income capitalization method. Although they likely have adjusted their production techniques to increase yields or decrease production costs (while still maintaining yield), and changed their marketing methods to increase prices received, the Robinsons could review those plans for additional efficiencies and opportunities. They could drop their income expectations from the land; if they lowered their estimate from $60 to $30 per acre and left the other figures unchanged, the income capitalization value becomes $2,560 per acre.

Perhaps their estimate for the capitalization rate is too high. Choosing the cap rate is definitely not as easy as calling to ask the price of diesel. Decreasing the capitalization rate from 5% to 4% would increase the income capitalization value to $2,450. The question now becomes whether they have chosen the right cap rate based on recent actual sales. For each sale, they could divide their estimate of the returns for those farms by the actual sales price—as described above. Averaging the estimated cap rate over several farms will provide an estimate of what the market is saying the cap rate is.

The Robinsons could also consider subsidizing the land purchase from other income and capital sources. There are several reasons they might want to do this. Established farmers with high equity in land they own may want to subsidize the purchase of new land to increase their holdings for retirement or other investment purposes. Other intangible business reasons include future expansion and investment plans and acquisition of land close to the base or home farm. They may have non-income reasons for the purchase, such as being able to control the use of the land, possibly to keep residential development away from an established livestock facility. Another control reason could be to keep a farmer from moving into the area and establishing a base for future expansion. Subsidizing the purchase may also be done due to anticipation of non-agricultural forces that may push the land value above the income capitalization value, such as non-agricultural policies affecting land values, future plans for new roads and thus development near the land, or potential expansion of businesses and communities near the land being considered.

One way to incorporate these other factors is to modify the income capitalization formula to evaluate a shorter time period (say, 10 years) and account for the present value of a forecasted price (say, 10 years in the future). In this modification, the land produces income for a specified number of years and has an estimated market value at the end of this period. The modified formula has the value of farming for a set number of years and adds the present value of the anticipated price at the end of the period:

$$PV = \sum_{t=1}^{n} \left[R_t / (1 + i)^t \right] + AP/(1 + i)^n$$

where R_t is the estimated net return in each year from 1 to n, AP is the anticipated price of land, n is the number of years the land will be held, and i is the discount rate (or weighted average cost of capital discussed in Chapter 20) and not the real cap rate.

As an example of using this modified formula, suppose a land auction is scheduled in the near future. A neighboring farmer wants to know the maximum bid price that is reasonable for this land. She determines that, for the standard corn-soybean crop mix, the expected annual net income per acre is $112.50. She decides the appropriate discount rate is 8%. If land prices continued to increase at the historical rate of 4% per year, she calculates that today's typical price of $1,150 per acre in her area will be $1,700 in 10 years.

Using the modified formula, the present value of farming for 10 years is $755 per acre and the present value of the anticipated land price in 10 years is $787. The maximum bid price is thus $1,542 per acre.

$$PV = \sum_{t=1}^{10} \left[112.5/(1 + .08)^t \right] + 1700/(1 + .08)^{10} = 755 + 787 = 1,542$$

Financial Feasibility

As described in the previous chapter, after evaluating the economic profitability of investing in land, the next step is to evaluate the after-tax financial feasibility of the land purchase using the price, estimated returns, and the available loan terms. The financial feasibility analysis will likely show the need for and magnitude of additional sources of capital to help pay the loan. These additional sources of capital can be farm or non-farm and family or non-family sources. A sensitivity analysis also needs to be done to determine the impact and importance of various factors affecting the land value and financial feasibility.

When viewed as a separate investment, farm land rarely pays for itself from production income. However, crop production does not capture the appreciation in land value, which is non-cash but can be a significant portion of the return to land ownership. An alternative way to evaluate a land purchase and to account for land value appreciation is to separate farm operations from land ownership (Example 21.2).

Example 21.2. Separating Farm Operations and Land Ownership

Separating land ownership from the use of the land can provide better information to the manager than keeping them together. This separation can be real in the form of different business entities or just on paper in terms of analysis.

"Requiring" crop and livestock enterprises to pay all land expenses including interest paid on loans and the opportunity cost of equity in the land is not a correct budgeting system. Crops and livestock produce grains, milk, meat, and so on. However, these enterprises do not produce the appreciation in land prices, so they should not be required to pay all land expenses.

One simple method to analyze the financial benefits of owning land separate from the production of crops or livestock is to create a separate land enterprise that receives rent from the crop and livestock enterprises and also pays all interest on land loans and the opportunity cost of the equity tied up in land. To make this comparison, a farm that produces only corn and soybeans would have not two but three enterprises: corn, soybeans, and land ownership. The corn and soybeans will "pay" the local cash rent to the land enterprise. The land enterprise will receive the rent from the crops and pay all taxes, interest, other land expenses, and be assessed the opportunity cost of the equity in the land. An estimate of the (non-cash) change in the market value of the land can be added to the land enterprise to reflect the other reason for owning land: appreciation in its price over time.

By separating the land enterprise from crops and livestock enterprises, the manager and investor can see both the true profitability of the crop and livestock and the anticipated profitability of land ownership.

Impact on the Balance Sheet

Buying land has a large impact on a farm's balance sheet. This impact needs to be considered before making the final decision to buy. When the purchase is financed with a loan, both asset value and liabilities increase. The increased debt load may hinder the ability to obtain financing for other investments and also increases the risk of not meeting cash flow obligations due to the increased loan payment.

Suppose the Gables (our example farm) decided to consider buying land in late December. The purchase would be 160 acres at $4,000 per acre; no buildings are on the land. The bank offers them loan terms of 7.5% interest and 25 years, and requires 15% down payment. These terms and the land price would require the Gables to use $96,000 in cash from their current business savings for the down payment. The value of their real estate land, a non-current asset, would increase by $640,000 (160 * 4,000). They would take out a loan of $544,000 ($640,000 − 96,000), which would result in an annual loan payment of $48,803. The current portion of this non-current loan due next year would be $8,003, leaving $535,997 to be paid in future years. (Since the loan is taken out in late December, we'll ignore the accrued interest for this simple example.)

This potential purchase would affect their previous projected ending balance sheet (see Table 17.6) in the following ways: Total current assets would decrease by $96,000 due to savings being used for the down payment. Total non-current assets would increase by $640,000 due to the market value of the land to be purchased. Total current liabilities would increase by $8,003 due to the additional principal due next year. Total non-current liabilities would increase by $535,997 due to the remaining principal from the new loan. (Deferred taxes would not increase, since the cost basis and market value are set at the same level this close to the purchase date.)

Even though the Gables are projected to be in good shape on their balance sheet, a purchase of this size would adversely affect their financial condition. If they were to purchase this land, their current ratio would decrease from 5.3 to 4.7 and their debt-to-asset ratio would increase from 25% to 30%. Although neither ratio indicates a change to a vulnerable position, the change is in the negative direction in terms of financial condition. If a farm with a less favorable balance sheet (such as a lower total asset value) were to make this land purchase, the change in the current ratio and debt-to-asset ratio would move the farm closer to a vulnerable position.

Leasing Land

Leasing or renting land is an alternative to owning. Renting allows a farmer to increase the size of his or her operation without having to commit (or even have) the money needed to buy the land. For beginning farmers, renting is a very good way to enjoy the benefits of a larger operation without taking on large amounts of debt. Renting also provides a farmer with more flexibility to move the operation to different geographical areas. For example, a young farmer could initially expand by renting land over a relatively large area and then, as land becomes available closer to the home farm, stop renting land at the farthest points in favor of land closer.

Over half of the cropland in the United States is rented. The landowners may be the tenant's parents or siblings, retired farmers, surviving spouses, or off-farm investors. Landowners either manage the rental arrangements themselves or hire a professional farm manager to handle part or all aspects of land management.

The two most common rental agreements for farmland are a cash lease and a crop share lease. Flexible cash rent agreements are also available but not as widely used as a fixed cash lease.

Cash Lease

With a cash lease or cash rental agreement, the tenant pays the owner a fixed amount per year and owns the entire crop to use or sell as the tenant determines. Under a cash lease, the tenant pays all the direct growing costs for that crop (seed, fertilizer, pest control, fuel, crop insurance, transportation, and so on); the landowner pays all the costs associated with owning the land (real estate taxes, land loan interest, general insurance, building depreciation, and so on). The landowner pays no production costs. With a cash lease, the tenant assumes all the risks of producing and marketing the crop; the landowner assumes only the risk of the tenant not paying the specified, fixed rent.

Compared to the share rent, the tenant with a cash rent agreement has more freedom to make production decisions. The tenant makes all crop marketing decisions. With a cash lease, the landowner does not participate in management decisions except perhaps in setting guidelines for crop rotations, fertility levels, erosion control and other concerns related to maintaining soil and environmental quality; these guidelines are usually written into the rental agreement. Landowners have less risk with cash rent; they do not have an immediate or direct worry about what the yield and price will be in the rental year. The only risk a landowner may have with a cash lease is the risk of the tenant not being able to pay the rent. Because they have less risk, the landowner should expect to receive less net return to land with a cash rent agreement than with a share rent agreement. Landowners who do not want the worry of making marketing decisions or the risk of a bad year may want a cash lease. Tenants who want more freedom in production decisions and who can take on the additional risk may appreciate a cash lease over a share rent agreement. Typical cash rents vary geographically and by soil quality.

Historically, the timing of cash rent payments has been half in the spring and half in the fall. However, some landowners, and perhaps an increasing number of them, are requiring payment of the entire rent in the spring to avoid the need to file a landlord's lien with the county in order to have protection if the tenant defaults. Having to make the full payment in the spring increases the cash flow needs and financing requirements of the tenant, who wouldn't be able to delay half of the cash rent until after harvest and the chance to sell some of the crop to pay rent.

Share Lease

With a share lease or share rental agreement, the owner agrees to share in some of the direct growing costs. Typically, the owner shares in the seed, fertilizer, crop insurance, drying, and transportation costs. With a typical share lease, the tenant pays for fuel, oil, repairs, hired labor, and machinery depreciation, and the owner pays the real estate taxes, general insurance, land loan interest, and so on. Some share owners also share in the costs of weed control; others say that the tenant pays for all weed control and decides whether to use chemical or mechanical weed control. With the improved efficacy of herbicides, the common approach today is to share weed control costs. Usually, the owner takes ownership and control of his or her share of the crop at harvest. In a traditional crop share lease, the tenant and owner are responsible for the storage and marketing of their own share in the crop. Since the owner is receiving the physical crop as the rental payment under a share lease, the owner is assuming some of the risk of the resulting value of the crop and the tenant is relieved of some of the risk. Thus, the owner can benefit from good weather and good prices with a share lease but is open to the problems caused by poor weather and poor prices. The tenant loses some of the potential benefit of good weather and good prices but, with a share lease, is able to give some of the risk to the owner.

In a share rent agreement, the tenant farms the land and the owner pays a share of the direct production costs and receives a share of the physical product. Once the physical yield is divided between tenant and owner after harvest, each is responsible for their own marketing decisions. Since he or she will benefit from good yields, a landowner usually takes a more active management role with a share rent agreement—that is, the landowner may want to help decide which varieties to plant, fertility levels, planting and harvesting schedules, and so on. Compared to a cash rent, the landowner takes on more risk of what the yields and prices will be, so in an average or typical year, the landowner should receive a higher return to land than a typical cash rent. Landowners are more likely to choose share rent if they like to be more involved in the farming operation; they do take on more of the risk of bad years, but they also have the chance to enjoy good years. Tenants, especially young farmers, may appreciate the decreased risk they face with share rent agreements since some of the price and yield risk is shifted to the landowner. Common shares or percentages in share rent agreements are 50-50 and 60-40 for the tenant and landowner, respectively, but these percentages do vary by locality.

For a share rental agreement to be fair, the tenant's and landowner's shares of production should be equal (or nearly equal) to their shares of yield determining expenses. If production is not shared in the same way as yield determining expenses, some inputs may not be applied at economically correct levels. For instance, if a tenant receives 50% of production but is expected to pay for 60% of the fertilizer expenses, the tenant will not realize the full benefit of the crop's response to fertilizer and may decide to apply less than the landowner may want. However, in tight land markets, tenants strive to keep renting the land they currently rent. Thus, they will likely apply fertilizers and other production inputs at levels to achieve good production and to keep landowners pleased.

Flexible Leases

Flexible or variable cash leases or agreements are also available for landowners and tenants. With these leases, the final cash rent is determined after harvest and the current year's yield and/or price are known. Landowners may enjoy this type of lease because they do not have to market their own crop but they can enjoy the higher returns in good years. Tenants may enjoy this type of lease because they can shift some risk to the landowner and maintain control over more of the production decisions. A tenant who wants all the grain for livestock but also wants to decrease his or her risk may want to consider a flexible cash lease. Some common variations of the flexible cash lease are described below.

Base Rent Multiplied by the Ratio of Current Year's Price to a Stated Base Price.   The tenant and landowner specify the base rent and base price in the lease using typical or expected prices, yields, and costs. The lease also specifies how the current year's price is to be determined. This could be done by choosing a certain period (September 15 to November 15, for example) and calculating the average price at a specific location such as the local elevator. Say the tenant and landowner agree that the base rent will be $90 per acre and the base price will be $2.00 for corn. If the current year price turns out to be $2.15, the rent is increased to $96.75 per acre ($96.75 = 90 * 2.15/2.00$). The procedure could be modified slightly to account for a typical crop rotation by specifying the base rent and base prices for each crop in the rotation and determining the annual rent based on each crop's price ratio. In a multiple-year lease, the base rent and base price would remain the same, but the annual cash rent would vary due to the current year's price varying.

Base Rent with Stated Adjustments for Price Changes.   Rather than changing the annual rent for any change in the current year's price, this form of the flexible cash lease describes how the base rent will be adjusted if the price moves out of a specified range. Perhaps the rent changes are made only when the price moves above a specified price. This form of flexibility results in less change in the annual rent than the first alternative. Some tenants and landowners may prefer to have the increased stability in their cash flows that this alternative provides compared to other flexible leases.

Fixed Amount of Commodity.   The lease defines the rent in terms of physical yield (bushels, kilograms, or tons, for example) and also defines a procedure for determining the current year's price. The rent for each year is the set physical yield multiplied by the current year's price. In a multiple year lease, the physical yield would remain the same, but the annual cash rent could vary as the current year's price varies.

Base Rent Multiplied by the Ratio of Current Year's Price to a Base Price and by the Current Year's Yield to a Base Yield.   This variation in flexibility is similar to the first option described except the yield is also included. As in the earlier example, say the tenant and landowner agree that the base rent will be $90 per acre and the base price will be $2.00 for corn, plus they also agree that the base yield for corn will be 150 bushels per acre. If the current year price turns out to be $2.15 but the actual yield is 145, the rent is increased to $93.53 per acre (= 90 * 2.15/2.00 * 145/150). This annual rent is lower than the earlier example because the actual current year's yield is lower than the base yield.

Stated Percentage of the Current Crop's Value.   This variation is very similar to a share rent agreement except a pricing procedure is specified rather than the landowner taking physical possession of the crop.

Minimum Base Rent plus a Percentage of Increased Value.   With this variation, the tenant agrees to pay a fixed, minimum base rent plus a specified percentage of an increase in value based on the current year's yield and price. Two similar but slightly different methods for determining the flexible portion in this lease are (1) as a percentage of the yield above a base yield with the price chosen on a certain day or period and (2) as a percentage of the current year's crop value over a specified base. In the first option, the bonus or variable portion is based on the actual yield exceeding a base and then valued using the current year's price. With this option, the variable portion will be positive if the yield is high and the price is low. If the yield is below the base and current prices are quite high, the landowner will not receive a higher payment even though farm income may be higher. With the second option, the bonus or variable portion of the rent is based on each year's combination of yields and prices. Thus, if low yields and high prices happen in the same year, the total value could still exceed the specified base value and the landowner still receive a positive variable rent payment.

Rent Negotiation

When negotiating to rent or lease land, astute farmers and landowners need the same three pieces of information. First, they need to know how competitive the market is for rental land. By knowing this, each side can decide how hard they can push the other party in the negotiations. In most areas, the land rental market is very competitive because many farmers are looking for more land than is available to rent. When the market is competitive, landowners have more power to negotiate better rental terms for themselves as owners. They have this power because they know other renters are looking for more land to rent and could be willing to pay more. If the land market is less competitive, the landowner does not have as much power as in a very competitive market so the tenant has more ability to negotiate rental terms. A recent survey in Germany identified the two main determinants of cash rent for farm land (Example 21.3).

Example 21.3. Determinants of Cash Rent

What determines cash rent? This question is asked by both the landowner and the renter. Recent research in Germany identifies two main determinants: the value of the land to the renter and the level of competition for land in the local geographical area.

Using data from Lower Saxony, Germany, researchers found that the farm characteristics that explained differences in cash rent were operating revenue per hectare, share of high-value crops, soil quality, share of rented acreage, share of arable land relative to rented acreage, and animal density. Characteristics that did not explain differences included labor and machinery/buildings per hectare as well as the size of the farm itself. The work also showed that higher competition for rented land was due to higher animal densities and public subsidies. These subsidies included set-aside programs and support for investments in livestock production and renewable energy. More recent work using the same data showed that a farmer's cash rent was quite sensitive to neighboring cash rents. If the rental price elsewhere in the neighborhood increased by €1, the farmer's rental price was pulled up by €0.57. This work also found that increases in EU payments per hectare increased cash rent more than the subsidy at the margin.

Sources: G. Breustedt and H. Habermann, "Determinants of Agricultural Cash Rents in Germany: A Spatial Econometric Analysis for Farm-Level Data." Contributed paper at the International Association of Agricultural Economists 2009 Conference, August 16–22, 2009, Beijing, China. Accessed on January 7, 2010, at http://purl.umn.edu/51685.

The second piece of information both parties need to know is their own expectations for revenues and costs, and the third is the other party's estimated revenues and costs. Although they may not know the other's revenue and costs perfectly, having an estimate allows each side to know which costs are hard, which costs are softer and could be changed, and which are desired returns to land, labor, management, and risk. This knowledge of revenues and costs allows each side to decide how hard to negotiate without breaking the negotiating process and losing a relationship. For example, how high can a landowner raise rent before no renter is willing to work for no pay? How much of a rent decrease can a tenant ask for and still keep a landowner's return to land at a reasonable rate? Also, by knowing their own costs, tenants know when the potential rent becomes too high for their desired profit levels and, thus, when they need to consider other options.

As an example, let us look at a recent estimate of the costs of producing corn in southwestern Minnesota (Table 21.1). The landowner wants to receive $180 per acre as an opportunity cost of owning the land, which is about a 4.0% return on the land value from production. The landowner also is expecting to have an additional return from land appreciation, but will realize that at the time of selling the land. For their unpaid labor and management, the tenants want to receive $50 per acre.

Table 21.1 An Example Comparison of Tenant's and Landowner's Costs for Producing Corn in Southwestern Minnesota

	Total Value	Units	Cash Rent Tenant's Share	Cash Rent Owner's Share	Share Rent Tenant's Share	Share Rent Owner's Share	Tenant's Share
Revenue							
Yield	175	bu./acre	175				
Price	4.00	$/bu.	4.00				
Gov't	25	$/acre	25				
Total	725	$/acre	725	0			
Direct Expenses							
Seed	90	$/acre	90		45	45	50%
Fertilizer	168	$/acre	168		84	84	50%
Chemicals	30	$/acre	30		15	15	50%
Crop insurance	22	$/acre	22		11	11	50%
Drying fuel	10	$/acre	10		5	5	50%
Fuel and oil	28	$/acre	28		28	0	100%
Repairs	38	$/acre	38		38	0	100%
Miscellaneous	12	$/acre	12		12	0	100%
Oper. interest	12	$/acre	12		12	7	prop.
Total	410	$/acre	410	0	245	165	
Overhead Expenses							
Hired labor	12	$/acre	12	0	12	0	
Real estate taxes	18	$/acre	0	18	0	18	
Farm insurance	8	$/acre	0	8	0	8	
Utilities	2	$/acre	2	0	2	0	
Interest (opp.)	180	$/acre	0	180	0	180	
Depreciation	40	$/acre	50	0	50	0	
Miscellaneous	6	$/acre	6	0	6	0	
Total	266	$/acre	60	206	60	206	
Labor and Management	50	$/acre	50	0	50	0	
Total Expenses	726	$/acre	520	206	355	371	
Net Return	−1	$/acre	205	−206			
From these cost estimates:							
Tenant's maximum cash rent =			205				
Landowner's minimum cash rent =				206			
Percentage share of the costs =					49%	51%	

By splitting the revenues and costs between the tenant and the landowner, the potential net returns to each can be estimated. If the tenant received the estimated yield and price and paid the estimated costs and desired labor and management returns, the tenant's maximum cash rent is the difference between estimated revenue and estimated costs or $205 per acre in this example. In order for the landowner to pay the estimated costs and receive the desired returns to the land investment, labor, and management, the minimum cash rent the owner could receive is the total of these costs, or $206 per acre. The tenant and landowner can use these estimates (1) to compare with the land rental market and (2) as starting points for rent negotiation.

For share rent negotiation, the fair share of the production is the share each party has in the total costs. For this example, the tenant and the landowner are sharing the costs of seed, fertilizer, crop chemicals, and crop insurance equally. Given the costs in this example, the fair share for the tenant is 49% and for the landowner is 51%. These percentages are quite close to the market in this area, where a 50-50 share rent agreement is common.

For both types of leases, these estimates would be the beginning positions. The dynamics of the local land market, the unique conditions of each party, and the negotiating power of each person would determine the final rental rates. If either or both parties want higher returns or the expected prices and yields are low, the tenant's maximum could be lower than the owner's minimum. In this case, a tenant could change production techniques to increase yields or decrease production costs (while still maintaining yield), change marketing methods to increase prices received, decrease income expectations, or use some combination of these ideas. Or the owner may have to adjust his or her desired returns.

Typical Contract Provisions

In addition to the names of the owners and tenants and the legal description of the land, written lease contracts also contain terms and clauses describing how the land will be farmed and who has what rights, obligations, and duties. Typical contract provisions are described in this section, but each lease agreement and pair of landowners and tenants may change the general lease agreement by adjusting standard terms and by adding new terms and clauses.

General terms include the time period covered, how long the lease is in effect, how it will or can be reviewed and terminated, and how it can be amended or altered. The landowner usually retains the right of entry and access at reasonable times and without interfering with the tenant's regular operations to consult with the tenant, to make repairs, and to perform farming operations after the agreement is terminated. Clauses are usually included that say the agreement does not create a partnership relationship, that the tenant does not have the right to sublease any part of the farm, that the owner can transfer the title of the farm subject to the provisions of the lease, and that the lease is binding upon the heirs, executors, administrators, and successors of both the landowner and the tenant. Additional clauses, such as a landlord's lien, may be added to cover specific situations and conditions.

Clauses are usually included to stipulate how the land can be used. The landowner may want to specify what crops can be grown and perhaps the acres of each, any restrictions on a tenant's crop choice, participation in government programs, and how government program payments will be shared. Permission and restrictions on livestock and pastures may be included as needed.

Several clauses cover the expectations of the tenant regarding the operation and maintenance of the farm. The tenant usually agrees to provide the labor to maintain the farm in good condition, control noxious weeds, control erosion, and repair erosion control structures. The tenant also agrees to pay all costs of operation except those specified to be shared in a share rental arrangement; those costs are specified elsewhere in the agreement. The tenant also agrees not to do several actions without written permission from the landowner: not to spend more than a specified amount for maintenance and repairs, not to plow pastures, not to cut live trees, not to pasture new seedlings in the year they are first seeded, not to cause violation of terms in the landowners' insurance policies, not to add improvements or incur expenses for the landowner, not to add plumbing or wiring, and not to damage erosion control structures. When leaving, the tenant agrees to pay reasonable compensation for any damages to the farm if the tenant is responsible for them.

The agreement also usually includes several expectations of the landowner regarding the operation and maintenance of the farm. The landowner is expected to replace or repair as promptly as possible any building or equipment regularly used by the tenant that is damaged or destroyed by causes beyond the control of the tenant, or the agreement may allow the landowner to make rental arrangements in lieu of repair and replacement. The landowner is also expected to provide materials to the tenant for normal maintenance and repairs to the fixed assets or fixtures on the land, to provide skilled labor that the tenant is unable to perform satisfactorily, and to reimburse the tenant for materials up to the limit specified in the agreement. The landowner is usually required to allow the tenant to make improvements (at the tenant's expense) that are removable and that do not mar the condition or appearance of the farm and to allow the tenant to remove the improvements upon the termination of the lease. In a share agreement, the landowner is expected to pay directly or to reimburse the tenant for the landowner's specified share of production expenses and for any field work done for crops to be harvested in the year following termination of the lease.

Both the tenant and the landowner agree not to obligate the other party for extension of credit or for payment of debts. How the costs of establishing permanent pastures and for lime and other long-lived fertilizers are to be shared by the tenant and landowner is specified in a typical agreement. Procedures for arbitration of differences are also specified in most agreements.

Other terms that may be included depend on the specific conditions of the farm and needs of the parties, the geographical area, and other unique characteristics. The rent for and use of dwellings and livestock facilities is specified as needed. The ownership of mineral rights may be specified in a rental agreement in areas where mineral rights are an important part of total land value.

This chapter presented the basic principles of purchasing and renting land. While owning land is a major goal of many farmers, renting is an affordable and wise choice for many.

Summary

- The value of land comes from several sources.
- Land value can be estimated by either the market value or income capitalization method.
- With the market value approach, the value of land is determined by comparing it with similar pieces of land that have sold recently.
- With the income capitalization method, the estimated income per year is assumed to last into perpetuity, and the present value of the land is estimated by dividing the estimated income by the capitalization rate.
- Land investment involves questions of both economic profitability and financial feasibility.
- Renting land is an alternative to owning.

- The two most common forms of rental agreements are the cash lease and share rent (or share lease).
- With a share lease, the landowner agrees to share in some of the direct growing costs and receives a share of the production.
- If costs are not shared in the same proportion as production, optimal levels of fertilizer and other inputs may not be applied.
- With a cash lease, the landowner receives a fixed cash payment, does not pay for any direct production costs, and does not receive any production.
- Various forms of flexible cash rents are available but not widely used.
- Estimating and comparing the costs and returns of both the landowner and the tenant, and knowing current market rental conditions, provides both parties a good base from which to negotiate land rental rates.
- The typical lease specifies the payment level and terms and also includes several clauses describing expectations of the landowner and the tenant concerning treatment of the land, ending the agreement, and other conditions.

Review Questions

1. What are the advantages and disadvantages of buying land versus renting land?
2. Why would a beginning farmer be interested in renting land?
3. Jeremy and Kathy Hansen are considering buying a farm they have been renting for several years. The farm has been offered to them privately for $2,050 per acre. Since they are very familiar with its yield history and production costs, they are confident their future net returns would be similar to those they have had in the past. They have had the 150 acres in a 50-50 corn-soybean rotation and expect to continue that rotation in the future. Their yield and financial records for the past six years are in the table below.

Corn yield, bu./acre	108	172	140	140	156	186
Corn price, $/bu.	2.06	2.21	2.32	3.31	2.67	3.08
Soybean yield, bu./acre	45	53	52	50	53	51
Soybean price, $/bu.	6.11	6.07	5.72	7.28	7.02	7.82
Production costs:*						
Corn, $/acre	193	212	248	296	353	411
Soybeans, $/acre	109	154	218	247	253	296

*These are their total production costs on the rented land. These costs do not include the rent they paid, but they do include the potential real estate taxes they would have had to pay as owners. Principal and interest payments are not included. Their own labor expenses are not included.

In addition to this land, the Hansens own and farm another 300 tillable acres. They have been striving to average $30,000 a year for living and debt repayment from their current cropping enterprises and want to continue that expectation. They are both 56 years old and are thinking of retiring within 10 years. Thus, they are considering the purchase as a potential part of their retirement plan.

    a. What is the average net return per acre for corn, for soybeans, and for the 50-50 corn-soybean rotation?

    b. What cost should they use for their own labor and management?

    c. Based on this information, what is your estimate of the annual return to land?

    d. Using a cap (or capitalization) rate of 5%, what is the value of the land using the income capitalization method?

    e. If the Hansens were considering selling the 150 acres in 10 years for their retirement, what is the value of the land? Assume that the asking price of $2,050 is an accurate reflection of the land market and that land prices will increase by an average of 6% per year for the next 10 years. Use a discount rate of 7% and the modified income capitalization method.

    f. Do you think the Hansens should buy the farm? Why or why not?

4. What are the differences between a cash lease and a share lease? How is risk shared between tenant and landowner in each?

5. What are flexible lease agreements? Describe three basic types of flexible leases. How is the payment determined in each? Which type would work best for a farm you are familiar with?

6. Why would tenants and landowners be interested in flexible leases? What are the advantages and disadvantages of using a flexible lease agreement compared to a cash lease and to a share lease? Which type would you prefer: cash, share, or flexible?

7. Why would the renter and the landowner want to set a maximum and minimum rent in a flexible lease agreement?

8. Carl Krill is debating whether to rent more land. He thinks some will be coming available close to his farm. Using the budget information below and the procedures described in the text, fill in the table below and decide whether Carl should rent this land or not.

    With a cash lease, Mr. Krill will receive all production and the full government payment and pay for all direct costs plus these overhead costs: hired labor, machinery depreciation, and miscellaneous expenses. Under a cash lease, the landowner will pay the real estate taxes and farm insurance, plus she wants $80 as the opportunity interest payment for the value of the land.

    Since a 50-50 share rent agreement is very common in his area, Mr. Krill uses those terms to evaluate a share lease. Under these terms, the landowner will receive 50% of the production and 50% of the government payment; the owner will pay 50% of the seed, fertilizer, chemical, and drying costs, as well as the overhead of real estate taxes, farm insurance, and wants the full $80 in opportunity interest on the land.

    a. What is the maximum cash rent feasible for the tenant?

    b. What is the minimum cash rent needed by the landowner?

    c. What are the tenant's and landowner's estimated shares in total expenses?

    d. If you were Mr. Krill, what would you do after you made these estimations?

    e. If you were the landowner and made similar estimations, what would you do next?

Carl Krill's Estimated Corn Production Costs and Rental Evaluation

	Owner-operator	Cash Rent Evaluation		Share Rent Evaluation	
		Tenant	Owner	Tenant	Owner
RECEIPTS					
Yield (bushels per acre)	145				
Price ($ per bushel)	3.85				
Gov't transition payment	25				
Total income ($/acre)	583				
DIRECT COSTS	($/acre)				
Corn seed	80				
Fertilizer	140				
Chemical	26				
Crop insurance	20				
Fuel and oil	16				
Repairs	36				
Drying fuel	43				
Miscellaneous	9				
Operating interest	12				
TOTAL DIRECT COSTS	382				
Interest on land					
OVERHEAD COSTS					
Hired labor	16				
Real estate taxes	14				
Farm insurance	7				
Utilities	3				
Interest (opp. cost)	140				
Depreciation	50				
Miscellaneous	6				
TOTAL OVERHEAD COSTS	236				
Operator labor and mgmt.	40				
TOTAL COSTS	658				
NET RETURN before rent ($/acre)	−75				
Estimated beginning negotiating positions (using the figures listed above):					
Maximum cash rent feasible for tenant:			xxx	xxx	xxx
Minimum cash rent needed by landowner:		xxx		xxx	xxx
Estimated share in total expenses:		xxx	xxx		

Further Reading

Barry, Peter J., Paul N. Elbinger, John A. Hopkin, and C. B. Baker. 2000. *Financial Management in Agriculture*. Danville, Illinois: Interstate Publishers.

22

Risk Management

In this chapter:

- Sources of risk
- Managing risk
- Making risky decisions
- Scenarios for management planning

Every decision in farm and ranch management involves some risk. By taking risks, we have the chance to accomplish our strategic and financial objectives, and ultimately our goals. Because risk cannot be avoided, the farm manager needs to incorporate it into his or her management process so risks can be considered explicitly.

The goal of risk management is to balance a farm's risk exposure and tolerance with the farm's strategic and financial objectives such as income, wealth, environmental quality, and personal goals. This balancing is done after considering the sources of risk, the methods of reducing risk, the ability and the willingness to take risks, and the income potential of alternative strategies. The goal of risk management is not solely to reduce risk; other objectives would not be met then. Risk management involves choosing how we use our resources—time, land, money, and so on—best to achieve our personal and business objectives.

This chapter has several parts. After presenting the main sources of risk faced by a farmer, many management options are identified and discussed briefly. Then crop insurance options are discussed in more depth. In the rest of the chapter, the methods for making risky decisions and the process of developing scenarios for assessing the future, analyzing different potential paths, and considering the impact of different scenarios on objectives are also presented.

For most of us, risk and uncertainty refer to the same thing: variation and change that cannot be completely controlled. Sometimes distinctions are made between risk and uncertainty. The term risk is used when the decision maker knows all the possible outcomes of an action and the objective probability of each outcome. Uncertainty is used when the decision maker knows part or all of the possible outcomes but cannot quantify the probabilities. In this book, risk and uncertainty are used interchangeably. For a working definition of risk, let us say that a manager faces risk when decisions must be made but the outcome of one or more alternative actions is unknown.

Sources of Risk

Any business or person faces risk coming from many sources, which can be grouped into five main categories: production, marketing, financial, legal, and human resources. Let us look at each of these briefly.

Production Risk.   Production risk involves not knowing what your crop yield, animal productivity, or other production will be. The major sources of production risk are weather, pests, diseases, technology, genetics, machinery efficiency and reliability, and the quality of inputs.

Marketing Risk.   We do not know with certainty what prices will be. Unanticipated forces, such as weather or government action, can lead to dramatic changes in crop and livestock prices.

Financial Risk.   Financial risk has four basic components: (1) the cost and availability of debt capital, (2) the ability to meet cash flow needs, (3) the ability to maintain and grow equity, and (4) the increasing chance of losing equity by larger levels of borrowing against the same net worth. The first three components are influenced by internal and external forces, and the fourth is very much affected by farmers' decisions on how much debt they take on compared with their equity.

Legal Risk.   Legal issues are involved with almost every aspect of farm management and day-to-day activities of farm operation. The legal issues most commonly associated with agriculture fall into four main areas: business structure and tax and estate planning, contractual arrangements, tort liability, and statutory compliance, including environmental issues. All these contribute to the potential for extensive risk exposure for a farm or ranch business.

   Legal risk includes political risk—that is, the risk of changing policies, both governmental and institutional. Changes in federal farm policy or in a bank's lending policy, for example, can increase the risk of not achieving a farm's objectives and goals. Policies are usually expressed through rules and regulations that farmers may follow and enjoy the benefits or violate and face penalties and lack of potential benefits. Risk can be present in the inability to follow the rules and in lack of knowledge of certain rules.

Human Resource Risk.   People can bring both increased risk exposure and increased ability to deal with risk. Death, divorce, injury, or illness of a principal owner, manager, or employee of a farm can disrupt how the farm performs or even survives. If people are not managed well, risk will increase due to improper operation and application of production and marketing procedures for example. However, the proper hiring of the right people for the right jobs and the use of training are examples of ways to use people to reduce risk exposure. Moral risk is due to the behavior of people inside and outside the business. Moral risk is caused not just by corrupt and criminal behavior; it also is caused by devious and less-than-truthful behavior by individuals and other companies.

Managing Risk

With all these possible sources of risk, how does a farmer decide which sources need attention first? One way is to rank the sources based on two criteria: (1) potential impact on the business and (2) the probability of the risk happening. The potential impact can range from small to catastrophic. The probability of happening ranges from low to high. By evaluating each possible source of risk on each criterion and putting the two criteria together, a farmer can group the sources into those that need immediate attention and action down to those that need no attention or action. The graph in Figure 22.1 can help a manager decide which sources of risk have the highest priorities and thus need attention before other sources.

An extreme example of using these criteria and prioritizing risk involves a lightning strike. If a person is struck by lightning, catastrophic results may occur. If the sky is clear while planting, for example, the chance of a lightning strike is extremely low. The combination of a potential catastrophic impact but extremely low probability of happening puts this occurrence in the lower right corner of Figure 22.1. Thus, very little action is needed to protect the farmer from a lightning strike. A farmer could continue to work in the field with little concern. However, suppose a thunderstorm is forecast. This raises the probability of a lightning strike out of the lower right corner but only enough, say, to require a farmer to be more attentive to the sky and potential development of a storm. Suppose a severe thunderstorm has developed and is heading directly at the farmer in the field; then the probability of a lightning strike is rather high. Catastrophic results may occur if a person is struck, so the situation is now in the upper right corner of Figure 22.1. Immediate action is needed. A farmer planting in this situation would most likely move to a protected area or at least into an area that reduces the chance of being struck by lightning.

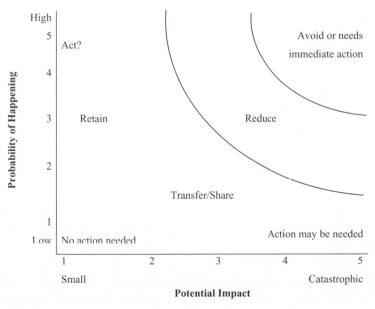

Figure 22.1 Prioritizing Risks
Source: Adapted from Boehlje, Gray, and Detre, 2005.

The problems of price and yield variability are not as dramatic as a lightning strike, but if a farmer suffers a poor yield in a low-price year, the results may be catastrophic for the farmer's finances. Based on current market information and past yield history, a farmer can decide how much protection is needed—that is, how much crop insurance to buy, how much hedging to do, or whether to buy a revenue insurance product that includes both yield and price protection. The cost of the crop insurance and hedging options will also have to be balanced with the potential losses.

Other examples show how farmers can be in different sections of Figure 22.1 and thus respond to similar risks in different ways. The destruction of a livestock confinement building due to fire would be catastrophic for most farmers, but fire usually has a low probability of occurring. Thus, the purchase of insurance to cover losses due to fire (and, within the same policy, several other potential causes) is probably sufficient. A farmer with buildings on a flood plain has a higher probability of being flooded and a higher need to buy flood insurance than a farmer on high ground. Crops on sandy soils have a greater chance of crop failure due to lack of moisture, so a farmer may consider the need for irrigation on those soils before irrigating loam and clay soils, for example. Farms with more employees have a higher probability of problems due to human resource risk and thus a higher need for good hiring and management procedures.

Once we have decided which sources of risk need our attention as managers, we can manage or handle this risk one of four ways, or in combinations of the four ways:

- Reduce
- Shift
- Self-insure
- Retain

Reduce Risk

An obvious way to reduce risk is to avoid it. This can be done, for example, by not selecting a specific, risky enterprise (such as fresh produce with its volatile weekly markets), not pushing either end of planting windows, not increasing your debt-to-asset ratio beyond your comfort level, and so on. Restricting visitors from the farm and especially livestock facilities can avoid the risk of disease being transmitted to your own livestock. Risk can also be avoided by proper maintenance of machinery and equipment and keeping fences in good repair to keep livestock off the highway. In some parts of the world, risk is avoided by corralling grazing livestock at night to keep them safe from roaming dogs, coyotes, hyenas, and other predators.

Diversification—that is, choosing a variety of enterprises—can reduce the risk of a bad year for one enterprise that would have a devastating impact on farm income. Diversification is, as the old saying goes, "not putting all your eggs in one basket." For diversification to have the highest impact on reducing the risk of income variation, the sources of revenue need to be diversified, not just the variety of enterprises. For example, a livestock farmer who raises all the feed needed but sells only one primary product (milk, for example) is not diversified in revenue sources even though the presence of a variety of crops makes the farm look diversified. Diversification decreases risk if enterprises are chosen that tend to have good and poor years in different years or have different levels of variability in prices and yields. The success of diversification depends upon the statistical correlations between the choices and the variations of the potential returns.

Selecting a diversity of crops and crop varieties can provide drought tolerance, disease and insect resistance, and other benefits that minimize crop failure risk. Different varieties of the same crop can have shorter or longer growing seasons needed to achieve maturity as well as differences in drought and disease resistance and other tolerances. Besides spreading out the time requirements for planting and harvesting, different growing season requirements can reduce risk by spreading out the times of pollination and harvest to avoid potential production problems caused by weather, insects, and diseases.

For fresh produce, different varieties and different planting dates can spread out the harvest dates and thus reduce the potential of having fresh products ready during a low-price period of the marketing window and increase the chance of having the same fresh product ready for a high-price period.

Diversification can also be increased by producing crops and livestock in different geographical locations. Putting distance between production sites reduces the risk of weather and disease problems affecting the whole enterprise.

Non-farm activities and investments can also diversify the sources of income for a family. Diversifying investments beyond farm land, for example, can improve the stability of potential retirement income. The value of land in a diversified investment portfolio was shown in a recent Canadian study (Example 22.1).

Example 22.1. Diversification with Land in the Investment Portfolio

Diversification can be a risk management strategy when selecting more than one or two major products for a farm to produce and sell. Diversification can also be a risk management strategy for investments.

A recent study found that international portfolio investment performance was significantly improved with the addition of Canadian farmland for the period 1990–2007. "Farmland in Canada is considered relatively low risk, enters the efficient portfolios at low risk levels and adds the most financial improvement to low and medium risk portfolios. Compared to T-bills and long bonds, farmland has higher risk and yield, but lower risk than stocks. Compared with stocks, farmland has income yields and risk that are similar or better than dividend yields and risk on stocks while farmland has capital gain yields and risk that are usually lower, on average, than stocks. The low and negative correlation of farmland yields with stocks and bonds make it a good candidate for portfolio diversification benefits."

Source: M. Painter, "Equity Financing and Investment, Opportunities in Canadian Primary Agriculture." Peer-reviewed paper at the 17th International Farm Management Congress, Illinois State University, Bloomington/Normal, Illinois, U.S., July 19–24, 2009, accessed on February 3, 2010, at http://www.ifmaonline.org/pdf/congress/09_Painter.pdf.

Risk can be reduced in others ways besides obvious diversification, but the concept of diversification can be seen in many of these alternative methods.

By renting or leasing instead of owning land, machinery, and livestock, a farmer reduces risk by increasing flexibility. Increased flexibility allows a farmer to more quickly adapt to changing market conditions by changing to new, more profitable strategies and enterprises that do not use the assets currently rented. Renting or leasing also decreases the long-term commitment of capital and thus decreases the risk of asset devaluation and the potential negative impact on a farmer's balance sheet. Although renting also means a farmer does not have the potential benefit of asset value appreciation, so the concept of diversification in asset control—that is, renting versus owning—needs to be considered.

Flexibility in plans means a farmer is willing and able to change to meet new conditions and opportunities. For example, buildings designed for flexibility, not specialty, can allow a farm to change enterprises. A basic pole barn customized for hog finishing could be easier to change to beef finishing compared with a specialized hog confinement building. Flexibility also means knowing where your decision points are, such as: Do I sell my calves now as planned or feed them until they are yearlings?

As discussed in the chapter on land use and control, different forms of rental agreements split the risk of crop production differently between landowner and tenant. A cash lease places all the risk of production and marketing on the tenant. A crop share lease transfers some production and price risk from the tenant to the landowner. Flexible cash leases offer different ways to share varying amounts of risk.

Risk reduction can be accomplished within production management. Environmental control can decrease risk by controlling the growing conditions of the enterprise. Examples include use of irrigation, frost control, hot caps, plastic mulch, greenhouses, strip farming, and contour plowing. Shortening lead times in production allows a farmer to reduce risk by recapturing costs sooner. Examples of shorter lead times are growing annual crops versus permanent crops, raising hogs versus cattle, selling feeder pigs instead of market-weight hogs, buying heavier feeders versus lighter feeders, and so on.

Redundancy of resources is also a risk management tool. For example, a farmer can decrease the chance of being without a working tractor by having two smaller tractors instead of one big tractor. Having a backup generator for livestock confinement buildings reduces the risk of being without electricity due to a system-wide outage.

Risk reduction can also occur within management activities. Hiring veterinarians, crop scouts, lawyers, financial advisors, management consultants, and other experts can increase management information, decrease surprises, and potentially improve decisions. Obtaining more and better information by subscribing to market news services, attending meetings, and talking with others can also reduce risk. Learning new skills and knowledge can cause earlier awareness of important internal and external changes and conditions. For example, attending classes to learn new marketing or risk management techniques can help reduce risk.

Shift Risk

The most obvious example of shifting risk is buying insurance. With insurance, a person pays the company to take on his or her risk in exchange for a premium. The more risk shifted, the higher the cost of the insurance or other contract and the lower the potential reward from taking on risk. Several types of insurance are available to cover different types of risk: crop, health, fire, life, and liability. The decision to buy insurance involves estimating potential losses and their probability, the cost of the insurance, and both the ability to bear the loss and the impact on the business. The ability to bear the loss considers whether a loss would cause business failure. This is different from the impact on the business, which looks at cash flow deviations and other changes that could cause deviations from the plans that are undesirable, but not complete failure.

In the United States, insurance is provided for many crops and recently for livestock by the federal government. These options are discussed in Appendix 22.1.

Shifting risk also takes place in pricing products. Hedging a commodity in the futures market shifts the risk of an unknown future cash price from the farmer to others in the market but leaves the farmer with the risk of changes in the basis and the risk of potential margin calls. The use of options can also shift risk from the farmer to others willing to take the risk or rewards of uncertain price movements. Options can be used to set a minimum product price needed to pay costs or set a maximum input price needed to preserve a profit. Forward contracts have a fixed quantity, a fixed price, or both in the contract. They remove the risk of uncertain prices but also remove the opportunities of beneficial movements in prices. A farmer usually does not contract his or her whole crop because of the potential of low production and the resulting need to buy replacement quantities at a price higher than the contract price to fulfill the contract.

Self-Insure against Risk

If they have the financial capacity, farmers can self-insure against risk. If they have enough equity or available credit, farmers can decide to not buy insurance, for example, and be ready to cover losses themselves. However, even farms with large equity levels will still insure major assets such as buildings due to the potential negative effect of having a large loss and the desire to allow more funds to be used for other, more productive uses. To stabilize family income, farmers can build up financial reserves in good years to reduce the financial impact of poor years; that is, they "save for a rainy day."

Retain Risk

In reality, risk and uncertainty cannot be reduced or avoided completely, so we retain risk by default. However, we can learn how to make decisions in the face of risk and uncertainty.

In some circumstances, farmers decide that the potential benefit of retaining risk is greater than the cost of protecting from risk. For example, a farmer may use hedge or buy options on part of the production (to pay for expenses, for example) but leave the rest with no protection from downside risk in the belief that the chances of a positive movement in prices are sufficiently greater than a negative movement.

Another way to deal with risk is to forecast returns if potential events occur and make a decision based on how likely good results may occur compared to the likelihood of bad results. Also, as discussed at the end of this chapter, scenarios of the future can be developed and used to deal with a lack of knowledge of the future and to analyze the success or failure of potential plans under each scenario. After forecasting and scenario development, the manager also needs to have a set of tools that help in making decisions in a risky environment. These methods and tools are discussed in the next section.

In actuality, combinations of the above methods are used. For example, one farmer may specialize in one product and use hedging, options, forward contracts, and cash reserves to reduce the risk and impact of unforeseen price changes. Another farmer may choose to be more diversified and reduce risk exposure in that way.

Making Risky Decisions

To choose between options in a risky environment, a manager has to have some framework or process to follow. This section presents several methods and rules for making risky decisions.

A risky decision has five parts:

- Actions: What are the choices available to us? We can choose which crops to grow, which livestock to raise.
- Events (states, conditions): What cannot be controlled, but will affect the results? What is random or unpredictable? What is the effect of the actions and decisions of others?
- Payoffs and regrets: What are the measured consequences of our actions under each event?
- Probabilities: What are the chances that the events will occur?
- Criteria on how to choose the best course of action.

For simple situations, there are three ways to organize the first four pieces of data: payoff matrices, regret matrices, and decision trees.

Payoff Matrices

When a decision involves a choice of action and a result (or payoff) depending upon an event (such as rainfall or price level), a **payoff matrix** may be useful for some people. This method usually involves only one decision and one set of events. The potential returns are called "payoffs" in games and game theory, so the name "payoff matrix" is used.

A payoff matrix could be used to answer the question of selling cattle now or selling them next week. Selling now means we will get a certain price and weight. Selling next week means the price may change, and we will pay more in feed costs. Are the chances that the price will rise worth the additional feed costs?

A payoff matrix such as the one in Table 22.1 can help order the information and help the manager make a decision. On the left side are the possible events: price down, steady, and up. On the top are the manager's two choices: sell now or sell next week. Within the table (or matrix) are the expected returns for each choice under each event (i.e., price level). In the example, if the manager decides to sell now, he will receive a net return of $31 per head regardless of what the price does during the next

Table 22.1   Example Payoff Matrix and Regret Matrix

Price Level	Probability	Payoff Matrix		Regret Matrix	
		Sell Now	Sell Next Week	Sell Now	Sell Next Week
		($/head)		($/head)	
Down 5 cents	.2	$31	−$20	$0	51
Steady	.5	31	30	0	1
Up 5 cents	.3	31	80	49	0
Minimum return		31	−20	xxx	xxx
Maximum regret		xxx	xxx	49	51
Simple average		31	30	16.3	17.3
Expected return or regret		31	35	14.7	9.7

week. If he decides to wait and sell next week and the price is steady, he will receive a net return of $30 after paying for the extra feed and other costs and benefitting from a heavier animal. If price would go down 5 cents, he would lose $20 per head. If the price goes up, he would receive $80 per head.

The data in a payoff matrix are evaluated by judging which action will provide the highest payoff or returns. The various methods of evaluating or deciding are presented in the later section on decision criteria.

Regret Matrices

A **regret matrix** uses the same information as a payoff matrix but looks at the decision in a different way. A payoff matrix shows the potential returns (or payoffs) for having chosen a particular action for each event. A regret matrix shows the potential lost return (or payoff) of not having chosen the best action for each event or, as in this example, the price level.

Using the data in the payoff matrix, a regret matrix can be formed (Table 22.1). First, consider the action of selling now. If the price were to go down, the regret would be 0 because selling now is the best action. Selling now is also the best option if the price were to remain steady, so the regret then is also 0. However, if the price were to go up, the manager would regret having sold now rather than waiting and selling next week. The size of the regret is the difference in potential returns: $80 minus $31 (or $49). In other words, the manager would regret selling now if the price were to go up because the return from selling next week at the higher price is $49 higher than the return from selling now.

The potential regret due to deciding to sell next week rather than now can be calculated in a similar way. If the manager decided to sell next week and the price went down, the manager would regret the decision because the return would be $51 lower than selling now. If the price remained steady, there is a regret of $1 if the manager waited to sell because the return would be $1 lower. If the price were to go up, there would be no regret for having waited to sell because the return would be higher.

Mechanically, regrets are calculated by looking at the payoff matrix one row at a time. For example, in the first event of the price going down, the maximum payoff is $31. The regrets are calculated as the maximum payoff in the row minus the estimated payoff for each action in that row. That is, the regret for selling now if the price goes down is $0 which is the maximum payoff in that row ($31) minus the estimated payoff for selling now ($31). The regret for selling next week is if the price goes down is $51 which is the maximum payoff in that row ($31) minus the estimated payoff for selling next week (−$20).

Similarly, the regret for selling now if the price were to go up is $49 which is the maximum payoff in that row ($80) minus the estimated payoff for selling now ($31). And the regret for selling next week if the price were to go up is $0 which is the maximum payoff in that row ($80) minus the estimated payoff for selling next week ($80).

The regret matrix is evaluated in a similar but opposite way from the payoff matrix. We want higher payoffs and lower regrets. As we will see in the section on decision criteria, we choose the action that we think will yield the minimum regret.

Decision Trees

When dealing with production and marketing risks, a decision tree may be the easiest way to organize the data. A **decision tree** consists of branches and nodes; it grows on its side. Square nodes are

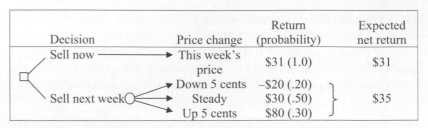

Decision	Price change	Return (probability)	Expected net return
Sell now ⟶	This week's price	$31 (1.0)	$31
Sell next week	Down 5 cents	−$20 (.20)	
	Steady	$30 (.50)	$35
	Up 5 cents	$80 (.30)	

Figure 22.2 An Example Decision Tree

used to denote decisions or alternative actions, and circular nodes denote the things that depend on chance—the events. The decision tree framework is illustrated by the cattle sale example (Figure 22.2).

The decision tree is drawn in chronological sequence from left to right with the alternative actions (e.g., selling now or next week) branching from the decision node denoted by a square and the events (price level) branching from events or chance nodes denoted by circles. At the decision node, it is the manager's choice whether to go down the "sell now" branch or the "sell next week" branch. The "sell next week" action branch has three event branches: price movements of "down," "steady," and "up." The estimated net returns are shown at the end of each branch.

The choice between using a payoff matrix, regret matrix, decision tree, or other information-organizing method depends on the question being studied and the personal preference of the manager. It could very well be that just going through the process of organizing the information will give the manager enough information to decide. Also having an idea of how to organize this information may allow a manager to sort things out mentally without having to draw a decision tree such as the one depicted in Figure 22.2.

Probabilities

There are many occasions when probabilities of certain events are needed to evaluate a decision fully. Probabilities are classified into three types based on the information source and how they are calculated. These types are:

1. Empirical Probabilities

    These probabilities are based on historical and/or experimental data and not on personal views of the future. Examples of empirical include the probability of rain or frost on a certain date, and the range of potential crop yields in a certain field. Usually they are preferred to subjective probabilities. However, when empirical probabilities are applied to future events, they become subjective probabilities because the assumption that historical data can predict the future is a subjective assumption.

2. Deductive Probabilities

    These probabilities can be deduced by the information or circumstances surrounding the event(s) under consideration. Without doing extensive genetic research, we deduce that the probability of having either male or female offspring is 0.5.

3. Subjective Probabilities

    Many times we have no or insufficient data to estimate probabilities empirically and we cannot deduce what the probabilities of certain events are. For these occasions, we need to have methods for developing a set of probabilities based on how we view the future. These methods involve subjective, not objective, views of the future and thus result in what are called subjective probabilities.

There are three basic rules to follow when estimating probabilities. These are simple rules, but must be adhered to or any resulting analysis is worthless.

The first rule says the probability of any event must be 0, 1, or any number between 0 and 1. An event with a probability of 0 is certain not to occur. An event with a probability of 1 is certain to occur. No event can have a probability lower than 0 or higher than 1. Mathematically, this is written:

$$0 \leq P(O_i) \leq 1$$

where O_i is the occurrence of the ith event, and $P(O_i)$ is the probability of the occurrence of the ith event.

The second rule requires that all possible events are included so that the list is collectively exhaustive of possible outcomes. If this rule is met, the sum of the probabilities of all possible events will be equal to 1:

$$\sum_i P(O_i) = 1, \text{ for } I = 1, \ldots, M$$

For example, next week the cattle price may go up, it may go down, or it may remain the same as this week. These are all the possible events that may happen to the cattle price, so the sum of the probabilities of these three events must be 1. If the sum is less than 1 or greater than 1, we have done something wrong in the way that we estimated the probabilities of the individual events. In a more complicated situation, the sum may be less than 1 because we have failed to include all possible events; the solution is to include all possible events and then re-add the probabilities to see whether this second rule is satisfied.

The third rule is that all events are mutually exclusive. That is, the events do not include parts of another event. For example, two events that are not mutually exclusive are a cattle price increase of 5 cents per pound and a positive price increase; the first event is included in the second event. Mathematically,

$$P(O_i \text{ or } O_j) = P(O_i) + P(O_j), \text{ for all i and j where } i \neq j$$

Several methods for estimating subjective probabilities are presented in Appendix 22.2.

Decision Criteria

Although we can organize our data with payoff matrices, regret matrices, and decision trees, we still need some process to sort it all out and some criteria by which we can make decisions. Several different rules or criteria are available for our use. We will look at seven of them.

The first three decision rules do not require probabilities: maximin, minimax, and simple average. Two decision rules do require probabilities: maximum expected returns and safety-first rules. The sixth rule evaluates the efficiency with which increases in expected returns are traded for increases in variability of those returns. The seventh rule compares the probability of success between alternatives.

Maximin (for returns or payoffs).   The manager chooses the action that has the largest of the minimum returns. When using the maximin rule and the data in the example payoff matrix (Table 22.1), the manager would choose to sell now because selling now has the largest minimum return: $31 versus −$20.

The advantage of this decision rule is that it protects the lower end of the income. The disadvantage is that it ignores the highest potential returns that may occur and the average returns that may occur. For example, it ignores the chance for $80 in Table 22.1.

Minimax (for regrets).   The manager chooses the action that has the smallest of the maximum regrets. When using the minimax rule and the data in the example payoff matrix (Table 22.1), the manager would choose to sell now because selling now has the smallest maximum regret: $49 versus $51.

The advantage of this rule is that it avoids those actions that would cause large regrets. The disadvantage is that it ignores high income potential.

Maximum Simple Average.   The manager cannot decide which events are most likely to happen; no probabilities are estimated. Thus, the manager chooses the action that has the largest simple average of all possible returns.

Using this decision rule, the feedlot manager chooses to sell now because it has a simple average return of $31 compared with the simple average of $30 for selling next week (Table 22.1).

Maximum Expected Returns (or minimum expected regrets).   With this decision rule, the manager weighs each potential return by the probability or chance of the event or combination of events occurring. The best action is chosen based on the largest total of these weighted potential returns. This method accounts for variability in returns and the potential that some events will be more likely to occur than others.

In the cattle selling example (Table 22.1), probabilities were chosen for each of the potential price events. These probabilities are 0.2, 0.5, and 0.3 for down, steady, and up, respectively. With these probabilities, the expected net return from selling next week is $35 (0.2 * −20 + 0.5 * 30 + 0.3 * 80). The expected return from selling now is $31. Using the maximum expected return rule, the feedlot manager would choose to sell next week.

In the example decision tree (Figure 22.2), the same potential returns and probabilities are used. Thus, the expected net return from selling next week is $35 and the expected return from selling now is $31. Again, using the maximum expected return rule, the feedlot manager will choose to sell next week.

The same estimated probabilities can also be used with the regret matrix (Table 22.1). With these probabilities, the expected regret from selling now is $14.7 (0.2 * 0 + 0.5 * 0 + 0.3 * 49). The expected regret from selling next week is $9.7 (0.2 * 51 + 0.5 * 1 + 0.3 * 0). Using the minimum expected regret rule, the feedlot manager would choose to sell next week.

Safety-First Rule.   The **safety-first decision rule** contains multiple objectives. The first objective is to obtain a minimum return with a certain probability. Any action that does not meet this minimum return with a certain probability is eliminated from further consideration. The second part of the safety-first rule is to choose the best action from those remaining. Usually the maximum expected returns rule is applied on the remaining actions. A manager may use a safety-first rule to say that minimum levels of cash flow and security are needed before risks can be taken. Using the safety-first rule in the cattle feeding example (Table 22.1), the manager may choose to sell now to avoid the chance of the negative return if the cattle are sold next week and the price declines.

Probability of Success. Another way to look at a risky decision and choose among alternatives is to evaluate the chances of successfully accomplishing the goal of paying all expenses or meeting income goals. The alternative with the highest probability of success is the one chosen. In Table 22.1, for example, the probability of having a positive return—that is, successfully covering all expenses— is 100% for selling now. However, due to the 20% chance of a loss, selling next week has an 80% chance of having success.

Mean and Variance. The statistical measures of mean and variance reveal considerable information about the riskiness and comparability of different alternatives. The mean or average is calculated as

$$\bar{x} = \frac{\sum_{i-1}^{n} x_i}{n}$$

where $\bar{x}$ is the average, x_i is the ith observation, and n is the number of observations. The sample variance is calculated as

$$v = \frac{\sum_{i-1}^{n} (x_i - \bar{x})^2}{n - 1}$$

and the standard deviation is the square root of the variance:

$$s = \sqrt{v}$$

The larger the variance, the greater the dispersion of the values of what is being measured. The coefficient of variation, or C.V., is often used to assess the variability of a measure compared to its mean:

$$\text{C.V.} = \frac{s}{\bar{x}}$$

As an example, consider the sample averages and standard deviations for the prices, yields, and gross revenue for three crops and two common rotations over the past 10 years in Minnesota (Table 22.2). The gross revenue per acre is calculated as the product of each year's average price and average yield. The C.V. of the net returns shows that corn has a more stable net return than the other crops since it has the lowest C.V. The C.V. of the standard rotation of 50% corn and 50% soybeans is lower than the C.V. for either crop by itself. If sugar beets are added on 10% of the acreage, the average net return is higher, but the C.V. for this rotation is slightly higher.

The tradeoff between expected net return and the variability of net returns can be shown in a mean–variance graph. The mean of the net return for each choice is plotted on the vertical axis and the variance on the horizontal axis. The mean and variance for the three crops and two rotations are shown in Figure 22.3. A farmer can use this graph by evaluating the tradeoffs between the mean return and its variance. Pragmatically, this means looking for those crops and rotations that are to

Table 22.2   Mean and Variance for Three Crops and Two Rotations 1998–2007, Minnesota

Crop or Rotation	Mean	Variance	Standard Deviation	Coefficient of Variation
Corn price ($/bu.)	2.20	0.6	0.8	0.35
Corn yield (bu./acre)	152.1	138.8	11.8	0.08
Corn net return ($/acre)	337.80	13,260.9	115.2	0.34
Soybean price	5.80	3.3	1.8	0.31
Soybean yield	40.3	22.1	4.7	0.12
Soybean net return	234.7	6,215.6	78.8	0.34
Sugarbeet price	40.2	20.8	4.6	0.11
Sugarbeet yield	21.0	4.2	2.0	0.10
Sugarbeet net return	848.30	25,631.9	160.1	0.19
Net return from rotation of 50% corn and 50% soybean	286.20	9,245.8	96.2	0.34
Net return from rotation of 45% corn, 45% soybean, and 10% sugarbeet	342.4	10,028.0	100.1	0.29

Source of data: Minnesota Agricultural Statistics

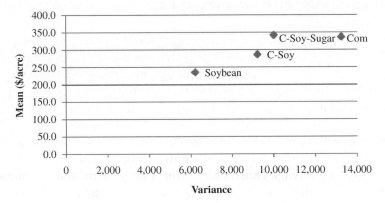

Figure 22.3   Mean–Variance of Crops and Rotations

the upper left of others. These can be pictured as drawing a line from the lower left up and then curving towards the upper right. In this example, the better choices are soybean and the corn-soybean-sugar beet rotation form this line and the farmer would choose between these two. The corn-soybean rotation and corn can be seen as less desirable in the mean-variance tradeoff since they lie below and to the right of that line.

Scenarios for Management Planning

Using only one view of the future to plan major directions and investments could be a mistake with devastating results. Instead, alternative scenarios or descriptions of the future can be developed to help understand the potential impacts of different paths that future events may take. These scenarios can be used to help estimate results and subjective scores for proposed strategies under different views of the future. Scenarios are useful for forecasting the future because they help us:

- Identify which factors and forces are and will be important
- Focus on the forces in the marketplace and other environments
- See the future even with imperfect information
- Not blindly accept one view of the future

The uncertain impact of potential changes in European farm policy was analyzed using scenarios because the actual direction was not known but farmers needed an estimate of what the impact on their farms could be (Example 22.2).

Example 22.2. Scenario Analysis for Dutch Dairy Farms

As in many countries, dairy farmers in the Netherlands are faced with uncertainty about future policy. To help farmers understand the impact of the different options, researchers developed scenarios describing three policy options and the resulting impact on milk prices and other factors. These scenarios were developed around the Common Agricultural Policy (CAP) in the European Union, the Doha Round of World Trade Organization (WTO) negotiations, and other changes in agricultural markets.

The first scenario, called "reference" or "baseline," described the situation if agricultural and rural policy continued to be developed as described in current European policy objectives, including a successful outcome of the Doha Round of trade negotiations. A second scenario, called "regionalization," was developed around the possibility of an unsuccessful conclusion of the Doha Round, continuing bilateral and multilateral trade negotiations, and more promotion of the internal market in the Netherlands. A third scenario, called "liberalization," described the movement toward open international markets and the gradual elimination of all forms of market and trade policies and income support in the European Union and the rest of the world.

Economic models of an average Dutch dairy farm, a large farm, and an intensive farm were used to calculate future farm income. The baseline scenario using current trends provided the highest levels of average farm income; regionalization provided the next highest income; and liberalization provided the lowest. The larger farm had higher average incomes but was the most vulnerable to price fluctuations.

As shown in this example, the use of scenarios can provide farmers with at least two different pieces of information. First, scenario analysis can show what policy option or options are the best for them in terms of farm income. Second, as political discussions proceed and one option seems more likely than the others, farmers can evaluate the need to change their strategy and operation for the future.

Source: J. van den Hengel, C. Ondersteijn, and A. Wisse, "Scenario Analysis on Farm Income of Dutch Dairy Farmers through 2020; the Effect of Regionalisation and Liberalisation on the Future of Dutch Dairying." Peer-reviewed paper at the 17th International Farm Management Congress, Illinois State University, Bloomington/Normal, Illinois, U.S., July 19–24, 2009, accessed on February 1, 2010, at http://www.ifmaonline.org/pdf/congress/09_vandenHengel_etal.pdf.

Developing and Utilizing Scenarios

The development of scenarios of the future requires a good understanding of the forces involved in the current situation and how those forces will affect trends and movements into the future. The procedures described below are adapted from Willis (1987) and begin by identifying the uncertain elements in the situation and the causal factors that will affect those uncertainties. Thus, rather than just choosing a set of variables in a seemingly random process, these procedures will help a manager develop a set of more rational, internally logical, and consistent scenarios.

1. Identify the uncertainties:
    a. Examine and classify each element in the situation as: *constant*: unlikely to change; *predetermined*: predictable; trends are stable; *uncertain*: depends on irresolvable uncertainty.
    b. All three elements are part of each scenario, but the uncertain elements are used to create and differentiate the scenarios.
    c. Evaluate both trends and discontinuities in the uncertainties. This involves using knowledge and expertise from many disciplines and fields.
2. Classify the uncertainties:
    a. *Independent uncertainties* are independent of other elements affecting the decision or they are essentially independent even if one could find some weak but plausible connection. For example, interest rates for farmers are essentially independent of other elements such as crop prices and labor availability.
    b. *Dependent uncertainties* are not known, but their value is determined by independent uncertainties. For example, the wheat price in Europe is a dependent uncertainty because it is largely determined by the production levels not only in Europe but also in the other major production areas in the world as well as shifts in the demand for wheat, changes in other markets such as livestock, and so on.
    c. Only independent uncertainties are used to develop scenarios. Dependent uncertainties can be estimated once assumptions about the independent uncertainties are made.
3. Identify causal factors for independent uncertainties:
    a. Decide what affects the independent uncertainties. For example, what determines how much corn is produced in Illinois and Iowa? What affects the performance of the general economy, which can affect the Federal Reserve's interest rate decisions? A manager needs to make assumptions about how these causal factors will behave.
    b. For reasons of practicality, we limit how "far back" we go to identify causal factors. For example, we may choose different levels of corn production in the main part of the Corn Belt rather than split that into different factors such as costs, weather, and others. Practicality says we can comprehend only so much detail; we deal with the lack of detail by the number of scenarios we analyze.
    c. These casual factors become the "scenario variables" from which we define the potential scenarios of future events.
4. Develop internally logical and consistent scenarios:
    a. To do this effectively, we need a knowledge of how the farm and its environment works.
    b. Estimate the "second-order" effects of assumptions. Variables may be interrelated. For example, if we assume bad weather in the Corn Belt and thus poor corn yields, we should not assume to have high soybean yields in the same area.
    c. A good scenario will not have conflicting assumptions and second-order effects.

5. Analyze scenarios for:
   a. Returns for each alternative action
   b. Future results on the industry or firm
   c. Implications for structural attractiveness (i.e., profit)
   d. Competitive advantages for the firm
   e. Impacts on the factors identified in the strategy tests listed earlier

Scenarios can be used in at least two ways. First, they can be used to help develop scores for proposed strategies as described earlier. Second, they can also be used within the decision framework of payoff and regret matrices: scenarios can be thought of as events and the different strategies as actions.

As an example of developing scenarios, let us consider a couple that produces hogs in the Midwest. Their farm has the capacity to farrow and finish about 4,000 hogs. They have and are willing to sell feeder pigs if the market suggests that is the best option. They also farm about 480 acres (160 owned and 320 rented) with the help of both full- and part-time employees.

They had done well in the past, but recent years have been rough on their operation. They have endured extremely low prices and have had disease problems that required them to depopulate and rebuild the herd. As a result, both productivity and profitability have been low and their financial position has eroded tremendously. The bank is threatening not to renew their operating loan unless they can show a high likelihood that the bank will be repaid and their financial position will improve.

Right now they are considering three main options. First, they could continue raising both hogs and crops. Second, since the hogs are the biggest financial drain, they could consider renting out their buildings, raising only crops, and taking off-farm jobs. Third, since the hogs are the biggest potential source of income, they also could consider the possibility of not renting the additional land and focusing on the hogs. These three options are broad definitions of what they could choose to do. They are also open to other options and to fine-tuning these three options if needed.

However, they are unsure of what the future will look like. They do not know what the prices may be, whether disease may hit them again, and so on. Using the steps outlined above, they have developed a set of scenarios to help evaluate their situation and the potential of alternative strategies for the future. The first three steps are shown in Table 22.3. This is not a complete list of elements and scenarios, but it does show the process of scenario development. This example also will need to be reviewed and likely changed for different producers and different years.

In step 4, several scenarios could be developed from the causal factors just identified. Five are described below. Others would be variations of these or perhaps different intensities of each factor.

Scenario A ("Most likely"): Some producers continue to expand faster than other producers exit, thus there is a net increase in production that is in balance with increases in pork demand so hog prices remain at current levels. Management can control disease, so farrowing productivity and production efficiencies are good. Weather is normal so yields are normal, therefore crop and feed prices are at normal levels.

Scenario B ("Lower prices"): This is also very likely, perhaps equally likely as scenario A. The net increase in hog production is greater than the increase in pork demand, so hog prices feel a downward pressure from current levels. Management can control disease, so farrowing productivity and production efficiencies are good. Weather is normal, so yields are normal, thus crop and feed prices are at normal levels.

Table 22.3   Identification of Causal Factors for Scenario Development for a Hog Farm

Step 1. Identify the uncertainties AND
Step 2. Divide the uncertainties into independent and dependent

Elements	Constant, Predetermined, or Uncertain?	Are Uncertainties Independent or Dependent?
Hog prices in market	Uncertain	Dependent on hog supply in market and pork demand
Hog supply in market	Uncertain	Dependent on other producers' actions
Other producers' actions	Uncertain	Independent
Pork demand	Predetermined	
This farm's hog supply	Uncertain	Dependent upon farrowing decisions and disease level
This farm's farrowing decisions	Uncertain	Dependent on hog prices in market and farrowing capacity
Farrowing capacity	Constant	
Disease level	Uncertain	Dependent upon following sanitation procedures with chance of occurrence anyway
Feed prices in market	Uncertain	Dependent upon market crop production and demand
Crop production	Uncertain	Dependent upon weather and expected crop prices
Weather	Uncertain	Independent
Labor supply and wages	Predetermined	
Government programs	Predetermined	

Step 3. Identify causal factors for uncertainties

Independent Uncertainty	Causal Factors
Other producers' actions	Long-run price expectations, expected processor behavior, changes in pork demand
Disease level	Infected visitors, wind, failed safety procedures
Weather	Position of jet streams

Scenario C ("Disease hits"): Despite management's efforts, disease breaks out pushing productivity and efficiency down. Other producers continue to expand faster than producers exit, thus production has a net increase in production that is in balance with increases in pork demand so hog prices remain at current levels. Weather is normal so yields are normal; therefore crop and feed prices are at normal levels.

Scenario D ("Widespread drought"): The potential for widespread drought is realized in the next year. Crop production is down and crop and feed prices are up considerably. Other producers continue to expand faster than producers exit, thus production has a net increase in production that is in balance with increases in pork demand so hog prices remain at current levels. Management can control disease, so farrowing productivity and production efficiencies are good.

Scenario E ("Good times"): The net increase in hog production is not as great as the increase in pork demand, so hog prices rise from current levels. Management can control disease, so farrowing productivity and production efficiencies are good. Weather is normal so yields are normal; therefore crop and feed prices are at normal levels.

Other variations could include drought over most of the Corn Belt but not on this farm. Another variation is the opposite: drought and poor yields on this farm but the drought is not widespread.

The number and need for more scenarios will vary with the need for details, the time available for analysis and interpretation, and so on. The number of scenarios needs to be balanced with the potential for information overload, rejection of alternative scenarios, and focusing on only one scenario, which would result in an incomplete picture of the future.

Choosing the Number of Scenarios

The number of scenarios needs to be limited due to the confusion and possible rejection of the whole process if too many options and alternatives are analyzed. One way to reduce the number of scenarios is to reduce the number of scenario variables to only those crucial variables with large impacts on the results being watched (say, net farm income or cash flow).

Another way to reduce the number of scenarios is to reduce the number of assumptions about each variable. The choice of assumptions is affected by four factors.

- The need to encompass the uncertainty to give credibility to the analysis. If we do not cover all the possible alternatives to what may happen, the analysis may be faulty due to incompleteness.
- The regularity of the impact of the variable. If the analysis is very sensitive to small changes in the scenario variable, more scenarios are needed. If the results are not very sensitive, fewer scenarios will be needed to analyze the impact of the variable.
- The owner's or manager's beliefs about the future or about the impact of variables will determine the number of scenarios needed. Some beliefs need to be tested and evaluated to see what impact they may have and whether that impact is important. As a result, some beliefs need to be changed.
- The practicality of analysis will restrict the number of scenarios. More scenarios means more work needs to be done. Time is needed for both doing the analysis and interpreting the results. The comprehension ability and endurance of the intended audience also need to be considered.

The number of scenarios can be kept to a minimum by choosing an analysis sequence that yields management insight for a selection of a strategy. For instance, the first scenario to be analyzed should be the one considered to be the most likely. Then a scenario polar to the most likely one should be analyzed. After that, analyze more scenarios until the impacts of the important scenario variables are understood. Limit the number of scenarios, but be sure to include major discontinuities in the variables (such as major shifts in demand or supply). Include enough scenarios to illuminate the range of possible futures that will affect strategy formulation and to communicate, educate, and stretch managers' thinking about the future. Willis (1987) suggests that we look for themes in the trends, variables, and other elements and then develop scenarios around those themes.

Another way to choose the number of scenarios is to evaluate the advantages and disadvantages of each number of scenarios. These are pointed out below.

One scenario: This is the "most likely" scenario. This option ignores other possibilities and may omit important events.

Two scenarios: Two scenarios are better than one, especially if they are polar opposites. Two can be very useful if they are equally likely to happen—that is, they are "deadly enemies." Trying to capture all possible events in two scenarios can be a problem.

Three scenarios: Three scenarios are also better than one, but they may become overly simplified to the most likely, optimistic, and pessimistic scenarios. In that case the optimistic and pessimistic scenarios are often "ignored," and the problems of having only one scenario return. Also, what is optimistic? What is pessimistic?

Four scenarios: Four scenarios can be useful if they are developed to have similar probabilities. This many scenarios can start to show and encompass uncertainty. Four also allows the evaluation of the opportunity costs of strategies (i.e., the regrets of choosing this strategy over another).

At what point does confusion start? What is too many? What can management comprehend? These questions need to be answered for each situation and each manager or management team.

Once strategies are planned, what might happen to change the plan? At this point in planning, scenarios can be developed and used in an iterative process. A manager or management team can play the "Devil's Advocate" on what may happen and evaluate the consequences for the business under a potentially final strategy. This iterative process can test specific questions about the impact of future events and what, if any, contingency plans are needed within the final chosen strategy.

Summary

- Every decision involves some risk, so risk needs to be incorporated into the decision process.
- The goal of risk management is to balance a farm's risk exposure and tolerance with its strategic and financial objectives.
- Risk can be described as coming from five main sources: production, marketing, financial, legal, and human resources.
- In order to decide which risks need attention first, sources of risk can be prioritized by considering their probability of happening along with the potential impact. Those risks that have a large potential impact and a high probability of happening need immediate attention.
- Risk can be managed or handled in one of five ways: retain risk, shift risk, reduce risk, self-insure, or avoid risk.
- A manager has many specific options for managing risks, including insurance, hedging, contracting, diversification, and financial reserves.
- Crop insurance has become an important risk management tool, especially in combination with the futures market so both yield and price are protected—Crop Revenue Coverage (CRC), for example.
- Payoff matrices, regret matrices, and decision trees can be used to organize information and thus help a manager make a risky decision.
- Decision criteria for risky decisions include maximin, minimax, maximum simple average, maximum expected returns, minimum expected regrets, safety-first rule, and probability of success.
- Managers can develop scenarios to better understand the impact of alternative views of the future and so make more informed decisions.

Review Questions

1. List at least two specific potential sources of risk that a farmer could encounter in each major risk category. If you are familiar with a specific farm, list the sources of risk for that farm.

a. Production risk

b. Marketing risk

c. Financial risk

d. Legal risk

e. Human resource risk

2. For each of the specific risks you listed in Question 1, consider their probability of happening and potential impact and place the letter of each in the graph below.

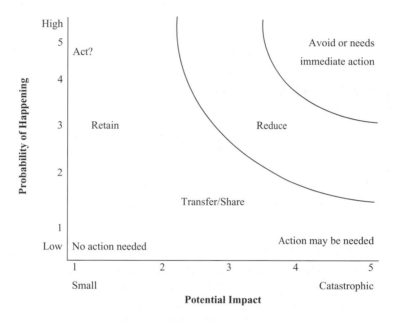

Source: Adapted from Boehlje, Gray, and Detre, 2005.

3. For two sources of risk you identified as high priority (that is, the upper right corner of the graph) in Question 2, choose two methods that could be used to reduce the farm's exposure to risk due to this source.

4. Compare and contrast a payoff matrix and a regret matrix. What information does a regret matrix provide that a payoff matrix does not?

5. For many years Glenda and Paul Christianson, like most of their neighbors, have been growing corn and soybeans in a 50-50 rotation using a chisel plow as their primary tillage. Now they were considering switching from this conventional tillage system to either an alternative system (which still uses the chisel plow but adds alfalfa to their rotation) or a ridge till system. The ridge till system does not include alfalfa. After talking with their neighbors who were using the other systems and researchers at the local university research center, they estimated their potential returns under the three tillage systems for each of the past 6 years. They put these estimates into a table with one row for each year and a column for each of their tillage choices. This table became their payoff matrix and is shown below. Develop the regret matrix for their decision.

Christianson's Estimated Payoff Matrix for Tillage Systems ($/year)

	PAYOFF MATRIX			REGRET MATRIX		
Year	Conventional	Alternative	Ridge Till	Conventional	Alternative	Ridge Till
1	1,563	2,765	13,505			
2	19,411	18,436	11,588			
3	20,025	15,774	15,749			
4	−25,274	4,894	−23,103			
5	16,783	12,174	14,762			
6	21,818	19,261	20,667			
Minimum payoff				xxx	xxx	xxx
Maximum regret	xxx	xxx	xxx			
Average						

6. For the tillage decision in Question 5, which alternative should be chosen using each of these decision criteria:

    a. Maximin:

    b. Minimax:

    c. Maximum expected returns:

    d. Safety-first: (use the safety rule of no more than a 10% chance of a negative payoff)

7. Based on the results in Question 6, which alternative would you choose and why?

8. How can the probability of success be used in making risky decisions?

9. Gene Meyer has estimated his variable costs of finishing feeder pigs to be $51 per head. He thinks the next group of feeder pigs will cost $45 per head (for a 45 lb animal). He sells his hogs at 230 lb and expects a 1% death loss. After listening to market analysts and looking at recent trading at the Chicago Mercantile, Gene has developed his conviction weights for finished hog prices in four months. These are shown in the table below.

    a. Using the conviction weight method described in Appendix 22.2, estimate the probability for each price interval.

    b. What is his estimated total cost per cwt for the finished market hog in four months? Include the cost of the feeder pig, variable costs, and death loss.

    c. What is the probability of success for covering the total cost of the feeder pig plus his variable costs?

    d. Do you think Gene should buy these pigs? Why or why not?

Estimating Price Probabilities Using Conviction Weights

Market Hog Price Intervals ($/cwt)	Midpoint	Conviction Weights	Estimated Interval Probabilities	Estimated Cumulative Probability
30–34.99	32.50	50		
35–39.99	37.50	90		
40–44.99	42.50	100		
45–49.99	47.50	70		
50–55.00	52.50	20		
TOTALS				

10. What are scenarios? How are they developed? How can scenarios be used in making risky decisions?

Further Reading

Hardaker, J. B., R. B. M. Huirne, J. R. Anderson, and G. Lien. 2004. *Coping with Risk in Agriculture.* 2nd ed. Wallingford, Oxfordshire, UK: CABI Publishing, 332 pp.

Hoag, Dana L., ed. 2010. *Applied Risk Management in Agriculture.* Boca Raton, Florida: CRC Press, Taylor and Francis Group, 403 pp.

Roucan-Kane, M., Boehlje, M., Gray, A., and Akridge, J. 2009. "Tools and Analytical Framework to Make Decisions in Turbulent Times." Working Paper 09-17. Department of Agricultural Economics, Purdue University. Accessed on January 8, 2010, at http://purl.umn.edu/55465.

Willis, R. E. 1987. *A Guide to Forecasting for Planners and Managers.* Englewood Cliffs, New Jersey: Prentice-Hall.

Appendix 22.1: Crop and Livestock Insurance in the United States

Currently, USDA's Risk Management Agency (RMA) provides several crop and livestock insurance programs through local insurance agents. USDA's Farm Service Agency (FSA) provides crop and livestock disaster programs. The major policies and programs are described briefly below.

These programs are not available in all states and in all counties in those states. The descriptions below are not official; the RMA is the final say on rules and policies. Rules and premiums do change, so check the RMA Web site (http://www.rma.usda.gov), the FSA Web site (www.fsa.usda.gov), and local agents and offices to obtain the latest information.

RMA provides policies for more than 100 crops and conducts studies to determine the feasibility of insuring other crops. USDA's Farm Service Agency (FSA) manages the Noninsured Crop Disaster Assistance Program (NAP), which provides to producers of noninsurable crops when low yields, loss of inventory, or prevented planted occurs.

Crop Insurance

Yield-Based (APH) Insurance Coverage

Actual Production History (APH) policies insure producers against yield losses due to natural causes such as drought, excessive moisture, hail, wind, frost, insects, and disease. The farmer selects the amount of average yield he or she wishes to insure, from 50% to 75% (in some areas to 85%). The farmer also selects the percent of the predicted price he or she wants to insure: between 55% and 100% of the crop price established annually by RMA. If the harvest is less than the yield insured, the farmer is paid an indemnity based on the difference. Indemnities are calculated by multiplying this difference by the insured percentage of the established price selected when crop insurance was purchased.

Group Risk Plan (GRP) policies use a county index as the basis for determining a loss. When the county yield for the insured crop, as determined by USDA's National Agricultural Statistics Service

(NASS), falls below the trigger level chosen by the farmer, an indemnity is paid. Payments are not based on the individual farmer's loss records. Yield levels are available for up to 90% of the expected county yield. GRP protection involves less paperwork and costs less than the farm-level coverage described above. However, individual crop losses may not be covered if the county yield does not suffer a similar level of loss. This insurance is most often selected by farmers whose crop losses typically follow the county pattern.

Dollar Plan provides protection against declining value due to damage that causes a yield shortfall. The amount of insurance is based on the cost of growing a crop in a specific area. A loss occurs when the annual crop value is less than the amount of insurance. The maximum dollar amount of insurance is stated on the actuarial document. The insured may select a percent of the maximum dollar amount equal to CAT (catastrophic level of coverage), or additional coverage levels.

Rainfall Index (RI) is a new pilot program based on weather data collected and maintained by NOAA's Climate Prediction Center. The index reflects how much precipitation is received relative to the long-term average for a specified area and timeframe. The program divides the country into six regions due to different weather patterns, with pilots available in select counties.

Vegetation Index (VI) is also a new program based on the U.S. Geological Survey's Earth Resources Observation and Science (EROS) normalized difference vegetation index (NDVI) data derived from satellites observing long-term changes in greenness of vegetation of the earth since 1989. The program divides the country into six regions due to different weather patterns, with pilots available in select counties.

Revenue Insurance Plans

Adjusted Gross Revenue (AGR) insures revenue of the entire farm rather than an individual crop by guaranteeing a percentage of average gross farm revenue, including a small amount of livestock revenue. The plan uses information from a producer's Schedule F tax forms and current year expected farm revenue to calculate policy revenue guarantee. The insurance covers income from agricultural commodities, as well as income from animals, animal products, and aquaculture species reared in a controlled environment. AGR protection is based on the farmer's choice of coverage level (65%, 75%, or 80%) and payment rate (75% or 90%). Loss payments are triggered when the adjusted income for the insured year is less than the loss inception point. The loss inception point is calculated by multiplying the approved AGR by the selected coverage level. Once a revenue loss it triggered, the payment is based on the payment rate selected: 75 or 90 cents for each dollar lost.

Adjusted Gross Revenue-Lite (AGR-Lite) is similar to AGR but not identical. AGR-Lite is a whole-farm, revenue protection plan of insurance. Most farm-raised crops, animals, and animal products are eligible for protection. AGR-Lite has a lower maximum payment limit and can be used in conjunction with other federal crop insurance plans (except AGR). Coverage levels and payment rates are the same as for AGR but the maximum indemnity is lower. Loss payments are calculated in the same way as for AGR.

Crop Revenue Coverage (CRC) provides revenue protection based on price and yield expectations by paying for losses below the guarantee at the higher of an early-season price or the harvest price. CRC protects against losses from both yield and price fluctuation by converting the bushel guarantee per acre to a dollar guarantee per acre. A loss results when the calculated revenue is less than the final guarantee. The difference between these two figures times the insured's share results in a payable indemnity. Losses are based on the minimum or harvest guarantee price (whichever is higher) and the calculated revenue. CRC yield coverage choices range from 50% to 75% (and 85% in some counties).

All price levels used in CRC calculations are average Chicago Board of Trade (CBOT) futures prices on specific contract months depending on the crop. Local prices have no impact on CRC coverage guarantees or payments, nor do the farmers' actual sales. Sale of the crop is not even required.

The minimum revenue guarantee with CRC coverage is established by the March 15 closing date. That guarantee cannot be reduced, but it can be increased if harvest CBOT futures prices are higher than the base CBOT price. The calculated production revenue is the actual production times the final calculated harvest price based on CBOT futures. It the calculated production revenue is lower than the final guaranteed revenue, an indemnity payment is made on the CRC policy.

Group Risk Income Protection (GRIP) makes indemnity payments only when the average county revenue for the insured crop falls below the revenue chosen by the farmer. The farmer's yields and prices do not affect the premium paid or the loss payment.

Revenue Assurance (RA) provides dollar-denominated coverage by the producer selecting a dollar amount of target revenue from a range defined by 65% to 75% of expected revenue. RA is similar to CRC and provides coverage to protect against loss of revenue caused by low yields, low prices, or a combination of both. The RA price reference is based on the CBOT options contract projected price. The insurance coverage guarantee may increase during the insurance coverage period. RA, unlike CRC, has no maximum upward price movement for the insurance coverage guarantee. Yield variability is based on APH rules and price variability is based on CBOT options contracts. Local elevator prices, basis levels, and individual farmer's grain sale prices have no impact on guarantees price levels for RA coverage.

Income Protection (IP) protects producers against reductions in gross income when either a crop's price or yield declines from early-season expectations. It is similar to CRC and RA but not identical.

Policy Endorsements

Catastrophic Coverage (CAT) pays 55% of the established price of the commodity on crop yield losses in excess of 50%. The premium on CAT coverage is paid by the federal government; however, producers must pay a $300 administrative fee (as of the 2008 Farm Bill) for each crop insured in each county. Limited-resource farmers may have this fee waived. CAT coverage is not available on all types of policies.

Organic Farming Practices

Organic farming practices are now recognized as good farming practices so organic growers can now insure their organically grown (insurable) crops. RMA currently provides coverage for (1) certified organic acreage, (2) transitional acreage being converted to certified organic acreage in accordance with an organic plan, and (3) buffer zone acreage. Insurance can only be provided for any crop grown using organic farming practices when a premium rate for the organic practice is contained within the actuarial documents or there is an approved written agreement. Insurable damage caused by insects, disease, or weeds is covered if recognized organic farming practices fail to provide an effective control. Any loss due to failure to comply with the organic standards is considered an uninsured cause of loss. Contamination by application or drift of prohibited substances onto land where crops are grown using organic farming practices is not an insured peril on any certified, transitional, or buffer zone acreage. Prevented planting acreage is considered organic practice acreage if it is identified as certified organic, transitional, or buffer zone acreage in the organic plan. The price elections or insurance dollar amounts will be the price elections or insurance dollar amounts published by RMA for the crop grown using conventional means, for the current crop year. Premiums are adjusted to recognize any additional risk associated with covering organic farming practices. AGR and AGR-Lite also cover organic crops.

Crop Disaster Assistance

Supplemental revenue assistance payments program (SURE) provides crop disaster assistance payments to eligible producers on farms that have incurred crop production or crop quality losses due to natural disasters. It is the 2008 Farm Bill's successor to prior ad hoc crop disaster programs. To be eligible for SURE, producers must have suffered at least a 10% production loss on at least one crop of economic significance. In addition, producers must meet the risk management purchase requirement by either obtaining a policy or plan of insurance, under the Federal Crop Insurance Act or Noninsured Crop Disaster Assistance Program (NAP) coverage, for all economically significant crops. There are limited exceptions to this rule, and SURE does not require coverage for forage crops intended for grazing.

In addition to meeting the risk management purchase requirement, a producer must have a farming interest physically located in a county that was declared a primary disaster county or contiguous county by the Agriculture Secretary under a Secretarial Disaster Designation. Regardless of a Secretarial Disaster Designation, individual producers may also be eligible for SURE if the actual production on the farm is less than 50% of the normal production on the farm due to a natural disaster. For SURE, a farm is defined as all crops in which a producer had an interest nationwide.

SURE provides assistance in an amount equal to 60% of the difference between the SURE farm guarantee and total farm revenue. The farm guarantee is based on the amount of crop insurance and Noninsured Crop Disaster Assistance Program (NAP) coverage on the farm. Total farm revenue takes into account the actual value of production on the farm as well as insurance indemnities and certain farm program payments.

Livestock Insurance

Livestock Gross Margin Insurance (LGM) provides protection to livestock producers (dairy, swine, and cattle) when feed costs rise or product prices drop. Gross margin is the market value of the livestock or milk minus feed costs. LGM uses futures prices for corn, soybean meal, livestock, and milk to determine the expected gross margin and the actual gross margin. The indemnity is the difference (if positive) between the gross margin guarantee and the actual gross margin. The price the producer receives at the local market is not used in these calculations. LGM is available only in selected states. LGM premiums depend on each producer's marketing plan, coverage selected, deductible level, futures, and price volatility. LGM covers the difference between the gross margin guarantee and the actual gross margin. LGM does not insure against death loss or any other loss or damage to the producer's livestock. Indemnity payments will equal the difference between the gross margin guarantee and the actual total gross margin for the insurance period. LGM rules vary slightly for each livestock type.

Livestock Risk Protection (LRP) is designed to insure against declining market prices. It is available for swine, feeder cattle, fed cattle, and lamb. Producers may select from a variety of coverage levels and insurance periods that match the time their livestock would normally be marketed. Coverage prices range from 70% to 100% of the expected ending value. At the end of the insurance period, if the actual ending value is below the coverage price, the producer will be paid an indemnity for the difference between the coverage price and the actual ending value. LRP rules vary slightly for each livestock type.

Livestock Disaster Assistance

Livestock Indemnity Program (LIP) provides benefits to livestock producers for livestock deaths in excess of normal mortality caused by adverse weather, including losses because of hurricanes, floods, blizzards, disease, wildfires, extreme heat, and extreme cold. The livestock death losses must have also occurred in the calendar year for which benefits are being requested. LIP provisions are similar to other livestock indemnity programs implemented by FSA in recent years except that an owner or contract grower's livestock do not have to be located in a county or contiguous county designated a natural disaster by the President or declared by the U.S. Secretary of Agriculture. Under the current LIP, an owner or contract grower's livestock payments will be based on individual producers' losses.

Livestock Forage Disaster Program (LFP) provides compensation to eligible livestock producers who have suffered grazing losses for covered livestock on land that is native or improved pastureland with permanent vegetative cover or is planted specifically for grazing. The grazing losses must be due to a qualifying drought condition during the normal grazing period for the county. LFP also provides compensation to eligible livestock producers who have suffered grazing losses on rangeland managed by a federal agency if the eligible livestock producer is prohibited by the federal agency from grazing the normal permitted livestock on the managed rangeland due to a qualifying fire.

Source: This appendix is based on information available at www.rma.usda.gov and www.fsa.usda.gov, accessed on February 12, 2010.

Appendix 22.2: Estimating Subjective Probabilities

In this appendix, the process of choosing data intervals and several methods for estimating subjective probabilities are presented.

Choosing Data Intervals for Probability Estimation

The intervals chosen for any probability estimation process are critical to the accuracy of the work, the complexity of the analysis, and the time required to complete the analysis. Important factors to consider are the relevant range of the entire distribution, the number of intervals, the width of the intervals, and, for ease of analysis, the midpoint of the intervals.

The relevant range for a set of prices, weather data, yields, and so on includes the values most likely to occur. It does not necessarily include all of the observed values. If we consider a set of soybean prices that ranged from $2 to $11 per bushel over a long time period, we may decide that the relevant range for this year's analysis is $3 to $9 per bushel. All values do not have to be included just because they have occurred in the past.

Observations that are "outliers" (that is, quite a distance from the main group of observations) do not have to be included in the relevant range because they may not add much information, but they may add more time and complexity to the analysis. For instance, suppose there are some very high soybean prices due to an export embargo in a past year and we do not expect to see another embargo this year; those high prices may be excluded from the relevant range of prices for the current year. However, the number of observations has to be fairly large before a value can be treated as a "true outlier" rather than part of a normal range.

The number and width of the intervals chosen are related. The necessary complexity of the analysis and the time required to do the analysis are components in deciding the width and number of intervals used. For instance, soybean prices could be divided into 10-cent intervals between $3 and $9 per bushel, but that would add unnecessary complexity and a large amount of computational time. A more reasonable interval may be 50 cents. This would result in 12 intervals between $3 and $9 per bushel.

Also, all intervals do not have to be equal in width. A soybean price interval of 50 cents may be correct in the $4 to $8 per bushel range and an interval of $1 may be correct from $3 to $4 and from $8 to $9 per bushel. This would result in 10 intervals between $3 and $9 per bushel.

Another factor used in determining the final set of intervals is the choice of the midpoint for each interval. Midpoints are used to represent the interval as a single number. For most intervals, the midpoint will be the average of the interval limits. That is, for the interval $5 to $6, the midpoint would be $5.50. For some intervals, such as the lowest and highest of the range, a "midpoint" may be the value most expected in that interval but not the mathematical midpoint. If the highest interval for the soybean price is from $8 to $11, a midpoint of $9 may be selected over $9.50 because $9 is more representative of the prices that may occur in that high price interval.

Since midpoints affect the understandability and computational ease of a set of prices or yields, intervals may be set so that "rounded" midpoints may be chosen. For instance, starting a 25-cent interval on a half cent can make a price distribution easier to use and understand. For example, a midpoint of $5.25 for an interval of $5.125 to $5.375 may be easier to use and understand than a midpoint of $5.375 for the interval $5.25 to $5.50.

Usually, interval boundaries are adjusted to avoid overlapping boundaries. Instead of having intervals such as $5.00 to $5.50 and $5.50 to $6.00 and wondering where to put a price of $5.50, the intervals could be redefined as $5.01 to $5.50 and $5.51 to $6.00. The midpoints can still be $5.25 and $5.75, respectively. If desired, the lower boundaries may be rounded numbers (for example, $6.00 rather than $5.99 or $6.01) rather than the upper boundaries.

Let us return to the soybean price example and choose a final set of intervals. After considering the information needed and the desire to have some understandable midpoints, a set of 10 intervals is chosen (Table 22.A1). In this set, the final intervals have uneven widths. Also, not every midpoint is the mathematical midpoint of the interval. Furthermore, it is not the only set of intervals that could be developed; other information, situations, and years may require another set of intervals.

In summary, the basic rules in choosing intervals are accuracy, understandability, and ease of calculations. These rules may compete with each other. Thus, to decide which rules are most important in a specific situation, we need to determine how much accuracy is required, what set of numbers are

Table 22.A1   Soybean Price Intervals and Midpoints

Soybean Price Interval ($/bushel)	Midpoint ($/bushel)
3.00–4.75	4.00
4.76–5.25	5.00
5.26–5.75	5.50
5.76–6.25	6.00
6.26–6.75	6.50
6.76–7.25	7.00
7.26–7.75	7.50
7.76–8.25	8.00
8.26–9.25	8.75
9.26–11.00	10.00

available, what we understand, and how we will be doing the calculations. The final choice depends upon the situation and the user.

Estimation Methods

While we always want to use all the objective information available, there are times when we do not have good, objective information, or the cost of obtaining the information relative to the potential benefits is too high, or there is insufficient time to find the information before a decision must be made.

Decisions still need to be made even without good, objective information so, for risky decisions we still need to be able to develop probabilities for analysis. Since these probabilities are based on subjective views and not objective data, they are called subjective probabilities.

There are several ways to develop subjective probabilities. The methods described in this Appendix are:

1. Direct estimation
2. Cumulative probabilities
3. Conviction weights
4. Sparse data methods
5. Triangular distribution

The choice of method depends upon the amount of information available and personal preference. When some information is available, it should be used even if subjective information is needed to complete the estimation of probabilities. If the quantity of historical information available is not sufficient to derive accurate empirical probabilities, the sparse data method is preferred. In situations when there is very little historical information, one of the other methods can be used. The choice of those methods also depends upon how well the manager knows and likes each method. With all of these methods, we should remember that the resulting probabilities can be adjusted to reflect better perceptions and to include new information.

Direct Estimation

The direct estimation method is just what its name says. Once the intervals are chosen, the manager starts assigning probabilities to each interval according to his perceptions of the marketplace, weather, and other conditions that may affect the distribution under consideration. There is no intermediate step; probabilities between and including 0 and 1 are specified and adjusted until they are satisfactory and the sum is equal to 1.0. An example of direct estimation is specifying the probabilities for the soybean price intervals in Table 22.A1 without consulting historical price frequencies.

The use of a pencil or a computer spreadsheet is recommended for this method since many changes may be made to the probabilities. Unless a person is very familiar with estimating probabilities and knows the events being considered, the conviction weight method is recommended over the direct estimation method.

Cumulative Probabilities

This method also involves estimating directly, but in a slightly different manner than the direct estimation method. The approach is to estimate the probability that, for example, a price equal to or less

Table 22.A2 Soybean Yield Probabilities

Yield Interval (bu./acre)	Midpoint (bu.)	Estimated Cumulative Probability	Interval Probability
15.0–22.4	19	.05	.05
22.5–27.4	25	.12	.12−.05 = .07
27.5–32.4	30	.25	.25−.12 = .13
32.5–37.4	35	.44	.44−.25 = .19
37.5–42.4	40	.72	.72−.44 = .28
42.5–47.4	45	.82	.82−.72 = .10
47.5–52.4	50	.90	.90−.82 = .08
52.5–57.4	55	.95	.95−.90 = .05
57.5–62.4	60	.98	.98−.95 = .03
62.5–67.4	65	1.00	1.00−.98 = .02
TOTAL			1.00

than a certain level will occur. It is cumulative in the sense that the probability of the price being below $5 is the probability of the price being below $4 plus the probability of the price being equal to or greater than $4, but still less than $5.

As with direct estimation, there are no preliminary steps other than specifying the intervals. The manager looks at the set of intervals, considers the market and other factors in the situation, and estimates the probability that the soybean price, for example, will be in the lowest interval, the lowest two intervals, the lowest three intervals, and so on, until there is a probability of 1.00 of the price being in the highest or lower interval.

There is no rule that says that the cumulative probability cannot reach 1.00 before the highest interval. If the cumulative probabilities are calculated for the wheat price in Table 22.A2, the cumulative probability will reach 1.00 in the next to highest interval. This indicates that the probability of a price occurring in that highest interval is zero, which is what the historical data show in this case.

Once the cumulative probabilities have been estimated, the probability for each interval is calculated. This is done by subtracting the cumulative probability for the next lower interval from the cumulative probability for each interval.

As an example, let us consider the probabilities of various soybean yields. A farmer considers his or her past yields, the county yields, and experimental yields and develops a set of intervals (Table 22.A2).

Using the cumulative probabilities method, the farmer specifies the cumulative probabilities for each interval. For the first interval, it's decided that the yield may be that low for 5% of the time. For the second interval, it's decided that the yield will be in that interval or the lower interval for 12% of the time. By the time the interval 37.5 to 42.4 bushels is considered, it is felt that the typical yield is included, so the cumulative probability should be over 0.5; thus, for that interval, the cumulative probability is set at 0.72. The cumulative probabilities are estimated for each interval from lowest to highest.

The probability for each interval is calculated by subtracting the cumulative probability of the next lower interval from the cumulative probability of the interval under consideration. For instance, the probability of the soybean yield being in the interval 32.5 to 37.4 is 0.19: this is the cumulative probability that the yield will be less than 37.5 bushels (that is, 0.44) minus the cumulative probability that the yield will be less than 32.5 bushels (that is, 0.25—from the next lower interval).

Conviction Weights

In this method, the estimation of probabilities depends upon how strongly we feel that one event will happen relative to another event happening. Specifically, we weight our conviction that an event will happen within a certain interval relative to all other intervals. These conviction weights are then used to estimate the probabilities of those events happening.

The use of conviction weights is useful for two reasons. First, they may be easier to use than estimating probabilities directly. Conviction weights are usually between 0 and 100; these may be easier to understand than numbers between 0 and 1. Second, the weights may disguise the process and, thus, keep some of our biases out of the resulting probabilities.

After the desired set of intervals is developed, we start by choosing the interval in which the price, for example, will most likely be. This interval is given a conviction weight of 100. The next step is to specify weights for the remaining intervals based on our conviction that the price will occur within that interval rather than the initial interval. More than one interval can have a conviction weight of 100, if we feel that they all have an equal chance of containing the final price or yield.

The conviction weight method has two nice features. Both of them have to do with decreasing our calculation time. First, conviction weights of over 100 are allowable. This is convenient for those occasions when, after starting, we decide an interval has a greater chance than the one we chose initially. We can give this new interval a conviction weight greater than 100 and not have to rescale all the other conviction weights. Second, when estimating our conviction weights, we do not have to be concerned with the rules of estimating probabilities; those are taken care of in the next step.

After specifying and adjusting our conviction weights to our satisfaction, we calculate the sum of the conviction weights. The probability of the final event (price, for example) being in a certain interval is that interval's conviction weight divided by the sum of all the conviction weights (just as if the conviction weights were frequencies and not weights.)

As an example of the conviction weights method, let us estimate the probabilities of a range of yields for corn in Minnesota. The range and intervals to be considered are specified in Table 22.A3.

Table 22.A3   Corn Yield Probabilities

Yield Interval (bu./acre)	Midpoint	Conviction Weight	Probability
75–85	80	15	15/455 = .03
85.1–95	90	35	35/455 = .08
95.1–105	100	65	65/455 = .14
105.1–115	110	85	85/455 = .19
115.1–125	120	100	100/455 = .22
125.1–135	130	80	80/455 = .18
135.1–145	140	50	50/455 = .11
145.1–155	150	25	25/455 = .05
TOTALS		455	1.00

Since the county average yield has been about 120 bushels per acre, the yield interval 115.1 to 125 bushels is chosen as the interval in which the yield is most likely to be found. That interval is given a conviction weight of 100. The rest of the intervals are given weights based on our conviction of the actual yield being in that interval relative to the first conviction weight of 100.

The conviction weights for all the intervals add up to 455. This sum is used to calculate the probability of the actual yield being in each interval. For example, the first interval (75 to 85 bu.) has a conviction weight of 15; the probability for that interval is .03 (15/455). The probability for the most likely interval (115.1 to 125 bu.) is .22 (100/455). The probabilities for the rest of the intervals are calculated in the same way. If rounding has caused the sum to be slightly under or over 1.0, the individual probabilities may need to be adjusted so that the sum is equal to 1.0.

Sparse Data

There are times when data are available, but there is not enough to estimate empirical probabilities satisfactorily. Often, this "sparse data" situation occurs with yields for a specific farm. The situation is not hopeless. The data are still useful to help guide a subjective approach to estimating probabilities.

The procedures for a "sparse data" situation are similar to the cumulative probability method. After the intervals are set, the available data are used to develop a preliminary set of probabilities. This preliminary set is refined to the final set of probabilities.

The crux of the sparse data method is ordering the available data from smallest to largest, and then dividing the cumulative probability over the range of the data. The division is made according to the ranking of the available data. The probability that the actual yield will be equal to or less than an observed yield is set at that yield's rank divided by the sum of the number of observations plus one. Mathematically, the probability that the sum will be equal to or less than an observed yield is expressed in the following equation:

$$\text{Cumulative probability} = k/(n+1)$$

where k is the rank of the specific yield in question, and n is the total number of observed yields.

For example, we have five soybean yields from two years and three similar fields: 39, 31, 45, 34, and 42. The ordering is done as shown in Table 22.A4. The preliminary cumulative probabilities are estimated from the five observed yields. The final set of probabilities is developed on the basis of the preliminary probabilities and our subjective views of what else may affect the actual distribution of yields.

In this example, the five observed yields are used as a guide to develop the final set of probabilities. The preliminary probabilities are refined by our knowledge of the circumstances surrounding these yields and where they are in relation to the interval boundaries. For instance, the observed yield of 34 is the second lowest, which causes a preliminary estimate of .33 for the interval 32.5 to 37.4 bushels. Since 34 is in the lower side of that interval, the final cumulative probability is increased to 0.40 to account for higher yields that may occur within that interval. Some of the other probabilities are modified by this same reasoning. The probabilities for the upper and lower intervals are developed by subjective views of yield potential.

If two or more observed yields are in the same interval, the preliminary cumulative probability is calculated on the basis of the highest rank in that interval. In this example, the third and fourth

Table 22.A4   Soybean Yield Probabilities, Revisited

Yield Interval (bu./acre)	Observed Yields (bu.)	Prelim. Cum. Probability	Refined Cum. Probability	Interval Prob.
15.0–22.4			.03	.03
22.5–27.4			.10	.07
27.5–32.4	31	$1/(5+1) = .17$	.20	.10
32.5–37.4	34	$2/(5+1) = .33$	.40	.20
37.5–42.4	39, 42	$4/(5+1) = .67$	.67	.27
42.5–47.4	45	$5/(5+1) = .83$	.83	.16
47.5–52.4			.92	.09
52.5–57.4			.98	.06
57.5–62.4			1.00	.02
62.5–67.4			1.00	.00

observed yields (out of five) were in the same interval. So the preliminary cumulative probability for this interval is 0.67 ($= 4/(5+1)$).

The reliability of the probabilities suggested by these methods depends upon our view of the situation surrounding the wheat yields. The cumulative probabilities estimated directly (Table 22.A2) are slightly different. Do the observed yields carry enough information to change our views? Only your opinion in the specific situation can answer that question.

Triangular Distribution

The triangular distribution method involves specifying three events: the lowest, most likely, and highest yields or prices that may occur. These three events are used to estimate the probabilities that the actual yield or price will be in each interval.

The range between the lowest and highest values should encompass almost all of the yields or prices that may occur, but it does not have to include every single possible yield that may occur in even the wildest situation. For instance, the lowest corn yield possible is zero, but if we ignored this utter failure, the lowest yield may be 75 bushels compared with a most likely yield of 115 bushels and a highest yield of 155 bushels per acre.

The triangular distribution method starts from the assumption that the probability is 0.5 that the actual value will be lower than the most likely value and .5 that the actual value will be higher than the most likely value (Figure 22.A1). This assumption is softened by two features of this method. First, the most likely yield or price does not have to be the midpoint between the lowest and highest values. Second, the number of intervals above and below the most likely value do not have to be equal. To use these procedures, the most likely value has to be one of the interval boundaries.

Once the intervals have been developed and the lowest, most likely, and highest values have been specified, the probabilities are calculated in three steps.

1. The interval boundaries are given values between zero and one. For the intervals below the most likely yield or price, the values are increments between 0 and 0.5. For the intervals above the most likely yield or price, the values are increments between 0.5 and 1. The increments for either side of

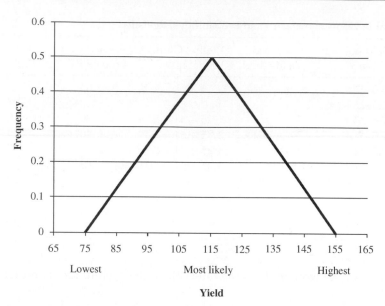

Figure 22.A1 Basic Depiction of the Example Triangular Distribution

the most likely value are calculated by dividing 0.5 by the number of intervals on that side of the most likely value. For instance, if there are four intervals on the lower side, the increment is 0.125 ($= 0.5/4$) and the values for the interval boundaries are 0.0, 0.125, 0.25, 0.375, and 0.5.

2. The interval boundary values are transformed into subjective probabilities that the event will actually be greater than that boundary. For example, the values of 0.125 and 0.25 are changed into the probability that the yield will be greater than the yields associated with those interval boundaries. (This is the reverse of the cumulative probability, which was the probability that the actual event will be less than a certain level.) This is done by different methods depending on where the boundary lies in relation to the most likely value.

   a. For the lowest boundary at the least likely value, the probability that the yield or price will be greater than that value is 1.0 by definition.

   b. For the interval boundaries less than the most likely value, the equation for the probability of the yield or price being greater than the boundary is:

$$\text{probability} = 1 - \left(x^2/0.5\right)$$

where x is the value between 0 and 0.5 for each interval boundary.

   c. For the interval boundary at the most likely value, the probability is 0.5 that the yield or price will be greater than the most likely value.

   d. For the intervals greater than the most likely value, the equation for the probability of the yield or price being greater than the boundary is:

$$\text{probability} = (1 - x)^2/0.5$$

where x is the value between 0.5 and 1 for each interval boundary.

Table 22.A5   Corn Yield Probabilities, Revisited

Steps 1 and 2:

Interval Boundary	Boundary Value (bu./acre)	Subjective Probability (bu.)
75	0.000	1.000
85	.125	$1 - (.125^2/0.5) = .969$
95	.250	.875
105	.375	.719
115	.500	.500
125	.625	$(1 - .625)^2/0.5 = .281$
135	.750	.125
145	.875	.031
155	1.000	0.000

Step 3:

Yield Interval (bu./acre)	Midpoint (bu.)	Interval Probability
75.0–85	80	$1.000 - .969 = .031$
85.1–95	90	$.969 - .875 = .094$
95.1–105	100	$.875 - .719 = .156$
105.1–115	110	$.719 - .500 = .219$
115.1–125	120	$.500 - .281 = .219$
125.1–135	130	$.281 - .125 = .156$
135.1–145	140	$.125 - .031 = .094$
145.1–155	150	$.031 - .000 = .031$
TOTAL		1.000

   e. For the highest boundary, the probability of a value greater than that boundary is 0.0.

3. The probability that the actual price or yield will be in a specific interval is the difference between the probability that the value will be greater than the lower boundary and the probability that it will be greater than the upper boundary.

For an example, let us reconsider the corn yields for the farmer in southwestern Minnesota. The intervals are the same as in Table 22.A3. The most likely yield is now 125 bushels per acre. The lowest and highest yields are 75 and 155 bushels, respectively. The three steps and the resulting probabilities are shown in Table 22.A5.

The triangular distribution method assumes what is called a "normal" distribution in statistics. If the data is not a normal distribution and the triangular distribution is used, the resulting probabilities may not be accurate. However, having probabilities that may be somewhat inaccurate is better than not having any information, so use this method if you like it and if better information is not available. Since these are subjective probabilities, they could be refined, after initial calculation, to reflect non-normality. However, this may require prior experience with calculating probabilities.

Summary

Probabilities are useful for many decisions. For example, they are useful when trying to decide what the actual market price will be to help determine your marketing strategy. Another example is predicting what the crop production will be to help determine the best rental rate.

This Appendix has been a brief description of some of the methods available for estimating probabilities. The choice of method is up to the person who will be using the probabilities and will be influenced by the amount of information available.

When estimating probabilities, having some data is better than having no data. However, although they may be biased, subjective probabilities may be better than not having any information on what potential prices or yields may be. And as stated earlier, empirical probabilities predict future probabilities only as well as the original data predict future data.

If we do not have enough data for estimating empirical probabilities, we should be collecting it. Using one of the subjective methods may suffice for now, but we need to improve our information by collecting data for future use.

Review Questions

1. How are historical or empirical probabilities different from subjective probabilities?
2. Describe how probabilities can be estimated from conviction weights.
3. Using her own personal convictions about what the beef price will do in six months, Cindy Green has formulated her conviction weights for the following intervals for market-weight beef. Calculate her resulting interval and cumulative probabilities.

Price Intervals ($/cwt)	Midpoint of Price Interval	Conviction Weights	Estimated Interval Probability	Estimated Cumulative Probability
65.1–70	67.5	60		
70.1–75	72.5	80		
75.1–80	77.5	100		
80.1–85	82.5	70		
85.1–90	87.5	40		
Total				1.00

4. Sam Vasquez has a dairy farm and wants to know how many acres of hay he needs to feed his herd in 7 out of 10 years (or close to that frequency). His yields in the past 7 years have been 3.7, 4.2, 4.6, 3.8, 5.5, 4.7, and 4.8 tons per acre. Using the sparse data method and the intervals listed below, estimate the interval probabilities for the hay yield as a first step.

Yield Intervals (tons/acre)	Midpoint	Observed Yields	Preliminary Cumulative Probability	Refined Cumulative Probability	Interval Probability
2.75–3.24	3.0				
3.25–3.74	3.5				
3.75–4.24	4.0				
4.25–4.74	4.5				
4.75–5.24	5.0				
5.25–5.74	5.5				
5.75–6.24	6.0				

5. Another way to estimate the distribution of hay yields is by using the triangular distribution method. A neighbor of Sam's says his most likely hay yield is 5.0 tons per acre, his lowest possible yield is 3.5, and his highest possible yield is 6.5. Use the intervals given below to estimate the probability distribution.

Steps 1 and 2:

Interval Boundary (tons/acre)	Boundary Value	Subjective Probability
3.5		
4.0		
4.5		
5.0		
5.5		
6.0		
6.5		

Step 3:

Yield Interval (ton/acre)	Midpoint	Interval Probability
3.5–3.99		
4.0–4.49		
4.5–4.99		
5.0–5.49		
5.5–5.99		
6.0–6.5		

23

Production Contract Evaluation

In this chapter:

- Types of production contracts
- Evaluating production contracts
- A production contract checklist

Contracts have been used in farming for a long time and in many ways: land rental agreements, marketing agreements, forward contracts, futures contracts, security agreements, loans, contracts for deed, labor contracts, contracts to produce vegetables and seed crops, contracts to deliver sugar beets as part of a processing cooperative, among others. In recent years, the use of production contracts has become increasingly common and important for livestock (especially hogs), grains to meet specific characteristics that meet consumer and/or processor needs, new venture cooperatives for grain processing, new products, and so on. Since production contracts are a relatively new phenomena for many farmers, this chapter concentrates on explaining and understanding them.

Production contracts can be made between two farmers or between farmers and agribusinesses. Contracts usually specify certain quality requirements, price, quantity, and services provided. Through combining both market and production functions, contracting generally reduces all participants' exposure to risk. Farmers enter into contracts for various reasons, including income stability, improved efficiency, market security, and access to capital. Processors enter into contracts to control input supplies, improve responses to consumer demand, and expand and diversify operations.

A **contract** is an agreement between two or more persons to do something or to not do something. Four basic requirements must be met for an agreement to be a legally enforceable contract.

- The parties to a contract must be identifiable and legally competent. If both parties are not known, there is no way to determine who is obligated to meet the terms of the agreement. Also, a party must be of legal age and mentally competent.
- The subject matter of the agreement must be legal. For example, a loan agreement that has a rate exceeding the legal maximum is not enforceable.

- There must be mutual agreement. One party must make an offer that is accepted by another party.
- There must be consideration given. Something is given for something received. This consideration may consist of money, goods, services, or merely the promise of future consideration.

A contract may be either verbal or written, but to be legally enforceable, the following contracts must be in writing:

- Contracts that cannot be completed within one year
- Contracts for transfers of interests in real estate
- Contracts to sell goods valued at $500 or more
- Credit agreements
- Loan guarantees

Even though not all contracts have to be written, putting an agreement in writing decreases the likelihood that the parties will misunderstand the agreement, their responsibilities, and what each party expects to receive. A written contract also provides tangible evidence of an agreement and the terms of that agreement. All terms and agreements should be made part of a written agreement. Verbal agreements made but not included in the written terms are rarely enforceable. The language of a contract must be very specific. Ambiguous language, such as "reasonable efforts," "best of one's ability," or "a timely manner," can easily mean different things to different people. Either avoid terms such as these or specify the criteria to define what these terms mean in the context of the contract.

Types of Production Contracts

Production contracts specify the quality and quantity of the commodity to be produced, the quality and quantity of production inputs to be supplied by the contracting firm (e.g., processor, feed mill, or other farm operation), the quality and quantity of services to be provided by the grower (i.e., contractee), and the type, magnitude, and schedule of compensation that the grower will receive. The manner in which contracts are constructed affects the legal relationship between the producer and the contractor.

Four types of production contracts are common in agriculture:

- Sales or market-specific production contracts
- Production-management contracts
- Bailments
- Personal service or resource providing contracts

Sales contracts or **market-specific production contracts** are very similar to forward contracts. With sales contracts, the farmer produces the crop or livestock and agrees to sell the product at harvest to the contractor. The farmer retains ownership until harvest and consequent sale. These contracts are usually subject to the provisions of the Uniform Commercial Code (UCC) relating to sales contracts. A buyer in a sales contract benefits because delivery schedules are specified and more stable. This allows the buyer to plan for further processing or transportation and take advantage of efficiencies not available when deliveries are not stable. The seller benefits from risk reduction of finding a market and usually receives premiums above a spot-market price. The market-specific or sales contract usually transfers minimal control across stages (that is, between the producer and processor).

A **production-management contract** increases the control of the buyer (say, a vegetable processor or seed company) over the production process. Production-management contracts are often used when the seller (i.e., producer), through production decisions, can affect the value of the product to the buyer or when the seller, through marketing decisions, can affect the value of the product to the buyer.

In these contracts, buyers usually gain control over decisions once made in open production, such as the timing of planting decisions, variety of seed planted, weed control methods, and harvest timing. By taking more control than assumed in a market-specific contract, the contractor or buyer usually takes on more of the producer's price risk. The buyer benefits from the control of the quality and timing of the product. For instance, a vegetable processor can gain control over the timing of the planting of specific seed varieties and the timing of harvest and thus, presumably, benefits from a more stable flow of a product with a more consistent quality.

Production-management contracts may be considered bailments. A **bailment** is the legal relationship that exists when someone else is entrusted with the possession of property but has no ownership interest in it. A common bailment is a grain storage contract in which the elevator stores but does not own the farmer's grain. Crop production contracts structured as bailments provide the contractor with additional protection against the unauthorized distribution of seeds, crops, livestock, and genetics that remain the property of the contractor.

Production contracts may also be structured as **personal service contracts** or **resource-providing contracts**. These contracts specify that the producer is to provide services, not commodities, to the contractor. For example, the producer will provide the services of a hog-finishing building and management knowledge to the owner of the hogs. The hogs will reside in the producer's building but the contractor will retain ownership of the hogs. The UCC provisions relating to sales of commodities will not be applicable to a personal sales contract. Some production contracts may be leases of facilities especially if the contracts relate to production of livestock.

Regardless of the type of contract, all contracts need to be checked and evaluated in terms of profitability, risk, and relationships. The process of evaluation and a checklist are the subjects of the next two sections.

Evaluating Production Contracts

Evaluating a contract involves answering three basic questions. First, does the contract improve profitability? Second, how does the contract change the risks that the farmer faces? Third, how does the contract change legal relationships and obligations? If the economic and legal implications of the contract are not fully understood, a farmer should seek expert advice to help evaluate the contract. That expert advice can be obtained from lawyers, business and financial consultants, and other farmers experienced with the same type of contract.

Before a farmer signs a contract, he or she should know and understand the following points. If there are questions on any of the points, the contract should not be signed.

- All of the terms and features and how they will affect the business.
- How profit will be affected.
- How risk is reduced; how risk is increased.
- How the contract works under extreme price and production conditions.
- The other party to the contract and, if possible, their financial condition and ability to meet their obligations within the contract.
- How prices and quantities will be determined. How any equations behave in extreme market conditions.
- Who will determine prices and quantities?
- The implications and obligations if production falls below contracted quantities.
- Whether and how the contract can be terminated by any party involved.
- Who, in the other parties, to communicate with before signing and throughout the life of the contract.

Profitability

The best and perhaps only way, to measure profitability is to estimate two sets of budgets: one for operating under the contract and another for operating independently. The procedures for estimating enterprise budgets are described in Chapter 15. Except for how prices, sales quantities, and costs are chosen, the same budgeting procedures should be used for evaluating contract profitability. The terms of the contract will specify product prices and quantity as well as the timing of the payments. Costs will be determined by either the product specifications described in the contract or by the production and capital investment specifications in the contract. If the contract is for several years and, especially if it requires capital investments, either a budget using long-term prices and costs or a budget for each year should be developed. The budgets developed using the terms of the contract should be compared to budgets developed as if the farmer(s) were operating independently. A partial budget can be used to evaluate the choice of changing from operating independently to operating under a contractual arrangement. The format and development of partial budgets are explained in Chapter 16.

Risk

Avoiding risk is a major reason for farmers to sign contracts, but contracts can introduce new risks too. The contract usually specifies a product or service price, a quantity that can be sold, or both. Signing a contract also usually means that the farmer will have a market for his or her product. However, the contract needs to be evaluated to see whether the farmer is exposed to other sources of risk that weren't present or were less important without the contract. These risks include manner and timing of payment, long-term capital investment, potential liabilities, greater moral risk, increased risk of not being able to meet product specifications, counterparty risk, and assumed risks. **Counterparty** risk is the risk that the other party in a contract will default—that is, not meet the obligations in the contract. Assumed risks are those assigned to each party of a contract, either stated explicitly or implied through contract language.

As an example of risk created by a contract, consider recent hog contracts that guarantee a certain cash price or a range of prices for the hogs sold under the contract. This sales price guarantee stabilizes cash flow and income for the length of the contract. These contracts also contain a clause about the packer maintaining an account and tracking the times the contract price was higher than the cash market price and when it was lower. Under this contract, the producers decreased the risk of price and income variation, but the producers were also exposed to a new risk of a large liability at the end of the contract. They became painfully aware of this when the cash hog market reached very low levels in 1998–99 and these packer accounts became very large against the producer.

Another example of risk is the risk of bankruptcy by the contractor. The ethanol industry in the United States was growing rapidly and then suffered from falling ethanol prices and high corn prices in 2008–09. Several ethanol producers encountered hard financial times. Bankruptcies occurred, and farmers with contracts saw their contracts either voided or renegotiated from high corn prices to lower prices. These farmers faced the counterparty risk of the ethanol producer not being able to pay the contract price and using the legal process of bankruptcy to cancel the original contract.

Risk also increases when a building is built as part of the contract. Livestock and poultry contracts often involve a building purchase. This is a fixed asset and a fixed financial obligation for many years. Before signing, a manager needs to evaluate how that fixed obligation may affect them if the other party does not perform as the contract says or encounters financial difficulties. This risk is sometimes called "hold up" (as in the owner cannot use the building) or asset fixity. The problem lies in having a single-purpose building and only one buyer of the product. If the other party does not perform, the building may be required to sit unused or empty. The asset is fixed or held up. Contracts usually do and should have a clause saying that the building expenses will be paid for during the life of the contract, but the farmer's expected return from that investment is nonexistent. The problem is exacerbated if the other party is not able to even pay the building costs. The farmer can be left with a financial obligation, a building, and not many options for its use. This type of risk can be evaluated by considering the financial status and reputation of the other party. If these are questionable or not available, this hold-up risk is higher.

Recent crop contracts for non-GMO grains may seem very good in terms of a better, more stable price and quantity. However, some contracts could expose producers to other forms of risk due to signing a guarantee that their grain is, for example, 95% free of GMO grain (or 99%, 99.5%, or even 100%). The risk is changed from one of market price fluctuations to one of potential contamination of the grain in storage and shipment, so that it does not meet the product specifications in the contract.

A payoff and regret matrix (as described in Chapter 22) can be useful to organize the potential profitability estimates under different scenarios of the future with and without a contract (Example 23.1).

Legal

Contracts have been used for centuries, and their terms have developed very specific legal meanings. These specific meanings can have large impacts on the potential profitability of a contract to a producer, the risks to which they are exposed, and the legal rights and obligations under the contract. Certain differences in wording, for example, can change a producer from a contractor to an employee, which can have major impacts on the legal obligations and responsibilities. The different types of production contracts also have different legal impacts on both the producer and contractor.

Example 23.1. A Simple Payoff/Regret Matrix for Evaluating a Production Contract

The potential profit and risk of a production contract can be evaluated using a payoff/regret matrix. As a simple example, consider the question of whether a farmer should sign a contract to provide space for someone else's pigs. The alternative is for the farmer to own and feed her own pigs in the building.

For this example, the contractor will pay the farmer $39 per pig. The farmer's costs are $29 per pig for a net return of $10 per pig. The contractor pays all feed, medicine, and other costs and takes all risk in changes in pig prices and feed prices. So the net return of $10 does not change as pig and feed prices change for the contractor.

If the farmer were to own and feed her own pigs, the three scenarios are combinations of pig prices and feed costs. As shown below, these combinations result in net returns per pig of $23, $−3, and $−38 per pig. These estimates show the farmer to be exposed to the risk of changing pig and feed prices with net return ranging from a high $23 per pig with a high pig price and low feed costs to a low of a loss of $−38 per pig with a low pig price and high feed costs.

Based on these estimates, the farmer has a choice of a contract with an average payoff of $10 per pig or feeding and selling on the open market with an average payoff of $4 per pig but a high of $32 and a low of $−28. The regret matrix shows the contract choice to have much lower regret. Between these two choices, many people would likely sign the contract. Other people may see the chance to earn $32 per pig instead of $10; if the whole matrix is not evaluated, the possible loss of $−28 may be overlooked.

(The farmer also has the third option of neither signing the contract nor feeding her own pigs. This choice would have to evaluate the time and other resources required for these two options compared to the potential income from other uses of that time and other resources.)

Scenario	Payoff per Pig:		Regret per Pig:	
	Contract	Open Market	Contract	Open Market
High hog price, low feed cost	10	32	22	0
Medium hog price, medium feed cost	10	7	0	3
Low hog price, high feed cost	10	−28	0	38
Average	10	4	7	14
Minimum payoff	10	−28	xxx	xxx
Maximum regret	xxx	xxx	22	38

This simple example shows how the payoff and regret matrix can be used to evaluate the tradeoff between payoffs and risk in contract evaluation. However, the matrix does not show the answer for every farmer. Each situation and decision will be different. Each contract will have different expectations and specifics, and each person will have different options.

Several of these legal concerns and specific wordings are noted in the checklist in the next section. As noted earlier, if the terms in the contract are not fully understood, outside expert advice is needed before signing any contract.

A Production Contract Checklist

The following checklist is developed to help farmers evaluate potential production contracts. The list is adapted and expanded from the lists developed by Gerhardson (1999) and by a task force established by the Production Contracts Task Force (1996a, 1996b). However, no checklist can raise every question and not every question will be relevant to every producer because times, conditions, and points of law change. The decision to sign a contract is each party's own responsibility.

In the following list, the term "producer" is used to identify the party who will be obligated to produce a product, provide a service, or buy an input. In this discussion of production contracts in farm management, the "producer" is usually thought of as the farmer. The term "contractor" is used to identify the party other than the producer or farmer. The contractor may be asking the producer to produce a certain product according to specifications in the contract, to provide a specified service, or to buy a certain input. The contractor may be a processor, a product buyer, an input supplier, or another farmer. If both parties are farmers, each farmer would evaluate the contract using this same checklist but from their own viewpoint as a producer or contractor.

The list consists of both items to check when done and questions to be answered. The first item, "I have read ALL the terms of the contract," for example, is an item to be checked as done. It isn't a question of how much has been read; it is a question of whether all of it has been read. Questions to be answered involve questions with simple answers, "Is the contract in writing?" for example, and questions requiring considerable analysis, such as "Does the contract improve the prospects for producer profitability?" By considering the items and answering the questions in this list, a producer will gather considerable information from which he or she can make a much more informed decision on whether to sign a contract—that is, enter into a contractual relationship.

First of All:
  I have read ALL the terms of the contract.
  I understand ALL the terms of the contract.
Get It in Writing:
  Is the contract in writing?
  Is the written agreement different from the verbal promises made?
  Is the ENTIRE agreement in writing?
  Were verbal agreements made during negotiations, but not written into the contract?
  Is the agreement clearly written?
  When does the agreement become an enforceable contract?
  How do you enforce the contract?
In General:
  What is the legal form of the contract?
  Can I negotiate the terms of the contract?
  Can I join a marketing association that will negotiate contract terms with the contractor?

Why is the contractor considering contracting?

Why is the producer considering contracting?

Does the contract fit into the producer's long-term goals and business strategy?

Have neighbors been informed and consulted if the contract involves livestock production, new genetically modified organisms, or other inputs and products that may affect them?

Parties to the Contract:

Who are the parties to the contract?

Is the contractor a subsidiary of a larger company?

What are the contractor's credentials?

If the producer has concerns about being paid, will the contractor provide a financial statement?

Will the contractor provide a list of producers with whom the contractor has contracted with in the past?

Does it appear that the contractor is committed to contracting in this area in the future?

Has the contractor made investments in fixed assets or relocated management to this region?

Is contracting part of the contractor's core business?

What are the producer's credentials?

How can they be verified?

If the contractor has questions about the producer's ability to perform the contract, is the producer required (and willing and able) to release a financial statement and names of individuals who will verify the producer's financial stability and management abilities?

Can the contract be assigned or transferred by the producer to other producers?

Can the contract be assigned or transferred by the contractor to others such as a lender?

Do other parties have to approve the contract, such as landlords, lenders, spouses?

Duration, Termination, and Renewal of the Contract:

What is the duration of the contract?

Is the duration of the contract adequate to recover any investments in facilities and equipment?

Can the contract be terminated early?

Under what conditions can the contractor terminate the contract?

Who determines whether those conditions are met?

Are there objective standards, or is termination at the discretion of the contractor?

How much notice must the contractor give to the producer before terminating the contract?

Is the producer given an opportunity to cure any problem before the contractor terminates? How much time is the producer given to cure a problem? What options are specified for the producer to cure a problem?

What are the producer's rights after termination of the contract?

Will the producer be paid for work done up to the date of termination?

In the event of termination, does the producer have an option to buy the product (livestock or crops) if it is owned by the contractor?

Can the contract be terminated before the producer's investment is fully recovered?

If so, what is specified to compensate the producer for any remaining, unrecovered investment?

Under what conditions can the producer terminate the contract?

If the producer gets sick, becomes disabled, or dies, can the contract be terminated?

Can the producer terminate the contract if the contractor fails to deliver inputs on time or make payments on time?

What happens if the contractor files for bankruptcy?

What happens if the producer files for bankruptcy?

Does the contract excuse non-performance on the part of the contractor caused by "acts of God," meaning occurrences out of human control?

Does the contract excuse non-performance on the part of the producer caused by "acts of God," meaning occurrences out of human control?

Legal Relationship Created by the Contract:

Does the contract describe a sale of goods or a sale of services?

Who owns the product during production?

If the contract describes a sale of goods, does the contract specifically address whether the Uniform Commercial Code applies to the contract?

Does the contract describe the producer as a "merchant who deals in goods of the kind"?

Does the contract make the claim that the producer holds himself out as having knowledge or skill particular to the practices of goods involved in the transaction?

If the contract describes a sale of services, does the contract address whether the producer is considered an independent contractor or an employee of the contractor?

Does it address whether the producer is a partner, joint venturer or agent of the contractor? Does the contract establish some other relationship, such as landlord/tenant?

Price, Payment, and Compensation:

On what basis is the producer being paid?

Are the terms describing pricing/compensation clear?

Is the method of calculating payment clearly defined?

Which payment criteria are out of the producer's control?

Is the schedule of payments firmly set?

Will this schedule satisfy the producer's need for cash flow?

May the contractor change the calculation of payments or the schedule of payments?

Are there penalties for late payments by the contractor?

If so, are they clearly defined with a firm schedule of when they would be paid?

Can the payments be assigned to a lender or other third party?

Will the full payment be made before the product leaves the producer's facilities?

Will the name of the producer's lender be on the payment checks?

Are the weighing and grading procedures outlined in the contract clearly defined?

Who has control over weighing and grading?

How may the producer verify weighing and grading if it is performed by the contractor?

Does the contract include incentive payments?

What does the producer have to do to receive the incentive payments?

How are the payments calculated and when are the payments made?

Can the producer examine the computations used to determine the incentive payments and verify any methods used?

What are the producer's costs of production?

When the costs of production are deducted from the payments, is the contract profitable?

If the producer does not have cost of production records, has the Extension Service or other professionals provided assistance in arriving at estimated production costs?

Does the contract improve the prospects for producer profitability?

Does the contract attempt to modify the producer's right to an agriculture production lien?

Production Issues:

What are the written obligations of the producer under the contract?

What specific production inputs and practices are required of the producer?

What are the written obligations of the contractor under the contract?

What specific production inputs and operations will be provided by the contractor?

What normal and necessary production inputs and operations are not specifically listed? And who supplies them?

Who is responsible for the quality of inputs (feed, animals, seed, equipment, and so on) and the delivery of these inputs?

Who is responsible for supplying labor and management?

Who is responsible for keeping records?

Who has access to the land, facilities, and records? When is access allowed?

What are the facility requirements? Do new facilities need to be built? Who provides financing for new facilities and on what terms?

Is there an "exclusivity of use" clause for any facilities?

Does a livestock contract allow the producer to have any other livestock on the farm?

Who is responsible for manure removal and facility cleaning?

Who is responsible for post-harvest tillage and other operations?

Is the risk of loss passed from one party to the other in the terms of the contract?

Disputes:

Does the contract require an alternative dispute resolution method in the event of a dispute?

Does it require mediation?

Does it require arbitration?

Does it specify or limit who may serve as a mediator or arbitrator?

Where will the mediation or arbitration take place?

Is the arbitration binding?

In the event mediation or non-binding arbitration is unsuccessful, what happens?

Does the contract specify that a certain state's law governs disputes under the contract?

How much would it cost to hire a lawyer licensed in that state?

Does the contract set a venue (i.e., location) for any lawsuit that might be filed?

How much would it cost to bring a claim in that location?

A Concluding Comment

As noted earlier, signing a contract, especially for the first time, creates a very different business environment for the farmer. Old relationships are not necessarily the same. New risks may be larger than envisioned. If the terms in the contract or its legal consequences are not fully understood, an attorney should be consulted. If the financial and tax consequences of the contract are not fully understood, a lender, tax professional, Extension educator, agricultural consultant, or other knowledgeable advisor should be consulted. Another usually good source of information and advice is other producers who have experience with contracts; talk to them.

Summary

- Contracts have been used in farming for a long time.
- Production contracts have increased in popularity and frequency of use in recent years.
- Contracting generally reduces all participants' exposure to risk by combining both market and production functions.
- Farmers enter into contracts for various reasons, including income stability, improved efficiency, market security, and access to capital.
- Processors enter into contracts to control input supplies, improve responses to consumer demand, and expand and diversify operations.
- Production contracts specify the quality and quantity of the commodity to be produced, the quality and quantity of production inputs to be supplied by the contracting firm, the quality and quantity of services to be provided by the grower, and the type, magnitude, and schedule of compensation that the grower will receive.
- The manner in which contracts are constructed affects the legal relationship between the producer and the contractor and, thus, the legal obligations of each party. There are four main types of production contracts.
- With sales contracts or market-specific production contracts, the farmer produces the crop or livestock and agrees to sell the product at harvest to the contractor. The farmer retains ownership until harvest and consequent sale.
- A production-management contract increases the control of the buyer over the production process.
- A production-management contract may be considered a bailment when someone else is entrusted with the possession of property but has no ownership interest in it.
- Personal service contracts or resource-providing contracts specify that the producer is to provide services, not commodities, to the contractor.
- Evaluating a contract involves answering three basic questions. First, does the contract improve profitability? Second, how does the contract change the risks that the farmer faces? Third, how does the contract change legal relationships and obligations?
- The best way to evaluate profitability is to develop two sets of budgets: one for operating under the contract and one without.
- Avoiding risk is a major reason for contracting, but contracts can introduce new risks.
- Signing a contract can change legal relationships, expectations, and obligations from established, yet informal, relationships.
- A checklist can help a farmer evaluate potential contracts.
- If economic and legal implications of a potential contract are not fully understood, a farmer should seek expert advice to help evaluate the contract.
- The decision to sign a contract is each party's own responsibility.

Review Questions

1. What are some reasons for a farmer to sign a contract? What are some reasons for a farmer not to sign a contract?

2. What are some reasons for a processor or other buyer to sign a contract? What are some reasons for a processor or other buyer not to sign a contract?
3. What are the four basic requirements for an agreement to be a legally enforceable contract?
4. What types of contracts must be in writing to be legally enforceable?
5. Even though a contract does not have to be in writing, what are the benefits of putting it in writing?
6. Describe and contrast the four types of production contracts.
7. What are the three basic questions involved in contract evaluation?
8. Using the checklist in this chapter, evaluate the example contract listed below.
9. Using estimated breakeven prices of $16 per head for variable costs and $30 per head for all costs of producing feeder pigs, evaluate the profitability and risk of signing the contract below compared to producing and selling the feeder pigs in the open market without a contract. Recently, the Chicago Mercantile price for lean hogs has been ranging from $50 to $75 per cwt. (Is this the meat price the contract refers to?) Cash prices have ranged from $25 to $50 per head recently. Using the techniques described in Chapter 22, Risk Management, for probability of success and the triangular distribution, what is the probability of a profit for this contract? For the Chicago Mercantile price for lean hogs, use a most likely price of $62 per cwt, a minimum of $40, and a maximum of $70. For the cash price, use a most likely price of $35 per head, a minimum of $25, and a maximum of $50.

THE FOLLOWING IS AN EXAMPLE CONTRACT. NAMES ARE FICTITIOUS.
IT IS NEITHER A LEGAL INSTRUMENT NOR A MODEL LEGAL INSTRUMENT.
LEGAL COUNSEL IS NEEDED TO CREATE A LEGAL INSTRUMENT.

Feeder Pig Purchase Agreement

THIS AGREEMENT made this 1st day of February, 2002, between Harold Smythe, of South-town, Anystate, herein after called Producer and Prairie Pigs, Inc., of Northtown, Anystate, herein after called Buyer.

1. Pig Prices. Pigs will be priced at 50% of the meat price on the next Monday close of the Chicago Mercantile five (5) months out with a floor of $25.00 and a ceiling of $35.00 per pig delivered to the Buyer. These pigs will be approximately fourteen (14) to nineteen (19) days old and weigh eight (8) pounds or more. Pigs that weigh less than eight (8) pounds will be priced according to Buyer's discount schedule. Pigs weighing 10 (10) pounds or more will receive an additional 50 cents per pound.

2. Payment. Buyer agrees to pay the agreed-upon price for the pigs upon delivery.

3. Delivery. Producer agrees to sell to Buyer and Buyer agrees to purchase from Producer approximately 250 head of early weaned pigs every four (4) weeks. Producer shall provide groups of approximately 250 head every four (4) weeks. Producer shall notify Buyer of expected delivery dates at least three (3) days prior to delivery.

(continued)

(*continued*)

4. Risk of Loss and Transfer of Ownership. The Producer shall bear all risk of loss while the pigs are in transport due to natural causes; for other death losses, cargo insurance will be provided by the carrier. Ownership of said pigs shall pass at the time of delivery to Buyer.

5. Health. Producer agrees to provide all health permits necessary to qualify the pigs for shipment, and to notify Buyer immediately if there are any production problems that may affect the pigs' delivery date, amount of delivery, or quality of pigs delivered.

6. Buyer's Right of Rejection. Buyer reserves the right to reject individual pigs at the time of delivery. The value of any pig in question will be adjusted according to Buyer's discount schedule. Any total discount greater than $250.00 per delivery group must be reported to Producer prior to acceptance of pigs by the Buyer. Buyer must notify Producer of any complaints within twenty-four (24) hours of delivery. The Producer reserves the right, at its sole discretion, to inspect and remove any pigs rejected and subject to discount schedule.

7. Duration of Contract. This agreement shall be effective immediately upon execution by the parties hereto and shall terminate five (5) years following the date of the first delivery of pigs to the Buyer's facility. This agreement, if not terminated in writing at least six (6) months prior to the end of said five (5) year period, will be deemed renewed until either party terminates the Agreement by giving the other party a six (6) month written notice of termination.

8. Notices. All notices that are required to be given pursuant to the Agreement or that are given pursuant to the relationship of the parties shall be in writing and shall be sent postage prepaid by certified or registered mail to the addresses as given below.

9. Acts of God. Neither party shall be liable for damages due to delay or failure to perform any obligations under the Agreement if such delay or failure results directly or indirectly from circumstances beyond the control of such party. Such circumstances shall include, but shall not be limited to acts of God, acts of war, civil commotions, riots, strikes, lockouts, acts of government in either its sovereign or contractual capacity, perturbation in telecommunications transmission, inability to obtain suitable equipment or components, accident, fire, water damages, flood, earthquake, or other natural catastrophes.

10. Arbitration. The parties agree that should any dispute arise as to the terms or execution of the contact, they will submit the controversy to arbitration in the manner as allowed by Anystate and that they will abide by the arbitrator's decision.

11. Independent Contractor. It is understood and agreed that the parties to the Agreement are independent contractors.

12. Governing Laws. It is agreed that this Agreement shall be governed by, construed, and enforced in accordance with the laws of Anystate.

13. Waiver. The waiver by either party of any breach or violation of this Agreement shall not operate or be construed as a waiver of subsequent breach or violation thereof.

14. Entire understanding. This Agreement constitutes the full understanding of the parties and supersedes any and all prior agreements relating thereto, whether written or oral, that may exist between the parties hereto:

_____   By: _____
Witness   Producer

_____   By: _____
Witness   Buyer

NOTE: THE PRECEDING IS AN EXAMPLE CONTRACT. NAMES ARE FICTITIOUS.
IT IS NEITHER A LEGAL INSTRUMENT NOR A MODEL LEGAL INSTRUMENT.
LEGAL COUNSEL IS NEEDED TO CREATE A LEGAL INSTRUMENT.

Further Reading

Gerhardson, B. 1999. *A Guide to Agricultural Production Contracting in Minnesota*. St. Paul: Minnesota Department of Agriculture, 1999.

Kunkel, Phillip L., Jeffrey A. Peterson, and Jessica A. Mitchell. 2009. "Agricultural Production Contracts." University of Minnesota Extension, University of Minnesota, St. Paul, 5 pp. Accessed on October 26, 2009, at http://www.extension.umn.edu/distribution/businessmanagement/DF7291.html.

Production Contracts Task Force. 1996a. "Grain Production Contract Checklist." Office of the Attorney General, Iowa Department of Justice. Accessed December 6, 2002, through Iowa State University Extension, http://www.exnet.iastate.edu/Pages/grain/tools/graincontract.html.

Production Contracts Task Force. 1996b. "Livestock Production Contract Checklist." Office of the Attorney General, Iowa Department of Justice, accessed December 6, 2002, through Iowa State University Extension, URL: http://www.exnet.iastate.edu/Pages/grain/tools/livecontract.html.

24

Human Resource Management

In this chapter:

- Human and employee needs
- Cultural diversity
- Human resource management

Managing the workforce (or human resource management) is becoming more important in agriculture since an increasing number of farms have employees. Farms with multiple partners and operators who may be related or unrelated; husband and wife; parents, children, or siblings; on-farm or off-farm also need to consider the issues surrounding human resource management. Not everyone needs, or can handle, the same levels of responsibility, authority, and accountability. Not everyone deserves the same level of compensation. Understanding the principles of human resource management will help improve communication among people and thus management of the whole farm. Understanding that human resource management practices can and need to change as the farm grows is critical; one example of the evolution to a good process is described in Example 24.1.

Example 24.1. Changing the Human Resource Management Process

"If I shook a prospective employee's hand and felt a pulse, I hired him," is how George Mueller described his hiring practices in the early years of managing his dairy farm. But the process had to change as the farm expanded. The farm needed high-quality workers who could share the management of operations, and it needed to maximize productivity and quality of non-management people. Pay and incentives had to be designed to encourage and reward behavior that helped the farm maintain and improve productivity and profitability. The farm also had to attract and retain good workers in jobs that held a less-than-positive view for many and in areas that had many workers moving away.

To accomplish these goals, the farm pays the non-management workers the same wage as available in other jobs locally, and adds a premium per hour for evening and other non-regular work hours. It offers paid vacation and personal days, health care, reduced cost housing, meat, birthday parties on work time, and annual business dinners with employees. It also has performance reviews twice a year, training on and off the farm, staff meetings, employee empowerment (through asking for and listening to ideas), and improved working conditions. The farm also has four compensation programs aimed at attraction, retention, quality, and productivity goals.

- Worker cow-ownership program (WCOP): Mueller noticed that workers who owned cows took better care of the cows and watched to be sure other workers took care of the animals. Productivity for the whole farm improved. He felt that WCOP also enhanced the reputation of the farm as an employer, which helped in attracting and retaining workers.
- Incentives for high-quality milk production: The milk buyer pays a bonus based on low bacteria, and somatic cell and sediment counts. Mueller divides the whole bonus evenly among the milkers. If the farm is fined due to poor-quality milk, the milkers are not paid the bonus until the penalty is paid back from the quality bonus. The workers want the bonus pay, so they strive to achieve high-quality milk and avoid mistakes that decrease quality.
- Incentives for noticing cows in heat: One major problem for dairies is the detection of cows in heat so they can be bred in a timely manner. Workers are paid for each cow they accurately detect in heat. This incentive is paid in a separate check so that it is an obvious bonus. Is it worth it? Mueller noted that "it is surprising how much sharper workers' eyesight gets" if they know they might get a bonus.
- Incentives for achieving field crop production goals: Field crew bonuses are based on achieving timeliness goals set by workers and management each year for planting and harvesting. The bonus is intended to encourage employees to work the long hours required during planting and harvest.

Source: M. E. Graham, R. Welsh, and G. Mueller, "In the Land of Milk and Money: One Dairy Farm's Strategic Compensation System," *Journal of Agribusiness*, 15-2 (Fall 1997): 171–188.

This chapter starts with some basic information about human needs and the roots of cultural diversity. The bulk of the chapter deals with the process of staffing or human resource management: assessing needs, designing jobs, recruiting, interviewing, hiring, training, motivating, leading, directing, evaluating, and compensating.

Human and Employee Needs

The first fact to remember in human resource management is that employees and all fellow workers are humans; they are intelligent adults. People are different, often very different, from each other but they are still human. We come from different cultures. These differences do not need to be avoided;

in fact they cannot be avoided, and we probably should not even try to avoid them. Managers need to accept differences in people and work with them through the differences. A stronger workforce and a stronger farm will result.

Human Needs

As humans, we have basic needs that need to be met. Maslow (1970) identified seven basic human needs. **Maslow's seven needs** are listed below in his order of priority. How they relate to workforce management is also described. For workforce management, meeting the highest priorities is obvious; paying attention to the other needs can create an even better workforce and improved employee loyalty and efficiency.

1. Physiological. We all need air, water, and food. We will instinctively and immediately fight anything or anyone that limits our ability to breathe. Our bodies will tell us we need to drink or eat. Our cultures have set up schedules for meals and breaks for water and food.

An employee's physiological needs are met by access to air, water, and food at work. By being paid, they can have these at home as well. Work rules need to allow time and space for water and food on the job. Sufficient ventilation is also critical. (These also relate to the second need, safety, but there is a point when the problem moves from an immediate life-threatening situation to a longer-term safety concern.) Providing access to retirement programs and disability insurance are also ways to meet physiological needs, although in a long-term sense.

2. Safety. We all want to avoid pain and danger, although we may have different pain and danger thresholds. We find comfort in being sheltered and not exposed to bad weather, potential harm, and so on.

An employee needs safety guards, tractor cabs, safe equipment, rest, protection from the weather, as they apply to the job. Again, work rules that allow for rest breaks provide for safety by decreasing the chance for accidents due to drowsiness or inattentiveness. Health insurance gives us access to medical care and protection from financial loss that may occur if medical bills are large.

3. Belonging and Love. We all need to be part of a group, although that need may be expressed in different degrees. Even a "loner" can feel a need to belong to a group albeit at a distance. We need the security and comfort of a close relationship or someone to talk with although we have different definitions of "close."

Belonging is a two-way street. The individual needs a group or a person. From the other direction, the group or other person needs to signal positively that the person does indeed belong to the group or to the relationship.

Employees need to feel they are part of the business. This may not be expressed directly, but at some level, the need to belong is present. An employee needs to have pride in the business, to receive respect from management, to be able to respect management, and to receive some communication about the business. A manager needs to avoid the "them vs. us" atmosphere.

Interpersonal relationships between employees can range from a very good relationship that creates a productive atmosphere to very bad relationship that can be devastating to morale, productivity, and safety. A manager needs to pay attention to how workers relate to each other and how to avoid problems that may occur due to interpersonal relationships.

4. Esteem and Self-esteem. We need to be accepted by others. At some level, we want the status and recognition by others that we have done well. We need to be able to look at what we have done and tell ourselves that we are satisfied with that effort.

An employee needs "company" esteem, which can come from promotions or merits, increases in responsibility, and awards (even little ones). Besides monetary awards and job changes, a manager can signal acceptance publicly in a variety of ways: certificates that signal management's recognition of accomplishments (e.g., 9.0 pigs/litter; 22,500 pounds of milk per cow); awards of hats or coats for productivity, safety, or other accomplishments; pictures and announcements in a local newspaper or company newsletter. Even things that seem small can be very good for self-esteem and desired by employees when done in a public, respectful way.

5. Self-actualization. We need to realize our potential and use it. We want to develop and expand our potential. We want to know what we are good at, use that skill or knowledge, and improve ourselves and our productivity. This skill or knowledge may be work related or it may not. Hobbies or avocations may be the place where this human need is met.

A good interview process can help fit the right person to the right job. This is the first step in allowing an employee to realize and use his or her potential. An employee also needs training to continue to improve skills. Future advancement within the company, or career ladders, can help an employee see how he or she can advance. By setting realistic goals, a manager can help employees realize accomplishment and the satisfaction of using their skills. However, a manager also needs to be cautious and not set unrealistic goals. Unrealistic goals could cause underachievement if an employee cannot see any possibility of accomplishing the goal.

6. Cognitive Understanding. We need to understand ourselves, our lives, our environment, and how they relate to each other. We need to understand "why we are here." This is the hardest human need to meet. Other needs obviously have a higher priority. We need to find this cognitive understanding only after all our other needs have been met.

Employees need to know where they fit within a company and the company's goals. This can be done through communications, training, and answers to questions such as, Why are we doing this? and What is the future direction of the company?

7. Aesthetic Needs. Although Maslow says this is hard to see, he believes that, after other needs are met satisfactorily, humans have a need for beauty. For employees this can be a need for clean, nice places to work.

Employee Needs

Although Maslow's list of needs provides a very good background for understanding people and their needs, his list is not the only way to classify workers' needs. When focusing directly on workforce management, employees' needs can be grouped into four areas: responsibility, authority, accountability, and compensation. These areas will be used to define jobs.

Responsibility. Whether a worker is an employee, a partner, or a family member, he or she needs to have the responsibility of assigned duties. Workers need to be responsible for something. These responsibilities may be called duties. Responsibility builds self-esteem, respect, belonging, and self-actualization.

Authority. A worker who has the responsibility for a job needs the authority to do the job. He or she needs to decide how to do it and to acquire the resources to do it. Perhaps the job and the resources are well-defined (feeding the cattle or driving the combine, for example), but the worker still has to have the authority to get and operate the needed equipment. If the person is trained to use the equipment, valuable time can be wasted if the worker is waiting for approval to use an obviously needed piece of equipment. Having authority helps build self-esteem, self-actualization, and career development.

Accountability. If you have the responsibility and authority to do a job, you should also be held accountable for getting the job done. If there is no accountability, you can have anarchy! A manager needs to describe the job and the standards against which the results will be measured. Having accountability and meeting standards help with esteem, self-actualization, career development, respect, and acceptance by management.

Compensation. Compensation can be more than money. Monetary compensation allows a worker to obtain food, housing, clothes, transportation, and other physiological needs. A residence on the farm or products from the farm (milk and meat, for example) can also be part of the compensation package. Compensation can also provide health and disability insurance to meet physiological and safety needs. Providing year-end bonuses can allow a worker to participate in the benefits of a good year and a good effort and show the worker that he or she does belong to the company and is not just an employee. Providing a vehicle to a worker provides not only physiological needs but also improves belonging and esteem if given as a reward for length of service or status of job, for example.

Is "all this stuff" about human needs and employee needs really important? IT IS! A survey by Agri Careers of New Hampton, Iowa, found that over 80% of the reasons that employees gave for quitting a job could have been prevented (Thomas and Erven, 1989). The reasons given for leaving and the percentage of respondents that gave that reason are listed below.

- 7% said: limited time off
- 8% said: lack of training
- 10% said: lack of recognition
- 13% said: lack of achievement
- 13% said: lack of responsibility
- 14% said: low salary
- 17% said: problems with the boss and the boss's family

Each one of these reasons could have been dealt with directly by management or by management realizing that it needed some better training.

Cultural Diversity

Another, increasingly important aspect of human resource management is the acceptance and understanding of the cultural diversity of the workforce. Acceptance and then understanding

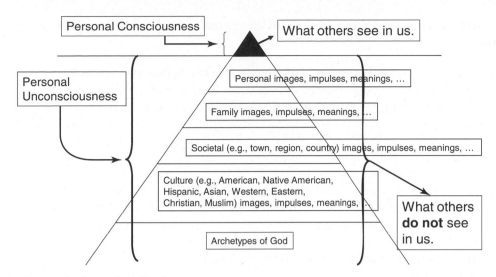

Figure 24.1 Jung's Geology of the Soul
Source: Personal communication with Dr Robert Hurlbut, who learned it from Dr John Villenski, who learned it from Dr Carl Jung. No published reference available.

of how to work with people from different cultures will greatly increase the chances of success for businesses in the future. A large part of understanding different cultures is the realization that people respond differently not because they are being obstinate or uneducated but because they have a whole set of different backgrounds, memories, and cultural history than others may have. We do not realize all that we have and we certainly don't know all that someone else has. One way to realize this difference and to start down the road to understanding is depicted by Dr Carl Jung's Geology of the Soul (Figure 24.1). The analogy struck by the use of the word geology is very appropriate. We can see only part of the background of another person, and they can see only part of what is in us. We do not know all the personal and family experiences that another person has had. We can see differences when we meet someone from another town or region but we don't know how they will react to certain events because we don't know all of their "geology." Even a long-time childhood friend from the same community and of the same age does not see and know all the experiences that you have had and thus cannot always predict the way you will react to events. Sometimes we don't even understand ourselves because parts of our "geology" are buried so deep.

When we add different cultures to our mix of friends and staff, we must expect that responses, initiatives, and mode of operation will be different. Since cultural diversity exists now and will be part of the future, we need to understand that our approach to human resource management needs to be different. It will take longer to understand how people of different cultures operate, what is positive and negative to them, what are better incentives for them, how they learn new skills, and so on. Realizing that they have a different "geology" from your culture is the place to start. Our deep "geology" cannot be changed, but we can choose to learn how to live and work with other cultures, and they with ours. Learning how to celebrate with other cultures can be one of the great benefits of taking time to understand each other.

Human Resource Management

Human resource management, or managing the workforce, can be described as the following steps or tasks.

1. Assessing the present situation
2. Developing tentative job descriptions
3. Matching present employees (or partners and family members) to those tentative job descriptions
4. Developing job descriptions for the remaining tasks
5. Recruiting, interviewing and hiring employees who fit those job descriptions
6. Training employees
7. Motivating, leading, and directing employees and colleagues
8. Evaluating performance
9. Compensating employees

These tasks can be classified in terms of the four broad functions of management introduced in Chapter 2: planning, organizing, directing, and controlling. By realizing where the different tasks fit in terms of functions, we can perform each more efficiently by knowing which "management hat" we need to be wearing. It also becomes very evident that some tasks of workforce management take place under different management functions. For example, the setting of wage rates and incentive structures is done as part of the planning function, but the actual compensation occurs under either directing or controlling (in terms of incentives to obtain the desired performance).

1. Planning
   Assessing the situation
   Setting wage scales and incentive plans
2. Organizing
   Estimating the type and number of people needed
   Writing job descriptions
   Setting employee goals and standards
   Recruiting
   Interviewing
   Hiring
   Training
3. Directing
   Leading
   Supervising
   Motivating
4. Controlling
   Evaluating employees and determining incentive pay
   Taking corrective actions: reassign, retrain, reevaluate, release

Assessing the Situation

Assessing the present situation involves determining the amount of labor available, listing the jobs that need to be done and the labor required for each job, and then comparing the amount available and amount required to estimate any hiring needs. A standard form such as the one in Table 24.1 can be helpful for organizing this information. This form classifies the labor available as operator, partner, family, hired, and custom. Off-farm work is listed as a need or demand for labor to (1) reflect the increasing frequency of farmers having off-farm employment and (2) emphasize the idea that this

Table 24.1 Labor Estimate Worksheet

	Total Hours for Year	Distribution of Hours			
		Dec. thru March	April May June	July August	Sept. Oct. Nov.
Suggested hours for full-time worker	2,400	600	675	450	675
My estimate for full-time worker					
LABOR HOURS AVAILABLE					
Operator (or Partner No. 1)					
Partner No. 2					
Family labor					
Hired labor					
Custom machine operators					
(1) TOTAL LABOR HOURS AVAILABLE					
(2) OFF-FARM WORK					
DIRECT LABOR HOURS NEEDED BY CROP AND ANIMAL ENTERPRISES					
Crop Enterprises	Acres	Total Hr/ Acre			
(3) TOTAL LABOR HOURS NEEDED FOR CROPS					
DIRECT LABOR HOURS NEEDED BY ANIMAL ENTERPRISES					
Animal Enterprises	No. of Units	Total Hr/ Unit			
(4) TOTAL LABOR HOURS NEEDED FOR ANIMALS					
(5) Total Hours of Indirect Labor Needed					
(6) TOTAL LABOR HOURS NEEDED (lines 2 + 3 + 4 + 5)					
(7) Additional Labor Hours Required (line 6 minus line 1 if >0)					
(8) Excess Labor Hours Available (line 1 minus line 6 if >0)					

choice is an allocation of labor resources very similar to the allocation of land to crops. Custom operators are included to be sure that all labor needs are covered and that nothing is forgotten; for example, harvest labor is still needed even though a custom operator will be hired and supplying that labor. Labor needs are separated into the labor needed for crops, for livestock, and for the whole farm (and not directly allocated to either crops or livestock). Identifying the amount available and needed by season will help determine whether any additional needed labor should be year round or seasonal.

Job Descriptions

After determining what and how much labor is needed, jobs need to be designed that include listing tasks that need to be done. In job design, a manager considers what tasks need to be done and what combination of tasks will be both complementary with each other and interesting to the worker. Putting all the "good" tasks in one job and the "distasteful" tasks in another job will likely create one job that a worker likes and stays in for a long time and a second job that no one likes and stays at. For example, the job that includes cleaning the barns should also include some more pleasant tasks. Jobs with "distasteful" tasks may need other benefits such as extra incentive payments, shorter work hours on "distasteful" days, and so on.

Part of job design (and thus developing good job descriptions) involves worrying about workers' job satisfaction. An employee needs to have a meaningful role in the firm to be happy and satisfied with a job. If an employee likes a job, he or she will probably perform well, which will improve the overall performance of the business. If an employee does not like the job, performance will suffer and perhaps the employee will leave—both actions will hurt the performance of the business.

Job satisfaction and job dissatisfaction are on two different scales. They are not the endpoints of the same continuum. Different factors affect these two concepts, so a worker can, at the same time, be both satisfied and dissatisfied with a job. Factors that are intrinsic to the job or the work itself are potential satisfiers. These include:

- Achievement—the ability to do a task well, to improve oneself
- Responsibility—the ability to have control, to be in charge of at least a small part of the job
- The work itself—a job design that is interesting, and can be seen as useful to the business and society

Factors that are extrinsic to the job or work itself are potential dissatisfiers. These include:

- Supervision—poor supervision, bad bosses, high stress, can make a good job unbearable
- Pay—low pay, both in absolute and relative terms, can make a worker unhappy
- Working conditions—unsafe conditions, poor equipment, poor ventilation, are examples of why workers can be unhappy and thus be "short-timers" in the job

A job description needs to be developed and written for advertising, interviewing, hiring, and evaluating the employee. The act of writing can help clarify the job and also serve as a communication tool within a multi-operator business. A job description should describe the job to be done as well as the authorities given to the employee and measures by which the employee will be evaluated. The evaluation measures should be both quantitative (i.e., measurable) and controllable by the employee. The amount of detail will depend on the job and the employee's knowledge. The job description should be clear enough that potential applicants, current employees, and management all understand what is to be done. Besides the title, a complete job description should include:

- Responsibilities
- Authorities
- Evaluation measures
- Required qualifications
- Desired qualifications
- Supervision (amount and, if applicable, who is direct supervisor)
- Time expectations (hours per day and per week, starting and ending times, overtime rules, seasonal differences, etc.)
- Beginning wage or salary and any bonuses and incentives
- Benefits (insurance, vacation, time off, etc.)

Required qualifications are minimal levels of training, knowledge, personal characteristics, physical abilities, flexibility in time, flexibility in tasks, and other minimal requirements for the employee to do the job. Required qualifications are used to determine whether an applicant can do the job.

Desired qualifications are additional levels of training, knowledge, and such that would allow an applicant to do the described job even better. Desired qualifications are used to compare and rank applicants.

An example job description for a farm operator assistant is shown in Table 24.2. Examples of quantitative measures for evaluation, potential interview questions, and possible tests of ability needed in the job are included with the description.

Recruiting, Interviewing and Selecting

The first job of recruiting is to obtain a good pool of applicants for a job opening. This usually begins with advertising the job. Advertising needs to be done in the proper places for the job needed and where appropriate applicants will see it. The advertisement needs to be written clearly with the minimum requirements listed. The application form should be written to show whether applicants meet minimal requirements and to provide enough additional information to help select the proper applicants to interview.

Interviewing is done with job-specific questions crafted to evaluate the candidates, their knowledge, and their ability to accomplish the job needed. Part of the interview should be a test of their skills needed for the job; just relying on an applicant's opinion of his or her skills will not always yield accurate assessments. These can be written tests or demonstrations of skills such as tractor driving, computer operation, livestock knowledge, pesticide application procedures, and plant identification. A general interview form is shown in Table 24.3, but job-specific questions and tests need to be crafted based on the job description and designed to complete the form.

Table 24.2   Example Job Description for a Farm Operator Assistant

This is a job description for a farm operator assistant on a 1,000-acre crop farm. We grow corn, soybeans, alfalfa, and wheat in east central Minnesota. We rent most of our land and are spread out across several counties.

Duties and responsibilities:
1. Plant and harvest crops
2. Apply chemicals
3. Cultivate row crops
4. Cut, rake, bale alfalfa
5. Drive grain truck as needed
6. Do general maintenance on equipment and tractors
7. Buy parts and supplies for general maintenance
8. Notify owner of needed repairs

Authorities:
1. Do general maintenance on schedule
2. Buy needed parts and supplies within budget provided by owner
3. Decide which fields need to be cultivated

Accountabilities:
   The employee will report to the owner
   Expenditures for parts and supplies have to be appropriate and within budget
   Machinery has to be maintained
   Row crop fields have to be cultivated

Evaluation standards:
1. Equipment and tractors properly maintained
2. Cultivation and chemical applications done in timely manner
3. Level of weed infestations in field
4. Quality of field work
5. Purchases within budget
6. Punctuality and regularity of work time
7. Maintains good relationships with owners, other employees, suppliers, and others

Minimum qualifications:
1. Able to drive a tractor in a straight line
2. Able to lift 80# from ground to height of pickup bed
3. Able to do general maintenance on machinery
4. Able to order and buy parts and supplies
5. Background knowledge of farming and agriculture

Desired qualifications:
1. Ability to operate combines and other machinery
2. Ability to keep maintenance records
3. Willingness to work long hours during planting and harvesting
4. License to drive grain truck
5. Ability to identify weeds
6. Ability to maintain good relationships with owners, other employees, suppliers, and others

Compensation package: $8 per hour, time and a half when over 50 hours per week, health benefits for worker, family benefits available at 1/2 cost, meals while working, pickup truck available.

Three quantitative measures for evaluating performance in this job:
   A.   Machinery maintained on schedule
   B.   Level of weed control in cultivated fields
   C.   Punctuality and regularity of work schedule

Five questions you might ask in an interview with an applicant:
   A.   What is your experience with driving large machinery?
   B.   What is your knowledge of weed control?
   C.   What would you check before starting and operating a tractor?
   D.   How deep should you run a cultivator?
   E.   How would you decide it is time to buy more oil for the machinery?

Three tests that would evaluate the applicant's abilities needed for this job:
   A.   Drive a tractor in a straight line for 200 yards
   B.   Lift a 80# bag from the ground to a pickup
   C.   Change oil and filter on a tractor

Training

Training is needed regardless of previous experience. Orientation—that is, the initial training session—can communicate expectations and process and instill the "team" feeling. For a new employee who worked elsewhere, training in the current job on the current farm can show how the new employer likes the job done. Even little details can be big factors in quality management and/or cost control. Training to review procedures is always good, especially for seasonal jobs (e.g., combine operation, pesticide application). Training promotes safety. It can also help in career advancement, personal development, and employee self-esteem. Training doesn't have to be directly related to the job. Going to a general meeting about new ideas, agricultural conditions, and so on can also be considered training. Also, training does not have to be done on the farm or by the employer. Certification of pesticide applicators is a very good example of training that is usually done off the farm and by certified trainers.

Employers and supervisors should not forget the positive effect of going to an outside meeting or training with their employees. The act of going together shows the importance of the training or meeting, helps in team building, and gives the employee some self-esteem because the boss is going to the same training and meeting.

Motivation, Leading, Directing

There are many aspects of motivation, and many books on the subject are available. Much of motivation is directly related to Maslow's list of basic needs and how those needs can be interpreted for employees. If the employer can learn the employee's needs and then design jobs and rewards to satisfy those needs as well as meet the needs of the farm, the job and the results will create a very satisfying relationship for both parties. Monetary reward is certainly one motivating factor but not the only one. Proper job design that provides a meaningful, satisfying role within the firm will be a great motivator for most employees. Removing the dissatisfiers, described earlier, is the first step toward creating motivated, loyal employees.

Table 24.3 General Interview Form

Date:
Interviewer:
Job being interviewed for:

Name of applicant:
Contact information: mailing address, phone(s), email address(es)
Past work experiences:
Reasons for leaving former job:
Present skills and certificates relevant to this job:
Other questions and information relevant to this job:
Personal goals and aspirations relative to farming:
Why are you applying for this job?
Results of tests relevant to this job:
Characteristics (rate those relevant to this job): 1 = Low and 5 = High

1. Leadership qualities	1	2	3	4	5
2. Ability to work with others	1	2	3	4	5
3. Receptiveness to receiving directions	1	2	3	4	5
4. Motivation to learn	1	2	3	4	5
5. Willingness to perform physical labor	1	2	3	4	5
6. Training and background in:					
Livestock production	1	2	3	4	5
Animal nutrition	1	2	3	4	5
Animal health	1	2	3	4	5
Crop production	1	2	3	4	5
Pesticide application	1	2	3	4	5
Mechanical skills	1	2	3	4	5
Machinery operation	1	2	3	4	5
Vehicle operation	1	2	3	4	5
Management concepts	1	2	3	4	5
Finance	1	2	3	4	5
Marketing	1	2	3	4	5
Ability to manage others	1	2	3	4	5
Ability to compromise	1	2	3	4	5
Ability to identify problems	1	2	3	4	5
Ability to analyze situations	1	2	3	4	5
Ability to make a decision	1	2	3	4	5
Ability to understand directions	1	2	3	4	5
7. Personal goals	1	2	3	4	5
8. Initiative and imagination	1	2	3	4	5
9. Motivation	1	2	3	4	5
10. Determination	1	2	3	4	5
11. Willingness to ask questions	1	2	3	4	5

Comments from references:
Comments by current employees:
Overall rating:

Source: Adapted from Thomas and Erven, 1989.

For aligning an employee with the goals of the firm, Tjan (2009) suggests the approach of asking the employee to list his or her top five priorities on the job prior to their review session. At the review session, Tjan then asks three questions:

1. Which of these priorities do you think will have the greatest impact for our firm?
2. Which of these priorities interest you the most?
3. Which of these priorities are you most likely to be successful with?

The "real magic," as Tjan calls it, is when the questions produce the same answer. The problem is that this seldom happens. Tjan says this can be corrected with communication, confidence, and aligning interests. An employer needs to consistently communicate the top three to five priorities for the firm and make sure people understand them. Tjan suggests asking employees to reshape what they do each day, week, month, and year into goals that match the firm's priorities. An employer needs to promote confidence in people. Besides commenting on good results and effort, another way to instill confidence is to say you expect them to try enough new ideas that a few of the ideas will fail because, the employer should say, "not failing a few times means you're not trying enough new ideas." An employer also needs to align employee interests to responsibilities where possible. Knowing what an employee's interests are helps an employer design jobs and reallocate tasks so the employee has a better chance of doing a task that he or she is passionate about.

Tjan ends with these comments: "It boils down to a simple three-step plan. Step one: get the right focus and relentlessly communicate it. Step two: align the priorities to areas. Step three: build employee confidence and exploit natural interests. Result: happier, harder working, and more loyal employees."

As an employer or supervisor, providing an employee with the knowledge of why the job needs to be done and how the job will be done can help that employee understand where he or she fits in the operation and business. The methods and styles of motivation, leading, and directing will vary with the individual employers and supervisors and, on the personal side of motivation, vary with the employee and how each will respond to various incentives and ideas.

Poor leadership and supervision can be costly. Intentional and unintentional disrespect of employees by the supervisor and/or the manager can be disastrous in terms of direct costs, poor productivity, and high employee turnover. Erven (2001a) says that leadership is not the simple question of whether to be autocratic or democratic. Good leadership is cognizant of the situation and the employee(s) involved. Erven describes the correct leadership behavior as a combination of directive behavior and supportive behavior that is mixed depending on an employee's knowledge, skills, abilities, experience, self-esteem, self-confidence, and commitment. Erven goes on to say that situational leadership is a combination of Blanchard's four leadership styles:

Directing: control and close supervision of the worker
Coaching: more explanation, seek input, stay in control
Supporting: team approach, support rather than control
Delegating: turn over authority and responsibility to the worker

The situational leader, Erven says, bases the choice of a leadership style on the competence and commitment of the person being led rather than on the leader's usual or preferred style.

Evaluation

Evaluation is a major source of control of employees. A private, formal evaluation session is needed at least annually and probably more frequently for new employees. However, corrections and commendations also need to be communicated to the employee whenever it is needed, not just once a year. A new employee needs evaluation very often at the beginning of employment to be sure both parties know what is being done and whether it is being done as expected. Small, frequent corrections of procedures by a close supervisor may help improve overall, long-run performance. Good training may decrease the need for close supervision and frequent evaluation. If there are signs of trouble, supervision and evaluation may need to be increased. If possible, evaluation should be frequent enough so each employee knows the expectations and standards and whether they are being met. A longer-term employee still needs evaluation both when something seems to be wrong and when a manager observes tasks being done well.

Evaluation should be done on the basis of quantitative standards or measures written in the job description, discussed in the job interview, and agreed to at the time of hire. These standards should be appropriate to the job and skill level required. They should be measurable and affected by actions controllable by the employee. Standards should not be vaguely worded, such as "exerts good effort." A better standard would be the amount of work done, the efficiency with which work is accomplished, production levels, and similar quantitative measures. Some examples include acres covered per day, fuel use per acre, bushels over area average crop yield, total production, downtime for machinery repairs, pigs weaned per litter, pounds of milk per cow, sanitation levels in milk, feed costs per unit of animal production, productivity increases over previous years, and so on.

The standards and measures should not be completely beyond the control of the employee. Other factors should not have a large impact on the measures. For example, if the farrowing house manager has no control over herd genetics, the average ham and loin percent should not be used as a standard, but the number of live pigs born per litter and weaned per litter are very appropriate measures.

Some jobs do not lend themselves well to quantitative measures as the only measure. The product of these jobs has both qualitative and quantitative aspects. Employees in these jobs can still be given some measure of quantitative evaluation by giving them a numerical qualitative score on a frequent basis and then using an average score to provide the employee a quantitative measure.

For example, one plant nursery's employee evaluation form had every employee ranked from 0 to 10 every day. The employees were evaluated on a moving three-week average of those scores to avoid daily fluctuations. The nursery used this system because the plants or trees needed to be potted, moved, pruned, and cared for in a high-quality manner otherwise sales were hurt. So employees needed to be evaluated on both the physical amount of work and the quality of their work. Because the tasks were very different, a quantified estimate of quality was difficult, if not impossible, to develop. Therefore, the subjective measure of both quality and quantity was adopted by the nursery. Crop and livestock farmers may benefit from a similar employee evaluation system if the needed tasks are also very different from one hour, one day, or one season to the next. This daily evaluation also provides an immediate evaluation of the employee's work and hopefully positive responses by the employee.

At the evaluation session, the basic question is whether the employee met the standards. As said earlier, both commendations and reprimands are needed. Commendations reinforce good behavior, show respect of the employee, build self-esteem and company-esteem, and build trust in management by the employee. Reprimands are needed to correct behavior and reinforce management's desired performance standards. The evaluation discussion should include points or ideas on why the standards were or were not met. Constructive criticism is a better motivation for improvement than are negative approaches.

An example performance appraisal is shown in Table 24.4. The supportive details and comments noted on the example form should contain references to the information in the job description. This written form and comments should be given to the employee and a copy placed in the employee's file whether the appraisal is positive or negative. If the appraisal is positive, the employee should benefit through compensation and/or additional authority. If the appraisal is negative, several steps are possible and are discussed next.

Negative evaluations should result in a written warning to the employee and then one of four actions. These are the four Rs:

- Retrain. Make sure the employee understands what is to be done and how it is to be done. Prepare a written performance improvement plan and give one to the employee and place a copy in the employee's file.
- Reassign. Give the employee new responsibilities. A faulty interview process may have caused a person to be placed in the wrong job. The reasons for reassignment should be written and provided to the employee with a copy put in his or her file.
- Reevaluate. Before the last option (firing) is used, reevaluate the person. Remember that the initial evaluation may be faulty. Perhaps the evaluator was having a bad day for reasons other than the employee's performance. Perhaps the manager and the employee just had a disagreement or a fight over a small part of the job. Perhaps the system in which the employee works needs redesign, not the employee. This reevaluation should be written also.
- Release. Firing should be the last option to be considered. Firing is the most expensive option due to the costs of firing and of recruiting, interviewing, hiring, and training a new employee. Firing can also create potential legal problems. For these reasons and for just a better base from which to make decisions, keeping a record of quantitative measures of job performance will help establish goals and a basis for releasing employees.

Compensation

Compensation involves the base salary and any incentives and benefits or fringes that the business provides. The overall level of compensation is determined by the local labor market—that is, the supply of and demand for labor in the local area. Workers usually have other potential employers, so farmers will have to pay similar wages and benefits as those jobs in order to attract employees. If those businesses provide health insurance for the employee and the employee's family, farmers will have to provide that also. Other factors that will affect pay levels and labor availability are the presence of unions, the cost of living in the area, and labor regulations.

Farmers, just like any other business, will have to evaluate the costs of labor in their local area versus the benefits of having the work done. If the cost of labor is deemed too expensive for the farm, alternatives to labor could be evaluated—alternatives such as mechanization or computerization to replace labor or to improve the productivity of labor. If productivity is improved, the benefits may then be high enough to compensate labor according to the local market demands.

Table 24.4 An Example Performance Appraisal Form

Employee name _____ Position _____

Rating descriptions:
Outstanding: Performance is exceptional in all areas and is recognizable as a major contribution.
Good: Results clearly exceed requirements. Performance is of high quality and is achieved on a consistent basis.
Satisfactory: Competent and dependable level of performance. Meets expectations.
Improvement Needed: Performance is deficient in certain areas. Improvement is needed.
Unsatisfactory: Results are generally unacceptable.

Rating point scale:

Outstanding:	90–100	Improvement Needed:	60–69
Good:	80–89	Unsatisfactory:	< 60
Satisfactory:	70–79		

1. Quality: The accuracy, thoroughness and acceptability of work performed.
   ☐ Outstanding ☐ Good ☐ Satisfactory ☐ Improvement Needed ☐ Unsatisfactory Points = _____
2. Quantity: The volume of work produced.
   ☐ Outstanding ☐ Good ☐ Satisfactory ☐ Improvement Needed ☐ Unsatisfactory Points = _____
3. Adaptability: The response to changing requirements and conditions.
   ☐ Outstanding ☐ Good ☐ Satisfactory ☐ Improvement Needed ☐ Unsatisfactory Points = _____
4. Cooperation: The relationship with supervisor and co-workers, including the willingness to help others with their overloads.
   ☐ Outstanding ☐ Good ☐ Satisfactory ☐ Improvement Needed ☐ Unsatisfactory Points = _____
5. Reliability: The extent to which the employee can be relied on to complete responsibilities in a timely manner.
   ☐ Outstanding ☐ Good ☐ Satisfactory ☐ Improvement Needed ☐ Unsatisfactory Points = _____
6. Attendance and punctuality
   ☐ Outstanding ☐ Good ☐ Satisfactory ☐ Improvement Needed ☐ Unsatisfactory Points = _____
                                        OVERALL PERFORMANCE SCORE = _____

Supporting details or comments:

Supervisor _____ Date _____

Employee Statement: I agree/disagree with this evaluation.
Comments:

Employee signature _____ Date _____

Source: Adapted from Erven, 2001a.

The basic rule of compensation is to reward what you want done. In addition to a base wage or salary, incentives and bonuses may be desirable. Incentives are usually based on volume of business, productivity, longevity, and profitability. Reaching a goal in business volume—for example, a certain amount of milk produced per month—can be a reason to pay a bonus to those involved in reaching that volume. Other incentives can be for overtime work and for achieving stated levels of productivity and efficiency. These may be based on, for example, acres covered per hour, animals detected in heat or sick, pigs saved per litter, feed conversion rates, milk per cow, crop yields, and so on. Some incentives may be based on the employee's length of employment with the farm to reward loyalty. If the farm has a profitable year, an astute manager will be sure that employees also share in the profit. Thomas and Erven (1989) suggest that normal incentives and bonuses should total 2–5% of the cash wages for semi-skilled workers, 4–10% for skilled workers, and 5–40% for supervisory and management employees.

Incentives may be informal. That is, bonuses, rewards and benefits are awarded when good work and efforts are shown but no sure expectation of receiving the bonus is felt by the employee. However, to be effective in improving and maintaining good performance by employees and for the business, incentives need to have formal structures. Then employees can understand and expect rewards for certain behaviors. Structured, formal incentive programs are most likely to succeed if they have (1) established standards, (2) clearly linked superior performance with pay or a valued reward, and (3) carefully considered what type of performance the incentive stimulates (Billikopf, 2000). Effective incentives are designed so that the larger the amount earned by the employee, the greater are the benefits obtained by the farmer.

Potential incentives can be evaluated in a partial budget framework before being implemented. For example, the value of increasing the number of pigs weaned per sow per year by 0.5 can be estimated for the farm and compared to what may have to be paid to employees to have them pay better attention to sow and piglet care and any additional expenses incurred for that care. The amount and cost of overtime needed to plant crops in a timely manner can be compared to either the additional cost of investing in bigger machinery for timely planting or the potential value of yield losses due to not planting in a timely manner.

As an example of evaluating the worth of an incentive program, consider a farmer evaluating whether to pay his milker $1 per cwt (or 100 lb) to raise the milk production of 300 cows from 21,000 to 23,000 lb per cow by taking better care of the cows. This farmer has to decide whether the incentive would be profitable for him and whether it is sufficient to encourage the milker to do the extra work. For the whole herd, the increase of 2,000 lb per cow would mean an increase of 600,000 lb per year. If this farmer's variable costs for this increase in milk production is $10 per 100 lb (which includes the proposed incentive of $1 per cwt to the milker) and milk is worth $13 per cwt, the additional value of the increase would be $3 per cwt for a total net value of $18,000 per year for the farmer. The farmer does have some ability, it appears, to increase the incentive, but needs to consider the risk of different costs and prices. Now the farmer must decide whether the $1 per cwt is enough incentive to encourage the milker to take extra care of the animals. Most likely, the farmer may need to talk to the milker, explain the process, and use the incentive program for a specified test period to see if the milker responds. The milker would, of course, have to understand the rules and that a test period was being used. If the farmer does not make sure the milker understands the incentive program or the milker is unable to obtain the desired gains in productivity, the milker could easily become dissatisfied with the job and performance could suffer—the opposite of the desired result.

To be effective in obtaining the desired results intended by incentives, employees must have a fair amount of control over the measures used. Incentives based on crop yield or animal genetics may not be of interest to employees because they cannot control weather or the choice of animals. However, if the incentives are to plant correctly or to observe animals in heat or sick, employees can control those activities. The incentive must also be large enough to create some interest in achieving the goal. However, care must be taken to provide incentives for good work but to design the incentives so that employees are not rewarded for behavior that is not good for the whole farm.

Fringes or benefits usually include health insurance for the employee and the employee's family. Housing, utilities, and food are also common benefits. If the employee has any supervisory duties or works somewhat unusual hours, a farm vehicle may be part of the compensation package. Vacations (with pay) have also become more common on farms. A survey of U.S. hog farms showed the most common benefit for paid employees was major medical coverage (Table 24.5). Other benefits listed in the table were also very common.

As an employer wrestles with the question of how much to pay, the question first raised in quality management should be considered again: Should inputs (labor in this case) be purchased or hired on the basis of the level of cash wages only? No, Deming would say; wages and the entire compensation package (as well as the entire labor management and production process) should be chosen on the basis of lowest costs to the business, not just the lowest cash cost per hour.

As an example, consider two real, neighboring farmers in California. The first farmer paid a low hourly wage, used poor (and cheap) labor management practices (e.g., a lot of yelling), had low productivity and a high turnover of employees, and thus had a high labor cost per unit of product.

Table 24.5   Percentage of Employees on U.S. Hog Farms Indicating the Availability of the Following Benefits, 2000 and 2006.

Benefit	2006	2000
Medical insurance	66%	70%
Dental insurance	36	35
Disability insurance	25	32
Life insurance	37	44
Paid vacation	72	86
Paid holidays	57	69
Workers' compensation	55	66
Unemployment insurance	34	36
Paid sick leave	44	60
Pension/retirement plan	54	50
Profit-sharing plan	18	24
Housing	21	30
Paid utilities	15	17
Vehicle	21	20
Processed meat	44	42
Continuing education	20	23
Other	6	10

Source: Kliebenstein et al., 2006.

The second farmer paid a high hourly wage for the area, used good labor management practices, had high productivity and a low turnover of employees, and as a result had a low labor cost per unit. Which farmer do you think had the better income statement?

Summary

- Human resource management is becoming ever more important for farm managers.
- Maslow's seven basic human needs are physiological, safety, belonging and love, esteem and self-esteem, self-actualization, cognitive understanding, and aesthetic needs.
- Since employees are human, these basic human needs are important to them and to managers also.
- An employee also needs responsibility, authority, accountability, and compensation.
- Jung's geology of the soul helps explain why people do not behave according to our expectations.
- Human resource management involves several steps: assessing the situation; developing tentative job descriptions; matching present employees with tentative job descriptions; developing job descriptions for remaining tasks; recruiting, interviewing, and hiring employees; training employees; motivating, leading, and directing employees; evaluating performance; and compensating employees.
- Assessing the situation involves determining and comparing the type, amount, and timing of available labor and the type, amount, and timing of labor needs.
- A job description needs to include the employee's responsibilities, authorities, evaluation standards, required and desired qualifications, supervision, time expectations, compensation information, and benefits.
- Proper recruiting, interviewing, and selection of employees helps ensure better fit with jobs and thus better productivity of the employees and higher profitability of the farm.
- Testing of applicants' skills is a much better method to ascertain their ability to perform a job compared with trusting applicants' and references' statements.
- Employers and supervisors should learn an employee's needs, interests, and abilities and then strive to match those needs, interests, and abilities by designing jobs that align these with the goals of the business.
- Training is needed regardless of previous experience.
- Monetary reward is one method for motivating employees but not the only method.
- Appropriate and effective methods for motivating, leading, and directing will vary with both the supervisor and the employee.
- Situational leadership mixes the styles of directing, coaching, supporting, and delegating depending on the competence and commitment of the employee, not the leader's preferred style.
- Evaluation is a major source of control of employees and should be done at least annually and more often if needed.
- The basic question in evaluation is whether the employee met the standards described in the job description. Both commendations and reprimands are needed.
- Negative evaluations should result in one of four actions: retrain, reassign, reevaluate, or release.
- Release or firing is the most expensive option and should be the last choice.
- Compensation involves the base salary, incentives, and benefits. It is set according to the local job market and the performance of the employee.

- Formal incentive programs allow an employee to anticipate and work toward specific goals that are desirable for both the employee and the farm.
- Low labor costs per unit of production are not directly related to low cash wages per hour.

Review Questions

1. What are the seven basic human needs according to Maslow? Describe what these are in terms of any human being and also in terms of an employee.
2. Describe the four basic needs of employees.
3. How can understanding Jung's geology help a manager of a culturally diverse workforce?
4. What are employees' main reasons for leaving jobs according to the survey cited in the text? How important is salary in their view?
5. Is all that stuff about human needs and employee needs really necessary? Why not just pay an employee well and expect him or her to perform well?
6. Describe the main steps in personnel management.
7. What are the three intrinsic job factors that are potential satisfiers for an employee?
8. What are the three extrinsic job factors that are potential dissatisfiers for an employee?
9. Why have job descriptions?
10. Why write a job description even for one employee or for a parent–child partnership?
11. What items should be included in a job description?
12. Describe what is involved in recruiting, interviewing, and selecting. Why are these so important?
13. Why should new employees be trained?
14. Why should "old" employees be trained?
15. How can an employee's interests be aligned with the goals of the farm business?
16. What is situational leadership?
17. How often does an employee need to be evaluated?
18. Against what standards should an employee be evaluated?
19. How can employees be given a quantitative but subjective evaluation?
20. If an employee has a negative evaluation, should he or she be fired immediately?
21. Is firing an employee always the cheapest way to improve performance? Why or why not?
22. What should be included in the basic compensation package?
23. Why should an incentive package be based mostly on those items that an employee can control?
24. If partial budget analysis shows that an incentive plan is profitable for an owner, will an employee respond as the owner wants him or her to respond? Why or why not?

Further Reading

Billikopf, G. E. 2000. "Labor Management in Ag: Cultivating Personnel Productivity." Agricultural Extension, Stanislaus County, University of California, http://www.cnr.berkeley.edu/ucce50/ag-labor/. Accessed October 22, 2002.

Blanchard, Ken. 1997. *The Color Model: A Situational Approach to Managing People*. Escondido, California: Blanchard Training and Development (quoted by Erven, 2001a).

Erven, Bernard L. 2001a. "Becoming an Effective Leader through Situational Leadership." Unpublished paper, Department of Agricultural, Environmental and Development Economics, Ohio State University. Accessed at http://aede.osu.edu/people/erven.1/HRM/Situaltional_Leadership.pdf on September 13, 2009.

Erven, Bernard L. 2001b. "Evaluating Performance and Providing Feedback to Employees." Unpublished paper, Department of Agricultural, Environmental and Development Economics, Ohio State University. Accessed at http://aede.osu.edu/people/erven.1/HRM/Employee Reviews.pdf on September 13, 2009.

Kliebenstein, James, Terrance Hurley, Peter Orazem, Dale Miller, and Steve May. 2006. "Employee Rosters Rise; Wages Continue to Climb." A.S. Leaflet R2167, Iowa State University Animal Industry Report 2006. Department of Economics, Iowa State University, Ames, Iowa. Accessed on December 21, 2009, at http://www.ans.iastate.edu/report/air/2006pdf/R2167.pdf.

Maslow, A. H. 1970. *Motivation and Personality*. 2nd ed. New York: Harper & Row.

Thomas, K. H., and B. L. Erven. 1989. *"Farm Personnel Management."* North Central Extension Publication 329-1989, Ag-BU-3613.

Tjan, A. 2009. "How to Align Employee and Company Interests." Upstarts and titans blog, August 2, 2009. Accessed at http://blogs.harvardbusiness.org/tjan/ on August 6, 2009.

25

Business Organization

In this chapter:

- Organizational structure
- Board of advisors
- Legal forms of business organization

In this chapter, we look at three questions. First, how do people involved in the farm business relate to each other—that is, what is the organizational or management structure? Simply stated, the question is, "Who is in charge?" Second, does a board of advisors for the farm business make sense? Third, how should the farm business be organized from a legal viewpoint: sole proprietorship, partnership, corporation, cooperative, or any of the other variations of those basic legal forms?

Organizational Structure

Is one person in charge or a committee? Who is in charge of what? How much responsibility and authority does each person have? For a single-person business, these are easy questions. For a multi-operator business, even a family business, they can be very involved and contentious. Considerable thought is needed to answer these questions well because the answers become part of the strategic plan of the farm. Good communication on these issues and an understanding by all parties will go a long way in helping any business achieve its strategic and financial objectives and goals. Resolving these issues can help a multi-operator, multi-employee business work more efficiently and more productively.

The complexity of the business plus the ownership and the knowledge and desires of those involved are important factors in designing an organizational chart. For example, a farmer who runs his cash corn-soybean farms as a sole proprietor with only one employee may not need an extensive chart. Even if the employee is in charge of the equipment and the repair shop, both the farmer and the employee probably know who is in charge of the whole operation.

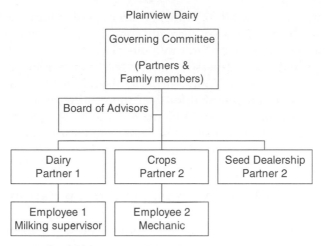

Figure 25.1 Example Organization Chart for a Farm

A farm that has several strategic parts and several people involved will have a more compli-cated chart. For example, consider two partners with two employees who operate a dairy and crop farm with a seed dealership "on the side." As part of their strategic planning and their staffing plan, these two partners should have discussed who has interest, knowledge, and skills needed in each part of the business. As an example of one possible result of this discussion, their organizational chart could have one partner in charge of the dairy and one in charge of both the crops and the seed dealership (Figure 25.1). This split in responsibility could be due to both interests and the seasonality of work demands: the dairy has a steady work demand throughout the year, while the crop farm and seed dealership have different seasonal work demand patterns. Through talking with their employees and evaluating their skills, the partners have decided that one of the employees can be in charge of milking and the milk house and one can be in charge of the machine shop and equipment maintenance. This split of responsibility can be part of their motivation and recognition of employees as well as the partners' realization that they can't make all decisions. If their families are involved closely in the business (perhaps as employees), they too should be involved in this discussion. This involvement is shown in the example, where the family is part of the governing committee.

Board of Advisors

Farming is a complicated business and will continue to become even more complicated in the future. A board of advisors can be a valuable management tool in understanding and preparing for this increasing business complexity. The members of a board of advisors could, but not nec-essarily, include the farm's banker, seed and/or fertilizer dealer, a non-farm business owner, another farmer perhaps, and others who have knowledge of farming, the locality, and the broader economy. Obviously, a farmer would include only those who could contribute manage-ment wisdom, are trusted by the farmer, and would keep business information confidential. In many ways, a farmer may already talk with this group of people individually at their businesses and in the coffee shops. The advantage of formally convening a board of advisors is to gain their collective concentration on this specific farm in a business atmosphere (rather than in the coffee shop). The board can provide a third-person view of the farm as a business without being emotionally or financially involved in the family, the farm history, or the business directly. The board members probably need to be compensated for their time and wisdom, but the cost may be small compared to the better decisions that could be made because of their advice. Other, large businesses have boards of directors and consultants; there is no reason not to use this source of management expertise in farm businesses of any size.

Legal Forms of Business Organization

A key issue involved with a farm or ranch operation is the legal form in which the business will operate. The most common forms of business organization for farms are presented in this section. A summary of the information is found in Table 25.1. While this section is written from the view of a U.S. entity, many of the same points, questions, and concerns can be found in other countries.

Choosing a business organization revolves around these primary issues: access to capital, liability, risk, management flexibility and control, continuity, permanence, taxation, and legal filing requirements and other costs. As will be noted in the rest of this section, each structure has advantages in some of these issues but not in all. Sole proprietorship, for example, is simple and thus desirable to many, but it has disadvantages in liability, continuity, and access to capital compared to other structures.

Sole Proprietorship

The sole proprietorship is the most common form of ownership in farming. Its main advantage is simplicity of formation and governance. In a sole proprietorship, the farmer is the sole owner, has legal title to the property, and is self-employed. Decision making and control are centralized in the owner, so these processes can be streamlined and run efficiently. However, growth is then limited to the abilities, skills, and interests of the owner.

A sole proprietorship is easy to start and has no reporting requirements through its life. If the business operates under the name of the owner (for example, Joe Smith or Smith Farms), no legal documents need to be drafted or filed with the government. In some states, if another name is used that is not close to the owner's name (such as Plainview Farms), a legal form does have to be filed stating the assumed name and the owner.

The sole proprietorship is limited to the life of the owner; the business ceases to exist upon the owner's death. That also means a sole proprietorship is the easiest to liquidate. The sole proprietor can decide to stop operating the business at any time. Transfer of ownership between generations is the most inefficient with a sole proprietorship due to having a single owner and death of the business upon death of the owner. If continuity of the business is desired, other forms of legal organization should be considered.

Income is reported as part of the individual's tax forms and taxed at individual rates. Business losses can be used to offset other income. Capital is limited to what the sole proprietorship has available. It may be difficult to obtain credit, thus limiting growth.

Table 25.1 Comparison of the Major Types of Business Arrangements

	Sole Proprietorship	Partnership	Corporation
Nature of entity	Single individual	Association of two or more individuals	Legal entity separate from shareholders
Source of capital	Personal funds or loans	Partners' contributions or loans	Contribution of shareholders for stock, sale of stock, or loans
Management decisions	Proprietor	Agreement of partners	Shareholders elect directors who manage business through officers
Liability	Personally liable	General partner(s) liable for all partnership obligations; limited partners' liability is limited to their investment	Shareholders not liable for corporate obligations (but individual shareholders or officers of small corporations may be asked to cosign loans)
Limits of business	Proprietor's discretion	Partnership agreement	Articles of incorporation and state law
Life of business	Terminates on death	Agreed term, but terminates on death of partner	Perpetual in most cases
Effect of death	Liquidation	Liquidation or sale to surviving partner	No effect; stock passes by will or inheritance
Transfer of interest	Terminates proprietorship	Dissolves partnership; but new partnership may be formed	No effect on continuity; stock transferable to anyone if not restricted
Income taxes	Business income is combined with other income on individual tax return	Partnership files IRS information report; each partner's share of partnership income is added to her or his individual taxable income	C: corporation files a tax return and pays income tax; salaries to shareholder employees are deductible; shareholders pay tax on dividends received S: corporation files IRS information report; shareholders report their shares of income, operating loss, and capital gains on individual returns
Alternative forms		General and limited partnerships; limited liability	Regular (C), tax option (subchapter S), limited liability

One of the biggest concerns with a sole proprietorship is that liability is not limited to business assets; both business and personal assets are at risk with a sole proprietorship. If the farm is sued for a farm accident, the farmer's home and personal assets may also be in jeopardy. The owner bears personal liability for all debts of the business as well as any other liabilities. That is, when the owner signs as the owner of a sole proprietorship, he or she also signs as an individual person. The owner is limited in the availability of fringe benefits and retirement benefits, as well as in the deductibility of health insurance on income taxes.

General Partnership

A general partnership consists of two or more partners who have joined to operate a business. Each partner is personally liable for all debts incurred by any of the other partners in the operation of the business. A general partnership is very flexible and fairly easy to establish, but forms do have to be filed with the government.

A general partnership passes all income and deductions to the partners. The partners pay any income taxes that are due at their personal tax rate. Business losses can be passed on to the partners. A general partnership does not pay income taxes but usually has to file tax forms to report income passed on to the partners. A partnership is unable to hold income; all income must pass through to the partners. This makes it difficult to hold income for tax management or deferral purposes.

A general partnership ceases to exist when the partners dissolve the partnership. A partnership ceases to exist upon the death of a partner, although termination agreements within the initial partnership agreement may spell out how surviving partners may buy the deceased's share and continue the business. If these terms are not spelled out, the partnership may have difficulty attracting external capital in some instances.

Partnerships can allow people to pool their financial, management, and other resources to create, hopefully, a better advantage in the marketplace than the partners would have with their own sole proprietorships. For some people, the disadvantage of this pooling is the loss of control over finances, management, and other resources. Now, two or more people are in control instead of just one.

A general partnership is a quasi-person in the law. It can own assets, enter into contracts, and so on. Resources can be pooled from all partners. This pool forms a larger base to attract more outside funding than may have been possible as individuals.

In a general partnership, partners are jointly responsible for debts and obligations of the business. Even if the partnership agreement spells out how they are shared, if one partner defaults or fails to meet their share of the obligation, all other general partners are liable for those obligations. Control and decision making are shared, but each partner can legally act on behalf of the business and obligate all partners. This points out the need to know and trust potential partners before the partnership is formed.

Limited Partnership

A limited partnership is similar to a general partnership except that one or more partners are liable only to the extent of their investment. A limited partnership consists of two or more partners who have joined to operate a business with at least one partner personally liable for any and all debts of the partnership and at least one partner limited in liability. The advantage of the limited partnership (over the general partnership) is its ability to attract outside capital from individuals who are willing to put some money at risk but do not want to become personally liable for all debts and other liabilities of the partnership. The disadvantage to general partners is their unlimited liability to the debts of a larger business. Limited partners have no voice in the management of the business; they are primarily investors who expect a return on their money.

The limited partnership does require formal organization, filing, and reporting because of its protection of the limited partners. This is a disadvantage due to complexity and cost of initial formation and increased accounting and reporting requirements.

The primary advantage of the limited partnership is the limited liability of the limited partner. The life of the limited partnership does not have to end with the death of any one partner, so continuity of life is possible under this structure.

A family limited partnership is allowed in many states. This allows a closely held business to continue without the disadvantages of other structures. The advantages and disadvantages are similar to general and limited partnerships; however, there are restrictions on who can participate as partners.

Corporation

Corporations are separate entities that, once formed, have unlimited life. They have shareholders, directors, and officers. The initial cost of forming a corporation is greater than a partnership or a sole proprietorship; taxation rules and forms are more involved; and the business must be run more formally. They must have meetings with recorded and filed minutes of those meetings. Since they are more complex to start, they are also more complex and costly to dissolve, making exit more difficult if circumstances change.

One or more shareholders own shares or stock in the corporation and their liability is limited to their investment. Shares are easily transferable, which facilitates the transfer of ownership between shareholders and eases estate planning. Different classes of shares or stock allow easier access to capital, so the corporation may find it easier to grow. One of the main advantages of a corporation is that the shareholders or owners are not personally liable for debts of the corporation—unless they also sign as individuals and not just as officers of the corporation.

Subchapter-C corporations can be publically held companies such as the corporations listed on stock exchanges, but they can also be privately held corporations. There is no limit on the number of shares, types of shareholders, or the number of owners of subchapter-C corporations. Subchapter-C corporations can be large (like major multinational companies), or they can be small (like some farm corporations).

Management of the corporation is held by the board of directors and officers. They may feel in control, but minority shareholders may feel left out and out of control.

Subchapter-C corporations can deduct health insurance costs for employees. Also, they can utilize many retirement and fringe benefits not available to other business forms.

One disadvantage of subchapter-C corporations is the double taxation of their profits. Subchapter-C corporations pay taxes on corporation income at corporate rates. The shareholders pay taxes at individual rates on any dividends paid to them. Dividends paid to the owners are not deductible by the corporation. Thus, the total tax rate can be quite high. However, owners can be employees of a subchapter-C corporation, and as long as the level of compensation is reasonable compared to the services provided, that compensation is most likely deductible. Income can also be held by the corporation and not passed to the shareholders each year; this allows the management of income and deferred income for tax purposes. With the subchapter-C corporation, it is also harder to use business losses to offset income from other sources.

This double taxation can be quite vexing if the corporation owns land that appreciates in value. In the past, many small subchapter-C corporations (such as farms) did not own land, but rented land owned personally by the owners of the corporation. The ability to form limited liability companies (discussed next) has eliminated the need for this separation of ownership and operation.

Subchapter-S corporations are limited in the number and type of shareholders. They are generally taxed as a partnership so they also have the disadvantage of limited deductibility of fringe benefits, retirement, and health insurance costs. Income, however, can be passed through to the owners—as in a partnership. Subchapter-S corporations were designed to help avoid double taxation problems but the design was not entirely successful. Land should not be held by subchapter-S corporations, since land appreciation could be double taxed.

Limited Liability Company (LLC)

Limited liability companies have the tax benefits of a partnership (no double taxation), the limited liability of a corporation, and the flexible management of a general partnership. Limited liability companies can hold land without any penalty of double taxation on the appreciation of that land (or any asset) because income is passed through to the owners. The owners of the business are called members, and "managers" run the business. The disadvantage of the limited liability company is the complexity and organizational cost. It is still required to have fairly complex accounting and reporting. It also can't fully utilize all fringe and retirement benefits. Ownership interests are not as liquid as shares of a corporation, making it more difficult to transfer ownership. Thus an LLC is not always attractive for estate planning.

This chapter has covered the basic ideas of how to organize a farm in terms of the responsibilities of the people involved in the farm and the alternative legal business organizations available (in the United States). Both of these aspects of organization (responsibilities and legal) can be used to aim the farm toward the vision and objectives developed and described in the strategic plan.

Summary

- The complexity of the farm business and the number of people involved increase the need for a formal description of how the farm and the people involved are organized and work together.
- A board of advisors can be a valuable management tool for a manager facing an increasingly complex business environment.
- Three common legal forms of business organization are the sole proprietorship, partnership, and corporation, with the sole proprietorship being the most common among farms in the United States.
- Other legal forms also used by some farmers include limited partnerships, subchapter-S corporations, and limited liability companies.
- Each legal form has different benefits and requirements and is appropriate in different situations.

Review Questions

1. Why and when should a farm manager develop an organizational chart?
2. What are the reasons a farm manager may want to have a board of advisors?
3. What are the three common forms of business organization in the United States? Which form is the most common?
4. What are the main legal forms of business organization available in your country?

5. What are the benefits of each form of organization?
6. What are the advantages of being a sole proprietor versus working with partners or as a corporation?
7. What types of farms would you expect to find using each of the legal forms?

Further Reading

Boehlje, Michael, and David Lins. 1995. "Alternative Financial/Organizational Structures of Farm and Agribusiness Firms." NCR-568, Cooperative Extension Service, Purdue University, West Lafayette, Indiana.

Hachfeld, Gary A., David B. Bau, C. Robert Holcomb, and James N. Kurtz. 2009. "Using Farm Partnerships or Corporations to Transfer Assets." University of Minnesota Extension (September). Accessed on October 7, 2009 and available at http://www.cffm.umn.edu/Publications/pubs/FarmMgtTopics/TransferringTheFarmSeries.pdf.

Harl, Neil. 2001. *Farm Estate and Business Planning*. 15th ed. Niles, Illinois: Century Communications, 488 pp.

Jones, Rodney, and Michael R. Langemeier. 2005. "Important Farm Business Terms Defined—Business Structures." MF-2696, Department of Agricultural Economics, Kansas State University.

26

Farm Transfer and Succession Planning

In this chapter:

- The farm business life cycle
- The process of farm transfer and succession planning
- The farm transfer and succession plan

The goal of many farming families is to see the family business continue into the future with the next generation owning and operating the farm. Transferring the farm from one generation to the next is a large step that requires considerable thought, discussion, and planning to be successful. This transfer involves not just the physical assets of land, buildings, machinery, and livestock. It also involves the transfer of knowledge, skills, labor, management, and control of the business. The transfer is also about changing the leadership of the farm business. That is why it is called a "farm transfer and succession plan."

People are involved in the transfer and leadership of the farm changes. To improve the chances for a successful transfer, a succession plan needs to be developed to identify who will assume leadership and how leadership will transfer. Current leadership needs to let go, and new leadership needs to be prepared to step in. Since farm families often live on the farm and farmers identify themselves very closely with the farm, each person has a lot of emotions tied up in the farm that have to be dealt with and settled in order to have a successful transfer of the business and its leadership. The impacts of having or not having a successor and a succession plan start earlier than is often realized (Example 26.1).

The first section of this chapter discusses the stages a farm business goes through as it "ages" and as the owners and operators age. Different generations have different goals, and need to understand how they can work together to develop common goals for the farm business. The second section identifies the process or steps needed to develop a transfer and succession plan. The last section describes the basic parts of the written documentation of the farm transfer and succession plan.

Example 26.1. Succession Decisions Impact Management Decisions Early

The presence or absence of a successor can affect management decisions long before the actual succession takes place. Using Belgian data, researchers found that the preparation of the farm transfer or farm exit is a process that starts in the consolidation stage of the farm life cycle. The results show that the succession effect plays a role from the age of 45. At that point, the decision to transfer the farm or not is made and management decisions are adjusted according to that decision. The more certain it is that a successor is identified, the more investment is made to maintain competitiveness of the farm into the future. If the successor is not known with certainty, less investment is made. Even less investment is made if it is known with certainty that there is no successor. The earlier a successor is identified, the greater the incentive is to invest and to improve the farm and its management.

Source: M. Calus and G. Van Huylenbroeck, "The Succession Effect within Management Decisions of Family Farms." Contributed paper at the European Association of Agricultural Economists 2008 International Congress, August 26–29, 2008, Ghent, Belgium. Accessed on January 7, 2010, at http://purl.umn.edu/44131.

The Farm Business Life Cycle

Businesses change as the ages of the people and the business change, along with goals, activities, and involvement. These changes and the reasons for them can be understood by considering the three stages of the life cycle.

1. Entry or establishment stage
2. Growth and survival stage
3. Exit or disinvestment stage

These stages are readily apparent with family farms, especially sole proprietorships. They are less apparent but are still evident in corporations and partnerships.

Entry or Establishment Stage

Before this stage starts, the prospective farmer evaluates farming as a career versus other career opportunities. If farming is chosen, the person must acquire a minimum set of capital resources and managerial skills necessary to establish an economically viable business. Historically, the entry stage has been characterized by a career progression known as the "agricultural career ladder." The traditional ladder consisted of the following steps.

- Begin as family labor or as a hired worker for a parent, relative, or unrelated farmer
- Gradually acquire a basic set of machinery or livestock
- Rent land or buildings

- Establish part ownership of farmed land
- Become the principal operator of the farm business

Another common variation of the ladder involves, first, part-time farming with an off-farm job for additional income and then, through growth, full-time farming. Sometimes part-time farming is the goal. This can be the rational choice of many due to personal and family goals and the situation in which the family finds themselves.

Other methods of starting may be necessary as the capital needed to start farming continues to increase. This increase is due to machinery and equipment being substituted for labor and increases in the investment needed for machinery, buildings, and land. Some examples of these other methods, which are not listed as a career ladder, include those listed below.

- Become a partner of an established farmer. This person may or may not be a relative.
- Obtain financial backing from a third party to purchase land, buildings, machinery, and livestock.
- Become a laborer or manager in an existing business and gradually invest in the business.
- Marry into a farming family.

The keys to entry are management skills, land tenure, and capital. Possessing strong management skills and having evidence of those skills is critical to gaining tenure and financial resources.

Corporations and partnerships also have an entry and establishment phase. It may be shorter than for a sole proprietorship, because in farming, corporations and partnerships are often formed from an established farm or farms. The establishment phase may be the learning phase for the owners and operators—learning how to manage together and communicate with each other.

Often a corporation or partnership is established to allow for growth of the farm or for transfer of ownership. In these cases, stakeholders in the business are not only in the establishment stage but are also in the growth or disinvestment stage.

In the entry and establishment phase, goals such as net worth accumulation and resource productivity usually have a higher priority than those of income and consumption. The basic goal is to establish both the business and a performance record on which to build the future.

Persons and businesses in this stage may be willing to take riskier actions for two reasons. First, since they likely have less money invested in the business, they have less to lose. Second, if the business is not successful in this stage, it will not be around for growth. Also, since this stage often involves younger people, they are more willing to take risks because they have more time to try something else if the venture does not work.

The Growth and Survival Stage

This stage involves expansion of the business and consolidation of the business' financial and operating base. The farm has been established, and now it builds on its niche in the industry. Managers look for strategies to improve efficiency and expand the resource base of the business. They recognize resource bottlenecks and inefficiencies and makes needed corrections. Financial considerations are important.

As the business grows, debt is maintained at a safe level relative to total asset value. Equity is protected. The ability to take on more risk grows, but the desire to avoid risk grows too. The survival of the farm requires risk management to avoid the adverse effects of the market, weather, disease, and so on. Depending on the persons and the business situation, goals such as income, community support, family and leisure time may increase in importance in this stage. A partnership or corporation will operate very similarly to a sole proprietor in this stage.

The Exit or Disinvestment Stage

In this stage, the farmer plans for and reaches retirement. Resources and managerial responsibilities are transferred to the next generation or other parties. The farmer may sell some assets but retain ownership of the land at least for a few years. Most people in this stage place a high priority on avoiding risk and providing for their retirement years—perhaps balanced by the goal to transfer the farm to the next generation.

A corporation or partnership may or may not go through this stage. If it were set up to transfer the farm from one generation to another, a corporation or partnership may remain. However, some owners may be going through exit and disinvestment and seek to avoid risk. The younger generation has already started and wants to keep the business itself in the growth and survival stage. Being younger, they may lean toward being more aggressive on growth now and will worry more about survival as they age. (The alert reader can already see how this mix of generations can lead to conflicts and the need for communication within the management team and all stakeholders.)

The Process of Farm Transfer and Succession Planning

The process of developing the plan is just as crucial to the success of the transfer as are the contents of the plan. While the main goal is a written plan, the family has to be involved in writing the plan and in agreement with the plan when it is finished. Having only one generation doing the planning and writing may sound efficient but will not result in acceptance and success. Therefore the first step in preparing a plan is to initiate and ensure communication so that all "own" the final plan. This is reinforced in a summary of farm succession steps from the northeast United States. (Example 26.2).

Communication

This first step is critical. In fact, a plan for communication is needed in order to prepare the best transfer plan possible. Communication is needed from both a family and a business perspective. Scheduling meetings with an agenda and a facilitator is important. Including family members not directly involved in the farm transfer can be critical to the success of the transfer.

Time. Setting aside a specific time for meetings will help communication. Specific beginning and ending times will help get the meeting started and allow those involved know when they can move on to other tasks. Physical and mental participation will be better when stakeholders know the time limits.

Example 26.2. Taking Over the Family Farm

"Start talking now!!" is how the New England Small Farm Institute (NESFI) starts answering the question: "I plan to take over my family's farm. What are the best ways to accomplish this?" After mentioning that good communication is one key to a successful family farm transfer and recommending that family meetings be scheduled, NESFI lists these things to think about:

- Decide whether the family farm business is right for both you and your family. What is each family member willing to "put up with"?
- Talk about your family's goals for the future of the farm. Are goals similar or conflicting?
- Clarify the family expectations for working together. The senior generation's need for respect has to balance with the junior generation's need for trust and responsibility.
- What are the expectations of farm life within the different generations? How much time off? What are income expectations? What is the best business arrangement to facilitate the transfer?
- Start the farm transfer process with a transfer team.

Source: The New England Small Farm Institute, "I Plan to Take over My Family's Farm. What Are the Best Ways to Accomplish This?" accessed on February 8, 2010, at http://www.smallfarm.org/main/for_new_farmers/new_farmer_q_and_a/taking_over_my_family_farm/.

Place. A lot of farm family meetings take place at the dinner table or in the shop. That is fine and appropriate for many issues and decisions. However, transferring the farm is a major event, and it deserves the attention of all, so meeting off the farm should be given serious consideration. A meal at a restaurant in a private meeting room is one option. Banks may allow the use of their conference room for their customers especially when they know the topic is continuing a business. The bank will likely want to maintain good relations with good customers and room use is one part of that relationship.

Facilitation.   The goal of these planning meetings is to find a common goal and develop a common plan to transfer a family business to the next generation. Success depends on all the parties agreeing to that plan. A leader can exert too much control either directly or indirectly just by being "the leader." Facilitating these meetings is a better approach than leading the meeting. The first meeting will likely be facilitated by the elder manager but not necessarily. To ensure that the thoughts, ideas, and concerns of others are heard and discussed, the role of facilitator should rotate through those directly involved in the farm business and transfer. In some situations, a "third-party" facilitator who is not a family member or a stakeholder may be needed to ensure that all voices are heard. In some states, Extension personnel may be available to serve as the facilitator.

Agenda.   Any of those affected by the business and plan should be able to add items to the agenda. Due to time limits, all issues will not be discussed in one meeting. Also, some issues will be discussed or introduced at one meeting and not resolved, answered, or finished until a later meeting. If one party wants to talk about an issue and another party does not, the issue is obviously one that needs to be discussed. Items listed in the outline in the next section should be placed on the agenda even though they are not explicitly asked for by anyone.

All of the people involved should be very strict about keeping the transfer planning meeting focused on the topic. Issues about the daily operation of the farm and family events will probably be raised, but they should be written down for discussion at another time. These meetings involve a long-run goal of the family, and that long-run goal is the only reason for the meetings.

"Read my mind" does not work! Don't assume that everyone thinks the same way. People need to talk about issues, even ones they feel uncomfortable bringing up. Even people from the same family will not know and understand thoughts and concerns that are not voiced. Raising an issue for discussion at a meeting can decrease the chances of yelling, family breakdown, divorce, and failure to obtain what was a common goal.

Before Beginning the Process

There are four questions a farm family should address before proceeding to developing a farm transfer and succession plan.

Does the entire family have the goal to transfer the farm business? All family members of all generations need to respond positively to this question. If the family cannot agree on an answer, the process and the transfer plan will have a low probability of success. Family members who are not farming but are concerned due to owning farm assets or being a potential heir to an estate of a farming member need to be involved. Even non-farming family members with no financial stake in the farm may have emotional ties to the business. These may need to be dealt with for the sake of family unity. Also, do not forget that non-farming members could be a source of critical financial assistance if they are able and so inclined to invest.

Who is the successor? Is there one or more successors identified? Is the potential successor truly interested in farming? Parents may be able to tell interested children by their actions and comments, but it is best to discuss openly and directly who is and isn't interested in farming. Are the parents willing to accept the successor as successor versus "permanent trainee"?

Is the farm profitable and viable now and into the future? Financial analysis of the farm and projections into the future are needed. The current financial condition and performance need to be evaluated in terms of liquidity, solvency, profitability, and efficiency. This evaluation should be done by or at least reviewed by a third party to improve the chance of acceptance and validity of the report by the direct participants. This evaluation and the financial statements need to be shared with those directly involved in the farming business—even if they are children who have never seen their parents' finances. Parents and children may not need to share all their information about non-farm assets and ventures, but they do need to share the farm information. To maintain good communication and avoid unspoken concerns, all participants need to share all sources of income so planning for the farm can be more open. This may start a discussion of lifestyle expectations and the income needed for that lifestyle, and that can be a good discussion to have. If there are disagreements about income and lifestyle of either generation, it is best to have these discussions early rather than too late.

Another part of this question is whether the farm is viable now and in the future. This is essentially a review of the farm's strategic position. The stakeholders need to know whether the farm is big enough for two or more families, whether it is in the right business for the market conditions now and in the future, and so on.

If the farm is not financially sound or viable for the future, the participants need to review the business and make decisions and steps to improve financial performance and viability. If this can't be done, then other decisions about the future of the people and the assets need to be made.

What is the timetable for transfer and succession? Before moving too far down the path to developing the details of the transfer plan, the stakeholders need to agree on a preliminary timetable for finishing the plan and the transfer. They need to agree whether they are looking at a process that will take several years or just a few. This preliminary timetable can and probably should include separate timetables for transferring labor expectations, management duties, machinery and livestock assets, and land assets. The timetable may also need to include expectations and timing of families moving off and on the farmstead.

Fair Is Not Necessarily Equal

When more than one heir is involved, the families need to discuss the issue of what fairness is and what equality is. When one or more heirs want to keep farming and others do not, splitting the farm assets equally may destroy the chance of transferring the farm business intact. When one heir or more has stayed on the farm and helped the older generation continue the farm, non-farm heirs should realize the value of that contribution to the current value of the business. They can have a discussion about what that value is, but they should realize that it is not zero. Sometimes financial fairness can be achieved by the older generation purchasing life insurance or other investments with the non-farm heirs as beneficiaries and giving farm assets to the farming heirs.

Developing the Plan

Developing the farm transfer and succession plan will not be a simple process. It will not be a straightforward completion of the outline in the next section. As a family works through that outline, discussions will take place and issues will be raised that cause other parts of the plan to be revised even after those parts were thought to be finished. This is normal.

Use Lawyers and Consultants

A successful farm business is a complicated web of ownership, management, and people. Transferring a successful farm business is even more complicated. Lawyers and other consultants can help the development of a transfer and succession plan by explaining different options such as legal business structures, trusts, wills, and so on. Estate planners can provide knowledge, advice, and experience with developing these plans. Financial experts can provide an outside evaluation of the plan so all parties can accept the results more easily. Facilitation consultants can help guide discussions so that all voices are heard and topics discussed. No one person knows all the options or all the potential problems. Outside experts can help fill the gaps in knowledge and experience.

The Farm Transfer and Succession Plan

The farm transfer and succession plan is a business plan; the outline for the documentation of the plan is similar to the business plan described in Chapter 3. However, a transfer and succession plan involves more sections to explain how assets, labor, management, and control will be transferred. Although not all points will be needed by all farms and families, each point should be discussed and settled at a business meeting to increase the chances for a successful transfer. This outline is adapted from Coughler (2004).

Business Overview

The business overview is a brief summary of the farm business. It describes the products of the farm, its size, and the location. The overview describes who is involved in the business and what their duties are. It specifies the legal business organization of the farm (such as sole proprietorship or different forms of partnerships or corporations). The overview can also include a brief description of the future plans for the farm and the transfer goals. As discussed in Chapter 3, this overview should emphasize four points: (1) the people involved, (2) the opportunity, (3) the context, and (4) the risks and rewards. Details on the numbers and financial analysis will come later; the overview should describe the bigger picture.

Description of Business and Personal Vision, Mission, Goals, and Expectations

The elements of vision, mission, and goals are described in Chapter 7; they are just as crucial here for the transfer plan as they are in an ongoing business. The vision for the farm will help develop the transfer plan, its implementation plan, and the measures for measuring success toward the goals of transferring the business. Obviously, the business side needs to be a shared vision by all stakeholders. The personal visions need to be shared in order to have a more transparent discussion and development of the shared business vision.

Retirement Plan

The retirement plans and expectations of the older generation need to be discussed as part of the transfer. This includes both financial and lifestyle plans. Lifestyle plans include how much the retiring generation wants to be involved in the farm as well as their other plans. Part of this retirement plan should be living arrangements and location. Financially, the plan should show how the retiring generation will be able to finance their lifestyle expectations through a statement of their income sources and assets.

Training and Development Plan for the Successors (and Future Retirees)

While the younger generation may think it is ready to take over leadership immediately, the retiring generation may not be ready to let go and will probably be right in thinking that more training and experience may be needed by the younger generation. The training and development plan should include a listing of the knowledge and skills needed and how future leadership measures up to these needs. A new, entry-level recruit in a general business should not expect to be in top management quickly; a new farmer cannot expect this either in most situations. The older and younger generations should discuss and create a plan for developing management skills and then allowing the younger generation to increase management decision making and control over time. The younger generation may start in the business by providing labor and participating in decision discussions but not by making final decisions. Over time, he or she may be given more management responsibilities for part of the farm business. For example, the younger generation may be given responsibility for choosing rations for the livestock, for breeding programs, or for machinery maintenance, but supervision is still done by the older generation. Eventually, the younger generation may be given the title of herd manager or crop manager with greater responsibility and independence of supervision by the older generation. General business uses this gradual step-by-step process continually. In some instances, the younger generation may have worked for another farm or business for a year or two with the explicit purpose of learning another way of operating and managing a farm. This alternative gives the younger person great experience from another "teacher" and allows the older generation to start the adjustment of letting go. The training and development plan should include opportunities for formal classes and workshops—even after a college degree. The training and development plan should also include some points and a timetable on how the older generation will recognize, acknowledge, and adjust to the experience and knowledge gained by the younger generation.

Both groups need to accept that while training and preparing the younger generation may be needed, information and training can flow in the other direction too. The older group needs to learn new techniques, methods, and ideas from the younger. The younger generation has new skills and will face new and different conditions, opportunities, and threats. The older generation needs to accept that the old ways of business may not work in the future. The plan is to have the younger generation take over, so the older generation needs to be open to new ideas, to the younger generation becoming the real owners and managers, and not just "permanent trainees" until the older generation dies. The older generation needs to accept that they are training themselves for retirement.

Farm Business Plan for the Future

This part of the transfer and succession plan will look very similar to any business plan. This business plan should be an expansion of the four points briefly discussed in the overview: (1) the people involved, (2) the opportunity, (3) the context, and (4) the risks and rewards. The plan should include vision and mission statements; the chosen strategy; production, marketing, and financing plans; personnel plans; and financial statements. It should specify how the needs of both the retiring generation and the younger generation will be met.

Transferring the business can start and take shape in several ways:

• Farming together for a trial period. This can help test compatibility and commitment. This step can involve a wage for the younger generation or the start of ownership.
• Farming together but apart. This strategy involves separate ownership but common operation of at least part of the business. The younger generation may rent machinery and other facilities from the

older generation. The two groups would keep separate financial records but work together in many ways.

- Multiple owners and joint ventures. The original business may remain as it is, but the two generations own and work together on new ventures. More land is purchased, for example, and owned jointly but separately from the original business. This may be the beginning step to full blending of the business and asset ownership.
- Partnerships and corporations. These legal structures can be used to more easily combine ownership of the business and its assets. Shares can be smaller financial commitments to transfer ownership. The partnership or corporation may be the operating entity while the ownership of land and building assets remains with individuals—the older generation, for example—and the partnership or corporation rents the asset.

Organization Plan

The organization plan describes how daily activities will be organized and managed. It will detail the roles, responsibilities, and authorities of everyone. An organizational chart may be appropriate. The plan should also describe how this will change over time as the transfer moves through implementation.

The organization plan should also describe how business meetings will be structured, when they will occur, how the agenda will be set, and who will lead the meetings. Who has a vote and the power of that vote should also be stated clearly. Whether and how voting power will change over time should be included.

Labor, Management, Control Transfer Plan

As described in other sections of the transfer plan, the timetable for transferring labor, management, and control needs to be specified and stated. Including this as a separate section will increase the need for and result in improved understanding of when these transfers will occur and, perhaps, whether the younger generation has enough experience to make the transfer.

Ownership Transfer Plan

Transferring ownership of assets will likely be the slowest part of the transfer. This part of the plan should start with a description of current ownership and the steps planned for the transfer in the future.

The plan for transferring ownership will depend on the legal structure of the business. If the business is a sole proprietorship, direct sale or gifting will be needed. If the farm is structured as a partnership or corporation, a different timing of sales in smaller shares can be made as the younger generation has the financial resources to make the purchases.

The ownership of different assets will likely be handled in different ways. Machinery and livestock turnover may be quicker and involve smaller financial commitments so the younger generation may be able to take ownership of these assets sooner. Land with its larger financial value will likely be on a longer timetable. For retirement income purposes, land ownership could be held by the retiring generation for a considerable time, with rental arrangements described in this and other sections of the plan.

Implementation Timetable

This section will be a complete listing of the steps required for implementing the transfer plan. It will include a compilation of the dates and plans mentioned in other sections of the plan, such as training and development dates and management transfer. It should also include other dates not mentioned specifically before, such as moving dates for families as retirement begins and management transfer proceeds. This complete implementation timetable could be presented as a Gantt chart, discussed in Chapter 18, Operations Management for the Farm.

Communications Plan

As discussed in a previous section, communications is very important to a successful transfer of the business and succession of leadership. The transfer plan should include the points above so that all parties can see the plans for meetings including scheduling, facilitating, agenda development, voting power, and so on.

Contingency Plan

Regretfully, real life does not always go according to our plans. The transfer plan needs to include a discussion of contingency plans if major events occur. The stakeholders need to discuss the potential impact of death or divorce. They should have in writing how disagreements will be resolved. If a major fire or other disaster happens, what steps will be taken in response? How can the plan be adjusted if a major change in the economy negatively affects financial profitability and viability and thus retirement and transfer plans? How are life, health, fire, and other insurance tools, plus other risk management tools, being used to mitigate the impact if these events were to occur?

Another part of the contingency plan should be the exit plan if either generation decides not to follow through on the full plan. The younger generation may realize that farming or farming together is not their career choice after all. The older generation may not like how the younger generation is managing the farm. A death, divorce, or a new marriage may change a lot of expectations and needs. The exit plan is a discussion of how assets and the business itself will be valued. It should have some discussion of how ownership shares will be determined. The exit plan should provide for either generation leaving earlier than initially planned. A good exit plan may keep the families together even though they are not farming together anymore.

As with any business plan, the stakeholders need to review, update, and adjust the plan. The contingency plan involves major changes, but small changes in people, the business, and in the business and physical environments can create the need to fine-tune and redirect the business succession plans.

As was said at the beginning of this chapter, the goal of many farming families is to see the family business continue into the future. This process needs to be planned and accepted by all involved. By following the steps and ideas in this chapter, the chances of a successful transfer will increase.

Summary

- The three stages of the business life cycle are entry or establishment, growth and survival, and exit or disinvestment.
- Each generation needs to realize that other generations will have different goals and needs.
- Transferring the farm is a major event that requires considerable discussion and planning. A written plan can be critical to a successful transfer.
- The process for developing a plan can help in the development of a good plan owned by all stakeholders. Communication between all generations and stakeholders is critical. "Read my mind" does not work.
- Before developing a plan, those involved should agree that the family wants to transfer the farm business, know who the successor(s) is, evaluate whether the farm is profitable and viable now and into the future, and agree on a timetable.
- Fair is not necessarily equal.
- The farm transfer and succession plan is a business plan with some additional sections.
- The older generation needs to acknowledge the younger generation's knowledge, training, and experience and adjust the management of the farm in response.
- The younger generation needs to acknowledge their need to gain knowledge and experience but also expect greater responsibility and independence as well.
- Plans for transferring management and ownership need to be developed, including an implementation timetable.
- Contingency plans are needed.

Review Questions

1. Describe the three stages in the farm business life cycle.
2. For the three different farming couples listed below, list some possible goals they would have for their farm. Even though you are not in each of these age groups, think of yourself as (a) a young, beginning farm couple; (b) an established, middle-aged farm couple; and (c) a farming couple planning to retire soon. Put yourself in each generation's position and write the goals you think "your" generation would have.
3. If the three couples were in the same family and operating the same farm, describe how you think they could come to a common set of goals and objectives for the farm. Whose goals should have the highest priority? How should competing goals be handled?
4. Why is communication so important to planning farm transfer and succession? What are the factors that contribute to good communication for planning?
5. What does a family need to agree on before they even begin to develop a transfer and succession plan?
6. Why is fair not necessarily equal?
7. Identify and describe the major parts of a complete transfer and succession plan.
8. Why is a timetable critical?
9. Why is a contingency plan needed?

10. What does the older generation need to acknowledge and adjust to in the younger generation?
11. What does the younger generation need to acknowledge and adjust to in the older generation?

Further Reading

Coughler, Peter. 2004. "Components of a Farm Succession Plan." Factsheet 04-073, Ontario Ministry of Agriculture, Food, and Rural Affairs. Accessed on September 14, 2009, at http://www.omafra.gov.on.ca/english/busdev/facts/04-073.htm.

Edwards, William. 2009. "Two-Generation Farming: Transferring Machinery and Livestock." Pm1474d (rev.). Ames, Iowa: Iowa State University Extension. 20 pp.

Hachfeld, Gary A., David B. Bau, C. Robert Holcomb, and James N. Kurtz. 2009. "Transferring the Farm Series: (1) Preparing to Transfer the Farm Business, (2) Farming Together as a Transfer Strategy, (3) Using Farm Partnerships or Corporations to Transfer Assets, (4) Transferring Livestock & Machinery, (5) Should You Sell Your Real Estate?, (6) Gifting Farm Assets, (7) Major Tax Considerations When Transferring Assets, (8) Treatment of the Heirs in the Transfer Process, (9) Financial Help for Beginning Minnesota Farmers, and (10) Developing a Written Transfer Plan." University of Minnesota Extension. September 2009. Accessed on October 7, 2009 and available at http://www.cffm.umn.edu/Publications/pubs/FarmMgtTopics/TransferringTheFarmSeries.pdf.

Harl, Neil. 2001. *Farm Estate and Business Planning*. 15th ed. Niles, Illinois: Century Communications. 488 pp.

Harl, Neil. 2000. "Estate Planning—Planning for Tomorrow." Pm-993 (rev.). Ames, Iowa: Iowa State University Extension. 56 pp.

Hofstrand, Don. 1998. "Two-Generation Farming: Step 1: Getting Started." Pm1474a (rev.). Ames, Iowa: Iowa State University Extension. 16 pp.

Hofstrand, Don. 1998. "Two-Generation Farming: Step 2: Selecting a Business Arrangement." Pm1474b (rev.). Ames, Iowa: Iowa State University Extension. 16 pp.

Hofstrand, Don. 1998. "Two-Generation Farming: Step 3: Making It Work." Pm1474c (rev.). Ames, Iowa: Iowa State University Extension. 16 pp.

Préfontaine, Serge. 2009. "60 Questions to Prepare the Succession of a Business." Longueuil, Quebec, Canada: Farm Management Groups. 4 pp. Accessed on December 9, 2009, at www.farmcentre.com/Resources/.

Winter, Mary, and Carol B. Volker. 2002. "Ready, Set, Retire: Farming with an Operating Heir." Pm1167f (rev.). Ames, Iowa: Iowa State University Extension. 4 pp.

Winter, Mary, and Carol B. Volker. 2002. "Ready, Set, Retire: Farming without an Operating Heir." Pm1167g (rev.). Ames, Iowa: Iowa State University Extension. 4 pp.

27

Farming in the Future

In this chapter:

- Opportunities and challenges
- Farmers' responses

In the first chapter we looked at our changed and changing world and the forces that are affecting farming. Since that first chapter, we have learned many tools that farmers have to evaluate their farms; their economic environment; and how they design, position, and manage their farms to accomplish their goals. Now in this last chapter, let's look at the major challenges and opportunities that face farmers today and discuss some ideas on how they can respond.

Opportunities and Challenges

As discussed in the first chapter, technology, communication, and ease of travel and transportation have brought the world to us and we to the world. We can enjoy this closer connection and expand the market for our products, but our competitors can also benefit just as easily. The challenge is to keep aware of what customers and potential customers want either directly or through our marketing organizations. Our opportunity is to respond to those needs even as they change.

The connectedness of the world also means we need to be aware of what may happen and is happening around the world and understand what that may mean for our farms. This knowledge may come from our own reading and interpretation or from a farm organization or consultant. The challenge is to gather this knowledge and filter it to distill what is important for a specific farm. The opportunity is to adapt quicker for survival and to take advantage of new opportunities.

The challenge of changing demographics is that the demand for our traditional products may be changing. The mirror of that challenge is the opportunity. Changing demographics can offer new opportunities for new products, new markets, and better profits.

Farm business expansion will continue and will call for corporate forms of ownership. As farm size increases, farms in the future will face the need for more capital, especially equity capital. They will need to acquire this equity capital from off-farm and non-farm sources. They will need to address the challenge of communicating and reporting to these equity holders to keep them abreast of the farm operation and satisfied with the returns and the progress. The needs for additional capital to finance larger operations will also involve more debt capital; however, the financial crisis of 2008–10 promises to increase the regulations and requirements for obtaining credit. The challenge of more rigorous requirements for obtaining credit brings with it the opportunity of taking more time and energy to evaluate the plans and risks and developing a better, more robust business plan for the future.

Changing demand levels, as economic growth and recession come and go, can allow farmers and processors to adjust their product mix for a balanced portfolio of products that can weather the increased uncertainty and volatility of prices and profit in the future. The challenge of increased uncertainty and volatility can be seen as an opportunity for farmers to learn new risk management tools for prices, interest rates, and currency exchange rates.

The opportunities of world trade will always bring with them the challenges of trade regulations, GMO and phytosanitary concerns, trade constraints, and different cultural customs. This will be true whether the trading is done directly by farmers or by other businesses. The opportunities of greater trade due to personal income growth in China, India, and other Southeast Asian countries bring with them the challenge of understanding what people want and then "meeting or exceeding those expectations" better than your competition.

Livestock producers will face challenges from several sources. The profit squeeze produced by rising feed prices will continue to cause adjustments in all areas of livestock production. Producers will adjust their production processes as well as their size to find new profitable business models. The issues surrounding animal rights and animal welfare will continue to force change from new government policies and regulations and, perhaps even more important, from the buyers of animals and animal products. Buyers will be and already are acting faster than governments in changing the way livestock is cared for and processed. The potential impact of climate change and the companion development of a carbon tax will affect livestock producers directly and indirectly. A carbon tax will have a direct impact on livestock production and producers' income; the size of the impact and the size of management changes will depend on how legislation is written. Even without a carbon tax, climate change will affect where grain production takes place and thus the supply and transportation costs of obtaining grain.

Local food production and organic production are opportunities for those who understand the market and the production and reporting requirements. In both of these opportunities, the market is much smaller than traditional markets for agricultural products. As with trade to other nations, the challenge is to understand what people in your locality want and then "meet or exceed those expectations" better than your competition.

The trials and tribulations of the biofuel industry are matched by the potential opportunities. As with all new ventures and markets, the challenge is having sufficient capital to weather the storms along the way. Current technologies will not be the technologies of the future, but current technologies have produced (and lost) a lot of equity for investors. The challenge for farmer-owners of biofuel businesses will be to balance ownership of production assets with the flexibility to switch as new technologies and products are introduced.

The challenge of climate change is increased variability and uncertainty of rainfall patterns and temperature levels. In the long run, production regions may change for some crops, but that is a long-run challenge. Meeting this challenge can be accomplished in similar ways of meeting other new uncertainties: adopting new technologies, producing different products, using different inputs, and learning new risk management tools. These new risk management tools will not be completely new; the tools of the future will be built on the current tools for using futures markets and insurance policies. The concern over carbon and its impact on climate change has already created new opportunities for farmers in carbon sequestration and the carbon credit market. These opportunities will only increase in the future.

The challenge of responding to new regulations and pressure to protect the environment may create new opportunities. Some production areas may lose their advantage (livestock production very close to concentrated urban areas, for example). At the same time, other areas may benefit—for example, from new products such as eco-tourism. Those producers who grasp and respond to what consumers are asking for in terms of animal welfare will be the first to enjoy the opportunities of new markets and new products.

Innovation and new technology are both opportunities and challenges. Early adopters can harvest the advantages of new innovations and technologies that will become a challenge to later adopters. However, since technology changes so quickly, an early adopter may at first benefit and then be challenged with old technology as others adopt newer technology. As noted in the first chapter, increased farm size is seen by some as the way to take full advantage of new technologies and avoid the cost of obsolescence by being able to replace at a faster rate as new technological advances are introduced.

The preceding list of challenges and opportunities is certainly not comprehensive, and it certainly cannot contain the events and changes that are in the future but not yet known. As in all competitive markets, the farms that benefit from these new challenges and opportunities will be those who can "meet or exceed the customers' expectations" better than the competition. In their work with farmers in different parts of the world, Napier and Nell found several areas where leading farmers were taking advantage of the opportunities and challenges before them (Example 27.1).

Example 27.1. Taking Advantage of Opportunities due to Change

According to Napier and Nell, leading farmers around the world are focusing on nine major areas as they seize opportunities from the changes occurring around them. Those areas and the strategies in each are:

Planning (strategic and operational): Leading farmers analyze their own strengths and weaknesses; make major changes if required; prepare written business, personal, and family goals; modify the goals as circumstances change; write and communicate business plans; develop operational manuals for key tasks; delegate to employees; focus on management and major determinants of business success; appoint boards of independent experts to regularly review their businesses; use more outside expertise; and improve continuously.

(continued)

(continued)

Environmental management: Leading farmers realize that demand for improved environmental management will only increase; are not defensive; see business opportunities for meeting these demands; develop their environmental credentials; become multifunctional in their objectives; and involve stakeholders.

New technologies: Leading farmers focus on achieving excellence in their production systems; adopt new technology early; work closely with researchers; work closely with each other; learn about new technologies; experiment for tomorrow; always look for the next technologies; and adopt new technology by outsourcing to expert contractors, which saves capital spent on new equipment.

Cooperation: Leading farmers work together to learn; to share expertise; to develop new management and marketing models; and to form purchasing, information sharing, marketing, and management groups.

Market-driven: Leading farmers recognize the opportunities and are learning to be marketers; develop the relationships necessary for success; transform their businesses to align with customer needs and demands; anticipate market changes and achieve rewards by participating with customers and monitoring market trends; understand that the real competition is between supply chains, so they coordinate within their supply chains to improve performance of all those; implement quality assurance and traceability systems in line with customer demands; constantly develop differentiated products with services that add value to their customers; grow their businesses to ensure sufficient volume for market access; and are better able to weather market shocks through market participation and excellence in risk management.

Business growth: Leading farmers grow their businesses but not necessarily through size. Leading farmers seek to increase profit margins and/or develop other businesses with their farms. They understand whether constraints are primarily due to the personal capacity of the manager, the organizational structure, limited resources, or a combination. Leading farmers have separated their land business from their operating business. They are determined to have a cash-rich balance sheet so they retain decision-making control. Leading farmers seldom seek to own all assets, but they do work through syndicates, leasing, shared-farming, equity partnerships, and franchises. They are able to attract outside capital by offering business propositions that meet both the investors' and farmer's goals. Leading farmers grow their management systems as their businesses grow.

Risk management: Leading farmers realize future risk involves more than production and marketing risk. Risk also involves business relationship breakdowns, personnel performance breakdowns, changing government policies, and changes in competition. Leading farmers learn how to develop comprehensive risk management plans.

Off-farm businesses: Leading farmers realize their farm management skills are the same skills needed to manage businesses, farm related and non-farm. Through these other businesses, they achieve better risk management, complementarities between the businesses, and more efficient use of managerial, financial, and physical resources. They do not see geographical distance as a hindrance to developing new businesses or in monitoring new and old businesses.

Managing people: Leading farmers realize their dependence on the performance of people: family, partners, employees, and others. They regard people as an investment, not a cost; focus on effectively employing all their human resources; accept the challenge of creating stimulating workplaces; develop their own and everyone's capabilities; and have learning plans driven by the goals of their business. Leading farmers realize the importance of planning, communicating, motivating, and delegating so they can spend more time managing the business rather than working in the business. Leading farmers realize the need to develop not-traditionally-farming skills in information management, marketing, human resource management, creative and critical thinking, planning, learning, and so on; these skills do not become redundant or obsolete over time compared to some traditional skills. Leading farmers regard succession planning and family teamwork as critical management tasks.

Source: R. Napier and W. T. Nell, "How the World's Leading Farmers Are Responding to Global Changes—A Consultant's Review." Applied paper at the 16th International Farm Management Congress, UCC, Cork, Ireland, July 15–20, 2007, accessed on February 3, 2010, at http://www.ifmaonline.org/pdf/congress/07Napier&Nell.pdf.

Farmers' Responses

As I travel to meetings, I like to visit with farmers to learn how they are responding to the trends and changes and their ideas for the future. I also talk to others close to farmers, such as extension educators, professional farm managers, bankers, and other advisors. I talked with and listened to farmers from a broad range of age, farm size, and geography. From these conversations, I have organized the common ideas into six themes or categories: (1) getting bigger or smaller, (2) focusing on commodity markets or on niche markets, (3) moving closer to the final consumer in the value chain, (4) redesigning the production system, (5) adopting new technologies, and (6) increasing management skills. These six ideas are related, and a mix of them can be seen on the same farm. They are separate ideas, however, so let us look at each idea.

Getting Bigger or Smaller

The admonition that a farm needs to get bigger to survive is still true in some ways but not as true as it once was. The pressures to increase size still come from the market pressure to decrease the product's cost per unit sold. The continual change comes from the changes in technologies that allow one person to manage and operate larger operations. These technologies include both physical technologies, such as auto steer for machinery, automatic milking machines, and health programs for livestock, and managerial technologies, such as data collection and reporting processes that allow improved management of crops and livestock. These farms are increasing in size to maintain or increase the family income obtained from the farm business.

Increasing size can come in a variety of ways. The traditional way of controlling more land through purchase or rental is still strong. Expanding the number of animals with or without building more facilities is also very common. I have learned of farmers who buy the neighboring farm business—not the land, but the business. The seller is perhaps at or approaching retirement age and the buyer sees the opportunity to increase the size of his or her business without having to buy all the assets separately. In addition, the arrangement usually has the seller staying on the farm (for a few years at least) to operate it almost independently and also enjoy the conversion of paper equity into real equity for retirement.

I also have talked to farmers who see opportunities to change (drastically for some) the way they do business. Their whole view and business model changes from a production and low-cost model to one that starts with understanding what potential customers want and then—once again we hear this phrase—"meeting or exceeding their expectations." These farmers are following the admonishment to sell more than their physical product, which is one of the secrets of best-managed farms listed in Chapter 2. The quote from that article is "Give the customer what he wants, when he wants it, and how he wants it, and they'll throw money at you." These farms have not necessarily gotten bigger; some of them have stayed the same size. But most of them have decreased size as measured by acres or production. What they have grown is their vision of what their farm is and their ability to produce for the customer. As a result, they have increased their gross sales and net income. These farms have also adopted strategies involving niche markets and moving down the value chain, which are discussed in the next two sections.

Focusing on Commodity Markets or on Niche Markets

The traditional view of farming is as a producer of commodities. Farmers produce commodities such as maize, wheat, pork, beef, milk, and barley; these products don't have brand names. Processors and retailers have brand names such as General Mills' Wheaties, Hormel's Spam, Heinz Tomato Ketchup, Finax Muesli, and Arla Milk.

If a farmer chooses a strategy to produce a commodity, the market forces him to become a low-cost producer because there is no way for him to identify his product from another farmer's product. That is true whether the other farmer is next door or across the ocean. The prudent farm manager, having chosen to produce a commodity, will then focus on improving productivity and efficiency in order to decrease and keep costs per unit sold at a level that allows a profit to be made at the price the market offers. The top farmers in this group are truly into lean management: waste is cut out whenever and wherever it is seen and all known ways to increase production profitably are utilized.

Another group of farmers have discovered, found, created, or made—the verb differs with the story—a niche market. The product may look like a commodity, such as the milk one farmer produces, packages, and sells to a small chain of small convenience stores. But the farmer has found what the customer wants and delivers that product. The definition of the product in all these stories includes timing, labeling, quality, and delivery, as well as the physical product. The niche market price for the product—milk, for example—is higher than the commodity market price, but the whole product delivered to the niche market is much different from the product delivered to the commodity market by another farmer. Other farmers and products I have heard of include pork delivered to a restaurant (with the farm named on the menu), organic milk and ice cream delivered to a grocery store, vegetables sold to local restaurants, and corn and soybeans produced in Iowa and sold to customers in Japan. Community-supported agriculture (CSA) farms would fall into this category also. These farmers follow the best-price strategy, not the low-cost strategy. Another niche market that some farmers are taking advantage is "agritainment" (Example 27.2).

Example 27.2. Agritainment

Farming is not necessarily just crops and livestock any more. New ventures and new ideas are contributing to the income of farm families around the world. Beyond farmers capturing more value through biofuels, direct marketing of crop and livestock products, ownership of processing facilities such as bread bakeries, a growing area is agricultural entertainment, or "agritainment," for non-farm public. This includes bed-and-breakfasts, hunting, farm tours, working vacations, and so on.

Another example is the maize mazes that are being designed in many countries. In England, one maize maze had a ticket price of £5 in 2009 with an expectation of "15,000 or so visitors over the summer." Plus, in October, 80% of the crop will still be good to sell as cattle feed. Other examples of "agritainment" include bed-and-breakfast accommodation, wedding venues, dance halls, and shooting ranges (both real and paintball). As reported by *The Economist* magazine, Great Britain's Department for Environment, Food and Rural Affairs (DEFRA) "reckons that a tenth of farms have diversified into sports and recreation activities. More still have exploited a fad for locally sourced food that has spawned scores of farmers' markets." In all, diversified enterprises accounted for 15% of farming income in the financial year 2007–08, according to DEFRA.

Imagination and marketing may be the tools for farmers to realize new ways to create income from the resources they already have.

Source: "Hedge-Fun Managers: From Mazes to Weddings, Farmers Are Making More Money out of the Public," *The Economist*, July 9, 2009, accessed last on January 31, 2010, at http://www.economist.com/research/articlesBySubject/displaystory.cfm?subjectid=478044&story_id=E1_TQDDGSNS

The management skills required for these two very different foci are also very different. The need to focus on cost of production and operating efficiencies requires a very dedicated attention to the details of production and purchase of inputs. The necessity to focus on the need of the customer in a niche market requires customer relations, marketing knowledge, sanitary regulations, prospecting and protecting skills, and production and operating skills as well. While the niche market farmer still needs to monitor and eliminate waste, she or he does not have to be as focused on eliminating waste (compared to a producer of commodities) because the customer is looking for more than just cost. And, while the commodity farmer needs to monitor the market and cultivate relationships with buyers, he does not have to be as focused on this because the buyer has cost per unit as the prime objective. Both strategies are demanding in their own way; both require top management skills to be successful.

Moving Down the Value Chain

"Moving down the supply chain" (that is, closer to the final consumer) is one of the most frequent ideas I hear. The knowledge of and desire to participate farther down the supply chain (or value chain) is widespread. As one farmer said, "Just producing and selling won't work." Another expressed it this way, "I don't want to hear about how to cut expenses. I want to hear about increasing equity." The idea and desire to capture more value was expressed by almost all the farmers. Most of them realize that they, as farmers, needed to be producing for the final consumers' needs, not for the farmers' own needs, wants, and advantages. They have heard the phrase of creating value for the consumer and want to capture more of that value for themselves.

As part of this desire to move down the chain (and, as will be discussed later, to reduce risk), production contracts will increase in frequency and importance. Production contracts will come in two different forms. The first form is the traditional contract. A farmer signs a contract with a company to produce a product of specified quality and quantity. Seed and vegetable production contracts are common examples of this type of contract. The recent increase in contracting for high oil corn and similar products are also examples of this type. Traditional production contracts will also be used for new products from genetic engineering (such as nutriceuticals).

A second form of production contract that we will see more of in the future is the contract between neighbors. While this has always existed, the formality of the contract will increase. Now we often hear of the crop grower, for example, agreeing verbally to produce a certain quantity of corn silage for the neighboring livestock producer. In the future, the producer and grower may develop a working agreement or contract that specifies which crop variety to plant, how much to plant, and how to value the crop based on the protein, energy, and other nutrient characteristics that create value for the livestock producer and, thus, the crop grower.

Preserving the identity of grains by variety provides the potential to capture greater value. Farmers are certainly aware of the value of and concern about genetically modified (GM) and non-GM varieties. They also know about the potential for niche markets with certain varieties and special crops. (Most are also aware of the small size of niche markets.) Research has shown processors (such as General Mills) that certain varieties possess characteristics that are better both for processing and for the consumers. These companies are aware of the increased value for the consumer and themselves, so they already provide an incentive to farmers to grow and deliver those desired varieties (if they are not mixed with other varieties). Thus, many farmers already participate in the value of identity preservation. Identity preservation does create problems for both the farmer and industry. These problems include increased logistics of keeping grains separate, moral risk of mixing different varieties, and so on. In spite of these problems, identity preservation is now required and is being done for many crop and livestock products. This practice will only increase. Those who do not segregate will not receive any of the potential premiums.

Organic farming usually moves a farmer down the supply chain and is also a new redesign of the production system. Organic products are a small but rapidly increasing area for the food market because consumers are asking for these products. Food retailers are responding faster than other parts of the food supply chain. Many farmers are seeing this as a way to achieve the multiple goals of income, environmental protection, and personal health.

A traditional way to capture more value is to market directly to consumers. A new and yet not so new idea that is being pursued is for farmers to form (new) marketing cooperatives rather than trying to contact the consumers as individual farmers. This is not a new idea, obviously; we have several large, established marketing cooperatives already in existence: CHS (Cenex Harvest States), Land O' Lakes, Arla, Sunkist, Diamond Walnut, and many more. The "newness" is in the recent formation and discussion of small, local cooperatives for the purpose of marketing directly with local consumers or retailers or for buying inputs for several farmers to increase purchasing and negotiation power. Slightly larger cooperative efforts have also formed in recent years, such as a group of farmers who own a rather small hog processing firm in southwest Minnesota that negotiated an export agreement with Japan.

In addition to cooperative marketing, I also hear farmers talking about cooperative production efforts or joint ventures with other farmers. These range from sharing machinery with neighbors to forming companies to build livestock facilities. This joint work is especially common in hog and dairy production but is also seen in specialty products such as fish production. In some of these joint efforts, the organizers saw local resources and developed the idea of how to use these resources to produce a product the consumers wanted.

I should note that while these are cooperative efforts in one definition of the word cooperative, the new entities and efforts may or may not be organized and filed legally as a cooperative. These new entities may also be various forms of partnerships and corporations.

Redesigning the Production System

Farmers will always seek to increase economic efficiency and productivity. They have cut costs many times and will continue to cut costs; this is part of being in a competitive industry. In recent years, they are talking again about how to cut costs. Sometimes this is expressed in terms of needing a lower capitalization level.

Others talk about the need to change the production system—perhaps slightly, perhaps radically. Converting or considering the conversion to organic production methods are mentioned often. Also mentioned are the need for less substitution of capital for labor, increasing productivity through tiling of wet areas, use of GIS technology (as discussed later), and the use of more efficient equipment in livestock buildings and for product handling.

This discussion is an appropriate reaction to the need to design a production system that delivers a product at a cost that can compete in the market. Farmers are looking for ways they can respond to the market instead of just wanting the market to supply a price that covers their current costs of production. The management expert, Peter Drucker, describes several companies and industries that failed to heed the warning against the dream of a market delivering a good price versus the reality of producing at a cost level that balances with the price supplied by the market.

Farm managers in the future will continue to be concerned about balancing increased productivity with the risks of higher costs due to investments for raising productivity. I heard some farmers and farm managers talking about the need to lower capitalization on farms. For example, they wanted to purchase fewer inputs (herbicides, for example) and use more on-farm resources (labor and mechanical cultivation, for example). This idea runs counter to the usual trend of increased substitution of capital for labor, and I don't think the new trend will reverse the old substitution in total. The concerns for timeliness and for "covering ground" remain. The idea of substituting labor for capital is due to the concern of covering cash costs in the current period of low prices. However, I suspect this current concern affects a current and young generation of farmers and, thus, will carry into the future. Future managers will more seriously consider alternatives that do not rely solely on purchased inputs.

Another idea for redesigning the production process is the expressed desire to share risk between landowners and tenants through flexible cash rents. Landowners may not want to take on the responsibility and risks of grain marketing required by share rental agreements. As cash rents increase, tenants may not want to take all the risks of both production and price. When both the owner and tenant see the need to share risk, new rental agreements will be written that establish a base cash rent and the rules by which the landowner is paid additional cash rent based on that year's yield and, perhaps, price.

Sharing machinery ownership is another old and, I found, newly fashionable way to reduce ownership costs as well as enjoy the potential benefits of better mechanical technology. If there is some geographic dispersion of the farms, they may also enjoy increased efficiency in the use of the machinery in response to differing weather and soil conditions. These shared ownership agreements appeared to be working well between farmers who had similar-sized farms. The agreements were not limited to relatives or legal partnerships. The farmers had agreed beforehand that repairs and maintenance costs would be shared in proportion to the land use regardless of where the machine broke down. They also felt that the decrease in ownership costs due to sharing were far larger than any yield losses due to a decrease in timeliness.

Adopting New Technologies

The precision farming tools (such as yield monitors, GPS, GIS, and auto steer) have been quickly adopted by many farmers. Equipment dealers are adding them as standard equipment to large machinery. Farmers are very interested in the ability to farm areas within a field via precision agriculture rather than the whole field. They had relatively small areas (bald areas, wet areas, etc.) that were not as productive as the rest of the field, but it was currently too expensive in terms of timeliness to change any seeding, fertilizer, or herbicide application as they passed through or drove around those areas using traditional machinery.

The farmers did express some concern over the spread of e-commerce and the potential impact on local communities. While lower input prices are desirable, that was not their only concern. They did not want to lose their local service and said they would be willing to pay somewhat higher prices to keep that local company in business. On the personal side of e-commerce, farmers also wanted local businesses to use the Internet to improve the local service, not to replace it. The local service they wanted the most on the Internet was the ability to check prices, order inputs, and leave messages after regular business hours.

These are not the only new technologies in which farmers are interested. Many other ideas were mentioned but not extensively or by large numbers of farmers. As discussed in an earlier section, farmers were interested in other new technologies such as genetically modified crops and animals and organic production methods. They were also interested in new techniques of the old technology paths such as mechanical guidance systems, computer-assisted field work, automated information collection and processing, and so on.

Increasing Management Skills

For the future, the farmers themselves could see the need to move beyond production management. Marketing will still be important and still could be improved by many farmers. However, more management time and skills will be needed in risk, strategic, and personnel management. Better information can be obtained through managerial accounting versus cash-based, whole-farm-only methods.

Risk management was described by farmers as protecting their income and protecting their farm resources. Forward contracts, hedging, options, and other marketing tools continue to increase in importance for farm managers. As production contracts become more prevalent, farmers were becoming more concerned about contract evaluation and negotiation techniques. With more farms having more employees, personnel selection and management become important not just for production management but also for risk management. The wrong employee or an improperly trained employee can quickly change the potential outcome in a negative direction. Job descriptions, selection tests, training, evaluation, and incentive packages will become important tools to the farm manager of the future. Another set of management tools for the future are those used for controlling the process to better ensure that it is proceeding as planned, to be ready to take corrective actions, and to alter plans in response to changes in the situation a farmer faces. Strategic management itself is seen as a risk management tool.

Strategic management involves positioning the farm for the future. It is "big picture" thinking. The farmers I talked to were very concerned about and taking some actions to move and change their farm into one ready for the future. Contracting with companies and neighbors, as mentioned earlier, is one example of strategic changes. Cooperating with others for livestock production is another option that has been taken and is still being looked upon as having good potential (with memories of bad results too). Another example of strategic change is the hog farmer who could not see a good future in hog farming for himself and his son, so they developed the business of cleaning pits and spreading manure for neighbors. Accomplishing this did not involve just the addition of manure hauling and dropping of hogs; they also had to change from corn and soybeans to alfalfa because the demand for hauling was highest in the spring and fall and that conflicted with planting and harvesting of the corn and soybeans. Alfalfa hay had a different time demand schedule that did not conflict with the manure hauling business. Also, the raising of alfalfa hay meant they had another product to sell some of their manure-hauling customers.

Some farmers were looking at their resources with new eyes once they thought of individual parts of the farm as profit centers. For example, the farm shop can be used for many activities in the off-season. One farmer used it as a base for a snow removal business; another as a place to assemble machinery for the local dealer. This is one example of how a resource became even more useful when it was viewed as a "mini-business" or profit center, and the manager asked, "How can this resource be better used?"

Farmers were also looking at how to respond to some unknown events in the future. They knew they are outnumbered both nationally (less than 2% of the population are farmers) and locally. The local decisions on county boards are being driven more and more by the non-farming rural population, who do not always have the same goals and ideas as farmers. Farmers are discussing and planning how to respond to this situation. They don't have all the solutions, but, as one farmer said, "It's odors now, dust and noise are next." The potential changes in national farm policy are also unknown, and farmers are trying to decide how to respond to the directions those changes may take.

Personnel management came up in our discussions; farms are losing the traditional source of workers because rural children were "going to the city" and there is a need to understand a new source or workers (and neighbors) from different cultures. However, not all children were going to the city. I also heard that some people wanted to live in rural areas and work on farms but did not want to own a farm and be responsible for all the decisions and financial risk that owning involved.

Some of the farmers described an open style of management that they had found very valuable. Instead of feeling they had to make all the decisions, these farmers were willing and sought out the ideas of employees and fellow farmers. They felt they ended up with more and better ideas than if they had not asked. I am sure the employees had a very different sense of belonging and loyalty to those farmers than they would to a dictatorial farmer.

Opportunities for Consultants

These conversations point to some opportunities for consultants and advisors to farmers. Some farmers could convert these opportunities into businesses to complement their farm businesses. First, the farmers themselves realized that they cannot be everything or do everything that needs to be done. Many, if not all, future farmers will still like the task of producing, but not all will like the business side of farming. Many farmers would probably agree with the one who said to me, ''I enjoy being in the field and doing something different every day. I don't like doing paperwork.'' They were interested in hiring some of the business work done for them while still maintaining ownership control over their farm. Another farmer described this interest as wanting to hire a ''CEO'' for his farm. However, a CFO, or chief financial officer, is a better title of what this farmer wanted. He described this person's duties as preparing financial information, finding and evaluating new opportunities and contracts, working with the various government agencies, and so on. The CFO would be responsible to the farmer/owner who would act more as the chair of the board (and still be able to drive the tractor, work with the animals, etc.). While hiring a CFO may seem too extreme to some farmers, farmers already hire financial advisors, tax accountants, bookkeepers, and other advisors. These people could use this farmer's desire to develop new lines of their businesses to help farmers doing the new paperwork in the future. I am sure this farmer is not alone in wanting to avoid paperwork.

The traditional jobs for consultants will continue: bookkeeping, crop consultants, veterinary services, marketing services, and so on. Some new ideas I heard about were contract identification and evaluation, evaluation of new ventures, and making market connections between geographically separated individuals. The list of potential opportunities will most certainly increase since the complexity of farming is not decreasing.

Another set of farmers discussed the future and came up with five critical themes or questions they needed to address in order to be successful in the future (Example 27.3).

Example 27.3. Crucial Questions for the Future

Dutch dairy farmers and experts were surveyed about how dairy farmers are going to anticipate changing circumstances in the future. The results lead to five central themes or questions that are important for all farmers in every country to consider.

1. How do I improve my entrepreneurship?
   A farmer needs to become an entrepreneur, not just a craftsman. How can a farmer utilize personal strengths and skills in better ways, evaluate outlook and developments in markets

---

and society to recognize opportunities and threats, develop a vision based on outlooks and trends, translate this vision into a business strategy, and increase the return on capital invested in farm assets?

2. How can I expand the farm?

Expansion is not just an increase in the physical number of animals and land. Expansion is really about the expansion of income due to improved efficiencies and/or physical expansion. Based on the outlook and trends, how and when can expansion occur?

3. How do I prepare for fluctuations in prices of milk and feed (or any product and input)?

A first step is the evaluation of the impact of low and high prices on cash flow. Increasing the gross margin per unit of product and decreasing the cost of production per unit should be emphasized in good times as well as hard times. They are strong tools for reducing the financial risk of low product prices. Repaying debt during good times will help survival during hard times.

4. How can I keep the farm system simple?

Keeping the farm safe and simple is needed for two reasons. Simple working methods are easier to explain to workers and mean lower risk of errors in operation and in safety. This is especially needed when more than one person does the same activity. Second, with a set of standard operating procedures and steering and monitoring on the basis of a limited number of important parameters, a manager can maintain better control of the whole farm.

5. How do I decide between personnel and automation?

Expansion and efficiency improvements can mean a choice between hiring more workers and investing in more equipment. Many farmers do not want to get involved in personnel management, but equipment can be costly. When expansion is done in relatively small steps, the need for more labor can be met through the hiring of part-time workers so personnel management techniques can be learned in smaller steps. The time and cost of learning the skills for managing people can be viewed as in investment in management skills that that will have future as well as immediate benefits.

Source: J. Zijlstra and M. de Haan, "Developing the Dairy Business in New Reality." Paper presented at the European Dairy Farmers Congress, Groningen, the Netherlands, June 20, 2008. Accessed on February 11, 2010, at http://library.wur.nl/way/bestanden/clc/1890621.pdf.

Concluding Comments

Success is defined in many ways and comes in many forms. Success is not just profit maximization, nor is it just getting bigger. Each farmer and farm family have their own views of what success is. In this text, we have looked at how to understand the wider industry and economy and how to position the farm within that wider industry and economy to best meet your definition of success. We have also covered a long list of management tools and techniques for you to use in implementing your chosen strategy. However, since the world is a risky place, we also discussed how to make risky decisions to increase the chances of accomplishing your goals and objectives.

Summary

- Change has always been part of agriculture.
- How farmers are responding to change can be grouped into six themes or categories: (1) getting bigger or smaller, (2) focusing on commodity markets or on niche markets, (3) moving closer to the final consumer in the value chain, (4) redesigning the production system, (5) adopting new technologies, and (6) increasing management skills.
- For farmers, "moving down the supply chain" means producing closer to the final consumer and capturing more of that value.
- Farmers will always seek more economic efficiency and increased productivity, and they will always be redesigning the production system to meet the current needs and demands of the marketplace.
- New technologies are being developed continually and, as part of their effort to improve efficiency and productivity, farmers will observe and test the latest technologies to see whether they are worth adopting.
- Farmers are and will be expanding their management skills and activities beyond production management. Many have already done so, and more will soon follow.
- The increasing complexity of farming and the demands of the marketplace are providing new opportunities for consultants.
- Success is defined in many ways and comes in many forms.
- Each farmer and farm family need to decide what their definition of success is and how it can be obtained in the future.

Review Questions

1. What are six themes or categories that describe how farmers are adapting to change?
2. Do you see some other ways to adapt that were not mentioned in these six categories?
3. Describe some other trends and changes you see affecting agriculture.
4. How do you think farmers can adapt to the trends and changes you just listed?
5. Will production management become more or less important (relative to other management activities) for the farmer in the future?
6. How do you see consultants fitting into your management plan?
7. What is your definition of success?

Appendices

Appendix Table 1   Amount of 1 at compound interest

	$V^f_n = (1 + i)^n$										
	2%	3%	4%	5%	6%	7%	8%	9%	10%	11%	12%
1	1.0200	1.0300	1.0400	1.0500	1.0600	1.0700	1.0800	1.0900	1.1000	1.1100	1.1200
2	1.0404	1.0609	1.0816	1.1025	1.1236	1.1449	1.1664	1.1881	1.2100	1.2321	1.2544
3	1.0612	1.0927	1.1249	1.1576	1.1910	1.2250	1.2597	1.2950	1.3310	1.3676	1.4049
4	1.0824	1.1255	1.1699	1.2155	1.2625	1.3108	1.3605	1.4116	1.4641	1.5181	1.5735
5	1.1041	1.1593	1.2167	1.2763	1.3382	1.4026	1.4693	1.5386	1.6105	1.6851	1.7623
6	1.1262	1.1941	1.2653	1.3401	1.4185	1.5007	1.5869	1.6771	1.7716	1.8704	1.9738
7	1.1487	1.2299	1.3159	1.4071	1.5036	1.6058	1.7138	1.8280	1.9487	2.0762	2.2107
8	1.1717	1.2668	1.3686	1.4775	1.5938	1.7182	1.8509	1.9926	2.1436	2.3045	2.4760
9	1.1951	1.3048	1.4233	1.5513	1.6895	1.8385	1.9990	2.1719	2.3579	2.5580	2.7731
10	1.2190	1.3439	1.4802	1.6289	1.7908	1.9672	2.1589	2.3674	2.5937	2.8394	3.1058
11	1.2434	1.3842	1.5395	1.7103	1.8983	2.1049	2.3316	2.5804	2.8531	3.1518	3.4785
12	1.2682	1.4258	1.6010	1.7959	2.0122	2.2522	2.5182	2.8127	3.1384	3.4985	3.8960
13	1.2936	1.4685	1.6651	1.8856	2.1329	2.4098	2.7196	3.0658	3.4523	3.8833	4.3635
14	1.3195	1.5126	1.7317	1.9799	2.2609	2.5785	2.9372	3.3417	3.7975	4.3104	4.8871
15	1.3459	1.5580	1.8009	2.0789	2.3966	2.7590	3.1722	3.6425	4.1772	4.7846	5.4736
16	1.3728	1.6047	1.8730	2.1829	2.5404	2.9522	3.4259	3.9703	4.5950	5.3109	6.1304
17	1.4002	1.6528	1.9479	2.2920	2.6928	3.1588	3.7000	4.3276	5.0545	5.8951	6.8660
18	1.4282	1.7024	2.0258	2.4066	2.8543	3.3799	3.9960	4.7171	5.5599	6.5436	7.6900
19	1.4568	1.7535	2.1068	2.5270	3.0256	3.6165	4.3157	5.1417	6.1159	7.2633	8.6128
20	1.4859	1.8061	2.1911	2.6533	3.2071	3.8697	4.6610	5.6044	6.7275	8.0623	9.6463
21	1.5157	1.8603	2.2788	2.7860	3.3996	4.1406	5.0338	6.1088	7.4002	8.9492	10.8038
22	1.5460	1.9161	2.3699	2.9253	3.6035	4.4304	5.4365	6.6586	8.1403	9.9336	12.1003
23	1.5769	1.9736	2.4647	3.0715	3.8197	4.7405	5.8715	7.2579	8.9543	11.0263	13.5523
24	1.6084	2.0328	2.5633	3.2251	4.0489	5.0724	6.3412	7.9111	9.8497	12.2392	15.1786
25	1.6406	2.0938	2.6658	3.3864	4.2919	5.4274	6.8485	8.6231	10.8347	13.5855	17.0001
26	1.6734	2.1566	2.7725	3.5557	4.5494	5.8074	7.3964	9.3992	11.9182	15.0799	19.0401
27	1.7069	2.2213	2.8834	3.7335	4.8223	6.2139	7.9881	10.2451	13.1100	16.7386	21.3249
28	1.7410	2.2879	2.9987	3.9201	5.1117	6.6488	8.6271	11.1671	14.4210	18.5799	23.8839
29	1.7758	2.3566	3.1187	4.1161	5.4184	7.1143	9.3173	12.1722	15.8631	20.6237	26.7499
30	1.8114	2.4273	3.2434	4.3219	5.7435	7.6123	10.0627	13.2677	17.4494	22.8923	29.9599
31	1.8476	2.5001	3.3731	4.5380	6.0881	8.1451	10.8677	14.4618	19.1943	25.4104	33.5551
32	1.8845	2.5751	3.5081	4.7649	6.4534	8.7153	11.7371	15.7633	21.1138	28.2056	37.5817
33	1.9222	2.6523	3.6484	5.0032	6.8406	9.3253	12.6760	17.1820	23.2252	31.3082	42.0915
34	1.9607	2.7319	3.7943	5.2533	7.2510	9.9781	13.6901	18.7284	25.5477	34.7521	47.1425
35	1.9999	2.8139	3.9461	5.5160	7.6861	10.6766	14.7853	20.4140	28.1024	38.5749	52.7996
36	2.0399	2.8983	4.1039	5.7918	8.1473	11.4239	15.9682	22.2512	30.9127	42.8181	59.1356
37	2.0807	2.9852	4.2681	6.0814	8.6361	12.2236	17.2456	24.2538	34.0039	47.5281	66.2318
38	2.1223	3.0748	4.4388	6.3855	9.1543	13.0793	18.6253	26.4367	37.4043	52.7562	74.1797
39	2.1647	3.1670	4.6164	6.7048	9.7035	13.9948	20.1153	28.8160	41.1448	58.5593	83.0812
40	2.2080	3.2620	4.8010	7.0400	10.2857	14.9745	21.7245	31.4094	45.2593	65.0009	93.0510

Appendix Table 2 Present value of 1 at compound interest

					$V^p_n = 1/(1+i)^n$						
	2%	3%	4%	5%	6%	7%	8%	9%	10%	11%	12%
1	0.9804	0.9709	0.9615	0.9524	0.9434	0.9346	0.9259	0.9174	0.9091	0.9009	0.8929
2	0.9612	0.9426	0.9246	0.9070	0.8900	0.8734	0.8573	0.8417	0.8264	0.8116	0.7972
3	0.9423	0.9151	0.8890	0.8638	0.8396	0.8163	0.7938	0.7722	0.7513	0.7312	0.7118
4	0.9238	0.8885	0.8548	0.8227	0.7921	0.7629	0.7350	0.7084	0.6830	0.6587	0.6355
5	0.9057	0.8626	0.8219	0.7835	0.7473	0.7130	0.6806	0.6499	0.6209	0.5935	0.5674
6	0.8880	0.8375	0.7903	0.7462	0.7050	0.6663	0.6302	0.5963	0.5645	0.5346	0.5066
7	0.8706	0.8131	0.7599	0.7107	0.6651	0.6227	0.5835	0.5470	0.5132	0.4817	0.4523
8	0.8535	0.7894	0.7307	0.6768	0.6274	0.5820	0.5403	0.5019	0.4665	0.4339	0.4039
9	0.8368	0.7664	0.7026	0.6446	0.5919	0.5439	0.5002	0.4604	0.4241	0.3909	0.3606
10	0.8203	0.7441	0.6756	0.6139	0.5584	0.5083	0.4632	0.4224	0.3855	0.3522	0.3220
11	0.8043	0.7224	0.6496	0.5847	0.5268	0.4751	0.4289	0.3875	0.3505	0.3173	0.2875
12	0.7885	0.7014	0.6246	0.5568	0.4970	0.4440	0.3971	0.3555	0.3186	0.2858	0.2567
13	0.7730	0.6810	0.6006	0.5303	0.4688	0.4150	0.3677	0.3262	0.2897	0.2575	0.2292
14	0.7579	0.6611	0.5775	0.5051	0.4423	0.3878	0.3405	0.2992	0.2633	0.2320	0.2046
15	0.7430	0.6419	0.5553	0.4810	0.4173	0.3624	0.3152	0.2745	0.2394	0.2090	0.1827
16	0.7284	0.6232	0.5339	0.4581	0.3936	0.3387	0.2919	0.2519	0.2176	0.1883	0.1631
17	0.7142	0.6050	0.5134	0.4363	0.3714	0.3166	0.2703	0.2311	0.1978	0.1696	0.1456
18	0.7002	0.5874	0.4936	0.4155	0.3503	0.2959	0.2502	0.2120	0.1799	0.1528	0.1300
19	0.6864	0.5703	0.4746	0.3957	0.3305	0.2765	0.2317	0.1945	0.1635	0.1377	0.1161
20	0.6730	0.5537	0.4564	0.3769	0.3118	0.2584	0.2145	0.1784	0.1486	0.1240	0.1037
21	0.6598	0.5375	0.4388	0.3589	0.2942	0.2415	0.1987	0.1637	0.1351	0.1117	0.0926
22	0.6468	0.5219	0.4220	0.3418	0.2775	0.2257	0.1839	0.1502	0.1228	0.1007	0.0826
23	0.6342	0.5067	0.4057	0.3256	0.2618	0.2109	0.1703	0.1378	0.1117	0.0907	0.0738
24	0.6217	0.4919	0.3901	0.3101	0.2470	0.1971	0.1577	0.1264	0.1015	0.0817	0.0659
25	0.6095	0.4776	0.3751	0.2953	0.2330	0.1842	0.1460	0.1160	0.0923	0.0736	0.0588
26	0.5976	0.4637	0.3607	0.2812	0.2198	0.1722	0.1352	0.1064	0.0839	0.0663	0.0525
27	0.5859	0.4502	0.3468	0.2678	0.2074	0.1609	0.1252	0.0976	0.0763	0.0597	0.0469
28	0.5744	0.4371	0.3335	0.2551	0.1956	0.1504	0.1159	0.0895	0.0693	0.0538	0.0419
29	0.5631	0.4243	0.3207	0.2429	0.1846	0.1406	0.1073	0.0822	0.0630	0.0485	0.0374
30	0.5521	0.4120	0.3083	0.2314	0.1741	0.1314	0.0994	0.0754	0.0573	0.0437	0.0334
31	0.5412	0.4000	0.2965	0.2204	0.1643	0.1228	0.0920	0.0691	0.0521	0.0394	0.0298
32	0.5306	0.3883	0.2851	0.2099	0.1550	0.1147	0.0852	0.0634	0.0474	0.0355	0.0266
33	0.5202	0.3770	0.2741	0.1999	0.1462	0.1072	0.0789	0.0582	0.0431	0.0319	0.0238
34	0.5100	0.3660	0.2636	0.1904	0.1379	0.1002	0.0730	0.0534	0.0391	0.0288	0.0212
35	0.5000	0.3554	0.2534	0.1813	0.1301	0.0937	0.0676	0.0490	0.0356	0.0259	0.0189
36	0.4902	0.3450	0.2437	0.1727	0.1227	0.0875	0.0626	0.0449	0.0323	0.0234	0.0169
37	0.4806	0.3350	0.2343	0.1644	0.1158	0.0818	0.0580	0.0412	0.0294	0.0210	0.0151
38	0.4712	0.3252	0.2253	0.1566	0.1092	0.0765	0.0537	0.0378	0.0267	0.0190	0.0135
39	0.4619	0.3158	0.2166	0.1491	0.1031	0.0715	0.0497	0.0347	0.0243	0.0171	0.0120
40	0.4529	0.3066	0.2083	0.1420	0.0972	0.0668	0.0460	0.0318	0.0221	0.0154	0.0107

Appendix Table 3 Annuity factors (Present value of 1 per annum at compound interest)

$$a = (1 - (1 + i)^{-n})/i$$

	2%	3%	4%	5%	6%	7%	8%	9%	10%	11%	12%
1	0.9804	0.9709	0.9615	0.9524	0.9434	0.9346	0.9259	0.9174	0.9091	0.9009	0.8929
2	1.9416	1.9135	1.8861	1.8594	1.8334	1.8080	1.7833	1.7591	1.7355	1.7125	1.6901
3	2.8839	2.8286	2.7751	2.7232	2.6730	2.6243	2.5771	2.5313	2.4869	2.4437	2.4018
4	3.8077	3.7171	3.6299	3.5460	3.4651	3.3872	3.3121	3.2397	3.1699	3.1024	3.0373
5	4.7135	4.5797	4.4518	4.3295	4.2124	4.1002	3.9927	3.8897	3.7908	3.6959	3.6048
6	5.6014	5.4172	5.2421	5.0757	4.9173	4.7665	4.6229	4.4859	4.3553	4.2305	4.1114
7	6.4720	6.2303	6.0021	5.7864	5.5824	5.3893	5.2064	5.0330	4.8684	4.7122	4.5638
8	7.3255	7.0197	6.7327	6.4632	6.2098	5.9713	5.7466	5.5348	5.3349	5.1461	4.9676
9	8.1622	7.7861	7.4353	7.1078	6.8017	6.5152	6.2469	5.9952	5.7590	5.5370	5.3282
10	8.9826	8.5302	8.1109	7.7217	7.3601	7.0236	6.7101	6.4177	6.1446	5.8892	5.6502
11	9.7868	9.2526	8.7605	8.3064	7.8869	7.4987	7.1390	6.8052	6.4951	6.2065	5.9377
12	10.5753	9.9540	9.3851	8.8633	8.3838	7.9427	7.5361	7.1607	6.8137	6.4924	6.1944
13	11.3484	10.6350	9.9856	9.3936	8.8527	8.3577	7.9038	7.4869	7.1034	6.7499	6.4235
14	12.1062	11.2961	10.5631	9.8986	9.2950	8.7455	8.2442	7.7862	7.3667	6.9819	6.6282
15	12.8493	11.9379	11.1184	10.3797	9.7122	9.1079	8.5595	8.0607	7.6061	7.1909	6.8109
16	13.5777	12.5611	11.6523	10.8378	10.1059	9.4466	8.8514	8.3126	7.8237	7.3792	6.9740
17	14.2919	13.1661	12.1657	11.2741	10.4773	9.7632	9.1216	8.5436	8.0216	7.5488	7.1196
18	14.9920	13.7535	12.6593	11.6896	10.8276	10.0591	9.3719	8.7556	8.2014	7.7016	7.2497
19	15.6785	14.3238	13.1339	12.0853	11.1581	10.3356	9.6036	8.9501	8.3649	7.8393	7.3658
20	16.3514	14.8775	13.5903	12.4622	11.4699	10.5940	9.8181	9.1285	8.5136	7.9633	7.4694
21	17.0112	15.4150	14.0292	12.8212	11.7641	10.8355	10.0168	9.2922	8.6487	8.0751	7.5620
22	17.6580	15.9369	14.4511	13.1630	12.0416	11.0612	10.2007	9.4424	8.7715	8.1757	7.6446
23	18.2922	16.4436	14.8568	13.4886	12.3034	11.2722	10.3711	9.5802	8.8832	8.2664	7.7184
24	18.9139	16.9355	15.2470	13.7986	12.5504	11.4693	10.5288	9.7066	8.9847	8.3481	7.7843
25	19.5235	17.4131	15.6221	14.0939	12.7834	11.6536	10.6748	9.8226	9.0770	8.4217	7.8431
26	20.1210	17.8768	15.9828	14.3752	13.0032	11.8258	10.8100	9.9290	9.1609	8.4881	7.8957
27	20.7069	18.3270	16.3296	14.6430	13.2105	11.9867	10.9352	10.0266	9.2372	8.5478	7.9426
28	21.2813	18.7641	16.6631	14.8981	13.4062	12.1371	11.0511	10.1161	9.3066	8.6016	7.9844
29	21.8444	19.1885	16.9837	15.1411	13.5907	12.2777	11.1584	10.1983	9.3696	8.6501	8.0218
30	22.3965	19.6004	17.2920	15.3725	13.7648	12.4090	11.2578	10.2737	9.4269	8.6938	8.0552
31	22.9377	20.0004	17.5885	15.5928	13.9291	12.5318	11.3498	10.3428	9.4790	8.7331	8.0850
32	23.4683	20.3888	17.8736	15.8027	14.0840	12.6466	11.4350	10.4062	9.5264	8.7686	8.1116
33	23.9886	20.7658	18.1476	16.0025	14.2302	12.7538	11.5139	10.4644	9.5694	8.8005	8.1354
34	24.4986	21.1318	18.4112	16.1929	14.3681	12.8540	11.5869	10.5178	9.6086	8.8293	8.1566
35	24.9986	21.4872	18.6646	16.3742	14.4982	12.9477	11.6546	10.5668	9.6442	8.8552	8.1755
36	25.4888	21.8323	18.9083	16.5469	14.6210	13.0352	11.7172	10.6118	9.6765	8.8786	8.1924
37	25.9695	22.1672	19.1426	16.7113	14.7368	13.1170	11.7752	10.6530	9.7059	8.8996	8.2075
38	26.4406	22.4925	19.3679	16.8679	14.8460	13.1935	11.8289	10.6908	9.7327	8.9186	8.2210
39	26.9026	22.8082	19.5845	17.0170	14.9491	13.2649	11.8786	10.7255	9.7570	8.9357	8.2330
40	27.3555	23.1148	19.7928	17.1591	15.0463	13.3317	11.9246	10.7574	9.7791	8.9511	8.2438

Appendix Table 4   Capital recovery or amortization factors (Annuity whose present value at compound interest is 1)

	\multicolumn{11}{c}{$1/a = i/(1 - (1 + i)^{-n})$}										
	2%	3%	4%	5%	6%	7%	8%	9%	10%	11%	12%
1	1.0200	1.0300	1.0400	1.0500	1.0600	1.0700	1.0800	1.0900	1.1000	1.1100	1.1200
2	0.5150	0.5226	0.5302	0.5378	0.5454	0.5531	0.5608	0.5685	0.5762	0.5839	0.5917
3	0.3468	0.3535	0.3603	0.3672	0.3741	0.3811	0.3880	0.3951	0.4021	0.4092	0.4163
4	0.2626	0.2690	0.2755	0.2820	0.2886	0.2952	0.3019	0.3087	0.3155	0.3223	0.3292
5	0.2122	0.2184	0.2246	0.2310	0.2374	0.2439	0.2505	0.2571	0.2638	0.2706	0.2774
6	0.1785	0.1846	0.1908	0.1970	0.2034	0.2098	0.2163	0.2229	0.2296	0.2364	0.2432
7	0.1545	0.1605	0.1666	0.1728	0.1791	0.1856	0.1921	0.1987	0.2054	0.2122	0.2191
8	0.1365	0.1425	0.1485	0.1547	0.1610	0.1675	0.1740	0.1807	0.1874	0.1943	0.2013
9	0.1225	0.1284	0.1345	0.1407	0.1470	0.1535	0.1601	0.1668	0.1736	0.1806	0.1877
10	0.1113	0.1172	0.1233	0.1295	0.1359	0.1424	0.1490	0.1558	0.1627	0.1698	0.1770
11	0.1022	0.1081	0.1141	0.1204	0.1268	0.1334	0.1401	0.1469	0.1540	0.1611	0.1684
12	0.0946	0.1005	0.1066	0.1128	0.1193	0.1259	0.1327	0.1397	0.1468	0.1540	0.1614
13	0.0881	0.0940	0.1001	0.1065	0.1130	0.1197	0.1265	0.1336	0.1408	0.1482	0.1557
14	0.0826	0.0885	0.0947	0.1010	0.1076	0.1143	0.1213	0.1284	0.1357	0.1432	0.1509
15	0.0778	0.0838	0.0899	0.0963	0.1030	0.1098	0.1168	0.1241	0.1315	0.1391	0.1468
16	0.0737	0.0796	0.0858	0.0923	0.0990	0.1059	0.1130	0.1203	0.1278	0.1355	0.1434
17	0.0700	0.0760	0.0822	0.0887	0.0954	0.1024	0.1096	0.1170	0.1247	0.1325	0.1405
18	0.0667	0.0727	0.0790	0.0855	0.0924	0.0994	0.1067	0.1142	0.1219	0.1298	0.1379
19	0.0638	0.0698	0.0761	0.0827	0.0896	0.0968	0.1041	0.1117	0.1195	0.1276	0.1358
20	0.0612	0.0672	0.0736	0.0802	0.0872	0.0944	0.1019	0.1095	0.1175	0.1256	0.1339
21	0.0588	0.0649	0.0713	0.0780	0.0850	0.0923	0.0998	0.1076	0.1156	0.1238	0.1322
22	0.0566	0.0627	0.0692	0.0760	0.0830	0.0904	0.0980	0.1059	0.1140	0.1223	0.1308
23	0.0547	0.0608	0.0673	0.0741	0.0813	0.0887	0.0964	0.1044	0.1126	0.1210	0.1296
24	0.0529	0.0590	0.0656	0.0725	0.0797	0.0872	0.0950	0.1030	0.1113	0.1198	0.1285
25	0.0512	0.0574	0.0640	0.0710	0.0782	0.0858	0.0937	0.1018	0.1102	0.1187	0.1275
26	0.0497	0.0559	0.0626	0.0696	0.0769	0.0846	0.0925	0.1007	0.1092	0.1178	0.1267
27	0.0483	0.0546	0.0612	0.0683	0.0757	0.0834	0.0914	0.0997	0.1083	0.1170	0.1259
28	0.0470	0.0533	0.0600	0.0671	0.0746	0.0824	0.0905	0.0989	0.1075	0.1163	0.1252
29	0.0458	0.0521	0.0589	0.0660	0.0736	0.0814	0.0896	0.0981	0.1067	0.1156	0.1247
30	0.0446	0.0510	0.0578	0.0651	0.0726	0.0806	0.0888	0.0973	0.1061	0.1150	0.1241
31	0.0436	0.0500	0.0569	0.0641	0.0718	0.0798	0.0881	0.0967	0.1055	0.1145	0.1237
32	0.0426	0.0490	0.0559	0.0633	0.0710	0.0791	0.0875	0.0961	0.1050	0.1140	0.1233
33	0.0417	0.0482	0.0551	0.0625	0.0703	0.0784	0.0869	0.0956	0.1045	0.1136	0.1229
34	0.0408	0.0473	0.0543	0.0618	0.0696	0.0778	0.0863	0.0951	0.1041	0.1133	0.1226
35	0.0400	0.0465	0.0536	0.0611	0.0690	0.0772	0.0858	0.0946	0.1037	0.1129	0.1223
36	0.0392	0.0458	0.0529	0.0604	0.0684	0.0767	0.0853	0.0942	0.1033	0.1126	0.1221
37	0.0385	0.0451	0.0522	0.0598	0.0679	0.0762	0.0849	0.0939	0.1030	0.1124	0.1218
38	0.0378	0.0445	0.0516	0.0593	0.0674	0.0758	0.0845	0.0935	0.1027	0.1121	0.1216
39	0.0372	0.0438	0.0511	0.0588	0.0669	0.0754	0.0842	0.0932	0.1025	0.1119	0.1215
40	0.0366	0.0433	0.0505	0.0583	0.0665	0.0750	0.0839	0.0930	0.1023	0.1117	0.1213

Glossary

Abilities: The abilities are availability, reliability, and maintainability.

Accountability: Being answerable for the completion of certain tasks.

Accounting values: Values of assets, incomes, costs determined by standard rules of accounting.

Actual cash flow: The cash flow that happened in reality. An actual cash flow is made after the time period is over and once the prices, quantities, and other cash flows are known with certainty.

Amortization: Allocation of a loan (or other value) over a specified number of periods and, at the same time, accounting for any interest that may also accrue.

Annuity: A series of uniform, periodic payments received (or paid) for either a fixed number of periods or in perpetuity.

Authority: The right and power to command, use, access, and so on.

Average income or expense value: Value per unit (acre, bushel, head, for example).

Bailment: A contract in which someone is entrusted with the possession of another's property, but has no ownership interest in it.

Balance sheet: Table that shows the value of assets, amount of liabilities, and a farm's net worth at a certain point in time.

Benchmarking: Identifying the best and then comparing costs and physical efficiencies between farms.

Budget: Projection of future income and expenses; used for planning.

Business life cycle: The stages that a business goes through from its beginning entry or establishment, through growth and survival, to exit or disinvestment.

Business model: A plan of how the business expects to make money.

Business plan: A structured statement of a business' strategic plan, marketing plan, production and operations plan, financial plan and statements, and organization and staffing plan.

Business organization: Both (1) how a business is organized in terms of how owners, managers, and workers relate to each other and (2) the legal form of organization (i.e., sole proprietorship, partnership, corporation, or cooperative).

Capital: Simply put, capital is money. Capital is one of the three main broad inputs for business; the other two are land and labor.

Capital asset: An asset that is not expected to be used up during production and thus has a multi-year useful life.

Cash cost or income: A cost or expense that involves an actual cash transfer.

Cash flow budget: A statement of cash inflows and cash outflows.

Cash flow deviations: Differences between the projected cash flow and the actual cash flow.

Cash flow management: Managing the flow of cash in and out of a business and analyzing when cash is needed and available for paying farm expenses, loan payments, and living expenses, for example.

Cash flow statement: Statement that shows the annual flow and timing of cash coming in and out of a business.

Cash rent: A fixed amount of money paid by the tenant to the landowner for the use of the land and(or) buildings.

Cause-and-effect diagram: A diagram that shows a problem or opportunity and the potential causes for the problem or opportunity.

Check sheets: Forms that merely require a check made in the appropriate column or spot to indicate the frequency of certain events that relate to quality or process characteristics.

Compensation: The payment or reimbursement to a worker for performing the tasks assigned.

Competitive advantage: Having a profit rate higher than the industry average.

Competitive forces: The forces that affect the level of competition within an industry.

Compounding: The mathematical process of calculating the future value of a known, present value. Interest is calculated on both the original amount and any accumulated interest.

Contract: An agreement between two or more persons or parties to do or not to do something.

Contractee: In common agricultural use, usually thought of as the person or party who does the work of producing the product or providing the service to the buyer, that is, the company or processor. (Contractee is not always commonly used. In other usage, a contractor is the one who does the work. So care must be taken to understand who or what the word refers to in the specific situation involved.) See Contractor.

Contractor: Usually thought of as the buyer in common agricultural use—that is, the company or processor who contracts with the seller, typically a farmer, to grow, raise, or provide a specific product or service. (In other usage, a contractor is the one who does the work. So care must be taken to understand who or what the word refers to in the specific situation involved.) See Contractee.

Controlling: Comparing actual results with goals and objectives and taking corrective actions, if needed.

Conviction weights: Weights or scores based on our personal, subjective opinion as to whether a certain event will occur.

Cooperative: An enterprise collectively owned and operated for mutual benefit.

Corporation: A group of persons granted a charter to form a separate entity having its own rights, privileges, and liabilities; a corporation is usually formed to operate a business.

Cost center: An enterprise that incurs costs, such as land ownership.

Costs of quality: Costs that are associated with not meeting the customer's requirements.

Counterparty risk: The risk that the other party in a contract will not perform according to the standards and expectations of the contract.

Crafting strategy: The managerial process of deciding how to achieve the targeted results within the farm's physical and economic environment and its prospects for the future.

Cumulative probability: The increasing probability that a certain event (price, yield, weight, and so on) will occur as the range of possible occurrences increases. The cumulative probability ranges from 0 to 1.

Debt capital: Capital from a liability or other financial obligation on which interest and other fees have to be paid.

Decision criteria: A set of rules that can be used to evaluate the information available and make a decision even though the end results are not known with certainty.

Decision-making: The process of gathering information, analyzing alternatives, and choosing the best alternative.

Diagnostic analysis: The process of identifying problems behind the symptoms and identifying potential solutions.

Direct costs: Costs that are used directly by a specific enterprise.

Directing: Coordinating resources, directing and scheduling activities, and managing personnel.

Discounting: The mathematical process of calculating the present value of a known, future value by subtracting potential interest. Discounting is the opposite of compounding.

Dispatching: Deciding which jobs or tasks need to be done next.

Dominate economic traits: Those economic traits or characteristics that drive and affect an industry and the firms within that industry.

Economic engineering: Use of data from manufacturers, university reports, and other sources to prepare a budget (instead of allocating whole-farm records).

Economic environment: All the external factors that affect the economic decisions and results on a farm. These factors are grouped into four areas: resources, markets, institutions, and technology.

Economic profitability: An investment's ability to return a reasonable profit on the initial investment. It is evaluated in one of three ways: the payback period, net present value, and internal rate of return.

Economic values: Values that take into account cash values, non-cash values, opportunity costs, and other methods not included in standard rules of accounting.

Employee: A person hired to do certain tasks for a business or organization.

Employee needs: Responsibility, authority, accountability, and compensation.

Enterprise: A common name for any activity, such as corn, dairy, or machinery.

Enterprise budget: A statement of what is expected if particular production practices are used to produce a specified amount of product.

Enterprise selection: The process of choosing enterprises or products for a farm.

Entry or establishment stage: Stage at which a business is started and established on a stable foundation.

Equity capital: Capital from the owner(s) of the business as well as from partners and other investors.

Exit or disinvestment: Planning for and reaching retirement through sale and transfer of resources and responsibilities.

Expense: A charge that is made, or is expected to be made, in return for receiving a product or service.

External analysis: Looking outside the firm; studying the forces operating in the general economy and in the industry to which the firm belongs.

Fail-safe plan: A process and product design tool that looks for ways to eliminate the possibility of problems or mistakes occurring.

Financial analysis: Evaluation of a farm's financial health—that is, its financial position and performance—on the basis of its profitability, solvency, liquidity, repayment capacity, and financial efficiency.

Financial condition and performance: An evaluation of a farm's profitability, solvency, liquidity, repayment capacity, and efficiencies.

Financial control: The process of determining and implementing the necessary actions to make certain that financial plans translate into desired results.

Financial efficiency: The ability to use financial resources and expenses well to produce profit.

Financial feasibility: An investment's ability to generate sufficient cash flow to cover any debt incurred to make the investment.

Financial management: The process of obtaining, using, and controlling the use of capital, both cash and credit.

Financial objectives: Targets established for the farm's financial performance.

Financial performance: The financial results of decisions over time.

Financial position: The financial resources controlled by a farm and the claims against those resources.

Financial risk: Financial risk has four components: (1) the cost and availability of debt capital, (2) the ability to meet cash flow needs in a timely manner, (3) the ability to maintain and grow equity, and (4) the increasing chance of losing equity by larger levels of borrowing against the same net worth.

Financial statements: Reports that organize a farm's financial information into four main parts: income statement, balance sheet, statement of cash flows, and statement of owner's equity.

Fixed cost: A cost that occurs no matter what or how much is produced.

Functions of management: Planning, organizing, directing, and controlling. (Compared to the functions of business: production, marketing, finance, personnel, and so on.)

Gantt chart: A chart showing (1) when jobs are to be done, (2) who is doing which jobs, and (3) which equipment is being used on which jobs, by whom, and on which days.

GIGO: Garbage in, garbage out.

Gross margin: Gross income minus variable costs.

Growth and survival stage: Improving and expanding the resource base and income generation while protecting the business from the risks in its economic environment.

Hazard Analysis and Critical Control Point (HACCP, pronounced "hassip"): A system to monitor and reduce contamination through preventive and corrective measures instituted at each stage of the food production process where food safety hazards could occur.

Human resource risk: Disruption in the business due to death, divorce, injury, illness, poor management, improper operation and application of production and marketing procedures, poor hiring decisions, improper training, and so on.

Income: A value that is received, or expected to be received, in return for providing a product or service.

Income capitalization: The value of real estate estimated as the present value of the future stream of income due to the productive capability of that real estate.

Income statement: Financial statement that reports income versus expenses for a specific period of time.

Information: Processed, interpreted data.

Initial analysis: A first-time analysis of a farm with the assumption of having no previous knowledge of the farm.

Input supply management: The process of identifying the quantity, timing, and source of the inputs needed to meet production output plans.

Internal analysis: Looking inside the firm; evaluating a farm's strengths, weaknesses, competitive capabilities, and its past and potential condition and performance.

Internal rate of return (IRR): The discount rate that sets the net present value of the investment to zero.

Interval probability: The probability or chance that a certain event (such as the actual price or yield being within a certain interval) will occur. An interval probability will range from 0 to 1. The sum of all the interval probabilities for a certain event will equal 0.

ISO 9000 standards: A set of guidelines (developed by the International Organization for Standards) on how to set up and operate a management system to ensure that products conform to the customer's requirements.

Job design: The process of developing jobs by combining tasks that are complementary to each other and interesting to the worker.

Legal risk: Unknown and unanticipated events due to business structure and tax and estate planning, contractual arrangements, tort liability, and statutory compliance, including environmental issues.

Liquidity: The ability of the firm to cover debt during the next 12 months from short-term assets, measured at a certain point in time.

Long-range objectives: The results to be achieved either within the next three to five years or else on an ongoing basis year after year.

Long-run: A planning horizon that is more than one year and probably many more years.

Low-cost strategy: The strategy of being the low-cost producer.

Macro environment: The four dimensions of macroeconomics: social, demographic, and the political and legal environments.

Macroeconomics: The study of economy-wide issues, including economic growth, inflation, changes in employment and unemployment, trade with other countries and the balance of payments, monetary and fiscal economic policy, the role of central banks, and so on.

Management: Making and implementing decisions that allocate limited resources in ways to achieve an organization's goals as best as possible.

Management by exception: Setting rules on what size of deviations need management's attention. These rules can be in terms of absolute deviations or percentage deviations.

Marginal input cost: The cost of an additional unit of input.

Marginal product: The product received due to an additional unit of input.

Marginal return or cost: The additional return or cost resulting from an additional unit of output.

Market pull: Make what one can sell; see the need and then fill it.

Market niche strategy: The strategy of producing a specialty product for a specific market.

Market value: The value or price assigned to real estate by the marketplace.

Market-specific production contract: A contract (also referred to as a sales contract) in which the farmer agrees to produce a specific crop or livestock and to sell the product at harvest to the contractor.

Marketing risk: Not knowing what prices will be. Unanticipated forces, such as weather or government action, can lead to dramatic changes in crop and livestock prices.

Maslow's seven basic human needs: Physiological, safety, belonging and love, esteem and self-esteem, self-actualization, cognitive understanding, and aesthetic needs.

Maximin: A decision criteria that chooses the action that, after identifying the minimum return of each possible action, has the largest minimum return. In other words, it chooses the maximum of the minimums.

Microeconomics: The study of the behavior of individual persons, individual businesses and organizations, and the markets they participate in.

Minimax: A decision criteria that chooses the action that, after identifying the maximum regret of each possible action, has the smallest maximum regret.

In other words, it chooses the minimum of the maximums.

Mission: A firm's definition of its current business directions and goals; it indicates what a farm is trying to do for its customers.

Modified internal rate of return (MIRR): A modification of the IRR to account for the assumption that all returns are reinvested at the same rate of return that the original investment is providing.

Moral risk: Devious and less-than-truthful behavior by individuals and other companies as well as corrupt and criminal behavior.

Net present value (NPV): The sum of the present values of future after-tax net cash flows minus the initial investment.

Non-cash cost or income: A real income or cost that does not involve a transfer of cash, such as depreciation and intra-farm transfers between enterprises (corn to livestock, for example).

Opportunity cost: The net value that could be received from the best alternative use of a resource.

Organizing: Acquiring and organizing the necessary resources to carry out the business' plan.

Overhead costs: Costs that are hard to assign directly to a particular enterprise.

Partial budget: Estimate of the net effects of only what changes in the business.

Partnership: Two or more parties who have joined to operate a business.

Payback period: The number of years required to recover the initial cost of the investment. The payback period can be estimated using either discounted or undiscounted future after-tax net returns.

Payoff matrix: A table of potential returns or payoffs that could be obtained if certain actions are taken and certain events occur.

Personal service contract: A contract (also referred to as a resource-providing contract) that specifies that the producer is to provide services, not commodities, to the contractor.

Planning: Determining the intended strategy and course of action for the business.

Political risk: Disruption in plans due to changing policies, both governmental and institutional (such as lending policies at a bank).

Porter's five forces: Five forces that shape the competitiveness within an industry. They are risk of entry by potential competitors, rivalry among established farms, bargaining power of buyers, bargaining power of suppliers, and substitute products.

Process: A series of actions designed to bring about a particular result.

Process control: The procedures used to monitor production for compliance with the original plan, and development of corrective actions designed to bring the process back into compliance.

Process design: Specifications for the inputs, actions, methods, jobs, machines, and steps to be used in the production process.

Process improvement: understanding the current process better and looking for potential ways to improve both the process and the product.

Process map: A description of a method or process of accomplishing a task.

Process quality: (1) How well a process produces a product within specification given by the consumer and (2) how well the process performs for the producer.

Product development: The process of choosing the specific characteristics of the items that could be produced.

Product quality: The extent to which a product meets the specifications given by the customer; it's "fitness of use."

Production contract: An agreement between two or more persons or parties to produce a specific product or provide a specific service.

Production risk: Not knowing what actual production levels will be. The major sources of production risk are weather, pests, diseases, technology, genetics, machinery efficiency and reliability, and the quality of inputs.

Production-management contract: A contract used when the seller (i.e., farmer or producer), through production decisions, can affect the value of the product to the buyer (say, a vegetable or meat processor or seed company) or when the seller, through marketing decisions, can affect the value of the product to the buyer.

Profit center: An enterprise that brings in income, such as soybeans or hogs.

Profitability: The ability to produce a profit over a period of time.

Projected cash flow: An estimate of what the cash flow may be for a future period of time. A projected cash flow or cash flow budget is made with information available before the time period under consideration.

Quality: The extent to which customer requirements are met or exceeded.

Quality control: The steps taken to control the already selected production process for the products already chosen and designed. Two major parts of quality control are process control and process improvement.

Quality management: A holistic view of the entire production process from initial design through input purchases and actual production to the service supplied after production.

Quality of conformance: How well the production process has done in producing a product that meets the specifications of the design.

Quality of design: The extent to which the product design meets consumer needs and wants.

Real estate: Landed property; usually referring to the land plus buildings and other improvements such as drainage tile, waterways, fences, and so on.

Regret matrix: A table of potential regrets for having chosen a certain action instead of having chosen any other alternative action. A regret matrix is calculated from a payoff matrix.

Repayment capacity: The ability to cover cash outflow from cash inflows over a period of time.

Resource-providing contract: A contract (also referred to as a personal service contract) that specifies that the producer is to provide services, not commodities, to the contractor.

Responsibility(ies): The duty(ies) or task(s) that a worker is obligated or expected to do.

Risk: The outcome of events is uncertain, but we know all the possible outcomes and the objective probability of each outcome occurring.

Safety-first rule: A decision criteria that first eliminates all possible actions that violate some safety-first imperative (such as, "no losses") and then chooses from the remaining actions using a decision rule such as the maximum expected return.

Sales contract: A contract (also referred to as a market-specific production contract) in which the farmer agrees to produce a specific crop or livestock and to sell the product at harvest to the contractor.

Scenarios: Descriptions of different views or possibilities of what the future may be like.

Scheduling: Deciding what activities are to be done, when they will be done, who will do them, and what equipment will be needed.

Sequencing: Specifying the exact order of operations or jobs.

Service after delivery: The warranty, repair, and replacement after a product has been sold.

Share rent: A percentage of the physical yield that the landowner receives in return for allowing the tenant to use the land. The value of the physical yield received by the landowner will vary with the price of the product. The landowner usually pays some of the production costs as well as receiving part of the yield.

Short-range objectives: The organization's near-term performance targets; the amount of short-term improvement signals how fast management is trying to achieve the long-range objectives.

Short-run: A planning horizon of one year or less.

Simple rate of return (SRR): The average annual net return divided by either the initial investment or the average investment.

Sole proprietorship: A business owned by one party.

Solvency: The ability to pay off all debts at a certain point in time.

Sparse data method: A method of estimating probabilities using only a few observations.

Stakeholders: The people, businesses, and institutions that have a claim or interest in the farm.

Strategic control: The process of monitoring a farm's strategic performance and its external environment and making adjustments in the strategy and its implementation as needed to accomplish the farm's objectives and vision.

Strategic objectives: Targets established for strengthening the farm's overall position and competitive vitality.

Strategic plan: A statement outlining an organization's mission and future direction, near-term and long-term performance targets, and strategy.

Strategic planning: The process of identifying stakeholders, objectives, vision, and mission; developing internal and external analysis; crafting strategy.

Strategy: The pattern of actions managers employ to achieve organizational objectives.

Strategy implementation: The full range of managerial activities associated with putting the chosen strategy into place, supervising its pursuit, and achieving the targeted results.

Structural change: Changes in the makeup of an industry: the number, size, and geographical location of buyers, suppliers, processors, producers, and all other firms as well as the physical, legal, and social network of connections between the firms in an industry.

Sunk costs: Variable costs that have become fixed once they have been used or committed to use.

SWOT analysis: A procedure that develops and analyzes a firm's strengths, weaknesses, opportunities, and threats.

Technology push: Sell what one can make; make it and then figure out how to sell it.

Time value of money: The value that money has by being used over time.

Total income or expense: income or expense summed over an entire farm or enterprise.

TQM, total quality management: A management philosophy that strives to involves everyone in a continual effort to improve quality and achieve customer satisfaction.

Trend chart: A running plot of measured quality characteristics: stored grain moisture, pigs born per litter, milk per cow per day, acres per day, bacteria or somatic cell counts, and so on.

Triangular distribution: Estimation of probabilities using only three values: most likely, lowest, and highest.

Uncertainty: The state in which we know some (or maybe all) of the possible outcomes of an event, but we cannot quantify the probabilities.

Value of additional product: The value of the marginal product.

Variable cost: A cost that changes as the volume of business changes.

Variable or flexible cash rent: Payment arrangement in which the landowner receives only cash, but the amount paid each year can vary due to changes in the physical crop yield, the productivity of the animals, or the market price. The entire payment may be variable or there may be a fixed base cash rent plus a variable portion.

Vision: The picture of what the stakeholders want the farm to look like in the future; a view of an organization's future direction and business course; a guiding concept for what the organization is trying to do and to become.

Whole farm: All of the enterprises on a farm.

Whole-farm budget: A summary of the major physical and financial features of the entire farm.

Workforce: The people who work for a business, farm, or any organization.

Index